2003 U.S. Master™ Finance Guide

Jae K. Shim, Ph.D., MBA

CCH INCORPORATED
Chicago

Editorial Staff

Technical Review: Sharie T. Dow, MST, CPA
Copyedit: Nancy McDonagh, Holly Porter
Production: Holly J. Porter, Christopher Zwirek
Index: Judith Brocks

This publication is designed to provide accurate and authoritative information in regard to the subject matter covered. It is sold with the understanding that the publisher is not engaged in rendering legal, accounting, or other professional service and that the author is not offering such advice in this publication. If legal advice or other expert assistance is required, the services of a competent professional person should be sought.

In the course of preparing this publication, the author has randomly selected names for use in providing examples and describing situations. Any similarity to persons living or dead, fictional or nonfictional is purely coincidental and the author and publisher disclaim any responsibility of liability therefor.

ISBN: 0-8080-0890-0

4025 W. Peterson Ave.
Chicago, IL 60646-6085
1 800 248 3248
http://tax.cchgroup.com

To Dr. Bill F. Roberts,

and Professor C.B. McGuire,

former mentors at the University of California at Berkeley.

Preface

The *U.S. Master Finance Guide* is a handy problem-solver for today's busy chief financial officer, controller, treasurer, accountant, financial analyst, banker, financial consultant, investment adviser, and business manager. Although the book examines many complex financial topics and techniques for experienced finance veterans, it also covers fundamentals and career topics that appeal to the novice. Substantial effort is made to explain and illustrate important concepts that represent the tools of the trade. The broad scope and generous size of the volume supports the overall goal, which is to be the premier financial reference for professionals at all stages of their careers. No easy feat, both author and publisher are committed to meeting our readers' needs and heeding their suggestions to make this happen. Annual editions are planned.

Displaying a penchant for practical use, the *Guide* seeks to answer the reader's most critical questions. What is it that the professional seeks in the financial areas covered? What are the objectives? What are the important signposts? What needs to be done? How do things get done? Whether the reader is interested in something as complex as understanding how a business is valued or something as straightforward as the price of a mutual fund share, the *Guide* delivers the answers.

Checklists, ratios, formulas, measures, guidelines, procedures, rules of thumb, illustrations, step-by-step instructions, real life examples, tables, charts, and exhibits help the reader analyze and evaluate any business-related problem.

The *Guide* contains approaches and techniques for understanding and solving problems of:

- Managerial accounting and financial analysis
- Financial statement analysis and financial metrics
- Financial forecasting, planning, and budgeting
- Management of assets and liabilities
- Financing the business
- Long-term capital budgeting decisions
- Business valuations
- Investments
- Risk management and financial engineering

- Mergers and acquisitions, divestitures, and spin-offs
- Multinational finance
- Personal financial planning

Part One (Chapters 1-2) is an overview of financial management. It also outlines the roundup and new developments in finance from the past year.

Part Two (Chapters 3-4) introduces a variety of certificates related to finance and its related fields. What types of fields can be adopted as a career in finance are listed and described. A list of major financial organizations is also presented.

Part Three (Chapters 5-8) addresses the foundations of financial management. It covers major tools and concepts vital to financial management—the types of business forms, the time value of money, risk and return, and valuation.

Part Four (Chapters 9-13) focuses on managerial accounting and financial decisions. It discusses what the financial officer should know about break-even cost-volume-profit (CVP) analysis, leverage and risks, budgeting and financial modeling, and capital budgeting. It also describes how to manage working capital and make decisions on cash, accounts receivable, and inventory.

Part Five (Chapters 14-16) is directed toward financial analysis areas including risk/reward relationships and financial statement analysis for internal evaluation. It addresses how to measure and improve managerial and segment performance. Heavy emphasis is placed on a celebrated financial metric—Economic Value Added (EVA). It ends with an examination on how to determine the value of businesses.

Part Six (Chapters 17-20) deals with how to adequately obtain financing for the business to meet its goals and financial needs. Short-term, intermediate-term, and long-term financing requirements are discussed as well as indicating under what circumstances each would be appropriate. Cost of capital determination and capital structure decisions are presented.

Part Seven (Chapter 21-25) surveys a variety of investment vehicles and discusses the pros and cons of each. It also covers investment portfolio selection so as to earn a satisfactory return while controlling risk. The global investing arena is taken up.

Part Eight (Chapters 26-30) address special topics in financial management. It begins with risk management and financial engineering. It presents the planning and financial aspects for mergers and acquisitions. The reasons and ways of divesting of business segments are discussed. The financial management issues of overseas operations crucial to multinational companies (MNCs) are addressed. Key elements of personal financial planning are summarized.

The Appendix provides some useful tools and information, including a finance glossary, financial tables, financial tools, and useful websites. Keep this book handy for easy reference throughout the year!

Jae K. Shim

January 2003

About the Author

Dr. Jae K. Shim is one of the most well-known and prolific accounting and finance experts in the world. He is a professor of finance and accounting at California State University in Long Beach, and president of Delta Consulting Company, a financial consulting and training firm. Professor Shim received his MBA and Ph.D. degrees from the University of California at Berkeley (Haas School of Business). He has been a consultant to commercial and nonprofit organizations for over 30 years.

Dr. Shim has over 50 college and professional books to his credit, including, *Financial Management, Investment Sourcebook, Dictionary of Real Estate, Dictionary of Economics, Dictionary of International Investment Terms, Dictionary of Personal Finance, Encyclopedic Dictionary of Accounting and Finance, Encyclopedic Dictionary of International Finance and Banking, Managerial Accounting, Vest-Pocket CPA, Vest-Pocket CFO,* and *Vest-Pocket MBA.*

Dr. Shim has been frequently quoted by such media as the *Los Angeles Times, Orange County Register, Business Start-ups, Personal Finance,* and *Money Radio.* Dr. Shim has also published numerous articles in professional and academic journals. He was the recipient of the *Credit Research Foundation Award* for his article on cash flow forecasting and financial modeling.

Acknowledgments

A special note of gratitude is extended to Jason Caan and Allison Shim for their skillful word processing and spreadsheet work. I also thank Stephanie Canavan for her review of several key chapters of the book.

All errors remain with the author, however. Comments and criticisms from readers are welcome and can be directed to jaeshim@csulb.edu or jshim@socal.rr.com.

Contents

Part 1

An Overview of Financial Management and Developments in Finance

Chapter 1

An Overview of Financial Management

¶ 101 Objectives of Managerial Finance

Financial management is the process of planning decisions in order to maximize the shareholders' wealth (or the firm's market value). Financial managers play a major role in cash management, the acquisition of funds, and in all aspects of raising and allocating financial capital, taking into account the trade-off between risk and return. Financial managers need accounting and financial information to carry out their responsibilities.

Company goals usually include (1) stockholder wealth maximization, (2) profit maximization, (3) managerial reward maximization, (4) behavioral goals, and (5) social responsibility. Modern finance theory operates on the assumption that the primary goal of the business is to maximize the wealth of its stockholders, which translates into maximizing the price of the firm's common stock. The other goals mentioned above also influence the company's policy but are less important than stock price maximization. Note that the traditional goal frequently stressed by economists—profit maximization—is not sufficient for most companies today.

.01 Profit Maximization v. Stockholder Wealth Maximization

Profit maximization is basically a single-period or, at most, a short-term goal, to be achieved within one year. It is usually interpreted to mean the maximization of profits within a given period of time. A corporation may maximize its short-term profits at the expense of its long-term profitability. In contrast, stockholder wealth maximization is a long-term goal, since stockholders are interested in future as well as present profits. Wealth maximization is generally preferred because it considers (1) wealth for the long term, (2) risk or uncertainty, (3) the timing of returns, and (4) the stockholders' return. Timing of returns is important; the earlier the return is received the better, since a quick return reduces the uncertainty about receiving the return, and the money received can be reinvested sooner.

Exhibit 1 summarizes the advantages and disadvantages of these two often conflicting goals.

Exhibit 1

Profit Maximization vs. Stockholder Wealth Maximization

Goal	*Objective*	*Advantages*	*Disadvantages*
Profit maximization	Large profits	1. Easy to calculate profits. 2. Easy to determine the link between financial decisions and profits.	1. Emphasizes the short term. 2. Ignores risk or uncertainty. 3. Ignores the timing of returns. 4. Requires immediate resources.
Stockholder wealth maximization	Highest share price of common stock	1. Emphasizes the long term. 2. Recognizes risk or uncertainty. 3. Recognizes the timing of returns. 4. Considers stockholders' return.	1. Offers no clear relationship between financial decisions and stock price. 2. Can lead to management anxiety and frustration. 3. Can promote aggressive and *creative* accounting practices

Following are examples of how profit maximization may affect wealth maximization.

Example 1: Profit maximization can be achieved in the short term at the expense of the long-term goal of wealth maximization. For example, a costly investment may create losses in the short term but yield substantial profits in the long term. Hence, a company that wants to show a short-term profit may postpone major repairs or replacement of vital company property, even though such postponement is likely to hurt its long-term profitability.

Example 2: Profit maximization, unlike wealth maximization, does not consider risk or uncertainty. Consider two products, A and B, and their projected earnings over the next five years, as shown below.

Year	*Product A*	*Product B*
1	$ 20,000	$ 22,000
2	$ 20,000	$ 22,000
3	$ 20,000	$ 22,000
4	$ 20,000	$ 22,000
5	$ 20,000	$ 22,000
	$100,000	$110,000

A profit maximization approach favors product B over product A because its total projected earnings after five years are higher. However, if product B is more risky than product A, then the decision is not as straightforward as the figures seem to indicate because of the trade-off between risk and return. Stockholders expect greater returns from investments with higher risk; they will demand a sufficiently larger return to compensate for the comparatively greater level of risk of producing product B.

.02 The Agency Problem

Even though the goal of the firm is the maximization of shareholder wealth, an obstacle known as the agency problem may interfere with the implementation of this goal. For example, managers will not work for the owners unless it is in their best interest. Major agency problems develop (1) between shareholders (owners) and managers and (2) between creditors and shareholders (owners).

Shareholders vs. managers. The agency problem arises when a manager owns less than 100 percent of the company's ownership. As a result of the separation between the managers and owners, managers may make decisions that are not in line with the goal of maximizing stockholder wealth. For example, they may work less eagerly and benefit themselves in terms of salary and perks. The costs associated with the agency problem, such as a reduced stock price and various "perks", are called agency costs. Several mechanisms are used to ensure that managers act in the best interests of the shareholders: (1) golden parachutes or severance contracts, (2) performance-based stock option plans, and (3) the threat of takeover.

Creditors vs. shareholders. Conflicts develop if (1) managers, acting in the interest of shareholders, take on projects with greater risk than creditors anticipated and (2) raise the debt level higher than was expected. These actions tend to reduce the value of the debt outstanding to creditors.

¶ 105 Finance Decisions and Risk-Return Trade-Off

The concept of risk-return trade-off is integral to the theory of finance. Additional risk is not acceptable unless there is an expectation of being compensated with additional return. Exhibit 2 illustrates this tradeoff.

Exhibit 2

Risk-Return Function

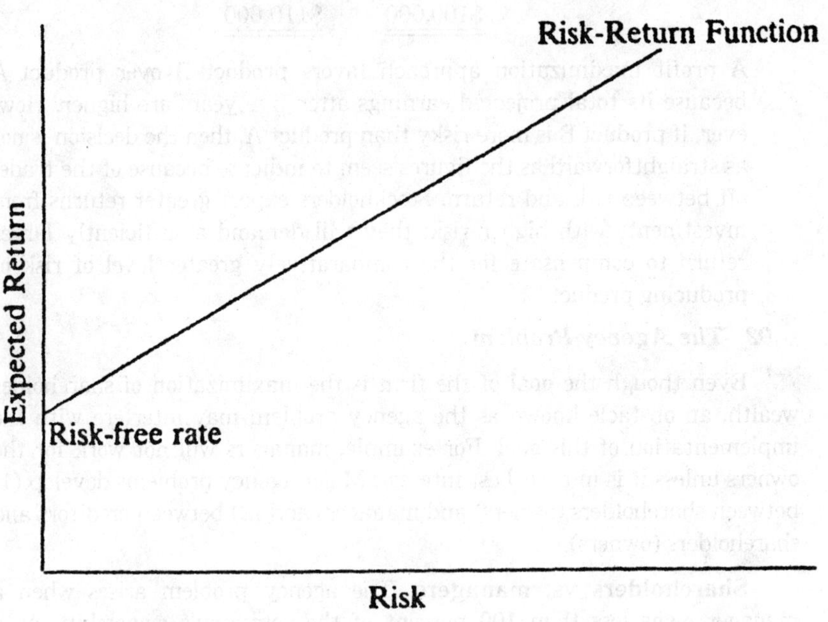

Risk refers to the variability of expected returns (sales, earnings, or cash flow) and is the probability that a financial problem will affect the company's operational performance or financial position. Typical forms of risk are economic risk, political uncertainties, and industry problems.

Risk analysis is a process of measuring and analyzing the risk associated with the financial and investment decisions. It is important to consider risk in making capital investment decisions because of the large amount of capital involved and the long-term nature of the investments. Analysts must also consider the rate of return in relation to the degree of risk involved. (Return, the reward for investing, consists of current income, in the form of either periodic cash payments or capital gain (or loss) from appreciation (or depreciation) in market value.)

Proper assessment and balance of the various risk-return trade-offs available is part of creating a sound stockholder wealth maximization plan. The risk-return trade-off is discussed in Chapters 7, 9, 13, and 26.

.01 Portfolio Risk and Return

Not all risk is created equal. Some risk can be diversified away, and some cannot. There is an old saying, "don't put all your eggs in one basket." For most securities and projects some risk can be reduced or eliminated through diversification. This issue, and how to measure portfolio return and risk, is discussed in Chapter 7.

.02 Time Value of Money

Today's dollars are not the same as tomorrow's. A dollar now is worth more than a dollar to be received later, because one can invest that dollar for a return and have more than a dollar at the specified later date. Further, receiving a dollar in the future has uncertainty attached to it; inflation might make the dollar received at a later time worth less in buying power.

Time value of money is a critical consideration in financial and investment decisions. For example, compound interest calculations can help one determine one's eventual return from an investment. Discounting, or the calculation of present value, which is inversely related to compounding, is used to evaluate future cash flow associated with long-term projects; the discounted value of receiving future cash flows from a proposal is an important consideration.

Time value of money has many applications in finance. For example, it can help one determine the periodic payout or interest rate on a loan or decide between leasing and buying equipment. The time value of money is fully discussed in Chapter 6.

¶ 111 Responsibilities of Financial Managers

Financial managers have a responsibility to understand all aspects of finance and related disciplines, such as accounting, that may impact the many decisions they make while carrying out their duties.

.01 Importance of Understanding Finance

Financial managers spend a good portion of their time on planning, setting objectives, and developing efficient courses of action to achieve their objectives. A financial manager must have a thorough understanding of finance and know how to apply it successfully, whether dealing with production, marketing, personnel, operations, or any other aspect of corporate functioning. Each of these is different, and all require some kind of financial knowledge. She should know where to look, what to ask, and where to get the answers to questions about her department or company operations. Further, financial and accounting knowledge is necessary in order to be able to understand the financial reports prepared by other segments of the organization.

Financial knowledge is critical in a wide number of areas. When involved in a decision whether to use debt or equity financing, it is necessary to have the knowledge to weigh the benefits and costs of each in order to meet or maintain the company's capital goals. A financial manager must understand financial statements and be able to analyze such information to make intelligent financial decisions. A financial manager may also be called upon to plan and analyze project performance if his company invests in capital projects (property, plant, and equipment) that are tied to plans for product development, marketing, and production.

Why and what of finance. Finance involves many interrelated functions, including obtaining funds, using funds, monitoring performance, and solving current and prospective problems.

Financial managers have to know product pricing, planning, and variance analysis (comparing actual to budgeted figures). They must know how to manage assets and optimize the rate of return. They have to be familiar with budgeting, effective handling of productive assets, and the financial strengths and weaknesses of the business.

Enhanced communication. Understanding finance allows for better communication among departments. For example, the corporate budget (financial plan) communicates overall company goals to department managers so they know what is expected of them and what financial parameters exist for their operations. A financial manager must be able to identify any problems with the proposed budget before it is finalized and to make recommendations for subsequent budgets. Further, she needs to be able to discuss the budget with other members of the company. Failure to understand the budget may mean failure to achieve corporate goals.

A financial manager has to present convincing information to upper management to obtain approval for activities and projects, such as new product lines. Here, knowledge of forecasting and capital budgeting (selecting the most profitable project among long-term alternatives) is essential. It is necessary to appraise monetary and manpower requests before submitting them; being ill prepared will create a negative impression and may result in denial of a request.

The language of finance. A financial manager must master the finance vocabulary in order to comprehend financial information, know how to utilize that information effectively, and communicate clearly the quantitative aspects of performance and results. Further, she must be able to clearly express what she needs in financial terms to perform her job effectively.

.02 The Relationship Between Accounting and Finance

Accounting provides financial information and includes financial accounting and managerial accounting. *Financial accounting* records the financial history of the business and involves the preparation of reports for use by external parties, such as investors and creditors. *Managerial accounting* provides financial information to be used in making decisions about the future of the company. Financial and managerial accounting are more fully discussed later in this chapter at ¶ 121.

Financial managers use accounting information to make decisions regarding the receipt and use of funds to meet corporate objectives and to forecast future financing needs. The finance function analyzes the accounting information to improve decisions affecting the company's wealth.

¶ 115 Controller vs. Treasurer

In a large company, the financial responsibilities are probably conducted by the controller, treasurer, and chief financial officer (financial vice-president). The activities of the controller and treasurer fall under the umbrella of finance.

There is no precise distinction between the job of the controller and treasurer, and the functions may differ slightly between organizations because of company policy and the personality of the office holder.

.01 Functions of the Controller

The controller's functions are primarily of an internal nature, and include record keeping, tracking, and controlling the financial effects of prior and current operations. The internal matters of importance to the controller include financial and managerial accounting, taxes, control, and audit functions. The controller is the chief accountant and is involved in the preparation of financial statements, tax returns, the annual report, and Securities and Exchange Commission (SEC) filing. The controller's function is primarily assuring that funds are used efficiently. He or she is primarily concerned with collecting and presenting financial information. The controller usually looks at what has occurred rather than what should or will happen.

Many controllers are involved with management information systems and review previous, current, and emerging patterns. They report their analysis of the financial implications of decisions to top management.

.02 Functions of the Treasurer

The treasurer's functions, in contrast, are primarily external. The treasurer obtains and manages the corporation's capital and is involved with creditors (e.g., bank loan officers), stockholders, investors, underwriters of equity (stock) and bond issuances, and governmental regulatory bodies (e.g., the SEC). The treasurer is responsible for managing corporate assets (e.g., accounts receivable, inventory) and debt, planning the finances and capital expenditures, obtaining funds, formulating credit policy, and managing the investment portfolio.

The treasurer concentrates on keeping the company afloat by obtaining cash to meet obligations and buying assets to achieve corporate objectives. While the controller concentrates on profitability, the treasurer emphasizes cash flow. Even though a company has been profitable, it may have a significant negative cash flow; for example, there may exist substantial long-term receivables (receivables having a maturity of greater than one year). Without adequate cash flow, even a profitable company may fail. By emphasizing cash flow, the treasurer strives to prevent bankruptcy and achieve corporate goals. The treasurer analyzes the financial statements, formulates additional data, and makes decisions based on the analysis.

.03 Financial Structure within a Company

The major responsibilities of controllers and treasurers are shown in Exhibit 3. The chief financial officer (financial vice-president), also known as the CFO, is involved with financial policy making and planning. He or she has financial and managerial responsibilities, supervises all phases of financial activity, and serves as the financial adviser to the board of directors.

Exhibit 3

Functions of Controller and Treasurer

Controller	*Treasurer*
1. Accounting	1. Obtaining Financing
2. Reporting financial information	2. Banking relationships
3. Custody of records	3. Investment of funds
4. Interpretation of financial data	4. Investor relations
5. Budgeting	5. Cash management
6. Controlling operations	6. Insuring assets
7. Appraisal of results and making recommendations	7. Fostering relationships with creditors and investors
	8. Credit appraisal and collecting funds
8. Preparation of taxes	9. Deciding on the financing Mix
9. Internal auditing	

Exhibit 4 shows an organization chart of the financial structure within a company. Note that the controller and treasurer report to the vice-president of finance.

Exhibit 4

Financial Structure

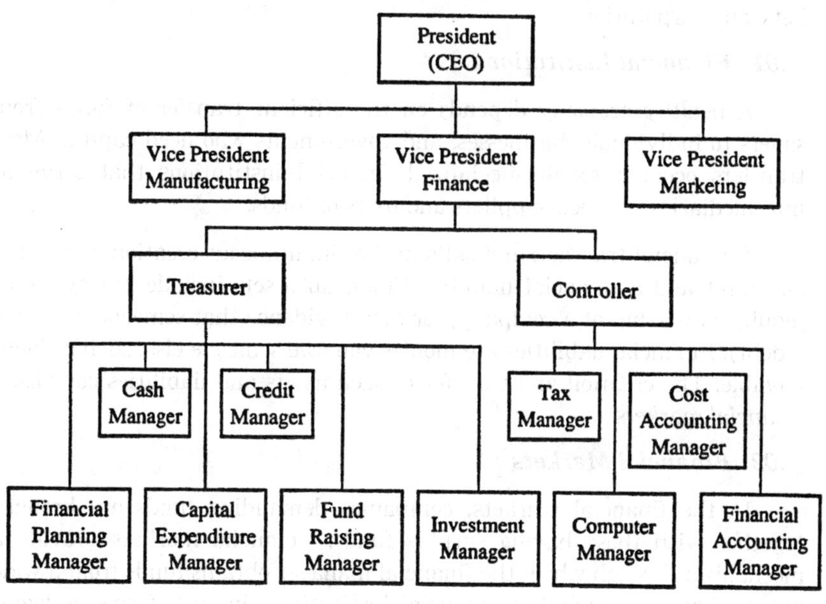

¶ 121 Relationship Between Accounting and Finance

Accounting and finance have different focuses. The primary distinctions between accounting and finance involve the treatment of funds and decision making. Accounting is a necessary subfunction of finance.

The control features of the finance function are referred to as managerial accounting. Managerial accounting includes the preparation of reports used by management for internal decision making, such as budgeting, costing, pricing, capital budgeting, performance evaluation, break-even analysis, transfer pricing (pricing of goods or services transferred between departments), and rate-of-return analysis. Managerial accounting depends heavily on historical data obtained as part of the financial accounting and emphasizes making the right decisions today to ensure future performance.

Managerial accounting information is important to the financial manager. For example, the break-event point analysis is useful in deciding whether to introduce a product line. Variance analysis is used to compare actual revenue and/or costs to standard revenue and/or costs for performance evaluation. Managerial accounting can help identify and suggest corrective action. Budgets provide manufacturing and marketing guidelines.

¶ 125 Financial Operating Environment

A financial manager operates in the financial environment and is indirectly affected by it. This section discusses financial institutions, markets, and corporations.

.01 *Financial Institutions*

A healthy economy depends on the efficient transfer of funds from savers to individuals, businesses, and governments who need capital. Most transfers occur through specialized financial institutions that serve as intermediaries between suppliers and users of funds.

A financial transaction results in the simultaneous creation of a financial asset and a financial liability. Financial assets include money, stock (equity ownership of a company), or debt (evidence that someone owes you a debt). Financial liabilities are monies you owe someone else, such as loans payable. The creation and transfer of such assets and liabilities constitute *financial markets.*

.02 *Financial Markets*

In the financial markets, companies demanding funds are brought together with those having surplus funds. Financial markets provide a mechanism through which the financial manager obtains funds from a wide range of sources, including financial institutions, in such forms as loans, bonds, and common stocks. The financial markets are composed of money markets and capital markets. Exhibit 5 depicts the general flow of funds among financial institutions and markets.

Money markets. *Money markets* are the markets for *short-term* debt securities (those with maturities of less than one year). Examples of money market securities include U.S. Treasury bills, commercial paper, and negotiable certificates of deposit issued by government, business, and financial institutions. Federal funds borrowings between banks, bank borrowings from the Federal Reserve Bank, and various types of repurchase agreements are also elements of the money market. These instruments have in common safety and liquidity. The money market, which operates through dealers, money center banks, and the New York Federal Reserve Bank, represents an outlet for both shortages and surpluses of liquidity, including those due to fluctuations in business.

Capital markets. *Capital markets* are the markets for *long-term* debt (that with a maturity of more than one year) and corporate stocks. The New York Stock Exchange, which handles the stocks of many large corporations, is a prime example of a capital market. The American Stock Exchange and the regional stock exchanges are other examples. In addition, securities are traded by thousands of brokers and dealers over-the-counter, a term used to denote all buying and selling activities in securities that do not occur in an organized stock exchange.

In the capital market, a distinction is made between the primary market, where new issues of securities are traded, and the secondary market, where previously issued securities are traded. The primary market is a source of new securities for the secondary market.

In practice, the boundaries between the money markets and capital markets are blurred, because most financial instruments deal with both kinds of financial instruments, both short and long term. In addition, revolving short-term loans become long-term loans in practice.

.03 The Corporate Connection

The financial manger has responsibility for obtaining funds and allocating them among alternative projects and specific uses, such as inventories and equipment. He or she must manage the cash flow cycle, payments for expenses and the purchases of capital goods, and sales of products and services to obtain cash inflows. In the management of cash flows, some cash is recycled and some is returned to financing sources as debt payment.

Financial market issues, including government regulation, are more fully discussed in Chapter 18.

Exhibit 5

General Flow of Funds Among Financial Institutions and Financial Markets

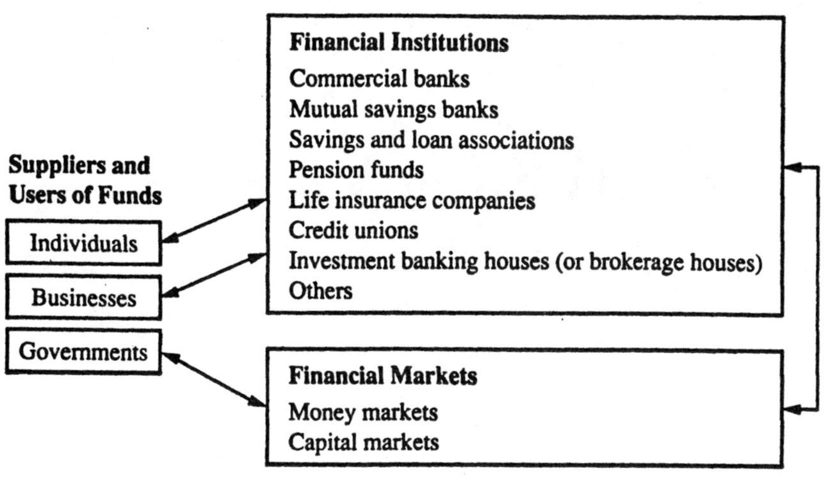

Chapter 2

Roundup and Developments in Finance

¶ 201 Accounting Scandals Bring About New Guidelines and Legislation

The past year has included a number of high-profile corporate scandals: Enron, Tyco International, K-mart, and WorldCom. While these are the most glaring, there are many more companies whose shareholders and employees have suffered as stock prices have fallen, such as Cisco, Nokia, Lucent Technologies, and most internet-related businesses. Following is a list of developments in finance and accounting and a series of corporate accounting scandals on the heels of the Enron debacle that have led to new sweeping accounting guidelines, proposals, and legislation. Each of these developments is discussed in detail in this chapter.

- Points of Controversy
- Recent Financial Restatements
- Stock Options Controversy: To Expense or Not to Expense
- FASB Proposes Consolidation Principles for Special-Purpose Entities (SPEs)

- FASB Proposes Guidelines for Stock Options
- The New York Stock Exchange's Corporate Governance Rules
- Corporate Responsibility Law
- SEC Approves Rules to Address Analyst Conflicts
- SEC Tightens its Deadlines for Disclosure
- The Association for Investment Management and Research's Proposal: the Objectivity of Analysts' Stock Research

¶ 205 Points of Controversy

During the past decade, the role of financial executives—primarily CFOs—has changed from that of primarily an accountant and controller to that of a "business partner" and "strategist." Due to the pressures on them in their emerging role as strategic partners, the CFO and finance team can also lose their objectivity and independence. This shift might have prompted the CFOs to use aggressive accounting and reporting practices. A CFO.com survey (www.cfo.com or *CFO Magazine*, August 13, 2002) reveals that 17 percent of all respondents report being pressured to misrepresent their results by their companies' CEOs during the past five years. A key factor in recent corporate scandals was a failure of financial functions to spot the signs of malpractice.

Over the past two years, volumes of shareholder wealth evaporated as the audited financial statements of certain companies were revealed as creative fiction. One of the most distressing examples is the scandal surrounding Enron Corp. The Houston-based energy trader overstated profits and hid debt from investors for years, its audit committee permitted obfuscation in public disclosures, and auditors at Arthur Andersen (one of the world's "Big Five" accounting firms, a group that also includes Ernst & Young, PricewaterhouseCoopers, Deloitte & Touche, and KPMG) approved Enron's false financial statements. After Enron's malady came to light, Andersen employees went so far as to destroy documents. The fact that Enron's imaginative accounting went on for so long exposes an end-to-end failure of the system and, predictably, the tab has been left with investors, creditors, and employees.

More detailed sources of accounting irregularities and scandals are summarized below.

.01 Moving Debt Off the Balance Sheet

The accounting technique made infamous by Enron (and the main reason for its downfall) was its use of special-purpose entities (SPE) to move debt off its balance sheet. A lot of debt was carried, but not reflected on its balance sheet. Much of it was collateralized with Enron stock. As the stock price fell, the house of cards came down.

Many U.S. companies have for a long time used special-purpose entities to finance projects in a way that allows tax benefits without visibly impairing balance sheets. This is perhaps the most dangerous accounting gimmick, because it is very difficult to determine from financial filings exactly when a company has entered into these agreements. The lack of disclosure makes it impossible for investors to determine how much the company must pay to fully service its debt or to fulfill other contractual obligations.

.02 Earnings "Management" and the Use of Pro Forma Results

Many companies have used the "complicated accounting legerdemain" to avoid disappointing investors and brokerage analysts from quarter to quarter, potentially at the expense of a long-term focus. Companies use so-called pro forma earnings to spruce up their results. The problem with pro forma results is that they are too often promotional, eliminating the negative and emphasizing the positive. Companies in the tech sector perfected the practice, but it has spread well beyond Silicon Valley.

.03 Overstated Pension Plan Assumptions

Pension plan accounting is complicated, esoteric, and not entirely logical. But what every shareholder needs to understand is that most companies have obligations to fund their pension plan to a certain level. Any shortfall must eventually be made up by contributions from the company's coffers. During the bull market of the past few years, companies were able to cut back on contributions, as gains in the stock market helped keep pension plans healthy. But even as stock prices stumbled, or fell dramatically, many firms kept on predicting robust growth of their pension investments to help boost their bottom line.

Some companies are using rosy projected returns for their employee pension plans to buff their financial statements. Many firms still assume 9 percent to 10 percent annual returns on their pension plans in coming years, when 5 percent would be more realistic. The higher the assumed long-term returns, the lower the annual pension plan contributions a company is required to make in the near term. Instead, money that would have been earmarked for a pension plan accrues to the company's bottom line.

.04 Underreporting of Executive Compensation

Most major companies do not treat the costs of employee stock options as an official expense on income statements. That has contributed to an overstatement of earnings in recent years. When options involve no charge to earnings, they are considered a cheap form of compensation, when in fact they represent a cost to shareholders. A recent survey found company after company that would have seen reported earnings slashed by as much as 200 percent had they been forced to expense stock option plans.

.05 Revenue Accounting

Basic accounting practices must be the bedrock of every finance department, and one of the most basic issues is revenue recognition—when to recognize revenue, at what amount, and the degree of provision for future reversals. Many of the recent failures came from this issue. Enron, acting as a broker between sellers and buyers of energy, took sales credits for the total size of the transaction rather than only the fee involved, which made the company's size and growth rate look much stronger than it really was. Global Crossing and Qwest Communications, among other companies, bought and sold capacity from each other and took sales credit at both ends, overstating both companies' revenues.

.06 Expense Accounting

The basic tenet of the matching principle in accounting is that expenses must be matched with their corresponding revenues. It does not always happen. For example, research and development expenditure is written off when incurred, even though the product sales to which it relates may occur many years later. However, the accounting intent is to match. WorldCom clearly violated the matching principle by considering the fees paid for line usage bought from local carriers every month as a capital expenditure, not an operating expense.

.07 Channel Stuffing

Another gray area involves "inventory management." Old tricks include "channel stuffing"—or shifting surplus finished goods to distributors' shelves. Nothing will destroy a company's ability to meet analysts' earnings expectations more than having a warehouse full of unsold goods. Rather than come clean and tell shareholders they have not met sales expectations, some companies are tempted to move their merchandise to the market knowing that much of it is going to come back unsold or will have to be sold at a massive discount. Investors looking for evidence of channel stuffing should look for large changes to stated inventory levels, or an increase in the contingencies set aside for bad accounts.

The most powerful example of the practice was the fall from grace of Al Dunlap, the former head of Sunbeam Corp. He allegedly moved millions of dollars in merchandise onto the hands of distributors and retailers using discounts and other inducements. That, along with the use of cash reserves to pump up the company's operating earnings, resulted in a record-breaking $189 million in reported earnings in fiscal 1992. But when the scheme was uncovered, Sunbeam was forced to restate its earnings from the fourth quarter of 1996 to the first quarter of 1998; the SEC alleges that $60 million of that record-breaking profit was the result of accounting fraud. CFO Magazine (January 15, 2002) stated that 'Chainsaw' Al Dunlap agreed to pay $15 million to settle a shareholder lawsuit alleging inflated stock prices. Sunbeam's auditor at the time was Anderson.

.08 *Auditor Independence*

Auditors must recognize that their ultimate client is not management. In fact, they are supposed to serve shareholders. But in practice, auditors are paid by the very companies whose books they are supposed to scrutinize. And in recent years, that relationship has become even more complicated. The Big Five routinely perform lucrative management, information technology, tax, and other consulting work for the companies they audit.

According to the Investor Responsibility Research Center (IRRC), a Washington D.C.-based advocacy group for institutional investors, large accounting firms receive just 28 percent of their fees from auditing work. Nonaudit fees significantly exceed the amount paid for auditing services.

.09 *Corporate Governance Issue*

A company's audit committee has myriad responsibilities, the most important being to oversee the presentation and honesty of financial statements. Members are appointed by the board of directors. The problem is, many company audit committees include directors who also serve on the executive team. Because management are insiders who are paid out of the funds of the company, there's a need for a check on management. Audit committees comprising directors should not be tied to management in any way. More corporations are complying in the wake of Enron, but until the guidelines become mandatory, some could continue to ignore them.

¶211 Recent Financial Restatements

Below is a list of recent earnings restatements.

- Household International, August 2002: The nation's No. 2 consumer finance concern (and a previous Anderson client) disclosed that it earned $386 million less than previously reported over the last nine years. The company, which issues MasterCard and Visa credit cards and makes home equity and car loans, said the restatement came after its new auditors reviewed its accounting for "complex" credit-card contracts.

- The Pantry Inc., August 2002: The convenience-store retailer said it had found an "inadvertent" $8 million accounting error in its reports for the first and second quarters.

- Interpublic Group of Companies, August 2002: A major advertising business, it said it had identified $68.5 million in expenses that had not been properly accounted for. The company is restating its earnings back to 1997 to reflect the overlooked expenses, mostly incurred in its European operations.

- Xerox, June 2002: The company disclosed that it inflated revenue by $6.4 billion over five years. Anne Mulcahy, CEO of

Xerox, announced a $1.9 billion reversal of revenues and a $1.4 billion restatement of profits for the past five years.

- WorldCom, August 2002: The telecommunications company announced that an internal audit found $7.1 billion in accounting irregularities. On July 21, 2002 it filed a voluntary petition for reorganization under Chapter 11.

- Qwest Communications International, June 2002: The company's chief executive was forced out because of concern that a federal investigation would result in a restatement of revenue for 2000 and 2001.

- Tyco International, June 2002: The company said it would restate its second-quarter earnings by $4.5 billion. In September 2002, Tyco filed an 8-K on improper conduct by former management, including its CFO.

- Adelphia Communications, May 2002: The cable television company, which filed for bankruptcy protection this month, announced that it would restate earnings for the last three years. Federal investigators also are looking into $3 billion in off-the-books loans made to the company's founders. In September 2002 Century Cable filed Chapter 11.

- CMS Energy, May 2002: The company announced it would restate $1 billion of "round-trip" trades for 2000 and $4.2 billion for 2001. CEO William T. McCormick, Jr. resigned.

- Network Associates, May 2002: The company restated results for 1998, 1999, and 2000, blaming the problems on intentional errors made by a single employee, who was fired. The errors overstated income by $4 million in 1998.

- Peregrine Systems, May 2002: The San Diego software maker, which fired its CEO and CFO, said it would restate downward its revenues by as much as $100 million for the last three years because of accounting irregularities uncovered by its new auditors. In August 2002 it was notified of its delisting by NASDAQ. In September 2002 it filed a voluntary petition for reorganization under Chapter 11.

- Reliant, May 2002: The Houston energy company admitted to $6 billion in sham trades that inflated revenue by about 10 percent.

- Homestore.com, March 2002: The Westlake Village company restated results for 2000, disclosing that revenue had been overstated.

- Enron, December 2001: The energy-trading company filed for bankruptcy protection after off-the-books accounting was uncovered.

- Rite Aid, October 1999: CEO Martin Grass was forced out when the company announced it would restate results for 1997 through 1999. The company overstated net income by $1.6 billion.

- Cendant, April 1998: The company said it would restate results because of inflated earnings. Two former top executives were indicted.

¶ 215 Stock Options Controversy: To Expense or Not to Expense

The whole premise behind expensing options is to further clarify a company's accounting, making its numbers more transparent to the public and thereby boosting investors' confidence, which has been ravaged by corporate scandals.

Executives involved in those scandals were often lavished with options that made them fabulously rich and allegedly prompted the financial abuses that were aimed at keeping the companies' profits—and stock prices—as high as possible. Options came under assault, and now treating them as a cost to be deducted from earnings is seen as one solution to curbing the abuses.

The debate primarily rages over the effect the accounting change might have on the companies' financial results, their stock prices, and their employees. The following summarizes the opposing views:

Arguments

To expense

- Since options are now all but free to companies, excessive grants to top executives have been encouraged. But options do have costs: they dilute shareholders' stakes and deprive companies of the funds they would otherwise get by selling those shares in the open market. Such costs should be reflected in earnings.

- Bringing more discipline to option grants will also reduce the incentives top executives now have to pump their stocks through short-term earnings maneuvers in hopes of cashing in big option gains.

- Some 75 percent to 80 percent of executive pay now comes in the form of options. Since all other forms of compensation must be deducted from earnings, options should be treated the same.

- Deducting the cost of options will yield more accurate earnings figures, which should help restore investor confidence.

Not to expense

- Unlike salaries or other perks, granting options requires no cash outlay from companies. Since there is no real cost for the company to deduct, doing so will unjustly penalize earnings.
- Deducting the cost of options will slash earnings, which is likely to drive down share prices.
- Companies will issue far fewer options. That will hurt morale, limit a key tool used to lure talent, and inhibit companies from aligning employee and shareholder interests.
- Tech firms contend that generous option grants have attracted and retained talent and spurred the risk-taking and entrepreneurship so crucial to innovation. Expensing options would sharply reduce their reported profits.
- There are no universal models for expensing options; all valuation methods require big assumptions and estimates. An unreliable estimate of the fair value of options in the income statement would distort earnings.

.01 Option Pricing Models

The big problem with option pricing is that corporations cannot predict what will happen to share prices, who will leave the company before their options vest, and which options will expire underwater—that is, with no value. Hence, they have no way of knowing what options will be worth when they are exercised many years after issue. Unlike shares, which have a market value at all times, the true value of options is only known when they are cashed in, in some cases long after the employees who received them provided their service to the company.

The well-known option-pricing formula, the Black-Scholes option pricing model, uses option terms such as the strike price and life span of the option, stock price, volatility, and dividend yield to estimate future value (to be discussed in detail in Chapter 23). The Black-Scholes model and its many variants have, over the years, become the most widely used methods of valuing employee options for disclosure in financial footnotes. However, they are far from perfect.

Designed for valuing options traded in open stock exchanges, the standard Black-Scholes model is not adjusted to account for the added restrictions of employee options, such as vesting and lack of transferability. Those limits make employee options worth considerably less than exchange-traded options. In fact, firms that use the model to expense options would take a much bigger charge to earnings than is necessary. For example, Bear,

Stearns & Co. estimates that using the Black-Scholes model to expense options would have trimmed 20 percent off the earnings per share of the Standard & Poor's 500-stock index last year. Also, 13 companies, including Microsoft Corp. and Cisco Systems Inc., would each have had to deduct pretax options expenses in excess of $1 billion in 2001 alone.

By waiting until employees exercise their options, then booking the difference between the exercise price and the stock price as an expense, companies would record the precise cost of the options. That sum would equal the amount the company would spend to buy those shares on the open market, or the amount the company is forgoing by not selling the shares and pocketing the funds itself. Also, options that never get exercised never get expensed. This is the only way of accurately stating the true cost of options to the company.

Simply waiting violates, however, most of the accounting principles about expense recognition. Companies are required to deduct expenses during the period in which they are incurred—that's why equipment is amortized over its useful life instead of being expensed when purchased or sold. Expensing options only when they are exercised violates that basic principal, sometimes requiring companies to deduct the option expense long after the employee's period of service. An executive who retires with a boatload of vested options would, in this scenario, create a huge expense when she exercises them—one that should properly have been taken throughout the period of employment.

To achieve much the same result of expensing at the time of exercising, the intrinsic value method can be employed. Under this approach, a firm expenses the difference between the exercise price and the stock price throughout the vesting life of the option, repeatedly updating it as the stock moves. As the stock price rises, options become more valuable, and that additional value is charged to earnings. If the stock declines, options decrease in value, and the charge to earnings evaporates.

Companies that use this method benefit greatly. Unlike Black-Scholes, the simplicity of intrinsic value makes it tough to manipulate. Since the charge to earnings is considerably lower than any of the Black-Scholes variants, it's less disruptive to earnings and the stock price. In a declining market, it is also the only accounting method that does not create a charge for underwater options. Further, the approach may discourage massive option grants to underperforming executives, who frequently get rewarded for failure with grants designed to match the Black-Scholes value of last year's grant.

Note: For volatile stocks the earnings charge is hard to predict, which is why this method is not widely used.

¶ 221 FASB Proposes Consolidation Principles for Special-Purpose Entities (SPEs)

On July 1, 2002, the Financial Accounting Standards Board (FASB) approved for issuance an Exposure Draft of a proposed Interpretation that establishes accounting guidance for consolidation of special-purpose entities (SPEs). The proposed Interpretation, Consolidation of Certain Special-Purpose Entities, will apply to any business enterprise—both public and private companies—that has an ownership interest, contractual relationship, or other business relationship with an SPE. The proposed guidance would not apply to not-for-profit organizations.

The objective of this proposed Interpretation is to improve financial reporting by enterprises involved with SPEs, not to restrict the use of SPEs. However, it is expected that when this proposal is implemented, more SPEs will be consolidated than in the past. Most SPEs serve valid business purposes. Examples include isolating assets or activities to protect the interests of creditors or other investors, or allocating risks among participants. Many SPEs that were unconsolidated prior to the issuance of this proposed Interpretation were reported according to the guidance and accepted practice that existed prior to this proposed Interpretation.

The Financial Accounting Standards Board's proposed rules on "special-purpose entities" would cover the partnerships that Enron created, but their greatest effect would be on "synthetic leases" used by many companies to finance property. In a synthetic lease arrangement, a financial institution sets up a special-purpose entity that borrows money to finance new construction or to purchase an existing building for a company. AOL Time Warner, for example, is financing construction of its new Manhattan headquarters with a synthetic lease arrangement set up by Bank of America Corp.

The FASB is calling for special-purpose entities to be included on a company's balance sheet if less than 10 percent of the equity in an entity is from outside investors. Under existing rules, Enron was able to keep its partnerships off its books even though outsiders' capital was less than 3 percent of the total.

Apart from a specific percentage of outside interest, special-purpose entities should have to be consolidated on companies' books if it is evident that the entities are not truly independent.

Note: The Exposure Draft may be accessed from the FASB's website at www.fasb.org.

¶ 225 FASB Proposes Guidelines for Stock Options

Until recently, nearly all companies granted options without having to officially subtract the options' value from the income statement. Under existing FASB rules, companies need only provide pro forma, or "as if" earnings statements in the footnotes of their annual reports. On August 14, 2002, the FASB proposed the following guidelines:

- Firms opting not to formally expense options require options footnotes to be disclosed quarterly instead of just once a year, and to be more prominent in a company's financial statements. Thus, investors would find it much easier to see those costs.

- Companies planning to treat employee stock options as a normal cost would have three methods for expensing the options under a proposal, expected to take effect in mid-December: The three alternatives are:

    1. Companies could expense options granted since the beginning of the fiscal year in which they decided to start the practice.

    2. They could expense options issued not only since the start of the year but also the unvested part of previous options awards.

    3. A retroactive restatement could be used, where companies would restate three years of prior financial results to reflect options granted during those years.

¶ 231 The New York Stock Exchange's Corporate Governance Rules

Buoyed by the flurry of corporate accounting scandals in recent months, the Corporate Accountability and Listing Standards Committee's report calls for a number of significant new listing requirements. They include:

- An independent majority on a company's board.

- A stricter definition of director independence.

- Regular executive sessions of nonmanagement directors.

- The appointment of a lead director solely to run those meetings.

- Investor approval of all equity-based pay plans.

- A ban on broker votes for such plans unless they get customers' approval.

The new rules would weaken the control that management currently enjoys at many companies. Stronger governance standards will give directors better tools to empower them.

¶ 235 Corporate Responsibility Law

On July 30, 2002, President Bush signed into law H.R. 3763, the "Sarbanes-Oxley Act of 2002" (www.whitehouse.gov/infocus/corporater-esponsibility). This act adopts tough new provisions to deter and punish corporate and accounting fraud and corruption, ensures justice for wrongdoers, and protects the interests of workers and shareholders.

This bill improves the quality and transparency of financial reporting, independent audits, and accounting services for public companies. It also:

- Creates a Public Company Accounting Oversight Board to enforce professional standards, ethics, and competence for the accounting profession;
- Strengthens the independence of firms that audit public companies;
- Increases corporate responsibility and the usefulness of corporate financial disclosure;
- Increases penalties for corporate wrongdoing;
- Protects the objectivity and independence of securities analysts; and
- Increases Securities and Exchange Commission resources.

Under this law, CEOs and chief financial officers must personally vouch for the truth and fairness of their company's disclosures. As a result, those financial disclosures will be broader and better than ever before.

Corporate officials will play by the same rules as their employees. In the periods when workers are prevented from buying and selling company stock in their pensions or 401(k)s, corporate officials will also be banned from any buying or selling.

Corporate misdeeds will be found and punished. This law authorizes new funding for investigators and technology at the SEC to uncover wrongdoing. The SEC will now have the administrative authority to bar dishonest directors and officers from ever again serving in positions of corporate responsibility. The penalties for obstructing justice and shredding documents are greatly increased.

¶ 241 SEC Approves Rules to Address Analyst Conflicts

On May 8, 2002, the SEC approved proposed changes to the rules of the National Association of Securities Dealers and the New York Stock Exchange to address conflicts of interest that are raised when research analysts recommend securities in public communications (www.sec.gov/news/press/2002-63.htm). These conflicts can arise when analysts work for firms that have investment banking relationships with the issuers of the recommended securities, or when the analyst or firm owns securities of the recommended issuer.

These rules include the following provisions, among others:

Promises of favorable research. The rule changes will prohibit analysts from offering or threatening to withhold a favorable research rating or specific price target to induce investment banking business from companies. The rule changes also impose "quiet periods" that bar a firm that is acting as manager or co-manager of a securities offering from issuing a report on a company within 40 days after an initial public offering or within 10 days after a secondary offering for an inactively traded company. Promising favorable research coverage to a company will not be as attractive if the research follows research issued by other analysts.

Limitations on relationships and communications. The rule changes will prohibit research analysts from being supervised by the investment banking department. In addition, investment banking personnel will be prohibited from discussing research reports with analysts prior to distribution, unless staff from the firm's legal/compliance department monitors those communications. Analysts will also be prohibited from sharing draft research reports with the target companies, other than to check facts after approval from the firm's legal/compliance department. This provision helps protect research analysts from influences that could impair their objectivity and independence.

Analyst compensation. The rule changes will bar securities firms from tying an analyst's compensation to specific investment banking transactions. Furthermore, if an analyst's compensation is based on the firm's general investment banking revenues, that fact will have to be disclosed in the firm's research reports. Prohibiting compensation from specific investment banking transactions significantly curtails a potentially major influence on research analysts' objectivity.

Firm compensation. The rule changes will require a securities firm to disclose in a research report if it managed or co-managed a public offering of equity securities for the company or if it received any compensation for investment banking services from the company in the past 12 months. A firm will also be required to disclose if it expects to receive or intends to seek compensation for investment banking services from the company during the next three months. Requiring securities firms to disclose compensation from investment banking clients can alert investors to potential biases in their recommendations.

Restrictions on personal trading by analysts. The rule changes will bar analysts and members of their households from investing in a company's securities prior to its initial public offering if the company is in the business sector that the analyst covers. In addition, the rule changes will require "blackout periods" that prohibit analysts from trading securities of the companies they follow for 30 days before and five days after they issue a research report about the company. Analysts will also be prohibited from trading against their most recent recommendations. Removing analysts' incentives to trade around the time they issue research reports should reduce conflicts arising from personal financial interests.

Disclosures of financial interests in covered companies. The rule changes will require analysts to disclose if they own shares of recommended companies. Firms will also be required to disclose if they own one percent or more of a company's equity securities as of the previous month's end. Requiring analysts and securities firms to disclose financial interests can alert investors to potential biases in their recommendations.

Disclosures in research reports regarding the firm's ratings. The rule changes will require firms to clearly explain in research reports the meaning of all ratings terms they use, and this terminology must be consistent with its plain meaning. Additionally, firms will have to provide the percentage of all the ratings that they have assigned to buy/hold/sell categories and the percentage of investment banking clients in each category. Firms will also be required to provide a graph or chart that plots the historical price movements of the security and indicates those points at which the firm initiated and changed ratings and price targets for the company. These disclosures will assist investors in deciding what value to place on a securities firm's ratings and provide them with better information to assess its research.

Disclosures during public appearances by analysts. The rule changes will require disclosures from analysts during public appearances, such as television or radio interviews. Guest analysts will have to disclose if they or their firm have a position in the stock and also if the company is an investment banking client of the firm. This disclosure will inform investors who learn of analyst opinions and ratings through the media, rather than in written research reports, of analyst conflicts. The SEC will request that the NASD and NYSE report within a year of implementing these rules on their operation and effectiveness, and whether they recommend any changes or additions to the rules.

These rules are part of an ongoing process by the SEC, NASD, NYSE, and the states to address conflicts of interest affecting the production and dissemination of research by securities firms. On April 24, 2002, the SEC announced that it had commenced a formal inquiry into market practices concerning research analysts and the conflicts that can arise from the relationship between research and investment banking. It is possible that this inquiry will indicate the need for further rulemaking by the NASD and NYSE or additional SEC action.

Provisions of these rule changes will take effect 60 to 180 days from issuance of the SEC's order, depending on the provision.

¶ 245 SEC Tightens Its Deadlines for Disclosure

The Securities and Exchange Commission voted on August 27, 2002 to shorten the amount of time companies have to report earnings and to require stock trades by corporate insiders to be disclosed within two days (www.sec.gov/news/press/2002-128.htm). The changes, approved unanimously by the five-member SEC, come on two fronts:

1. Detailed quarterly and annual financial statements will have to be filed more quickly with the SEC. That will reduce the risk that companies will issue rosy news releases about their earnings, only to reveal problems important to investors months later in their official SEC filings.
2. The rules will require company insiders—high-ranking executives, directors, and major shareholders—to report the details of their stock trades more quickly.

¶ 251 The Association for Investment Management and Research's Proposal: The Objectivity of Analysts' Stock Research

On August 19, 2002, the AIMR proposed some of the key ideas to improve the objectivity of analysts' stock research (www.aimr.org/pdf/standards/aimr-ros.pdfll-side). They are:

- Brokerages should establish "three-dimensional" stock rating systems that incorporate measures of risk and a time horizon to help investors assess the suitability of a security for their own circumstances, rather than rely on simple "buy," "sell," or "hold" ratings.
- When discontinuing coverage of a stock, a brokerage should issue a "final" research report and recommendation, explaining the reasons for dropping the issue. Many brokerages have preferred to quietly end coverage of stocks to avoid offending the issuing companies.
- Brokerages should prohibit research analysts from participating in marketing activities, including "road shows," for corporate clients that are issuing new shares.
- Analysts who give media interviews or make other public appearances discussing their stock recommendations should make the full research reports available to the public at a reasonable price.
- Corporations should refrain from making accusations against research analysts in the media. Some companies have publicly criticized analysts when the firms have not liked an analyst's rating of the company.

- Fund managers and other "buy side" investment professionals should be prohibited from threatening to reduce their companies' trading business with a brokerage in an effort to secure a more favorable rating on a security they hold.
- News media should establish formal policies for disclosing conflicts of interest, or potential conflicts, when interviewing analysts or portfolio managers.

Exhibit 1 summarizes points of controversy and related proposals and legislation.

Exhibit 1

Points of Controversy and Related Proposals and Legislation

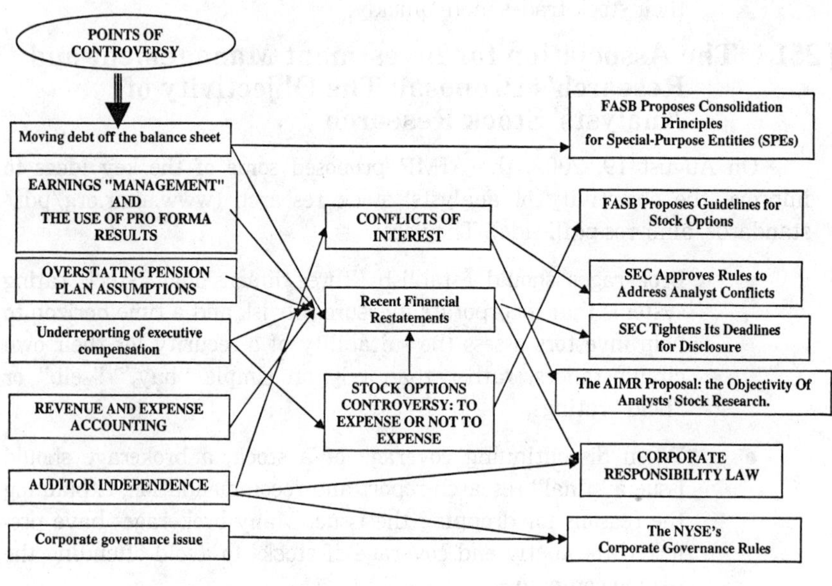

Part 2

Certificates, Associations, and Fields in Finance

Chapter 3

Certifications and Associations in Finance

¶ 301 Overview

There are numerous certifications in the areas of finance, accounting, taxes, insurance, fraud, investments, banking, personal financial planning, and information systems and technology. More are coming.

This chapter briefly describes each of the certifications and associations listed below. (This is by no means an exhaustive list.) Readers may visit the website listed for each entry for more details.

- Certified Public Accountant (CPA)
- Certified Management Accountant (CMA)
- Certified in Financial Management (CFM)
- Certified Cash Manager (CCM)
- Certified Internal Auditor (CIA)

- Certified Cost Estimator/Analyst (CCEA)
- Chartered Financial Analyst (CFA)
- Certified Fraud Examiner (CFE)
- Certified Information Systems Auditor (CISA)
- Certified Bank Auditor (CBA)
- Enrolled Agent (EA)
- Certified Financial Planner (CFP)
- Chartered Financial Consultant (ChFC)
- Personal Financial Specialist (PFS)
- Registered Investment Adviser (RIA)
- Chartered Life Underwriter (CLU)
- Chartered Mutual Fund Counselor (CMFC)
- Financial Management Association (FMA)
- Association for Investment Management and Research (AIMR)
- Mortgage Banking Association (MBA)

¶ 305 Certified Public Accountant (CPA)

CPAs must have a bachelor's degree, pass a national exam, and continually keep up with changing tax laws. The CPA examination consists of the following four parts:

1. Business Law & Professional Responsibilities (3 hours)
2. Auditing (4 1/2 hours)
3. Accounting & Reporting—Taxation, Managerial, & Governmental and Not-for-Profit Organizations (3 1/2 hours)
4. Financial Accounting & Reporting—Business Enterprises (4 1/2 hours)

Note:

1. For more information, call the AICPA at (888) 777-7077 or (201) 938-3750 or visit its website: www.aicpa.org.

American Institute of Certified Public Accountants (AICPA)
Harborside Financial Center
201 Plaza III
Jersey City, NJ 07311-3881

2. The exam is given in the 1st week of May and November (Wednesday and Thursday).

¶ 311 Certified Management Accountant (CMA)

Management accounting has expanded in scope to cover a wide variety of business disciplines such as finance, economics, organizational behavior, and quantitative methods. In line with this development, the Institute of Management Accountants (IMA) created the Institute of Certified Management Accountants, which offers a program leading to the *Certified Management Accountant (CMA)* examination.

The objectives of the CMA program are fourfold: (1) to establish management accounting as a recognized profession by identifying the role of the management accountant and financial manager, the underlying body of knowledge, and a course of study by which such knowledge is acquired; (2) to encourage higher educational standards in the management accounting field; (3) to establish an objective measure of an individual's knowledge and competence in the field of management accounting; and (4) to encourage continued professional development by management accountants.

The CMA program requires candidates to pass a series of uniform examinations covering a wide range of subjects. The examination consists of the following four parts:

1. Economics, Finance, and Management (3 hours)
2. Financial Accounting and reporting (3 hours)
3. Management Reporting, Analysis, and Behavioral Issues (3 hours)
4. Decision Analysis and Information Systems (3 hours)

Note:

1. For more information, call the IMA at (800) 638-4427, ext. 265 or (201) 573-9000 or visit their website: www.imanet.org.

   Institute of Management Accountants (IMA)
   10 Paragon Drive
   Montvale, NJ 07645-1759

2. The exam is given on demand.

¶ 315 Certified in Financial Management (CFM)

The IMA has also created the new CFM (Certified in Financial Management) designation to provide an objective measure of knowledge and competence in the field of financial management. The examination consists of the following four parts:

1. Economics, Finance, and Management (3 hours)
2. Corporate Financial Management (3 hours)

3. Management Reporting, Analysis, and Behavioral Issues (3 hours)
4. Decision Analysis and Information Systems (3 hours)

Note:

1. The CFM is co-sponsored by the prestigious *Financial Management Association International,* whose website is www.fma.org.

2. For more information, call the IMA at (800) 638-4427, ext. 265 or (201) 573-9000 or visit their website: www.imanet.org.

   Institute of Management Accountants (IMA)
   10 Paragon Drive
   Montvale, NJ 07645-1759

3. Review programs on the CMA/CFM exams are offered by Lambers (www.lamberscpa.com, 1-800-272-0707) and MicroMash (www.micromash.com, 1-800-272-pass, ext. 2229).

4. The IMA publishes two important journals: *Management Accounting* (quarterly) and *Strategic Finance* (monthly).

¶ 321 Certified Cash Manager (CCM)

The Certified Cash Manager (CCM) is an examination-based certification and is widely regarded by treasury managers as one of the leading credentials in the field. The CCM program is a professional certification program designed to measure an individual's knowledge of the fundamentals of cash/treasury management and to augment career development through continuing professional education.

The CCM credential serves as a benchmark in the industry and increases the visibility of cash/treasury managers in the corporate workplace. To date, more than 14,000 individuals have earned the CCM credential by successfully passing the CCM examination. CCMs represent corporate, governmental, and institutional professionals with broad responsibility in the treasury profession. CCM certification also enhances customer relations for bankers, cash management consultants, and providers of related services.

Note:

1. The 150 question multiple-choice exam was developed based upon the body of knowledge in Essentials of Cash Management, Seventh Edition published by the Association for Financial Professionals, Inc.

2. The exam is given twice a year.

3. For more information, visit www.afponline.org/Professional_Development/Certification

Association for Financial Professionals, Inc.
7315 Wisconsin Avenue, Suite 600 West
Bethesda, MD 20814

¶ 325 Certified Internal Auditor (CIA)

The Institute of Internal auditors (IIA) created this certification in 1974. The CIA exam is broader than the CPA exam because it covers a broad range of areas, including management, economics, finance, and quantitative methods. The CIA exam lasts 14 hours and covers the following areas:

1. Internal Audit Process (3 1/2 hours)
2. Internal Audit Skills (3 1/2 hours)
3. Management Control and Information Technology (3 1/2 hours)
4. The Audit Environment (3 1/2 hours)

Note:

1. For more information, call the IIA at (407) 830-7600 or visit their website: www.theiia.org.

Institute of Internal auditors (IIA)
249 Maitland Avenue
Altamonte Springs, FL 32701

2. The exam is given in May and November on a Wednesday and Thursday.

¶ 331 Certified Cost Estimator/Analyst (CCEA)

The Society of Cost Estimating and Analysis (SCEA) administers a professional certification program to award the designation of Certified Cost Estimator/Analyst (CCEA) to qualified applicants. Applicants meeting the criteria of education and/or job experience in the area of cost analysis and satisfactorily passing a written examination conducted by the Society are awarded the CCEA designation. The test is a four-hour, two-part examination intended to allow the candidates the opportunity to demonstrate their knowledge of both general theory and quantitative methods applicable to cost estimating or analysis. According to the SCEA, the body of knowledge of cost analysis includes:

1. Basic skills—background knowledge.
2. Cost concepts.
3. Cost theory.
4. Data and measurement.
5. Estimation and testing statistical theory.
6. Analysis techniques.

Note: For more information, call the SCEA at (703) 751-8069, fax them at (703) 461-7328, or visit their website: www.erols.com/scea.

Director of Certification
SCEA National Office
101 South Whiting Street, Suite 201
Alexandria, VA 22304

¶ 335 Chartered Financial Analyst (CFA)

Awarded by the Association for Investment Management and Research (AIMR), the Chartered Financial Analyst (CFA®) Program is a globally recognized standard for measuring the competence and integrity of financial analysts. Three levels of examination measure a candidate's ability to apply the fundamental knowledge of investment principles at a professional level. Two features of the candidate's body of knowledge (CBOK) are especially relevant to the CFA exams. First, the curriculum for each level of the exams is organized primarily around a functional area:

1. The Level I study program emphasizes tools and inputs and includes an introduction to asset valuation and portfolio management techniques.

2. The Level II study program emphasizes asset valuation and includes applications of the tools and inputs (including economics, accounting, and quantitative techniques) in asset valuation.

3. The Level III study program emphasizes portfolio management and includes strategies for applying the tools and inputs in managing equity and fixed-income securities.

The second important feature of the CBOK is that ethical and professional standards are an integral part of all three functional areas of investment management and, hence, are covered at all three levels of the curriculum.

What does it mean to be awarded the CFA charter? Increasingly, employers are recognizing the value of this designation and the potential benefits that an employee with this designation can offer to a company. The CFA charter represents a combination of academic achievement and professional experience along with a commitment to a stringent code of professional and ethical standards. CFAs must annually renew their pledge to abide by the code, and violations of the code can carry severe sanctions.

The investments profession, like many others, involves life-long learning. After receiving the CFA designation, investment professionals can participate in the CFA Accreditation Program in order to remain current on investment issues. This program allows them to earn continuing education credits through a variety of means, including workshops, seminars, and reading on their own.

The AIMR has done an outstanding job of fostering a professional environment for investment practitioners and academics and is the professional organization for investment professionals. Similarly, the CFA professional designation is the designation for serious investment professionals committed to the highest standards of professionalism in investing activities and to the highest possible standards of ethical and professional conduct. All individuals interested in a serious career in the investments field should investigate the possibility of being awarded a CFA charter.

Note: For more information, call the AIMR at 800-247-8132 or visit their website: www.aimr.com.

Association for Investment Management and Research (AIMR)
P.O. Box 3668
560 Ray C. Hunt Dr.
Charlottesville, VA 22903-0668

¶ 341 Certified Fraud Examiner (CFE)

The Association of Certified Fraud Examiners, established in 1988, is based in Austin, Texas. The 25,000-member professional organization is dedicated to educating qualified individuals (Certified Fraud Examiners) who are trained in the highly specialized aspects of detecting, investigating, and deterring fraud and white-collar crime. Each member of the Association designated a Certified Fraud Examiner has earned certification after an extensive application process and upon passing the uniform CFE Examination.

Certified Fraud Examiners come from various professions, including auditors, accountants, fraud investigators, loss prevention specialists, attorneys, educators, and criminologists. CFEs gather evidence, take statements, write reports, and assist in investigating fraud in its varied forms. CFEs work in most major corporations and government agencies and also provide consulting and investigative services.

The exam consists of 500 objective and true/false questions in a Windows format. There are four sections of 125 questions each:

1. Fraudulent Financial Transactions
2. Legal Elements of Fraud
3. Fraud Investigation
4. Criminology and Ethics

Note: For more information, visit the Association of Certified Fraud Examiners at their website: www.cfenet.com/home.asp.

¶ 345 Certified Information Systems Auditor (CISA)

Founded in 1969, the Information Systems Audit and Control Association & Foundation (ISACA) sponsors international conferences, administers the globally respected CISA (Certified Information Systems Auditor) designation earned by more than 26,000 professionals worldwide, and develops globally applicable information systems (IS) auditing and control standards. The examination consists of the following seven parts:

1. Management, Planning, and Organization of IS (11%)
2. Technical Infrastructure and Operational Practices (13%)
3. Protection of Information Assets (25%)
4. Disaster Recovery and Business Continuity (10%)
5. Business Application System Development, Acquisition, Implementation, and Maintenance (16%)
6. Business Process Evaluation and Risk Management (15%)
7. The IS Audit Process (10%)

Note: For more information, visit the ISACA website: www.isaca.org.

The Information Systems Audit and Control Association & Foundation
(ISACA)
3701 Algonquin Road, Suite 1010
Rolling Meadows, Illinois, 60008

¶ 351 Certified Bank Auditor (CBA)

The Bank Administration Institute (BAI) offers the Certified Bank Auditor (CBA) designation, which is recognized throughout the financial services industry as the only certification program that thoroughly tests candidates in four distinct bank-specific areas:

1. Accounting
2. Auditing Principles and Bank Laws/Regulations
3. Auditing Practices
4. General Business

Those who pass the exam will join a network of over 5,000 CBAs from across the United States and abroad. This prestigious network gives CBAs access to key professionals in the financial services industry, as well as the latest information and trends in the business.

Note: For more information, call the BAI at (800) 224-9889 or (312) 683-2464 or visit their website: www.bai.org/cba.

Bank Administration Institute
One North Franklin, Suite 1000
Chicago, Illinois 60606-3421

¶ 355 Enrolled Agent (EA)

To attain the Enrolled Agent designation an individual must pass a two-day tax exam and background check—both administered by the IRS. Or, an individual may become an enrolled agent if he or she has worked for the IRS for at least five years in a job where he or she applied and interpreted IRS provisions, codes, and regulations. The enrollment examination is generally given in September or October. The exact dates, determined in January of each year, are scheduled to avoid religious holidays.

The 11-hour written examination covers federal taxation and tax accounting and the use of tax return forms for individuals, partnerships, corporations, trusts, estates, and gifts. It also covers ethical considerations and procedural requirements. The exam consists of four parts and takes two days to complete. Parts 1 and 2 (3 hours each) are given on the morning (9:00 a.m.–Noon) and afternoon (1:30–4:30 p.m.) of the first day. Parts 3 (3 hours) and 4 (2 hours) are given on the morning (9:00 a.m.–Noon) and afternoon (1:30–3:30 p.m.) of the second day. The questions on the examination are directed toward the tasks that enrolled agents must perform to complete and file forms and tax returns and to represent taxpayers before the IRS. The examination includes true/false and multiple-choice questions and covers the following tax topics:

- Part 1—Individuals.
- Part 2—Sole Proprietorships and Partnerships.
- Part 3—Corporations, Fiduciaries, Estate and Gift Tax, and Trusts.
- Part 4—IRS Administration and Ethics, Recordkeeping Procedures, Appeal Procedures, Exempt Organizations, Retirement Plans, Practitioner Penalty Provisions, Research Materials, and Collection Procedures.

Note:

1. Apply for the Special Enrollment Examination through the IRS on Form 2587. The application form is revised every year to reflect the scheduled examination date. Forms are available after June 1 each year. Obtain the application form by calling the IRS to request Form 2587. You may also obtain this form via the IRS website. Visit www.irs.ustreas.gov/formspubs/index.html and follow the instructions.

2. Also visit the IRS Enrolled Agent Program website: www.irs.gov/taxpros/agents/index.html.

3. For more information, contact the National Association of Enrolled Agents at (800) 424-4339 or visit their website: www.naea.org.

¶ 361 Certificates in Business Valuation

Business valuation is a specialized field that employs sophisticated financial theories and techniques. Rules and guidelines that must be followed come from a diverse group of authorities. There are several valuation methods and each valuation must be performed based on the specific purpose of the valuation. The business model, such as manufacturing, service, sales, etc., must also be taken into account when selecting the methods. Because financial theories and techniques are of paramount importance, business valuations have been historically the domain of professionals with strong finance backgrounds, such as Certified Financial Analysts. Because, the application of such techniques and theories must also take into account the tax law, financial accounting considerations and other topics of keen interest to accountants, there is also a strong association between CPAs and valuation. Because business valuations are often challenged in the courts and contested by the IRS, attorneys are often involved and there is a strong history as well with professionals with litigation support skills.

Unfortunately, for the uninitiated, especially the small business owner, business valuation is often viewed as a relatively simple process. The truth is that business valuation is one of the more challenging fields for finance professionals. There are many books, newsletters, software packages, financial services and databases dedicated to helping business valuators perform their difficult task. For comprehensive practical guidance on business valuation, refer to CCH Business Valuation Guide by George Hawkins and Michael Pachall. The discussion below on accreditation and certifications is adapted from this publication.

.01 Business Appraisal Accreditations

There are four national certifications, each one developed by one of four national accrediting organizations, with each organization providing its own education and testing programs. The designations are as follows:

1. Accredited Senior Appraiser (ASA) and Accredited Member (AM) awarded by the American Society of Appraisers (ASA).

2. Certified Business Appraiser (CBA) awarded by The Institute of Business Appraisers (IBA).

3. Certified Valuation Analyst (CVA) awarded by the National Association of Certified Valuation Analysts (NACVA).

4. Accredited in Business Valuation (ABV) awarded by the American Institute of Certified Public Accountants (AICPA).

All four organizations provide excellent training for prospective business appraisers, and their certifications enhance valuation professionalism. Each group offers an array of introductory and advanced valuation courses, along with continuing education programs, seminars, and conferences. These groups also work together in various ways to develop valuation standards and terminology.

In addition, the Chartered Financial Analyst (CFA) awarded by the Association for Investment Management and Research (AIMR), parent organization of the Institute of Chartered Financial Analysts, is another important accreditation. While not specifically a business valuation certification, the CFA covers valuation in depth, both of public and private companies, along with a broad-based, inclusive study of other investment subjects. It is among the most prestigious of all certifications in the field of corporate finance and on Wall Street.

.02 The Five Accrediting Organizations

Each of the accrediting organizations and the benefits, certification requirements, and educational programs they offer to prospective business appraisers are discussed below. Because of the variety and excellence of the organizations' offerings, many valuators are members of more than one.

American Society of Appraisers. The American Society of Appraisers (ASA) is the oldest multidisciplinary appraisal society in the United States (originating in 1936). The ASA's 6,500 members have or are candidates for certification in the five fields:

1. Business valuation (including patents, trademarks, copyrights, and other intangible assets);
2. Real property;
3. Machinery and technical specialties;
4. Personal property; and
5. Gems and jewelry.

ASA valuation certifications. The ASA offers two certifications in the field of business valuation to candidates who first pass an extensive approval and certification process:

1. Accredited Senior Appraiser (ASA)
2. Accredited Member (AM)

The difference between the ASA and AM designations is the experience requirement. The ASA candidate must possess at least five years full-time experience preparing business valuations, while the AM candidate needs only two years.

ASA years of experience requirement. The ASA uses a full-time equivalent basis to determine each candidate's years of experience. For example, if a CPA spends 20 percent of his or her typical year preparing business valuations and the other 80 percent on financial statement and tax return preparation, only 20 percent of the year would count toward meeting the experience requirement. However, the ASA does exempt CPAs with five or more years of practice experience, even if not in the area of valuation, from one year of the minimum experience requirements. Similarly, it exempts holders of the CFA certification from one year of the minimum experience requirements.

ASA courses. All candidates for either designation must take and pass four four-day courses, each of which includes a comprehensive examination. ASA's courses are offered on a rotating basis throughout the year and at various cities throughout the country. The courses provide a comprehensive treatment of business valuation, starting at a basic level and proceeding to advanced valuation topics such as estate and gift tax, Employee Stock Ownership Plans (ESOPs), dissenting minority shareholder cases, and other issues.

As a prerequisite to taking the advanced courses, an individual must already have a solid grounding in accounting and finance and pass the four basic courses listed below:

- BV 201-Introduction to Business Valuation, Part One
- BV 202-Introduction to Business Valuation, Part Two
- BV 203-Business Valuation Case Study
- BV 204-Business Valuation—Selected Advanced Topics

As an alternative to taking the basic courses above, a candidate may attempt to take and pass the examination for each course without attending class. Unless one is extremely experienced and well read in business valuation, these exams will be difficult to pass.

Taking the courses themselves is highly beneficial and is the preferred route for even the most experienced professional. The courses provide a detailed treatment of many complex issues, including a number of techniques that are evolving and to which the individual may have had no previous exposure. Just as important, the interplay with other business appraisers in the class leads to the sharing of different approaches and views to which the professional might otherwise not be exposed. A typical class might have representatives from large and small valuation and accounting practices, investment banking firms, and the IRS, each with different valuation viewpoints.

ASA ethics and standards exams. Once the candidate meets the experience and education requirements, he or she must also pass an exam on ethics, as well as one concerning the Uniform Standards of Professional Appraisal Practice.

The ASA actively promotes standards and ethics for the business valuation profession. Candidates, members, and accredited senior members of the ASA are required to adhere to the ASA's rigorous Business Valuation Standards, which set forth the mandated report content and definitions. The ASA also has a rigorous code of ethics that establishes a high degree of professionalism. In addition, the American Society of Appraisers is the only society representing business appraisers that is a member of The Appraisal Foundation, the body mandated by Congress to issue and enforce appraisal standards.

ASA report requirements. After successfully meeting the ASA experience, course, and exam requirements, the candidate must submit two actual valuation reports to the ASA's International Board of Examiners for review for technical competency. This Board carefully reviews the valuations to ensure that they meet the ASA's Business Valuation Standards and the Uniform Standards of Professional Appraisal Practice (USPAP), compliance with which is mandated by federal law. They also check that the valuations are sound, well supported, and professionally prepared.

The ASA and The Institute of Business Appraisers, Inc. (IBA) are the only two bodies certifying business appraisers that have any report review requirement. Many experts suggest that the report is where "the rubber meets the road" in business valuation. A candidate with a great deal of experience and training must also show his or her competency in preparing a professional, supported business valuation.

ASA continuing education programs. Once professionals earn the ASA designation, their education does not end. Every five years ASAs must recertify by demonstrating that they have met a continuing education requirement and are actively involved and experienced in business valuation.

The ASA has an outstanding continuing education program to maintain and enhance skills. It offers two courses:

- BV 205-Valuation of Small Businesses and Professional Practices
- BV 206-Valuation of Employee Stock Ownership Plans

In addition, the ASA holds an advanced business valuation conference each year. Attended by valuators from throughout the nation, this two-day conference features seminars and workshops on a variety of contemporary valuation topics by leaders in the field.

ASA publications. The Business Valuation Committee of the ASA publishes *Business Valuation Review,* a quarterly journal covering a variety of business valuation issues, techniques, controversies, and studies. Readers also submit challenging letters to the editor debating positions elicited in prior articles, making it easy for valuators to see many alternative points of view. As one of the oldest valuation publications, it is a must-read for any valuation professional and an important tool in research for specific valuation assignments. *Business Valuation Review* has been published since 1982, and it is possible to purchase a complete set of all prior issues, a high priority for any new valuation library.

ASA candidates, members, and nonmembers are welcome to subscribe. For information, contact:

Business Valuation Review
2777 South Colorado Boulevard, Suite 200
Denver, CO 80222
Phone: (303) 758-6148
Fax: (303) 758-6164

The ASA also publishes *Valuation*, a multi-disciplinary appraisal journal, on a periodic basis varying from one to two times per year. *Valuation* typically includes high-quality articles on contemporary valuation topics authored by leaders in the valuation field. For information, contact:

Valuation
P.O. Box 17265
Washington, DC 20041
Phone: (703) 478-2228

Contacting the ASA. To learn more about the American Society of Appraisers, its education programs, and publications, contact:

American Society of Appraisers
555 Herndon Parkway, Suite 125
Herndon, VA 20170
Phone: (800) ASA-VALU
Internet: www.appraisers.org

The Institute of Business Appraisers, Inc. Established in 1978, The Institute of Business Appraisers, Inc. (IBA) is the oldest appraisal society focusing solely on business appraisal. It was the first organization to certify business appraisers and establish a dedicated training program. The IBA's membership of more than 3,000 includes business appraisers, accountants, attorneys, and business brokers, most of whom value smaller businesses and professional practices.

The IBA offers its members the potential to earn accreditation as a Certified Business Appraiser (CBA) after demonstrating competence and professionalism in business valuation. In addition, it offers a less rigorous professional designation, Accredited by IBA (AIBA). This designation was developed to encourage IBA members and others in the appraisal community to obtain additional education and to start members on the road to the

Certified Business Appraiser (CBA) designation. Finally, it offers the Business Valuator Accredited for Litigation (BVAL) designation. The IBA indicates that "the designation is designed to recognize experienced business appraisers who demonstrate their ability to competently present expert testimony which supports their objective conclusion of value."

IBA courses. IBA's educational offerings include the following:

- IBA 2001-Fundamentals of Valuing Midsize and Smaller Businesses (two-day seminars)
- IBA 2002-Advanced Theory and Applications of Business Valuation (two-day seminars)
- IBA 8001-Mastering Appraisal Skills for Valuing the Closely Held Business (eight-day workshop)
- IBA 7001-Litigation Support and Expert Witness Training for the Business Appraiser (seven-day workshop)

In addition to their extensive education program, IBA also offers seminars and conventions.

IBA Market Database. All IBA members have access to IBA's Market Database, a proprietary database of private transaction and comparable sales information. Market Database is the largest database of guideline transactions for valuing midsized and smaller businesses, and it is worth the price of membership alone. The database includes information on more than 12,500 actual sales of closely held businesses in more than 600 industries. Access to the database is free to IBA members in good standing. IBA members may request data by SIC Codes in hard copy as well as electronic format (Excel spreadsheet). Data requests are delivered by e-mail, or by mail if requesting a disk.

IBA technical assistance and other resources. IBA members may also ask questions to technical assistance; valuators who are experts on the particular topic involved will answer. In addition, a valuation bibliographic database exists along with the IBA's website (www.instbusapp.org). The IBA website contains an especially helpful web page with links to a variety of useful Internet resources, including business valuation organizations, accounting and public company information, economic data, industry research and regulations, and demographic data.

Business Appraisal Reports Library. The Institute of Business Appraisers makes available to members and interested parties its Business Appraisal Reports Library. Produced on CD-Rom, and in hard copy, the library provides full sample business valuation reports of a variety of types and for various purposes.

Business Appraisal Practice. The Institute of Business Appraisers publishes an outstanding semi-annual journal on business valuation issues, entitled *Business Appraisal Practice.* In addition to articles on contemporary valuation issues and techniques, the journal has an interesting experts' corner where tricky valuation issues are posed to various experts who provide their own (and often differing) views as to how the issue at hand should be dealt with and why.

IBA exam. To earn accreditation as a Certified Business Appraiser (CBA), candidates must pass a 3.5-hour written examination covering the theory and practice of business appraisal. The exam is given at selected sites in the spring and fall of each year and at IBA's national conference. Applicants may be exempt from the exam if they:

- Hold an Accredited Senior Appraiser (ASA) designation in business valuation from the American Society of Appraisers;
- Have earned the Certificate of Educational Achievement (CEA) certificate in business valuation or the Accredited in Business Valuation (ABV) designation from the American Institute of Certified Public Accountants; or
- Hold the Certified Valuation Analyst (CVA) designation from the National Association of Certified Valuation Analysts.

IBA report requirements and standards. After passing the examination, the applicant must submit two business appraisal reports for review. The reports must demonstrate the applicant's ability to perform original appraisal work of good quality, and they must conform to the requirements of IBA's Business Appraisal Standards. The IBA was the first to establish business valuation standards and has been an important force in fostering professionalism in business valuation.

Business appraisers new to the field and with less experience may want to consider obtaining the IBA's Accredited by IBA (AIBA) designation. The designation was developed to provide an entry into the field for those who do not have two suitable appraisal reports to submit for review (as required by the CBA designation), or who wish to obtain more business valuation education before becoming a candidate for the CBA designation.

To achieve the AIBA designation, the IBA indicates that the candidate must:

- Attend all sessions of the 8-day Appraisal Workshop;
- Complete all Workshop assignments;
- Pass the written exam, which concludes the Workshop;
- Submit for peer review a completed appraisal based on the Workshop problem, or another appraisal (the appraisal report must pass the scrutiny of the AIBA Qualifications Review Committee).

Pass a character and fitness screening. Passage of the above requirements entitles an IBA member to use the AIBA designation for three years as a transitional period in the individual's move towards the CBA designation. By the end of the three years, the member is required to have entered the full CBA process, which requires a new application, application fee, and peer review of two appraisal reports by IBA's Qualifications Review Committee.

Contacting the IBA. For more information, contact the IBA at any of the following:

The Institute of Business Appraisers, Inc.
P.O. Box 17410
Plantation, FL 33318
Phone: 954-584-1144
Fax: 954-584-1184
Internet: www.instbusapp.org

National Association of Certified Valuation Analysts. The National Association of Certified Valuation Analysts (NACVA) is one of the youngest of the bodies accrediting business appraisers, having been formed in 1990. Despite its young age, NACVA has grown rapidly and has more than 3,300 members, most of them CPAs.

NACVA valuation certifications. NACVA offers its members the opportunity to earn the following accreditations in business valuation:

1. Certified Valuation Analyst (CVA)
2. Government Valuation Analyst (GVA)
3. Accredited Valuation Analyst (AVA)

To earn the CVA certification, the candidate must attend a five-day training program, then pass a take-home examination. In addition, the candidate must hold a valid CPA certificate.

In the year after the exam, the new CVA must attend (or take by self-study) a course on report writing, ethics, and standards. There is no business valuation experience requirement for candidates to submit copies of actual business valuations for review for technical competency. NACVA does require its members to prepare an analysis based on a valuation case study. Similarly, there is no requirement for candidates to submit copies of actual business valuations for review for technical competency, as is required by the American Society of Appraisers and The Institute of Business Appraisers, Inc.

NACVA is the first society to seize the opportunity to establish a new Government Valuation Analyst (GVA) certification for members of governmental bodies who must either perform or review business valuations. Its requirements are similar to the CVA's.

NACVA also offers the Accredited Valuation Analyst (AVA) designation, which offers certification in the field for those who do not hold a CPA certificate, but have demonstrated experience and training in business valuation. To obtain the AVA designation, NACVA indicates that the applicant must:

1. Hold a business degree (i.e., management, economics, finance, marketing, accounting, or other business field) and/or an MBA (Masters in Business Administration) or higher Business Degree from an accredited college or university.

2. Be able to demonstrate with business references or attestations from previous employers and/or partners substantial experience in business valuation. For this purpose, substantial could mean:

   a. Two (2) years or more full-time or equivalent experience in business valuation and related disciplines (such as mergers and acquisition work, securities analyst for a major brokerage concern, economic loss analysis, etc.); or

   b. Having performed ten (10) or more business valuations where the applicant's role was significant enough such that they were referenced in the valuation report or a signatory on the report; or

   c. Being able to demonstrate substantial knowledge of business valuation concepts having: published works on the subject; completed graduate work in the field; obtained accreditation from another recognized business valuation accrediting organization.

3. Pass a pre-qualification examination focused mostly on subject matter related to accounting fundamentals and forensic accounting concepts as might be applicable in business valuation theory and practice. The proctored exam requires a fee and will take up to eight hours to complete. It is offered at nationwide testing centers. Applicants holding a CFA (Chartered Financial Analyst) or CMA (Certified Management Accountant) designation or those having obtained a Masters (or higher) degree in accounting can exempt out of the pre-qualification examination. Applicants may request an exemption from the exam in writing, explaining their reasons and justification for such exemption. Requests will be submitted to the Certification Board for approval.

4. Be a member in good standing with NACVA.

5. Complete a program of training as prescribed by the Association.

6. Submit three (3) personal and three (3) business references.

7. Pass a comprehensive two-part examination. Part 1 is a half-day proctored exam and Part 2 is a take-home/in-office exam that incorporates essay questions and a standardized case study (provided by NACVA) that requires performing a complete business valuation. Part 2 of the exam takes 30-50 hours to complete.

An application to take the examination must be submitted prior to issuance of the exam. To hold an active AVA certification individuals must maintain current membership in NACVA. AVA's who allow their membership to lapse will lose their certification and must reapply to become an AVA if they later choose to reinstate their membership.

An exciting aspect of the AVA designation is that it gives the ability for the non-CPA business appraiser to obtain a NACVA certification.

NACVA benefits. Although young, NACVA has been among the most innovative and aggressive of all of the valuation societies at seeking to provide valuable support and services to business appraisers. These include:

- Training and education programs.
- Telephone counseling.
- Mentor support for valuation problems and issues.
- Newsletters and publications including the *Valuation Examiner*, a bimonthly journal on contemporary business valuation issues.
- Comparable sales database.
- Proprietary valuation software package, Valuation Master, for purchase.

In addition, NACVA has an extensive national network of local member chapters that are actively involved in hosting local and regional valuation conferences. Members also have access to extensive resources on NACVA's Internet site, as well as the ability to request resources from the association's library. Finally, NACVA has been among the most responsive to providing its members extensive tools, brochures, prepared seminar packages, and other products to help market their business valuation practices.

Contacting NACVA. For more information on NACVA, contact:

National Association of Certified Valuation Analysts
1245 East Brickyard Road
Suite 110
Salt Lake City, UT 84106

Phone: (801) 486-0600
Fax: (801) 486-7500
Internet: www.nacva.com.

American Institute of Certified Public Accountants. The American Institute of Certified Public Accountants (AICPA) is the national society of certified public accountants.

Accredited in Business Valuation (ABV). Beginning in the late fall of 1997, AICPA offered the first ABV certifying exam for CPAs. To earn the ABV designation, a candidate must hold a valid CPA certificate or license and pass an all-day examination on business valuation theory.

AICPA substantial experience requirement. In addition, the candidate must fill out an application with a paragraph description of ten valuation assignments in which he or she demonstrated substantial experience and competence. AICPA defined "substantial experience" as:

> [s]ufficient research and analysis to arrive at a conclusion or estimate of value of an entity, instrument or economic benefit requiring a documented conclusion.

AICPA continuing education requirement. To maintain accreditation, every three years the ABV holder must demonstrate substantial involvement in five new business valuation assignments and complete a 60-hour continuing education requirement.

The AICPA does not presently have a set of valuation report standards, although as of this edition it is presently working on developing them.

Comparisons. A weakness of the AICPA's ABV designation is its lack of a requirement to submit actual valuation reports for review for technical competency. Additionally, its requirement of substantial experience (ten valuation assignments) is very modest. Furthermore, the substantial experience requirement for accreditation does not require that the person actually had full responsibility for the engagement; a person might have played a minor role in the assignment. The AICPA defines participating in a valuation as:

> [d]efining the engagement/project objectives, planning the specific procedures appropriate to the engagement/project, developing a basis for a conclusion, and documenting a conclusion.

Contacting the AICPA. For more information on the AICPA ABV program, contact:

American Institute of Certified Public Accountants
Coordinator, ABV Program
1211 Avenue of the Americas
New York, NY 10036-8775
Phone: (212) 596-6254
Fax: (212) 596-6268

Association for Investment Management and Research. Another important certification, while not directly aimed at business valuation, is applicable in many ways. It is the Chartered Financial Analyst (CFA).

The CFA certification is issued by the Association of Investment Management and Research (AIMR), created in 1990 from the merger of the Financial Analysts Federation and the Institute of Chartered Financial Analysts. AIMR currently represents more than 50,000 investment professionals in over 100 countries.

The CFA reputation. The CFA is considered by many to be the premiere certification in the fields of investment banking, mergers and acquisitions, investment management, and securities analysis. In these fields, the CFA program is so highly regarded that it is difficult or impossible to advance in a career without it. Because of the quality of the program, many states now exempt CFA holders from having to pass securities licensing exams. Many business valuators also hold the CFA designation, and among many national business valuation firms either the CFA and/or the ASA is typically required to hold a senior business valuation position. Since 1963 thousands of CFA charters have been issued, and the CFA program is one of the fastest growing financial certifications worldwide, experiencing explosive growth.

AIMR requirements and training. To earn the CFA, candidates must pass a grueling, but intellectually rewarding, three-year program of study in:

- Financial analysis,
- Corporate finance,
- The valuation of equities (stocks), fixed income (bonds) and derivative securities (options and futures),
- Investment analysis,
- Economic analysis, and
- Portfolio management.

Successful candidates must pass three comprehensive all-day examinations, one held each year. The CFA program, while it is more focused on publicly traded companies, has a heavy emphasis on valuation and also covers privately held company topics.

Skill building. The CFA is a superb program that any valuation professional should strongly consider undertaking. In addition to providing a solid grounding in valuation techniques like the other certifications, the CFA program goes much further. In particular, it provides analysts the tools to meet the challenges of dealing with the rapidly increasing complexity of corporate finance arrangements. Closely held businesses now have many of the same financial tools at their disposal as do larger public companies, including derivative securities (options, futures, swaps, swap-options, interest rate caps, collars, and so on), and off-balance-sheet financing arrangements. These investments can directly and significantly affect the financial results, risks, and values of private companies and are important for the analyst to understand and assess. The CFA program helps build these skills.

Career flexibility. Additionally, the CFA program provides comprehensive training in financial, economic and industry analysis, and forecasting, and requires extensive readings from leading researchers in the fields of finance, economics, and portfolio management. Beyond stocks, bonds, and derivative securities, the program exposes the CFA candidate to extensive readings concerning investments in real estate, real estate securities, venture capital, and international securities. One noteworthy plus to having a CFA charter is that it adds career flexibility extending well beyond the field of business valuation.

AIMR benefits. Membership in AIMR also brings a number of valuable benefits, particularly in the area of financial research, seminars, and other continuing education programs. Financial Analysts Journal, a highly regarded research publication, is published quarterly by AIMR, and it includes many articles of use to business valuators. Additionally, AIMR holds seminars throughout the nation each year on finance, valuation, economics, industry research, investing, and portfolio management topics. Even though the CFA might not be able to attend, proceedings are published and distributed to AIMR members. Many of these publications are valuation-related and represent valuable resources for any valuation practice.

Contacting the AIMR. For more information on the CFA program, contact the Association for Investment Management and Research at:

The CFA Program
Association for Investment Management and Research
5 Boar's Head Lane
P.O. Box 3668
Charlottesville, Virginia 22903
Phone: (804) 980-3668 or (800) 247-8132
Fax: (804) 980-9755
Internet: www.aimr.org

¶ 365 Personal Financial Planning Certifications

.01 Credentials

Financial planners come from a variety of backgrounds and, therefore, may hold a variety of degrees and licenses. Some take specialized training in financial planning and earn credentials such as certified financial planner (CFP) or chartered financial consultant (ChFC). Others may hold degrees or registrations such as attorney (JD), chartered life underwriter (CLU), or certified public accountant (CPA). For information on personal financial planning careers, see ¶ 421.

Certified financial planner (CFP). To become a CFP, a designation conferred by the Certified Financial Planners Board of Standards, a candidate must take a two-year course. The six parts of the course, each capped by a three-hour test, are the following:

1. Introduction to financial planning
2. Risk management (insurance)
3. Investments
4. Tax planning and management
5. Retirement planning and employee benefits
6. Estate planning

The candidate must pass a two-day exam covering more than 100 financial planning topics. Three to five years of financial planning work experience is also required.

Note: For more information, contact the Certified Financial Planners Board of Standards at (303) 830-7500 or (888) CFP-MARK, fax them at (303) 860-7388, or visit their website: www.CFP-Board.org.

CFP Board
1700 Broadway, Suite 2100
Denver, Colorado 80290-2101

Other financial planning and investment designations are described below.

Chartered financial consultant (ChFC). A candidate must have three years of experience in financial services and must complete a 10-course curriculum that focuses on comprehensive financial planning issues. This designation is awarded by American College in Bryn Mawr, Pa. For information, call the Society of Financial Service Professionals. (Phone: (610) 526-2500. Website: www.financialpro.org.)

Personal financial specialist (PFS). This designation is awarded to CPAs who have at least three years of financial planning experience, pass a six-hour financial planning exam, and complete 72 hours of continuing education every three years. The candidate must be a member of the American Institute of Certified Public Accountants. (Phone: (888) 777-7077. Website: www.aicpa.org/members/div/pfp/index.htm.)

Registered representative. To become a stockbroker, the candidate must pass exams administered by the National Association of Securities

Dealers as well as any exams required by the state. All registered representatives—including financial planners—who execute, buy, or sell orders for mutual funds, stocks, bonds, commodities, or other securities for clients for compensation must be licensed by the appropriate state securities agency and registered with the NASD. (Phone: (800) 289-9999. Website: www.nasdr.com.)

Registered investment adviser (RIA). Anyone can become an RIA by registering with the Securities and Exchange Commission, filing a form, and paying a fee. An RIA who only manages money in a no-load mutual fund for a percentage of assets is not required to register with the National Association of Securities Dealers or the state. (Phone: (800) 289-9999. Website: www.nasdr.com.)

Chartered life underwriter (CLU). This designation is awarded to life insurance agents who complete 10 insurance-related courses. It is awarded by American College in Bryn Mawr, Pa. For information, call the Society of Financial Service Professionals. (Phone: (610) 526-2500. Website: www.financialpro.org.)

Chartered mutual fund counselor (CMFC). This new designation offered by the National Endowment for Financial Education enhances the ability of financial advisors to speak directly to their clients' mutual fund questions and concerns. (Website: www.financial-planning.com/wwwboard5/messages/1703.html.)

¶ 371 Professional Finance Associations

.01 Financial Management Association International

Financial Management Association International, established in 1970, is a global leader in developing and disseminating knowledge about financial decision making.

FMA's members include finance practitioners, academicians, and students who are interested in the techniques and advances that define the field of finance.

The mission of FMA International is to serve the global finance community by:

- Broadening the common interests between academics and practitioners.
- Providing opportunities for professional interaction between and among academics, practitioners, and students.
- Promoting the development and understanding of basic and applied research and of sound financial practices.
- Enhancing the quality of education in finance.

Note: For more information, call the FMA at (813) 974-2084, fax them at (813) 974-3318, e-mail them at fma@coba.usf.edu, or visit their website: www.fma.org.

Financial Management Association International
University of South Florida
College of Business Administration
Tampa, FL 33620-5500

.02 The Association for Investment Management and Research (AIMR)

The Association for Investment Management and Research, which was fully described earlier at ¶ 361.02, is an international, nonprofit organization of more than 50,000 investment practitioners and educators in over 100 countries.

Founded in January 1990, AIMR was created from the merger of the Financial Analysts Federation (FAF) and the Institute of Chartered Financial Analysts (ICFA). The FAF was originally established in 1947 as a service organization for investment professionals in its societies and chapters. The ICFA was founded in 1959 to examine candidates and award the Chartered Financial Analyst (CFA) designation.

AIMR's mission is to serve its members and investors as a global leader in educating and examining investment managers and analysts and sustaining high standards of professional conduct. AIMR's membership is global in scope, and its activities are worldwide.

The Research Foundation of the AIMR sponsors practitioner-oriented research through funding and publishing a diverse assortment of monographs, tutorials, and research papers to broaden investment professionals' knowledge and understanding of their field.

AIMR offers services in three broad categories: Education through seminars and publications; Professional Conduct and Ethics; and Standards of Practice and Advocacy.

AIMR's members are employed as securities analysts, portfolio managers, strategists, consultants, educators, and other investment specialists. These professionals practice in a variety of fields, including investment counseling and management, banking, insurance, and investment banking and brokerage firms.

Note: For more information, visit the AIMR website: www.aimr.com.

.03 Mortgage Bankers Association of America (MBA)

Mortgage Bankers Association of America is the preeminent association representing the real estate finance industry. MBA serves its membership by representing their legislative and regulatory interests before the United States Congress and federal agencies, by meeting their educational needs through programs and a range of periodicals and publications, and by supporting their business interests with a variety of research initiatives and other products and services.

The industry MBA represents plays a vital role in the national economy and in building and sustaining the communities in which Americans live, work, shop, and play. The mortgage finance industry is the engine that generates the capital to build and own homes, apartments, offices, hotels, shops, and theaters—almost all of our physical surroundings. The MBA industry links the housing and community financing needs of a rapidly changing marketplace to the capital markets of the nation and the world. It is an industry that has continued to grow and adapt to ever-changing economic, demographic, technological, and political realities. Today, the real estate finance industry is the largest segment of the U.S. capital markets. It holds a central place in the everyday lives of all Americans, and in the well being of our nation.

Though the objectives of MBA and its members are many and varied, there are a few overriding goals that remain constant, and that provide focus and continuity to what they do. These are to:

- Achieve the lowest possible cost of credit for homebuyers and other real estate borrowers.
- Maintain a stable, efficient, and assured source of mortgage credit.
- Create an environment for an efficient, profitable real estate finance industry.
- Work in partnership with the Federal National Mortgage Association (Fannie Mae), the Federal Home Loan Mortgage Corporation (Freddie Mac), and the Government National Mortgage Association (Ginnie Mae) to preserve an efficient secondary mortgage market.
- Ensure that federal legislation and regulation provides for safety and soundness and consumer protection, without undue burdens and costs on private industry or on consumer choice.

The industry MBA represents, mortgage banking, is involved in making, selling, and servicing mortgages secured by residential or commercial (i.e., income-producing) real estate. Mortgage bankers serve as middlemen, arranging and making loans using short-term funding, and then selling these loans to other lenders and investors, both within the U.S. secondary market and abroad. The buyers of mortgages include private conduits, commercial banks, thrifts, life insurance companies, pension funds, and, most significantly, the secondary market agencies—Fannie Mae, Freddie Mac and Ginnie Mae—through various securitization programs. Though some mortgage banking companies may be subsidiaries of depository institutions or their holding companies, mortgage companies themselves do not receive money from individual depositors.

Mortgage bankers are the primary suppliers of loans to the secondary market through programs administered by Fannie Mae, Freddie Mac and Ginnie Mae. Fannie Mae and Freddie Mac purchase primarily conventional mortgage loans, while Ginnie Mae is involved with government loans exclusively. All three agencies were created with a mission to provide liquidity to the mortgage market and affordable housing to homebuyers and renters. They currently channel approximately two-thirds of total home mortgage credit and, working with their mortgage banker partners, they have reduced the interest rate cost of credit by as much as 1/2 percent, according to housing experts.

Mortgage bankers also make use of a number of federal and state government programs to provide more affordable housing credit. For example, the U.S. Federal Housing Administration (FHA) provides mortgage insurance for residential mortgages. Over the course of its over 60-year history, FHA has insured home loans for some 20 million Americans. The U.S. Department of Veterans' Affairs (VA) administers the VA Home Loan Guaranty program, which enables mortgage lenders to offer long-term, low down payment mortgage financing to eligible veterans. Mortgage bankers have long been the primary originators of FHA and VA loans. In addition, through a wide variety of state programs, mortgage bankers are the delivery vehicles for providing low interest rate financing to moderate-income homebuyers.

Mortgage bankers, in conjunction with their lending partners, serve a critical need in the United States. They make homeownership possible for tens of millions of Americans. They also help to build communities by providing financing for places where people can work and shop and play. And, they create important investment opportunities for the world's capital markets.

Note: For more information, visit the MBA website: www.mbaa.org.

Chapter 4

Fields in Finance

¶ 401 Overview

The fields in finance are perhaps more diverse than any other fields in business administration. A variety of organizations—commercial, non-profit, service, merchandising, and manufacturing—employ finance professionals as financial managers, financial analysts, and financial executives, such as the controller, treasurer, and the Chief Financial Officer (CFO). Financial professionals are also engaged in financial services as financial advisors, financial planners, financial consultants, brokers, bankers, and investment representatives. Following is a list of some areas of finance.

- Financial Management
- Financial Analysis
- Cash/Credit Management
- Commercial Banking
- Investments
- Investment Banking
- Personal Financial Planning
- Mortgage Banking

¶ 405 Careers in Financial Management

Among a variety of areas of finance, financial management offers the greatest number of career opportunities. Financial management is important to commercial businesses as well as nonprofit and governmental agencies.

.01 Financial Managers

The financial manager—the controller, treasurer, or CFO— plays an important role in the company's goals, policies, and financial success. The financial manager's responsibilities include the following:

- *Financial analysis and planning.* Determining the proper amount of funds to employ in the firm; that is, designating the size of the firm and its rate of growth.
- *Investment decisions.* Allocating funds to specific assets (things owned). The financial manager makes decisions regarding the mix and type of assets acquired, as well as modification or replacement of assets.
- *Financing and capital structure decisions.* Raising funds on favorable terms; that is, determining the nature of the company's liabilities (obligations). For instance, should funds be obtained from short-term or long-term sources?
- *Management of financial resources.* Managing cash, receivables, and inventory to accomplish higher returns without undue risk.

The financial manager affects stockholder wealth maximization by influencing:

1. Present and future earnings per share (EPS).
2. Timing and risk of earnings.
3. Dividend policy.
4. Manner of financing.

Exhibit 1 presents the functions of the financial manager.

Exhibit 1

Functions of the Financial Manager

A. Planning

Long- and short-range financial and corporate planning

Budgeting for operations and capital expenditures

Evaluating performance

Pricing policies and sales forecasting

Analyzing economic factors

Appraising acquisitions and divestment

B. Provision of capital

Short-term sources; cost and arrangements

Long-term sources; cost and arrangements

Internal generation

C. Administration of Funds

Cash management

Banking arrangements

Receipt, custody, and disbursement of companies' securities and moneys

Credit and collection management

Managing pension moneys

Investment portfolio management

D. Accounting and Control

Establishing accounting policies

Development and reporting of accounting data

Cost accounting

Internal auditing

Systems and procedures

Government reporting

Reporting and interpretation of results of operations to management

Comparison of performance with operating plans and standards

E. Protection of Assets

Providing for insurance

Establishing sound internal controls

F. Tax Administration

Establishing tax policies

Preparation of tax reports

Tax planning

G. Investor Relations

Acting as liaison with the investment community

Providing public financial information to stock analysts

H. Evaluation and Consulting

Consulting with and advising other corporate executives on company policies, operations, objectives, and their degree of effectiveness

I. Management Information Systems

Development and use of computerized facilities
Development and use of management information systems
Development and use of systems and procedures

.02 Financial Analysts

Financial analysts, usually working for the controller, are employed by almost any business organization—for-profit, nonprofit, service, merchandising, and manufacturing.

Their responsibilities include the following:

- Provide financial analysis and business decision support to upper level management.
- Develop financial plans and capital and operating budgets.
- Recommend budget adjustments and other cost improvement measures.
- Analyze complex financial data for the purpose of evaluating past financial performance and/or to project a financial probability.
- Perform cost estimates and projections and cost benefit analysis related to projects and/or programs.
- Lead in the building of financial models to aid in forecasting cost estimating, pricing, and evaluating investment proposals.
- Assist with contract negotiations.
- Perform the role of financial business partner.

The educational qualifications are a Bachelor's degree in Accounting or Finance and an MBA or equivalent. CPA or CMA/CFM is a plus. Three years or more accounting and financial analysis experience is often required.

.03 Cash/Treasury Managers

Cash/treasury managers, usually working for the treasurer, are employed by almost any business organization—for-profit, nonprofit, service, and manufacturing. Their responsibilities include the following:

- *Management of a company's cash investments.* Compare the returns on short-term securities, purchase short-term securities, and monitor the investments to ensure the company remains fully invested at all times. This involves diversification of maturities so as not to run out of operating funds.

- *Cash flow forecasting.* Responsible for the development and management of long- and short-term cash forecasts, utilizing historical trends, seasonal influences, and future projections. Determine cash requirements and maintain appropriate cash flows with banking and investment institutions to ensure adequate liquidity to meet all obligations and optimization of excess balances.

- *Cash management/modeling.* Develop and implement cash management systems, including policies, procedures, and internal controls. Oversee daily cash management process: setting cash position, wire transfer operations, and deposit and disbursement accounts. Act as key liaison and customer service advocate for business units for all cash management-related duties.

- *Insurance.* Review, analyze, and determine advantages and costs as they relate to management of corporate property and casualty insurance programs. Responsible for supporting the Treasurer in analysis of risk, selection of limits and retentions, negotiation of terms and conditions, and payment and allocation of premium.

- *Business analysis.* Analyze moderate to complex financial information, including trends and forecasts.

The educational qualifications are a Bachelor's degree in Accounting, Finance, or Business. Professional certification, such as CCM, is a plus.

.04 Corporate Risk Managers

More and more companies are employing corporate risk managers to quantify the interest rate, foreign exchange, and commodity risks the company faces. They are responsible for designing and implementing strategies for managing these risks.

.05 Pension Fund Managers

This individual manages the company's pension fund investments or selects and monitors the performance of outside investment managers.

.06 Directors of Financial Reporting

Publicly traded companies must meet the financial reporting requirements imposed by the securities laws. The director of financial reporting ensures compliance with these standards.

¶411 Banking Careers

Banks are institutions that take care of the money of individuals and corporations. Banks pay interest on the deposited money and provide loans to people for business or personal use. They also offer a wide range of services, such as exchanging foreign currency, giving advice related to investment and insurance, and acting as trustees.

With the information technology boom, banking is computerized to provide more efficient service to the customers. Banks with facilities that allow customers to use ATM cards for 24-hour cash withdrawals or deposits and credit card facilities are commonplace. With such widespread access to the Internet, many banks offer online information to customers. Certain banks provide home banking as a service, wherein a bank representative visits the customer's home to open an account for him/her.

There is tremendous competition in the banking sector to come up with innovative and customer-friendly schemes. Banks have all their branches connected via the computer network. There is a growing need for better and better banking facilities due to international trade and industrial liberalization, contributing to the change in the banking environment. All this has created an increase in opportunities in banking jobs and a requirement for people with marketing and technological skills apart from financial background.

With computerized banking, it has become absolutely necessary for a person to be computer literate in order to use the software packages to perform the daily transactions. A bank clerk is involved in various operations, such as keeping a record of accounts, loans, and mortgages, and providing services, such as payrolls and inventory accounting to the customers.

.01 Bank Managers

As a bank manager, a person is responsible for profit, people and resource management, and strategic planning to generate more profits. Various foreign banks and financial institutions are entering the market, which increases competition. Aggressive marketing and innovative policies hold the key to the success of bank operations. A manager should be able to judge this based on the area where the operations are carried on and the type of customers that the bank is catering to. A manager should provide constant support and motivation to the staff so that they give the best possible service to their customers. Managers need to interact and communicate with CEOs of corporations who are interested in getting their operations funded and then follow up on the big customers who make use of loans from the bank.

.02 *Merchant Banking*

Merchant banking implies investment management. This includes management of mutual funds, public issues, trusts, securities, and international funds. It involves dealing with corporate clients and advising them on various issues, such as mergers, acquisitions, public issues, capital structure decisions, etc. With so many mergers and acquisitions (M&A), the scope of merchant banking has grown to a large extent.

.03 *Treasury and Foreign Exchange (Forex) Functions*

This aspect of banking is becoming increasingly important as the forex flow is increasing and the international markets are funding the operations of the multinational corporations (MNCs). The success of any business is measured by the fund management, this making treasury management a very critical finance function. Management of a treasury profit center requires a wide variety of knowledge in the area of global money markets and financial instruments, such as deposit certificates, treasury bills, forecasting, source evaluation, and cost of domestic and foreign currency funds. Treasury and risk management ensures cost effectiveness in planning strategies in this era of deregulation.

The currency values, interest rates, share index, and commodities affect the financial derivatives, such as futures, swaps, and other tools of risk management. Corporations, therefore, employ well-trained professionals to manage treasury and forex functions, so that they can ensure competent management.

In a forex marketing job, which is an interbank job, a person needs to assess various markets on the behalf of the bank to advise corporations or other banks that need foreign currency. The job requires one to be constantly updated about the policies of the regulatory bodies, as well as monitoring the current prices and making predictions based on analysis of trends, etc.

.04 *Lending Officers*

Lending officers work for banks and other financial institutions that lend money. They help design and negotiate the loan arrangements and monitor the borrower's performance while the loan is outstanding.

.05 *Debt-Rating Analysts*

The debt-rating agencies employ credit analysts who participate in the debt-rating process. Usually these analysts specialize in an industry or particular type of security. Debt-rating analyst positions offer a good opportunity to learn about particular industries as well as to sharpen credit skills.

.06 *Branch Managers*

Branch managers are responsible for the day-to-day operations of brokerage house branch offices or insurance sales offices. These are usually persons who have excelled at the respective entry-level positions and earned greater management responsibility.

¶ 415 Investments as a Profession

The world of investments offers several rewarding careers, both professionally and financially.

.01 *Investment Bankers*

Investment bankers, who arrange the sale of new securities and assist in mergers and acquisitions, enjoyed phenomenal financial rewards in the booming 1990s. Although there is comparatively less activity of this type today, an experienced merger and acquisition specialist still can earn compensation in the $1 million range. Even someone with limited experience of a few years can earn $200,000 to $400,000 in this area.

.02 *Securities Traders*

Brokerage houses, banks, money management companies, and many other types of financial institutions employ individuals who actively trade securities. They play an important role in helping the capital markets function. Stockbrokers help investors make investments. They usually make investment recommendations as well as place orders to buy or sell securities on behalf of their clients.

Top traders and salespeople seem to do best on Wall Street. A "junior" bond trader on Wall Street can earn $300,000 to $400,000 or more, while an experienced bond trader can earn in the neighborhood of $750,000. A bond salesperson who sells to institutional investors can earn $200,000 or more if relatively inexperienced and $600,000 to $700,000 if experienced. Some 80,000 registered representatives (stockbrokers) are employed in cities across the country.

.03 *Security Analysts*

For those interested in doing research, which is less glamorous and less profitable for the firms involved, the good jobs on Wall Street still pay well. A security analyst on Wall Street with a few years of experience can earn $200,000 or more, while one with 10 years of experience can earn up to $500,000.

A range of financial institutions, including brokerage firms, investment bankers, banks, and insurance companies, need the services of investment analysts. Brokerage houses need them to support their registered representatives (who in turn serve the public) by, for example, preparing the research reports provided to customers. Investment bankers need analysts to assist in the sale of new securities and in the valuation of firms as possible merger or acquisition candidates. Banks and insurance companies own portfolios of securities that must be evaluated in order to be managed. Mutual funds need analysts to evaluate securities for possible purchase or sale.

.04 *Portfolio Managers*

All the financial firms mentioned above need portfolio managers to manage the portfolios of securities handled by these organizations. Portfolio managers are responsible for making the actual portfolio buy and sell decisions—what to buy and sell, when to buy and sell, and so forth. Portfolio performance is calculated for these managers, and their jobs may depend on their performance relative to other managed portfolios and to market averages.

Individuals interested in careers in the investments field should consider seeking a *Chartered Financial Analyst (CFA)* designation, which is fully discussed in Chapter 3 at ¶ 335 and ¶ 361.02. This is a professional designation for people in the investments area, like the CPA designation for accountants. The CFA designation is widely recognized in the investments industry today. It serves as an indication that areas of knowledge relevant to investing have been studied and that high ethical and professional standards have been recognized and accepted.

¶ 421 Personal Financial Planning

There is a great demand for personal financial planning by individuals, as money management is of primary importance to the "average person."

.01 *Major Areas of Concern*

The major areas of personal financial planning include:

- Proper insurance coverage to protect against personal risk such as death, disability, and losses. For example, adequate life insurance is needed for dependents.
- Capital accumulation. There should be a regular savings and investment program. A balanced investment portfolio should exist (for example, certificates of deposit, equity securities, fixed-income securities), taking into account financial goals and risk tolerance.
- Investment and property management. This involves managing assets for high return without undue risk.
- Tax planning. Tax saving techniques should be employed.
- Debt and credit management. One should not be overextended.
- Planning for retirement. Adequate retirement income should be provided for.

- Estate planning. Proper estate planning is needed to assure assets are transferred to beneficiaries as desired.

.02 Education and Certification

Though financial planners come from all types of educational and professional backgrounds, most have attained a four-year college degree in financial planning, accounting, finance, law, economics, business, math, or marketing. Certification—such as the Certified Financial Planner and Chartered Financial Consultant designations—is not required, but is recommended by many financial companies. The number of financial planners continues to grow. Because no standard credentials for financial planners exist, anyone can claim to be a financial planner. Although most planners must register with the Securities and Exchange Commission as a *Registered Investment Advisor (RIA)*, this involves only filling out a form providing information on education and background and paying a $150 registration fee. Otherwise, financial planners are bound only by the job requirements of professional organizations to which they belong. Individuals seeking a financial planner may wish to contact these organizations. (They include the National Association of Personal Financial Advisors (800-366-2732); the International Association for Financial Planning (800-945-4237); and the Institute of Certified Financial Planners (800-282-7526).)

Designations that do connote training in the financial planning field include: *Certified Financial Planner (CFP)*, awarded by the Certified Financial Planning Board of Standards (an industry group), which requires coverage of a financial planning curriculum and successful completion of a ten-hour examination; *Chartered Financial Consultant (ChFC)*, which requires a comprehensive examination; and *Personal Financial Specialist*, awarded by the American Institute of Certified Public Accountants, which requires experience in personal financial planning and a comprehensive examination. All three designations require continuing education. Financial planning certifications are also discussed at ¶ 365.

.03 Types of Compensation

Financial planners are compensated by three methods: fee-based, commission-based, or fee-and-commission-based, which is the most common form of compensation. According to the Wall Street Journal's *Career Journal* (www.careerjournal.com/myc), the financial planner working in the United States now earns an average salary of $64,630, and with bonuses and benefits added, a total compensation of $82,654. These figures are national averages and actual cost-of-living in various locations affect what one might expect for his or her own situation.

.04 Employment Outlook

According to the U.S. Bureau of Labor Statistics, financial planners held about 95,600 jobs in 2000. About one-fourth are self-employed and run small firms. The rest work in companies such as banks, insurance companies, and brokerage firms. The bureau predicts faster-than-average growth for financial planners through 2010, as a better-educated, wealthier, and longer-living population requires more investment advice and financial guidance.

¶ 425 Financial Middlemen

.01 *Loan Brokers*

The independent financial broker is in an excellent position today due to the tremendous demand for working capital in the business community. This demand provides the loan broker with an unlimited opportunity for monetary success and personal satisfaction. Nearly all business firms need additional working capital. Lack of adequate working capital may seriously limit the true potential of many firms. The financial broker is in a position to assist these business firms in their financing needs and at the same time enjoy generous earnings for himself.

.02 *Mortgage Brokers*

Mortgage brokers are not direct or primary suppliers of capital. However, they do play an important and necessary role in the financing process. A mortgage broker is a person who serves to bring together the supplier and user of capital (borrower or mortgagee). For this service, the borrower normally pays a finder's fee equal to one percent or so of the amount borrowed. The financial success of the mortgage brokerage firm depends upon the ability to locate available funds and to match these funds with creditworthy borrowers.

Certain sources of funds, particularly insurance companies, do not always deal directly with the person looking for capital; rather, they work through a mortgage broker. Thus, a person wishing to borrow from certain lenders would need to go through a mortgage broker. Normally, the mortgage broker is not involved in servicing the loan once it is made, and the transaction is closed.

.03 *Mortgage Bankers*

The mortgage banker is a financial middleman. Unlike mortgage brokers, however, the services offered include more than simply bringing borrowers and investors together. Mortgage bankers normally make mortgage loans, package these loans, and then sell these packages as both primary loans and to secondary investors. Financial help is often sought from a lender, typically a commercial bank.

The bank becomes a warehouse for mortgage money, and the mortgage banker draws on these funds until payment is received from the investors. Usually the mortgage banker continues to service the loan (collect debt service, pay property taxes, handle delinquent accounts, etc.) even after the loan has been packaged and sold. For this management service, a small percentage of the amount collected is retained before forwarding the balance to the investor. Obviously, the success of the mortgage banker depends upon the ability to generate new loans. In some geographic areas, mortgage bankers are the primary source for financing real estate. All mortgage bankers try to stay in constant touch with investors and are aware of changing market conditions and lender requirements. Quite often the loan origination fee or finder's fee charged the borrower is more than offset by a lower interest rate from a lender not directly accessible to the borrower. Mortgage bankers are involved in both commercial and residential financing and also carry out related activities, such as writing hazard insurance policies, appraising, and investment counseling. As with mortgage brokers, state law regulates mortgage bankers. For more information, visit www.mbaa.org.

Mortgage Bankers Association of America (MBAA)
1919 Pennsylvania Ave, NW
Washington, DC 20006-3438
(202) 557-2700

.04 Insurance Agents

A great number of insurance products are in existence today, such as life, disability, casualty, medical, and long-term care insurance. Life insurance agents help their clients determine how much life insurance is appropriate and which life insurance products are most suitable for them. A Chartered Life Underwriter (CLU) designation, awarded to life insurance agents, would be helpful. For more information, visit www.financialpro.org.

Part 3

Foundations of Finance

Chapter 5
Understanding Entities

¶ 501 Overview

Finance is applicable to both economic entities, such as business firms, and nonprofit organizations, such as schools, governments, hospitals, churches, and so on.

Selecting the most appropriate structure for an organization is a difficult decision. What form to choose in terms of type of ownership, capital formation, management, and tax considerations will affect every aspect of its operation. Financial managers need to be familiar with the pros and cons of the various forms under which a business might be set up.

The seven basic types of business entity are: sole proprietorship, general partnership, limited partnership (LP), limited liability partnership (LLP), limited liability company (LLC), C corporation, and Subchapter S corporation. Of the seven, corporations are usually of the largest size (in terms of sales, total assets, or number of employees), whereas proprietorships and partnerships emphasize entrepreneurship to a greater degree.

¶ 505 Sole Proprietorship

A sole proprietorship is owned by one individual. Sole proprietorships are the most numerous of the seven types of organizations. The typical sole proprietorship is a small business; usually, only the proprietor and a few employees are involved. Funds are raised from personal resources or through borrowings. The sole proprietor is responsible for all the decisions. Sole proprietorships are common in the retail, wholesale, and service industries.

The advantages of a sole proprietorship are:

- No formal charter is required.
- Organizational costs are minimal.
- It can be inexpensively switched to a different structure if future tax reform alters a tax advantage. Further, it is perhaps the least risky business form from which to change.
- Profits and control are not shared with others.
- The income of the business is taxed as personal income.
- Confidentiality is maintained.
- Easy to discontinue business.
- Losses may offset other income.

The disadvantages are:

- The ability to raise large sums of capital is limited.
- Unlimited liability exists for the owner.
- The life of the business is limited to the life of the owner.
- The sole proprietor must be a "jack-of-all-trades."

Recent tax legislation has been benefiting sole proprietorships. Health insurance premiums paid by proprietors and other self-employed persons, for example, are now scheduled to become fully deductible by the year 2003.

Note: Consult tax accountants and lawyers about major tax legislation.

¶ 511 General Partnership

A partnership is similar to the sole proprietorship except that the business has more than one owner. Partnerships are often formed to bring together different skills or talents, or to obtain the necessary capital. Although partnerships are generally larger than sole proprietorships, they are not typically large businesses. Partnerships are common in finance, real estate, insurance, public accounting, brokerage, and law.

The partnership contract (articles of partnership) spells out the rights of each partner concerning such matters as profit distribution and fund withdrawal. Partnership property is *jointly* owned. Each partner's interest in the property is based on his or her proportionate capital balance. Profits and losses are divided in accordance with the partnership agreement. If nothing about distribution is stated, they are distributed equally.

Each partner acts as an *agent* for the others. The partnership (and thus each individual partner) is legally responsible for the acts of any partner. However, the partnership is not bound by acts committed beyond the scope of the partnership.

Forming a partnership creates these advantages:

- Partnerships can be easily established, with minimal organizational effort.
- Partnerships are free from special governmental regulation, at least compared to corporations.
- Income of the partnership is taxed as personal income to the partners.
- More funds are typically obtained than by a sole proprietorship.
- Better credit standing results from the availability of partners' personal assets to meet creditor claims.
- Partnerships attract good employees because of potential partnership opportunity.
- Expertise is increased through additional partners.

Its disadvantages are as follows:

- It carries unlimited liability for the partners; each member is held *personally* liable for all partnership debts.
- It dissolves upon the withdrawal or death of any partner.
- Because it cannot sell stock, its ability to raise significant capital is limited, which may restrict growth.

Note: The partners may avoid being personally liable for the partnership's debts and obligations by registering the partnership as a *limited liability partnership (LLP).*

¶ 515 Limited Partnership (LP)

A limited partnership (LP) is owned by one or more limited partners and at least one general partner. The mandatory general partner(s) has unlimited liability for partnership torts and debts, while the limited partner(s) has protection similar to that of a corporation's shareholders. Although limited partners can lose their entire investment, their personal assets are not subject to creditors' claims. In addition, limited partners are not liable for other partners' wrongdoing when they do not participate in managing the business.

¶ 521 Limited Liability Partnership (LLP)

A limited partnership must have at least one general partner who is personally liable for the debts and obligations of the limited partnership. Limited partners are not personally liable for the limited partnership's debts and obligations, provided they are not involved in the management and operations of the limited partnership. Frequently, a limited partnership uses a corporation or other limited liability entity as the general partner. This serves to limit the liability of the general partner. Some states allow a limited partnership to register as a limited liability partnership (LLP). By registering as an LLP, the general partner is provided with the same liability shield as the limited partners. Tax considerations are unlikely to determine the choice of entity between an LLP and a limited partnership, because they are both subject to partnership tax rules.

Note: An LLP is different from a limited partnership (LP) in that all the LLP's owners have some degree of limited liability. An LP, on the other hand, is owned by one or more limited partners and at least one general partner.

¶ 525 Limited Liability Company (LLC)

A limited liability company (LLC) has characteristics of both limited partnerships and corporations. The LLC members are not personally liable for the debts and obligations of the LLC, but they are allowed to run the day-to-day operations of the business. LLCs are a relatively recent development. Most states permit the establishment of LLCs. LLCs are typically not permitted to carry on certain service businesses (e.g., law, medicine, and accounting). An LLC provides limited personal liability, as a corporation does. Owners, who are called members, can be other corporations. The members run the company unless they hire an outside management group. The LLC can choose whether to be taxed as a regular corporation or pass through to members. Profits and losses can be split among members any way they choose.

LLCs are relatively new in the U.S., but an equivalent has been widely used in other countries. Hence, LLCs are useful for international businesses, especially because S corporations must be domestic, and nonresident aliens cannot own S corporation stock (to be discussed later).

Note: The LLC rules vary by state.

¶ 531 C Corporation

A corporation is a legal entity existing apart from its owners (stockholders). Ownership is evidenced by possession of shares of stock. The corporate form is not the most numerous type of business, but it is the most important in terms of total sales, assets, profits, and contribution to national income. Corporations are governed by a distinct set of state or federal laws and come in two forms: a state *C corporation or federal Subchapter S corporation.*

The advantages of a C corporation are:

- Unlimited life.

- Limited liability for its owners, as long as no personal guarantee on a business-related obligation such as a bank loan or lease exists.
- Ease of transfer of ownership through transfer of stock.
- Ability to raise large sums of capital.

Its disadvantages are:

- Difficult and costly to establish, as a formal charter is required.
- Subject to double taxation on its earnings and dividends paid to stockholders.
- Bankruptcy, even at the corporate level, does not discharge tax obligations.
- Subject to more legal control.

¶ 535 Subchapter S Corporation

A Subchapter S corporation is a form of corporation whose stockholders are taxed similarly to partners.

To qualify as an S corporation, the following is necessary:

- A corporation cannot have more than 75 shareholders.
- It cannot have any nonresident foreigners as shareholders.
- It cannot have more than one class of stock.
- It must properly elect Subchapter S status.

The S corporation can distribute its income directly to shareholders and avoid the corporate income tax while enjoying the other advantages of the corporate form.

Note: Not all states recognize Subchapter S corporations.

¶ 541 Summary of Entity Characteristics

Exhibit 1 summarizes general entity characteristics.

Exhibit 1

Choice of Entity

Characteristic	*C Corp*	*S Corp*	*Proprie-torship*	*General Part-nership*	*Limited Liability Company*
Centralization of authority	Yes	Yes	Yes	No	No
Ease of creation of entity	No	No	Yes	Yes	No
Ease of division through subsidiaries	Yes	Yes	No	No	No
Limited personal liability	Yes	Yes	No	No	Yes
Ease of ownership transferability	Yes	Yes	No	No	No
Income taxed to owner	No	Yes	Yes	Yes	Yes
Ease of operation of entity	Yes	Yes	Yes	Yes	Yes
Personal holding company income tax	Yes	No	No	No	No
Underpayment of estimated taxes penalty	Yes	Yes	Yes	Yes	Yes
Ease of changing tax year	Yes	No	No	No	No
Second tax on distributions to owners	Yes	No	No	No	No
Organization expense deductions	Yes	Yes	No	Yes	Yes
Losses available to offset owner's income	No	Yes	Yes	Yes	Yes
Charitable contributions deduction (limited)	Yes	No	No	No	No
Accumulated earnings tax	Yes	No	No	No	No
Income adjusted for reasonable salary	Yes	No	No	No	No
Indefinite life—continuity of existence	Yes	Yes	No	No	No

Chapter 6

Time Value of Money and Its Application

¶ 601 Overview

A dollar now is worth more than a dollar to be received later. This statement sums up an important principle: money has a time value. The truth of this principle is that by investing the dollar now, one will have more than a dollar at the specified later date.

Time value of money is a critical consideration in financial and investment decisions. For example, compound interest calculations are needed to determine future sums of money resulting from an investment. Discounting, or the calculation of present value, which is inversely related to compounding, is used to evaluate the future cash flow associated with capital budgeting projects. There are many applications of time value of money in finance.

¶ 605 Calculating Future Values/Money Growth

A dollar in hand today is worth more than a dollar to be received tomorrow because of the interest it could earn from putting it in a savings account or placing it in an investment account. Compounding interest means that interest earns interest. The following definitions apply to the discussion of the concepts of compounding and time value:

F_n = future value = the amount of money at the end of year n

P = principal

i = annual interest rate

n = number of years

Then,

F_1 = the amount of money at the end of year 1

= principal and interest = P + iP = P(1+i)

F_2 = the amount of money at the end of year 2
$= F_1(1+i) = P(1+i)(1+i) = P(1+i)^2$

The future value of an investment compounded annually at rate i for n years is:

$F_n = P(1+i)^n = P \times T_1(i,n)$

Where T_1 (i,n) is the compound amount of $1 and can be found in Table 1 in Appendix B.

Example 1: John Doe places $1,000 in a savings account earning eight-percent interest compounded annually. How much money will he have in the account at the end of four years?

$F_n = P(1+i)^n$

$F_4 = \$1,000\,(1 + 0.08)^4 = \$1,000\ T_1(8\%,4 \text{ years})$

From Appendix B, Table 1, the T_1 for four years at eight percent is 1.361. Therefore,

$F_4 = \$1,000\,(1.361) = \$1,361.$

Example 2: Jane Smith invested a large sum of money in the stock of Delta Corporation. The company paid a $3 dividend per share. The dividend is expected to increase by 20 percent per year for the next three years. Jane wishes to project the dividends for years 1 through 3.

$F_n = P(1+i)^n$

$F_1 = \$3(1+0.2)^1 = \$3\ T_1(20\%,1) = \$3\,(1.200) = \$3.60$

$F_2 = \$3(1+0.2)^2 = \$3\ T_1(20\%,2) = \$3\,(1.440) = \$4.32$

$F_3 = \$3(1+0.2)^3 = \$3\ T_1(20\%,3) = \$3\,(1.728) = \$5.18$

.01 Intrayear Compounding

Interest is often compounded more frequently than once a year. Banks, for example, compound interest quarterly, daily, and even continuously. If interest is compounded m times a year, then the general formula for solving the future value becomes:

$$F_n = P\left(1 + \frac{i}{m}\right)^{n \times m} = P \times T_1(i/m, n \times m)$$

The formula reflects more frequent compounding (n×m) at a smaller interest rate per period (i/m). For example, in the case of semiannual compounding (m = 2), the above formula becomes:

$$F_n = P(1 + i/2)^{n \times 2} = P \times T_1(i/2, n \times 2)$$

Example 3: Andy Walsh deposits $10,000 in an account offering an annual interest rate of 20 percent. Andy will keep the money on deposit for five years. The interest rate is compounded quarterly. The accumulated amount at the end of the fifth year is calculated as follows:

$$F_n = P(1 + \frac{i}{m})^{n \times m} = P \times T_1(i/m, n \times m)$$

Where:

P = $10,000

i/m = 20%/4 = 5%

n×m = 5 × 4 = 20

Therefore,

F_5 = $10,000(1 +.05)^{20} = $10,000 T_1 (5%,20) = $10,000 (2.653) = $26,530

Example 4: Assume that P = $1,000, i = 8%, and n = 2 years. Then for annual compounding (m=1):

F_2 = $1,000(1+0.08)^2 = $1,000 T_1 (8%, 2) = $1,000(1.166) = $1,166.00

Semiannual compounding (m=2):

$$F_2 = \$1,000\ (1 + \frac{0.08}{2})^{2 \times 2}$$

=$1,000 (1 + .04)^4 = $1,000 T_1 (4%, 4)
=$1,000 (1.170)
=$1,170.00

Quarterly compounding (m=4):

$$F_2 = \$1,000\ (1 + \frac{0.08}{4})^{2 \times 4}$$

=$1,000 (1 + .02)^8 = $1,000 T_1 (2%, 8)
=$1,000 (1.172)
=$1,172.00

As the example shows, the more frequently interest is compounded, the greater the amount accumulated. This is true for any interest for any period of time.

.02 Future Value of an Annuity

An annuity is defined as a series of payments (or receipts) of a fixed amount for a specified number of periods. Each payment is assumed to occur at the end of the period. The future value of an annuity is that of a compound annuity, which involves depositing or investing an equal sum of money at the end of each year for a certain number of years and allowing it to grow.

Let S_n = the future value on an n-year annuity

A = the amount of an annuity

Thus:

$$S_n = A(1+i)^{n-1} + A(1+i)^{n-2} + \ldots + A(1+i)^0$$
$$= A[(1+i)^{n-1} + (1+i)^{n-2} + \ldots + (1+i)^0]$$
$$= A \times \sum_{t=0}^{n-1} (1+i)^t = A\left[\frac{(1+i)^n - 1}{i}\right] = A \times T_2(i,n)$$

Where T_2 (i,n) represents the future value of an annuity of $1 for n years compounded at i percent and can be found in Table 2 in Appendix B.

Example 5: Joe Brown wants to determine the sum of money he will have in a savings account after depositing $1,000 at the end of each year for the next six years. The annual interest rate is eight percent. The T_2 (8%,6 years) is given in Appendix B, Table 2 as 7.336. Therefore,

S_6 = $1,000 T_2 (8%,6) = $1,000 (7.336) = $7,336

Example 6: Mary Brooks deposits $30,000 semiannually into a fund for 10 years. The annual interest rate is eight percent. The amount accumulated at the end of the tenth year is calculated as follows:

$S_n = A \times T_2 (i, n)$

Where A = $30,000

i = 8%/2 = 4%

n = 10 × 2 = 20

Therefore,

S_n = $30,000 T_2 (4%, 20)

= $30,000 (29.778) = $893,340

¶ 611 Calculating Present Value of Money

Present value is the present worth of future sums of money. The process of calculating present value, or discounting, is actually the opposite of finding the compounded future value. In connection with present value calculations, the interest rate i is called the discount rate. The discount rate used is more commonly called the cost of capital, which is the minimum rate of return required by the investor. Chapter 17 discusses in detail how to determine the cost of capital.

Recall that $F_n = P(1+i)^n$

Therefore,

$$P = \frac{F_n}{(1+i)^n} = F_n \left[\frac{1}{(1+i)^n}\right] = F_n \times T_3\,(i,n)$$

Where T_3 (i,n) represents the present value of $1 and is given in Appendix B, Table 3.

Example 7: William Burns has been given an opportunity to receive $20,000 six years from now. If he can earn 10 percent on his investments, what is the most he should pay for this opportunity? To answer this question, he must compute the present value of $20,000 to be received six years from now at a 10 percent rate of discount. F_6 is $20,000, i is 10 percent, and n is six years. T_3 (10%,6) from Appendix B, Table 3 is 0.565.

$$P = \$20{,}000 \left[\frac{1}{(1+0.1)^6}\right] = \$20{,}000\ T_3\,(10\%, 6) = \$20{,}000\ (0.565) = \$11{,}300$$

This means that he can earn 10 percent on his investment, and he would be indifferent to receiving $11,300 now or $20,000 six years from today, since the amounts are time equivalent. In other words, he could invest $11,300 today at 10 percent and have $20,000 in six years.

.01 Present Value of Mixed Streams of Cash Flows

The present value of a series of mixed payments (or receipts) is the sum of the present value of each individual payment. We know that the present value of each individual payment is the payment times the appropriate T_3 value.

Example 8: Carol Jones is thinking of starting a new product line that initially costs $32,000. Her annual projected cash inflows are:

Year 1	$10,000
Year 2	$20,000
Year 3	$5,000

If she must earn a minimum of 10 percent on her investment, should she undertake this new product line?

The present value of this series of mixed streams of cash inflows is calculated as follows:

Year	*Cash Inflows*	*X T_3 (10%, n)*	*Present Value*
1	$10,000	0.909	$ 9,090
2	$20,000	0.826	$16,520
3	$ 5,000	0.751	$ 3,755
			$29,365

Since the present value of her projected cash inflows is less than the initial investment, she should not undertake this project.

.02 Present Value of an Annuity

Interest received from bonds, pension funds, and insurance obligations all involve annuities. To compare these financial instruments, one needs to know the present value of each. The present value of an annuity (P_n) can be found by using the following equation:

$$P_n = A\left[\frac{1}{(1+i)^1}\right] + A\left[\frac{1}{(1+i)^2}\right] + \ldots + A\left[\frac{1}{(1+i)^n}\right]$$

$$= A\left[\frac{1}{(1+i)^1} + \frac{1}{(1+i)^2} + \ldots + \frac{1}{(1+i)^n}\right]$$

$$= A \times \sum_{t=1}^{n} \frac{1}{(1+i)^t} = A \times \frac{1}{i}\left[1 - \frac{1}{(1+i)^n}\right]$$

$$= A \times T_4(i,n)$$

Where T_4 (i,n) represents the present value of an annuity of $1 discounted at i percent for n years and is found in Appendix B, Table 4.

Example 9: Assume that the cash inflows in the previous example form an annuity of $10,000 for three years. Then the present value is:

$P_n = A \times T_4$ (i,n)

P_3 = $10,000 T_4 (10%, 3 years) = $10,000 (2.487) = $24,870

.03 Perpetuities

Some annuities go on forever, called perpetuities. An example of a perpetuity is preferred stock that yields a constant dollar dividend indefinitely. The present value of a perpetuity is found as follows:

$$\text{Present value of a perpetuity} = \frac{\text{receipt}}{\text{discount rate}} = \frac{A}{i}$$

Example 10: Assume that a perpetual bond has an $80-per-year interest payment and that the discount rate is 10 percent. The present value of this perpetuity is:

$$P = \frac{A}{i} = \frac{\$80}{0.10} = \$800$$

¶ 615 Applications of Future Values and Present Values

Future and present values have numerous applications in financial and investment decisions. Six of these applications are presented below.

.01 Deposits to Accumulate a Future Sum (Sinking Fund)

A financial manager might wish to find the annual deposit (or payment) that is necessary to accumulate a future sum. To find this future amount (or sinking fund) one can use the formula for finding the future value of an annuity.

$$S_n = A \times T_2(i,n)$$

Solving for A, one obtains:

$$\text{Annual deposit amount} = A = \frac{S_n}{T_2(i,n)}$$

Example 11: Ann Kelly wishes to determine the equal annual end-of-year deposits required to accumulate \$5,000 at the end of five years in a fund. The interest rate is 10 percent. The annual deposit is:

$S_5 = \$5{,}000$

T_2 (10%, 5 years) = 6.105 (from Table 2 in Appendix B)

$$A = \frac{\$5{,}000}{6.105} = \$819$$

In other words, if Ann deposits \$819 at the end of each year for five years at 10-percent interest, she will have accumulated \$5,000 at the end of the fifth year.

Example 12: Alex White needs a sinking fund for the retirement of a bond 30 years from now. The interest rate is 10 percent. The annual year-end contribution needed to accumulate \$1,000,000 is:

$S_{30} = \$1{,}000{,}000$

$T_2(10\%, 30\text{ years}) = 164.49$

$$A = \frac{\$1{,}000{,}000}{164.49} = 6{,}079.40$$

.02 Amortized Loans

An amortized loan is a loan that is repaid in equal periodic amounts. Examples include auto loans, mortgage loans, and most commercial loans. The periodic payment can easily be computed as follows:

$$P_n = A \times T_4(i,n)$$

Solving for A, one obtains:

$$\text{Amount of loan} = A = \frac{P_n}{T_4(i,n)}$$

Example 13: Patrick Byrne borrows $200,000 for five years at an interest rate of 14 percent. The annual year-end payment on the loan is calculated as follows:

P_5 = $200,000

T_4 (14%, 5 years) = 3.433 (from Table 4 in Appendix B)

$$\text{Amount of loan} = A = \frac{P_5}{T_4(14\%,5 \text{ years})} = \frac{\$200{,}000}{3.433}$$
$$= \$58{,}258.08$$

Example 14: Ted Anderson takes out a 40-month bank loan of $5,000 at a 12 percent annual interest rate. He wants to find out the monthly loan payment.

i = 12% / 12 months = 1%

P_{40} = $5,000

T_4 (1%, 40 months) = 32.835 (from Table 4 in Appendix B)

Therefore,

$$A = \frac{\$5{,}000}{32.835} = \$152.28$$

To repay the principal and interest on a $5,000, 12-percent, 40-month loan, Ted has to pay $152.28 a month for the next 40 months.

Example 15: Acme Insurance Co. borrows $2,000 to be repaid in three equal installments at the end of each of the next three years. The bank charges 12-percent interest. The amount of each payment is:

P_3 = $2,000

T_4 (12%, 3 years) = 2.402

Therefore,

$$A = \frac{\$2{,}000}{2.402} = \$832.64$$

.03 Loan Amortization Schedule

Each loan payment consists partly of interest and partly of principal. The breakdown is often displayed in a loan amortization schedule. The interest component of the payment is largest in the first period (because the principal balance is the highest) and subsequently declines, whereas the principal portion is smallest in the first period (because of the high interest) and increases thereafter, as shown in the following example.

Example 16: The following amortization schedule is set up using the same data as in the previous example.

Year	*Payment*	*Interest*	*Repayment of principal*	*Remaining Balance*
0	......	......	......	$2,000.00
1	$832.64	$240.00 (a)	$592.64 (b)	$1,407.36
2	$832.64	$168.88	$663.76	$ 743.60
3	$832.64	$ 89.23	$743.41 (c)	

(a) Interest is computed by multiplying the loan balance at the beginning of the year by the interest rate. Therefore, interest in year 1 is $2,000(0.12) = $240; in year 2 interest is $1,407.36(0.12) = $168.88; and in year 3 interest is $743.60(0.12) = $89.23. All figures are rounded.

(b) The reduction in principal equals the payment less the interest portion ($832.64 – $240.00 = $592.64).

(c) Not exact because of accumulated rounding errors.

.04 *Annual Percentage Rate (APR)*

Different types of investments use different compounding periods. For example, most bonds pay interest semiannually; banks generally pay interest quarterly. If a financial manager wishes to compare investments with different compounding periods, he or she needs to put them on a common basis. The annual percentage rate (APR), or effective annual rate, is used for this purpose and is computed as follows:

$$APR = (1 + \frac{i}{m})^m - 1.0$$

Where i = the stated, nominal, or quoted rate and m = the number of compounding periods per year.

Example 17: If the nominal rate is six percent, compounded quarterly, the APR is:

$$APR = (1 + \frac{i}{m})^m - 1.0 = (1 + \frac{0.06}{4})^4 - 1.0 = (1.015)^4 - 1.0$$

$$= 1.0614 - 1.0 = 0.0614 = 6.14\%$$

This means that if one bank offered six percent with quarterly compounding, while another offered 6.14 percent with annual compounding, they would both be paying the same effective rate of interest.

Annual percentage rate (APR) is also a measure of the cost of credit, expressed as a yearly rate. It includes interest as well as other financial charges, such as loan origination and certain closing fees. The lender is required to tell the borrower the APR. It provides the borrower with a good basis for comparing the cost of loans, including mortgage plans.

.05 *Rate of Growth*

In finance, it is necessary to calculate the compound annual rate of growth associated with a stream of earnings. Using the future value of investment formula, the compound annual growth rate in earnings per share is computed as follows:

$$F_n = P \times T_1 (i,n)$$

Solving this for T_1, one obtains:

$$T_1(i,n) = \frac{F_n}{P}$$

Example 18: Assume that XYZ Company has earnings per share of $2.50 in 20X1, and 10 years later the earnings per share has increased to $3.70. The compound annual rate of growth in earnings per share is computed as follows:

F_{10} = $3.70 and P = $2.50

Therefore,

$$T_1(i, 10) = \frac{\$3.70}{\$2.50}$$

From Table 1 in Appendix B, the T_1 value of 1.48 at 10 years is at i = four percent. Therefore, the compound annual rate of growth is four percent.

.06 *Bond Values*

Bonds call for the payment of a specific amount of interest for a stated number of years and the repayment of the face value at the maturity date. Thus, a bond represents an annuity plus a lump sum. Its value is found as the present value of the payment stream. The interest is usually paid semiannually.

$$V = \sum_{t=1}^{n} \frac{I}{(1+i)^t} + \frac{M}{(1+i)^n}$$
$$= I \times T_4(i,n) + M \times T_3(i,n)$$

Where:

I = interest payment per period

M = par value, or maturity value, usually $1,000

i = investor's required rate of return

n = number of periods

Example 19: Michael Brown has a 10-year bond with a 10-percent coupon that pays interest semiannually and has a face value of $1,000. Since interest is paid semiannually, the number of periods involved is 20, and the semiannual cash inflow is $100/2 = $50.

Michael has a required rate of return of 12 percent for this type of bond. Therefore, the present value (V) of this bond is:

$V = \$50 \times T_4 (6\%, 20) + \$1{,}000 \times T_3 (6\%, 20)$

$= \$50(11.470) + \$1{,}000(0.312) = \$573.50 + \$312.00 = \$885.50$

Note: $1,000 × T_3 (6%, 20) represents the present value of the bond at maturity in 20 years. The required rate of return (12 percent) is higher than the coupon rate of interest (10 percent), and so the bond value (or the price investors are willing to pay for this particular bond) is less than its $1,000 face value.

¶ 621 Using Computer Software for Calculations

This chapter discussed manual calculations using future and present value tables. These calculations also can be done using:

a. Financial calculators.

b. Spreadsheet software such as Excel.

Depending on the method one uses, rounding errors in answers are unavoidable. Computer software can be extremely helpful in making these calculations. For example, PV(rate,nper,pmt,fv,type) of Excel determines the present value of an investment, based on a series of equal payments, discounted at a periodic interest rate over the number of periods. To calculate the present value of an annuity due, use the following formula: PV(rate,nper,pmt,fv,type)×(1 + rate).

Chapter 7
Risk and Return

¶ 701 Overview

The outcome of any financial or investment decision is not known with certainty. In fact, the financial manager never makes decisions under conditions of certainty. Each decision presents certain risks and return characteristics.

Hence, all major decisions must be viewed in terms of expected return, expected risk, and their combined impact on the market value of the company. An understanding of the trade-off between the return expected from the decision and the degree of risk assumed to earn it is perhaps the most important key to successful financial and investment decisions.

¶ 705 Return

.01 Return Defined

Return is a key consideration in financial and investment decisions. Return is the reward for investing. *Total return on an investment* equals:

1. Periodic cash payments, called current income.

2. Appreciation (or depreciation) in market value, called capital gains (or losses).

Current income, which is received on a periodic basis, may take the form of interest, dividends, rent, and the like. Capital gains or losses represent changes in market value. A capital gain is the amount by which the proceeds from the sale of an investment exceeds its original purchase price. If the investment is sold for less than its purchase price, then the difference is a capital loss.

.02 Measuring Return

The way to measure the return on a given investment depends primarily on the definition of the relevant period over which the investment is held, called the holding period. The term holding period return (HPR) refers here to the total return that is earned from holding an investment for that period of time. It is computed as follows:

$$\text{HPR} = \frac{\text{Current income} + \text{Capital gain (or loss)}}{\text{Purchase price}}$$

Example 1: Consider the investment in stocks A and B over a one-year period of ownership:

	Stock	
	A	*B*
Purchase price (beginning of year)	$100	$100
Cash dividend received (during the year)	$ 13	$ 18
Sales price (end of year)	$107	$ 97

The current income from the investment in stocks A and B over the one-year period are $13 and $18, respectively. For stock A, a capital gain of $7 ($107 sales price − $100 purchase price) is realized over the period. In the case of stock B, a $3 capital loss ($97 sales price − $100 purchase price) results.

Combining the capital gain return (or loss) with the current income, the total return on each investment is summarized below:

	Stock	
Return	*A*	*B*
Cash dividend	13	18
Capital gain (loss)	7	(3)
Total return	$ 20	$ 15

Thus, the return on investments A and B are:

$$\text{HPR (Stock A)} = \frac{\$13 + (\$107 - \$100)}{\$100} = \frac{\$13 + \$7}{\$100} = \frac{\$20}{\$100} = 20\%$$

$$\text{HPR (Stock B)} = \frac{\$18 + (\$97 - \$100)}{\$100} = \frac{\$18 - \$3}{\$100} = \frac{\$15}{\$100} = 15\%$$

Measuring return over time: Arithmetic average return v. geometric average return. It is one thing to measure the return over a single holding period and quite another to describe a series of returns over time. When a financial manager holds an investment for more than one period, it is important to understand how to compute the average of the successive rates of return. There are two types of multi-period average (mean) returns. They are the *arithmetic average return* and *geometric average return.*

The arithmetic return is simply the arithmetic average of successive one-period rates of return. It is defined as:

$$\text{Arithmetic return} = 1/n \, \Sigma \, r_t$$

Where n = the number of time periods and r = the single holding period return in time t. The arithmetic average return, while simpler to calculate, can be quite misleading in multi-period return calculations.

A more accurate measure of the actual return generated by an investment over multiple periods is the *geometric average return,* commonly called the *compounded annual rate of return.* The geometric return over n periods is computed as follows:

$$\text{Geometric return} = \sqrt[n]{(1 + r_1)(1 + r_2) \ldots (1 + r_n)} - 1$$

The following example illustrates why the geometric return is an accurate measure in the multiple-period situation.

Example 2: Consider the following data where the price of a stock doubles in one period and depreciates back to the original price. Dividend income (current income) is zero.

Time periods

	t=0	*t=1*	*t=2*
Price (end of period)	$80	$160	$80
HPR	—	100%	– 50%

The arithmetic average return is the average of 100 percent and -50 percent, which is 25 percent, as shown below:

$$\frac{100\% + (-50\%)}{2} = 25\%$$

Note, however, that the stock purchased for $80 and sold for the same price two periods later did not earn 25 percent; it clearly earned zero return. This can be shown by computing the geometric average return. Note that n = 2, r1 = 100% = 1, and r2 = -50% = -0.5

Then,

$$\begin{aligned} \text{Geometric return} &= \sqrt{(1 + 1)(1 - 0.5)} - 1 \\ &= \sqrt{(2)(0.5)} - 1 \\ &= \sqrt{1} - 1 = 1 - 1 = 0 \end{aligned}$$

Example 3: Applying the formula discussed above to the data below indicates a compound average of 11.63 percent, somewhat less than the arithmetic average of 26.1 percent.

(1) Time	(2) Price	(3) Dividend	(4) Total Return	(5) Holding Period Return (HPR)
0	$100	$ —	$ —	—
1	60	10	− 30 (a)	− 0.300 (b)
2	120	10	70	1.167
3	100	10	− 10	− 0.083

(a) $10 + ($60 − $100)=$ − 30

(b) *HPR* =$ − 30/$100= − 0.300

The arithmetic average return is (-0.300+1.167−0.083)/3 = .261 = 26.1%, but the compound return is $[(1-0.300)(1+1.167)(1-0.083)]^{1/3} - 1 = 0.1163$, or 11.63%.

Effective annual yield. Different kinds of investments use different compounding periods. For instance, most bonds pay interest semiannually, and some banks offer interest quarterly. To compare investments with different compounding periods one must put them on a relative basis. The effective annual yield, commonly referred to as annual percentage rate (APR), is used for this purpose:

$$APR = (1 + r/m)^m - 1.0$$

Where r= the stated, nominal, or quoted rate

m= the number of compounding periods per year.

Example 4: If a bank offers six-percent interest, compounded quarterly, the annual percentage rate is:

$$APR = (1 - .06/4)^4 - 1.0 = (1.015)^4 - 1.0 = 1.0614 - 1.0 = 0.0614 = 6.14\%$$

Thus, if one bank offered six percent with quarterly compounding, but another offered 6.14 percent with annual compounding, they would both be offering the same yield.

Expected rate of return. A financial manager is primarily concerned with predicting future returns from an investment in a security. No one can state precisely what these future returns will be. At best, he/she can state the most likely expected outcome. This outcome is the expected rate of return. Of course, historical (actual) rates of return can provide a useful basis for formulating these future expectations. Probabilities may be used to evaluate the expected return. The expected rate of return ($\bar{r}$) is the weighted average of possible returns from a given investment, weights being probabilities.

Mathematically,

$\bar{r} = \Sigma\, r_i\ p_i$ for i = 1 to n

Where r_i is the ith possible return, p_i is the probability of the ith return, and n is the number of possible returns.

Example 5: Consider the possible rates of return, depending upon the state of the economy (recession, normal, or prosperity), that one might earn next year on a $50,000 investment in stock A or on a $50,000 investment in stock B:

Stock A

State of economy	*Return (r)*	*Probability (p)*
Recession	– 5%	.2
Normal	20	.6
Prosperity	40	.2

Stock B

State of economy	*Return (r)*	*Probability (p)*
Recession	10%	.2
Normal	15	.6
Prosperity	20	.2

The expected rates of return can be calculated as follows:

For stock A,

$\bar{r} = (-5\%)(.2) + (20\%)(.6) + (40\%)(.2) = 19\%$

For stock B,

$\bar{r} = (10\%)(.2) + (15\%)(.6) + (20\%)(.2) = 15\%$

¶ 711 Risk and the Risk-Return Trade-Off

Risk refers to the variation in earnings. It includes the chance of losing money on an investment. Integral to the subject of finance is the concept of a risk-return trade-off. All financial decisions involve some sort of risk-return trade-off. The greater the risk associated with any financial decision, the greater the return expected from it. Proper assessment and balance of the various risk-return trade-offs available is part of creating a sound financial and investment plan.

Example 6: An investor in stock would demand higher return from a speculative stock to compensate for the higher level of risk. In the case of working capital management, the less inventory one keeps, the higher the expected return (since less of the current assets are tied up). However, the risk of running out of stock and, thus, losing potential revenue is also greater.

.01 Measuring Risk

Standard deviation. The standard deviation, which is a statistical measure of dispersion of the probability distribution of possible returns of an investment, is used to measure risk. The smaller the deviation, the tighter the distribution and, thus, the lower the riskiness of the investment. Mathematically,

$$\sigma = \sqrt{\Sigma (r_i - \bar{r})^2 \; p_i}$$

To calculate σ, proceed as follows:

Step 1. First compute the expected rate of return ($\bar{r}$).

Step 2. Subtract each possible return from $\bar{r}$ to obtain a set of deviations ($r_i - \bar{r}$).

Step 3. Square each deviation, multiply the squared deviation by the probability of occurrence for its respective return, and sum these products to obtain the variance (σ^2):

$$\sigma^2 = \Sigma (r_i - \bar{r})^2 p_i$$

Step 4. Finally, take the square root of the variance to obtain the standard deviation ($\sqrt{\sigma^2}$).

Example 7: To follow this step-by-step approach, it is convenient to set up a table, as follows:

Stock A

Return (r_i)	*Probability* (p_i)	*(step 1)* r_ip_i	*(step 2)* $(r_i - \bar{r})$	*(step 3)* $(r_i - \bar{r})^2$	$(r_i - \bar{r})^2p_i$
− 5%	.2	− 1%	− 24%	.0576	.01152
20%	.6	12%	1%	.01	.00006
40%	.2	8%	21%	.0441	.00882
		$\bar{r}$ =19%			σ^2=.0204
				(step 4)	$\sigma = \sqrt{.0204}$
					=14.28%

Stock B

Return (r_i)	*Probability* (p_i)	*(step 1)* r_ip_i	*(step 2)* $(r_i - \bar{r})$	*(step 3)* $(r_i - \bar{r})^2$	$(r_i - \bar{r})^2p_i$
10%	.2	2%	− 5%	.0025	.0005
15%	.6	9%	0%	0.00	0
20%	.2	4%	5%	.0025	.0005
		$\bar{r}$ =15%			σ^2=.001
				(step 4)	$\sigma = \sqrt{.001}$
					=3.16%

Coefficient of variation. The financial manager must be careful in using the standard deviation to compare risk, since it is only an absolute measure of dispersion (risk). In other words, it does not consider the risk in relationship to an expected return. In comparisons of securities with differing expected returns, the *coefficient of variation* is commonly used. The coefficient of variation is computed simply by dividing the standard deviation for a security by its expected rate of return, i.e.,

$\sigma / \bar{r}$

The higher the coefficient, the more risky the security.

Example 8: Based on the following data, one can compute the coefficient of variation for each stock:

	Stock A	*Stock B*
$\bar{r}$	19%	15%
σ	14.28%	3.16%

The coefficient of variation is computed as follows:

For stock A,

$\sigma / \bar{r} = 14.28/19 = .75$

For stock B,

$\sigma / \bar{r} = 3.16/15 = .21$

Although stock A produces a considerably higher return than stock B, stock A is overall more risky than stock B, based on the computed coefficient of variation. Note, however, that if investments have the same expected returns, there is no need for the calculation of the coefficient of variation.

.02 Types of Risk

The following different sources of risk are involved in investment and financial decisions. Investors and decision makers must take into account the type of risk underlying an asset.

1. *Financial risk.* A type of investment risk associated with excessive debt.
2. *Industry risk.* The uncertainty of the inherent nature of the industry, such as high technology, product liability, and accidents.
3. *Economic risk.* The negative impact of a company from economic slowdowns. For example, airlines have lower business volume during a recession.
4. *Business risk.* This is caused by fluctuations of earnings before interest and taxes (operating income). Business risk depends on variability in demand, sales price, input prices, and amount of operating leverage.
5. *Financial leverage risk.* The risk to the shareholders from the use of financial leverage.

6. *Liquidity risk.* This represents the possibility that an asset may not be sold on short notice for its market value. If an investment must be sold at a high discount, then it is said to have a substantial amount of liquidity risk.

7. *Default risk.* This is the risk that a borrower will be unable to make interest payments or principal repayments on debt. For example, there is a great amount of default risk inherent in the bonds of a company experiencing financial difficulty.

8. *Market risk.* Market risk refers to changes in a stock's price that result from changes in the stock market as a whole, regardless of the fundamental change in a firm's earning power. Prices of all stocks are correlated to some degree with broad swings in the stock market.

9. *Interest rate risk.* This refers to the fluctuations in the value of an asset as the interest rates and conditions of the money and capital markets change. Interest rate risk relates to fixed income securities such as bonds. For example, if interest rates rise (fall), bond prices fall (rise).

10. *Inflation (purchasing power) risk.* This risk relates to the possibility that one will receive a lesser amount of purchasing power than was originally invested. Bonds are most affected by this risk, since the issuer will be paying back in cheaper dollars during an inflationary period.

11. *Systematic and unsystematic risk.* Many investors hold more than one financial asset. The portion of a security's risk called unsystematic risk can be controlled through diversification. This type of risk is unique to a given security. Business, liquidity, and default risks fall in this category. Unsystematic risk is also called diversifiable risk, nonmarket risk, or company-specific risk. Nondiversifiable risk, more commonly referred to as systematic risk, results from forces outside of the firm's control, and are, therefore, not unique to the given security. Purchasing power, interest rate, and market risks fall into this category. Systematic risk is also called market risk, which is measured by the beta coefficient.

12. *International and political risks.* The risks stemming from foreign operations in politically unstable foreign countries. An example is a U.S. company having a location and operations in a hostile country.

13. *Currency risk.* The risk that a foreign currency transaction will be negatively exposed to fluctuations in foreign exchange rates.

This is also called foreign exchange risk, exchange risk, or exchange rate risk.

14. *Social risk.* Problems facing the company due to ethnic boycott, discrimination cases, and environmental concerns.

.03 Risk Analysis

Risk analysis is the process of measuring and analyzing the risks associated with financial and investment decisions. It is especially important in making capital investment decisions because of the large amount of capital involved and the long-term nature of the investment being considered. The higher the risk associated with a proposed project, the greater the return that must be earned to compensate for that risk. There are several methods for the analysis of risk, including risk-adjusted discount rate, certainty equivalent, Monte Carlo simulation, sensitivity analysis, and decision trees. (For more information, see Chapter 20).

.04 Diversification Reduces Risk

Diversification is usually a good way to reduce risk. "Diversify" means "Don't Put All Your Eggs in One Basket." With a diversified portfolio (e.g., stocks, bonds, real estate, and savings accounts), the value of all these investments do not increase or decrease at the same time or in the same magnitude. Thus, one can protect oneself against fluctuations. One's company may diversify into different lines of businesses that are not subject to the same economic and political influences. Thus, it can protect itself against fluctuations in earnings.

¶ 715 Portfolio Theory

The central theme of the portfolio theory is that rational investors behave in a way that reflects their aversion to taking increased risk without being compensated by an adequate increase in expected return. Also, for any given expected return, most investors will prefer a lower risk, and for any given level of risk, they will prefer a higher return to a lower return. Nobel laureate economist Harry Markowitz showed how to calculate a set of "efficient" portfolios. An investor then will choose from among a set of efficient portfolios the best that is consistent with the risk profile of the investor.

Most financial assets are not held in isolation but, rather, are held as part of a portfolio. Therefore, the risk-return analysis should not be confined to single assets only. It is important to look at portfolios and the gains from diversification. What is important is the return on the portfolio, not just the return on one asset, and the portfolio's risk.

.01 Portfolio Return

The expected return on a portfolio (r_p) is simply the weighted average return of the individual sets in the portfolio, the weights being the fraction of the total funds invested in each asset:

$$r_p = w_1r_1 + w_2r_2 + ... + w_nr_n = \sum_{j=1}^{n} w_jr_j$$

Where r_j = expected return on each individual asset

w_j = fraction for each respective asset investment

n = number of assets in the portfolio

$$\sum_{j=1}^{n} w_j = 1.0$$

Example 9: A portfolio consists of assets A and B. Asset A makes up one-third of the portfolio and has an expected return of 18 percent. Asset B makes up the other two-thirds of the portfolio and is expected to earn nine percent. The expected return on the portfolio is:

Asset	*return* (r_j)	*fraction* (w_j)	w_jr_j
A	18%	1/3	1/3 × 18% = 6%
B	9%	2/3	2/3 × 9% = 6%
			r_P = 12%

.02 Portfolio Risk

Unlike returns, the risk of a portfolio (σ_p) is not simply the weighted average of the standard deviations of the individual assets in the contribution. A portfolio's risk is also dependent on the correlation coefficients of its assets. The correlation coefficient (ρ) is a measure of the degree to which two variables "move" together. It has a numerical value that ranges from -1.0 to 1.0. In a two-asset (A and B) portfolio, the portfolio risk is defined as:

$$\sigma_P = \sqrt{W_A^2\sigma_A^2 + W_B^2\sigma_B^2 + 2\rho_{AB}W_AW_B\sigma_A\sigma_B}$$

Where σ_A and σ_B = standard deviations of assets A and B, respectively

W_A and W_B = weights, or fractions, of total funds invested in assets A and B

ρ_{AB} = the correlation coefficient between assets A and B

Incidentally, the correlation coefficient is the measurement of joint movement between two securities.

.03 Diversification

As can be seen in the above formula, the portfolio risk, measured in terms of σ, is not the weighted average of the individual asset risks in the portfolio. Note that in the formula there is a third term, (ρ), which makes a significant contribution to the overall portfolio risk. What the formula basically shows is that portfolio risk can be minimized or completely eliminated by diversification. The degree of reduction in portfolio risk depends upon the correlation between the assets being combined. Generally speaking, by combining two perfectly negatively correlated assets (ρ =-1.0), one is able to eliminate the risk completely. In the real world, however, most securities are negatively, but not perfectly correlated. In fact, most assets are positively correlated. One could still reduce the portfolio risk by combining even positively correlated assets. An example of the latter might be ownership of two automobile stocks or two housing stocks.

Example 10: Assume the following:

Asset	σ	*w*
A	20%	1/3
B	10%	2/3

The portfolio risk then is:

$$\sigma_P = \sqrt{W_A^2\sigma_A^2 + W_B^2\sigma_B^2 + 2\rho_{AB}W_AW_B\sigma_A\sigma_B}$$

$$=[(1/3)^2(0.2)^2 + (2/3)^2(0.1)^2 + 2\rho_{AB}(1/3)(2/3)(0.2)(0.1)]^{1/2}$$

$$=[0.0089 + 0.0089\rho_{AB}]^{1/2}$$

(a) Now assume that the correlation coefficient between A and B is +1 (a perfectly positive correlation). This means that when the value of asset A increases in response to market conditions, so does the value of asset B, and it does so at exactly the same rate as A. The portfolio risk when ρ_{AB} = +1 then becomes:

$$\sigma_P = [0.0089 + 0.0089\rho_{AB}]^{1/2} = [0.0089 + 0.0089(+1)]^{1/2} = 0.1334 = 13.34\%$$

(b) If ρ_{AB} = 0, the assets lack correlation and the portfolio risk is simply the risk of the expected returns on the assets, i.e., the weighted average of the standard deviations of the individual assets in the portfolio. Therefore, when ρ_{AB} = 0, the portfolio risk for this example is:

$$\sigma_P=[0.0089 + 0.0089\rho_{AB}]^{1/2}=[0.0089 + 0.0089(0)]^{1/2}=0.094=9.4\%$$

(c) If $\rho_{AB} = -1$ (a perfectly negative correlation coefficient), then as the price of A rises, the price of B declines at the very same rate. In such a case, risk would be completely eliminated. Therefore, when $\rho_{AB} = -1$, the portfolio risk is:

$$\sigma_P=[0.0089 + 0.0089\rho_{AB}]^{1/2}=[0.0089 + 0.0089(-1)]^{1/2}= [0.0089 - 0.0089]^{1/2}=0=0$$

When comparing the results of (a), (b), and (c), one sees that a positive correlation between assets increases a portfolio's risk above the level found at zero correlation, while a perfectly negative correlation eliminates that risk.

Example 11: To illustrate the point of diversification, assume data on the following three securities are as follows:

Year	*Security X (%)*	*Security Y (%)*	*Security Z (%)*
20X1	10	50	10
20X2	20	40	20
20X3	30	30	30
20X4	40	20	40
20X5	50	10	50
r_j	30	30	30
σ_j	14.14	14.14	14.14

Note here that securities X and Y have a perfectly negative correlation, and securities X and Z have a perfectly positive correlation. Notice what happens to the portfolio risk when X and Y, and X and Z are combined. Assume that funds are split equally between the two securities in each portfolio.

Year	*Portfolio XY (50% – 50%)*	*Portfolio XZ (50% – 50%)*
20X1	30	10
20X2	30	20
20X3	30	30
20X4	30	40
20X5	30	50
r_P	30	30
σ_P	0	14.14

Again, see that the two perfectly negative correlated securities (XY) result in a zero overall risk.

¶ 721 Measuring Risk by Beta

Many investors hold more than one financial asset. A portion of a security's risk (called *unsystematic risk*) can be controlled through diversification. This type of risk is unique to a given security. Business, liquidity, and default risks, which were discussed earlier, fall in this category. Nondiversifiable risk, more commonly referred to as *systematic risk*, results from forces outside of the firm's control, and are, therefore, not unique to the given security. Purchasing power, interest rate, and market risks fall into this category. This type of risk is measured by *beta*.

Beta (b) measures a security's volatility relative to an average security. A particular stock's beta is useful in predicting how much the security will go up or down, provided that one knows which way the market will go.

Most of the unsystematic risk affecting a security can be diversified away in an efficiently constructed portfolio. Therefore, this type of risk does not need to be compensated with a higher level of return. The only relevant risk is systematic risk, or beta risk, for which the investor should expect to receive compensation, because it cannot be controlled.

.01 The Capital Asset Pricing Model (CAPM)

Under the *capital asset pricing model* (CAPM), in general, there is a relationship between a stock's expected (or required) return and its beta. The following formula is very helpful in determining a stock's expected return.

$$r_j = r_f + b(r_m - r_f)$$

In words,

Expected return = risk – free rate + beta × (market risk premium)

Where r_j = the expected (or required) return on security j; r_f = the risk-free rate on a security such as a T-bill; r_m = the expected return on the market portfolio (such as Standard and Poor's 500 Stock Composite Index or Dow Jones 30 Industrials); and b = beta, an index of systematic (nondiversifiable, uncontrollable) risk.

The market risk premium ($r_m - r_f$) equals the expected market return (r_m) minus the risk-free rate (r_f). The market risk premium is the additional return above that which one could earn on, say a T-bill, to compensate for assuming a given level of risk (as measured by beta).

Thus, the formula shows that the required (expected) return on a given security is equal to the return required for securities that have no risk plus a risk premium required by the investor for assuming a given level of risk. The key idea behind the formula is that the relevant measure of risk is the risk of the individual security, or its beta. The higher the beta for a security, the greater the return expected (or demanded) by the investor.

Example 12: Assume that $r_f = 6\%$, and $r_m = 10\%$. If a stock has a beta of 2.0, its risk premium should be 14 percent:

$r_j = r_f + b(r_m - r_f)$

$6\% + 2.0\,(10\% - 6\%) = 6\% + 8\% = 14\%$

This means that one would expect (or demand) an extra eight percent (risk premium) on this stock on top of the risk-free return of six percent. Therefore, the total expected (required) return on the stock should be 14 percent:

$6\% + 8\% = 14\%$

Example 13: The higher a stock's beta, the greater the return expected (or demanded) by the investor as follows:

Stock	*Beta*	*Required return*
Mobil	.85	6% + .85(12% − 6%)=11.1%
Bristol-Myers	1.0	6% + 1.0(12% − 6%)=12%
Neiman-Marcus	1.65	6% + 1.65(12% − 6%)=15.9%

.02 Reading Beta

Beta (b) measures a security's volatility relative to an average security. Putting it another way, it is a measure of a security's return over time to that of the overall market. For example, if a company's beta is 2.0, it means that if the stock market goes up 10 percent, the company's common stock goes up 20 percent; if the market goes down 10 percent, the company's stock price goes down 20 percent. Here is how to read betas:

Beta	*Meaning*
0	The security's return is independent of the market. An example is a risk-free security (e.g., T-Bill).
0.5	The security is half as volatile as the market.
1.0	The security is as volatile or risky as the market (i.e., average risk). This is the beta value of the market portfolio (e.g., Standard & Poor's 500).
2.0	The security is twice as volatile or risky as the market.

Exhibit 2 shows examples of betas for selected stocks.

Exhibit 2

Betas for Selected Corporations

Company	*Ticker Symbol*	*Beta*
IBM	IBM	1.3
Wal-Mart	WMT	1.0
Microsoft	MSFT	1.7
McDonald's	MCD	0.7
Pfizer	PFE	0.6
Nokia	NOK	2.1

Source: MSN Money Central Investor (moneycentral.msn.com/investor/home.asp), *Company Report,* August 21, 2002.

¶ 725 The Arbitrage Pricing Model (APM)

The CAPM assumes that required rates of return depend only on one risk factor, the stock's beta. The Arbitrage Pricing Model (APM) disputes this and includes any number of risk factors:

$$r = r_f + b_1 \ RP_1 + b_2 \ RP_2 + \ldots + b_n \ RP_n$$

Where r = the expected return for a given stock or portfolio

r_f = the risk-free rate

b_i = the sensitivity (or reaction) of the returns of the stock to unexpected changes in economic forces i (i = 1, . . .n)

RP_i = the market risk premium associated with an unexpected change in the ith economic force

n = the number of relevant economic forces

The following five economic forces are often suggested:

1. Changes in expected inflation.
2. Unanticipated changes in inflation.
3. Unanticipated changes in industrial production.
4. Unanticipated changes in the yield differential between low- and high-grade bonds (the default-risk premium).
5. Unanticipated changes in the yield differential between long-term and short-term bonds (the term structure of interest rates).

The importance of industry factors, investor confidence, exchange rates, oil prices, and a host of other variables are forces that cannot always be measured with accuracy.

Example 14: Suppose a three-factor APM holds and the risk free rate is six percent. An investor is interested in two particular stocks: A and B. The returns on both stocks are related to factors 1 and 2 as follows:

$r = 0.06 + b_1 (0.09) - b_2 (0.03) + b_3 (0.04)$

The sensitivity coefficients for the two stocks are given below.

Stock	b_1	b_2	b_3
A . . .	0.70	0.80	0.20
B . . .	0.50	0.04	1.20

One can calculate the expected returns on both stocks as follows:

For stock A:

$r = 0.06 + (0.70)(0.09) - (0.80)(0.03) + (0.20)(0.04)$

$r = 0.06 + 0.63 - 0.24 + 0.008$

$= 10.70\%$

For stock B:

$r = 0.06 + (0.50)(0.09) - (0.04)(0.03) + (1.20)(0.04)$

$r = 0.06 + 0.045 - 0.0012 = 0.048$

$= 15.18\%$

Stock B requires a higher return, indicating it is the riskier of the two. Part of the reason is that its return is substantially more sensitive to the third economic force than stock A's is.

Chapter 8
Valuation of Bonds and Stocks

¶ 801 Overview

Valuation is the process of determining the worth (or value) of an asset. Just like a company's investors, the company's financial managers must have a good understanding of how to value its stocks, bonds, and other securities to judge whether or not they are a "good buy." Failure to understand the concepts and computational procedures in valuing a security may preclude sound financial decisions and hinder a company's objective of maximizing the value of its common stock.

The concept of the time value of money can be used to analyze the values of bonds and stocks. This chapter discusses basic bond valuation and stock valuation models under varying assumptions. In all cases, bond and stock values are found to be the present value of the future cash flows expected from the security.

¶ 805 Valuing a Security

The process of valuing a security involves finding the present value of an asset's expected future cash flows using the investor's required rate of return. Thus, the basic security valuation model can be defined mathematically as follows:

$$V = \sum_{t=1}^{n} \frac{C_t}{(1+r)^t}$$

Where:

V = intrinsic value or present value of a security

C_t = expected future cash flows in period t = 1, . . . , n

r = the investor's required rate of return

¶ 811 Bonds

A bond is a certificate or security showing loaned funds to a company in return for fixed future interest and repayment of principal.

There are certain terms and features of bonds one should be familiar with, including:

1. *Par value.* The par value of a bond is the face value (maturity value), usually $1,000.

2. *Coupon rate.* The coupon rate is the nominal interest rate that determines the actual interest to be received on a bond. It is an annual interest based on par value. For example, if one owns a $1,000 bond having a coupon rate of six percent, the annual interest payment one will receive is $60.

3. *Maturity date.* The maturity date is the final date on which repayment of the bond principal is due.

4. *Yield.* The yield is different than the coupon interest rate. It is the effective interest rate one is earning on the bond investment. If a bond is bought below its face value (i.e., purchased at a discount), the yield is higher than the coupon rate. If a bond is acquired above face value (i.e., bought at a premium), the yield is below the coupon rate.

.01 Valuing Bonds

The valuation process for a bond requires knowledge of three basic elements: (1) the amount of the cash flows to be received by the investor, which is equal to the periodic interest to be received and the par value to be paid at maturity; (2) the maturity date of the bond; and (3) the investor's required rate of return.

Incidentally, the periodic interest may be received annually or semiannually. The value of a bond is simply the present value of these cash flows. Two versions of the bond valuation model are presented below:

If the interest payments are made annually, then

$$V = \sum_{t=1}^{n} \frac{I}{(1+r)^t} + \frac{M}{(1+r)^n} = I \times T_4(r,n) + M \times T_3(r,n)$$

Where:

I = interest payment each year = coupon interest rate × par value

M = par value, or maturity value, typically $1,000

r = the investor's required rate of return

n = number of years to maturity

T_4 = present value interest factor of an annuity of $1 (which can be found in Table 4 in Appendix B).

T_3 = present value interest factor of $1 (which can be found in Table 3 in Appendix B).

Both T_4 and T_3 were discussed in detail in Chapter 6.

Example 1: Consider a bond, maturing in 10 years and having a coupon rate of eight percent. The par value is $1,000. Investors consider 10 percent to be an appropriate required rate of return in view of the risk level associated with this bond. The annual interest payment is $80 (8% × $1,000). The present value of this bond is:

$$V = \sum_{t=1}^{n} \frac{I}{(1+r)^t} + \frac{M}{(1+r)^n}$$

$$= I \times T_4(r,n) + M \times T_3(r,n)$$

$$= \sum_{t=1}^{10} \frac{\$80}{(1+0.1)^t} + \frac{\$1,000}{(1+0.1)^{10}}$$

$$= \$80 \times T_4(10\%,10) + \$1,000 \times T_3(10\%,10)$$

$$= \$80\,(6.145) + \$1,000\,(0.386)$$

$$= \$491.60 + 386.00$$

$$= \$877.60$$

If the interest is paid semiannually, then

$$V = \sum_{t=1}^{2n} \frac{I/2}{(1+2/r)^t} + \frac{M}{(1+r/2)^{2n}} = \frac{I}{2} \times T_4(r/2,2n) + M \times T_3(r/2,2n)$$

Example 2: Assume the same data as in the above example, except the interest is paid semiannually.

$$V=\sum_{t=1}^{2n}\frac{I/2}{(1+2/r)^{t}}+\frac{M}{(1+r/2)^{2n}}=\frac{I}{2}\times T_4(r/2,2n)+M\times T_3(r/2,2n)$$

$$=\sum_{t=1}^{20}\frac{\$40}{(1+0.05)^{t}}+\frac{\$1{,}000}{(1+0.5)^{20}}$$

$= \$40 \times T_4\,(5\%,20) + \$1{,}000 \times T_3\,(5\%,20)$

$= \$40\,(12.462) + \$1{,}000\,(0.377)$

$= \$498.48 + \$377.00$

$= \$875.48$

.02 Calculating Yield (Effective Rate of Return) on a Bond

Bonds are evaluated on many different types of returns, including current yield and yield to maturity.

Current yield. The current yield is the annual interest payment divided by the current price of the bond. This is reported in the Wall Street Journal, among other places.

Example 3: Assume a 12-percent coupon rate $1,000 par value bond selling for $960. The current yield is:

$120/$960 = 12.5%

The problem with this measure of return is that it does not take into account the maturity date of the bond. A bond with 1 year to run and another with 15 years to run would have the same current yield quote if interest payments were $120 and the price were $960. Clearly, the one-year bond would be preferable under this circumstance, because one would not only get $120 in interest, but also a gain of $40 ($1000 − $960) with a one-year time period, and this amount could be reinvested.

Yield to maturity. The expected rate of return on a bond, better known as the bond's yield to maturity, is computed by solving the following equation (the bond valuation model) for r:

$$V=\sum_{t=1}^{n}\frac{I}{(1+r)^{t}}+\frac{M}{(1+r)^{n}}=I\times T_4(r,n)+M\times T_3(r,n)$$

The yield to maturity takes into account the maturity date of the bond. It is the real return one would receive from interest income plus capital gain, assuming the bond is held to maturity.

Finding the bond's yield r, involves trial and error. It is best explained by an example.

Example 4: Assume a 10-year, eight-percent coupon, $1,000 par value bond at a price of $877.60. What rate of return could one earn if one bought the bond and held it to maturity? Recall that in the previous example the value of the bond, $877.60, was obtained using the required rate of return of 10 percent. Compute this bond's yield to see if it is 10 percent.

First, set up the bond valuation model:

$$V = \sum_{t=1}^{10} \frac{\$80}{(1+r)^t} + \frac{\$1{,}000}{(1+r)^{10}} =$$

$= \$80 \times T_4\,(r,10) + \$1{,}000 \times T_3\,(r,10)$

Since the bond is selling at a discount under the par value ($877.60 versus $1,000), the bond's yield is above the going coupon rate of eight percent. Therefore, try a rate of nine percent. Substituting factors for nine percent in the equation, we obtain:

V = $80 (6.418) + $1,000 (0.422) = $513.44 + $422.0 = $935.44

The calculated bond value, $935.44, is above the actual market price of $877.60, so the yield is not nine percent. To lower the calculated value, the rate must be raised. Trying 10 percent, we obtain:

V = $80 (6.145) + $1,000 (0.386) = $491.60 + $386.0 = $877.60

This calculated value is exactly equal to the market price of the bond; thus, 10 percent is the bond's yield to maturity.

The formula that can be used to find the approximate yield to maturity on a bond is:

$$\text{Yield} = \frac{I + (M - V)/n}{(M + V)/2}$$

Where:

I = dollars of interest paid per year

M = the par value, typically $1,000 per bond

V = a bond's current value (price)

n = number of years to maturity

This formula can also be used to obtain a starting point for the trial-and-error method discussed in the previous example.

Example 5: Using the same data as in the previous example and the short-cut method, the rate of return on the bond is:

$$\text{Yield} = \frac{\$80 + (\$1{,}000 - \$877.60)/10}{(\$1{,}000 + \$877.60)/2}$$

$$= \frac{\$80 + \$12.24}{\$938.80} = \frac{\$92.24}{\$938.80} = \$9.8\%$$

As can be seen, since the bond was bought at a discount, the yield (9.8 percent) came out greater than the coupon rate of eight percent.

¶815 Preferred Stock

Preferred stock carries a fixed dividend that is paid quarterly. The dividend is stated in dollar terms per share, or as a percentage of par (stated) value of the stock. Preferred stock is considered a hybrid security because it possesses features of both common stock and a corporate bond. It is like common stock in that:

- It represents equity ownership and is issued without stated maturity dates;
- It pays dividends.

Preferred stock is also like a corporate bond in that:

- It provides for prior claims on earnings and assets;
- Its dividend is fixed for the life of the issue;
- It can carry call and convertible features and sinking fund provisions.

Since preferred stocks are traded on the basis of the yield offered to investors, they are, in effect, viewed as fixed income securities and, as a result, are in competition with bonds in the marketplace. Convertibles, however, trade more like common stock, depending on conversion prices.

.01 Valuing Preferred Stock

The value of preferred stock is the present worth of a series of equal cash flow streams (dividends), continuing indefinitely. The calculation is similar to the present value of a perpetuity discussed in Chapter 6. Since the dividends in each period are equal for preferred stock, the valuation model can be reduced to the following relationship:

$V = D/r$

Where:

V = present value of a preferred stock

D = annual dividend

r = the investor's required rate of return

Example 6: ABC preferred stock pays an annual dividend of $4.00. An investor requires a 16-percent return on his investment. The value of the ABC preferred stock can be determined as follows:

V = D/r = $4.00/.16 = $25

.02 Calculating Expected Return on Preferred Stock

In computing the preferred stockholder's expected rate of return, one uses the valuation equation for preferred stock presented above. Simply solving it for r,

r = D/V

This indicates that the expected rate of return of a preferred stock equals the dividend yield (annual dividend/market price).

Example 7: A preferred stock paying $5.00 a year in dividends and having a market price of $25 would have a current yield of 20 percent, computed as follows:

r = D/V = $5/$25 = 20%

¶ 821 Common Stock

Common stock is an equity investment that represents the ownership of a corporation. It corresponds to the capital account for a sole proprietorship or capital contributed by each partner for a partnership.

The corporation's stockholders have certain rights and privileges, including:

1. *Control of the firm.* The stockholders elect the firm's directors, who in turn select officers to manage the business.

2. *Preemptive rights.* This is the right to purchase new stock. A preemptive right entitles a common stockholder to maintain his or her proportional ownership through the opportunity to purchase, on a pro rata basis, any new stock being offered or any securities convertible into common stock.

.01 Valuing Common Stock

The value of a common stock is the present value of all future cash inflows expected to be received by the investor. The cash inflows expected to be received are dividends and the future price at the time of the sale of the stock.

Single holding period. For an investor holding a common stock for only one year, the value of the stock would be the present value of both the expected cash dividend to be received in one year (D_1) and the expected market price per share of the stock at year-end (P_1). If r represents an investor's required rate of return, the value of common stock (P_0) would be:

$$P_0 = \frac{D_1}{(1 + r)^1} + \frac{P_1}{(1 + r)^1}$$

Example 8: Assume an investor is considering the purchase of stock A at the beginning of the year. The dividend at year-end is expected to be \$1.50, and the market price by the end of the year is expected to be \$40. If the investor's required rate of return is 15%, the value of the stock would be:

$$P_0 = \frac{D_1}{(1 + r)^1} + \frac{P_1}{(1 + r)^1} = \frac{\$1.50}{(1 + 0.15)} + \frac{\$40}{(1 + 0.15)}$$

$= \$1.50\ T_3\ (15\%,1) + \$40\ T_3\ (15\%,1)$

$= \$1.50\ (0.870) + \$40\ (0.870)$

$= \$1.31 + \$34.80 = \$36.11$

Multiple holding period. Since common stock has no maturity date and is held for many years, a more general, multiperiod model is needed. The general common stock valuation model is defined as follows:

$$P_0 = \sum_{t=1} \frac{D_t}{(1+r)^t}$$

Where D_t = dividend in period t.

Two cases of growth in dividends are explained below. They are: (a) Zero growth, and (b) constant growth.

(a) Zero Growth Case

In the case of zero growth (i.e., $D_0 = D_1 = \ldots = D$), then the valuation model reduces to the formula:

$$P_0 = \frac{D}{r}$$

This is the case with a perpetuity. This model is most applicable to the valuation of preferred stocks, as was discussed earlier, or the common stocks of very mature companies, such as large utilities.

Example 9: Assuming dividends (D) equals \$2.50 and r equals 10 percent, then the value of the stock is:

$$P_0 = \frac{\$2.50}{0.1} = \$25$$

(b) Constant Growth Case

In the case of constant growth, assuming that dividends grow at a constant rate of g every year [i.e., $D_t = D_0 (1 + g)^t$], then the general model is simplified to:

$$P_0 = \frac{D_1}{r - g}$$

In words,

$$\text{Common stock value} = \frac{\text{Dividend in year 1}}{\text{(Required rate of return)} - \text{(Growth rate)}}$$

This formula is known as the Gordon's Growth Formula. This model is most applicable to the valuation of the common stocks of very large or broadly diversified firms.

Example 10: Consider a common stock that paid a $3 dividend per share at the end of the last year and is expected to pay a cash dividend every year at a growth rate of 10 percent. Assume the investor's required rate of return is 12 percent. The value of the stock would be:

$$D_1 = D_0 (1 + g) = \$3(1 + 0.10) = \$3.30$$

$$P_0 = \frac{D_1}{(r - g)} = \frac{\$3.30}{0.12 - 0.10} = \$16$$

.02 *Calculating Expected Return on Common Stock*

The formula for computing the expected rate of return on common stock can be derived easily from the valuation models.

The single-holding-period return formula is derived from:

$$P_0 = \frac{D_1}{(1 + r)^1} + \frac{P_1}{(1 + r)^1}$$

Solving for r gives:

$$r = \frac{D_1 + (P_1 - P_0)}{P_0}$$

In words,

$$\text{Rate of return} = \frac{\text{Annual dividend + Capital gain}}{\text{Beginning price}}$$

$$= \frac{\text{Annual dividend}}{\text{Beginning price}} + \frac{\text{Capital gain}}{\text{Beginning price}}$$

$$= \text{Dividend yield + Capital gain yield}$$

This formula is the same as the holding period rate of return (HPR), which was introduced in Chapter 7.

Example 11: Consider a stock that sells for $50. The company is expected to pay a $3 cash dividend at the end of the year, and the stock market price at the end of the year is expected to be $55 a share. Thus, the expected return would be:

$$r = \frac{D_1 + (P_1 - P_0)}{P_0} = \frac{\$3.00 + (\$55 - \$50)}{\$50} = \frac{\$3.00 + \$5.00}{\$50} = 16\%$$

Or:

$$\text{Dividend yield} = \frac{\$3.00}{\$50} = 6\%$$

$$\text{Capital gain yield} = \frac{\$5.00}{\$50} = 10\%$$

r = dividend yield + capital gain yield

= 6% + 10% = 16%

Assuming a constant growth in dividends, the formula for the expected rate of return on an investment in stock can be derived as follows:

$$P_0 = \frac{D_1}{r - g}$$

Solving for r gives:

$$r = \frac{D_1}{P_0} + g$$

= dividend yield + annual growth rate

Example 12: Assume that a company's dividend per share is $4.50 and is expected to grow at a constant rate of six percent. The current market price of the stock is $30. Therefore, the expected rate of return is:

$$r = \frac{D_1}{P_0} + g$$

$$= \frac{\$4.50}{\$30} + 6\% = 15\% + 6\% = 21\%$$

¶ 825 Price/Earnings Ratio

.01 Price/Earnings Ratio Approaches to Valuing Common Stock

A more popular pragmatic approach to valuing a common stock is to use the P/E ratio (or multiple). One may use the simple formula:

Expected stock price = a selected P/E ratio × projected earnings per share (EPS) (E_1)

Comparing the current price against the computed expected value price could help indicate if the stock is under- or overvalued.

> ***Example 13:*** The XYZ Corporation had EPS of $5. The EPS is expected to grow at 20 percent. The company's normal P/E ratio is estimated to be 7, which is used as the multiplier. Estimated EPS =$5 (1 + .20) = $6.00. The value of the stock is:
>
> 7 × $6.00 = $42

It is important to realize that for the P/E method to be effective in forecasting the future value of a stock, (a) earnings need to be correctly projected, and (b) the appropriate P/E multiple must be applied. Forecasting EPS is not an easy task. Furthermore, there is no agreed upon method of picking a meaningful P/E ratio. Some analysts use an average of historical earnings, some normalize earnings, some come up with a P/E ratio relative to the market's P/E ratio, and so on. A discussion of these methods follows.

Historical P/E ratios. The first approach is simply to look at historical P/E ratios. A 5- or 10-year average price-earnings ratio is a useful benchmark, because it will smooth out fluctuating earnings and prices during both economic expansions and recessions. Exhibit 1 illustrates this approach. It shows the calculated high, low, and average P/E ratios of each of the last five years. One can estimate a range of stock values by using these five-year average high, low, and average P/Es with an earning estimate.

Exhibit 1

Normalized Price-Earnings Ratio Example

Stock Price ($)

	1997	1998	1999	2000	2001	2002
High	24.50	40.90	45.40	45.00	51.30	—
Low	16.30	21.30	35.60	37.50	38.90	—

Earnings Per Share ($)

	1997	1998	1999	2000	2001	2002
	—	1.22	1.43	1.68	2.00*	2.30*

Normalized Price-Earnings Ratio

(Stock Price ÷ Next Year's Earnings Per Share)

	1997	1998	1999	2000	2001	2002
High	20.1	28.6	27.0	22.5	22.3	—
Low	13.4	14.9	21.2	18.8	16.9	—

Average Relative Price-Earnings Ratios:

24.1 = Five-Year High

17.0 = Five-Year Low

20.6 = Five-Year Average

Stock Valuation

High	$2.30 × 24.1 = $55.4
Low	$2.30 × 17.0 = $39.1
Average	$2.30 × 20.6 = $47.4

* Value Line estimated earnings.

This approach, however, does not take into account market factors, and one should adjust for them.

Market-relative P/E ratios. The second approach gets around the problem of market factors by looking at market-relative P/E ratios. The relative price-earnings ratio examines the relative relationship of the price-earnings ratio of a stock to the price-earnings ratio of the overall market or the stock's industry. It simply compares them with the overall market's price-earnings ratio by dividing a company's price-earnings ratio by the market's (S&P 500 or Value Line Index), as shown below. *Note:* A relative price-earnings ratio of 1.0 would indicate a price-earnings ratio that is equal to the market's price-earnings ratio. A relative price-earnings ratio above 1.0 would indicate that a company's price-earnings ratio is above the market's price-earnings ratio. By tracking the price-earnings relative over a number of years, one can estimate a price-earnings relative that a stock tends to follow.

$$\text{Relative P/E ratio} = \frac{\text{Company P/E}}{\text{Market P/E}}$$

Company P/E = relative P/E ratio × current market P/E

Exhibit 2 illustrates this approach. In this example, the relative ratio is based upon the most recent 12 months of earnings divided by the year-end market price-earnings ratio.

Exhibit 2

Relative Price-Earnings Ratio Example

Trailing Price-Earnings Ratio

(Stock Price ÷ Earnings Per Share)

	1997	*1998*	*1999*	*2000*	*2001*	*2002*
High	24.0	33.5	31.7	26.8	25.7	____
Low	16.0	17.5	24.9	22.3	19.5	____

S&P Trailing Price-Earnings Ratio

(Stock Price ÷ Earnings Per Share)

	1997	*1998*	*1999*	*2000*	*2001*	*2002*
High	17.3	26.1	21.1	21.5	17.6	____
Low	13.9	19.5	18.0	19.6	16.1	____

Relative Price-Earnings Ratio

(Company P/E ÷ S&P 500 P/E)

	1997	*1998*	*1999*	*2000*	*2001*	*2002*
High	1.4	1.3	1.5	1.2	1.5	____
Low	1.1	0.9	1.4	1.1	1.2	____

Average Relative Price-Earnings Ratios:

1.4 = Five-Year High

1.2 = Five-Year Low

1.3 = Five-Year Average

Also Note:

24.9 = Current Price-Earnings Ratio Of Market

$2.30 = Expected Next Annual Earnings Per Share

Price-Earnings Ratio, Based On A Relative Ratio And Current Market Ratio:

High: . . . . 1.4 × 24.9 = 34.9

Low: . . . . 1.2 × 24.9 = 30.0

Average: . . . . 1.3 × 24.9 = 32.4

Stock Valuation:

High: . . . . 34.9 × $2.30 = $80.3

Low: . . . . 30.0 × $2.30 = $69.0

Average: . . . . 32.4 × $2.30 = $74.5

Note: All the computation results are somewhat different from the spreadsheet figures due to rounding.

Graham and Dodd market-adjusted P/E approach. The third approach, developed by Graham and Dodd, is another market-adjusted P/E approach. The adjustment is based on (1) a statistical relationship between P/Es and growth, which is P/E = 8.5 + 2g, and (2) an interest adjustment, which is 4.4%/Y, where Y = corporate AAA bond yield. The adjusted P/E ratio is:

$$P/E \times \frac{4.4\%}{Y}$$

$$(8.5 + 2g) \times \frac{4.4\%}{Y}$$

Example 14: Assume:

E = $2.30, expected next annual earnings per share

g = 15%, annual growth in earnings per share

Y = 8%, current AAA corporate bond yield

For proper calculation, the percentages are removed from the Graham Dodd formula:

[8.5 + (2 × 15)] × 4.4/8 = 21.2

Expected stock price = a P/E ratio × projected EPS (E_1)

= 21.2 × $2.30 = $48.76

.02 Determinants of the Price-Earnings Ratio

The factors that determine the P/E multiple are very complex. Empirical evidence seems to suggest the following factors:

1. Historical growth rate in earnings.
2. Forecasted earnings.
3. Average dividend payout ratio.
4. Beta, the company's systematic (uncontrollable) risk.
5. Instability of earnings.
6. Financial leverage.
7. Other factors such as competitive position, management ability.
8. Economic conditions.

.03 Selling Stock on a High or Low Price-Earnings Ratio

To address this issue, the Gordon's Growth Formula can be helpful. If a company's dividends are expected to grow at a constant rate, then:

$$P_0 = \frac{D_1}{r-g}$$

Where P_0 = the current price of stock, D_1 = the expected dividend next year, r = the return required by investors from similar investments, and g = the expected growth in dividends. In order to find the P/E ratio, dividing through by expected EPS yields:

$$\frac{P_0}{EPS} = \frac{D_1}{EPS} \times \frac{1}{r-g}$$

Thus, a high P/E ratio may indicate that:

1. Investors expect high dividend growth (g), or
2. The stock has low risk and, therefore, investors are content with a low prospective return (r), or
3. The company is expected to achieve average growth while paying out a high proportion of earnings (D_1 /EPS).

Exhibit 3 shows price-earnings ratios of certain companies. Online computer investment databases such as cbs.marketguide.com contain such information.

Exhibit 3

P/E Ratios

Company	*Industry*	*2002*
Boeing	Aerospace	13
General Motors	Cars & Trucks	30
Phillip Morris	Consumer Products	14
Nordstrom	Retailing	27
Intel	Semiconductor	150
Safeway	Food	17

Source: Adapted from *The Business Week 50,* by Business Week, McGraw-Hill, Spring 2002, pp. 87-113.

¶ 831 Other Pragmatic Approaches to Valuing Stock Investments

In valuing a stock investment, there are several pragmatic techniques one may employ: price-sales (P/S), price-dividends, and price-book (P/B) value ratios.

.01 The Price-Sales (P/S) Ratio

This is an increasingly popular tool for determining underlying stock value. It is computed as:

$$\frac{\text{Market Price Per Share}}{\text{Sales Per Share}}$$

A P/S of, say, 0.83 means that one is paying 83 cents for every dollar of sales. The P/S ratio reflects a company's underlying strength. A company with a low P/S ratio is more attractive while one with a high ratio is less attractive. *Note:* As a rule of thumb, one should avoid stocks with a P/S ratio of 1.5 or more. Further, one should sell a stock when the ratio is between 3 and 6.

The following simple formula may be used:

Expected price = projected sales per share × average P/S ratio

> ***Example 15:*** The XYZ corporation projects sales to be $3.5 per share. The company's 5-year average P/S ratio is 14.4, which is used as the multiplier. The value of the stock is $51.0 ($3.5 × 14.4)

.02 The Price-Dividends (P/D) Ratio

This is another popular tool for determining underlying stock value. It is computed as:

$$\frac{\text{Market Price Per Share}}{\text{Dividends Per Share}}$$

The following simple formula may be used:

Expected price = projected dividends per share × average P/D ratio

> ***Example 16:*** The XYZ corporation projects dividends to be $0.88 per share. The company's 5-year average P/S ratio is 61.3, which is used as the multiplier. The value of the stock is $53.94 ($0.88 × 61.3)

.03 The Price-Book (P/B) Ratio

Book value (net asset, liquidation value) per share is the amount of corporate assets for each share of common stock. One may benefit by uncovering stock that is selling below book value or whose assets are significantly undervalued. A stock may represent a good value when its market price is below or close to book value, because the security is undervalued. Companies with lower ratios of market price to book value have historically earned better returns than those with higher ratios.

$$\frac{\text{Market Price Per Share}}{\text{Book Value Per Share}}$$

Where book value per share = total stockholders' equity/total shares outstanding.

Example 17: An investor is thinking of investing in a company that has a market price per share of $40. The book value per share is $50. This may be a buying opportunity, since market price ($40) is well below book value ($50), or P/B ratio of .9 ($40/$50), and an upward movement in prices may occur.

The following simple formula may be used:

Expected price = projected book value per share × average P/B ratio

Example 18: The XYZ corporation projects sales to be $5.50 per share. The company's 5-year average P/S ratio is 10.4, which is used as the multiplier. The value of the stock is $57.20 ($5.50 × 10.4).

Note: Various financial services track industries and companies. They offer expectations as to future earnings, sales, dividends, book value, and even market prices of stock. For example, reference may be made to Standard and Poor's *Stock Reports* and Value Line's *Investment Survey. Institutional Brokers Estimate System* (I/B/E/S) is a database available on CompuServe that provides consensus earnings estimates on over 3,400 publicly traded corporations. *Zack's* performs a similar service, and is available through Dow Jones News/Retrieval. These provide a thorough analysis of companies and provide clues as to future expectations and a source of earnings estimates.

.04 Choosing the Best Valuation Model

Several valuations were presented so far. The key is to decide which valuation model or models is best suited for a company an investor is interested in. For example, if a company is a mature, dividend-paying stock, such as a public utility, which is generally a low-growth stock, the dividend-based models make sense. If a company is a growth-oriented company, one should use an earnings-based model, since the earnings potential, rather than dividends, will drive the stock's price. Nonetheless, it is a good idea to perform sensitivity analysis and obtain a range of estimates. Any final decision on valuation estimates should, however, be based on a better understanding of the company, its management, and its competitive environment.

Part 4

Financial Decision-Making and Planning

Chapter 9

Financial Decision-Making: Tools and Concepts

¶ 901 Overview

Financial managers must consider several important concepts, including *return, risk, leverage,* and *cash flow.* A firm wants to be profitable and it wants to continue in business. Also, it may want to decide how much of other people's money to use to increase return to its owners. There exists, however, a trade-off between return and risk associated with a decision. Further, it is possible to be profitable, yet fail to continue because of lack of cash flow.

¶ 905 Finance Decisions and Risk-Return Trade-off

The concept of risk-return trade-off is integral to the theory of finance, which was discussed in Chapters 1 and 7. One will not bear additional risk unless one expects to be compensated with additional return. In maximizing return, there is always a trade-off with risk. For example, in the case of inventory management, the less inventory one keeps, the higher the expected return (since less of the firm's current assets are tied up). However, the risk of running out of stock and, thus, losing potential revenue is also greater.

Obviously, given two equally risky projects, one would choose the one with a greater expected return. In many business decisions, however, decision-makers are faced with the risk-return trade-off, and must ask themselves, "Is the extra return worth the risk?"

.01 Risk and Risk Analysis Defined

Risk refers to the variability of expected returns (sales, earnings, or cash flow) and is the probability that a financial problem will affect the company's operational performance or financial position. Typical forms of risk are economic risk, political uncertainties, and industry problems.

Risk analysis is a process of measuring and analyzing the risk associated with financial and investment decisions. It is important to consider risk in making capital investment decisions because of the large amount of capital involved and the long-term nature of the investments. Analysts must also consider the rate of return in relation to the degree of risk involved. (Return, the reward for investing, consists of current income, in the form of either periodic cash payments or capital gain (or loss) from appreciation (or depreciation) in market value.)

Proper assessment and balance of the various risk-return trade-offs available is part of creating a sound stockholder wealth maximization plan.

¶ 911 Return vs. Liquidity

There also exists a trade-off between liquidity and return. Greater liquidity results in more safety, but lower return.

As a means of increasing its liquidity, a business may choose to invest additional monies in cash and/or marketable securities, such as T-bills and commercial papers. Such action involves a trade-off, since such assets are likely to earn little return.

Example 1: Companies A and B are identical in every respect but one: Company B has invested $20,000 in T-bills, which has been financed with equity. Assume a 50-percent tax rate. The balance sheets and earnings of the two companies are shown below.

	Company A	*Company B*
Cash	$ 2,000	$ 2,000
Marketable Securities		20,000
Other Current Assets	50,000	50,000
Fixed Assets	100,000	100,000
Total	152,000	172,000
Current Liabilities	$ 30,000	$ 30,000
Long-Term Debt	50,000	50,000
Owner's Equity	72,000	92,000
Total	152,000	172,000
Net Income	$ 20,000	$ 20,800[(a)]

Current ratio

$$\frac{\$52{,}000}{\$30{,}000} = 1.73 \qquad \frac{\$72{,}000}{\$30{,}000} = 2.4$$

Return on total assets (ROA)

$$\frac{\$20{,}000}{\$152{,}000} = 13.16\% \qquad \frac{\$20{,}800}{\$172{,}000} = 12.09\%$$

(a) During the year, Company B held $20,000 in T-bills, which earned an eight-percent return, or $1,600 for the year, or $800 after taxes.

Note that Company A has a current ratio of 1.73 and earns 13.16-percent return on its total assets. Company B, on the other hand, has a higher liquidity as expressed by a current ratio of 2.4, but earns only 12.09 percent.

¶ 915 Leverage

One of the most important financial decisions faced by any business is how much leverage (use of other people's money) it should employ; i.e., the degree to which it incurs fixed costs. As sales increase, fixed costs do not increase. As a result, earnings can rise rapidly during good times. On the other hand, during bad times fixed costs do not decline, so profits fall sharply.

As stated, leverage refers to the degree to which a firm commits itself to high levels of fixed costs. The more leverage a firm has the riskier it is, because of the obligations on fixed costs that must be met regardless of good times or bad times. By the same token, the more highly leveraged, the greater the profits during good times. Here again, there is a trade-off between risk and return that the firm must consider in making a financial decision. There are two types of leverage, operating and financial, which will be discussed later at ¶ 1045.

¶ 921 Cash vs. Accrual Basis of Accounting

To measure an entity's operating performance it is necessary to match the revenue and the expense items applicable to a specific time period. There are two ways of recognizing revenue and expenses in financial reporting: cash basis and accrual basis. With a cash basis, revenue is recorded only as cash is received, and expenses are recorded only as paid. With an accrual system, revenue is recognized and recorded when it is earned, even though it may not be billed or received for some time. Expenses are recorded when incurred, even though they may not be paid for some time.

Accountants generally recommend the accrual basis as giving the best indication of actual performance. Inherent in the accrual method of accounting is the matching principle, which states that expenses should be matched against the revenue to which they are directly related, regardless of the timing of cash collections and payments. It poses a difficult problem, however, since the bottom line income figure does not represent cash flow. This problem is well illustrated in the following section.

.01 The Difference Between Cash Flow and Earnings

Cash flow is quite different from earnings (profit, net income) reported on the income statement. Earnings is an accounting concept created by accounting convention, while cash flow is based on the timing of the receipts and disbursements of cash. Under the accrual basis, revenue is recognized when earned and expenses are recognized when incurred; net income equals revenue less expenses. Net income measured on the accrual basis does not reflect the receipt or payment of cash. On the other hand, under the cash basis of accounting, revenue is recognized only when cash is actually received and expenses are recorded only when cash is actually paid; the difference between cash revenue and cash expense is cash earnings.

A small business moves on cash rather than profits. It must have cash, not net income, to pay bills or loans; it must pay workers money, not earnings. A small business needs cash to finance growth and to provide stability in downward markets. Even if the business has high profits, it does not necessarily mean it is generating cash flow from operations; net income must be converted to cash earnings when considering the cash flow from operations of the business. For example, positive earnings during the years 1966 to 1974, but negative cash flow from 1971 to 1974 preceded the W.T. Grant Company bankruptcy in 1975.

The following items make earnings and cash two entirely different concepts:

Sales/accounts receivable. Sales made on credit represent revenue that increases profit. However, cash flow is affected only when the receivable is collected. Accounts receivable becomes money only when received.

Inventory. The accountant's matching concept requires that inventory be charged to cost of sales (which reduces earnings) when a sale takes place. Money used in purchasing inventory of raw materials, work-in-process (partially completed goods on the assembly line), and finished goods (completed goods available for sale) cannot be used for anything else.

Noncash charges. Noncash charges such as depreciation and amortization are deducted from sales revenue to arrive at earnings. But they do not involve cash outlays. They are periodic charges created by accounting convention.

Prepaid items. Prepaid items such as insurance, rents, and service contracts are cash payments made in advance. They reduce earnings in future periods, not in the period of payment.

Fixed assets. Fixed assets such as property, plant, and equipment reduce cash by both the initial down payment and all subsequent installments. Earnings, on the other hand, are affected only by depreciation (the yearly decline in value of a fixed asset arising from wear and tear, natural deterioration, and obsolescence). Land is an exception since it is not depreciable.

Constant payments on interest-bearing obligations. Most interest-bearing obligations require monthly payments of principal and interest until the obligation is fully paid. Only the interest portion of the payment is reflected in earnings, whereas cash flow is affected by both principal and interest.

The following example illustrates the difference between the cash basis and accrual basis.

Example 2: Sarah Cohen started a consulting practice on January 1. For the month of January she rendered professional services and billed out $5,000. These bills were not paid until February. She also received $2,500 in January for other services. During January, she incurred expenses of $1,500 but paid out only $1,250. Based on this information, her cash earnings for January were $1,250, but her net income was $6,000, as shown below.

January 2002

	Cash Basis	*Accrual Basis*
Fee income . . .	$2,500	$7,500
Less: Expenses	1,250	1,500
Cash Earnings	$1,250	
Net income . .		6,000

Example 3: Assume a small business owner wants to determine his or her cash earnings (cash flow from operations) based on the following income statement data: net income $170,000, depreciation expense $5,000, and amortization expense $2,000. The cash earnings are $177,000, as computed below.

Net income	$170,000
Add: Noncash expenses	
Depreciation	5,000
Amortization	2,000
	$177,000

.02 Going Broke While Making a Profit

If one is to manage cash flows, one must understand (1) the difference between the profits one sees on the bottom line of the income statement and economic profits, and (2) how accounting profits differ from economic profits, which is cash flows.

The following example illustrates an important point: One can go broke even while showing accounting profits.

Example 4: As the year started, Mr. Davidson of the Office Products Company was in fine shape. His company made ballpoint pens for 75 cents each and sold them for $1. He kept a 30-day supply in inventory, paid his bills promptly, and billed his customers 30 days net. Sales were right on target, with the sales manager predicting a steady increase. It felt like his lucky year, and it began this way:

Office Products Company
Balance Sheet
January 1, 2002

Cash	$1,000	Liabilities	0
Inventory	750		
Receivables	1,000	Retained Earnings	$2,750
Total Assets	2,750	Total Liabilities & Equity	$2,750

In January, he sold 1,000 ballpoint pens, shipped them at a cost of $750, collected his receivables—winding up with a tidy $250 profit—and his books looked like this:

January 31, 2002

Cash	$1,250	Liabilities	0	
Inventory	750			
Receivables	1,000	Retained Earnings	$3,000	($2,750 + $250)
Total Assets	$3,000	Total Liabilities & Equity	$3,000	

February's sales jumped to 1,500 ballpoint pens. With a corresponding step-up in production to maintain his 30-day inventory, he made 2,000 pens at a cost of $1,500. All receivables from January were collected. The profit so far is: $625 ($250 + $375). Now his books looked like this:

February 28, 2002

Cash	$ 750	Liabilities	0	
Inventory	1,125			
Receivables	1,500	Retained Earnings	$3,375	($3,000 + $375)
Total Assets	$3,375	Total Liabilities & Equity	$3,375	

March sales were even better, with 2,000 units sold. Collections were also on time. Production, to adhere to his inventory policy, was 2,500 units. Operating results for the month: $500 profit. Profit to date: $1,125. His books now show:

March 31, 2002

Cash	$ 375	Liabilities	0	
Inventory	1,500			
Receivables	2,000	Retained Earnings	$3,875	($3,375 + $500)
Total Assets	$3,875	Total Liabilities & Equity	$3,875	

In April, sales jumped another 500 units to 2,500—and Davidson patted his sales manager on the back. His customers were paying right on time. Production was pushed to 3,000 units, and the month's business netted him $625, for a profit to date of $1,750. He took off to Florida before he saw the accountant's report:

April 30, 2002

Cash	$ 125	Liabilities	0	
Inventory	1,875			
Receivables	2,500	Retained Earnings	$4,500	($3,875 + $625)
Total Assets	$4,500	Total Liabilities & Equity	$4,500	

May saw Davidson's small business really taking off—sales of 3,000 units, production of 3,500, and a five-month profit of $2,500. But, suddenly, he got a phone call from his bookkeeper: "Come home! We need money!" His books had caught up with him:

May 31, 2002

Cash	$ 0	Liabilities	0	
Inventory	2,250			
Receivables	3,000	Retained Earnings	$5,250	($4,500 + $750)
Total Assets	$5,250	Total Liabilities & Equity	$5,250	

To capture the critical interactions and relationships between net income and cash flow, the following table lists the sources and uses of cash. The message is clear: you can go broke while making a profit. Davidson's cash was down to zero, while the business made a five-month profit of $2,500.

Office Products Company
Statement of Cash Flows
For the Month Ended June 30, 2002

	Feb.	*March*	*April*	*May*	*June*	*Total*
Cash Balance (a)	1,000	1,250	750	375	125	1,000
Sources of Cash						
Profits (b)	$ 250	$375	$500	$625	$750	$2,500
Uses of Cash						
Inventory	0	500	500	500	500	2,000
Receivables	0	375	375	375	375	1,500
Total (c)	0	875	875	875	875	3,500
Increase (Decrease) (d)	250	($500)	($375)	($250)	($125)	($1,000)
Cash Balance (e)	$1,250	$750	$375	$125	$0	$0

Note: (d) = (b) − (c) and (e) = (a) + (d)

In appraising his cash flow from operations, the small business owner must determine which income statement items generate or use cash. For example, even though credit sales increase profit, they do not increase cash until collected.

¶ 925 Profit Maximization and Marginal Analysis

Marginal analysis that utilizes the concepts of marginal revenue and marginal cost is a key principle in decision making that can be applied to financial and investment decisions. The analysis suggests that financial and investment decisions should be made and actions taken only when marginal revenues exceed marginal costs. If this condition exists, a given decision should maximize the firm's profits.

Managers at any level who have to make their functional (such as marketing, operational, production, purchasing, financing, investment, personnel, and so on) decisions must always weigh the marginal cost to be incurred against the marginal revenue to be derived from that decision. In actual practice, since chances are that decision-makers work with incremental data (rather than marginal data), they will have to weigh the incremental cost associated with the decision against the incremental revenue.

The goal of a firm is to maximize its profit. This is the traditional theory of the firm, which is distinguished from the behavioral theory of the firm. Marginal analysis suggests that business decisions should be made and actions taken only when marginal revenues (MR) exceed marginal costs (MC). MR is the additional revenue resulting from the sale of an additional unit of output, and MC is the cost of the inputs used to make an additional unit of output.

If MR > MC, a given decision should maximize the firm's profits.

In a discrete range of activity, which firms operate in actual business, MR is equivalent to incremental (or differential) revenue (IR). By the same token, MC is viewed as being equivalent to incremental (or differential) cost (IC), which is the increment in cost between the two alternatives or two discrete volumes of output. Therefore, in reality, the decision should be made only when IR > IC.

Example 5: Let TR(Q) denote the total revenue a firm generates from producing Q units of output, and let TC(Q) represent the total costs to the firm of producing Q units of output. The profit (π) then is:

$$\pi(Q) = TR(Q) - TC(Q)$$

The manager facing a situation like the one summarized in columns 1 through 3 in Exhibit 1 wishes to determine the output quantity that will maximize his profits.

Exhibit 1

Marginal Analysis

Q	*TR(Q)*	*TC(Q)*	*π(Q)*			
(1)	*(2)*	*(3)*	*(4) = (2) − (3)*	*MR*	*MC*	
0	0	0	0	—	—	
1	90	10	80	90	10	MR>MC
2	170	30	140	80	20	
3	240	60	180	70	30	
4	300	100	200	60	40	
5	350	150	200	50	50	MR=MC
6	390	210	180	40	60	
7	420	280	140	30	70	
8	440	360	80	20	80	
9	450	450	0	10	90	
10	450	550	−100	0	100	MR<MC

The profits are given in column 4. Note from Exhibit 1 that:

1. So long as MR exceeds MC, an increase in Q adds more to total revenues than it does to total costs.

2. The profits in column 4 are maximized when profits equal $200, which occurs when 5 units of Q are chosen by the manager.

3. At the profit maximizing level of Q (5 units), MR = MC (both are equal to $50 in this example). Note that the profit is maximized at 4 units. This situation occurs since we are dealing with discrete output units. In a continuous case, which is assumed throughout the book, the profit is maximized always when MR = MC.

Unfortunately, the profit-maximization goal, as operationally defined, suffers from some technical flaws: (1) In its practical application, it provides no explicit way of considering the risk associated with alternative decisions, (2) it provides no basis for comparing varying flows of revenues and costs over time, and (3) instead of seeking to "maximize" some objective such as profits, the firm is said to *satisfice*, or seek acceptable levels of performance, which is another model of the firm known as the *behavioral theory* of the firm. Furthermore, profit maximization is a short-term goal, which is simply the maximization of profits within a given period of time.

Note: A firm may maximize its short-term profits at the expense of its long-term profitability (stockholder wealth maximization), which was discussed in Chapter 1.

Chapter 10

Cost-Volume Profit (CVP) Analysis, Leverage, and Other Decision-Making Tools

¶ 1001 Overview

Cost-volume-profit (CVP) analysis, together with cost behavior information, helps financial managers and accountants perform many useful analyses. CVP analysis deals with how profits and costs change with a change in volume. More specifically, it looks at how changes in such factors as variable costs, fixed costs, selling prices, volume, and mix of products sold affect profits. By studying the relationships of costs, sales, and net income, management is better able to cope with many planning decisions. The concept of leverage, and figuring out what portion of the fixed costs represents a risk to the firm, is closely related to CVP analysis.

Break-even analysis, a branch of CVP analysis, determines the break-even sales. The break-even point—the financial crossover point when revenues exactly match costs—does not show up in corporate earnings reports, but financial managers find it an extremely useful measurement in a variety of ways.

¶1005 CVP Analysis

CVP analysis tries to answer the following questions:

1. What sales volume is required to break even?
2. What sales volume is necessary to earn a desired profit?
3. What profit can be expected on a given sales volume?
4. How would changes in selling price, variable costs, fixed costs, and output affect profits?
5. How would a change in the mix of products sold affect the break-even and target income volume and profit potential?

.01 *Applications of the CVP Model*

There are many actual and potential applications of the CVP approach. Some of these include:

1. *Economic analysis of new product.* Based on demand forecasts and estimates of production costs (variable and fixed), the economic impact of a new product can be estimated.
2. *Labor contract negotiations.* The effect of increased variable costs resulting from higher wages on the break-even level of output can be analyzed.
3. *Choice of production process.* The choice of reducing variable costs at the expense of incurring higher fixed costs can be evaluated. Management might decide to become more capital-intensive by performing tasks in the production process through use of equipment rather than labor. Application of the CVP model can indicate what the effects of this trade-off will be on the break-even output for the given product.
4. *Pricing policy.* The sales price of a new product can be set to achieve a target income level. Furthermore, should market penetration be a prime objective, the price could be set that would cover slightly more than the variable costs of production and provide only a partial contribution to the recovery of fixed costs.
5. *Location selection.* Some of the costs of having a facility in a location will be fixed, and some will vary with the volume of business. The cost structure and the volume of sales will probably be different for each location being considered. It is important to realize that the lowest-cost location will always be the maximum-profit location.
6. *Financing decisions.* Analysis of the firm's cost structure will reveal the proportion that fixed operating costs bear to sales. If

this proportion is high, the firm might reasonably decide not to add any fixed financing costs on top of the high fixed operating costs.

7. *Make or buy decision.* Break-even analysis can often be used to determine volume requirements in deciding whether to purchase from suppliers or manufacture in-house a certain component part.

8. *Capital budgeting analysis.* As a complementary technique to discounted cash flow (DCF) techniques, the CVP model locates in a rough way the sales volume needed to make a project economically beneficial to the firm. It should not be used to replace the DCF methodology.

.02 Contribution Margin (CM) Concepts

For accurate CVP analysis, costs must be distinguished as being either variable or fixed. Mixed costs must be separated into their variable and fixed components.

In order to compute the break-even point and perform various CVP analyses, note the following important concepts.

Contribution margin (CM). The contribution margin is the excess of sales (S) over the variable costs (VC) of the product or service. It is the amount of money available to cover fixed costs (FC) and to generate profit. Symbolically, CM = S − VC.

Unit CM. The unit CM is the excess of the unit-selling price (p) over the unit variable cost (v). Symbolically, unit CM = p − v.

CM Ratio. The CM ratio is the contribution margin as a percentage of sales, i.e.,

$$\text{CM Ratio} = \frac{\text{CM}}{\text{S}} = \frac{(\text{S} - \text{VC})}{\text{S}} = 1 - \frac{\text{VC}}{\text{S}}$$

The CM ratio can also be computed using per-unit data as follows:

$$\text{CM Ratio} = \frac{\text{Unit CM}}{\text{p}} = \frac{(\text{p} - \text{v})}{\text{p}} = 1 - \frac{\text{v}}{\text{p}}$$

Note that the CM ratio is 1 minus the variable cost ratio. For example, if variable costs are 40 percent of sales, then the variable cost ratio is 40 percent and the CM ratio is 60 percent.

Example 1: To illustrate the various concepts of CM, consider the following data for Porter Toy Store:

	Total	*Per Unit*	*Percentage*
Sales (1,500 units)	$37,500	$25	100%
Less: Variable costs	15,000	10	40
Contribution margin	$22,500	$15	60%
Less: Fixed costs	15,000		
Net income	$ 7,500		

From the data listed above, CM, unit CM, and the CM ratio are computed as:

CM = S − VC = $37,500 − $15,000 = $22,500

Unit CM = p − v = $25 − $10 = $15

CM Ratio = CM/S = $22,500/$37,500 or 1 − ($15,000/$37,500) = 1 − 0.4 = 0.6 = 60%

Or,

= Unit CM/p = $15/$25 = 0.6 = 60%

¶ 1011 Break-Even Analysis and Target Income Volume

The break-even point represents the level of sales revenue that equals the total of the variable and fixed costs for a given volume of output at a particular capacity use rate. For example, one might want to ask the break-even occupancy rate (or vacancy rate) for a hotel or the break-even load rate for an airliner.

Generally, the lower the break-even point, the higher the profit and the less the operating risk, other things being equal. The break-even point also provides managerial accountants with insights into profit planning.

The break-even point can be computed in two different ways: the equation approach and the graphical approach.

.01 The Equation Approach

The equation approach is based on the cost-volume-profit equation that shows the relationships among sales, variable and fixed costs, and net income.

S = VC + FC + Net Income

At the break-even volume, S = VC + FC + 0. Defining x = volume in units, the above relationship can be written in terms of x:

$px = vx + FC$

$(p - v)x = FC$

Solving for x yields the following formula for break-even sales volume:

$$x = \frac{FC}{(p - v)} = \frac{\text{Fixed Costs}}{\text{Unit CM}}$$

Or,

$$\text{Break-even point in dollars (S)} = \frac{\text{Fixed Costs}}{\text{CM Ratio}}$$

Note: The sales revenue needed to break even is that point at which the company covers all costs but generates no income.

$S = VC + FC + 0$

$S = (VC/S)S + FC$

$(1 - VC/S)S = FC$

$$S = \frac{FC}{(1 - VC/S)} = \frac{\text{Fixed Costs}}{(1 - \text{Variable Cost Ratio})} = \frac{\text{Fixed Costs}}{\text{CM Ratio}}$$

Example 2: Using the same data given in Example 1, where unit CM = \$25 − \$10 = \$15 and CM ratio = 60%, we get:

Break-even point in units = \$15,000/\$15 = 1,000 units

Break-even point in dollars = \$15,000/0.6 = \$25,000

Or, alternatively, 1,000 units × \$25 = \$25,000

.02 Graphical Approach in a Spreadsheet Format

The graphical approach to obtaining the break-even point is based on the so-called break-even (B-E) chart, as shown in Exhibit 1 at ¶ 1011.05. Sales revenue, variable costs, and fixed costs are plotted on the vertical axis, while volume, x, is plotted on the horizontal axis. The break-even point is the point where the total sales revenue line intersects the total cost line. The chart can also effectively report profit potentials over a wide range of activities and, therefore, be used as a tool for discussion and presentation.

The *profit-volume* (P-V) *chart*, as shown in Exhibit 2 at ¶ 1011.05, focuses directly on how profits vary with changes in volume. Profits are plotted on the vertical axis while units of output are shown on the horizontal axis. The P-V chart provides a quick condensed comparison of how alternatives on pricing, variable costs, or fixed costs may affect net income as volume changes. The P-V chart can be easily constructed from the B-E chart. Note that the slope of the chart is the unit CM.

.03 Determination of Target Income Volume

Besides determining the break-even point, CVP analysis determines the sales required to attain a particular income level or target net income. There are two ways in which target net income can be expressed:

Case 1. As a specific dollar amount

Case 2. As a percentage of sales

Case 1

As a specific dollar amount, the formula is:

$$\text{Target income sales volume} = \frac{\text{Fixed Costs} + \text{Target Income}}{\text{Unit CM}}$$

Case 2

Specifying target income as a percentage of sales, the cost-volume equation is:

$$px = vx + FC + \%(px)$$

Solving this for x yields:

$$\frac{FC}{p - v - \%(p)}$$

In words:

$$\text{Target income sales volume} = \frac{\text{Fixed Costs}}{\text{Unit CM} - (\text{\% of Unit Sales Price})}$$

Example 3: Using the same data given in Example 1, assume that Porter Toy Store wishes to attain:

Case 1. A target income of $15,000 before tax

Case 2. A target income of 20 percent of sales

In Case 1, the target income volume would be:

($15,000 + $15,000) / ($25 − $10) = $30,000 / $15 = 2,000 Units

In Case 2, the target income volume required is:

$15,000/[($25 − $10 − (20%)($25)] = $15,000/($15 − $5) = 1,500 Units

.04 Impact of Income Taxes

If target income (expressed as a specific dollar amount) is given on an after-tax basis, an adjustment is necessary before using the previous formula. The reason is that the profit target is expressed in before-tax terms. Therefore, the after-tax target income must first be converted to a before-tax target, as follows:

$$\text{Before-tax target income} = \frac{\text{After-tax Target Income}}{(1 - \text{Tax Rate})}$$

Example 4: Assume in Example 1 that Porter Toy Store wants to achieve an after-tax income of $6,000. The tax rate is 40 percent. The first step is:

$$\frac{\$6{,}000}{(1 - 0.4)} = \$10{,}000$$

The second step is to plug this figure into the regular formula as follows:

Target income volume = ($15,000 + $10,000) / 15 = 1,667 Units

Example 5: Using the same data given in Example 1, assume that Porter Toy Store wishes to attain a target income of $15,000 before tax.

Then, the target income volume would be:

($15,000 + $15,000) / ($25 − $10) = $30,000 / $15 = 2,000 Units

.05 Cash Break-Even Point

If a company has a minimum of available cash or the opportunity cost of holding excess cash is too high, management may want to know the volume of sales that will cover all cash expenses during a period. This is known as the cash break-even point. Not all fixed operating costs involve cash payments. For example, depreciation expenses are noncash fixed charges. Another example is prepaid expenses such as prepaid insurance and prepaid rent. The time period for which the break-even analysis is being performed might not involve an actual cash outlay for insurance coverage. To find the cash break-even point, the noncash charges must be subtracted from fixed costs. Therefore, the cash break-even point is lower than the usual break-even point. The formula is:

Cash break-even point = (Fixed costs − Noncash expenses)/Unit CM

Exhibit 1

Break-Even Chart

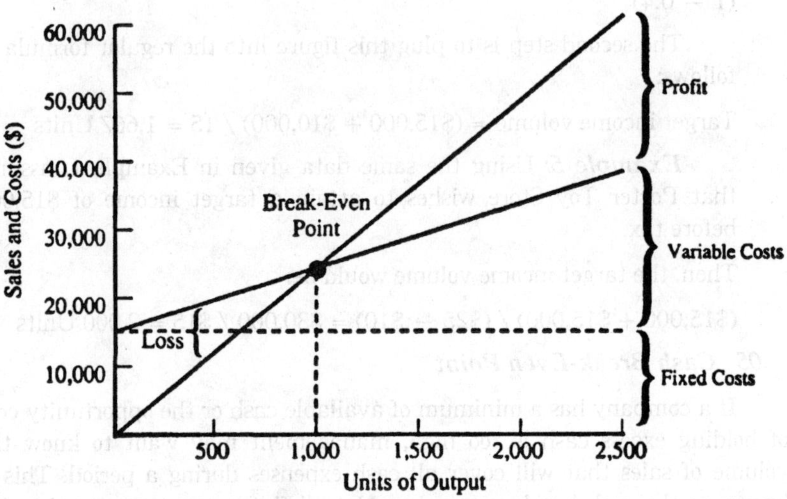

Exhibit 2

Profit-Volume (P-V) Chart

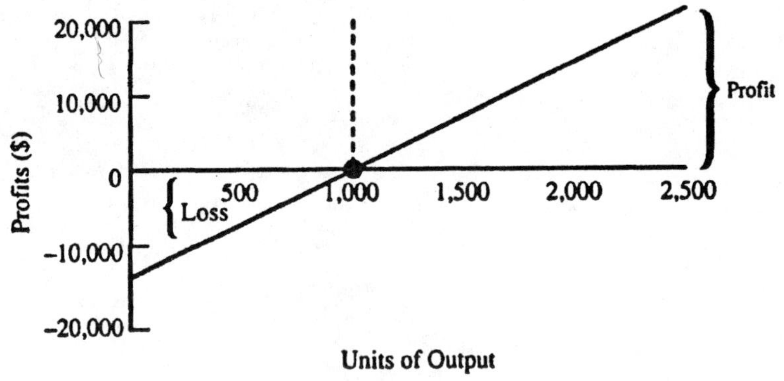

Example 6: Assume from Example 1 that the total fixed costs of $15,000 include depreciation of $1,500. Then the cash break-even point is:

($15,000 – $1,500) / ($25 – $10) = $13,500 / $15 = 900 Units

Porter Toy Store has to sell 900 units to cover only the fixed costs involving cash payments of $13,500 to break even.

.06 Margin of Safety

The margin of safety is a measure of difference between the actual sales and the break-even sales. It is the amount by which sales revenue may drop before losses begin, and is expressed as a percentage of expected sales:

Margin of Safety = Expected sales – Break-even sales/Expected sales

The margin of safety is used as a measure of operating risk. The larger the ratio, the safer the situation, since there is less risk of reaching the break-even point.

Example 7: Assume Porter Toy Store projects sales of $35,000 with a break-even sales level of $25,000. The projected margin of safety is:

($35,000 – $25,000) / $35,000 = 28.57%

¶ 1015 Applications of CVP Analysis and "What-If" Analysis

The concepts of contribution margin and the contribution income statement have many applications in profit planning and short-term decision making. Many what-if scenarios can be evaluated using them as planning tools, especially utilizing a spreadsheet program such as *Excel.* Some applications are illustrated in Examples 8 through 12, using the same data as in Example 1.

Example 8: Recall from Example 1 that Porter Toy Store has a CM of 60 percent and fixed costs of $15,000 per period. Assume that the store expects sales to go up by $10,000 for the next period. How much will income increase?

Using the CM concepts, one can quickly compute the impact of a change in sales on profits. The formula for computing the impact is:

Change in net income = Dollar change in sales X CM ratio

Thus:

Increase in net income = $10,000 × 60% = $6,000

Therefore, the income will go up by $6,000, assuming there is no change in fixed costs.

If there is a change in unit sales instead of dollars, then the formula becomes:

Change in net income = Change in unit sales × Unit CM

Example 9: Assume that the store expects sales to go up by 400 units. How much will income increase? From Example 1, the store's unit CM is $15.

Again, assuming there is no change in fixed costs, the income will increase by $6,000.

400 units × $15 = $6,000

Example 10: What net income is expected on sales of $47,500?

The answer is the difference between the CM and the fixed costs:

CM: $47,500 × 60%	$28,500
Less: Fixed costs	15,000
Net income	$13,500

Example 11: Porter Toy Store is considering increasing the advertising budget by $5,000, which would increase sales revenue by $8,000. Should the advertising budget be increased?

The answer is no, since the increase in the CM is less than the increased cost:

Increase in CM: $8,000 × 60%	$4,800
Increase in advertising	5,000
Decrease in net income	$ (200)

Example 12: Consider the original data. Assume again that Porter Toy Store is currently selling 1,500 units per period. In an effort to increase sales, management is considering cutting its unit price by $5 and increasing the advertising budget by $1,000.

If these two steps are taken, management feels that unit sales will go up by 60 percent. Should the two steps be taken?

A $5 reduction in the selling price will cause the unit CM to decrease from $15 to $10. Thus,

Proposed CM: 2,400 units × $10	$24,000
Present CM: 1,500 units × $15	22,500
Increase in CM	$ 1,500
Increase in advertising outlay	1,000
Increase in net income	$ 500

The answer, therefore, is yes. Alternatively, the same answer can be obtained by developing comparative income statements in a contribution format:

	(A) Present (1,500 units)	*(B) Proposed (2,400 units)*	*(B - A) Difference*
Sales	$37,500 (@$25)	$48,000 (@$20)	$10,500
Less: Variable cost	15,000 (@$10)	24,000 (@$10)	9,000
CM	$22,500	$24,000	$ 1,500
Less: Fixed costs	15,000	16,000	1,000
Net income	$ 7,500	$ 8,000	$ 500

¶ 1021 Elasticity of Demand

Whether or not price cutting or an increase in advertising dollars is desirable depends largely on the elasticity of demand for the product. Elasticity, one of the most important concepts in demand, tells one how sensitive quantity demanded is to the change in a factor in the demand function. The principal factors involved with demand elasticity are:

1. The price of the good (in the case of price elasticity)
2. Income (in the case of income elasticity)
3. The price of a substitute-product (in the case of cross elasticity)
4. Advertising (in the case of promotional elasticity)

Only price elasticity is discussed explicitly here, since other elasticity concepts are similar with respect to their calculations and implications.

Price elasticity, denoted with e_p, is the ratio of a percentage change in quantity demanded (Q) to a percentage change in price (p).

$$e_p = \frac{\%\text{ change in Q}}{\%\text{ change in p}} = \frac{dQ/Q}{dp/p} \times \frac{dQ}{dp}\,\frac{p}{Q}$$

Where dQ/dp is the slope of the demand function Q = (p).

The price elasticity demand is classified into three categories:

If $e_p > 1$, elastic

$e_p = 1$, unitary

$e_p < 1$, inelastic

Example 13: The demand function is given as Q = 200 − 6p. The price elasticity at p= 4 is computed as follows:

First, Q = 200 − 6(4) = 176

Since dQ/dp = -6, the e_p at p = 4 is:

$e_p = -6 \times (4/176) = -0.136$

Which means that a one-percent change in price will bring about a 0.14-percent change in demand. The product under study is considered price inelastic, since the e_p is less than 1 in absolute value.

Economists have established the following relationships between price elasticity (e_p) and sales revenue (S), which can aid a firm in setting its price.

Price	$e_p > 1$	$e_p = 1$	$e_p < 1$
Price rises	S falls	No change	S rises
Price falls	S rises	No change	S falls

1. Firms need to be aware of the elasticity of their own demand curves when they set product prices. For example, a profit maximizing firm would never choose to lower its price in the inelastic range of its demand curve—such a price decrease would only decrease total sales (see the above chart) and at the same time increase costs, since output would be rising. The result would be a drastic decrease in profits. In fact, when costs are rising and the product is inelastic, the firm would have no difficulty passing on the increases by raising the price to the customer.

2. When there are many substitutes and demand is quite elastic, increasing prices may lead to a reduction in total revenue rather than an increase. The result may be lower profits rather than higher profits.

3. Similarly, managers are sometimes surprised by a lack of success of price reductions, this merely being a reflection of the fact that demand is relatively inelastic. In such a case, they may have to rely on other marketing efforts, such as advertising and sales promotion, in an attempt to increase market share.

4. Various elasticity measures will allow marketing managers to see how effective each of the demand determinants (i.e., advertising, price change, and external factors) is going to be. In this way, marketing resources may be utilized more profitably and efficiently.

5. The concept of elasticity aids managers in setting the price.

¶ 1025 Sales Mix Analysis

Break-even and cost-volume-profit analysis requires some additional computations and assumptions when a company produces and sells more than one product. In multi-product firms, sales mix is an important factor in calculating an overall company break-even point.

Different selling prices and different variable costs result in different unit CM and CM ratios. As a result, the break-even points and cost-volume-profit relationships vary with the relative proportions of the products sold, called the sales mix.

.01 *Assumption of Stable Sales Mix*

In break-even and CVP analysis, it is necessary to predetermine the sales mix and then compute a weighted average unit CM. It is also necessary to assume that the sales mix does not change for a specified period. The break-even formula for the company as a whole is:

$$\text{Break-even sales in units (or in dollars)} = \frac{\text{Fixed Costs}}{\text{Weighted Average Unit CM (or CM Ratio)}}$$

Example 14: Assume that Knibex, Inc. produces cutlery sets out of high-quality wood and steel. The company makes a deluxe cutlery set and a standard set that have the following unit CM data:

	Deluxe	*Standard*
Selling price	$15	$10
Variable cost per unit	12	5
Unit CM	$ 3	$ 5
Sales mix	60%	40%
	(based on sales volume)	
Fixed costs	$ 76,000	

The weighted average unit CM = ($3)(0.6) + ($5)(0.4) = $3.80. Therefore, the company's break-even point in units is:

$76,000/$3.80 = 20,000 units

Which is divided as follows:

Deluxe:	20,000 units × 60% =	12,000 units
Standard:	20,000 units × 40% =	8,000
		20,000 units

Note: An alternative is to build a package containing three deluxe models and two economy models (3:2 ratio). By defining the product as a package, the multiple-product problem is converted into a single-product one. Then use the following three steps:

Step 1: Compute the package CM as follows:

	Deluxe	*Standard*
Selling price	$15	$10
Variable cost per unit	12	5
Unit CM	$ 3	$ 5
Sales mix	3	2
Package CM	$ 9	$10
		$19 package total

Step 2: Determine the number of packages that need to be sold to break even, as follows:

$76,000/$19 per package = 4,000 packages

Step 3: Multiply this number by the respective mix units:

Deluxe:	4,000 packages × 3 units =	12,000 units
Standard:	4,000 packages × 2 units =	8,000 units
		20,000 units

Example 15: Assume that Dante, Inc. is a producer of recreational equipment. It expects to produce and sell three types of sleeping bags—the Economy, the Regular, and the Backpacker. Information on the bags is given below:

Budgeted

	Economy	*Regular*	*Backpacker*	*Total*
Sales	$30,000	$ 60,000	$10,000	$100,000
Sales mix	30%	60%	10%	100%
Less VC	24,000	40,000	5,000	69,000
VC ratio	(80%)	(66 2/3%)	(50%)	
CM	$ 6,000	$ 20,000	$ 5,000	$ 31,000
CM ratio	20%	33 1/3%	50%	31%
Fixed costs				$ 18,600
Net income				$ 12,400

The CM ratio for Dante, Inc. is $31,000/$100,000 = 31%.

Therefore, the break-even point in dollars is:

$18,600/0.31 = $60,000

Which will be split in the mix ratio of 3:6:1 to give the following break-even points for the individual products:

Economy:	$60,000 × 30% =	$18,000
Regular:	$60,000 × 60% =	36,000
Backpacker:	$60,000 × 10% =	6,000
		$60,000

.02 *Sales Mix Changes*

One of the most important assumptions underlying CVP analysis in a multi-product firm is that the sales mix will not change during the planning period. If the sales mix does change, the break-even point will also change.

Example 16: Assume that total sales from Example 15 was achieved at $100,000 but that an actual mix came out differently from the budgeted mix (i.e., 30% to 55% for Economy, 60% to 40% for Regular, and 10% to 5% for Backpacker).

Actual

	Economy	*Regular*	*Backpacker*	*Total*
Sales	$55,000	$ 40,000	$ 5,000	$100,000
Sales mix	55%	40%	5%	100%
Less: VC	44,000	26,667*	2,500**	73,167
CM	$11,000	$ 13,333	$ 2,500	$ 26,833
CM ratio	20%	33 1/3%	50%	26.83%
Fixed Costs				$ 18,600
Net income				$ 8,233

* $26,667 = $40,000 × (VC ratio) = $40,000 × 66 2/3%
** $2,500 = $5,000 × (VC ratio) = $5,000 × 50%

Note: The shift in sales mix toward the less profitable line, Economy, has caused the CM ratio for the company as a whole to drop from 31 percent to 26.83 percent.

The new break-even point will be $18,600/0.2683 = $69,325.

The break-even dollar volume has increased from $60,000 to $69,325.

The deterioration (improvement) in the mix caused net income to go down (up). It is important to note that generally, the shift of emphasis from low-margin products to high-margin ones will increase the overall profits of the company.

¶ 1031 CVP Analysis with Step-Function Costs

The introduction of step-function costs is somewhat more difficult than it might first appear. It would be ideal to assume that, for any given relevant range, one could simply add together the step-function costs and the fixed costs to get the total applicable fixed costs. One could then utilize the formula as described above. Unfortunately, the process is not quite that simple, as the following example illustrates.

Example 17: Amco Magazine Company publishes a monthly magazine. The company has fixed costs of $100,000 a month, variable costs per magazine of $.80, and charges $1.80 per magazine. In addition, the company also has supervisory costs. These costs behave as follows:

Volume	*Costs*
0 – 50,000	$10,000
50,001 – 100,000	20,000
100,001 – 150,000	30,000

Amco's monthly break-even volume (number of magazines) can be calculated, step by step, as follows:

If one attempts to solve the break-even formula at the first level of fixed costs, the following equation applies:

$$x = FC/(p - v)$$
$$= (\$100{,}000 + 10{,}000)/(\$1.80 - \$.80)$$
$$= \$110{,}000/\$1$$
$$= 110{,}000 \text{ units}$$

The problem with this solution is that while the break-even volume is 110,000 magazines, the relevant range for the step-function costs was only 0 to 50,000 magazines. Thus, a break-even volume of greater than 50,000 magazines is invalid, and one must move to the next step on the step function, which gives the following equation:

$$x = FC/(p - v)$$
$$= (\$100{,}000 + 20{,}000)/(\$1.80 - \$.80)$$
$$= \$120{,}000/\$1$$
$$= 120{,}000 \text{ units}$$

This solution is also invalid. Only at the third level does one encounter a valid solution, as follows:

$$x = FC/(p - v)$$
$$= (\$100{,}000 + 30{,}000)/(\$1.80 - \$.80)$$
$$= \$130{,}000/\$1$$
$$= 130{,}000 \text{ units}$$

The conclusion one must draw is that the incorporation of step-function costs in the CVP formula requires a trial-and-error process to reach the break-even volume.

From a profit-seeking perspective, a 150,000-unit level is most profitable.

	50,000	*100,000*	*150,000*
CM(@1)	$50,000	$100,000	$150,000
FC	100,000	120,000	130,000
NI	($50,000)	($20,000)	$ 20,000

¶ 1035 Cost-Volume-Revenue Analysis and Nonprofit Organizations

Cost-volume-profit (CVP) analysis and break-even analysis are not limited to profit firms. CVP is appropriately called cost-volume-revenue (CVR) analysis as it pertains to nonprofit organizations. The CVR model not only calculates the break-even service level, but also helps answer a variety of "what-if" decision questions.

Example 18: AMC, Inc., a Los Angeles county agency, has a $1,200,000 lump-sum annual budget appropriation to help rehabilitate mentally ill clients. On top of this, the agency charges each client $600 a month for board and care. All of the appropriation and revenue must be spent. The variable costs for rehabilitation activity average $700 per client per month. The agency's annual fixed costs are $800,000. The agency manager wishes to know how many clients can be served.

Let x = number of clients to be served.

Revenue = Total expenses

Lump sum appropriation + $600 (12) x = Variable expenses + Fixed costs
$1,200,000 + $7,200 x = $8,400 x + $800,000
($7,200 − $8,400) x = $800,000 − $1,200,000
− $1,200 x = − $400,000
x = $400,000/$1,200
x = 333 clients

Let's investigate the following two "what-if" scenarios:

(1) Suppose the manager of the agency is concerned that the total budget for the coming year will be cut by 10 percent to a new amount of $1,080,000. All other things remain unchanged. The manager wants to know how this budget cut affects the next year's service level.

$1,080,000 + $7,200 x = $8,400 x + $800,000
($7,200 − $8,400) x = $800,000 − $1,080,000
− $1,200 x = − $280,000
x = $280,000/$1,200
x = 233 clients

(2) The manager does not reduce the number of clients served despite a budget cut of 10 percent. All other things remain unchanged. How much more does he/she have to charge his/her clients for board and care?

In this case, x = board and care charge per year

$$\$1{,}080{,}000 + 333\,x = \$8{,}400\,(333) + \$800{,}000$$
$$333\,x = \$2{,}797{,}200 + \$800{,}000 - \$1{,}080{,}000$$
$$333\,x = \$2{,}517{,}200$$
$$x = \$2{,}517{,}200/333 \text{ clients}$$
$$x = \$7{,}559$$

Thus, the monthly board and care charge must be increased to $630 ($7,559/12 months).

¶ 1041 Cost-Volume-Profit Analysis under Conditions of Uncertainty

The basic break-even and CVP models are subject to a number of limiting assumptions. They are:

1. The selling price per unit is constant throughout the entire relevant range of activity.
2. All costs are classified as fixed or variable.
3. The variable cost per unit is constant.
4. There is only one product or a constant sales mix.
5. Inventories do not change significantly from period to period.
6. Volume is the only factor affecting variable costs.

Although the CVP analysis discussed so far assumed that the variables listed above, which determine profit or contribution margin, are known with certainty, this is not a realistic assumption.

If one or more of these variables are subject to uncertainty, the managerial accountant should analyze the potential impact of this uncertainty. This additional analysis is required in evaluating alternative courses of action and in developing contingency plans. If management must choose between two products, expected profitability and risk should be considered before a choice is made. For example, if both products have the same expected profits, management might want to select the less risky product (less variation in profits).

One way of handling the conditions of uncertainty is to use "what-if" analysis, which was discussed at ¶ 1015.

.01 *Statistical Method*

Another approach to dealing with uncertainty is to use a statistical (probability) model. Suppose that sales volume is subject to uncertainty and, in fact, is normally distributed.

Note: The normal distribution is one of the most widely used probability distributions. It is bell-shaped and, hence, its shape is completely summarized by two statistics, i.e., the mean and the standard deviation.

With the normality assumption, one can utilize the standard statistical method to summarize the effect of the uncertainty in sales volume on a dependent variable, such as profit or contribution margin. Also, one can answer the following planning questions:

1. What is the probability of breaking even?
2. What is the chance that profits from the proposal would be at least a certain amount?
3. What are the chances that the proposal would cause the company to lose as much as a specified amount?

Any uncertainty in sales volume affects the total contribution margin (CM) and profit (P). The expected contribution margin, E(CM), is the unit CM times the expected volume, E(x):

$$E(CM) = \text{unit CM} \times E(x)$$

$$= (p - v)\,E(x)$$

The expected profit, E(p), is the expected contribution margin minus the fixed costs (FC):

$$E(p) = E(CM) - FC = (p - v)\,E(x) - FC$$

Because of the uncertainty in sales volume, the expected contribution margin and profit are also uncertain. The standard deviation of the expected contribution margin and profit is equal to the unit CM times the standard deviation of the sales volume. In equation form,

$$s_p = (p - v)\,s_x$$

Where s_p = standard deviation of expected profits

s_x = standard deviation of sales volume

Example 19: Rodeo Corporation has annual fixed costs of $1,500,000 and variable costs of $4.50 per unit. The selling price per unit is stable at $7.50, but the annual sales volume is uncertain and normally distributed with mean expected sales of 600,000 units and a standard deviation of 309,278 units. Management expects this pattern to continue in the future. The normal distribution of profits is illustrated in Exhibit 3, below.

The expected contribution is $1,800,000:

$$E(CM) = (\$7.50 - \$4.50) \times 600{,}000 \text{ units}$$

$$= \$3 \times 600{,}000 = \$1{,}800{,}000$$

The expected profits are $300,000:

$$E(p) = \$1{,}800{,}000 - \$1{,}500{,}000 = \$300{,}000$$

The standard deviation of the expected profits is $927,834:

$$s_p = \$3 \times 309{,}278 = \$927{,}834$$

Example 20: From the results obtained in Example 19, one can answer the following questions:

1. What is the probability of breaking even?

2. What is the probability of obtaining a profit of $500,000 or more?

3. What is the probability of losing at least $250,000?

In each case, one must determine the standard normal variate, better known as z, which is the number of standard deviations from any profit to the expected (mean) profit.

To determine the probability of at least breaking even, one must first determine z, as follows:

$$z = \frac{0 - E(p)}{S_p} = \frac{\$0 - \$300{,}000}{\$927{,}834} = -0.32$$

In Table 5 of Appendix B (Normal Distribution), the probability of obtaining a z value of -.32 or less is 0.3745, which means there is only a 37.45-percent chance that the company would lose money or about a 62.55-percent chance the company will at least break even. *Note:* Here, we are looking at the shaded area in Exhibit 4, below. Table 5 in Appendix B gives the area of the other side of the curve.

To find the probability of obtaining a profit of at least $500,000, one must first determine the number of standard deviations $500,000 is from the expected profit:

$$z = \frac{\$500{,}000 - \$300{,}000}{\$927{,}834} = \frac{\$200{,}000}{\$927{,}834} = 0.22$$

From Table 5, one can calculate that the chances are only .5871 of earning less than $500,000; thus, one can conclude that the chances of bettering a $500,000 profit are .4129 or 41.29 percent (1 − .5871 = .4129).

To find the probability of losing at least $250,000, again one calculates the value for z:

$$z = \frac{-\$250{,}000 - \$300{,}000}{\$927{,}834} = \frac{-\$550{,}000}{\$927{,}834} = -0.59$$

Table 5 indicates that there is only a 0.2776 (1 − .7224 = .2776) chance of losing at least $250,000.

To summarize:

1. The chance of breaking even is better than 62.55 percent.

2. The chance of making at least $500,000 is 41.29 percent.

3. The chance of losing at least $250,000 is only about 27.76 percent.

A caveat. In the previous example, sales volume was considered to be subject to uncertainty—a random variable. It is also possible to consider fixed costs, variable costs, and selling price as random variables to test the effect of their uncertainty on profits. When one of these four variables—sales volume, price, variable cost, and fixed cost—is allowed to be uncertain, the analysis is accomplished exactly as illustrated above. However, if they become random variables simultaneously, the analysis is complicated and reserved for a more advanced statistical text.

Exhibit 3

Probability Distribution of Profits

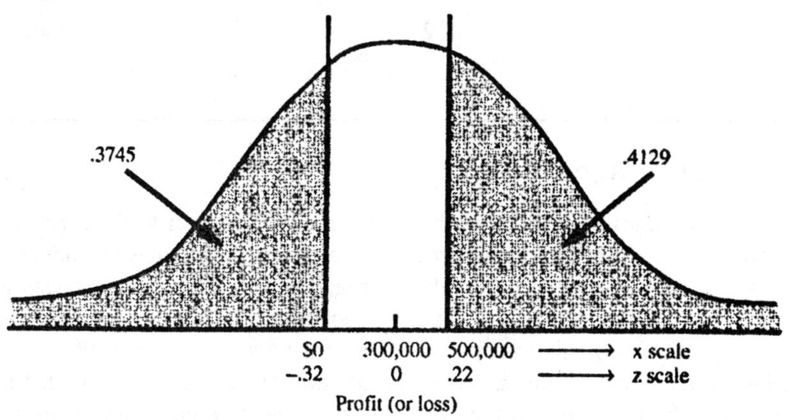

Exhibit 4

Probability of Losing Money

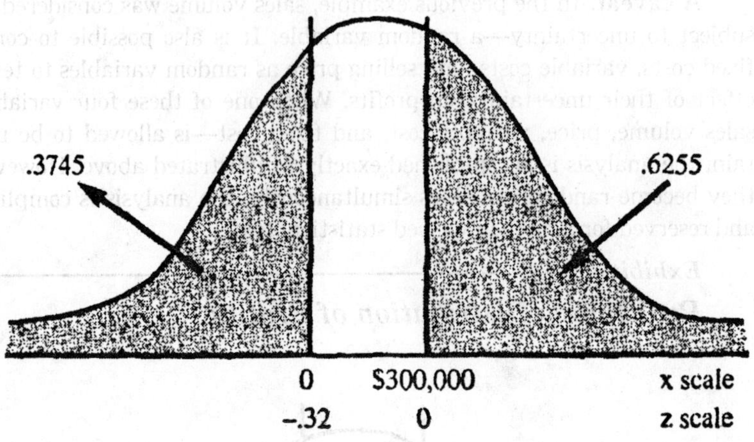

¶ 1045 Leverage

Companies wish to know where they are with respect to the break-even point. If they are operating around break-even point sales, management may be more conservative in its approach to implementing changes and mapping out new strategies. On the other hand, if they are operating well away from the break-even point, management will be more liberal, since the downside risk is not as great. A measure that relates to this distance between break-even sales and the current or planned sales volume is *leverage.*

Leverage is that portion of the fixed costs that represents a risk to the firm. Operating leverage, a measure of operating risk, refers to the fixed operating costs found in the firm's income statement. Financial leverage, a measure of financial risk, refers to financing a portion of the firm's assets, bearing fixed financing charges in hopes of increasing the return to the common stockholders. The higher the financial leverage the higher the financial risk, and the higher the cost of capital. Cost of capital rises because it costs more to raise funds for a risky business. Total leverage is a measure of total risk.

.01 Operating Leverage

Operating leverage is a measure of operating risk and arises from fixed operating costs. A simple indication of operating leverage is the effect that a change in sales has on earnings.

The formula is:

Operating leverage at a given level of sales (x)

$$= \frac{\text{Percentage change in EBIT}}{\text{Percentage change in sales}}$$

$$= \frac{\Delta EBIT/EBIT}{\Delta x / x} = \frac{(p - v)\,\Delta x\,/\,(p - v)x - FC}{\Delta x / x}$$

$$= \frac{(p - v)x}{(p - v)x - FC}$$

Where EBIT = earnings before interest and taxes (operating income in accounting)

$= (p - v)x - FC$

Example 21: The Shawn Company manufactures and sells doors to homebuilders. The doors are sold for $25 each. Variable costs are $15 per door, and fixed operating costs total $50,000. Assume further that the Shawn Company is currently selling 6,000 doors per year. Its operating leverage is:

$$\frac{(p - v)}{(p - v)x - FC} = \frac{(\$25 - \$15)(6{,}000)}{(\$25 - \$15)(6{,}000) - \$50{,}000} = \frac{\$60{,}000}{\$10{,}000} = 6$$

Which means if sales increase (decrease) by one percent, the company can expect its net income to increase (decrease) by six times that amount, or six percent.

.02 *Financial Leverage*

Financial leverage is a measure of financial risk and arises from fixed financial costs. One way to measure financial leverage is to determine how earnings per share are affected by a change in EBIT (or operating income).

Financial leverage at a given level of sales (x)

$$= \frac{\text{Percentage in change in EPS}}{\text{Percentage in change in EBIT}} = \frac{(p - v)x - FC}{(p - v)x - FC - IC}$$

Where EPS is earnings per share and IC is fixed finance charges, i.e., interest expense or preferred stock dividends. [Preferred stock dividend must be adjusted for taxes, i.e., preferred stock dividend/ (1 − t).]

Example 22: Using the data in Example 21, the Shawn Company has total financial charges of $2,000, half in interest expense and half in preferred stock dividend. Assume a corporate tax rate of 40 percent.

First, the fixed financial charges are:

$$IC = \$1{,}000 + \frac{\$1{,}000}{(1 - 0.4)} = \$1{,}000 + \$1{,}667 = \$2{,}667$$

Therefore, Shawn's financial leverage is computed as follows:

$$\frac{(p - v)x - FC}{(p - v)x - FC - IC} = \frac{(\$25 - \$15)(6{,}000) - \$50{,}000}{(\$25 - \$15)(6{,}000) - \$50{,}000 - \$2{,}667} = \frac{\$10{,}000}{\$7{,}333} = 1.36$$

Which means that if EBIT increases (decreases) by one percent, Shawn can expect its EPS to increase (decrease) by 1.36 times, or by 1.36 percent.

.03 Total Leverage

Total leverage is a measure of total risk. The way to measure total leverage is to determine how EPS is affected by a change in sales.

$$\text{Total leverage at a given level of sales (x)} = \frac{\text{Percentage in change in EPS}}{\text{Percentage in change in sales}}$$

$$= \text{operating leverage} \times \text{financial leverage}$$

$$= \frac{(p - v)x}{(p - v)x - FC} \times \frac{(p - v)x - FC}{(p - v)x - FC - IC}$$

$$= \frac{(p - v)x}{(p - v)x - FC - IC}$$

Example 23: From Examples 21 and 22, the total leverage for Shawn company is:

Operating leverage × financial leverage = 6 × 1.36 = 8.16

Or,

$$\frac{(p - v)X}{(p - v)x - FC - IC} = \frac{(\$25 - \$15)(6{,}000)}{(\$25 - \$15)(6{,}000) - \$50{,}000 - \$2{,}667}$$

$$= \frac{\$60{,}000}{\$7{,}333} = 8.18 \text{ (due to rounding error)}$$

Which means that if sales increase (decrease) by one percent, Shawn can expect its EPS to increase (decrease) by 8.18 percent.

¶ 1051 Linear Programming and Opportunity Costs

Linear programming (LP) is a mathematical technique designed to determine an optimal decision (or an optimal plan) chosen from a large number of possible decisions. The optimal decision is the one that meets the specified objective of the company, subject to various restrictions or constraints. It concerns itself with the problem of allocating scarce resources among competing activities in an optimal manner. The optimal decision yields the highest profit, contribution margin (CM), or revenue, or the lowest cost. A linear programming model consists of two important ingredients:

1. *Objective function.* The company must define the specific objective to be achieved.

2. *Constraints.* Constraints are in the form of restrictions on availability of resources or meeting minimum requirements. As the name linear programming indicates, both the objective function and constraints must be in *linear* form.

Example 24: A firm wishes to find an optimal product mix. The optimal mix would be the one that maximizes its total profit or contribution margin (CM) within the allowed budget and production capacity. Or, the firm may want to determine a least-cost combination of input materials while meeting production requirements, employing production capacities, and using available employees.

.01 Applications of LP

Applications of LP are numerous. They include:

1. Developing an optimal budget.
2. Determining an optimal investment portfolio (or asset allocation).
3. Allocating an advertising budget to a variety of media.
4. Selecting least-cost mix of ingredients for manufactured products.
5. Scheduling jobs to machines.
6. Determining a least-cost shipping pattern.
7. Scheduling flights.
8. Gasoline blending.
9. Optimal manpower allocation.
10. Selecting the best warehouse location to minimize shipping costs.

.02 Formulation of LP

To formulate an LP problem, certain steps are followed. They are:

1. Define what is called decision variables that you are trying to solve for.

2. Express the objective function and constraints in terms of these decision variables. All the expressions must be in linear form.

In the following example, this technique is used to find the optimal product mix.

Example 25: The Omni Furniture Manufacturing Company produces two products: desk and table. Both products require time in two processing departments, Assembly Department and Finishing Department. Data on the two products are as follows:

Processing	*Products*		*Available*
	Desk	*Table*	*Hours*
Assembly	2 hours per unit	4	100 hours
Finishing	3	2	90
CM unit	$25	$40	

The company wants to find the most profitable mix of these two products.

Step 1: Define the decision variables as follows:

A = Number of units of desk to be produced

B = Number of units of table to be produced

Step 2: The objective function to maximize total CM is expressed as:

$CM = 25A + 40B$

Then, formulate the constraints as inequalities:

$2A + 4B \leq 100$ (Assembly constraint)

$3A + 2B \leq 90$ (Finishing constraint)

In addition, implicit in any LP formulation are the constraints that restrict A and B to be nonnegative, i.e.,

$A, B \geq 0$

Maximize: $CM = 25A + 40B$

Subject to: $2A + 4B \leq 100$

$3A + 2B \leq 90$

$A, B \geq 0$

.03 Computation Methods of LP

There are solution methods available to solve LP problems. They include:

1. The simplex method.

2. The graphical method.

The simplex method is the technique most commonly used to solve LP problems. It is an algorithm, which is an iteration method of computation to move from one solution to another until it reaches the best solution.

The graphical solution is easier to use but limited to the LP problems involving two (or at most three) decision variables. The graphical method follows these steps:

Step 1: Change inequalities to equalities.

Step 2: Graph the equalities. To graph the equality, (1) set one variable equal to zero and find the value of the other and connect those two points on the graph, and (2) mark these intersections on the axes and connect them with a straight line.

Step 3: Identify the correct side for the original inequalities by shading. Repeat steps 1-3 for each constraint.

Step 4: After all this, identify the feasible region, the area of feasible solutions.

Step 5: Solve the constraints (expressed as equalities) simultaneously for the various corner points of the feasible region.

Step 6: Determine the profit or contribution margin at all corners in the region.

Note: Feasible solutions are values of decision variables that satisfy all the constraints simultaneously. They are found on and within the boundary of the feasible region. The graphical approach is based on two important LP properties:

1. The optimal solution lies on the boundary of the feasible region, which implies that one can ignore the (infinitely numerous) interior points of the feasible region when searching for an optimal solution.

2. The optimal solution occurs at one of the corner points (basic feasible solutions) of the feasible region.

Example 26: Using the data and the LP model from Example 25, follow steps 1 through 4 to obtain the following feasible region (shaded area).

Step 1: Change inequalities to equalities.

$2A + 4B = 100$

$3A + 2B = 90$

Step 2: Graph the equalities. To graph the equality, set one variable equal to zero, find the value of the other, mark the points on the axes, and connect those two points with a straight line.

For equation 1: If A = 0, B = 25; if B = 0, then A = 50, connect B = 25 and A = 50.

For equation 2: If A = 0, B = 30; if B = 0, then A = 45, connect B = 30 and A = 45.

Step 3: Identify the correct side for the original inequalities. The correct side is the line and the area below it for less-than or equal-to constraints.

Step 4: After all this, identify the feasible region, the area of feasible solutions. The area of feasible solutions is the duplicated area as indicated by the shaded area in Exhibit 5.

Step 5: Solve the constraints (expressed as equalities) simultaneously for the various corner points of the feasible region.

Step 6: Determine the profit or contribution margin at all corners in the feasible region.

All of the corner points are evaluated as follows:

	Corner Points		CM
	A	*B*	*\$25A + \$40B*
(a)	30	0	\$25(30) + \$40(0) = \$750
(b)	20	15	25(20) + 40(15) = 1,100
(c)	0	25	25(0) + 40(25) = 1,000
(d)	0	0	25(0) + 40(0) = 0

The corner point (b) (A = 20, B = 15) produces the most profitable solution (CM* = \$1,100). This point can be found by solving two equations that created it simultaneously, as shown below.

$$2A + 4B = 100 \quad (1)$$

$$3A + 2B = 90 \quad (2)$$

Multiplying the second equation (2) through by 2 and subtracting from (1) produces:

$$\begin{array}{rcl} 2A + 4B & = & 100 \quad (1) \\ -\ (6A + 4B & = & 180) \\ \hline -\ 4A & = & -\ 80 \\ A & = & 20 \end{array}$$

Substituting A = 20 into (1) or (2) yields B = 15.

Exhibit 5

The Feasible Region and Corner Points

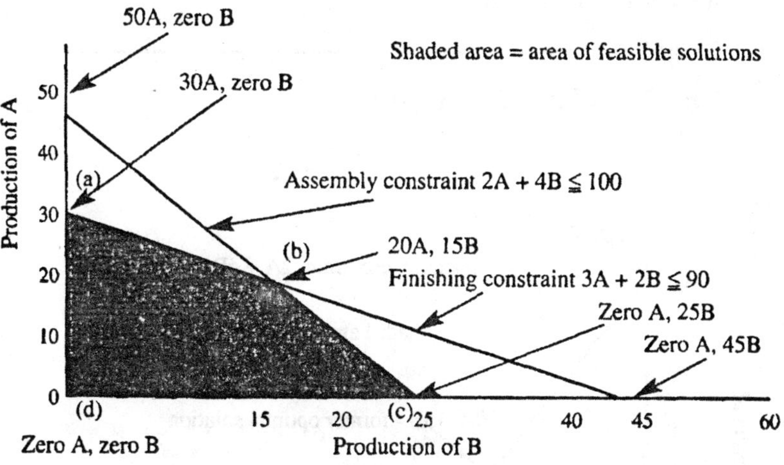

.04 *Opportunity Costs (Shadow Prices)*

A financial manager who has solved an LP problem might wish to know whether it pays to add capacity in hours in a particular department. The analyst might be interested in the monetary value to the firm of adding, say, an hour per week of assembly time. This monetary value is usually the additional profit that could be earned. This amount is the *opportunity cost* (also known as the *shadow price*), the profit that would be lost by not adding an additional hour of capacity. To justify a decision in favor of a short-term capacity decision, the manager must be sure that the shadow price exceeds the actual price of that expansion. For example, suppose that the shadow price of an hour of assembly capacity is $6.50, while the actual market price is $8.00. That means it does not pay to obtain an additional hour of the assembly capacity.

Shadow prices are computed, step by step, as follows:

1. Add one hour (preferably, more than one hour to make it easier to show graphically) to the constraint of a given LP problem under consideration.

2. Resolve the problem and find the maximum CM.

3. Compute the difference between the CM of the original LP problem and the CM determined in step 2, which is the shadow price.

Example 27: Using the data in Example 25, compute the shadow price of the assembly capacity. To make it easier to show graphically, add 8 hours of capacity to the assembly department, rather than one hour. The new assembly constraint and the resulting feasible region are shown in Exhibit 6.

Exhibit 6

The New Feasible Region

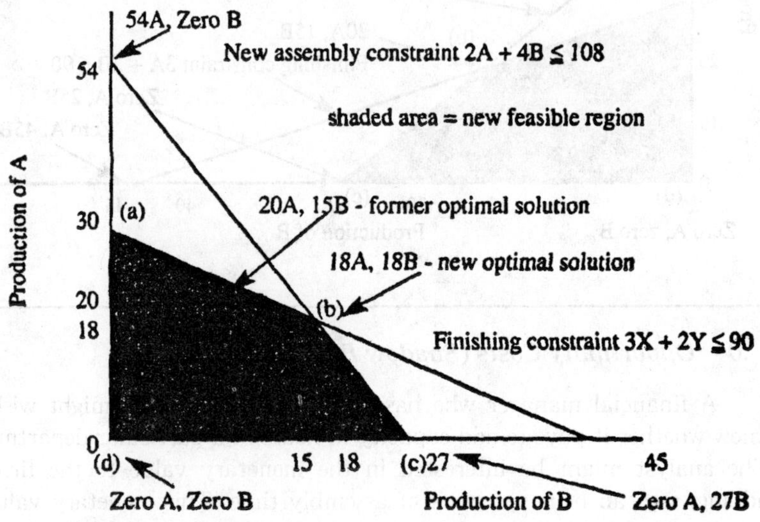

Then evaluate all of the corner points in the *new* feasible region in terms of their CM, as follows:

	Corner Points		CM
	A	*B*	*$25A + $40B*
(a)	30	0	$25(30) + $40(0) = $750
(b)	18	18	25(18) + 40(18) = 1,170
(c)	0	27	25(0) + 40(227) = 1,080
(d)	0	0	25(0) + 40(0) = 0

The new optimal solution of 18A, 18B has total CM of $1,170 per week. Therefore, the shadow price of the assembly capacity is $70 ($1,170 – $1,100 = $70), or $8.75 per hour ($70/8 hours = $8.75). The firm would be willing to pay up to $70 to obtain an additional 8 hours of the assembly capacity per week, or $8.75 per hour per week.

In other words, the firm's *opportunity cost* of not adding an additional hour is $8.75.

.05 Use of Computer LP Software

Computer LP software packages such as LINDO (*Linear Interactive and Discrete Optimization*) (www.lindo.com) and *What's Best!* (www.AnalyCorp.com) can quickly solve an LP problem.

Exhibit 7 shows a LINDO output by an LP program for the LP model set up in Example 25.

Note: The printout shows the following optimal solution:

A = 20 units

B = 15 units

CM = 1,100

Shadow prices are:

Assembly capacity = $8.75

Finishing capacity = $2.50

Exhibit 7

Computer Printout for LP

```
                    **INFORMATION ENTERED**
NUMBER OF CONSTRAINTS              2
NUMBER OF VARIABLES                2
NUMBER OF ≦ CONSTRAINTS            2
NUMBER OF = CONSTRAINTS            0
NUMBER OF ≧ CONSTRAINTS            0

MAXIMIZATION PROBLEM
             25 X 1         +40 X 2

SUBJECT TO
             2 X 1          + 4 X 2        ≦ 100
             3 X 1          + 2 X 2        ≦ 90

   **RESULTS**
             VARIABLE       ORIGINAL       COEFF.
VARIABLE      VALUE          COEFF.        SENS.

X1             20              25            0
X2             15              40            0

CONSTRAINT   ORIGINAL       SLACK OR       SHADOW
NUMBER         RHS          SURPLUS        PRICE

1              100             0            8.75
2               90             0            2.5

OBJECTIVE FUNCTION VALUE: 1100 = CM
    SENSITIVITY ANALYSIS
    OBJECTIVE FUNCTION COEFFICIENTS
              LOWER         ORIGINAL       UPPER
VARIABLE      LIMIT        COEFFICIENT     LIMIT

X1             20              25            60
X2             16.67           40            50

    RIGHT HAND SIDE
CONSTRAINT    LOWER         ORIGINAL       UPPER
NUMBER        LIMIT          VALUE         LIMIT

1              60             100           180
2              50              90           150
```

Note:
$X_1 = A$
$X_2 = B$

Solution:
$X_1 = A = 20$
$X_2 = B = 15$

Shadow price of the assembly capacity

Example 28: The Doubtfire Company produces and sells two products: snowmobiles (A) and outdoor motors (B). Each model requires the use of both the assembly department and the testing department. Production and contribution data are presented below.

Department	*Available Capacity Machine Hrs.*	*Daily Maximum Production of Product*			*Use of Capacity in Hours Per Unit*	
		A		*B*	*A*	*B*
Assembly	600 mhs	200	or	150	3.0	4.0
Testing	240	120	or	240	2.0	1.0
Unit CM		$400		$500		

Suppose a department works exclusively on a single product. The table indicates, for example, that the assembly department can assemble a maximum of 200 snowmobiles (600 machine hours/3.0 machine hours per unit = 200 output units) or 150 outdoor motors (600 machine hours/4 machine hours per unit = 150 output units). The problem can be formulated as follows:

Maximize: Total CM = 400A + 500B

Subject to: 3.0A + 4.0B ≤ 600 (or A + 4/3B ≤ 200 or 3/4A + B ≤ 150)

2.0A + 1.0B ≤ 240 (or A + 1/2B ≤ 120)

A, B ≥ 0

Chapter 11

Financial Forecasting, Budgeting, and Planning

¶ 1101 Overview

Financial forecasting, an essential element of planning, is the basis for *budgeting* activities. It is also needed when estimating future financing requirements. A company may look either internally or externally for financing. Internal financing refers to cash flow generated by the company's normal operating activities. External financing refers to capital provided by parties external to the company. One needs to analyze how to estimate *external* financing requirements. Basically, forecasts of future sales and related expenses provide the firm with the information to project future external financing needs.

¶ 1105 The Percent-of-Sales Method

The basic steps in projecting financing needs are:

1. Project the firm's sales. The sales forecast is the initial and most important step. Most other forecasts (budgets) follow the sales forecast.

2. Project additional variables, such as expenses.

3. Estimate the level of investment in current and fixed assets required to support the projected sales.

4. Calculate the firm's financing needs.

The most widely used method for projecting the company's financing needs is the *percent-of-sales method.* This method involves estimating the various expenses, assets, and liabilities for a future period as a percent of the sales forecast and then using these percentages, together with the projected sales, to construct forecasted balance sheets. The following example illustrates how to develop a pro forma balance sheet and determine the amount of external financing needed.

Example 1: Assume that sales for 20X0 = \$20, projected sales for 20X1 = \$24, net income = 5% of sales, and the dividend payout ratio = 40%. Exhibit 1, below, illustrates the method, step by step. All dollar amounts are in millions.

The steps for the computations are outlined as follows:

Step 1. Express those balance sheet items that vary directly with sales as a percentage of sales. Any item such as long-term debt that does not vary directly with sales is designated "n.a." or "not applicable."

Step 2. Multiply these percentages by the 20X1 projected sales = \$24 to obtain the projected amounts as shown in the last column.

Step 3. Simply insert figures for long-term debt, common stock, and paid-in-capital from the 20X1 balance sheet.

Step 4. Compute 20X1 retained earnings as shown in footnote (a).

Step 5. Sum the asset accounts, obtaining total projected assets of \$7.2, and also add the projected liabilities and equity to obtain \$7.12, the total financing provided. Since liabilities and equity must total \$7.2, but only \$7.12 is projected, we have a shortfall of \$0.08 "external financing needed."

Although the forecast of additional funds required could be made by setting up pro forma balance sheets as described above, it is often easier to use the following formula:

External funds needed (EFN)	=	Required increase in assets	–	Spontaneous increase in liabilities	–	Increase in retained earnings
EFN	=	$(A/S)\Delta S$	–	$(L/S)\Delta S$	–	$(PM)(PS)(1\text{-}d)$

Where A/S = Assets that increase spontaneously with sales as a percentage of sales.

L/S = Liabilities that increase spontaneously with sales as a percentage of sales.

ΔS = Change in sales.

PM = Profit margin on sales.

PS = Projected sales

d = Dividend payout ratio.

Example 2: In Example 1,

A/S = \$6/\$20 = 30%

L/S = \$2/\$20 = 10%

ΔS = (\$24 − \$20) = \$4

PM = 5% on sales

PS = \$24

d = 40%

Plugging these figures into the formula yields:

EFN = 0.3(\$4) − 0.1(\$4) − (0.05)(\$24)(1 − 0.4)

= \$1.2 − \$0.4 − \$0.72 = \$0.08

Thus, the amount of external financing needed is \$800,000, which can be raised by issuing notes payable, bonds, stocks, or any combination of these financing sources.

The major advantage of the percent-of-sales method of financial forecasting is that it is simple and inexpensive to use. One important assumption behind the use of the method is that the firm is operating at full capacity. This means that the company has no sufficient productive capacity to absorb a projected increase in sales and, thus, requires additional investment in assets. Therefore, the method must be used with extreme caution if excess capacity exists in certain asset accounts.

To obtain a more precise projection of the firm's future financing needs, however, the preparation of a cash budget (to be presented later at ¶ 1115.09) is required.

Exhibit 1

Pro Forma Balance Sheet in Millions of Dollars

	Present (20X0)	% of Sales (20X0 Sales=$20)	Projected (20X1 Sales=$24)	
Assets				
Current assets	2	10	2.4	
Fixed assets	4	20	4.8	
Total assets	6		7.2	
Liabilities and stockholders' equity				
Current liabilities	2	10	2.4	
Long-term debt	2.5	n.a.	2.5	
Total liabilities	4.5		4.9	
Common stock	0.1	n.a.	0.1	
Paid-in-capital	0.2	n.a.	0.2	
Retained earnings	1.2		1.92	(a)
Total equity	*1.5*		2.22	
Total liabilities and stockholders' equity	6		7.12	Total financing provided
			0.08	(b) External financing needed
			7.2	Total

(a) 20X1 retained earnings = 20X0 retained earnings + projected net income − cash dividends paid

= $1.2 + 5%($24) − 40%[5%($24)]

= $1.2 + $1.2 − $0.48 = $2.4 − $0.48 = $1.92

(b) External financing needed = projected total assets − (projected total liabilities + projected equity)

= $7.2 − ($4.9 + $2.22) = $7.2 − $7.12 = $0.08

¶ 1111 The Sustainable Rate of Growth

The sustainable rate of growth (g*) represents the rate at which a firm's sales can grow if it wants to maintain its present financial ratios and does not want to resort to the sale of new equity shares. A simple formula can be derived for g* where one assumes that a firm's assets and liabilities all grow at the same rate as its sales, that is:

Sustainable rate of growth (g*) = ROE (1 − b)

Recall that ROE is the firm's return on equity:

$$\text{ROE} = \frac{\text{Net profit after taxes}}{\text{Stockholders' equity}} = \frac{\text{Net profit after taxes}}{\text{Total assets}} \times \frac{\text{Total assets}}{\text{Stockholders' equity}}$$

$$= \text{Return on Investment (ROI)} \times \text{Equity multiplier}$$

And b is the firm's dividend payout ratio, that is, $\frac{\text{Dividends per share}}{\text{Earnings per share}}$

The term (1 − b) is sometimes referred to as the plowback ratio, since it indicates the fraction of earnings that are reinvested or plowed back into the firm. Consequently, a firm's sustainable rate of growth is determined by its ROE (i.e., its anticipated net profit margin, asset turnover, and capital structure), as well as its dividend policy.

.01 Calculating the Sustainable Rate of Growth

Consider the three firms:

Firm	*ROI*	*Equity Multiplier*	*Plowback Ratio*	*g**
A	10%	3.33	50%	16.65%
B	10%	3.33	100%	33.30%
C	10%	2.00	100%	20.00%

Comparing Firms A and B, note that the only difference is that Firm A pays out half its earnings in common dividends (i.e., plows back half its earnings), whereas Firm B retains or plows back all of its earnings. The net result is that Firm B, with its added source of internal equity financing, can grow at twice the rate of Firm A (33.30 percent compared to 16.65 percent).

Likewise, comparing Firms B and C, note that they differ only in that Firm B finances only 30 percent (1/3.33) of its assets with equity, whereas Firm C finances 50 percent (1/2.00) of its assets with equity. The result is that Firm C's sustainable rate of growth is 20 percent compared to 33.30 percent for Firm B. This example indicates that Firm B was using leverage (debt) favorably.

For this equation to accurately depict a firm's sustainable rate of growth, the following assumptions must hold: First, the firm's assets must vary as a constant percent of sales (i.e., even fixed assets expand and contract directly with the level of firm sales). Second, the firm's liabilities must all vary directly with firm sales. This means that the firm's management will expand its borrowing (both spontaneous and discretionary) in direct proportion with sales to maintain its present ratio of debt to assets. Finally, the firm pays out a constant proportion of its earnings in common stock dividends regardless of the level of firm sales. Since all three of these assumptions are only rough approximations to the way that firms actually behave, the equation provides a crude approximation of the firm's actual sustainable rate of growth. However, an estimate of g* using the equation can be a very useful first step in the firm's financial planning process.

¶ 1115 Preparing a Budget

A company's annual financial plan is called a *budget*. A comprehensive (master) budget is a formal statement of management's expectations regarding sales, expenses, volume, and other financial transactions of an organization for the coming period. Simply put, a budget is a set of *pro forma* (projected or planned) financial statements. It consists basically of a pro forma income statement, pro forma balance sheet, and cash budget.

A budget is a tool for both planning and control. At the beginning of the period, the budget is a plan or standard; at the end of the period, it serves as a control device to help management measure its performance against the plan so that future performance may be improved.

With the aid of computer technology, budgeting is an effective device for evaluation of "what-if" scenarios. Management is able to find the best course of action among various alternatives through simulation. If budgeted financial statements in terms of various financial ratios such as liquidity, activity (turnover), leverage, profit margin, and market value ratios are not acceptable, altering their contemplated decision and planning set is relatively easy.

The budget is classified broadly into two categories:

1. Operating budget, reflecting the results of operating decisions.

2. Financial budget, reflecting the financial decisions of the firm.

The *operating budget* consists of:

- Sales budget
- Production budget
- Direct materials budget
- Direct labor budget
- Factory overhead budget
- Selling and administrative expense budget
- Pro forma income statement

The financial budget consists of:

- Cash budget
- Pro forma balance sheet

The major steps in preparing the budget are:

1. Prepare a sales forecast.
2. Determine expected production volume.
3. Estimate manufacturing costs and operating expenses.
4. Determine cash flow and other financial effects.
5. Formulate projected financial statements.

Exhibit 2 shows a simplified diagram of the various parts of the comprehensive (master) budget—the master plan of the company.

.01 Comprehensive Illustration

To illustrate how all these budgets are put together, the following sections focus on a manufacturing company called the Johnson Company, which produces and markets a single product. Assume that the company develops the master budget on a quarterly basis. The variable cost and fixed cost breakdown is used throughout the illustration. Note that variable costs are those costs that vary in proportion to sales or production volume, while fixed costs remain constant regardless of volume.

Exhibit 2

A Master (Comprehensive) Budget

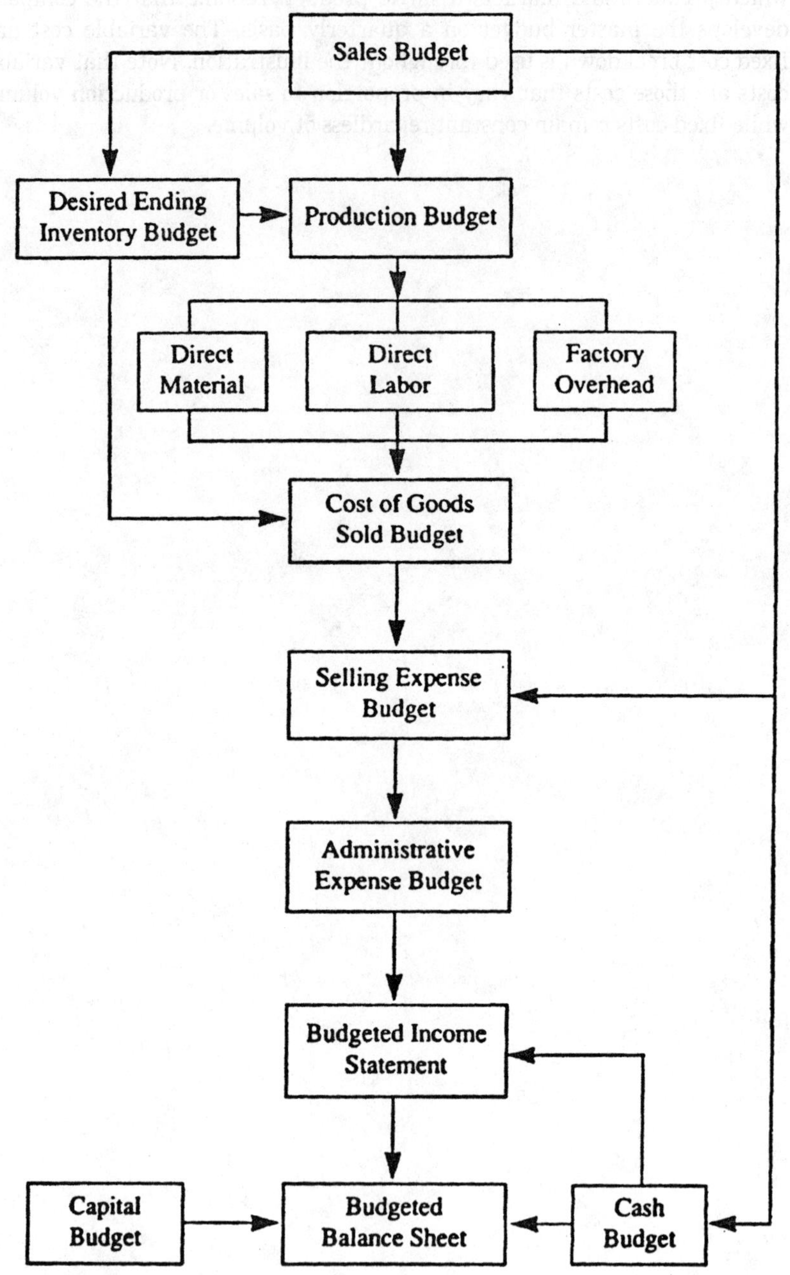

.02 The Sales Budget

The sales budget is the starting point in preparing the master budget, since estimated sales volume influences nearly all other items appearing throughout the master budget. The sales budget ordinarily indicates the quantity of each product expected to be sold. After sales volume has been estimated, the sales budget is constructed by multiplying the expected sales in units by the expected unit selling price. Generally, the sales budget includes a computation of expected cash collections from credit sales, which will be used later for cash budgeting.

Example 3:

THE JOHNSON COMPANY
Sales Budget
For the Year Ending December 31, 20B

	Quarter				
	1	*2*	*3*	*4*	*Total*
Expected sales in units	800	700	900	800	3,200
Unit sales price	×$80	×$80	×$80	×$80	×$80
Total sales	$64,000	$56,000	$72,000	$64,000	$256,000

Schedule of Expected Cash Collections

Accounts receivable, 12/31/20A	9,500*	. . . . . .	. . . . . .	. . . . . .	$9,500
1st quarter sales ($64,000).	44,800 +	$17,920 ++			62,720
2d quarter sales ($56,000)		39,200	$15,680		54,880
3d quarter sales ($72,000)			50,400	$20,160	70,560
4th quarter sales ($64,000)				44,800	44,800
Total cash collections	$54,300	$57,120	$66,080	$64,960	$242,460

* All of the $9,500 accounts receivable balance is assumed to be collectible in the first quarter.
\+ 70 percent of a quarter's sales are collected in the quarter of sale.
\+ + 28 percent of a quarter's sales are collected in the quarter following, and the remaining 2 percent are uncollectible.

.03 The Production Budget

After sales are budgeted, the production budget is determined. The number of units expected to be manufactured to meet budgeted sales and inventory requirements is set forth in the production budget. The expected volume of production is determined by subtracting the estimated inventory at the beginning of the period from the sum of the units expected to be sold and the desired inventory at the end of the period. The production budget is illustrated as follows:

Example 4:

THE JOHNSON COMPANY
Production Budget
For the Year Ending December 31, 20B

	Quarter				
	1	*2*	*3*	*4*	*Total*
Planned sales (Example 3)	800	700	900	800	3,200
Desired ending inventory*	70	90	80	100+	100
Total Needs	870	790	980	900	3,300
Less: Beginning inventory ++	80	70	90	80	80
Units to be produced	790	720	890	820	3,220

* 10 percent of the next quarter's sales.
+ Estimated.
+ + The same as the previous quarter's ending inventory.

.04 The Direct Materials Budget

When the level of production has been computed, a direct materials budget should be constructed to show how much material will be required and how much material must be purchased to meet this production requirement. The purchase will depend on both expected usage of materials and inventory levels. The formula for computing the amount of the purchase is:

Purchase in units = Usage + Desired ending material inventory units − Beginning inventory units

The direct materials budget is usually accompanied by a computation of expected cash payments for materials.

Example 5:

THE JOHNSON COMPANY
Direct Materials Budget
For the Year Ending December 31, 20B

	Quarter				
	1	*2*	*3*	*4*	*Total*
Units to be produced (Ex.4)	790	720	890	820	3,220
Material needs per unit(lbs)	× 3	× 3	× 3	× 3	× 3
Material needs for production	2,370	2,160	2,670	2,460	9,660
Desired ending inventory of materials*	216	267	246	250 +	250
Total needs	2,586	2,427	2,916	2,710	9,910
Less: Beginning inventory of materials+ +	237	216	267	246	237
Materials to be purchased	2,349	2,211	2,649	2,464	9,673
Unit price	× $2	× $2	× $2	× $2	× $2
Purchase cost	$4,698	$4,422	$5,298	$4,928	$19,346

* 10 percent of the next quarter's units needed for production.
+ Estimated.
+ + The same as the prior quarter's ending inventory.

Schedule of Expected Cash Disbursements

	1	2	3	4	Total
Accounts payable, 12/31/20A	$2,200				$2,200
1st quarter purchases($4,698)	2,349	2,349 **			4,698
2d quarter purchases($4,422)		2,211	2,211		4,422
3d quarter purchases($5,298)			2,649	2,649	5,298
4th quarter purchases ($4,928)				2,464	2,464
Total disbursements	$4,549	$4,560	$4,860	$5,113	$19,082

** 50 percent of a quarter's purchases are paid for in the quarter of purchase; the remainder are paid for in the following quarter.

.05 The Direct Labor Budget

The production requirements in the production budget also provide the starting point for the preparation of the direct labor budget. To compute direct labor requirements, expected production volume for each period is multiplied by the number of direct labor hours required to produce a single unit. The direct labor hours to meet production requirements is then multiplied by the direct labor cost per hour to obtain budgeted total direct labor costs.

Example 6:

THE JOHNSON COMPANY
Direct Labor Budget
For the Year Ending December 31, 20B

	Quarter				
	1	*2*	*3*	*4*	*Total*
Units to be produced (Example 4)	790	720	890	820	3,220
Direct labor hours per unit	× 5	× 5	× 5	× 5	× 5
Total hours	3,950	3,600	4,450	4,100	16,100
Direct labor cost per hour	×$5	×$5	×$5	×$5	×$5
Total direct labor cost	$19,750	$18,000	$22,250	$20,500	$80,500

.06 *The Factory Overhead Budget*

The factory overhead budget provides a schedule of all manufacturing costs other than direct materials and direct labor, such as depreciation, property taxes, and factory rent. In developing the cash budget, one must remember that depreciation does not entail a cash outlay and, therefore, must be deducted from the total factory overhead in computing cash disbursement for factory overhead.

Example 7: To illustrate the factory overhead budget, assume that:

- Total factory overhead budgeted — $6,000 fixed (per quarter), plus $2 per hour of direct labor.
- Depreciation expenses are $3,250 each quarter.
- All overhead costs involving cash outlays are paid for in the quarter incurred.

THE JOHNSON COMPANY
Factory Overhead Budget
For the Year Ending December 31, 20B

	Quarter				
	1	*2*	*3*	*4*	*Total*
Budgeted direct labor hours (Example 6)	3,950	3,600	4,450	4,100	16,100
Variable overhead rate	×$2	×$2	×$2	×$2	×$2
Variable overhead budgeted	7,900	7,200	8,900	8,200	32,200
Fixed overhead budgeted	6,000	6,000	6,000	6,000	24,000
Total budgeted overhead	13,900	13,200	14,900	14,200	56,200
Less: Depreciation	3,250	3,250	3,250	3,250	13,000
Cash disbursement for overhead	10,650	9,950	11,650	10,950	43,200

.07 *The Ending Inventory Budget*

The desired ending inventory budget provides the information required for the construction of budgeted financial statements. Specifically, it will help compute the cost of goods sold on the budgeted income statement. Secondly, it will give the dollar value of the ending materials and finished goods inventory to appear on the budgeted balance sheet.

Example 8:

THE JOHNSON COMPANY
Ending Inventory Budget
For the Year Ending December 31, 20B
Ending Inventory

	Units	*Unit Cost*	*Total*
Direct materials	250 pounds (Example 5)	$ 2	$ 500
Finished goods	100 units (Example 4)	$41 *	$4,100

* The unit variable cost of $41 is computed as follows:

	Unit Cost	*Units*	*Total*
Direct materials (Ex. 5)	$2	3 pounds	$ 6
Direct labor (Ex. 6)	5	5 hours	25
Variable overhead (Ex. 7)	2	5 hours	10
Total variable manufacturing cost			$41

.08 The Selling and Administrative Expense Budget

The selling and administrative expense budget lists the operating expenses in selling the products and in managing the business. To complete the budgeted income statement in contribution format, variable selling and administrative expense per unit must be computed.

Example 9:

THE JOHNSON COMPANY
Selling and Administrative Expense Budget
For the Year Ending December 31, 20B

	Quarter				
	1	*2*	*3*	*4*	*Total*
Expected sales in units	800	700	900	800	3,200
Variable selling and administrative expense per unit *	×$4	×$4	×$4	×$4	×$4
Budgeted variable expense	$3,200	$2,800	$3,600	$3,200	$12,800
Fixed selling and administrative expenses:					
Advertising	1,100	1,100	1,100	1,100	4,400
Insurance	2,800				2,800
Office salaries	8,500	8,500	8,500	8,500	34,000
Rent	350	350	350	350	1,400
Taxes			1,200		1,200
Total budgeted selling and administrative expenses+	$15,950	$12,750	$14,750	$13,150	$56,600

* Assumed. It includes sales agents' commissions, shipping, and supplies.
+ Paid for in the quarter incurred.

.09 The Cash Budget

The cash budget is prepared for the purpose of cash planning and control. It presents the expected cash inflow and outflow for a designated time period. The cash budget helps management keep cash balances in reasonable relationship to its needs. It aids in avoiding unnecessary idle cash and possible cash shortages. The cash budget consists typically of four major sections:

1. The *receipts* section, which is the beginning cash balance, cash collections from customers, and other receipts.
2. The *disbursements* section, which comprises all cash payments that are planned during the budget period.
3. The *cash surplus or deficit* section, which simply shows the difference between the cash receipts section and the cash disbursements section.
4. The *financing* section, which provides a detailed account of the borrowings and repayments expected during the budgeting period.

Example 10: To illustrate, assume the following:

- The company desires to maintain a $5,000 minimum cash balance at the end of each quarter.
- All borrowing and repayment must be in multiples of $500 at an interest rate of 10 percent per annum. Interest is computed and paid as the principal is repaid. Borrowing takes place at the beginning of each quarter and repayment is at the end of each quarter.

THE JOHNSON COMPANY
Cash Budget
For the Year Ending December 31, 20B

	From Example	*Quarter* 1	2	3	4	*Total*
Cash balance, beginning		10,000*	9,401	5,461	9,106	10,000
Add: Receipts:						
Collections from customers	3	54,300	57,120	66,080	64,960	242,460
Total cash available		64,300	66,521	71,541	74,066	252,460
Less: Disbursements:						
Direct materials	5	4,549	4,560	4,860	5,113	19,082
Direct labor	6	19,750	18,000	22,250	20,500	80,500
Factory overhead	7	10,650	9,950	11,650	10,950	43,200
Selling and Admin.	9	15,950	12,750	14,750	13,150	56,600
Machinery purchase	Given	—	24,300	—	—	24,300
Income tax	Given	4,000	—	—	—	4,000
Total disbursements		54,899	69,560	53,510	49,713	227,682
Cash surplus (deficit)		9,401	(3,039)	18,031	24,353	24,778
Financing:						
Borrowing		—	8,500	—	—	8,500
Repayment		—	—	(8,500)	—	(8,500)
Interest		—	—	(425)	—	(425)
Total financing		—	8,500	(8,925)	—	(425)
Cash balance, ending		9,401	5,461	9,106	24,353	24,353

*From balance sheet 20A.

.10 The Budgeted Income Statement

The budgeted income statement summarizes the various component projections of revenue and expenses for the budgeting period. However, for control purposes, the budget can be divided into quarters, or even months, depending on the need.

Example 11:

THE JOHNSON COMPANY
Budgeted Income Statement
For the Year Ending December 31, 20B

	From Example		
Sales (3,200 units @ $80)	3		$256,000
Less: Variable expenses			
Variable cost of goods sold (3,200 units @ $41)	4	$131,200	
Variable selling & administrative	9	12,800	144,000
Contribution margin			112,000
Less: Fixed expenses			
Factory overhead	7	24,000	
Selling and administrative	9	43,800	67,800
Net operating income			44,200
Less: Interest expense	10		425
Income before taxes			43,775
Less: Income taxes	20%		8,755
Net income			35,020

.11 The Budgeted Balance Sheet

The budgeted balance sheet is developed by beginning with the balance sheet for the year just ended and adjusting it, using all the activities that are expected to take place during the budgeting period. Some of the reasons why the budgeted balance sheet must be prepared are:

1. It could disclose some unfavorable financial conditions that management might want to avoid.

2. It serves as a final check on the mathematical accuracy of all the other schedules.

3. It helps management perform a variety of ratio calculations.

4. It highlights future resources and obligations.

Example 12: The following balance sheet for the year 20A will help illustrate.

THE JOHNSON COMPANY
Balance Sheet
As of December 31, 20A

Assets		*Liabilities and Stockholders' Equity*	
Current Assets:		Current Liabilities:	
Cash	10,000	Accounts Payable	2,200
Accounts Receivable	9,500	Income Tax Payable	4,000
Material Inventory	474	Total Current Liabilities	6,200
Finished Goods Inventory	3,280		
Total Current Assets	23,254		
Fixed Assets:		Stockholders' Equity:	
Land	50,000	Common Stock, No-Par	70,000
Building and Equipment	100,000	Retained Earnings	37,054
Accumulated Depreciation	(60,000)		
	90,000		
Total Assets	113,254	Total Liabilities and Stockholders' equity	113,254

THE JOHNSON COMPANY
Budgeted Balance Sheet
As of December 31, 20B

Assets		*Liabilities and Stockholders' Equity*	
Current Assets:		Current Liabilities:	
Cash	24,353 (a)	Accounts Payable	2,464 (h)
Accounts Receivable	23,040 (b)	Income Tax Payable	8,755 (i)
Material Inventory	500 (c)	Total Current Liabilities	11,219
Finished Goods Inventory	4,100 (d)		
Total Current Assets	$51,993		
Fixed Assets:		Stockholders' Equity:	
Land	50,000 (e)	Common Stock, No-Par	70,000 (j)
Building and Equipment	124,300 (f)	Retained Earnings	72,074 (k)
Accumulated Depreciation	(73,000)(g)		
	101,300		
Total Assets	153,293	Total Liabilities and Stockholders' Equity	153,293

Computations:

(a) From Example 10 (cash budget).

(b) $9,500 (from balance sheet 20A) + $256,000 sales (from Example 3) – $242,460 receipts (from Example 3) = $23,040.

(c) and (d) From Example 8 (ending inventory budget).

(e) No change.

(f) $100,000 (from balance sheet 20A) + $24,300 (from Example 10) = $124,300.

(g) $60,000 (from balance sheet 20A) + $13,000 (from Example 7) = $73,000.

(h) $2,200 (from balance sheet 20A) = $19,346 (from Example 5) – $19,082 (from Example 5) = $2,464 (all accounts payable relate to material purchases), or 50% of 4th quarter purchase = 50% ($4,928) = 2,464.

(i) From Example 11 (budgeted income statement).

(j) No change.

(k) $37,054 (from balance sheet 20A) + $35,020 net income (from Example 11) = $72,074.

.12 *Financial Ratio Calculations*

To see what kind of financial condition the Johnson Company is expected to be in for the budgeting year, a sample of financial ratio calculations are in order: (Assume 20A after-tax net income was $15,000.)

	20A	*20B*
Current ratio (Current assets/current liabilities)	= $23,254/$6,200 = 3.75	= $51,993/$11,219 = 4.63
Return on total assets (Net income after taxes/ total assets)	= $15,000/$113,254 = 13.24%	= $35,020/$153,293 = 22.85%

Sample calculations indicate that the Johnson Company is expected to have better liquidity as measured by the current ratio. Overall performance will be improved as measured by return on total assets. This could be an indication that the contemplated plan may work out well.

¶ 1121 Budgeting with the Aid of Computer Technology

.01 *Using an Electronic Spreadsheet to Develop a Budget Plan*

Examples 3 to 12 showed a detailed procedure for formulating a master budget. However, in practice, a short-cut approach to budgeting is quite common using computer technology. An electronic spreadsheet may be used to efficiently and quickly develop a budget (examples of available software are Lotus 1-2-3 and Excel). Such software carry out tedious, mechanical calculations, including addition, subtraction, multiplication, and division. More importantly, if a budgetary figure is changed (e.g., sales), the electronic spreadsheet will change all other budgetary amounts related to it (e.g., cost of sales, selling expenses). Hence, it is easy to make different sales projections and see what the resulting costs and profitability will be.

A discussion of spreadsheet programs follows. Three examples of projecting an income statement are presented.

Example 13: Given:

Sales for 1st month = $60,000

Cost of sales = 42% of sales, all variable

Operating expenses = $10,000 fixed plus 5% of sales

Taxes = 30% of net income

Sales increase by 5% each month

(a) Based on this information, Exhibit 3 presents a spreadsheet for the contribution income statement for the next 12 months and in total.

(b) Exhibit 4 shows the same information, assuming that sales increase by 10 percent and operating expenses = $10,000 plus 10 percent of sales. This is an example of "what-if" scenarios.

Exhibit 3
Projected Income Statement

	1	2	3	4	5	6	7	8	9	10	11	12	Total	Percent
Sales	$60,000	$63,000	$66,150	$69,458	$72,930	$76,577	$80,406	$84,426	$88,647	$93,080	$97,734	$102,620	$955,028	100%
Less: VC														
Cost of sales	$25,200	$26,460	$27,783	$29,172	$30,631	$32,162	$33,770	$35,459	$37,232	$39,093	$41,048	$43,101	$401,112	42%
Operating ex.	$3,000	$3,150	$3,308	$3,473	$3,647	$3,829	$4,020	$4,221	$4,432	$4,654	$4,887	$5,131	$47,751	5%
CM	$31,800	$33,390	$35,060	$36,812	$38,653	$40,586	$42,615	$44,746	$46,983	$49,332	$51,799	$54,389	$506,165	53%
Less: FC														
Op. expenses	$10,000	$10,000	$10,000	$10,000	$10,000	$10,000	$10,000	$10,000	$10,000	$10,000	$10,000	$10,000	$120,000	13%
Net income	$21,800	$23,390	$25,060	$26,812	$28,653	$30,586	$32,615	$34,746	$36,983	$39,332	$41,799	$44,389	$386,165	40%
Less:Tax	$6,540	$7,017	$7,518	$8,044	$8,596	$9,176	$9,785	$10,424	$11,095	$11,800	$12,540	$13,317	$115,849	12%
NI after tax	$15,260	$16,373	$17,542	$18,769	$20,057	$21,410	$22,831	$24,322	$25,888	$27,533	$29,259	$31,072	$270,315	28%

Exhibit 4
Projected Income Statement

	1	*2*	*3*	*4*	*5*	*6*	*7*	*8*	*9*	*10*	*11*	*12*	*Total*	*Percent*
Sales	$60,000	$66,000	$72,600	$79,860	$87,846	$96,631	$106,294	$116,923	$128,615	$141,477	$155,625	$171,187	$1,283,057	134%
Less: VC														
Cost of sales	$25,200	$27,720	$30,492	$33,541	$36,895	$40,585	$44,643	$49,108	$54,018	$59,420	$65,362	$71,899	$538,884	56%
Operating ex.	$6,000	$6,600	$7,260	$7,986	$8,785	$9,663	$10,629	$11,692	$12,862	$14,148	$15,562	$17,119	$64,153	7%
CM	$28,800	$31,680	$34,848	$38,333	$42,166	$46,383	$51,021	$56,123	$61,735	$67,909	$74,700	$82,170	$615,867	64%
Less: FC														
Op. expenses	$10,000	$10,000	$10,000	$10,000	$10,000	$10,000	$10,000	$10,000	$10,000	$10,000	$10,000	$10,000	$120,000	13%
Net income	$18,800	$21,680	$24,848	$28,333	$32,166	$36,383	$41,021	$46,123	$51,735	$57,909	$64,700	$72,170	$495,867	52%
Less:Tax	$5,640	$6,504	$7,454	$8,500	$9,650	$10,915	$12,306	$13,837	$15,521	$17,373	$19,410	$21,651	$148,760	16%
NI after tax	$13,160	$15,176	$17,394	$19,833	$22,516	$25,468	$28,715	$32,286	$36,215	$40,536	$45,290	$50,519	$347,107	36%

Example 14: Delta Gamma Company wishes to prepare a three-year projection of net income using the following information:

1. 2001 base year amounts are as follows:

Sales revenues	$4,500,000
Cost of sales	2,900,000
Selling and administrative expenses	800,000
Net income before taxes	800,000

2. Use the following assumptions:

   - Sales revenues increase by six percent in 2002, seven percent in 2003, and eight percent in 2004.
   - Cost of sales increase by five percent each year.
   - Selling and administrative expenses increase only one percent in 2002 and will remain at the 2003 level thereafter.
   - The income tax rate = 46 percent.

Exhibit 5 presents a spreadsheet for the income statement for the next three years.

Exhibit 5

Delta Gamma Company
Three-Year Income Projections (2001-2004)

	2001	*2002*	*2003*	*2004*
Sales	$4,500,000	$4,770,000	$5,103,900	$5,512,212
Cost of sales	$2,900,000	$3,045,000	$3,197,250	$3,357,112
Gross margin	$1,600,000	$1,725,000	$1,906,650	$2,155,100
Selling & adm. exp.	$800,000	$808,000	$808,000	$808,000
Earnings before tax	$800,000	$917,000	$1,098,650	$1,347,100
Tax	$368,000	$421,820	$505,379	$619,666
Earnings after tax	$432,000	$495,180	$593,271	$727,434

.02 Using Computer-Based Models for Financial Planning and Budgeting

A computer-based quantitative model may be used to construct a profit-planning budget and to help answer a variety of "what-if" questions. Its calculations provide a basis for choice among alternatives under conditions of uncertainty. There are primarily two approaches to modeling the corporate budgeting process: simulation and optimization.

There are many user-oriented software systems specifically designed for corporate planners, treasurers, budget preparers, CFOs, and business analysts. Several popular ones are described briefly below.

Adaytum Planning. Adaytum e.Planning by Adaytum Software (www.adaytum.com) (1-866-232-9886) is a multi-user budgeting, planning, and forecasting system.

Comshare's Planning Module (MPC). In Comshare MPC, all key finance functions such as corporate performance management, integrating budgeting, planning, forecasting, financial consolidation, and management reporting and analysis are handled by a single application. Integration allows management to set goals, implement strategy, track performance, and take corrective action when needed, all based on timely, accurate data. Comshare MPC gives real-time access to business critical information across the business organization.

1. With Comshare's planning solution, you can:
   - Extend the central application to meet specific end-user analysis needs.
   - Forecast using actual data for more accurate planning and budgeting.
   - Use "Goal-seeking" to work backwards and find the numbers needed to reach your goal.
   - Use "What-if" Analysis to model and test alternative budgeting or financing scenarios.
   - Perform specialized analysis and save individual views without affecting the core data.
   - Create multiple views showing different business perspectives.
   - Store completed plans in a central, secure repository.
   - Plan by management structure (division, department, etc.), activity, project, product, or strategic initiative.
2. With Comshare's budgeting solution, you can:
   - Quickly prepare budgets and rolling forecasts.
   - Analyze performance from any defined business perspective.
   - Perform asset and salary planning.
   - Receive proactive alerts indicating out-of-range data and exceptions.
   - Automatically load data from all popular sources.
   - Support multiple currency structures (EMU compliant).
   - Annotate numbers with text to show the thinking behind them.
   - Track which budget holders have or haven't entered their numbers.

- Budget for employees by unit, version, and one additional dimension.

For more, log on to the Comshare website (www.comshare.com/planning-software/index.cfm and www.comshare.com/budgeting-software/index.cfm, 1-800-922-7979, 3001 S. State St., P.O. Box 1588, Ann Arbor, Michigan 48106).

Encore and Webfact. This package was developed by Ferox Microsystems. The analytical functions are similar to Comshare and Hyperion, but Encore has more model building capability. For example, it is stronger in its risk analysis than Comshare, and even includes a Monte Carlo Simulator. Since Encore and Webfact are more powerful at the application development level than, say, Comshare, they require a higher level of programming ability. The Windows version is much easier to use than the previous versions. For more information log on to the Ferox Microsystems, Inc. website (www.ferox.com) or call 1-903-684-1660.

Budget Maestro. Planet's Budget Maestro is probably the best answer to distributed budgeting, strategic planning, and financial control. Budget Maestro shortens one's budgeting cycle and puts one into control of the process. Its information-driven environment guides the user through budgeting, planning, modeling, forecasting, resource management, consolidation, analysis, and reporting. CFOs and budget managers can plan, analyze, and manage, in ways never before possible. It allows one to look at a user's screen and make changes directly without ever being there. It can deliver budget models and deploy reconfigured software updates to many users at once, as well as manage budgetary information, even enterprise-wide information systems, with a single consistent interface. Planet's Budget Maestro is designed to put CFOs and financial managers in control of all aspects of managing budgets, creating financial models, and building and deploying financial plans. Budget Maestro allows business managers unparalleled flexibility in analyzing cash flow and business performance throughout the enterprise. Budget Maestro significantly shortens budgeting and planning cycles and eliminates re-keying and formatting of data. It increases data accuracy and integrity, allowing the user time to manage and analyze their business. It is available in both Desktop and Enterprise Edition. Budget Maestro Enterprise Edition enables multiple independent budgets and plans to be consolidated into a unified enterprise model. The Desktop Edition can be upgraded to the Enterprise Edition at any time. For more information, see Planet's website (www.planetcorp.com).

.03 The Latest Generation of Budgeting and Planning (B&P) Software

The new budgeting and planning (B&P) software represents a giant step forward for accountants. Finance managers can use these robust, Web-enabled programs to scan a wide range of data, radically speed up the planning process, and identify managers who have failed to submit budgets.

More often known as *active financial planning software*, these software include applications and the new level of functionality that combine budgeting, forecasting analytics, business intelligence, and collaboration. Exhibit 6 lists popular B&P software.

Exhibit 6

Active Financial Planning Software— Next Generation Budgeting and Planning (B & P) Software

Companies	*Websites*	*Software*
Active Strategy	www.activestrategy.com	ActiveStrategy Enterprise
Actuate	www.actuate.com	e.Reporting Suite
Adaytum Software	www.adaytum.com	e.planning
Applix	www.applix.com	iPlanning, iTM1
Brio Technology	www.brio.com	Brio.ONE, Brio. Impact, Brio. Inform
Business Objects	www.businessobjects.com	e-BL, BusinessObjects, Auditor, BusinessObjects BW Connect, Webintelligence
Cartesis	www.cartesis.com	Cartesis Budget Planning, Cartesis Carat, Cartesis Magnitude
Closedloop Solutions	www.closedloopsolutions.com	BizPlan Manager, SpendCap Manager, TopLine Manager
Cognos	www.cognos.com	Cognos Finance, Cognos Visualizer, Cognos Enterprise, Business Intelligence
Comshare	www.comshare.com	Management Planning and Control (MPC) Application, Comshare Decision
Corvu	www.corvu.com	CorManage, CorVu Rapid Scorecard, CorBusiness, CorPortfolio
E.Intelligence	www.eintelligence-inc.com	e.intelligence Suite
Epicor	www.epicor.com	Epicor eintelligence Suite
Geac	www.geac.com	Geac Smartstream Financials, Enterprise Solutions Expert Series, FRx
Great Plains Software	www.greatplains.com	eEnterprise, FRx Budget Controller, Dynamics
Hyperion	www.hyperion.com	Hyperion Financial Management, Hyperion Planning, Hyperion Essbase
J.D. Edwards	www.jdedwards.com	J.D. Edwards Financial Planning and Budgeting, Business Intelligence, Oneworld XE
Lawson Software	www.lawson.com	Enterprise Budgeting SEA Applications- Including E-Scorecard: Analytic Extensions
Longview Solutions	www.longview.com	Khalix
MIS-AG	www.misag.com	MIS Alea Decisionware, MIS DeltaMiner
NextStrat	www.nextstrat.com	NextStrat Strategic Implementation Portal (NextSIP)
Oracle	www.oracle.com	Oracle Strategic Enterprise Management (SEM)

Companies	*Websites*	*Software*
OutlookSoft	www.outlooksoft.com	OutlookSoft Financial Planning and Analysis (FPA), OutlookSoft Enterprise Analytic Portal
PeopleSoft	www.peoplesoft.com	Enterprise Performance Managment (EPM), PeopleSoft Balanced Scorecard, PeopleSoft Enterprise Warehouse, PeopleSoft eBusiness Analytics, PeopleSoft Activity-Based Management
SAP	www.sap.com	SAP Stategic Enterprise Managment (SEM), SAP Financial Analyzer Business Intelligence with mySAP.com
SAS Institute	www.sas.com	SAS Total Financial Management, Stategic Vision, SAS/Warehouse Administrator, SAS Enabling Technology (OLAP)
Silvon	www.silvon.com	Stratum
SRC Software	www.srcsoftware.com	Budget Advisor, Payroll Planner, Information Advisor

Chapter 12
Managing Working Capital

¶ 1201 Overview

Effective management of working capital (current assets less current liabilities) improves returns and minimizes the risk that the company will run short of cash. By optimally managing cash, receivables, and inventory, a company can maximize its rate of return and minimize its liquidity and business risk. The amount invested in each current asset may change daily and should be monitored carefully to ensure that funds are used in the most productive way possible. Large account balances may also indicate risk; for example, inventory may not be salable and/or accounts receivable may not be collectible. On the other hand, maintaining inadequate current asset levels may be costly; business may be lost if inventory is too low.

Cash refers to currency and demand deposits; excess funds may be invested in marketable securities. Cash management involves accelerating cash inflow and delaying cash outflow. Accounts receivable management involves selecting customers with good credit standing and speeding up customer collections. Inventory management involves having the optimal order size at the right time.

¶ 1205 Evaluating Working Capital

Working capital equals current assets less current liabilities. If current assets are $6,500,000 and current liabilities are $4,000,000, working capital equals $2,500,000. Managing working capital—regulating the various types of current assets and current liabilities—requires making decisions on how assets should be financed (e.g., by short-term debt, long-term debt, or equity); net working capital increases when current assets are financed through noncurrent sources.

Managing working capital is also evaluating the trade-off between return and risk. If funds are transferred from fixed assets to current assets, liquidity risk is reduced, greater ability to obtain short-term financing is enhanced, and the company has greater flexibility in adjusting current assets to meet changes in sales volume. However, it also receives reduced return, because the yield on fixed assets exceeds that of current assets. Financing with noncurrent debt carries less liquidity risk than financing with current debt, because the former is payable over a longer period. However, long-term debt often has a higher cost than short-term debt because of its greater uncertainty.

Using the *hedging* approach to financing, in which assets are financed by liabilities with similar maturity, may reduce liquidity risk. When a company needs funds to purchase seasonal or cyclical inventory, it uses short-term financing, which gives it flexibility to meet its seasonal needs within its ability to repay the loan. On the other hand, the company's permanent assets should be financed with long-term debt. Because the assets last longer, the financing can be spread over a longer time, helping to ensure the availability of adequate funds with which to meet debt payments.

The less time that it takes between purchase and delivery of goods, the less working capital needed. For example, if the company can receive a raw material in two weeks, it can maintain a lower level of inventory than if two months' lead time is required. One should purchase material early if by doing so one can pay significantly lower prices and if the material's cost savings exceed inventory carrying costs.

¶ 1211 Cash Management

.01 Maintaining a Proper Cash Balance

The goal of cash management is to invest excess cash for a return and at the same time have adequate liquidity. A proper cash balance, neither excessive nor deficient, should exist. For example, companies with many bank accounts may be accumulating excessive balances. Proper cash forecasting is particularly crucial in a recession and is required to determine (1) the optimal time to incur and pay back debt, and (2) the amount to transfer daily between accounts. A daily computerized listing of cash balances and transaction reporting keeps an up-to-date cash balance to determine how best to use the funds. One should also assess the costs one is paying for banking services, looking at each account's cost.

When cash receipts and cash payments are highly synchronized and predictable, a company may keep a smaller cash balance; if quick liquidity is needed, it can invest in marketable securities. Any additional cash should be invested in income producing securities with maturities structured to provide the necessary liquidity.

Financially strong companies that are able to borrow at favorable rates, even in difficult financial markets, can afford to keep a lower level of cash than companies that are highly leveraged or considered poor credit risks.

At a minimum, a company should hold in cash the greater of (1) compensating balances (deposits held by a bank to compensate it for providing services) or (2) precautionary balances (money held for emergency purposes) plus transaction balances (money to cover checks outstanding). It must also hold enough cash to meet its daily requirements.

A number of factors go into the decision of how much cash to hold. These include the company's liquid assets, business risk, debt levels and maturity dates, ability to borrow on short notice and on favorable terms, rate of return, economic conditions, and the possibility of unexpected problems, such as customer defaults.

.02 Acceleration of Cash Inflow

To improve cash inflow, one should evaluate the causes of, and take corrective action for, delays in having cash receipts deposited. One should ascertain the origin of cash receipts, how they are delivered, and how cash is transferred from outlying accounts to the main corporate account. One should also investigate banking policy regarding availability of funds and the length of the time lag between when a check is received and when it is deposited.

The types of delays in processing checks are: (1) "mail float," which is the time required for a check to move from debtor to creditor; (2) "processing float," which is the time needed for the creditor to render the payment; and (3) "deposit collection float," or "transit float," which is the time it takes for a check to clear.

Exhibit 1 depicts the total float of a check.

Exhibit 1

Total Float Time

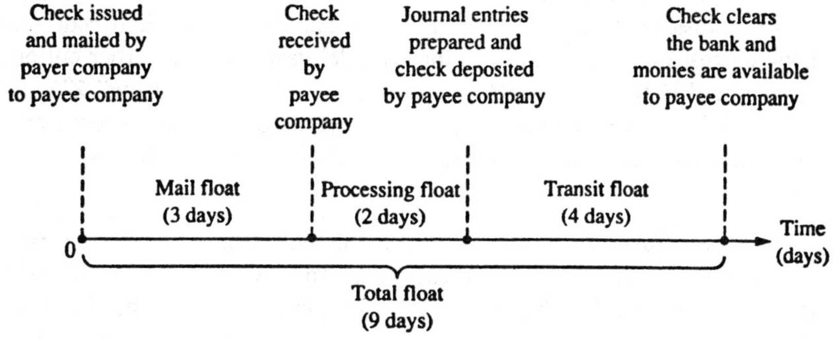

One should try out all possible ways to accelerate cash receipts, including the use of lockboxes, pre-authorized debits (PADs), wire transfers, and depository transfer checks.

Lockbox. A lockbox represents a way to place the optimum collection point near customers. Customer payments are mailed to strategic post office boxes geographically situated to reduce mailing and depositing time. Banks make collections from these boxes several times a day and deposit the funds to the corporate account. They then prepare a computer listing of payments received by account and a daily total, which is forwarded to the corporation.

To determine the effectiveness of using a lockbox, one should determine the average face value of checks received, the cost of operations eliminated, reducible processing overhead, and the reduction in "mail float" days. Because per-item processing costs for lockboxes is typically significant, it makes the most sense to use one for low-volume, high-dollar collections. However, as technological advances lower their per-item cost, businesses with high-volume, low-dollar receipts are also finding them cost effective.

Wholesale lockboxes are used for checks received from other *companies.* As a rule, the average dollar cash receipts are large, and the number of cash receipts is small. Many wholesale lock boxes result in mail time reductions of no more than one business day and check-clearing time reductions of only a few tenths of one day. They are, therefore, most useful for companies that have gross revenues of at least several million dollars and that receive large checks from distant customers.

A retail lockbox is the best choice if the company deals with the *public* (retail customers as distinguished from companies). Retail lockboxes typically receive many transactions of nominal amounts. The lockbox reduces float and transfers workload from the company to the bank, resulting in improved cash flow and reduced expenses.

Return envelopes. Providing return envelopes can accelerate customer remissions. On the return envelope, bar codes, nine-digit code numbers, or post office box numbers increase delivery speed. Another option is Accelerated Reply Mail (ARM), in which a unique "truncating" ZIP code is assigned to payments such as lockbox receivables. The coded remittances are removed from the postal system and processed by banks or third parties.

Pre-authorized debits. Cash from customers may be collected faster if you obtain permission from customers to have pre-authorized debits (PADs) automatically charged to the customers' bank accounts for repetitive charges. This is a common practice among insurance companies, which collect monthly premium payments via PADs. These debits may take the form of pre-authorized checks (PACs) or paperless automatic clearing house entries. PADs are cost-effective, because they avoid the process of billing the customer, receiving and processing the payment, and depositing the check. Using PADs for variable payments is less efficient, because the amount of the PAD must be changed each period and the customer generally must be advised by mail of the amount of the debit. PADs are most effective when used for constant, relatively nominal periodic payments.

Wire transfers. To accelerate cash flow, one may transfer funds between banks by wire transfers through computer terminals and telephones. Such transfers should be used only for significant dollar amounts, because both the originating and receiving banks assesses wire transfer fees. Wire transfers are best for intraorganization transfers, such as transfers to and from investments, deposits to an account made the day checks are expected to clear, and deposits made to any other account that requires immediate availability of funds. They may also be used to fund other types of checking accounts, such as payroll accounts. In order to avoid unnecessarily large balances in the account, one may fund it on a staggered basis. However, to prevent an overdraft, one should make sure balances are maintained in another account at the bank.

There are two types of wire transfers—preformatted (recurring) and free-form (nonrecurring). Recurring transfers do *not* involve extensive authorization and are suitable for ordinary transfers in which the company designates issuing and receiving banks and provides its account number. Nonrecurring transfers require greater control, including written confirmations instead of telephone or computer terminal confirmations.

Depository transfer checks (DTCs). Paper or paperless depository checks may be used to transfer funds between the company's bank accounts. They do not require a signature, since the check is payable to the bank for credit to the company's account. DTCs typically clear in one day. *Manual* DTCs are preprinted checks that include all information except the amount and date; *automated* DTCs are printed as needed.

Alternate methods. There are other ways to accelerate cash inflow. A company can send bills to customers sooner than is the practice, perhaps immediately after the order is shipped. A company can also require deposits on large or custom orders or submit progress billings as the work on the order progresses. It can charge interest on accounts receivable that are past due and offer cash discounts for early payment; it can also use cash-on-delivery terms. In any event, one should deposit checks immediately.

> ***Example 1:*** C Corporation obtains average cash receipts of \$200,000 per day. It usually takes 5 days from the time a check is mailed until the funds are available for use. The amount tied up by the delay is:
>
> 5 days × \$200,000 = \$1,000,000
>
> One can also calculate the return earned on the average cash balance.

Example 2: A company's weekly average cash balances are as follows:

Week	*Average Cash Balance*
1 . . .	$12,000
2 . . .	17,000
3 . . .	10,000
4 . .	15,000
Total	$54,000

The weekly average cash balance is:

$$\frac{\$54{,}000}{4} = \$13{,}500$$

If the annual interest rate is approximately 12 percent, the monthly return earned on the average cash balance is:

$$\$13{,}500 \times \frac{0.12}{12} = \$135$$

If one is thinking of establishing a lockbox to accelerate cash inflow, one will need to determine the maximum monthly charge one will incur for the service.

Example 3: It takes Travis Corporation about seven days to receive and deposit payments from customers. Therefore, it is considering establishing a lockbox system. It expects the system to reduce the float time to five days. Average daily collections are $500,000. The rate of return is 12 percent.

The reduction in outstanding cash balances arising from implementing the lockbox system is:

2 days × $500,000 = $1,000,000

The return that could be earned on these funds in a year is:

$1,000,000 × 0.12 = $120,000

The maximum monthly charge the company should pay for this lockbox arrangement is therefore:

$$\frac{\$120{,}000}{12} = \$10{,}000$$

One should compare the return earned on freed cash to the cost of the lockbox arrangement to determine if using the lockbox is financially advantageous.

Example 4: A company's financial officer is determining whether to initiate a lockbox arrangement that will cost $150,000 annually. The daily average collections are $700,000. Using a lockbox will reduce mailing and processing time by two days. The rate of return is 14 percent.

Annual return on freed cash (14%×2×$700,000)	$196,000
Annual cost	$150,000
Net advantage of lockbox system	$46,000

Sometimes one needs to determine whether to switch banks in order to lower the overall costs associated with a lockbox arrangement.

Example 5: ABC Company now has a lockbox arrangement in which Bank A handles $5 million a day in return for an $800,000 compensating balance. ABC's financial officer is thinking of canceling this arrangement and further dividing his western region by entering into contracts with two other banks. Bank B will handle $3 million a day in collections with a compensating balance of $700,000, and Bank C will handle $2 million a day with a compensating balance of $600,000. Collections will be half a day quicker than they are now. The return rate is 12 percent.

Accelerated cash receipts ($5 million per day×0.5 day)	$2,500,000
Increased compensating balance	500,000
Improved cash flow	$2,000,000
Rate of return	×0.12
Net annual savings	$240,000

.03 Delay of Cash Outlay

Delaying cash payments can help a company earn a greater return and have more cash available. The financial officer should evaluate the payees and determine to what extent the company can reasonably stretch time limits without incurring finance charges or impairing its credit rating.

There are many ways to delay cash payments, including centralizing payables, having zero balance accounts, and paying by draft.

Centralize payables. A company should centralize its payable operation—that is, make one center responsible for making all payments—so that debt may be paid at the most profitable time and so that the amount of disbursement float in the system may be ascertained.

Zero balance account (ZBA). Cash payments may be delayed by maintaining zero balance accounts in one bank in which the company maintains zero balances for all of its disbursing units, with funds being transferred in from a master account as needed. The advantages of ZBAs are that they allow better control over cash payments and reduce excess cash balances in regional banks. Using ZBAs is an aggressive strategy that requires the company to put funds into its payroll and payables checking accounts only when it expects checks to clear. However, the company must watch out for overdrafts and service charges.

Drafts. Payment drafts are another strategy for delaying disbursements. With a draft, payment is made when the draft is presented for collection to the bank, which in turn goes to the issuer for acceptance. When the draft is approved, the company deposits the funds to the payee's account. Because of this delay, the company can maintain a lower checking balance. Banks usually impose a charge for drafts, and one must endure the inconveniences of formally approving them before payment. Drafts can provide a measure of protection against fraud and theft because they must be presented for inspection before payment.

Delay in mail. One can delay cash payments by drawing checks on remote banks (e.g., a New York company might use a Texas bank), thus ensuring that checks take longer to clear. One may also mail checks from post offices that offer limited service or at which mail must go through numerous handling points. If one utilizes the mail float properly, one can maintain higher actual bank balances than book balances. For instance, if one writes checks averaging $200,000 per day and they take three days to clear, one will have $600,000 ($200,000 × 3) in one's checking account for those three days, even though the money has been deducted in one's records. When one uses this method, one should keep one's money in some kind of interest bearing account.

Check clearing. One can use probability analysis to determine the expected date for checks to clear. Probability is defined as the degree of likelihood that something will happen and is expressed as a percentage from 0 to 100. For example, it's likely that not all payroll checks are cashed on the payroll date, so one can deposit some funds later and earn a return until the last minute.

Delay payment to employees. A company can reduce the frequency of payments to employees (e.g., expense account reimbursements and payrolls). For example, a company can institute a monthly payroll rather than a weekly one. In this way, it will have the use of the cash for a greater period of time. A company can also disburse commissions on sales when the receivables are collected, rather than when sales are made. Finally, it can utilize noncash compensation and remuneration methods (e.g., distribute stock instead of bonuses).

Alternate methods. Other ways exist to delay cash payments. Instead of making full payment on an invoice, one can make partial payments. One can also delay payment by requesting additional information about an invoice from the vendor before paying it. Another strategy is to use a charge account to lengthen the time between when one buys goods and when one pays for them. In any event, never pay a bill before its due date.

Example 6: Every two weeks XYZ Company disburses checks that average $500,000 and take three days to clear. The company's financial officer wants to find out how much money can be saved annually if the transfer of funds is delayed from an interest-bearing account that pays 0.0384-percent interest per day (annual rate of 14 percent) for those three days.

$500,000 × (0.000384 × 3) = $576

The savings per year is $576 × 26 (yearly payrolls) = $14,976

A cash management system is shown in Exhibit 2.

Exhibit 2

Cash Management System

Acceleration of Cash Receipts	*Delay of Cash Payments*
Lockbox System	Pay by Draft
Concentration Banking	Requisition More Frequently
Preauthorized Checks	Disbursing Float
Preaddressed Stamped Envelopes	Make Partial Payments
Obtain Deposits on Large Orders	Use Charge Accounts
Charge Interest on Overdue Receivables	Delay Frequency of Paying Employees

.04 Cash Models

Conditions of certainty—The William Baumol model. A number of mathematical models have been developed to assist the financial manager in distributing a company's funds so that they provide a maximum return to the company. A model developed by William Baumol can determine the optimum amount of cash for a company to hold under conditions of certainty. The objective is to minimize the sum of the fixed costs of transactions and the opportunity cost (return forgone) of holding cash balances that do not yield a return. These costs are expressed as:

$$F \frac{(T)}{C} + i \frac{(C)}{2}$$

Where:

F = the fixed cost of a transaction

T = the total cash needed for the time period involved

i = the interest rate on marketable securities

C = cash balance

The optimal level of cash is determined using the following formula:

C* = optimal level of cash

$$C^* = \sqrt{\frac{2FT}{i}}$$

Example 7: Acme Company estimates a cash need for $4,000,000 over a one-month period during which the cash account is expected to be disbursed at a constant rate. The opportunity interest rate is six percent per annum, or 0.5 percent for a one-month period. The transaction cost each time Acme borrows or withdraws is $100.

The optimal transaction size (the optimal borrowing or withdrawal lot size) and the number of transactions Acme should make during the month follow:

$$C^* = \sqrt{\frac{2FT}{i}} = \sqrt{\frac{2(100)(4,000,000)}{0.0005}} = \$400,000$$

The optimal transaction size is $400,000.

The average cash balance is:

$$\frac{C^*}{2} = \frac{\$400,000}{2} = \$200,000$$

The number of transactions required is:

$$\frac{4,000,000}{\$400,000} = 10 \text{ transactions during the month.}$$

Conditions of uncertainty—The Miller-Orr model. There is also a model for cash management when cash payments are uncertain. The Miller-Orr model places upper and lower limits on cash balances. When the upper limit is reached, a transfer of cash to marketable securities is made; when the lower limit is reached, a transfer from securities to cash occurs. No transaction occurs as long as the cash balance stays within the limits.

Factors taken into account in the Miller-Orr model are the fixed costs of a securities transaction (F), assumed to be the same for buying as well as selling; the daily interest rate on marketable securities (i); and the variance of daily net cash flows (σ^2 – σ is sigma). The objective is to meet cash requirements at the lowest possible cost. A major assumption of this model is the randomness of cash flows. The control limits in the Miller-Orr model are "d" dollars as an upper limit and zero dollars at the lower limit. When the cash balance reaches the upper level, d less z dollars (optimal cash balance) of securities are bought, and the new balance becomes z dollars. When the cash balance equals zero, z dollars of securities are sold and the new balance again reaches z. Of course, in practice, the minimum cash balance is established at an amount greater than zero because of delays in transfer; the higher minimum, in effect, acts as a safety buffer.

The optimal cash balance z is computed as follows:

$$Z=\sqrt[3]{\frac{3F\sigma^2}{4i}}$$

The optimal value for d is computed as 3z.

The average cash balance approximates:

$$\frac{(z+d)}{3}$$

Example 8: Jones Company wishes to use the Miller-Orr model. The following information is supplied:

Fixed cost of a securities transaction	\$10
Variance of daily net cash flows	\$50
Daily interest rate on securities (10%/360)	0.000277

The optimal cash balance, the upper limit of cash needed, and the average cash balance follow:

$$z=\sqrt[3]{\frac{3(10)(50)}{4(0.000277)}}=\sqrt[3]{\frac{3(10)(50)}{0.001108}}=\sqrt[3]{\frac{1{,}500}{0.001108}}=\sqrt[3]{1{,}353{,}790}$$
$$=\$108$$

The optimal cash balance is \$108; the upper limit is \$324 (3 ×\$108); and the average cash balance is:

$$\$144=\frac{(\$108+\$324)}{3}$$

When the upper limit of \$324 is reached, \$216 of securities (\$324 − \$108) will be purchased to bring the account to the optimal cash balance of \$108. When the lower limit of zero dollars is reached, \$108 of securities will be sold to again bring it to the optimal cash balance of \$108.

.05 Banking Relationships

Before establishing a relationship with a bank, one should appraise its financial soundness by checking the ratings compiled by financial advisory services such as Moody's and Standard & Poor's. A company may want to limit its total deposits at any one bank to no more than the amount insured by the Federal Deposit Insurance Corporation, especially if the bank is having difficulties.

One may also decide to use different banks for different services. In selecting a bank, consider location (which affects lockboxes and disbursement points), type and cost of services, and availability of funds.

One may undertake a bank account analysis by comparing the value of the company balance maintained at the bank to the service charges imposed. Banks will provide such analysis if one wishes, but one should scrutinize the bank's analysis closely to be sure it is accurate.

Most checks clear in one business day; clearing time of three or more business days is rare. One should try to arrange for the financial institution to give same-day credit on deposits received prior to a specified cutoff time. If the deposit is made over the counter, the funds may not be immediately available; if the deposit is made early enough, especially through a lockbox, they may be.

.06 Investing in Marketable Securities

Cash management requires knowing the amount of funds the company has available for investment and the length of time for which they can be invested. Such investments earn a return for the company. Marketable securities include:

- *Time deposits.* Savings accounts that earn daily interest, long-term savings accounts, and certificates of deposit.
- *Money market funds.* Managed portfolios of short-term/high-grade debt instruments such as Treasury bills and commercial paper.
- *Interest-paying demand deposits.* U.S. Treasury securities.

Automatic short-term money market investments immediately deposit excess cash in money market securities in order to earn a return on the funds. Holding marketable securities serves as protection against cash shortages; companies with seasonal operations may purchase marketable securities when they have excess funds and then sell the securities when cash deficits occur. Companies may also invest in marketable securities when they are holding funds temporarily in expectation of short-term capital expansion. In selecting an investment portfolio, one should consider return, default risk, marketability, and maturity date.

One should monitor coupon and security collection to ensure that the company receives any interest it is entitled to and that securities that mature or are sold are properly collected and deposited.

¶ 1215 Accounts Receivable Management

Accounts receivable management directly impacts the profitability of the firm. It includes determining discount policy and credit policy for marginal customers, investigating ways of speeding up collections and reducing bad debts, and setting terms of sale to assure ultimate collection.

As part of accounts receivable management, one should appraise order entry, billing, and accounts receivable activities to be sure that proper procedures are being followed from the time an order is received until ultimate collection. Among the points to consider is how the average time lag between completing the sales transaction and invoicing the customer can be reduced. One should also consider the opportunity cost of holding receivables, that is, the return lost by having funds tied up in accounts receivable instead of invested elsewhere.

Accounts receivable management involves two types of float—invoicing and mail. *Invoicing float* is the number of days between the time goods are shipped to the customer and the time the invoice is sent out. Obviously, the company should mail invoices on a timely basis. *Mail float* is the time between the preparation of an invoice and the time it is received by the customer. Mail float may be reduced by decentralizing invoicing and mailing, coordinating outgoing mail with post office schedules, using express mail services for large invoices, enforcing due dates, and offering discounts for early payment.

.01 Credit Policies

A key concern in accounts receivable management is determining credit terms to be given to customers, which affects sales volume and collections. For example, offering longer credit terms will probably increase sales. Credit terms have a direct bearing on the costs and revenue generated from receivables. If credit terms are tight, the company will have a lower investment in accounts receivable and incur fewer bad-debt losses, but it may also experience lower sales, reduced profits, and adverse customer reaction. On the other hand, if credit terms are lax, the company may enjoy higher sales and gross profit, but it risks increased bad debts and a higher opportunity cost of carrying the investment in accounts receivable, because marginal customers take longer to pay. Receivable terms should be liberalized when one wants to get rid of excessive inventory or obsolete items or if one operates in an industry in which products are sold in advance of retail seasons (e.g., swimsuits). If one's products are perishable, one should impose short receivable terms and possibly require payment on delivery.

In granting trade credit, one should consider the competition and current economic conditions. In a recession, one may want to relax one's credit policy in order to stimulate additional business. For example, a company may not rebill customers who take a cash discount even after the discount period has elapsed. On the other hand, a company may decide to tighten credit policy in times of short supply, because at such times the company, as the seller, has the upper hand.

In evaluating a potential customer's ability to pay, one should consider the customer's integrity, financial soundness, and collateral. A customer's credit soundness may be appraised through quantitative techniques such as regression analysis, which examines the change in a dependent variable that occurs as an independent (explanatory) variable changes. Such techniques are particularly useful when one needs to evaluate a large number of small customers. One should be able to estimate bad debt losses reliably if one's company sells to many customers and has not changed its credit policies for a long time.

One may find it useful to obtain references from retail credit bureaus and professional credit reference services as part of one's customer credit evaluation. Dun and Bradstreet (D&B) reports contain information about a company's nature of business, product line, management, financial statements, number of employees, previous payment history as reported by suppliers, current debts, including any past due, terms of sale, audit opinion, lawsuits, insurance coverage, leases, criminal proceedings, banking relationships and account information (e.g., current bank loans), location, and seasonal fluctuations, if applicable.

Keep in mind that extending credit involves additional expenses—the administrative costs of operating the credit department, computer services, and fees paid to rating agencies.

.02 Monitoring Receivables

There are many ways to maximize profitability from accounts receivable and keep losses to a minimum. These include proper billing, factoring, and evaluating the customers' financial health.

Billing. Cycle billing, in which customers are billed at different time periods, can smooth out the billing process. In such a system, customers with last names starting with A may be billed on the first of the month, those with last names beginning with B on the second day, and so on. Customer statements should be mailed within twenty-four hours of the close of the billing period.

To speed up collections, one can send invoices to customers when their order is processed at the warehouse instead of when the merchandise is shipped. One can also bill for services at intervals when work is performed over a period of time or charge a retainer, rather than receiving payment when the work is completed. In any event, one should bill large sales immediately.

When business is slow, seasonal datings, in which one offers delayed payment terms to stimulate demand from customers who are unable to pay until later in the season, can be used.

Customer evaluation process. Before giving credit, carefully analyze customer financial statements and obtain ratings from financial advisory services. Try to avoid high-risk receivables, such as customers who are in a financially troubled industry or region. Be careful of customers who have been in business less than one year, since about 50 percent of businesses fail within the first two years. As a rule, consumer receivables carry a greater risk of default than do corporate receivables. One should modify credit limits and accelerate collections based on changes in a customer's financial health; one may want to withhold products or services until payments are made and ask for collateral in support of questionable accounts (the collateral value should equal or exceed the account balance). If necessary, one can use outside collection agencies to try to collect from recalcitrant customers.

One should age accounts receivable (that is, rank them by the time elapsed since they were billed) to spot delinquent customers and charge interest on late payments. After one compares current aged receivables to those of prior years, industry norms, and the competition's, one can prepare a Bad Debt Loss Report showing cumulative bad debt losses by customer, terms of sale, and size of account. The report can then be summarized by department, product line, and type of customer (e.g., industry). Bad debt losses are typically higher for smaller companies than for larger ones.

Insurance protection. One may want to have credit insurance to guard against unusual bad debt losses. In deciding whether to acquire this protection, one should consider expected average bad debt losses, the company's financial ability to withstand the losses, and the cost of insurance.

Factoring. One should factor (sell) accounts receivable if that results in a net savings. However, one should realize that confidential information might be disclosed in a factoring transaction.

.03 Determining the Investment in Accounts Receivable

To determine the dollar investment tied up in accounts receivable, one may use a computation that takes into account the annual credit sales and the length of time receivables are outstanding.

Example 9: A company sells on terms of net/30, meaning payment is required within 30 days. The accounts are on average 20 days past due. Annual credit sales are $600,000. The investment in accounts receivable is:

$$\frac{50}{360} \times \$600{,}000 = \$83{,}333.28$$

The investment in accounts receivable represents the cost tied up in those receivables, including both the cost of the product and the cost of capital.

Example 10: The cost of a product is 30 percent of selling price, and the cost of capital is 10 percent of selling price. On average, accounts are paid four months after sale. Average sales are $70,000 per month.

The *investment* in accounts receivable from this product is:

Accounts receivable (4 months×$70,000)	$280,000
Investment in accounts receivable [$280,000×(0.30 + 0.10)]	112,000

Example 11: Accounts receivable are $700,000. The average manufacturing cost is 40 percent of the selling price. The before-tax profit margin is 10 percent. The carrying cost of inventory is three-percent of selling price. The sales commission is eight-percent of sales. The investment in accounts receivable is:

$$\$700{,}000\ (0.40 + 0.03 + 0.08) = \$700{,}000\ (0.51) = \$357{,}000$$

The average investment in accounts receivable may be computed by multiplying the average accounts receivable by the cost/selling price ratio.

Example 12: If a company's credit sales are $120,000, the collection period is 60 days, and the cost is 80 percent of sales price, the average accounts receivable balance and the average investment in accounts receivable are calculated by the following:

$$\text{Accounts receivable turnover} = \frac{360}{60} = 6$$

$$\text{Average accounts receivable} = \frac{\text{Credit sales}}{\text{Turnover}} = \frac{\$120{,}000}{6} = \$20{,}000$$

$$\text{Average investment in accounts receivable} = \$20{,}000 \times 0.8 = \$16{,}000$$

.04 Discount Policy

In order to determine if customers should be offered a discount for the early payment of account balances, the financial manager has to compare the return on freed cash resulting from customers paying sooner to the cost of the discount.

Example 13: The following data is provided:

Current annual credit sales:	$14,000,000
Collection period:	3 months
Terms:	net/30
Minimum rate of return:	15%

The company is considering offering a 3/10, net/30 discount (That is, if the customer pays within 10 days of the date of sale, the customer will receive a three percent discount. If payment is made after 10 days, no discount is offered. Total payment must be made within 30 days.). The company expects 25 percent of the customers to take advantage of the discount. The collection period will decline to two months.

The discount should be offered, as indicated in the following calculations.

Advantage of discount

Increased profitability:

Average accounts receivable balance before a change in policy:

$$\frac{\text{Credit sales}}{\text{Accounts receivable turnover}} \quad \frac{\$14{,}000{,}000}{12 \div 3 = 4} = \$3{,}500{,}000$$

Average accounts receivable balance after change in policy:

$$\frac{\text{Credit sales}}{\text{Average receivable turnover}} \quad \frac{\$14{,}000{,}000}{12 \div 2 = 6} = \$2{,}333{,}333$$

Reduction in average accounts receivable balance	$1,116,667
Rate of return	×.15
Return	$175,000

Disavantage of discount

Cost of the discount (0.03 × 0.25 × $14,000,000)	$105,000
Net advantage of discount	$70,000

.05 Changing Credit Policy

To decide whether a company should give credit to marginal customers, one needs to compare the earnings on the additional sales obtained to the added cost of the receivables. If the company has idle capacity, the additional earnings are the contribution margin on the new sales, since fixed costs are constant. The additional cost of the receivables results from the likely increase in bad debts and the opportunity cost of tying up funds in receivables for a longer time period.

Example 14:

Sales price per unit	$120
Variable cost per unit	80
Fixed cost per unit	15
Annual credit sales	$600,000
Collection period	1 month
Minimum return	16%

If the company liberalizes the credit policy, it projects that:

- Sales will increase by 40 percent.

- The collection period on total accounts will increase to two months.
- Bad debts on the increased sales will be five percent.

Advantage of the change in policy

Additional profitability:

Incremental sales volume	2,000 units
× Contribution margin per unit (Selling price − variable cost) $120 − $80	×$40
Incremental profitability	$80,000

Disadvantage of the change in policy

Incremental bad debts:

Incremental units×Selling price (2,000×$120)	$240,000
Bad debt percentage	×0.05
Additional bad debts	$12,000

The first step in determining the opportunity cost of the investment tied up in accounts receivable is to compute the new average unit cost as follows:

	Units	×	Unit Cost	=	Total Cost
Current units	5,000	×	$95	=	$475,000
Additional units	2,000	×	$80	=	160,000
Total.........	7,000				$635,000

$$\text{New average unit cost} = \frac{\text{Total cost}}{\text{Units}} = \frac{\$635{,}000}{7{,}000} = \$90.71$$

Note that at idle capacity, fixed cost remains constant; therefore, the incremental cost is only the variable cost of $80 per unit. Therefore, the average unit cost will drop.

One may now compute the opportunity cost of funds placed in accounts receivable:

Average investment in accounts receivable after change in policy:

$$\frac{\text{Credit sales}}{\text{Accounts receivable turnover}} \times \frac{\text{Unit cost}}{\text{Selling price}}$$

$$\frac{\$840{,}000@}{6} \times \frac{\$90.71}{\$120} = \$105{,}828$$

(@7,000 units × $120 = $840,000)

Current average investment in accounts receivable:

$$\frac{\$600{,}000}{12} \times \frac{\$95}{\$120} = 39{,}583$$

Additional investment in accounts receivable		$66,245
Minimum return		×0.16
Opportunity cost of funds tied up		$10,599
Net advantage of relaxation in credit standards:		
Additional earnings		$80,000
Less:		
Additional bad debt losses	$12,000	
Opportunity cost	10,599	22,599
Net savings		$57,401

The company may have to decide whether to extend full credit to presently restricted credit customers or no-credit customers. Full credit should be given only if net profitability occurs.

Example 15:

Category	*Bad Debt Percentage*	*Collection Period*	*Credit Policy*	*Increase in Annual Sales if Credit Restrictions are Relaxed*
X	2%	30 days	Unlimited	$80,000
Y	5%	40 days	Restricted	600,000
Z	30%	80 days	No credit	850,000

Gross profit is 25 percent of sales. The minimum return on investment is 12 percent.

As one decides whether credit standards should be loosened, one should consider the gross profit on increased sales versus the opportunity cost associated with higher receivable balances and collection expenses.

Example 16: Apex Company is considering liberalizing the credit policy to encourage more customers to purchase on credit. Currently, 80 percent of sales are on credit, and there is a gross margin of 30 percent. The return rate on funds is 10 percent. Other relevant data are:

	Currently	*Proposal*
Sales	$300,000	$450,000
Credit sales	240,000	360,000
Collection expenses	4% of credit sales	5% of credit sales
Accounts receivable turnover	4.5	3

An analysis of the proposal yields the following results:

Gross profit:	
Expected increase in credit sales $360,000 – $240,000	$120,000
Gross profit rate	×.30
Increase in gross profit	$36,000
Opportunity cost:	
Average accounts receivable balance (credit sales/accounts receivable turnover)	
Expected average accounts receivable $360,000/3	$120,000
Current average accounts receivable $240,000/4.5	53,333
Increase in average accounts receivable	$66,667
× Return rate	×10%
Opportunity cost of funds tied up in accounts receivable	$6,667
Collection expenses:	
Expected collection expenses 0.05 × $360,000	$18,000
Current collection expenses 0.04 × $240,000	9,600
Increase in collection expenses	$8,400

Apex Company would profit from a more liberal credit policy as follows:

Increase in gross profit	$36,000
Opportunity cost in accounts receivable	(6,667)
Increase in collection expenses	(8,400)
Net advantage	$20,933

To determine whether it is advantageous to engage in a sales campaign, one should consider the gross margin earned, the sales discount, and the opportunity cost of higher receivable balances.

Example 17: B&B Company is planning a sales campaign in which it will offer credit terms of 3/10, net/45. It expects the collection period to increase from 60 days to 80 days. Relevant data for the contemplated campaign follows:

	Percent of Sales Before Campaign	*Percent of Sales During Campaign*
Cash sales	40%	30%
Payment from (in days)		
1-10	25	55
11-100	35	15

The proposed sales strategy will probably increase sales from $8 million to $10 million. There is a gross margin rate of 30 percent. The rate of return is 14 percent. Sales discounts are given on cash sales.

	Without Sales Campaign			With Sales Campaign		
Gross margin	(0.3×$8,000,000)		$2,400,000	(0.3×$10,000,000)		$3,000,000
Sales subject to discount						
(0.65×$8,000,000)		$5,200,000				
(0.85×$10,000,000)					$8,500,000	
Sales discount		×0.03	− 156,000		×0.03	− 255,000
Investment in average accounts receivable						
(60/360×$8,000,000×0.7)		$933,333				
		×0.14				
(80/360×$10,000,000×0.7)					$1,555,555	
					×0.14	
Return rate			− 130,667			− 217,778
Net profit			$2,113,333			$2,527,222

The company should undertake the sales campaign, because earnings will increase by $413,889 ($2,527,222 − $2,113,333).

¶ 1221 Inventory Management

One of the most common problems facing financial managers is inventory planning. This is understandable, since inventory usually represents a sizable portion of a firm's total assets and, more specifically, averages more than 30 percent of total current assets in the U.S. industry. Excessive money tied up in inventory is a drag on profitability.

Inventories may contain materials that have either *dependent demand* or *independent demand.* Dependent demand inventories consist of items whose demand depends on the demands for other items also held in inventory. Demand (or usage) of subassemblies and component parts is derived from the number of finished units that will be assembled. A classic example is demand for wheels for new automobiles. Independent demand items are the finished goods or other end items. Their demand is independent of the demand for any other item carried in inventory. Only management of independent demand items is discussed here.

The purpose of inventory planning is to develop policies that will achieve an optimal investment in inventory. This objective is achieved by determining the optimal level of inventory necessary to minimize inventory-related costs.

Inventory related costs fall into three categories:

1. *Ordering costs,* which include all costs associated with preparing a purchase order.

2. *Carrying (holding) costs,* which include storage costs for inventory items plus the cost of money tied up in inventory.

3. *Shortage (stockout) costs,* which include costs incurred when an item is out of stock. These include the lost contribution margin on sales plus lost customer goodwill.

There are many inventory planning models available that try to answer the following two questions:

1. How much to order?

2. When to order?

These models include the economic order quantity (EOQ) model, the reorder point, and the determination of safety stock.

.01 Basic Economic Order Quantity (EOQ) Model

The economic order quantity (EOQ) determines the order quantity that results in the lowest sum of carrying and ordering costs. The EOQ is computed as:

$$EOQ = \sqrt{\frac{2DO}{C}}$$

Where C = carrying cost per unit, O = ordering cost per order, D = annual demand (requirements) in units.

If the carrying cost were expressed as a percentage of average inventory value (say, 12 percent per year to hold inventory), then the denominator value in the EOQ formula would be 12 percent times the price of an item.

Example 18: Assume the Los Alamitos Store buys sets of steel at $40 per set from an outside vendor. It will sell 6,400 sets evenly throughout the year. The store's carrying cost is $8.00 per unit per year. The ordering cost is $100 per order. Therefore:

$$EOQ = \sqrt{\frac{2DO}{C}} = \sqrt{\frac{2(6{,}400)(\$100)}{\$8.00}} = \sqrt{160{,}000} = 400 \text{ units}$$

Total number of orders per year = D/EOQ = 6,400/400 = 16 orders

Total inventory costs = Carrying cost + Ordering cost

= C × (EOQ/2) + O (D/EOQ)

= ($8.00)(400/2) + ($100)(6,400/400)

= $1,600 + $1,600 = $3,200

Based on these calculations, the Los Alamitos Store's inventory policy should be the following:

1. The store should order 400 sets of steel each time it places an order and order 16 times during a year.
2. This policy will be most economical and cost the store $3,200 per year.

Note: When an item is made instead of purchasing it, the EOQ model is used to determine the economic production run size where O = setup cost per setup.

.02 Reorder Point

Reorder point (ROP), or the point at which to place a new order, requires a knowledge about the lead time, which is the time interval between placing an order and receiving delivery. Reorder point can be calculated as follows:

Reorder point = (average demand per unit of lead time × lead time) + safety stock

First, multiply average daily (or weekly) demand by the lead time in days (or weeks), yielding the lead time demand. Then add safety stock to this to provide for the variation in lead time demand to determine the reorder point. If average demand and lead time are both certain, no safety stock is necessary and should be dropped from the formula.

Example 19: Assume in Example 18 that lead time is constant at one week, and that there are 50 working weeks in a year.

Then the reorder point is 128 sets = (6,400 sets/50 weeks) × 1 week.

Therefore, when the inventory level drops to 128 sets, the new order should be placed. Suppose, however, that the store is faced with variable demand for its steel and requires a safety stock of 150 additional sets to carry. Then the reorder point will be 128 sets plus 150 sets, or 278 sets.

Exhibit 3 shows this inventory system when the order quantity is 400 sets and the reorder point is 128 sets.

Exhibit 3

Basic Inventory System with EOQ and Reorder Point

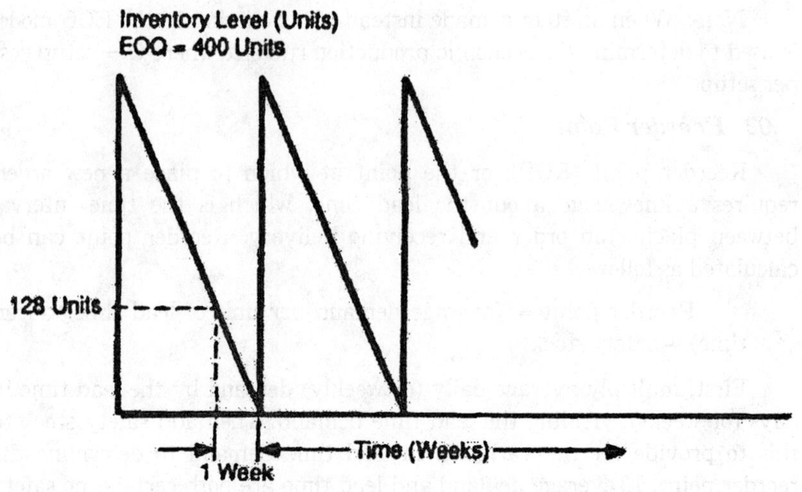

.03 EOQ Assumptions and Applications

The EOQ model makes some strong assumptions. They are:

1. Demand is fixed and constant throughout the year.
2. Lead time is known with certainty.
3. No quantity discounts are allowed.
4. No shortages are permitted.

Note: The assumptions may be unrealistic. However, the model still proves useful in inventory planning for many firms. In fact, many situations exist where a certain assumption holds or nearly holds. For example, subcontractors who must supply parts on a regular basis to a primary contractor face a constant demand. Even where demand varies, the assumption of uniform demand is not unrealistic. Demand for automobiles, for example, varies from week to week over a season, but the weekly fluctuations tend to cancel out each other so that seasonal demand can be assumed constant.

.04 EOQ with Noninstantaneous Replenishment

The discussion so far assumed that the inventory replenishment is instantaneously received. Now consider the case where the inventory is being manufactured while demands are being met. The following is assumed:

1. The product held in inventory is not purchased from an outside source, but manufactured.
2. Units are continuously being added to inventory during the production run.
3. When this inventory is completely depleted, a new production run is started.

The following definitions apply:

S= setup cost, C= carrying costs, D= annual demand, p= production rate, u= usage rate, Q= order quantity, and p> u.

The costs associated with operating this system are the carrying costs and the production setup costs (instead of ordering costs). Note that during a production run, inventory accumulates at a rate of (p − u) units per period. Afterwards, it is depleted at a rate of u units. The situation is depicted in Exhibit 4.

Exhibit 4

EOQ with Noninstantaneous Replenishment

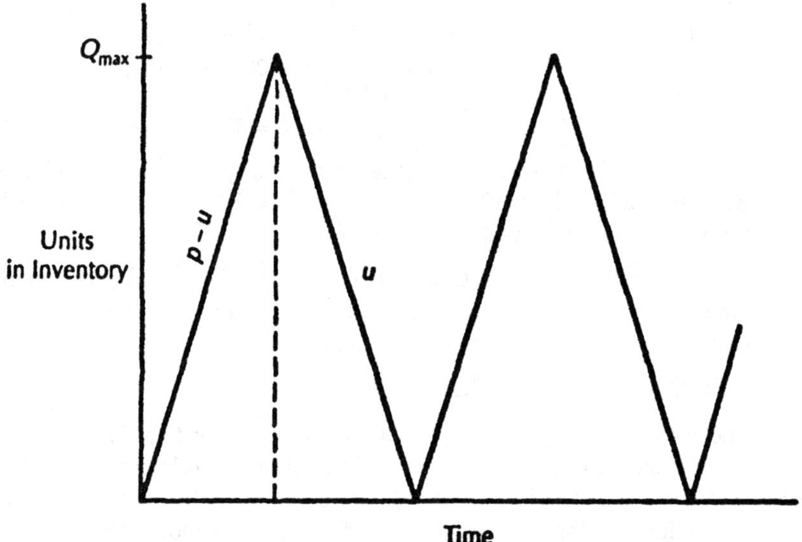

Then setup costs = S (D/Q)

Maximum inventory level = Inventory buildup rate × Period of delivery = (p − u)(Q/p)

Minimum inventory level = 0

$$\text{Average inventory level} = \frac{\text{Maximum inventory} + \text{Minimum inventory}}{2}$$

$$= 1/2[(p - u)(Q/p) + 0] = Q/2[(p - u)p]$$

Total annual inventory costs = C Q/2[(p– u)p] + S(D/Q). Using the calculus yields:

$$EOQ = \sqrt{[(2DS/C)[p/(p - u)]]} = \sqrt{[2DS/C\,(1 - u/p)]}$$

Example 20: Jog Plumbing, Inc. developed the following estimates for the #123 valves.

D = 800 valves per year, C = $.05 per valve per year, S = $1.00 per order or setup, p = 100 valves per week, and u = 60 valves per week. Then:

$$EOQ = \sqrt{\frac{2DS}{C}\ \frac{p}{(p - u)}} = \sqrt{\frac{2(800)(1)}{(.05)}\ \frac{100}{(100 - 60)}} = 283 \text{ valves}$$

The maximum inventory level = (p – u)(Q/p) = (100 – 60)(283/100) = 113.2 valves

Total annual inventory costs = C Q/2[(p – u)p] + S(D/Q)
= $.05(283/2)[(100 – 60)/100] + $1(800/283)
= $2.83 + $2.83 = $5.66 per year.

The production run time (the production phase of the cycle) = EOQ/p = 283 valves/100 valves per week = 2.83 weeks. Thus, each run will require 2.83 weeks to complete.

The cycle time (the time between orders or between the beginnings of runs) = EOQ/u = 283 valves/60 valves per week = 4.72 weeks. Thus, a run of valves will be made every 4.72 weeks.

.05 EOQ with Quantity Discounts

The economic order quantity (EOQ) model does not take into account quantity discounts, which is not realistic in many real world cases. Usually, the more one orders the lower the unit price one pays. Quantity discounts are price reductions for large orders offered to buyers to induce them to buy in large quantities. If quantity discounts are offered, the buyer must weigh the potential benefits of reduced purchase price and fewer orders that will result from buying in large quantities against the increase in carrying costs caused by higher average inventories. Hence, the buyer's goal in this case is to select the order quantity that will minimize total costs, where total cost is the sum of carrying cost, ordering cost, and product cost:

Total cost = Carrying cost + Ordering cost + Product cost
= C×(Q/2) + O×(D/Q) + PD

Where P = unit price, and Q = order quantity.

There are two general cases:

1. Carrying costs are constant.

2. Carrying costs are stated as a percentage of purchase price.

When carrying costs are constant there will be a single EOQ that is the same for all of the cost curves. When carrying costs are stated as a percentage, each curve will have a different EOQ.

Case 1: Constant carrying costs

A step by step approach in computing economic order quantity with quantity discounts is summarized below.

1. Compute the common EOQ when price discounts are ignored.

2. Only one of the curves will have the EOQ in its feasible range. Identify that curve.

   a. If the feasible EOQ is the lowest price curve, this is the overall EOQ.

   b. If the EOQ is on any other curve, compute the total cost for the EOQ and for the quantities for which price reductions will occur.

3. Select the value of Q that will result in the lowest total cost.

Example 21: In Example 18, assume that the Los Alamitos Store was offered the following price discount schedule:

Order quantity (Q)	*Unit price (P)*
1 to 499	$40.00
500 to 999	39.90
1000 or more	39.80

First, the EOQ with no discounts is computed as follows:

$$\text{EOQ} = \sqrt{\frac{2DO}{C}} = \sqrt{\frac{2(6{,}400)(\$100)}{\$8.00}} = \sqrt{160{,}000} = 400 \text{ units}$$

Total cost = $8.00(400/2) + $100(6,400/400) + $40.00(6,400)
= $1,600 + 1,600 + 256,000 = $259,200

We see that the value that minimized the sum of the carrying cost and the ordering cost but not the purchase cost was EOQ = 400 sets. The further we move from the point 400, the greater the sum of the carrying and ordering costs. Thus, 400 is obviously the only candidate for the minimum total cost value within the first price range. Q = 500 is the only candidate within the $39.90 price range, and Q = 1,000 is the only candidate within the $39.80 price bracket. These three quantities are evaluated in Exhibit 5.

Exhibit 5

Annual Costs with Varying Order Quantities

Order Quantity (Q)	*400*	*500*	*1,000*
Purchase price (P)	$ 40	$ 39.90	$ 39.80
Carrying cost (C×Q/2) $8×(order quantity/2)	$ 1,600	$ 2,000	$ 4,000
Ordering cost (O×D/Q)			
$100×(6,400/order quantity)	1,600	1,280	640
Product cost (PD) Unit price×6,400	256,000	255,360	254,720
Total cost	$259,200	$258,640	$259,360

Note that C = $8.00, O = $100, and D = 6,400 for all possible orders.

We find that the EOQ with price discounts is 500 sets. Hence, the Los Alamitos Store is justified in going to the first price break, but the extra carrying cost of going to the second price break more than outweighs the savings in ordering and in the cost of the product itself.

Case 2: Carrying costs stated as a percentage of purchase price

The procedure is follows:

1. Calculate EOQs for each price. Reject any EOQ that is not within the allowable quantity range for the price used.
2. Calculate total annual cost for feasible EOQs
   a. If the feasible EOQ is the lowest price curve, this is the overall EOQ.
   b. If the EOQ is not the lowest price range, compute the total cost for the EOQ and for the next quantities for which price reductions will occur.
3. Select the value of Q that will result in the lowest total cost.

Example 22: Discount Plumbing Industries, Inc., a maker of the No. 510 valve, has offered quantity discounts. The volumes and prices are:

Order quantity (Q)	*Unit price (P)*
1 to 399	$2.20
400 to 699	2.00
700 or more	1.80

The company developed the following estimates: D = 10,000 valves per year, S = \$5.50 per order, and C = 20% of unit price (P).

First, the EOQs are computed for each of the prices:

$$EOQ_{2.20} = \sqrt{2(10,000)(5.5)/.2(2.20)} = 500 \text{ (reject—too large)}$$

$$EOQ_{2.00} = \sqrt{2(10,000)(5.5)/.2(2.00)} = 524.4 \text{ (feasible)}$$

$$EOQ_{1.80} = \sqrt{2(10,000)(5.5)/.2(1.80)} = 552.8 \text{ (reject—too small)}$$

The total annual cost at two quantities is, therefore, investigated: 524.4 and 700 units per order:

At Q = 524.4,
total annual cost = (.2)(\$2)(524.4/2) + \$5.5(10,000/524.4) + \$2(10,000)
= \$104.88 + \$104.88 + \$20,000 = \$20,209.76

At Q = 700,
total annual cost = (.2)(\$1.8)(700/2) + \$5.5(10,000/700) + \$1.8(10,000)
= \$126 + \$78.57 + \$18,000 = \$18,204.57

700 valves are a more economical order quantity, since the total annual cost is lower than that associated with the EOQ.

Note: Buying in large quantities has some favorable and some unfavorable features. The advantages are lower unit costs, lower ordering costs, fewer stockouts, and lower transportation costs. On the other hand, there are disadvantages, such as higher inventory carrying costs, greater capital requirement, and higher probability of obsolescence and deterioration.

.06 Determination of Safety Stock

When lead time and demand are not certain, the firm must carry extra units of inventory called safety stock as protection against possible stockouts. To determine the optimal level of safety stock size, one might want to measure costs of not having enough inventory, or stockout costs. Also, one might want to consider the service level. Stockouts can be quite expensive. Lost sales and disgruntled customers are examples of external costs. Idle machines and disrupted production scheduling are examples of internal costs.

Service level can be defined as the probability that demand will not exceed supply during the lead time. Thus, a service level of 90 percent implies a probability of 90 percent that demand will not exceed supply during lead time. Exhibit 6 shows a service level of 90 percent.

Here are four cases for computing the safety stock. The first three do not recognize stockout costs; the fourth case does.

Case 1: Known maximum demand rate, constant lead time

A simple way to determine the size of safety stock is to deduct average demand from the maximum demand that can reasonably be expected during a period and then multiply the difference by the lead time.

Example 23: Assume that the economic order quantity is 500 units, that the lead time is 4 weeks, that the average weekly demand is 60 units, and that the maximum expected weekly demand is 70 units.

The owner of a small manufacturing business would compute a safety stock as follows:

Maximum expected demand	70 units
Average demand	60
Excess	10 units
Lead time	×4 weeks
Safety stock	40 units

Reorder point (ROP) = Expected demand during lead time + safety stock
= lead time×average demand per unit of time + safety stock
= 4 weeks×60 + 40
= 240 + 40
= 280 units

Case 2: Variable demand rate, constant lead time

ROP = Expected demand during lead time + safety stock

$$= \bar{d}\,LT + z\sqrt{LT}\,(\sigma_d)$$

Where:

$\bar{d}$ = average demand

LT = lead time

σ_d = standard deviation of demand rate

z = standard normal variate (See Table 5— Normal Distribution table in Appendix B)

Exhibit 6

Service Level of 90 Percent

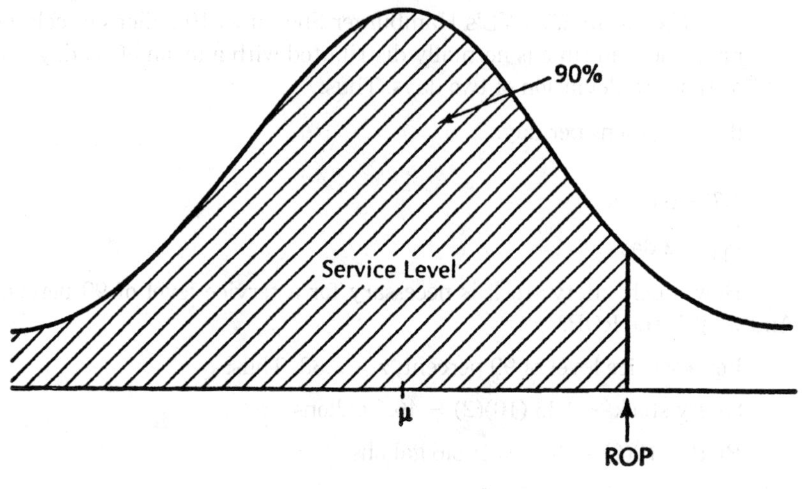

Example 24: Norman's Pizza uses large cases of tomatoes at an average rate of 50 cans per day. The demand can be approximated by a normal distribution with a standard deviation of five cans per day. Lead time is four days. Thus:

$\bar{d}$ = 50 cans per day.

LT = 4 days

σ_d = 5 cans

For a service level of 99 percent, safety stock and ROP are determined as follows:

For a service level of 99 percent, z = 2.33 (from Table 5 in Appendix B). Thus:

Safety stock = $2.33\sqrt{4}\,(5)$ = 23.3 cans

ROP = 50(4) + 23.3 = 223.3 cans

Case 3: Constant demand, variable lead time

ROP = Expected demand during lead time + safety stock

$= d\,\overline{LT} + z\,d\,(\sigma_{LT})$

Where:

d = constant demand

$\overline{LT}$ = average lead time

σ_{LT} = standard deviation of lead time

Example 25: SVL's Hamburger Shop uses 10 gallons of cola per day. The lead time is normally distributed with a mean of six days and a standard deviation of two days. Thus:

d = 10 gallons per day.

$\overline{LT}$ = 6 days

σ_{LT} = 2 days

How much safety stock is necessary for a service level of 99 percent? And what is the ROP?

For a service level of 99 percent, z = 2.33. Thus:

Safety stock = 2.33 (10)(2) = 46.6 gallons

ROP = 10(6) + 46.6 = 106.6 gallons

Case 4: Incorporation of stockout costs

The probability approach is illustrated below to show how the optimal stock size can be determined in the presence of stockout costs.

Example 26: In Examples 18 and 19, suppose that the total usage over a one-week period is expected to be:

Total usage	*Probability*
78	0.2
128	0.4
178	0.2
228	0.1
278	0.1
	1.00

Suppose further that a stockout cost is estimated at $12.00 per set. Recall that the carrying cost is $8.00 per set.

Exhibit 7 shows the computation of safety stock. The computation shows that the total costs are minimized at $1,200, when a safety stock of 150 sets is maintained. Therefore, the reorder point is: 128 sets+ 150 sets= 278 sets.

Exhibit 7

Computation of Safety Stock

Safety stock levels in units	*Stockout and probability*	*Average stockout in units*	*Average stockout costs*	*No. of orders*	*Total annual stockout costs*	*Carrying costs*	*Total*
0	50 with .2 100 with .1 150 with .1	35*	\$420 +	16	\$6720 ++	0	\$6720
50	50 with .1 100 with .1	15	180	16	2880	400 §	3290
100	50 with .1	5	60	16	960	800	1760
150	0	0	0	16	0	1200	1200

* 50(.2) + 100(.1) + 150(.1) = 10 + 10 + 15 = 35 units;
+ 35 units × \$12.00 =\$ 420
++ \$420 × 16 times = \$6,720
§ 50 units × \$8.00 = \$400

.07 The Single Period Inventory Problem—Marginal Analysis

Unlike the basic EOQ model, the marginal approach to inventory introduces the concept of uncertainty. The basic rule is to add inventory as long as the expected reduction in penalty cost for a shortage is greater than the expected cost of stocking the unit.

Define:

p = probability of selling an additional unit

MP = marginal profit from selling a unit

(1 − p) = probability of not selling a unit

ML = marginal loss from turning away a customer

As along as the expected marginal (incremental) profit is greater than the expected marginal (incremental) loss, the order quantity will be added. Net profits will be maximized when:

$p(MP) = (1 - p)(ML)$ for the last unit in order.

Solving for p, we obtain:

$$p = \frac{ML}{ML + MP}$$

The probability of selling a unit must be at least ML/(ML + MP) in order to justify the stocking of the unit.

Example 27: Home Holiday Store wishes to stock Christmas wreaths for sale during the holiday season. Assume that the store knows the probability distribution of demand to be:

Demand	Probability of Demand Equal to the Given Number	Probability of At Least the Given Number
6	.05	1.00
7	.15	.95
8	.20	.80
9	.40	.60
10	.10	.20
11	.10	.10
	1.00	

The store pays $2.00 for each item and sells it for $6.00. It must dispose of each item not sold by December 25 at a cost of $.50 per wreath. The ordering cost is fixed for all courses of action.

Note that MP = $6.00 – $2.00 = $4.00, ML = $2.00 + $.50 = $2.50

$$p = \frac{ML}{ML + MP} = \frac{\$2.50}{\$2.50 + \$4.00} = 3.85$$

From the demand distribution, p for unit 6 = 1.00, since demand will always be at least 6 units, p for unit 7 = .95, p for unit 8 = .8, p for unit 9 = .6, p for unit 10 = .2. Thus, the best course of action is to order 9 wreaths.

Note: p in the marginal analysis formula essentially represents the service level, i.e., the probability that demand will not exceed the stocking level.

.08 Computers and Inventory Planning

One of the first areas in business to benefit from computerization was inventory planning. Today, inventory stock records are routinely maintained with the use of computers. As changes in inventory levels occur, the computer files are modified to reflect the latest inventory transactions. Managers can query these files and instantaneously determine how much of a material is in inventory, how much of a material is on order, when certain orders are expected to be received, and other information critical to inventory management. Computing order quantities, determining when orders should be placed, and printing purchase requisitions and purchase orders are routinely performed by computers. Frederick's (www.fredrickgroup.com/products/tfg2000.html) *Communications Oriented Production and Control System (COPICS)* is a prime example of Enterprise Resource Planning (ERP) solutions with embedded inventory packages.

.09 Using the ABC System for Inventory Control

ABC analysis focuses on the most critical items—gross profitability, sensitive price or demand patterns, and supply excesses or shortages. The ABC method requires the classification of inventory into one of three groups—A, B, or C—according to the potential savings associated with a proper level of inventory control. In the exhibit below, Class A items, needing close control, are the high-dollar-volume group. They may include 80 percent of total inventory cost but only one percent of total items stocked. Class B is an intermediate-dollar-volume group—perhaps 15 percent of dollars and 30 percent of items. Class C is the rest—five percent of dollars and 69 percent of items. Exhibit 8 illustrates an ABC distribution.

Exhibit 8

ABC Inventory Distribution

Inventory Classification	*Population (percent)*	*Dollar Usage (percent)*
A	1	80
B	30	15
C	69	5

To institute the ABC method:

1. Compute annual dollar volume by inventory type anticipated (annual demand times unit cost).
2. Segregate merchandise into components based on annual dollar value.
3. Rank inventory in terms of annual dollar volume, ranging from high to low (e.g., A's in the top 80 percent, B's in the next 15 percent and C's in the last 5 percent). Tag inventory with the appropriate classification and record the classifications in the inventory records.

The following example illustrates the ABC system.

Example 28: Garner Auto Supply Co. has arranged its 9 inventory items in order of annual dollar volume. Exhibit 9 shows the ordered list, with dollar-volume expressed in percentages. The ordered list is examined in order to arrive at an ABC classification of the items.

Exhibit 10 shows the same 9 items grouped into classes A, B, and C. The two A items account for over 80 percent of total dollar usage—almost 5 times as much annual dollar-volume as the two B items, while the two B items account for almost 6 times as much as the 5 C items. Exhibit 11 graphically illustrates the ABC classification for this example.

Exhibit 9

Inventory Items in Annual Dollar Volume Order

Item Number	*Annual Dollar Usage*	*Percent of Total Dollar Usage*
113	130,000	47.6%
103	90,000	32.9%
123	31,000	11.3%
134	14,500	5.3%
301	6,200	2.3%
721	650	0.2%
764	525	0.2%
402	325	0.1%
520	300	0.1%
Total	273,500	100.0%

Exhibit 10

ABC Classification

Classification	*Item Number*	*Annual Dollar Usage*	*Percent of Total Dollar Usage*	*Number of Items*	*Percent of Total Number of Items*	*Cumulative Percent of Total Number*
A	103, 113	220,000	80.5%	2	22.2%	22.2%
B	123, 134	45,500	16.6%	2	22.2%	44.4%
C	301, 721, 520, 402, 764	8,000	2.9%	5	55.6%	100.0%
Total		273,500	100.0%	9	100.0%	

Exhibit 11

ABC Classification Percent Versus Percent of Items

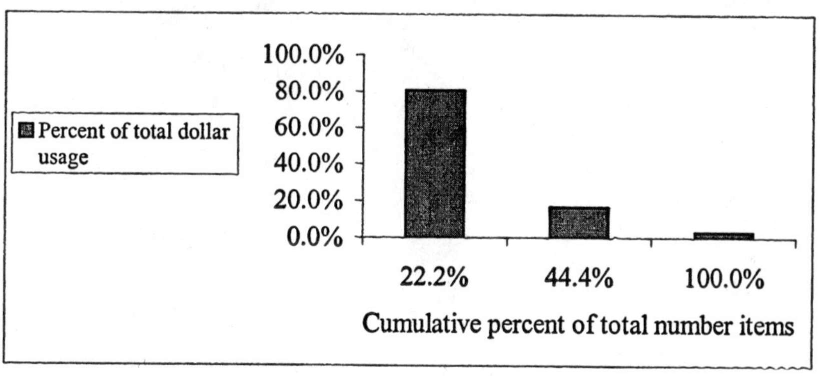

It is clear that A items should receive major attention, B items moderate attention, and C items little attention. Perpetual inventory records should be maintained for class A items, which require accuracy and frequent, often daily, attention. Class B items are less expensive than A items but are still important and require intermediate control. Class C items include most of the inventory items. Since they are usually less expensive and less used, they require less attention. There is usually a high safety stock level for C items. Blanket purchase orders should exist for A items and only "spot buys" for Bs and Cs.

Examples of inventory controls that may be based on ABC classification are:

- *Purchasing.* A purchase order for a class A item might be signed by the president, for a class B item by the head of the purchasing department, and for a class C item by any purchasing agent.

- *Physical Inventory Check.* Count A items monthly, B items twice a year, and C items annually.

- *Forecasting.* Forecast A items by several methods with resolution by a prediction committee, B items by simple trend projection, and C items by best guess of the responsible purchasing agent.

- *Safety Stock.* No safety stock for A items, one month's supply for B items, and three months' supply for C items.

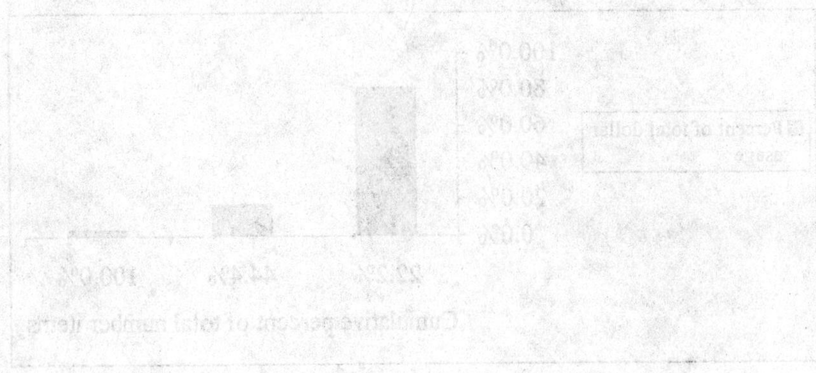

Chapter 13
Capital Budgeting Decisions

¶ 1301 Overview

Capital budgeting is the process of making long-term investment decisions. These decisions should be made in light of the goals of the company. The stockholders have entrusted the company with their money and they expect the firm to invest their money wisely. Investments in fixed assets should be consistent with the goal of maximizing the market value of the firm.

There are many investment decisions that the company may have to make in order to grow. Examples of capital budgeting applications are product line selection, whether to keep or sell a business segment, whether to lease or buy, and which assets to invest in. To make long-term investment decisions in accordance with a goal, three tasks must be performed in evaluating capital budgeting projects: (1) estimate cash flows, (2) estimate the cost of capital (or required rate of return), and (3) apply a decision rule to determine if a project is "good" or "bad."

¶ 1305 Types and Features of Investment Projects

There are typically two types of long-term investment decisions made by a company:

1. *Expansion decisions,* in terms of obtaining new facilities or expanding existing facilities. Examples include:
   a. Investments in property, plant, and equipment, as well as other types of assets.
   b. Resource commitments in the form of new product development, market research, introduction of information technology (IT), refunding of long-term debt, etc.
   c. Mergers and acquisitions in the form of buying another company to add a new product line.
2. *Replacement decisions,* in terms of replacing existing facilities with new facilities. Examples include replacing an old machine with a high-tech machine.

Long-term investments have three important features:

1. They typically involve a large amount of initial cash outlay, which tends to have a long-term impact on the firm's future profitability. Therefore, this initial cash outlay needs to be justified on a cost-benefit basis.
2. There are expected recurring cash inflows (for example, increased revenues, savings in cash operating expenses, etc.) over the life of the investment project. This frequently requires considering the time value of money.
3. Income taxes could make a difference in the accept or reject decision. Therefore, income tax factors must be taken into account in every capital budgeting decision.

¶ 1311 Measuring Investment Worth

Several methods of evaluating investment projects are as follows:

1. Payback period.
2. Accounting rate of return (ARR).
3. Internal rate of return (IRR).
4. Net present value (NPV).
5. Profitability index (or cost/benefit ratio).

The NPV method and the IRR method are called discounted cash flow (DCF) methods. Each of these methods is discussed below.

.01 Payback Period

The payback period measures the length of time required to recover the amount of initial investment. It is computed by dividing the initial investment by the expected annual cash inflows through increased revenues or cost savings.

Example 1: Assume:

Cost of investment	$18,000
Annual after-tax cash savings	$ 3,000

Then, the payback period is:

$$\text{Payback period} = \frac{\text{initial investment}}{\text{cost savings}} = \frac{\$18{,}000}{\$3{,}000} = 6 \text{ years}$$

Decision rule: Choose the project with the shorter payback period as it will be less risky and have greater liquidity.

Example 2: Consider the two projects in the chart below whose after-tax cash inflows are not even. Assume each project costs $1,000.

	Cash Inflow	
Year	*A($)*	*B($)*
1	100	500
2	200	400
3	300	300
4	400	100
5	500	
6	600	

When cash inflows are not even, the payback period has to be found by trial and error. The payback period of project A is ($1,000 = $100 + $200 + $300 + $400) four years. The payback period of project B is ($1,000 = $500 + $400 + $100):

$$2 \text{ years} + \frac{\$100}{\$300} = 2\tfrac{1}{3} \text{ years}$$

Project B is the project of choice in this case, since it has the shorter payback period.

Only $100 of $300 in year three in project B is actually used. Therefore, the payback period is two years plus the fraction.

The advantages of using the payback period method of evaluating an investment project are that it is simple to compute, easy to understand, and it handles investment risk effectively. The shortcomings of this method are that it does not recognize the time value of money, and it ignores the impact of cash inflow received after the payback period; essentially, cash flows after the payback period determine profitability of an investment.

.02 Accounting Rate of Return

Accounting rate of return (ARR), also called simple or unadjusted rate of return, measures profitability from the conventional accounting standpoint by relating the required initial investment (I)—or sometimes the average investment—to the future average annual income.

$$\text{ARR} = \frac{\text{Project's Average Annual Income}}{\text{Initial (or Average) Investment}}$$

Average investment is defined as follows:

$$\text{Average investment} = \frac{(I - S)}{2} + S$$

Where I = initial (original) investment and S = salvage value.

When there is no salvage value, the Average Investment = I/2

Decision rule: Under the ARR method, choose the project with the higher rate of return.

Example 3: Consider the following investment:

Initial investment	$6,500
Estimated life	20 years
Cash inflows per year	$1,000
Depreciation per year (using straight line method).......	$ 325

The accounting rate of return for this project is:

$$\text{APR} = \frac{\text{net income}}{\text{investment}} = \frac{\$1000 - \$325}{\$6,500} = 10.4\%$$

If average investment (usually assumed to be one-half of the original investment) is used, then:

$$\text{APR} = \frac{\$1,000 - \$325}{\$3,250} = 20.8\%$$

The advantages of this method are that it is easily understandable, simple to compute, and recognizes the profitability factor.

The shortcomings of this method are that it fails to recognize the time value of money, and it uses accounting data instead of cash flow data.

.03 *Internal Rate of Return*

Internal rate of return (IRR) is defined as the rate of interest that equates I with the present value (PV) of future cash inflows. In other words, at IRR,

I = PV

or

NPV = 0

Decision rule: Accept the project if the IRR exceeds the cost of capital. Otherwise, reject it.

Example 4: Consider the following investment:

Initial investment	$37,910
Estimated life	5 years
Annual cash inflows after taxes	$10,000
Cost of capital (minimum required rate of return)	8%

We set the following equality (I = PV):

$$\$37{,}910 = \$10{,}000.\ T_4\ (i{,}5\ \text{years})$$

$$T_4\ (i{,}5\ \text{years}) = \frac{\$37{,}910}{\$10{,}000} = 3.791$$

Which is right on 10 percent in the five-year line of Table 4 in the Appendix B.

Since the IRR of the investment is greater than the cost of capital (8%), accept the project.

The advantage of using the IRR method is that it considers the time value of money and, therefore, is more exact and realistic than the ARR method.

The shortcomings of this method are that the IRR Method is time-consuming to compute, especially when the cash inflows are not even, and it fails to recognize the varying sizes of investment in competing projects.

When cash inflows are not even, IRR is computed by the trial and error method, which is not discussed here. Best estimates can be obtained by using a financial calculator.

Can a computer help? Spreadsheet programs can be used in making IRR calculations. For example, *Excel* has a function IRR (*values, guess*). Excel considers negative numbers as cash outflows, such as the initial investment, and positive numbers as cash inflows. Many financial calculators have similar features. As in Example 4, assume one wants to calculate the IRR of a $37,910 investment (the value—37910—is entered in year 0 and is followed by five monthly cash inflows of $10,000). Using a guess of eight percent (the value of 0.08), which is in effect the cost of capital, the formula would be @IRR (values, 0.08) and Excel would return 10 percent, as shown below.

Year 0	*1*	*2*	*3*	*4*	*5*
-37910........	10000	10000	10000	10000	10000

IRR= 10%

NPV= $2,017.10

Note: The *Excel* formula for NPV is NPV (discount rate, cash inflow values) + I, where I is given as a negative number.

.04 Net Present Value

Net present value (NPV) is the excess of the present value (PV) of cash inflows generated by the project over the amount of the initial investment (I):

$$NPV = PV - I$$

The present value of future cash flows is computed using the so-called cost of capital (or minimum required rate of return) as the discount rate. In the case of an annuity, the present value would be:

$$PV = A \times T_4 (i,n)$$

Where A is the amount of the annuity. The value of T_4 is found in Table 4 in Appendix B.

Decision rule: If NPV is positive, accept the project. Otherwise, reject it.

Example 5: Assume the same data given in Example 4 and the net present value of the cash inflows is:

Present value of the cash inflows is:

$PV = A \times T_4$ (i, n)

= \$10,000. T_4 (8%,5 years)

= \$10,000 (3.993) \$39,930

Initial investment (I) 37,910

Net present value (NPV=PV − I) .... \$ 2,020

Since the NPV of the investment is positive, the investment should be accepted.

The advantages of the NPV method are that it obviously recognizes the time value of money and it is easy to compute, whether the cash flows are in the form of an annuity or vary from period to period.

.05 *Summary of Decision Rules Using Both IRR and NPV Methods*

Internal Rate of Return (IRR)

- Using the present-value tables, financial calculator, or Excel, compute the IRR.
- If the IRR exceeds the cost of capital, accept the project; if not, reject the project.

Net Present Value (NPV)

- Calculate the NPV, using the cost of capital as the discount rate.
- If the NPV is positive, accept the project; otherwise, reject the project.

.06 *Equivalent Uniform Annual Cost*

A replacement decision typically involves two mutually exclusive projects. When these two mutually exclusive projects have significantly different lives, an adjustment is necessary. It may require a comparison of annual costs, which means the conversion of cash flows into an equivalent uniform annual series. This procedure may be thought of as the inverse of finding present values. The so-called capital recovery factor, which is the reciprocal of the present value of an annuity factor (T_4), is used for this purpose. One calculates uniform annual cost (UAC) by using the following formula:

$$UAC = \{I - S_N [T_3 (i,T)]\} \, CRF(i,N) + c$$

Where:

S_N = salvage value at terminal period N

CRT(i,N) = capital recovery factor = $1/T_4$

c = uniform operating cost

Example 6: A company considers two equipment modules: Plan A and Plan B. Plan A, which requires an initial investment of $44,000, has expected annual operating costs of $24,400 and no terminal salvage value.

Plan B, which requires an initial investment of $70,000, is expected to reduce operating costs to $20,900 per year and have a salvage value of $9,500. Both equipment modules have a useful life of 10 years. Assume that the firm has determined a cost of capital of 22 percent.

Using the UAC formula gives the following results:

$$UAC_A = \{\$44,000 - 0 \, [T_3 (22\%, 10)]\} \, CRF(22\%, 10) + \$24,400$$

$= \$44{,}000\ (1/T_4\ (22\%, 10)) + \$24{,}400$

$= \$44{,}000\ (1/3.923) + \$24{,}400$

$= \$44{,}000\ (0.255) + \$24{,}400 = \$35{,}620$

$UAC_B = [\$70{,}000 - \$9{,}500\ [T_3\ (22\%, 10)]]\ CRF(22\%, 10) + \$20{,}900$

$= [\$70{,}000 - \$9{,}500\ (.137)]\ (1/T_4\ (22\%, 10) = \$20{,}900$

$= (\$70{,}000 - \$1{,}302)\ (1/3.293) + \$20{,}900$

$= \$68{,}698\ (0.255) + \$20{,}900 = \$38{,}418$

Based on equivalent uniform annual cost comparison, Plan A is more economical than Plan B.

.07 Profitability Index

The profitability index is the ratio of the total PV of future cash inflows to the initial investment, that is, PV/I. This index is used as a means of ranking projects in descending order of attractiveness.

Decision rule: If the profitability index is greater than one, accept the project.

Example 7: Using the data in Example 5, the profitability index is:

$$\frac{PV}{I} = \frac{\$39{,}930}{\$37{,}910} = 1.05$$

Since this project generates $1.05 for each dollar invested (i.e., its profitability index is greater than 1), accept the project.

The profitability index has the advantage of putting all projects on the same relative basis regardless of size.

¶ 1315 Selecting the Best Mix of Projects with a Limited Budget

Many firms specify a limit on the overall budget for capital spending. Capital rationing is concerned with the problem of selecting the mix of acceptable projects that provides the highest overall NPV. The profitability index is used widely in ranking projects competing for limited funds.

Example 8: A company with a fixed budget of $250,000 needs to select a mix of acceptable projects from the following:

Projects	*I($)*	*PV($)*	*NPV($)*	*Profitability Index*	*Ranking*
A	70,000	112,000	42,000	1.60	1
B	100,000	145,000	45,000	1.45	2
C	110,000	126,500	16,500	1.15	5
D	60,000	79,000	19,000	1.32	3
E	40,000	38,000	-2,000	0.95	6
F	80,000	95,000	15,000	1.19	4

The ranking resulting from the profitability index shows that the company should select projects A, B, and D.

	I	*PV*
A	\$ 70,000	\$112,000
B..................................	100,000	145,000
D	60,000	79,000
	\$230,000	\$336,000

Therefore,

NPV = \$336,000 – \$230,000 = \$106,000

.01 Zero-One Programming

A more general approach to solving capital rationing problems is the use of *zero-one programming,* which is a special case of *linear programming.* Here the objective is to select the mix of projects that maximizes the net present value (NPV) subject to a budget constraint.

Using the data given in Example 8, we can set up the problem as a zero-one programming problem such that:

$$X_j = \begin{cases} 1 \text{ if project j is selected} \\ 0 \text{ if project j is not selected} \end{cases}$$

$$(j = 1,2,3,4,5,6)$$

The problem then can be formulated as follows:

Maximize

$NPV = \$42{,}000x_1 + \$45{,}000x_2 + \$16{,}500x_3 + \$19{,}000x_4 - \$2{,}000x_5 + \$15{,}000x_6$

Subject to

$\$70{,}000x_1 + \$100{,}000x_2 + \$110{,}000x_3 + \$60{,}000x_4 + \$40{,}000x_5 + \$80{,}000x_6 \leq \$250{,}000$

$x_j = 0,1 \ (j = 1,2,\ldots,6)$

Using the zero-one programming solution routine, the solution to the problem is:

$x_1 = A = 1, x_2 = B = 1, x_4 = D = 1$

And the NPV is $106,000. Thus, projects A, B and D should be selected.

The strength of zero-one programming is its ability to handle mutually exclusive and interdependent projects.

Example 9: Suppose that exactly one project can be selected from the set of projects 1, 3, and 5. Since either 1, 3, or 5 must be selected and only one can be selected, exactly one of the three variables x_1, x_3, or x_5 must be equal to 1 and the rest must be equal to 0. The constraint to be added is:

$x_1 + x_3 + x_5 = 1$

Note that, for example, if $x_3 = 1$, then $x_1 = 0$ and $x_5 = 0$ in order for the constraint to hold.

Example 10: Suppose that projects 2 and 4 are mutually exclusive, which means that only one or neither may be selected. The constraint to be added:

$x_2 + x_4 \leq 1$

Note that the following three pairs satisfy this constraint:

$x_2 = 0$ and $x_4 = 0$

$x_2 = 1$ and $x_4 = 0$

$x_2 = 0$ and $x_4 = 1$

But $x_2 = 1$ and $x_4 = 1$ violates this constraint, since $1 + 1 = 2 > 1$

Example 11: Suppose if project 3 is selected, then project 4 must be selected. In other words, a mutual dependence exists between projects 3 and 4. An example might be a project such as building a second floor that requires the first floor to precede it. Then the constraint to be added is:

$x_3 \leq x_4$

Note that if $x_3 = 1$, then x_4 must be equal to 1. However, x_4 can be equal to 1 and x_3 can be equal to either 1 or 0. That is, the selection of project 4 does not imply that project 3 must be selected.

Example 12: Maximize:

$NPV = \$42{,}000x_1 + \$45{,}000x_2 + \$16{,}500x_3 + \$19{,}000x_4 - \$2{,}000x_5 + \$15{,}000x_6$

Subject to

$\$70{,}000x_1 + \$100{,}000x_2 + \$110{,}000x_3 + \$60{,}000x_4 + \$40{,}000x_5 + \$80{,}000x_6 \leq \$250{,}000$

$x_1 + x_4 \leq 1$ (Projects 1 and 4 are mutually exclusive)

$x_j = 0,1$ (j = 1,2,. . . ,6)

Using the zero-one programming solution routine, the solution to the problem is, as shown in the LINDO (Linear Interactive and Discrete Optimization) (www.lindo.com) output (Exhibit 1):

$x_1 = 1, x_2 = 1, x_6 = 1$

And the NPV is $102,000. Thus, projects 1, 2, and 6 should be accepted.

Exhibit 1

LINDO's Zero-One Programming Output

```
: MAX 42000X1+45000X2+16500X3+19000X4-2000X5+15000X6
? ST
? 70000X1+100000X2+110000X3+60000X4+40000X5+80000X6<250000
? X1+X4=1
? END
: INTEGER 6
: INTEGER X1
: INTEGER X2
: INTEGER X3
: INTEGER X4
: INTEGER X5
: INTEGER X6
: GO
          OBJECTIVE FUNCTION VALUE

 1)          102000.000       <-------- NPV

VARIABLE          VALUE            REDUCED COST        Solution:
      X1        1.000000              .000000
      X2        1.000000         -30000.000000          X1 = 1
      X3         .000000              .000000
      X4         .000000          21500.000000          X2 = 1
      X5         .000000           8000.000000
      X6        1.000000          -3000.000000          X6 = 1

     ROW    SLACK OR SURPLUS       DUAL PRICES
      2)         .000000              .150000
      3)         .000000         31500.000000

NO. ITERATIONS=        4
BRANCHES=     0 DETERM= 11.000E   4
BOUND ON OPTIMUM:   102000.0
ENUMERATION COMPLETE. BRANCHES=      0  PIVOTS=      4
```

¶ 1321 Handling Mutually Exclusive Investments

A project is said to be mutually exclusive if the acceptance of one project automatically excludes the acceptance of one or more other projects (for example, two alternative uses of a single plot of land). In the case where one must choose between mutually exclusive investments, the NPV and IRR methods may result in contradictory indications. The conditions under which contradictory rankings can occur are:

1. Projects that have different life expectancies.
2. Projects that have different sizes of investment.
3. Projects whose cash flows differ over time. For example, the cash flows of one project increase over time, while those of another decrease.

The contradictions result from different assumptions with respect to the reinvestment rate on cash flows from the projects.

1. The NPV method discounts all cash flows at the cost of capital, thus implicitly assuming that these cash flows can be reinvested at this rate.
2. The IRR method assumes that cash flows are reinvested at the often unrealistic rate specified by the project's internal rate of return. Thus, the implied reinvestment rate will differ from project to project.

Thus, the relative desirability of mutually exclusive projects depends on what rate of return the subsequent cash flows can earn. The NPV method generally gives correct ranking, since the cost of capital is a more realistic reinvestment rate. The cost of capital tends to give a close approximation for the market rate of return.

Example 13: Assume the following:

	Cash Flows					
	0	*1*	*2*	*3*	*4*	*5*
A	(100)	120				
B	(100)					201.14

Computing IRR and NPV at 10% gives the following different rankings:

	IRR	*NPV at 10%*
A	20%	9.01
B	15%	24.90

The difference in ranking between the two methods is caused by the methods' reinvestment rate assumptions. The IRR method assumes Project A's cash inflow of $120 is reinvested at 20 percent for the subsequent four years and the NPV method assumes $120 is reinvested at 10 percent. The correct decision is to select the project with the higher NPV (that is, Project B), since the NPV method assumes a more realistic reinvestment rate, that is, the cost of capital (10 percent in this example).

The net present values plotted against various discount rates (costs of capital) results in the NPV profiles for projects A and B (Exhibit 2). An analysis of Exhibit 2 indicates that at a discount rate larger than 14 percent, A has a higher NPV than B. Therefore, A should be selected. At a discount rate less than 14 percent, B has the higher NPV than A and, thus, should be selected.

Exhibit 2

The NPV Graph

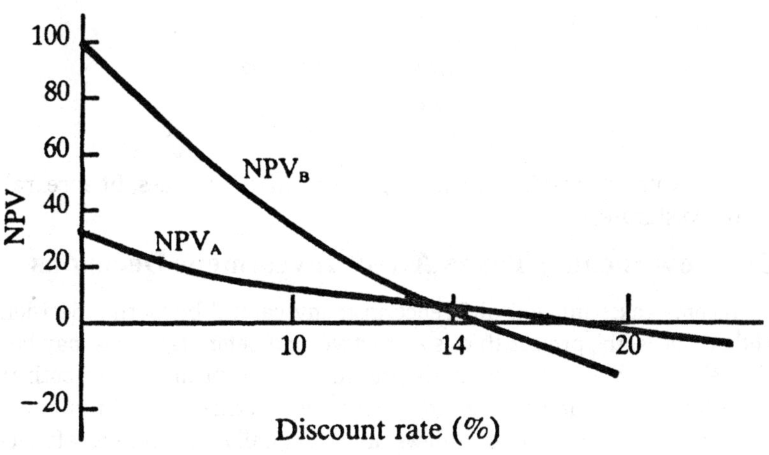

.01 *Modified Internal Rate of Return*

The modified internal rate of return (MIRR) is defined as the discount rate which forces the Initial cash outlay = present value of terminal (future) value compounded at the cost of capital.

The MIRR forces cash flow reinvestment at the cost of capital rather than at the project's own IRR, which was the problem with the IRR. MIRR avoids the problem of multiple IRRs. However, conflicts can still occur in ranking mutually exclusive projects with differing sizes. NPV should again be used when this occurs.

Example 14: Refer back to Example 13, where computing IRR and NPV at 10 percent gives the following different rankings:

Projects	*IRR*	*NPV at 10%*
A..................	20%	$ 9.01
B..................	15%	24.90

As noted, the correct decision is to select the project with the higher NPV (Project B), since the NPV method assumes a more realistic reinvestment rate, that is, the cost of capital (10 percent in this example). The MIRR overcomes this problem.

Project A's MIRR:

First, compute the project's terminal value at a 10% cost of capital.

$120 \times T_1$ (10%, 4 years) = 120×1.4641 = 175.69

Next, find the IRR by setting:

100 = 175.69 T_3 (MIRR, 5 years)

T_3 = 100/175.69 = 0.5692, which gives MIRR = about 12%

Now we see the consistent ranking from both the NPV and MIRR methods.

Projects	*MIRR*	*NPV at 10%*
A	12%	$ 9.01
B	15%	24.90

Note: Microsoft Excel has a function MIRR (values, finance_rate, reinvest_rate).

¶ 1325 How Income Taxes Affect Investment Decisions

Income taxes make a difference in many capital budgeting decisions. In other words, the project that is attractive on a before-tax basis may have to be rejected on an after-tax basis. Income taxes typically affect both the amount and the timing of cash flows. Since net income, not cash inflows, is subject to tax, after-tax cash inflows are not usually the same as after-tax net income.

Let us define:

S = Sales

E = Cash operating expenses

d = Depreciation

t = Tax rate

Then, before-tax cash inflows (or before-tax *cash savings*) = S − E and net income = S − E − d.

By definition:

After-tax cash inflows = Before-tax cash inflows − Taxes

= (S − E) − (S − E − d) (t)

Rearranging gives the short-cut formula:

After-tax cash inflows = (S − E) (1 − t) + (d)(t)

As can be seen, the deductibility of depreciation from sales in arriving at net income subject to taxes reduces income tax payments and, thus, serves as a tax shield.

Tax shield = Tax savings on depreciation = (d)(t)

Example 15: Assume:

S = \$12,000

E = \$10,000

d = \$500 per year using the straight-line method

t = 30%

Then,

After-tax cash inflow = (\$12,000 − \$10,000) (1 − 0.3) + (\$500)(0.3)

= (\$2,000)(.7) + (\$500)(0.3)

= \$1,400 + \$150 = \$1,550

Note that a tax shield = tax savings on depreciation = (d)(t)

= (\$500)(.3) = \$150

Since the tax shield is dt, the higher the depreciation deduction, the higher the tax savings on depreciation. Therefore, an accelerated depreciation method (such as double-declining balance) produces higher tax savings than the straight-line method. Accelerated methods produce higher present values for the tax savings, which may make a given investment more attractive.

Example 16: The Shalimar Company estimates that it can save \$2,500 a year in cash operating costs for the next 10 years if it buys a special-purpose machine at a cost of \$10,000. No salvage value is expected. Assume that the income tax rate is 30%, and the after-tax cost of capital (minimum required rate of return) is 10%. After-tax cash savings can be calculated as follows:

Note that depreciation by straight-line is \$10,000/10 = \$1,000 per year. Here, before-tax cash savings = (S − E) = \$2,500. Thus,

After-tax cash savings = (S − E) (1 − t) + (d)(t)

= \$2,500(1 − 0.3) + \$1,000(0.3)

= \$1,750 + \$300 = \$2,050

To see if this machine should be purchased, the net present value can be calculated.

PV = \$2,050 T_4 (10%, 10 years) = \$2,050 (6.145) = \$12,597.25

Thus, NPV = PV − I = \$12,597.25 − \$10,000 = \$2,597.25

Since NPV is positive, the machine should be bought.

Example 17: The CFO of a small appliance maker estimates the sales revenue, cash operating expenses, and cash inflows before taxes (shown in columns 1, 2, and 3 of the table below) if it buys a high tech machine at a cost of \$1,000,000. No residual value is expected. The life expectancy of the machine is five years. Depreciation is by straight-line. Assume that the income tax rate is 35 percent, and the after-tax cost of capital (minimum required rate of return) is 10 percent. Should the company buy the machine? Use the NPV method.

The process of arriving at net cash flow after taxes is shown in columns 4, 5, 6, 7, and 8.

Year	Sales (S) (1)	Cash Operating Expenses (E) (2)	Cash Inflow Before Taxes (S-E) (3)=(1) − (2)	Depreciation (noncash Expense) (d) (4)=1,000,000/5	Net Income Before Taxes (5)=(3) − (4)	Income Taxes (6)=.35×(5)	Net Income After Taxes (7)=(5) − (6)	Cash Inflow After Taxes (8)=(3) − (6) or (7) + (4)
1	$1,000,000	$625,000	$375,000	$200,000	$175,000	$61,250	$113,750	$313,750
2	$ 900,000	$610,000	$290,000	$200,000	$ 90,000	$31,500	$ 58,500	$258,500
3	$ 925,000	$635,000	$290,000	$200,000	$ 90,000	$31,500	$ 58,500	$258,500
4	$ 930,000	$605,000	$325,000	$200,000	$125,000	$43,750	$ 81,250	$281,250
5	$ 825,000	$557,000	$268,000	$200,000	$ 68,000	$23,800	$ 44,200	$244,200

The NPV of the machine can be calculated using Table 3 in Appendix B as shown below.

Year	*Cash Inflow After Taxes*	*T_3 at 10% Table value*	*PV*
1	$313,750	0.909	$ 285,199
2	$258,500	0.826	$ 213,521
3	$258,500	0.751	$ 194,134
4	$281,250	0.683	$ 192,094
5	$244,200	0.621	$ 151,648
			$1,036,596

Thus, NPV = PV − I = $1,036,596 − $1,000,000 = $36,596. Since NPV is positive, the machine should be bought.

Example 18: Shalimar Corporation has provided its revenues and cash operating costs (excluding depreciation) for the old and the new machine, as follows:

	Revenue	*Annual Cash Operating Costs*	*Net Profit before Depreciation and Taxes*
Old machine	$150,000	$70,000	$ 80,000
New machine	$180,000	$60,000	$120,000

Assume that the annual depreciation of the old machine and the new machine will be $30,000 and $50,000, respectively. Assume further that the tax rate is 46 percent.

To arrive at net profit after taxes, we first have to deduct depreciation expense from the net profit before depreciation and taxes, as follows:

	Net Profits after Taxes	*Add Depreciation*	*After-Tax Cash Inflows*
Old machine	($80,000−$30,000)(1−0.46)=$27,000	$30,000	$57,000
New machine	($120,000−$50,000)(1−0.46)=$37,800	$50,000	$87,800

Subtracting the after-tax cash inflows of the old machine from the cash inflows of the new machine results in the relevant, or incremental, cash inflows for each year.

Therefore, in this example, the relevant or incremental cash inflows for each year are $87,800 – $57,000 = $30,800.

Alternatively, the incremental cash inflows after taxes can be computed, using the following simple formula:

After-tax incremental cash inflows = (increase in revenues)(1 – tax rate)

– (increase in cash charges)(1 – tax rate)

+ (increase in depreciation expenses)(tax rate)

Example 19: Using the data in Example 18, after-tax incremental cash inflows for each year are:

Increase in revenue × (1 – tax rate):	
($180,000 – $150,000)(1 – 0.46)	$16,200
– Increase in cash charges × (1 – tax rate):	
($60,000 – $70,000)(1 – 0.46)	–(–5,400)
+ Increase in depreciation expense × tax rate:	
($50,000 – $30,000)(0.46)	9,200
	$30,800

¶ 1331 After-Tax Cash Flows

In general, a project's cash flows will fall into one of three categories: (1) the initial investment, (2) the differential flows over the project's life, or (3) the terminal cash flow. The capital-budgeting criteria will use these cash flows as inputs.

.01 Initial Investment—Incremental Investment

The initial investment involves the immediate cash outlay necessary to purchase the asset and put it in operating order. This amount includes the cost of installing the asset (the asset's purchase price plus any expenses associated with transportation or installation) and any nonexpense cash outlays, such as increased working capital requirements. If we are considering a new sales outlet, there might be additional cash flows associated with investment in working capital in the form of increased inventory and cash necessary to operate the sales outlet. While these cash flows are not included in the cost of the asset or even expensed on the books, they must be included in the analysis.

The after-tax cost of expense items incurred as a result of new investment must also be included as cash outflows—for example, any training expenses or special engineering expenses that would not have been incurred otherwise. Finally, if the investment decision is a replacement decision, the cash inflow associated with the selling price of the old asset, in addition to any tax effects resulting from its sale, must be accounted for.

Items included in the initial outlay calculation are summarized in Exhibit 3.

Exhibit 3

Initial Investment

1. Purchase price of asset and installation cost.
2. Additional expenses on an after-tax basis (for example, training expenses).
3. Additional nonexpense outlays incurred (for example, working capital investments).
4. In a replacement decision, the after-tax cash flow associated with the disposal of the old asset.

Tax effects of disposal. In general, gains and losses (i.e., the disposal value minus the book value) on disposal of equipment are taxed in the same way as ordinary gains and losses. Immediate disposal of the old equipment results in a loss that is fully tax deductible from current income. The loss (the excess of the book value over the disposal value) must be computed to isolate its effect on current income tax, but the total cash inflow is the sales price *plus* the current income tax effect.

In short, there are three possible tax situations dealing with the sale of an old asset:

1. The old asset is sold for a price above the depreciated value. This is considered recapture of depreciation (or gain) and taxed at the corporate tax rate. If, for example, the old machine was originally purchased for $15,000, had a book (undepreciated) value of $10,000, and was sold for $14,000, assuming the firm's tax rate is 40 percent, the taxes on gain (due from recapture of depreciation) would be ($14,000 − $10,000)(.40), or $1,600. The after-tax cash inflow then is $14,000 − $1,600 = $12,400.
2. The old asset is sold for its depreciated value. In this case no taxes result, as there is neither a gain nor a loss in the asset's sale. The after-tax cash inflow is the selling price (disposal value) or $10,000.
3. The old asset is sold for less than its depreciated value. In this case the difference between the depreciated book value and the salvage value of the asset is used to offset ordinary income and, thus, results in tax savings. Assume that the machine was sold

for $8,000, while its book value is $10,000. Two cash inflows are connected with this sale.

a. An $8,000 cash inflow in the form of the sales price, and

b. An $800 cash inflow in the form of a reduction in income taxes, resulting from the tax shield provided by the loss sustained on the sale, just like the tax shield provided by depreciation deduction, as computed as follows:

Book value		$10,000
Selling price		8,000
Loss		2,000
Tax shield	×.40	$ 800

Thus, the total cash inflow from the disposal is $8,800 ($8,000 + $800).

Example 20: Assume a company in the 40-percent tax bracket is contemplating the purchase of a new machine to be used in oil and gas drilling for $30,000. It has a useful life of five years and will be depreciated using the straight-line method. The new machine will replace an existing machine originally purchased for $30,000 10 years ago, which currently has five more years of expected useful life. The existing machine will generate $2,000 of depreciation expenses for each of the next five years, at which time the book value will be equal to zero. To put the new machine in running order, it is necessary to pay shipping charges of $2,000 and installation charges of $3,000. Because the new machine will work faster than the old one, it will require an increase in goods-in-process inventory of $3,000. Finally, the old machine can be sold to a scrap dealer for $15,000.

The installed cost of the new machine would be the $30,000 cost plus $2,000 shipping and $3,000 installation fees, for a total of $35,000. Additional outflows are associated with taxes incurred on the sale of the old machine and with increased investment in inventory. Although the old machine has a book value of $10,000, it could be sold for $15,000. The increased taxes on a gain (from recapture of depreciation) will be equal to the sales price of the old machine less its book value times the firm's tax rate, or ($15,000 − $10,000)(.4), or $2,000.

The increase in goods-in-process inventory of $3,000 must also be considered part of the initial outlay, which will be recovered at the termination of the project. In effect, the firm invests $3,000 in inventory now, resulting in an initial cash outlay, and liquidates this inventory in five years, resulting in a $3,000 cash inflow at the end of the project. The total outlays associated with the new machine are $35,000 for its installed cost, $2,000 in increased taxes, and $3,000 in investment in inventory, for a total of $40,000. This is somewhat offset by the sale of the old machine for $15,000. Thus, the initial investment associated with this project is $25,000, as shown in Exhibit 4.

Exhibit 4

Calculation of Initial Investment

Out-of-pocket outlays:	
Installed cost of machine	$35,000
Increased taxes from sale of old machine (15,000-$10,000)(.4)	2,000
Increased investment in inventory	3,000
Total Outlays	$40,000
Inflows:	
Salvage value of old machine	15,000
Initial outlay	$25,000

.02 Differential Flows over the Project's Life

The differential cash flows over the project's life involve the incremental after-tax cash flows resulting from increased revenues, plus labor or material savings, and reductions in selling expenses. Any major repair and overhaul costs must be included. Furthermore, an adjustment for the incremental change in taxes should be made, including any increase in taxes that might result from increased profits or any tax savings from an increase in depreciation expenses. Increased depreciation expenses affect tax-related cash flows by reducing taxable income and, thus, lowering taxes. Exhibit 5 lists some of the factors that might be involved in determining a project's differential cash flows.

Exhibit 5

Differential Cash Flows on an After-Tax Basis

1. Incremental revenue.
2. Labor and material savings.
3. Increases in overhead or overhaul incurred.
4. In a replacement decision, depreciation tax shield on an incremental basis.

In Example 20, assume further that purchasing the machine is expected to reduce salaries by $10,000 per year and fringe benefits by $1,000 annually because it will take only one man to operate, whereas the old machine requires two operators. In addition, the cost of defects will fall from $8,000 per year to $3,000. However, maintenance expenses will increase by $4,000 annually. The annual depreciation on this new machine is $7,000 per year, while the depreciation expense lost with the sale of the old machine is $2,000 for each of the next five years. Annual depreciation on the new machine is calculated using the straight-line method.

Since the depreciation on the old machine is $2,000 per year, the increased depreciation will go from $2,000 per year to $7,000 per year, or an increase of $5,000 per year. Although this increase in depreciation expenses is not a cash flow item, it does affect cash flows by reducing taxable income, which in turn reduces taxes.

To determine the annual net cash flows resulting from the acceptance of this project, the net savings before taxes using both book income and cash flows must be found. The additional taxes are then calculated based upon the before-tax book profit. Exhibit 6 shows the determination of the differential cash flows on an after-tax basis. Thus, the differential cash flows over the project's life are $9,200.

Exhibit 6

Calculation of Differential Cash Flows

	Book Income	*Cash Flow*
Savings: Reduced salary	$ 10,000	$ 10,000
Reduced fringe benefits	1,000	1,000
Reduced defects ($8,000 – $3,000)	5,000	5,000
Costs: Increased maintenance expense	– 4,000	– 4,000
Increased depreciation expense ($7,000 – $2,000)	– 5,000	
Net savings before taxes	$ 7,000	$ 12,000
Taxes (40%)	– 2,800	– 2,800
Net cash flow after taxes		$ 9,200

.03 Terminal Cash Flow

The calculation of the terminal cash flow is much simpler than the preceding two calculations. Flows associated with the project's termination generally include the salvage value of the project plus or minus any taxable gains or losses associated with its sales. In addition to the salvage value, there may be a cash outlay associated with the project termination, such as shutdown costs. Finally, any working capital outlay—inventory investments—required at the initiation of the project will be recovered by liquidating the inventory. Exhibit 7 lists some of the factors that might affect a project's terminal cash flow.

In Example 20, the depreciated book value and salvage value of the machine both are equal to zero. However, there will be a cash flow associated with the recapture of the initial outlay of work-in-process inventory of $3,000. This flow is generated from the liquidation of the $3,000 investment in work-in-process inventory. Therefore, the expected total terminal cash flow equals $3,000.

In summary, the company would have (1) an initial outlay of $25,000, (2) differential cash flows during years 1 through 5 of $9,200, and (3) a terminal cash flow at the end of year 5 of $3,000.

Exhibit 7

Terminal Cash Flow on an After-Tax Basis

1. The after-tax salvage value of the project.
2. Any cash outlays necessary to terminate the project.
3. Recapture of nonexpense outlays required at the project's outset (for example, working capital investments).

¶1335 Types of Depreciation Methods

We saw that depreciation provided the tax shield in the form of (d)(t). Among the commonly used depreciation methods are straight-line and accelerated methods. The two major accelerated methods are sum-of-the years'-digits (SYD) and double-declining-balance (DDB).

.01 Straight-line Method

This is the easiest and most popular method of calculating depreciation. It results in equal periodic depreciation charges. The method is most appropriate when an asset's usage is uniform from period to period, as is the case with furniture. The annual depreciation expense is calculated by using the following formula:

$$\text{Depreciation expense} = \frac{\text{Cost} - \text{Salvage value}}{\text{Number of years of useful life}}$$

Example 21: An auto is purchased for $20,000 and has an expected salvage value of $2,000. The auto's estimated life is eight years. Its annual depreciation is calculated as follows:

$$\text{Depreciation expense} = \frac{\text{cost} - \text{salvage value}}{\text{number of years of useful life}}$$

$$= \frac{\$20{,}000 - \$2{,}000}{8 \text{ years}} = \$2{,}250 \text{ / year}$$

An alternative means of computation is to multiply the *depreciable* cost ($18,000) by the annual depreciation rate, which is 12.5 percent in this example. The annual rate is calculated by dividing the number of years of useful life into one (1/8 = 12.5%). The result is the same: $18,000 × 12.5% = $2,250.

.02 Sum-of the Years'-Digits (SYD) Method

In this method, the number of years of life expectancy is enumerated in reverse order in the numerator, and the denominator is the sum of the digits. For example, if the life expectancy of a machine is eight years, write the numbers in reverse order: 8, 7, 6, 5, 4, 3, 2, 1. The sum of these digits is 36 (or 8 + 7 + 6 + 5 + 4 + 3 + 2 + 1). Thus, the fraction for the first year is 8/36, while the fraction for the last year is 1/36. The sum of the eight fractions equals 36/36, or 1. Therefore, at the end of eight years, the machine is completely written down to its salvage value.

The following formula may be used to quickly find the sum-of-the-years' digits (S):

$$S = \frac{(N)(N + 1)}{2}$$

Where N represents the number of years of expected life.

Example 22: In Example 21, the *depreciable* cost is $18,000 ($20,000 – $2,000). Using the SYD method, the computation for each year's depreciation expense is:

$$S = \frac{(N)(N + 1)}{2} = \frac{8(9)}{2} = \frac{72}{2} = 36$$

Year	*Fraction*	*X Depreciation Amount($)*	*= Depreciation Expense*
1	8/36	$18,000	$ 4,000
2	7/36	18,000	3,500
3	6/36	18,000	3,000
4	5/36	18,000	2,500
5	4/36	18,000	2,000
6	3/36	18,000	1,500
7	2/36	18,000	1,000
8	1/36	18,000	500
Total..			$18,000

.03 Double-Declining-Balance (DDB) Method

Under this method, depreciation expense is highest in the earlier years and lower in the later years. First, a depreciation rate is determined by doubling the straight-line rate. For example, if an asset has a life of 10 years, the straight-line rate is 1/10 or 10 percent, and the double-declining rate is 20 percent. Second, depreciation expense is computed by multiplying the rate by the book value of the asset at the beginning of each year. Since book value declines over time, the depreciation expense decreases each successive period.

This method *ignores* salvage value in the computation. However, the book value of the fixed asset at the end of its useful life cannot be below its salvage value.

Example 23: Assume the same data as in Example 21. Since the straight-line rate is 12.5 percent (1/8), the double-declining-balance rate is 25 percent (2 × 12.5%). The depreciation expense is computed as follows:

Year	*Book Value at Beginning of Year*	×	*Rate (%)*	=	*Depreciation Expense*	*Year-end Book Value*
1	$20,000		25%		$5,000	$15,000
2	15,000		25		3,750	11,250
3	11,250		25		2,813	8,437
4	8,437		25		2,109	6,328
5	6,328		25		1,582	4,746
6	4,746		25		1,187	3,559
7	3,559		25		890	2,669
8	2,669		25		667	2,002

Note: If the original estimated salvage value had been $2,100, the depreciation expense for the eighth year would have been $569 ($2,669 – $2,100) rather than $667, since the asset cannot be depreciated below its salvage value.

.04 Modified Accelerated Cost Recovery System (MACRS)

Although the traditional depreciation methods still can be used for computing depreciation for book purposes, 1981 brought a new way of computing depreciation deductions for tax purposes. The new rule is called the Modified Accelerated Cost Recovery System (MACRS) rule, as enacted by Congress in 1981 and then modified somewhat in 1986 under the Tax Reform Act of 1986. This rule is characterized as follows:

1. It abandons the concept of useful life and accelerates depreciation deductions by placing all depreciable assets into one of eight age property classes. It calculates deductions, based on an allowable percentage of the asset's original cost (See Exhibits 8 and 9, below). With a shorter life than useful life, the company would be able to deduct depreciation more quickly and save more in income taxes in the earlier years, thereby making an investment more attractive. The rationale behind the system is that this way the government encourages the company to invest in facilities and increase its productive capacity and efficiency. (Remember that the higher depreciation (d), the larger the tax shield (d)(t)).

2. Since the allowable percentages in Exhibit 9 add up to 100 percent, there is no need to consider the salvage value of an asset in computing depreciation.

3. The company may elect the straight-line method. The straight-line convention must follow what is called the half-year convention. This means that the company can deduct only half of the regular straight-line depreciation amount in the first year. The reason for electing to use the MACRS optional straight-line method is that some firms may prefer to stretch out depreciation deductions using the straight-line method rather than to accelerate them. This applies to firms that are just starting out or that have little or no income and wish to show more income on their income statements.

Example 24: Assume that a machine falls under a three-year property class and costs $3,000 initially. The straight-line option under MACRS differs from the traditional straight-line method in that under this method the company would deduct only $500 depreciation in the first year and the fourth year ($3,000/3 years = $1,000; $1,000/2 = $500). The Exhibit below compares the straight-line with half-year convention with the MACRS.

Year	*Straight line (half-year) Depreciation*	*Cost*		*MACRS%*	*MACRS Deduction*
1.............	$ 500	$3,000	×	33.3%	$ 999
2.............	1,000	3,000	×	44.5	1,335
3.............	1,000	3,000	×	14.8	444
4.............	500	3,000	×	7.4	222
	$3,000				$3,000

Example 25: A machine costs $10,000. Annual cash inflows are expected to be $5,000. The machine will be depreciated using the MACRS rule and will fall under the three-year property class. The cost of capital after taxes is 10 percent. The estimated life of the machine is five years. The salvage value of the machine at the end of the fifth year is expected to be $1,200. The tax rate is 30 percent. Should you buy the machine? Use the NPV method.

The formula for computation of after-tax cash inflows (S − E)(1 − t) + (d)(t) needs to be computed separately. The NPV analysis can be performed as follows:

				Present value Factor @ 10%	Present value
(S – E)(1 – t):					
	$ 5,000 for 5 years	$5,000(1 – .3)=$3,500 for 5 years	$3,500	3.791[(a)]	$13,268.50
(d)(t):					

Year	*Cost*	*MACRS%*	*d*	*(d)(t)*		
1	$10,000 ×	33.3%	$3,330	$ 999	.909[(b)]	908.09
2	$10,000 ×	44.5	4,450	1,335	.826[(b)]	1,102.71
3	$10,000 ×	14.8	1,480	444	.751[(b)]	333.44
4	$10,000 ×	7.4	740	222	.683[(b)]	151.63

Salvage value:					
	$ 1,200 in year 5	$1,200(1 – .3)=$840[(c)] in year 5	$ 840	.621[(b)]	521.64
		Present value (PV)			$16,286.01

[(a)] T_4 (10%, 4 years)=3.170 (from Table 4 in Appendix B).
[(b)] T_3 values (year 1, 2, 3, 4, 5) obtained from Table 3 in Appendix B.
[(c)] Any salvage value received under the MACRS rules is a *taxable gain* (the excess of the selling price over book value, $1,200 in this example), since the book value will be zero at the end of the life of the machine.

Since NPV = PV – I = $16,286.01 – $10,000 = $6,286.01 is positive, the machine should be bought.

Exhibit 8

Modified Accelerated Cost Recovery System Classification of Assets

Property class

Year	*3-year*	*5-year*	*7-year*	*10-year*	*15-year*	*20-year*
1	33.3%	20.0%	14.3%	10.0%	5.0%	3.8%
2	44.5	32.0	24.5	18.0	9.5	7.2
3	14.8a	19.2	17.5	14.4	8.6	6.7
4	7.4	11.5a	12.5	11.5	7.7	6.2
5		11.5	8.9a	9.2	6.9	5.7
6		5.8	8.9	7.4	6.2	5.3
7			8.9	6.6a	5.9a	4.9
8			4.5	6.6	5.9	4.5[a]
9				6.5	5.9	4.5
10				6.5	5.9	4.5
11				3.3	5.9	4.5
12					5.9	4.5
13					5.9	4.5
14					5.9	4.5
15					5.9	4.5
16					3.0	4.4
17						4.4
18						4.4
19						4.4
20						4.4
21						2.2
Total	100%	100%	100%	100%	100%	100%

---

[a] *Denotes the year of changeover to straight-line depreciation.*

Exhibit 9

MACRS Tables by Property Class

Property Class & Depreciation Method	*Useful Life (ADR Midpoint Life)*[a]	*Examples of Assets*
3-year property 200% declining balance	4 years or less	Most small tools are included; the law specifically excludes autos and light trucks from this property class.
5-year property 200% declining balance	More than 4 years to less than 10 years	Autos and light trucks, computers, typewriters, copiers, duplicating equipment, heavy general-purpose trucks, and research and experimentation equipment are included.
7-year property 200% and declining balance	10 years or more to less than 16 years	Office furniture and fixtures—Most items of machinery and equipment used in production are included.
10-year property 200% declining balance	16 years or more to less than 20 years	Various machinery and equipment, such as that used in petroleum distilling and refining and in the milling of grain, are included.
15-year property 150% declining balance	20 years or more to less than 25 years	Sewage treatment plants, telephone and electrical distribution facilities, and land improvements are included.
20-year property 150% declining balance	25 years or more	Service stations and other real property with an ADR midpoint life of less than 27.5 years are included.
27.5-year property straight-line	Not applicable	All residential rental property is included
39-year property straight-line	Not applicable	All nonresidential property is included.

[a] The term ADR midpoint life means the "useful life" of an asset in a business sense; the appropriate ADR midpoint lives for assets are designated in the tax regulations.

¶ 1341 The Lease-Purchase Decision

Firms considering the acquisition of new assets commonly confront the lease-purchase decision. It is a hybrid capital budgeting decision that forces a company to compare the leasing and financing (purchasing) alternatives.

.01 Leasing Benefits

There are tax benefits from leasing equipment rather than financing it with a term loan. Depending upon one's needs and the nature of one's business, the entire lease payment may be fully deductible as a business expense, thereby reducing one's taxable income. With a loan, only the interest and depreciation can be used for deductions. Another benefit a lease offers is 100 percent financing plus additional amounts on the equipment's costs to cover "soft costs," such as taxes, shipping, and installation. Some term loans offer 100 percent financing but, typically, they cover the cost of equipment only.

A lease can help one manage one's cash flow. The payments are usually lower than for a term loan. Since a lease payment often requires no down payment or deposit, one can get the equipment one needs without depleting one's reserve capital. The types of business that most often lease equipment to generate revenue are manufacturing, transportation, printing, and professional corporations, such as medical, law, or accounting firms. Leasing works well for such companies since they can keep their equipment current without having to dip into capital to do it. Since the business' capital is not being used for equipment, they can use it for business development and expansion.

.02 Loan Benefits

A loan is one's best choice, however, if one wishes to keep the equipment and build equity quickly. Loans can be structured so one can own the equipment outright at the end of the term.

Note: If one is sure one wants to retain one's equipment beyond the lease term and prefers to know the full cost of the financing up front, one may choose a Lease Purchase option. As its name implies, this option requires no additional payment to own the equipment at the end of the lease.

.03 Preparing a Present Value Comparison

To make an intelligent financial decision on a lease-purchase, an after-tax, cash outflow, present value comparison is needed. There are special steps to take when making this comparison. When considering a lease, take the following steps:

1. Find the annual lease payment. Since the annual lease payment is typically made in advance, the formula used is:

$$\text{Amount of lease} = A + A.T_4\,(i,n-1) \text{ or } A = \frac{\text{Amount of lease}}{1 + T_4\,(i,n-1)}$$

Notice we use n − 1 rather than n.

2. Find the after-tax cash outflows.

3. Find the present value of the after-tax cash outflows.

When considering a purchase, take the following steps:

1. Find the annual loan amortization by using:

$$A = \frac{\text{Amount of loan for the purchase}}{T_4\,(i, n - 1)}$$

The step may not be necessary since this amount is usually available.

2. Calculate the interest. The interest is segregated from the principal in each of the annual loan payments because only the interest is tax deductible.

3. Find the cash outflows by adding interest and depreciation (plus any maintenance costs), and then compute the after-tax outflows.

4. Find the present value of the after-tax cash outflows, using Table 3 in Appendix B.

Example 26: A firm has decided to acquire a computer system costing $100,000 that has an expected life of five years, after which the system is not expected to have any residual value. The system can be purchased by borrowing or it can be leased. If leasing is used, the lessor requires a 12-percent return. As is customary, lease payments are made in advance, that is, at the end of the year prior to each of the 10 years. The tax rate is 50 percent and the firm's cost of capital, or after-tax cost of borrowing, is eight percent.

First compute the present value of the after-tax cash outflows associated with the leasing alternative.

1. Find the annual lease payment:

$$A = \frac{\text{Amount of lease}}{1 + T_4\,(i, n - 1)}$$

$$= \frac{\$100{,}000}{1 + T_4\,(12\%, 4\text{ years})} = \frac{\$100{,}000}{1 + 3.3073} = \frac{\$100{,}000}{4.3073} = \$23{,}216\text{ (rounded)}$$

Steps 2 and 3 can be done in the same schedule, as follows:

Year	(1) Lease Payment($)	(2) Tax Savings($)	(3)=(1) − (2) After-Tax Cash Outflow($)	(4) PV at 8%	(5)=(3)×(4) PV of Cash Outflow ($,Rounded)
0	23,216		23,216	1.000	23,216
1-4	23,216	11,608[a]	11,608	3.3121[b]	38,447
5		11,608	(11,608)	0.6806[a]	(7,900)
					53,763

[a] $23,216 × 50%
[b] From Table 4 in Appendix B.
[c] From Table 3 in Appendix B.

If the asset is purchased, the firm is assumed to finance it entirely with a 10-percent unsecured term loan. Straight-line depreciation is used with no salvage value. Therefore, the annual depreciation is $20,000 ($100,000/5 years).

1. In this alternative, first find the annual loan payment by using:

$$A = \frac{\text{Amount of loan}}{T_4\,(i,n)}$$

$$= \frac{\$100{,}000}{T_4\,(10\%, 5\text{ years})} = \frac{\$100{,}000}{3.7906} = \$26{,}381\ (\text{rounded})$$

2. Calculate the interest by setting up a loan amortization schedule.

Year	(1) Loan Payment($)	(2) Beginning-of-Year Principal($)	(3)=(2)(10%) Interest($)	(4)=(1)−(3) Principal($)	(5)=(2)−(4) End-of-Year Principal
1	26,381	100,000	10,000	16,381	83,619
2	26,381	83,619	8,362	18,019	65,600
3	26,381	65,600	6,560	19,821	45,779
4	26,381	45,779	4,578	21,803	23,976
5	26,381	23,976[a]	2,398	23,983[a]	

[a] Because of rounding errors, there is a slight difference between (2) and (4)

Steps 3 (cash outflows) and 4 (present values of those outflows) can be done as shown below.

The sum of the present values of the cash outflows for leasing and purchasing by borrowing shows that purchasing is preferable because the PV of borrowing is less than the PV of leasing ($52,087 versus $53,761). The incremental savings are $1,674.

Exhibit 10

Lease Versus Purchase Evaluation Report

	Leasing		Purchase/Borrow							
Year	Lease Payments	Net After-Tax Cash Flow	Loan Payments	Interest Expense	Depreciation Expense	Net After-Tax Cash Flow	Present Value Factor	Discounted Cash Flow Leasing	Discounted Cash Flow Purchase
0	$ 23,216	$ 23,216					1	$ 23,216	
1	23,216	11,608	$ 26,381	$ 10,000	$ 20,000	$ 11,381	0.9259	10,748	10,538
2	23,216	11,608	26,381	8,362	20,000	12,200	0.8573	9,952	10,459
3	23,216	11,608	26,381	6,560	20,000	13,101	0.7938	9,214	10,400
4	23,216	11,608	26,381	4,578	20,000	14,092	0.735	8,532	10,358
5		(11,608)	26,381	2,398	20,000	15,182	0.6806	(7,900)	10,333
	$ 116,080	$ 58,040	$ 131,905	$ 31,898	$ 100,000	$ 65,956		$ 53,761	$ 52,087

	Lease Proposal	Purchase Proposal
Cost of machine	$ 100,000	$ 100,000
Terms of payment	5 years	5 years
Interest rate	12%	10%
Downpayment		
Monthly lease payment at the end of the year	$ 23,216	
Monthly loan payment		$ 26,381
Depreciation		Straight line
Residual purchase price	0%	0
Corporate tax bracket	50%	50%
After-tax cost of capital	8%	8%

¶ 1345 Economic Feasibility Study for A New Information System

Determining economic feasibility requires a careful investigation of the costs and benefits of a proposed information system. The basic framework for feasibility analysis is the capital budgeting model, in which cost savings and other benefits, as well as initial outlay costs, operating costs, and other cash outflows, are translated into dollar estimates.

The estimated benefits are compared with the costs to determine whether the system is cost beneficial. Where possible, benefits and costs that are not easily quantifiable should be estimated and included in the feasibility analysis. If they cannot be accurately estimated, they should be listed and the likelihood of their occurring and the expected impact on the organization evaluated. Some of the tangible and intangible benefits a company might obtain from a new system are cost savings, improved customer service, productivity, decision making, and data processing, better management control, and increased job satisfaction and employee morale.

Equipment costs are an initial outlay cost if the system is purchased and an operating cost if rented or leased. Equipment costs vary from a few thousand dollars for microcomputer systems to millions of dollars for enormous mainframes. Equipment costs are usually less than the cost of acquiring software and maintaining, supporting, and operating the system.

Software acquisition costs include the purchase price of software as well as the time and effort required to design, program, test, and document software. The personnel costs associated with hiring, training, and relocating staff can be substantial. Site preparation costs may be incurred for large computer systems. There are costs involved in installing the new system and converting files to the appropriate format and storage media.

The primary operating cost is maintaining the system. There may be significant annual cash outflows for equipment replacement and expansion and software updates. Human resource costs include the salaries of systems analysts, programmers, operators, data entry operators, and management. Costs are also incurred for supplies, overhead, and other operating costs. Initial cash outlay and operating costs are summarized in Exhibit 11.

Exhibit 11

Initial Cash Outlay and Operating Costs

Hardware
- Central processing unit
- Peripherals
- Special input/output devices
- Communications hardware
- Upgrade and expansion costs

Software
- Application, system, general-purpose, utility, and communications software
- Updated versions of software
- Application software design, programming, modification, and testing

Installation
- Freight and delivery charges
- Setup and connection fees

Conversion
- Systems testing
- File and data conversions
- Parallel operations

Documentation
- Systems documentation
- Training program documentation
- Operating standards and procedures

Site preparation
- Air-conditioning, humidity, and dust controls
- Physical security (access)
- Fire and water protection
- Cabling, wiring, and outlets
- Furnishing and fixtures

Staff
- Supervisors
- Analysts and programmers

Computer operators
Input (data conversion) personnel
Recruitment and staff training

Maintenance/backup
Hardware/software maintenance
Backup and recovery operations
Power supply protection

Supplies and overhead
Preprinted forms
Data storage devices
Supplies (paper, ribbons, toner)
Utilities and power

Others
Legal and consulting fees
Insurance

During systems design, several alternative approaches to meeting system requirements are developed. Various feasibility measures such as technical, operational, legal, and scheduling feasibility are then used to narrow the list of alternatives. Economic feasibility and capital budgeting techniques, which were discussed earlier, are used to evaluate the benefit-cost aspects of the alternatives.

Example 27: Sophie Wells, an information systems (IS) project manager for the MYK chain of discount stores, is contemplating installation of a new IS system that is flexible, efficient, timely, and responsive to user and customer needs. The new system aims at improving the company's business processes. After the analysis of the new system Sophie's IS project team decided they wanted the corporate office to gather daily sales data from each store. Analyzing the prior day's sales will help the company adapt quickly to customer needs. Providing sales data to suppliers will help avoid stockouts and overstocking.

Coordinating buying at the corporate office will help MYK to minimize inventory levels and negotiate lower wholesale prices. Stores will send orders electronically the day they are prepared. Based on store orders, the previous day's sales figures, and warehouse inventory, MYK will send purchase orders to suppliers. Suppliers will process orders and ship goods to regional warehouses or directly to the stores the day orders are received. Each store will have the flexibility to respond to local sales trends and conditions by placing local orders. Accounts payable will be centralized so the firm can make payments electronically.

Sophie's team conducted an economic feasibility study and determined that the project makes excellent use of funds. As shown in Exhibit 12, they estimated that initial outlay costs for the system are

$4.66 million (initial systems design and new hardware are $1.8 million each, software is $375,000, training is $185,000, and site preparation and conversion are $250,000 each).

The team estimated what it would cost to operate the system for its estimated six-year life, as well as what the system would save the company. The following recurring costs were identified: hardware expansion, additional software and software updates, systems maintenance, added personnel to operate the system, communication charges, and overhead. The system will also save the company money by eliminating clerical jobs, generating working capital savings, increasing sales and profits, and decreasing warehouse costs. The costs and savings for years 1 through 6, which are expected to rise from year to year, are shown in Exhibit 12.

Sophie calculated the annual savings minus the recurring additional costs and then calculated the annual after-tax cash savings under the MACRS tax rule. The $4.66 million system can be depreciated over the six-year period. For example, the depreciation in year 1 of $932,000 reduces net income by that amount. Since the company does not have to pay taxes on the $1 million, at their tax rate of 34 percent they end up saving an additional $316,880 in year 1. Finally, Sophie calculated the net savings for each year.

Sophie used MYK's cost of capital of 10 percent to calculate the net present value (NPV) of the investment, which is over $3 million. The internal rate of return (IRR) is a respectable 26 percent. Sophie realized how advantageous it would be for the company to borrow the money (at 10-percent interest rates) in order to produce a 26-percent return on that borrowed money. In addition, payback (the point at which the initial cost is recovered) occurs in the fourth year. NPV and IRR are calculated as shown in Exhibit 12.

Sophie presented the system and its cost-benefit calculations to top management. Challenges to her estimates (various "what-if" scenarios) were plugged into the Excel model so that management could see the effect of the changed assumptions. This spreadsheet analysis was intended to ensure a positive return of the new system under future uncertainty.

Exhibit 12

Economic Feasibility Study for a New Information System

	Outlay	Years					
	0	1	2	3	4	5	6
Initial outlay costs (I)							
Initial system design	$ 1,800,000						
Hardware	1,800,000						
Software	375,000						
Training	185,000						
Site preparation	250,000						
Conversion	250,000						
Total	$ 4,660,000						
Recurring costs							
Hardware expansion			$ 250,000	$ 290,000	$ 330,000	$ 370,000	$ 390,000
Software			160,000	210,000	230,000	245,000	260,000
Systems maintenance		$ 70,000	120,000	130,000	140,000	150,000	160,000
Personnel costs		485,000	800,000	900,000	1,000,000	1,100,000	1,300,000
Communication charges		99,000	160,000	180,000	200,000	220,000	250,000
Overhead		310,000	420,000	490,000	560,000	600,000	640,000
Total		$ 964,000	$ 1,910,000	$ 2,200,000	$ 2,460,000	$ 2,685,000	$ 3,000,000
Cash savings							
Clerical cost savings		$ 500,000	$ 1,110,000	$ 1,350,000	$ 1,500,000	1,700,000	1,950,000
Working capital savings		1,000,000	1,200,000	1,500,000	1,500,000	1,500,000	1,500,000
Increased sales and profits			500,000	900,000	1,200,000	1,500,000	1,800,000
Reduced warehouse costs			400,000	800,000	1,200,000	1,600,000	2,000,000
Total		$ 1,500,000	$ 3,210,000	$ 4,550,000	$ 5,400,000	$ 6,300,000	$ 7,250,000
Cash savings minus recurring costs		536,000	1,300,000	2,350,000	2,940,000	3,615,000	4,250,000
Less income taxes (34%)	34%	(182,240)	(442,000)	(799,000)	(999,600)	(1,229,100)	(1,445,000)
Cash savings (net of tax)		$ 353,760	$ 858,000	$ 1,551,000	$ 1,940,400	$ 2,385,900	$ 2,805,000
Tax shield from depreciation		316,880	507,008	304,205	182,206	182,206	91,895
Net cash inflows (net savings) after taxes	$ (4,660,000)	$ 670,640	$ 1,365,008	$ 1,855,205	$ 2,122,606	$ 2,568,106	$ 2,896,895

Tax savings from depreciation deduction

Year	*MACRS*	*Depreciation*	*Tax savings*
1	20.00%	$ 932,000	$ 316,880
2	32.00%	1,491,200	507,008
3	19.20%	894,720	304,205
4	11.50%	535,900	182,206
5	11.50%	535,900	182,206
6	5.80%	270,280	91,895

Net present value calculations @ a cost of capital of 10%

Year	*Net savings*	*PV factor*	*PV*
0	$ (4,660,000)	1.0000	$ (4,660,000)
1	670,640	0.9091	609,679
2	1,365,008	0.8265	1,128,179
3	1,855,205	0.7513	1,393,815
4	2,122,606	0.6830	1,449,740
5	2,568,106	0.6209	1,594,537
6	2,896,895	0.5645	1,635,297
		NPV	$ 3,151,248
		IRR	26.26%

¶ 1351 Capital Budgeting and Inflation

The accuracy of capital budgeting decisions depends on the accuracy of the data regarding cash inflows and outflows. For example, failure to incorporate price-level changes due to inflation in capital budgeting situations can result in errors in the predicting of cash flows and, thus, in incorrect decisions.

Typically, an analyst has two options when dealing with a capital budgeting situation with inflation: (1) either restate the cash flows in nominal terms and discount them at a nominal cost of capital (minimum required rate of return), or (2) restate both the cash flows and cost of capital in constant terms and discount the constant cash flows at a constant cost of capital. The two methods are basically equivalent.

Example 28: A company has the following projected cash flows estimated in real terms:

Real Cash Flows (000s)

Period	0	1	2	3
	−100	35	50	30

The nominal cost of capital is 15 percent. Assume that inflation is projected at 10 percent a year. Then the first cash flow for year 1, which is $35,000 in current dollars, will be 35,000 × 1.10 = $38,500 in year 1 dollars. Similarly, the cash flow for year 2 will be 50,000 × $(1.10)^2$ = $60,500 in year 2 dollars, and so on. If one discounts these nominal cash flows at the 15 percent nominal cost of capital, one has the following net present value (NPV) in thousands of dollars:

Period	*Cash Flows*	*T_3 (Table 3)*	*Present Values*
0	−100	1.000	−100.00
1	38.5	.870	33.50
2	60.5	.756	45.74
3	39.9	.658	26.25
		NPV=	5.49 or $5,490

Instead of converting the cash-flow forecasts into nominal terms, one could convert the cost of capital into real terms by using the following formula:

$$\text{Real cost of capital} = \frac{1 + \text{nominal cost of capital}}{1 + \text{inflation rate}} - 1$$

In the example, this gives:

Real cost of capital = (1 + .15)/(1 + .10) − 1

= 1.15/1.10 − 1

= 1.045 − 1

= .045 or 4.5%

One will obtain the same answer except for rounding errors ($5,490 vs. $5,580).

Period	*Cash Flows*	$T_3 = 1/(1+.045)^n$	*Present Values*
0	−100	1.000	−100.00
1	35	1/(1+.045)=.957	33.50
2	50	1/(1.045)2=.916	45.80
3	30	1/(1.045)3=.876	26.28
		NPV=	5.58 or $5,580

¶ 1355 Risk Analysis in Capital Budgeting

Risk analysis is important in making capital investment decisions because of the large amount of capital involved and the long-term nature of the investments being considered. The higher the risk associated with a proposed project, the greater the rate of return that must be earned on the project to compensate for that risk. Since different investment projects involve different risks, it is important to incorporate risk into the analysis of capital budgeting. There are several methods for incorporating risk, including:

1. Probability distributions.
2. Risk-adjusted discount rate.
3. Certainty equivalent.
4. Simulation.
5. Sensitivity analysis.
6. Decision trees (or probability trees).

.01 Probability Distributions

Expected values of a probability distribution may be computed. Before any capital budgeting method is applied, compute the expected cash inflows, or in some cases, the expected life of the asset.

Example 29: A firm is considering a $30,000 investment in equipment that will generate cash savings from operating costs. The following estimates regarding cash savings and useful life, along with their respective probabilities of occurrence, have been made:

Annual cash savings		*Useful life*	
$ 6,000	0.2	4 years	0.2
$ 8,000	0.5	5 years	0.6
$10,000	0.3	6 years	0.2

Then, the expected annual saving is:

\$6,000 (0.2)	=	\$1,200
\$8,000 (0.5)	=	4,000
\$10,000 (0.3)	=	3,000
		\$8,200

The expected useful life is:

4 (0.2)	=	0.8
5 (0.6)	=	3.0
6 (0.2)	=	1.2
		5.0 years

The expected NPV is computed as follows (assuming a 10-percent cost of capital):

$NPV = PV - I = \$8,200\ T_4\ (10\%,5) - \$30,000$

$= \$8,200\ (3.7908) - \$30,000 = \$31,085 = \$1,085$

The expected IRR is computed as follows: By definition, at IRR, I=PV

$\$30,000 = \$8,200\ T_4\ (r,5)$

$$T_4\ (r,5) = \frac{\$30,000}{\$8,200} = 3.6585$$

Which is about halfway between 10 and 12 percent in Table 4 in Appendix B, so that we can estimate the rate to be ~ 11 percent. Therefore, the equipment should be purchased, since (1) NPV = \$1,085, which is positive, and/or (2) IRR = 11 percent, which is greater than the cost of capital of 10 percent.

.02 Risk-Adjusted Discount Rate

This method of risk analysis adjusts the cost of capital (or discount rate) upward as projects become riskier. Therefore, by increasing the discount rate from 10 percent to 15 percent, the expected cash flow from the investment must be relatively larger or the increased discount rate will generate a negative NPV, and the proposed acquisition/investment would be turned down.

The use of the risk-adjusted discount rate is based on the assumption that investors demand higher returns for riskier projects. The expected cash flows are discounted at the risk-adjusted discount rate and then the usual capital budgeting criteria such as NPV and IRR are applied.

Example 30: A firm is considering an investment project with an expected life of three years. It requires an initial investment of

$35,000. The firm estimates the following data in each of the next three years:

After-tax Cash Inflow	*Probability*
$ 5,000	0.2
$10,000	0.3
$30,000	0.3
$50,000	0.2

Assuming a risk-adjusted required rate of return (after taxes) of 20 percent is appropriate for the investment projects of this level or risk, compute the risk-adjusted NPV.

First,

A = $5,000(0.2) + $10,000(0.3) + $30,000(0.3) + $50,000(0.2) = $23,000

The expected NPV = $23,000 T_4 (20%,3) – $35,000

= 23,000 (2.107) – $35,000 = $48,461 – $35,000 = $13,461

.03 Certainty Equivalent

The certainty equivalent approach to risk analysis is drawn directly from the concept of utility theory. This method forces the decision maker to specify at what point the firm is indifferent to the choice between a certain sum of money and the expected value of a risky sum.

Once certainty equivalent coefficients are obtained, they are multiplied by the original cash flow to obtain the equivalent certain cash flow. Then, the accept-or-reject decision is made, using the normal capital budgeting criteria. The risk-free rate of return is used as the discount rate under the NPV method and as the cutoff rate under the IRR method.

Example 31: XYZ, Inc., with a 14 percent cost of capital after taxes is considering a project with an expected life of four years. The project requires an initial certain cash outlay of $50,000. The expected cash inflows and certainty equivalent coefficients are as follows:

Year	*After-Tax Cash Flow ($)*	*Certainty Equivalent Coefficient*
1	10,000	0.95
2	15,000	0.80
3	20,000	0.70
4	25,000	0.60

The risk-free rate of return is five percent; compute the NPV and IRR. The equivalent certain cash inflows are obtained as follows:

Year	After-Tax Cash Inflow ($)	Certainty Equivalent Coefficient	Equivalent Certain Cash Inflow ($)	PV at 5%	PV ($)
1	10,000	0.95	9,500	0.9524	9,048
2	15,000	0.80	12,000	0.9070	10,884
3	20,000	0.70	14,000	0.8638	12,093
4	25,000	0.60	15,000	0.8227	12,341
					44,366

NPV = $44,366 − $50,000 = −$5,634

By trial and error, we could obtain four percent as the IRR. Therefore, the project should be rejected, since (1) NPV = −$5,634, which is negative, and/or (2) IRR = four percent, which is less than the risk-free rate of five percent.

.04 Simulation

This risk analysis method is frequently called Monte Carlo simulation. It requires that a probability distribution be constructed for each of the important variables affecting the project's cash flows.

.05 Sensitivity Analysis

Forecasts of many calculated NPVs under various alternative functions are compared to see how sensitive NPV is to changing conditions. It may be found that a certain variable or group of variables, once their assumptions are changed or relaxed, drastically alters the NPV. This results in a much riskier asset than was originally forecast.

.06 Decision Trees

Some firms use decision trees (probability trees) to evaluate the risk of capital budgeting proposals. A decision tree is a graphical method of showing the sequence of possible outcomes. A capital budgeting tree would show the cash flows and NPV of the project under different possible circumstances. The decision tree method has the following advantages: (1) It visually lays out all the possible outcomes of the proposed project and makes management aware of the adverse possibilities, and (2) the conditional nature of successive years' cash flows can be expressly depicted.

The primary disadvantage is that most problems are too complex to permit year-by-year depiction. For example, for a 3-year project with three possible outcomes following each year, there are 27 paths. For a 10-year project (again with three possible outcomes following each year) there will be about 60,000 paths.

Example 32: A firm has an opportunity to invest in a machine that will last two years, initially cost $125,000, and has the following estimated possible after-tax cash inflow pattern: In year 1, there is a 40-percent chance that the after-tax cash inflow will be $45,000, a 25-percent chance that it will be $65,000, and a 35-percent chance that it will be $90,000. In year 2, the after-tax cash inflow possibilities depend on the cash inflow that occurs in year 1; that is, the year 2 after-tax cash inflows are conditional probabilities.

Assume that the firm's after-tax cost of capital is 12 percent. The estimated conditional after-tax cash inflows (ATCI) and probabilities are given below.

If ATCI1 = $45,000		*If ATCI1 = $65,000*		*If ATCI1 = $90,000*	
ATCI2($)	*Probability*	*ATCI2($)*	*Probability*	*ATCI2($)*	*Probability*
30,000	0.3	80,000	0.2	90,000	0.1
60,000	0.4	90,000	0.6	100,000	0.8
90,000	0.3	100,000	0.2	110,000	0.1

Then the decision tree that shows the possible after-tax cash inflow in each year, including the conditional nature of the year 2 cash inflow and its probabilities, can be depicted as follows:

Time 0	*Time 1*	*Time 2*	*NPV at 12%*	*Joint Probability*	*Expected NPV*
		$ 30,000	– $60,905[a]	0.12[b]	– $7,309
	$45,000	$ 60,000	– $36,995	0.16	– 5,919
		$ 90,000	– $13,085	0.12	– 1,570
		$ 80,000	– $3,195	0.05	– 160
– $125,000	$65,000	$ 90,000	$4,775	0.15	716
		$100,000	$12,745	0.05	637
		$ 90,000	$27,100	0.035	949
	$90,000	$100,000	$35,070	0.28	9,820
		$110,000	$43,040	0.035	1,506
				1.00	– 1,330

[a] NPV = PV – I $= \dfrac{\$45{,}000}{(1+0.12)} + \dfrac{\$30{,}000}{(1+0.12)^2} - \$125{,}000$

$= \$45{,}000\ T_3\,(12\%,1) + \$30{,}000\ T_3\,(12\%,2) - \$125{,}000$

$= \$45{,}000\,(0.893) + \$30{,}000\,(0.797) - \$125{,}000$

$= \$40{,}185 + \$23{,}910 - \$125{,}000 = -\$60{,}905$

[b] Joint probability = (0.4)(0.3) = 0.120

The last column shows the calculation of expected NPV, which is the weighted average of the individual path NPVs where the weights are the path probabilities. In this example, the expected NPV of the project is –$1,330, and the project should be rejected.

.07 Correlation of Cash Flows over Time

When cash inflows are independent from period to period, it is fairly easy to measure the overall risk of an investment proposal. In some cases, however, especially with the introduction of a new product, the cash flows experienced in early years affect the size of the cash flows in later years. This is called the time dependence of cash flows, and it has the effect of increasing the risk of the project over time.

Example 33: Janday Corporation's after-tax cash inflows (ATCI) are time-dependent, so that year 1 results (ATCI1) affect the flows in year 2 (ATCI2) as follows:

If ATCI1 is $8,000 with a 40-percent probability, the distribution for ATCI2 is:

0.3	$ 5,000
0.5	$10,000
0.2	$15,000

If ATCI1 is $15,000 with a 50-percent probability, the distribution for ATCI2 is:

0.3	$10,000
0.6	$20,000
0.1	$30,000

If ATCI1 is $20,000 with a 10-percent probability, the distribution for ATCI2 is:

0.1	$15,000
0.8	$40,000
0.1	$50,000

The project requires an initial investment of $20,000 and the risk-free rate of capital is 10 percent.

The company uses the expected NPV from decision tree analysis to determine whether the project should be accepted. The analysis is as follows:

Time 0	*Time 1*	*Time 2*	*NPV at 10%*	*Joint Probability*	*Expected NPV*
		$ 5,000	– $8,595[a]	0.12[b]	– $1,031
	$ 8,000	$ 10,000	– $4,463	0.2	– 893
		$ 15,000	– $331	0.08	– 26
		$ 10,000	$1,901	0.15	285
– $20,000	$15,000	$ 20,000	$10,165	0.30	3,050
		$ 30,000	$18,429	0.05	921
		$ 15,000	$10,576	0.01	106
	$20,000	$ 40,000	$31,238	0.08	2,499
		$ 50,000	$39,502	0.01	395
				1.00	$5,306

[a] NPV=PV – I = $8,000 T_3 (10,1) + $5,000 T_3 (10,2) – $20,000
= $8,000 (0.9091) + $5,000 (0.8264) – $20,000 = – $8,595

[b] Joint probability of the first path=(0.4) (0.3)=0.12

Since the NPV is positive ($5,306), Janday Corporation should accept the project.

.08 *Normal Distribution and NPV Analysis*

With the assumption of independence of cash flows over time, the expected NPV would be:

$$NPV = PV - I$$

$$= \sum_{t=1}^{n} \frac{\overline{A_t}}{(1+r)^t} - I$$

The standard deviation of NPVs is:

$$\sigma = \sqrt{\sum_{t=1}^{n} \frac{\sigma_t^2}{(1+r)^{2t}}}$$

The expected value ($\bar{A}$) and the standard deviation (σ) give a considerable amount of information by which to assess the risk of an investment project. If the probability distribution is normal, some probability statement regarding the project's NPV can be made. For example, the probability of a project providing NPV of less or greater than zero can be computed by standardizing the normal variate x as follows:

$$z = \frac{x - NPV}{\sigma}$$

Where:

x = the outcome to be found

NPV = the expected NPV

z = the standardized normal variate whose probability value can be found in Table 5 in Appendix B.

Example 34: Assume an investment with the following data:

	Period 1	*Period 2*	*Period 3*
Expected cash inflow ($\bar{A}$)	$5,000	$4,000	$3,000
Standard deviation (σ)	1,140	1,140	1,140

Assume that the firm's cost of capital is eight percent and the initial investment is $9,000. Then the expected NPV is:

$$NPV = PV - I$$

$$= \frac{\$5,000}{(1 + 0.08)} + \frac{\$4,000}{(1 + 0.08)^2} + \frac{\$3,000}{(1 + 0.08)^3} - \$9,000$$

$= \$5{,}000\ T_3\ (8\%,1) + \$4{,}000\ T_3\ (8\%,2) + \$3{,}000\ T_3\ (8\%,3) - \$9{,}000$

$= \$5{,}000(0.9259) + \$4{,}000\ (0.8573) + \$3{,}000(0.7938) - \$9{,}000$

$= \$4{,}630 + \$3{,}429 + \$2{,}381 - \$9{,}000 = \$1{,}440$

The standard deviation about the expected NPV is:

$$\sigma = \sqrt{\sum_{t=1}^{n} \frac{\sigma_t^2}{(1+r)^{2t}}} = \sqrt{\frac{\$1{,}140^2}{(1+0.08)^2} + \frac{\$1{,}140^2}{(1+0.08)^4} + \frac{\$1{,}140^2}{(1+0.08)^6}} = \sqrt{\$2{,}788{,}411} = \$1{,}670$$

The probability that the PV is less than zero is then:

$$z = \frac{x - NPV}{\sigma} = \frac{0 - \$1{,}440}{\$1{,}670} = -0.86$$

The area of normal distribution that is z standard deviations to the left or right of the mean may be found in Table 5 in Appendix B. A value of z equal to -0.86 is 0.8051. Therefore, there is approximately a 19-percent chance (1 − 0.8051 = 0.1949) that the project's NPV will be zero or less. Putting it another way, there is a 19-percent chance that the IRR of the project will be less than the risk-free rate.

.09 CAPM in Capital Budgeting

Portfolio considerations play an important role in the overall capital budgeting process. Through diversification, a firm can stabilize earnings, reduce risk, and thereby increase the market price of the firm's stock. The beta coefficient can be used for this purpose.

The capital asset pricing model (CAPM) can be used to determine the appropriate cost of capital. The NPV method uses the cost of capital as the rate to discount future cash flows. The IRR method uses the cost of capital as the cutoff rate. The required rate of return, or cost of capital according to the CAPM, or security market line (SML), is equal to the risk-free rate of return (r_f) plus a risk premium equal to the firm's beta coefficient (b) times the market risk premium ($r_m - r_f$):

$$r_j = r_f + b\,(r_m - r_f)$$

Example 35: A project has the following projected cash flows:

Year 0	*Year 1*	*Year 2*	*Year 3*
− $400	$300	$200	$100

The estimated beta for the project is 1.5. The market return is 12 percent, and the risk-free rate is six percent. Then the firm's cost of capital, or required rate of return is:

$$r_j = r_f + b\,(r_m - r_f) = 6\% + 1.5(12\% - 6\%) = 15\%$$

The project's NPV can be computed using 15% as the discount rate:

Year	*Cash Flow ($)*	*PV at 15%*	*PV ($)*
0	– 400	1.000	– 400
1	300	0.870	261
2	200	0.756	151
3	100	0.658	66
		NPV=	78

The project should be accepted since its NPV of $78 is positive. Also, the project's IRR can be computed by trial and error. It is almost 30 percent, which exceeds the cost of capital of 15 percent. Therefore, by that standard the project should also be accepted.

¶ 1361 Capital Budgeting Software

There are many software packages such as ready-to-use Excel worksheets, called templates. The following are samples of such software.

1. Investment-Calc PRO 2002Version 5.0 (www.mlnsoft.com/software/most_popular/index.php)

With Investment-Calc PRO Version 5.0 you can create and manipulate ready to use cash flow Excel worksheets to analyse business, capital, share, lease purchase cash flow forecasts for internal use, for acquisitions, and for calculating best valuation for sale. The program calculates Net Present Values, Internal Rate of Return, Accounting Rate of Return, Share Valuation and Economic Valuations over any forecast period to 15, 20, 30 or 50 years. Investment-Calc incorporates self generating tables that calculate yearly asset depreciation values for any yearly capital purchase program, prepares tax calculations, calculates annual lease and loan finance costs and repayments, compounds money values, and transfers all values automatically into the user's spreadsheets to help save time.

2. Budget-Calc PRO 2002 (www.mlnsoft.com/software/most_popular/index.php)

Budget-Calc PRO provides ten budgeting templates plus dynamic (self-adjusting) Excel tables for depreciation and loan amortization for preparing investment forecasts, profit/loss budgets, cash flow forecasts, capital budgets, sales, 91 day AP/AR forecasts, and annual employee productivity plans quickly and accurately. (FASB 141 and 142 goodwill & intangible variable depreciation tables included).

Part 5

Financial Statement Analysis and Financial Metrics

Chapter 14
Financial Statement Analysis

¶ 1401 How Financial Statement Analysis is Used

Financial statement analysis attempts to answer the following basic questions:

1. How well is the business doing?
2. What are its strengths?
3. What are its weaknesses?
4. How does it fare in the industry?
5. Is the business improving or deteriorating?

Financial statement analysis tools that one can use in evaluating the firm's present and future financial condition include horizontal, vertical, and ratio analysis, which give relative measures of the performance and financial condition of the company.

The analysis of financial statements means different things to different people. It is of interest to creditors, present and prospective investors, and the firm's own management.

A *creditor* is primarily interested in the firm's debt-paying ability. A short-term creditor such as a vendor or supplier is ultimately concerned with the firm's ability to pay its bills and, therefore, wants to be assured that the firm is liquid. A long-term creditor such as a bank or bondholder, on the other hand, is interested in the firm's ability to repay interest and principal on borrowed funds.

An *investor* is interested in the present and future level of return (earnings) and risk (liquidity, debt, and activity). An investor evaluates a firm's stock based on an examination of its financial statements. This evaluation considers overall financial health, economic and political conditions, industry factors, and the future outlook of the company. The analysis attempts to ascertain whether the stock is overpriced, underpriced, or priced in proportion to its market value. A stock is valuable to an investor only if they can predict the future financial performance of the business. Financial statement analysis gives one much of the data one will need to forecast earnings and dividends.

Management must relate the analysis to all of the questions raised by creditors and investors, since these interested parties must be satisfied for the firm to obtain capital as needed.

¶ 1405 Horizontal and Vertical Analysis

.01 Horizontal Analysis

Comparison of two or more years' financial data is known as *horizontal analysis (trend analysis).* Horizontal analysis concentrates on the trend in the accounts in dollar and percentage terms over the years. It is typically presented in comparative financial statements (see MYRA, Inc. financial data in Exhibits 1 and 2). In annual reports, comparative financial data are usually shown for five years.

Through horizontal analysis one can pinpoint areas of wide divergence requiring investigation. For example, in the income statement shown in Exhibit 2, the significant rise in sales returns taken with the reduction in sales for 20X0-20X1 should cause concern. One might compare these results with those of competitors.

It is essential to present both the dollar amount of change and the percentage of change, since the use of one without the other may result in erroneous conclusions. The interest expense from 20X0-20X1 went up by 100.0 percent, but this represented only $1,000 and may not need further investigation. In a similar vein, a large number change might cause a small percentage change and not be of any great importance.

.02 Vertical Analysis

Key changes and trends can also be highlighted by the use of *common-size statements.* A common-size statement is one that shows the separate items appearing on it in percentage terms. Preparation of common-size statements is known as vertical analysis. In *vertical analysis,* a material financial statement item is used as a base value, and all other accounts on the financial statement are compared to it. In the balance sheet, for example, total assets equal 100 percent. Each asset is stated as a percentage of total assets. Similarly, total liabilities and stockholders' equity is assigned 100 percent with a given liability or equity account stated as a percentage of the total liabilities and stockholders' equity, respectively. Exhibit 3 shows a common-size income statement based on the data provided in Exhibit 2.

Placing all assets in common-size form clearly shows the relative importance of the current assets as compared to the noncurrent assets. It also shows that significant changes have taken place in the composition of the current assets over the last year. Notice, for example, that receivables have increased in relative importance and that cash has declined in relative importance. The deterioration in the cash position may be a result of inability to collect from customers.

For the income statement, 100 percent is assigned to net sales with all other revenue and expense accounts related to it. It is possible to see at a glance how each dollar of sales is distributed between the various costs, expenses, and profits. For example, notice from Exhibit 3 that 64.8 cents of every dollar of sales was needed to cover cost of goods sold in 20X2, as compared to only 57.3 cents in the prior year; also notice that only 9.9 cents out of every dollar of sales remained for profits in 20X2—down from 13.6 cents in the prior year.

One should also compare the vertical percentages of the business to those of the competition and to the industry norms. Then one can determine how the company fares in the industry.

Exhibit 1

MYRA, Inc.
Comparative Balance Sheet (in Millions of Dollars)

December 31, 20X2, 20X1, 20X0

				Increase/Decrease		*% Increase/Decrease*	
	20X2	*20X1*	*20X0*	*20X2-20X1*	*20X1-20X0*	*20X2-20X1*	*20X1-20X0*
Assets							
Current Assets:							
Cash	$ 28	$ 36	$ 36	(8.00)	0.00	−22.2%	0.0%
Short-term Investments	22	15	7	7.00	8.00	46.7%	114.3%
Accounts Receivable	21	16	10	5.00	6.00	31.3%	60.0%
Inventory	53	46	49	7.00	(3.00)	15.2%	−6.1%
Total Current Assets	124	113	102	11.00	11.00	9.7%	10.8%
Plant And Equip.	103	91	83	12.00	8.00	13.2%	9.6%
Total Assets	227	204	185	23.00	19.00	11.3%	10.3%
Liabilities							
Current Liabilities	56	50	51	6.00	(1.00)	12.0%	−2.0%
Long-term debt	83	74	69	9.00	5.00	12.2%	7.2%
Total Liabilities	139	124	120	15.00	4.00	12.1%	3.3%
Stockholders' Equity							
Common Stock, $10 par, 4,600 shares	46	46	46	0.00	0.00	0.0%	0.0%
Retained Earnings	42	34	19	8.00	15.00	23.5%	78.9%
Total Stockholders' Equity	88	80	65	8.00	15.00	10.0%	23.1%
Total Liabilities and Stockholders' Equity	$227	$204	$185	$23.00	$19.00	11.3%	10.3%

Exhibit 2

MYRA, Inc.

Comparative Income Statement (in Millions of Dollars)

For the Years Ended December 31, 20X2, 20X1, 20X0

				Increase/Decrease		*% Increase/Decrease*	
	20X2	*20X1*	*20X0*	*20X2-20X1*	*20X1-20X0*	*20X2-20X1*	*20X1-20X0*
Sales	$98.3	$120.0	$56.6	($21.7)	$63.4	−18.1%	112.0%
Sales Return & Allowances	18.0	10.0	4.0	8.0	6.0	80.0%	150.0%
Net Sales	80.3	110.0	52.6	(29.7)	57.4	−27.0%	109.1%
Cost of Goods Sold	52.0	63.0	28.0	(11.0)	35.0	−17.5%	125.0%
Gross Profit	28.3	47.0	24.6	(18.7)	22.4	−39.8%	91.1%
Operating Expenses							
Selling Expenses	12.0	13.0	11.0	(1.0)	2.0	−7.7%	18.2%
Administrative Expenses	5.0	8.0	3.0	(3.0)	5.0	−37.5%	166.7%
Total Operating Expenses	$17.0	$ 21.0	$14.0	($4.0)	$ 7.0	−19.0%	50.0%
Income from Operations	$11.3	$ 26.0	$10.6	($14.7)	$15.4	−56.5%	145.3%
Nonoperating Income	4.0	1.0	2.0	3.0	(1.0)	300.0%	−50.0%
Income before Interest & Taxes	15.3	27.0	12.6	(11.7)	14.4	−43.3%	114.3%
Interest Expense	2.0	2.0	1.0	0.0	1.0	0.0%	100.0%
Income before Taxes	13.3	25.0	11.6	(11.7)	13.4	−46.8%	115.5%
Income Taxes (40%)	5.3	10.0	4.6	(4.7)	5.4	−46.8%	115.5%
Net Income	$ 8.0	$ 15.0	$ 7.0	($7.0)	$ 8.0	−46.8%	115.5%

Exhibit 3

Income Statement and Common-Size Analysis MYRA, Inc. (in Millions of Dollars)

For the Years Ended December 31, 20X2 and 20X1

	20X2 Amount	*%*	*20X1 Amount*	*%*
Sales	$98.30	122.40%	$120.00	109.10%
Sales Return & Allowances	18.00	22.40%	10.00	9.10%
Net Sales	80.30	100.00%	110.00	100.00%
Cost of Goods Sold	52.00	64.80%	63.00	57.30%
Gross Profit	28.30	35.20%	47.00	42.70%
Operating Expenses				
Selling Expenses	12.00	14.90%	13.00	11.80%
Administrative Expenses	5.00	6.20%	8.00	7.30%
Total Operating Expenses	$17.00	21.20%	$ 21.00	19.10%
Income from Operations	$11.30	14.10%	$ 26.00	23.60%
Nonoperating Income	4.00	5.00%	1.00	0.90%
Income before Interest & Taxes	15.30	19.10%	27.00	24.50%
Interest Expense	2.00	2.50%	2.00	1.80%
Income before Taxes	13.30	16.60%	25.00	22.70%
Income Taxes (40%)	5.30	6.60%	10.00	9.10%
Net Income	$ 8.00	9.90%	$ 15.00	13.60%

¶ 1411 Calculating and Interpreting Financial Ratios

Horizontal and vertical analysis compares one figure to another within the same category. It is also vital to compare two figures applicable to different categories. This is accomplished by ratio analysis. Financial ratios, along with common-size and trend statements, provide powerful tools for tracking a company's performance over time, for making comparisons among different companies, and assessing compliance with contractual benchmarks. This section discusses how to calculate the various financial ratios and how to interpret them. The results of the ratio analysis allow one to:

1. Appraise the position of a business,
2. Identify trouble spots that need attention, and
3. Provide the basis for making projections and forecasts about the course of future operations.

Think of ratios as measures of the relative health or sickness of a business. Just as a doctor takes readings of a patient's temperature, blood pressure, heart rate, etc., one can take readings of a business's liquidity, profitability, leverage, efficiency in using assets, and market value. Whereas the doctor compares the readings to generally accepted guidelines such as a temperature of 98.6 degrees as normal, one compares the ratios to the accepted norms.

To obtain useful conclusions from the ratios, one must make two comparisons:

1. *Industry (benchmark) comparison.* This will allow one to answer the question "how does a business fare in the industry?" One must compare the company's ratios to those of competing companies in the industry or with industry standards (averages). One can obtain industry norms from financial services such as:

    a. *Risk Management Association (RMA).* RMA, also known as Robert Morris Associates, has been compiling statistical data on financial statements for more than 75 years. The RMA Annual Statement Studies provide statistical data from more than 150,000 actual companies on many key financial ratios, such as gross margin, operating margins, and return on equity and assets. If one wishes to put real authority into the industry average numbers that one's company is comparing to, the Statement Studies are the way to go. They're organized by SIC codes, and one can buy the financial statement studies for one's industry for $59.95 in report form or over the Internet (www.rmahq.org).

    b. *Dun and Bradstreet.* Dun and Bradstreet publishes Industry Norms and Key Business Ratios, which covers over 1 million firms in over 800 lines of business.

    c. *Value Line.* Value Line Investment Service provides financial data and rates stocks of over 1,700 firms.

    d. *The Department of Commerce.* The Department of Commerce Financial Report provides financial statement data and includes a variety of ratios and industry-wide common-size vertical financial statements.

    e. *Others.* Standard and Poor's, Moody's Investment Service, and various brokerages compile industry studies. Further, numerous online services such as AOL and MSN Money Central, to name a few, also provide these data.

2. *Trend analysis.* To see how the business is doing over time, one can compare a given ratio for one company over several years to see the direction of financial health or operational performance. To do a trend analysis, one simply plots a ratio over time, as

shown in Exhibit 4. This graph shows the rate of return on common equity (ROE) of XYZ Company versus the industry average. All the other ratios could be analyzed similarly.

Exhibit 4

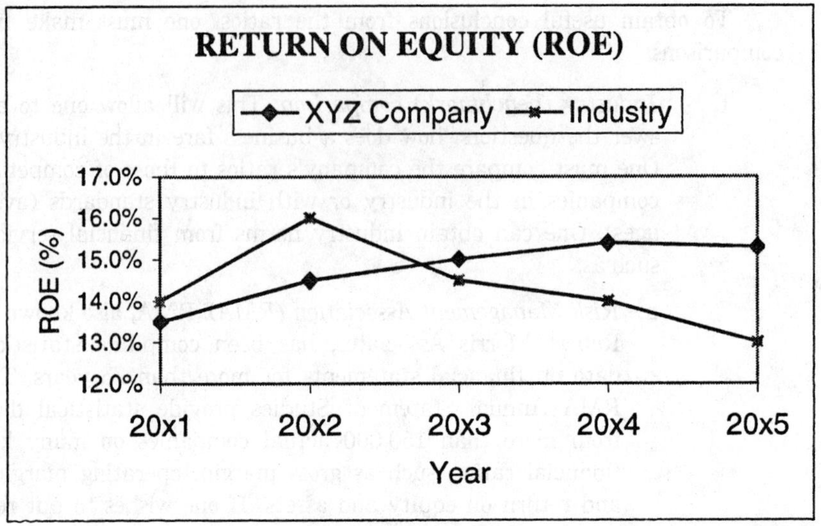

Financial ratios can be grouped into the following types: liquidity, asset utilization (activity), solvency (leverage and debt service), profitability, and market value.

.01 Liquidity

Liquidity is the firm's ability to satisfy maturing short-term debt. Liquidity is crucial to carrying out the business, especially during periods of adversity. It relates to the short term, typically a period of one year or less. Poor liquidity might lead to a higher cost of financing and an inability to pay bills and dividends. The three basic measures of liquidity are (a) net working capital, (b) the current ratio, and (c) the quick (acid-test) ratio.

The numbers in the following discussion are taken from Exhibits 1 and 2.

Net working capital equals current assets minus current liabilities. Net working capital for 20X2 is:

Net working capital = current assets − current liabilities

= $124 − $56

= $68

In 20X1, net working capital was $63. The rise over the year is favorable.

The *current ratio* equals current assets divided by current liabilities. The ratio reflects the company's ability to satisfy current debt from current assets.

$$\text{Current ratio} = \frac{\text{Current assets}}{\text{Current liabilities}}$$

For 20X2, the current ratio is:

$$\frac{\$124}{\$56} = 2.21$$

In 20X1, the current ratio was 2.26. The ratio's decline over the year points to a slight reduction in liquidity.

General rule: A declining ratio might be a sign of a deteriorating liquidity problem. On the other hand, it might be the result of a paring out of obsolete inventory or other stagnant assets.

A more stringent liquidity test can be found in the quick (acid-test) ratio. Inventory and prepaid expenses are excluded from the total of current assets, leaving only the more liquid (or quick) assets to be divided by current liabilities.

$$\text{Acid-test ratio} = \frac{\text{Cash + Short-term investments + Accounts receivable}}{\text{Current liabilities}}$$

The quick ratio for 20X2 is:

$$\frac{\$28+\$21+\$22}{\$56} = 1.27$$

In 20X1, the ratio was 1.34. A small reduction in the ratio over the period points to less liquidity.

The overall liquidity trend shows a slight deterioration as reflected in the lower current and quick ratios, although it is better than the industry norms (see Exhibit 5 at ¶ 1411.07 for industry averages). However, a mitigating factor is the increase in net working capital.

.02 Asset Utilization

Asset utilization (activity, turnover) ratios reflect the way in which a company uses its assets to obtain revenue and profit. One example is how well receivables are turning into cash. The higher the ratio, the more efficiently the business manages its assets.

Accounts receivable ratios comprise the accounts receivable turnover and the average collection period.

The *accounts receivable turnover* provides the number of times accounts receivable are collected in the year. Dividing net credit sales by average accounts receivable produces the accounts receivable turnover. One can calculate average accounts receivable by the average accounts receivable balance during a period.

$$\text{Accounts receivable turnover} = \frac{\text{Net credit sales}}{\text{Average accounts receivable}}$$

For 20X2, the average accounts receivable is:

$$\frac{\$21+\$16}{2} = \$18.5$$

The accounts receivable turnover for 20X2 is:,

$$\frac{\$80.3}{\$18.5} = 4.34$$

In 20X1, the turnover was 8.46. There is a sharp reduction in the turnover rate pointing to a collection problem.

The average collection period, also called days sales outstanding (DSO), is the length of time it takes to collect receivables. It represents the number of days receivables are held.

$$\text{Average collection period} = \frac{\text{365 days}}{\text{Accounts receivable turnover}}$$

In 20X2, the collection period is:

$$\frac{365}{4.34} = \text{84.1 days}$$

It takes this firm about 84 days to convert receivables to cash. In 20X1, the collection period was 43.1 days. The significant lengthening of the collection period may be a cause for some concern. The long collection period may be a result of the presence of many doubtful accounts, or it may be a result of poor credit management.

Inventory ratios are useful, especially when a buildup in inventory exists. Inventory ties up cash. Holding large amounts of inventory can result in lost opportunities for profit as well as increased storage costs. Before extending credit or lending money, one should examine the firm's *inventory turnover* and *average age of inventory.*

$$\text{Inventory turnover} = \frac{\text{Costs of goods sold}}{\text{Average inventory}}$$

The inventory turnover for 20X2 is:

$$\frac{\$52}{\$49.5} = 1.05$$

For 20X1, the turnover was 1.33.

$$\text{Average age of inventory} = \frac{365}{\text{Inventory turnover}}$$

In 20X2, the average age is:

$$\frac{365}{1.05} = 347.6 \text{ days}$$

In the previous year, the average age was 274.4 days.

The reduction in the turnover and increase in inventory age points to a longer holding of inventory. One should ask why the inventory is not selling as quickly.

The *operating cycle* is the number of days it takes to convert inventory and receivables to cash.

Operating cycle = Average collection period + Average age of inventory

In 20X2, the operating cycle is:

$$84.1 \text{ days} + 347.6 \text{ days} = 431.7 \text{ days}$$

In the previous year, the operating cycle was 317.5 days. An unfavorable direction is indicated because additional funds are tied up in noncash assets. Cash is being collected more slowly.

By calculating the *total asset turnover*, one can find out whether the company is efficiently employing its total assets to obtain sales revenue. A low ratio may indicate too high an investment in assets in comparison to the sales revenue generated.

$$\text{Total asset turnover} = \frac{\text{Net sales}}{\text{Average total assets}}$$

In 20X2, the ratio is:

$$\frac{\$80.3}{(\$204 + \$227)/2} = \frac{\$80.3}{\$215.5} = 0.37$$

In 20X1, the ratio was .57 ($110/$194.5). There has been a sharp reduction in asset utilization.

MYRA, Inc. has suffered a sharp deterioration in activity ratios, pointing to a need for improved credit and inventory management, although the 20X2 ratios are not far out of line with the industry averages (See Exhibit 5 at ¶ 1411.07). It appears that the problems are inefficient collection and obsolescence of inventory.

.03 Solvency (Leverage and Debt Service)

Solvency is the company's ability to satisfy long-term debt as it becomes due. One should be concerned about the long-term financial and operating structure of any firm in which one might be interested. Another important consideration is the size of debt in the firm's capital structure referred to as *financial leverage*. (Capital structure is the mix of the *long-term* sources of funds used by the firm).

Solvency also depends on earning power; in the long run, a company will not satisfy its debts unless it earns profit. A leveraged capital structure subjects the company to fixed interest charges, which contributes to earnings instability. Excessive debt may also make it difficult for the firm to borrow funds at reasonable rates during tight money markets.

The *debt ratio* reveals the amount of money a company owes to its creditors. Excessive debt means greater risk to the investor. The debt ratio is:

$$\text{Debt ratio} = \frac{\text{Total liabilities}}{\text{Total assets}}$$

In 20X2, the ratio is:

$$\frac{\$139}{\$227} = 0.61$$

The *debt-equity ratio* will show if the firm has a great amount of debt in its capital structure. Large debts mean that the borrower has to pay significant periodic interest and principal. Also, a heavily indebted firm takes a greater risk of running out of cash in difficult times. The interpretation of this ratio depends on several variables, including the ratios of other firms in the industry, the degree of access to additional debt financing, and stability of operations.

$$\text{Debt-equity ratio} = \frac{\text{Total liabilities}}{\text{Stockholders' equity}}$$

In 20X2, the ratio is:

$$\frac{\$139}{\$88} = 1.58$$

In the previous year, the ratio was 1.55. The trend is relatively static.

Times interest earned (interest coverage ratio) tells how many times the firm's before-tax earnings would cover interest. It is a safety margin indicator in that it reflects how much of a reduction in earnings a company can tolerate.

$$\text{Times interest earned} = \frac{\text{Income before interest and taxes}}{\text{Interest expense}}$$

For 20X2, the ratio is:

$$\frac{\$15.3}{\$2.0} = 7.65$$

In 20X1, interest was covered 13.5 times. The reduction in coverage during the period is a bad sign. It means that less earnings are available to satisfy interest charges.

One must also note liabilities that have not yet been reported in the balance sheet by closely examining footnote disclosure. For example, one should find out about lawsuits, noncapitalized leases, and future guarantees.

As was shown in Exhibit 3, the company's overall solvency is poor relative to the industry averages, although it has remained fairly constant. There has been no significant change in its ability to satisfy long-term debt. Note that significantly less profit is available to cover interest payments.

.04 Profitability

A company's ability to earn a good profit and return on investment is an indicator of its financial well being and the efficiency with which it is managed. Poor earnings have detrimental effects on market price of stock and dividends. Total dollar net income has little meaning unless it is compared to the input in getting that profit.

The *gross profit margin* shows the percentage of each dollar remaining once the company has paid for goods acquired. A high margin reflects good earning potential.

$$\text{Gross profit margin} = \frac{\text{Gross profit}}{\text{Net sales}}$$

In 20X2, the ratio is:

$$\frac{\$28.3}{\$80.3} = 0.35$$

The ratio was .43 in 20X1. The reduction shows that the company now receives less profit on each dollar of sales. Perhaps higher relative cost of merchandise sold is at fault.

Profit margin shows the earnings generated from revenue and is a key indicator of operating performance. It gives an idea of the firm's pricing, cost structure, and production efficiency.

$$\text{Profit margin} = \frac{\text{Net income}}{\text{Net sales}}$$

The ratio in 20X2 is:

$$\frac{\$8}{\$80.3} = 0.10$$

For the previous year, profit margin was .14. The decline in the ratio shows a downward trend in earning power. (Note that these percentages are available in the common-size income statement as given in Exhibit 2).

Return on investment is a prime indicator, because it allows one to evaluate the profit one will earn if one invests in the business. Two key ratios are the *return on total assets* and the *return on equity.*

The *return on total assets* shows whether management is efficient in using available resources to get profit.

$$\text{Return on total assets} = \frac{\text{Net income}}{\text{Average total assets}}$$

In 20X2, the return is:

$$\frac{\$8}{(\$227+\$204)/2} = 0.037$$

In 20X1, the return was .077. There has been a deterioration in the productivity of assets in generating earnings.

The *return on equity* (ROE) reflects the rate of return earned on the stockholders' investment.

$$\text{Return on common equity} = \frac{\text{Net income available to stockholder}}{\text{Average stockholders' equity}}$$

The return in 20X2 is:

$$\frac{\$8}{(\$88+\$80)/2} = 0.095$$

In 20X1, the return was .207. There has been a significant drop in return to the owners.

The overall profitability of the company has decreased considerably, causing a decline in both the return on assets and return on equity. Perhaps lower earnings were due in part to higher costs of short-term financing arising from the decline in liquidity and activity ratios. Moreover, as turnover rates in assets go down, profit will similarly decline because of a lack of sales and higher costs of carrying higher current asset balances. As indicated in Exhibit 5 at ¶ 1411.07, industry comparisons reveal that the company is faring very poorly in the industry.

.05 Market Value

Market value ratios relate the company's stock price to its earnings (or book value) per share. Also included are dividend-related ratios.

Earnings per share (EPS) is the ratio most widely watched by investors. EPS shows the net income per common share owned. One must reduce net income by the preferred dividends to obtain the net income available to common stockholders. Where preferred stock is not in the capital structure, one determines EPS by dividing net income by common shares outstanding. EPS is a gauge of corporate operating performance and of expected future dividends.

$$\text{EPS} = \frac{\text{Net income} - \text{Preferred dividend}}{\text{Common shares outstanding}}$$

EPS in 20X2 is:

$$\frac{\$8{,}000}{4{,}600 \text{ shares}} = \$1.74$$

For 20X1, EPS was $3.26. The sharp reduction over the year should cause alarm among investors. As was seen in Exhibit 4, the industry average EPS in 20X2 is much higher than that of MYRA, Inc. ($4.51 per share vs. $1.74 per share).

The *price/earnings (P/E) ratio,* also called *earnings multiple,* reflects the company's relationship to its stockholders. The P/E ratio represents the amount investors are willing to pay for each dollar of the firm's earnings. A high multiple (cost per dollar of earnings) is favored, since it shows that investors view the firm positively. On the other hand, investors looking for value would prefer a relatively lower multiple (cost per dollar of earnings) as compared with companies of similar risk and return.

$$\text{Price/earnings ratio} = \frac{\text{Market price per share}}{\text{Earnings per share}}$$

Assume a market price per share of $12 on December 31, 20X2, and $26 on December 31, 20X1. The P/E ratios are:

20X2:

$$\frac{\$12}{\$1.74} = 6.90$$

20X1:

$$\frac{\$26}{\$3.26} = 7.98$$

From the lower P/E multiple, one can infer that the stock market now has a lower opinion of the business. However, some investors argue that a low P/E ratio can mean that the stock is undervalued. Nevertheless, the decline over the year in stock price was 54 percent ($14/$26), which should cause deep investor concern.

Book value per share equals the net assets available to common stockholders divided by shares outstanding. By comparing it to market price per share one can get another view of how investors feel about the business.

The book value per share in 20X2 is:

$$\text{Book value per share} = \frac{\text{Total stockholders' equity} - \text{Preferred stock}}{\text{Common shares outstanding}}$$

$$= \frac{\$88{,}000 - 0}{4{,}600} = \$19.13$$

In 20X1, book value per share was $17.39.

The increased book value per share is a favorable sign, because it indicates that each share now has a higher book value. However, in 20X2, market price is much less than book value, which means that the stock market does not value the security highly. In 20X1, market price did exceed book value, but there is now some doubt in the minds of stockholders concerning the company. However, some analysts may argue that the stock is underpriced.

The price/book value ratio shows the market value of the company in comparison to its historical accounting value. A company with old assets may have a high ratio whereas one with new assets may have a low ratio. Hence, one should note the changes in the ratio when appraising the corporate assets.

The ratio equals:

$$\text{Price/book value} = \frac{\text{Market price per share}}{\text{Book value per share}}$$

In 20X2, the ratio is:

$$\frac{\$12}{\$19.13} = 0.63$$

In 20X1, the ratio was 1.5. The significant drop in the ratio may indicate a lower opinion of the company in the eyes of investors. Market price of stock may have dropped because of a deterioration in liquidity, activity, and profitability ratios. The major indicators of a company's performance are intertwined (i.e., one affects the other), so that problems in one area may spill over into another. This appears to have happened to the company in this example.

The *Q-ratio* is the market value of all securities (not just equity) divided by the replacement cost (*not* book value) of all assets. The Q-ratio reflects the market's valuation of new investment. A ratio greater than one means that a firm is earning returns greater than the amount invested. For this reason, the higher the Q-ratio, the greater the industry attractiveness and/or the competitive advantage.

Dividend ratios help one determine the current income from an investment. Two relevant ratios are:

$$\text{Dividend yield} = \frac{\text{Dividends per share}}{\text{Market price per share}}$$

$$\text{Dividend payout} = \frac{\text{Dividends per share}}{\text{Earnings per share}}$$

There is no such thing as a "right" payout ratio. Stockholders look unfavorably upon reduced dividends because it is a sign of possible deteriorating financial health. However, companies with ample opportunities for growth at high rates of return on assets tend to have low payout ratios.

.06 An Overall Evaluation—Summary of Financial Ratios

As indicated, a single ratio or a single group of ratios is not adequate for assessing all aspects of the firm's financial condition. Exhibit 5 summarizes the 20X1 and 20X2 ratios calculated in the previous sections, along with the industry average ratios for 20X2. The exhibit also shows the formula used to calculate each ratio. The last three columns of the exhibit contain subjective assessments of MYRA's financial condition, based on trend analysis and 20X2 comparisons to the industry norms. (five-year ratios are generally needed for trend analysis to be more meaningful, however.)

By appraising the trend in the company's ratios from 20X1 to 20X2, one sees from the drop in the current and quick ratios that there has been a slight detraction in short-term liquidity, although they have been above the industry averages. However, working capital has improved. A material deterioration in the activity ratios has occurred, indicating that improved credit and inventory policies are required. They are not terribly alarming, however, because these ratios are not way out of line with industry averages. Also, total utilization of assets, as indicated by the total asset turnover, shows a deteriorating trend.

Leverage (amount of debt) has been constant. However, there is less profit available to satisfy interest charges. MYRA's profitability has deteriorated over the year. In 20X2, it is consistently below the industry average in every measure of profitability. In consequence, the return on the owner's investment and the return on total assets have gone down. The earnings decrease may be partly due to the firm's high cost of short-term financing and partly due to operating inefficiency. The higher costs may be due to receivable and inventory difficulties that forced a decline in the liquidity and activity ratios. Furthermore, as receivables and inventory turn over less, profit will fall off from a lack of sales and the costs of carrying more in current asset balances.

The firm's market value, as measured by the price-earnings (P/E) ratio, is respectable as compared with the industry. But it shows a declining trend.

In summary, it appears that the company is doing satisfactorily in the industry in many categories. The 20X1-20X2 period, however, seems to indicate that the company is heading for financial trouble in terms of earnings, activity, and short-term liquidity. The business needs to concentrate on increasing operating efficiency and asset utilization.

.07 Limitations of Ratio Analysis

While ratio analysis is an effective tool for assessing a business's financial condition, one must also recognize the following limitations:

1. Accounting policies vary among companies and can inhibit useful comparisons. For example, the use of different depreciation methods (straight-line vs. double declining balance) will affect profitability and return ratios.

2. Management may "fool around" with ("window-dress") the figures. For example, it can reduce needed research expense just to bolster net income. This practice, however, will almost always hurt the company in the long run.

3. A ratio is static and does not reveal future flows. For example, it will not answer questions such as "How much cash do you have in your pocket now?" or "Is that sufficient, considering your expenses and income over the next month?"

4. A ratio does not indicate the quality of its components. For example, a high quick ratio may contain receivables that may not be collected.

5. Reported liabilities may be undervalued. An example is a lawsuit on which the company is contingently liable.

6. The company may have multiple lines of business, making it difficult to identify the industry group the company is a part of.

7. Industry averages cited by financial advisory services are only approximations. Hence, one may have to compare a company's ratios to those of competing companies in the industry.

Exhibit 5

MYRA, Inc.
Summary of Financial Ratios—Trend and Industry Comparisons

Ratios	*Definitions*	*20X1*	*20X2*	*Industry*[a]	*Evaluation*[b] *Ind*	*Trend*	*Overall*
LIQUIDITY							
Net working capital	Current assets/current liabilities	63	68	56	good	good	good
Current Ratio	Current assets/current liabilities	2.26	2.21	2.05	OK	OK	OK
Quick (Acid-test) ratio	(Cash + short-term investments + accounts receivable)/current liabilities	1.34	1.27	1.11	OK	OK	OK
ASSET UTILIZATION							
Accounts receivable turnover	Net credit sales/average accounts receivable	8.46	4.34	5.5	OK	poor	poor
Average collection period	365 days/accounts receivable turnover (days)	43.1	84.1	66.4	OK	poor	poor
Inventory turnover	Cost of goods sold/average inventory	1.33	1.05	1.2	OK	poor	poor
Average age of inventory	365 days/inventory turnover (days)	274.4	347.6	N/A	N/A	poor	poor
Operating cycle	Average collection period + average age of inventory (days)	317.5	431.7	N/A	N/A	poor	poor
Total asset turnover	Net sales/average total assets	0.57	0.37	0.44	OK	poor	poor
SOLVENCY							
Debt ratio	Total liabilities/total assets	0.61	0.61	N/A	N/A	OK	OK
Debt-equity ratio	Total liabilities/stockholders' equity	1.55	1.58	1.3	poor	poor	poor
Times interest earned	Income before interest and taxes/interest expense (times)	13.5	7.65	10	OK	poor	poor

Exhibit 5 (continued)

MYRA, Inc.

Summary of Financial Ratios—Trend and Industry Comparisons

Ratios	*Definitions*	*20X1*	*20X2*	*Industry*[a]	*Evaluation*[b]		
					Ind	*Trend*	*Overall*
PROFITABILITY							
Gross profit margin	Gross profit/net sales	0.43	0.35	0.48	poor	poor	poor
Profit margin	Net income/net sales	0.14	0.1	0.15	poor	poor	poor
Return on total assets	Net income/average total assets	0.077	0.037	0.1	poor	poor	poor
Return on equity (ROE)	Earnings available to common stockholders/ avg. stockholders' equity	0.207	0.095	0.27	poor	poor	poor
MARKET VALUE							
Earnings per share (EPS)	(Net income -preferred dividend)/common shares outstanding	3.26	1.74	4.51	poor	poor	poor
Price/earnings (P/E) ratio	Market price per share/EPS	7.98	6.9	7.12	OK	poor	poor
Book value per share	(Total stockholders' eqty - Preferred stock)/ common shrs outstanding	17.39	19.13	N/A	N/A	good	good
Price/book value ratio	Market price per share/book value per share	1.5	0.63	N/A	N/A	poor	poor
Dividend yield	Dividends per share/market price per share						
Dividend payout	Dividends per share/EPS						

([a]) Obtained from sources not included in this chapter

([b]) Represent subjective evaluation

¶ 1415 The Power of Cash Flow Ratios

Both the current and quick ratios have been criticized on the ground that they do not incorporate information about the timing and magnitude of future cash flows and outflows. The following two ratios get around this problem.

1. *Defensive interval measure* estimates the number of days the defensive assets could service the projected daily operating expenditures of the firm. The ratio is:

$$\frac{\text{Total defensive assets}}{\text{Projected daily operating expenditures}}$$

$$= \frac{\text{Cash} + \text{Short-term investments} + \text{Accounts receivable}}{\text{Cost of goods sold} + \text{Selling and administrative expenses} + \text{Interest expense}} \times 365 \text{ days}$$

2. *Cash ratio* is a more appropriate measure when inventory and accounts receivable are of questionable value, such as with companies whose receivables are collected on an installment basis. The ratio is:

$$\frac{\text{Cash} + \text{Short-term investments}}{\text{Current liabilities}}$$

The traditional liquidity ratios rely exclusively on balance sheet or income statement information, not on cash flow information. To fully understand a company's viability as an ongoing concern, an analyst should calculate ratios from data on the company's cash flow statement (the statement of sources and uses of cash). This is especially true in predicting bankruptcy and financial distress. Cash flow ratios can be viewed in terms of sufficiency and efficiency. Sufficiency describes the adequacy of cash flows for meeting a company's needs; efficiency describes how well a company generates cash flows relative both to other years and to other companies. Exhibit 6 summarizes related cash flow ratios.

Exhibit 6

Cash Flow Ratios

Sufficiency Ratios

1. Cash flow adequacy:

$$\frac{\text{Cash flow from operations}}{\text{Long-term debt paid} + \text{Purchases of assets} + \text{Dividends paid}}$$

2. Long-term debt payment:

$$\frac{\text{Long-term debt payments}}{\text{Cash flow from operations}}$$

3. Dividend payout:

$$\frac{\text{Dividends}}{\text{Cash flow from operations}}$$

4. Reinvestment:

$$\frac{\text{Purchase of assets}}{\text{Cash flow from operations}}$$

5. Debt coverage:

$$\frac{\text{Total debt}}{\text{Cash flow from operations}}$$

6. Depreciation-amortization impact:

$$\frac{\text{Depreciation} + \text{Amortization}}{\text{Cash flow from operations}}$$

Efficiency Ratios

7. Cash flow to sales:

$$\frac{\text{Cash flow from operations}}{\text{Sales}}$$

8. Operations index:

$$\frac{\text{Cash flow from operations}}{\text{Income from continuing operations}}$$

9. Cash flow return on assets:

$$\frac{\text{Cash flow from operations}}{\text{Total assets}}$$

.01 *Sufficiency Ratios*

The cash flow adequacy ratio directly measures a company's ability to generate cash sufficient to pay its debts, reinvest in its operations, and make distributions (dividends) to owners. A value of one over a period of several years shows satisfactory ability to cover these primary cash requirements. The long-term debt payment, dividend payout, and reinvestment ratios provide further insight for investors and creditors into the individual importance of these three components. When expressed as percentages and added together, these three ratios show the percentage of cash from operations available for discretionary uses.

Although a company could use cash generated from financing and investing activities to retire debt, cash from operations represents the main source of long-term funds. The debt coverage ratio can be viewed as a payback period; that is, it estimates how many years, at the current level of cash from operations, it will take to retire all debt.

The depreciation-amortization impact ratio shows the percentage of cash from operations resulting from add-backs of depreciation and amortization. Comparing this ratio to the reinvestment ratio provides insight into the sufficiency of a company's reinvestment and the maintenance of its asset base. Over several years, the reinvestment ratio should exceed the depreciation-amortization impact ratio to ensure sufficient replacement of assets at higher current costs. This ratio also can be used as an efficiency evaluation. A company would be considered more efficient if depreciation and amortization have a relatively low impact on cash from operations.

.02 *Efficiency Ratios*

Investors, creditors, and others concerned with a company's cash flows are especially interested in the income statement and earnings measures. The cash flow to sales ratio shows the percentage of each sales dollar realized as cash from operations. Over time, this ratio should approximate the company's return on sales. The operations index compares cash from operations to income from continuing operations. It measures the cash-generating productivity of continuing operations. Cash flow return on assets is a measure of the return on assets used to compare companies on the basis of cash generation (as opposed to income generation) from assets.

Sufficiency and efficiency ratios are examples of information available to financial statement users from the cash flow statement. It's important to remember that, as in all ratio analysis, isolated ratios provide limited information about a single period. The ratios become more useful when computed for a period of years to determine averages and trends and when compared to industry averages.

Note: From the *statement of cash flows,* cash flow from operations is defined as:

Net income
Add: Noncash expenses (e.g., depreciation, amortization)
Less: Noncash revenue (e.g., amortization of deferred revenue)

Cash flow from operations

¶ 1421 The Predictive Power of Financial Ratios

A number of empirical studies have been taken that test the predictive power of financial ratios. There is evidence that a selected group of financial ratios proved to be successful in predicting business failures or corporate bond ratings. The Z score model (to be illustrated below in detail) is one such example. Further, there have been attempts to develop (a) quantitative scoring models for loan decisions and (b) models consisting of various financial ratios that can discriminate between corporate debt securities in different rating categories.

.01 The Z Score Model: Forecasting Business Failures

The Z score is a quantitative model that Edward Altman developed in an effort to predict bankruptcy (financial distress) of a business, using a blend of the traditional financial ratios and a statistical method known as *multiple discriminant analysis* (MDA).

The Z score is known to be about 90 percent accurate in forecasting business failure one year in the future and about 80 percent accurate in forecasting it two years in the future.

The model is:

$$Z = 1.2 \times X_1 + 1.4 \times X_2 + 3.3 \times X_3 + 0.6 \times X_4 + 0.999 \times X_5$$

Where:

X_1 = Working capital/Total assets

X_2 = Retained earnings/Total assets

X_3 = Earnings before interest and taxes (EBIT)/Total assets

X_4 = Market value of equity/Book value of debt

X_5 = Sales/Total assets

Altman also established the following guidelines for classifying firms:

Z score	Probability of Short-Term Illiquidity
1.8 or less	Very high
1.81 - 2.99	Not sure
3.0 or higher	Unlikely

Example: Davidson Company has the following financial data selected from its financial statements:

Total assets = \$2,000 Retained earnings =\$750

EBIT = \$266 Sales =\$3,000

Market value of common and preferred stock = \$1,425

Book value of debt = \$1,100

Working capital = 400

The calculation of Davidson's Z score is shown below:

$$
\begin{aligned}
X_1 &= 400/2{,}000 && \times 1.2 = 0.240 \\
X_2 &= 750/2{,}000 && \times 1.4 = 0.525 \\
X_3 &= 266/2{,}000 && \times 3.3 = 0.439 \\
X_4 &= 1{,}425/1{,}100 && \times 0.6 = 0.777 \\
X_5 &= 3{,}000/2{,}000 && \times 0.999 = \underline{1.499} \\
& && Z = 3.480
\end{aligned}
$$

Since Davidson's Z score of 3.480 is well into the "unlikely" zone, there is virtually no chance that Davidson will go bankrupt within the next two years.

.02 Case Study

Spreadsheet models have been developed to calculate the prediction of bankruptcy using data extracted from *Moody's* and *Standard & Poor's.* Two companies—Navistar International (formerly International Harvester), which continues to struggle in the heavy and medium truck industry, and Best Products, Inc., which declared bankruptcy as of January 1991—have been selected for this study. Financial data has been collected for the period 1979 through 1990 for Best and for the period 1981 through 2001 for Navistar. Exhibit 7 shows the 20-year financial history and the Z scores of Navistar. Exhibit 8 presents the corresponding graph.

The graph shows that Navistar International performed at the edge of the ignorance zone ("unsure area") for the year 1981. In 1982, though, the company started showing signs of failure. However, by selling stock and assets, the firm managed to survive. Since 1985, the company showed an improvement in its Z scores, although the firm continually scored in the danger zone. Note that the 1991-2001 *Z*-scores are in the high probability range of < 1.81, except the year 1999.

Best Products, Inc. had a Z score in the 2.44 to 2.98 range from 1984 to 1988. The strong decline in 1989 may have correctly indicated the pending bankruptcy of Best that they filed for in January 1991. (See Exhibit 9 and Exhibit 10.)

Exhibit 7

Z Score—Navistar International

	Balance Sheet						Income Statement		Stock Data	Calculations					Misc Graph Value		
Year	Current Assets (CA)	Total Assets (TA)	Current Liability (CL)	Total Liability (TL)	Retained Earnings (RE)	Working Capital (WC)	SALES	EBIT	Market Value or Net Worth (MKT-NW)	WC/ TA (X1)	RE/ TA (X2)	EBIT/ TA (X3)	MKT-NW/TL (X4)	SALES/ TA (X5)	Z Score	TOP GRAY	BOTTOM GRAY
1981	2672	5346	1808	3864	600	864	7018	-16	376	0.1616	0.1122	-0.0030	0.0973	1.3128	1.71	2.99	1.81
1982	1656	3699	1135	3665	-1078	521	4322	-1274	151	0.1408	-0.2914	-0.3444	0.0412	1.1684	-0.18	2.99	1.81
1983	1388	3362	1367	3119	-1487	21	3600	-231	835	0.0062	-0.4423	-0.0687	0.2677	1.0708	0.39	2.99	1.81
1984	1412	3249	1257	2947	-1537	155	4861	120	575	0.0477	-0.4731	0.0369	0.1951	1.4962	1.13	2.99	1.81
1985	1101	2406	988	2364	-1894	113	3508	247	570	0.0470	-0.7872	0.1027	0.2411	1.4580	0.89	2.99	1.81
1986	698	1925	797	1809	-1889	-99	3357	163	441	-0.0514	-0.9813	0.0847	0.2438	1.7439	0.73	2.99	1.81
1987	785	1902	836	1259	-1743	-51	3530	219	1011	-0.0268	-0.9164	0.1151	0.8030	1.8559	1.40	2.99	1.81
1988	1280	4037	1126	1580	150	154	4082	451	1016	0.0381	0.0372	0.1117	0.6430	1.0111	1.86	2.99	1.81
1989	986	3609	761	1257	175	225	4241	303	1269	0.0623	0.0485	0.0840	1.0095	1.1751	2.20	2.99	1.81
1990	2663	3795	1579	2980	81	1084	3854	111	563	0.2856	0.0213	0.0292	0.1889	1.0155	1.60	2.99	1.81
1991	2286	3443	1145	2866	332	1141	3259	232	667	0.3314	0.0964	0.0674	0.2326	0.9466	1.84	2.99	1.81
1992	2472	3627	1152	3289	93	1320	3875	-145	572	0.3639	0.0256	-0.0400	0.1738	1.0684	1.51	2.99	1.81
1993	2672	5060	1338	4285	-1588	1334	4696	-441	1765	0.2636	-0.3138	-0.0872	0.4119	0.9281	0.76	2.99	1.81
1994	2870	5056	1810	4239	-1538	1060	5337	233	1469	0.2097	-0.3042	0.0461	0.3466	1.0556	1.24	2.99	1.81
1995	3310	5566	1111	4696	-1478	2199	6342	349	966	0.3951	-0.2655	0.0627	0.2057	1.1394	1.57	2.99	1.81
1996	2999	5326	820	4410	-1431	2179	5754	188	738	0.4091	-0.2687	0.0353	0.1673	1.0804	1.41	2.99	1.81
1997	3203	5516	2416	4496	-1301	787	6371	316	1374	0.1427	-0.2359	0.0573	0.3055	1.1550	1.37	2.99	1.81
1998	3715	6178	3395	5409	-1160	320	7885	515	1995	0.0518	-0.1878	0.0834	0.3688	1.2763	1.57	2.99	1.81
1999	3203	5516	2416	4496	-1301	787	8642	726	2494	0.1427	-0.2359	0.1316	0.5547	1.5667	2.17	2.99	1.81
2000	2374	6851	2315	5409	-143	59	8451	370	2257	0.0086	-0.0209	0.0540	0.4173	1.2335	1.64	2.99	1.81
2001	2736	7067	2273	5409	-170	463	6722	114	1900	0.0655	-0.0241	0.0161	0.3513	0.9512	1.26	2.99	1.81

Note: (1) To calculate "Z" score for private firms, enter Net Worth in the MKT-NW column. (For public-held companies, enter Market value of Equity.)
(2) EBIT= Earnings before Interest and Taxes.

Exhibit 8

"Z" Score Graph

(Navistar)

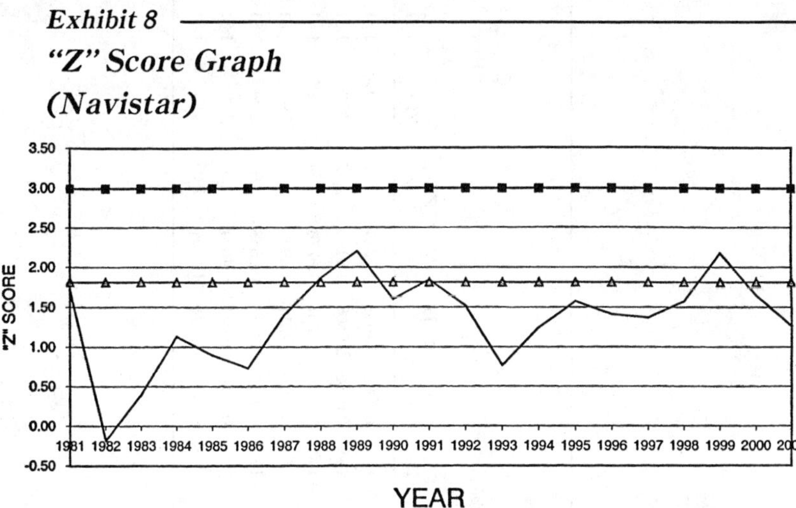

Exhibit 9

Best Product's Z Score

	Balance Sheet						Income Statement			Stock Data	Calculations						Misc Graph Values	
Year (X)	Current Assets (CA)	Total Assets (TA)	Current Liability (CL)	Total Liability (TL)	Retained Earnings (RE)	Net Worth (NW)	Working Capital (WC)	SALES	EBIT	Market Value (MKT)	WC/ TA	RE/ TA	EBIT/ TA	MKT/ TL	SALES/ TA	Z Score (A)	TOP GRAY (B)	BOTTOM GRAY (C)
1984	745228	1202138	468590	787135	186486	415003	276628	2081328	106952	319048	0.2301	0.1551	0.0890	0.4053	1.7314	2.76	2.99	1.81
1985	723684	1178424	443752	759278	193568	419146	279932	2252656	66705	407604	0.2375	0.1643	0.0566	0.5368	1.9116	2.93	2.99	1.81
1986	840686	1331975	529690	916579	189306	415396	310996	2234768	47271	253041	0.2335	0.1421	0.0355	0.2761	1.6778	2.44	2.99	1.81
1987	816853	1265637	400403	878479	160455	387158	416450	2142118	25372	202988	0.3290	0.1268	0.0200	0.2311	1.6925	2.47	2.99	1.81
1988	811314	1239860	426065	836956	190960	402904	385249	2066589	93226	672300	0.3107	0.1540	0.0752	0.8033	0.6668	2.98	2.99	1.81
1989	877937	1735595	738837	1646302	39293	89293	139100	809457	96440	672300	0.0801	0.0226	0.0556	0.4084	0.4664	1.02	2.99	1.81
1990	583773	1438208	412732	1366974	-14516	71234	171041	2094570	73512	672300	0.1189	-0.0101	0.0511	0.4918	1.4564	2.05	2.99	1.81

Exhibit 10

Best Product's Z Score Graph

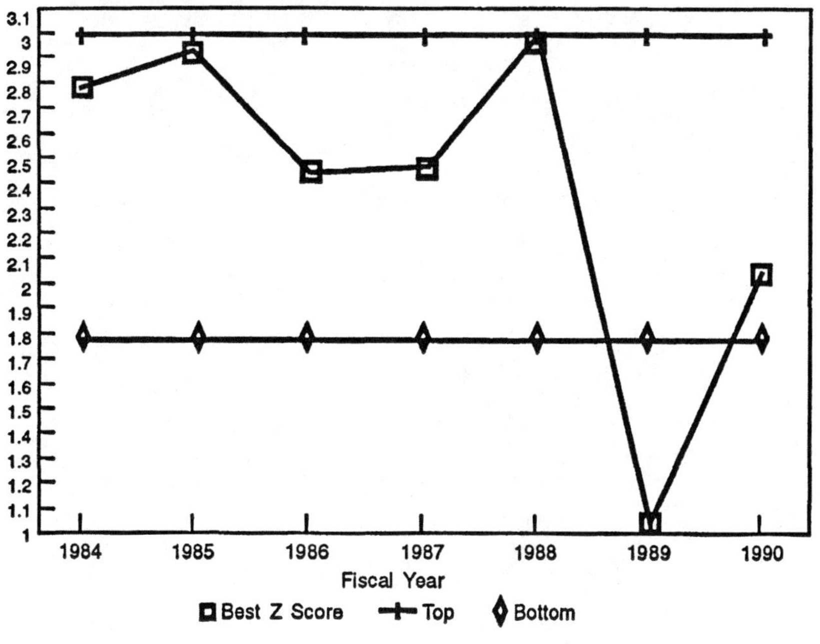

Chapter 15

Measuring and Improving Financial Performance

¶ 1501 Overview

The ability to measure managerial performance is essential in controlling operations toward the achievement of organizational goals. Perhaps the most widely used single measure of success of an organization and its subunits is the rate of return on investment (ROI). Related is the return to stockholders, known as the return on equity (ROE). Economic Value Added (EVA(r)) is an alternative metrics that received a great deal of attention. EVA is regarded as the financial performance measure that comes closer than any other to capturing the true economic profit of an enterprise. EVA also is the performance measure most directly linked to the creation of shareholder wealth over time.

¶ 1505 Return on Investment (ROI)

ROI relates net income to invested capital (total assets). ROI provides a standard for evaluating how efficiently management employs the average dollar invested in a firm's assets, whether that dollar came from owners or creditors. Furthermore, a better ROI can also translate directly into a higher return on the stockholders' equity.

ROI is calculated as:

$$\text{ROI} = \frac{\text{Net profit after taxes}}{\text{Total assets}}$$

Example 1: Consider the following financial data:

Total assets = $100,000

Net profit after taxes = $18,000

Then,

$$\text{ROI} = \frac{\text{Net profit after taxes}}{\text{Total assets}} = \frac{\$18{,}000}{\$100{,}000} = 18\%$$

The problem with this formula is that it only tells you about how a company did and how well it fared in the industry. It has very little value from the standpoint of profit planning.

.01 What Does ROI Consist Of?—Du Pont Formula

ROI can be broken down into two factors—profit margin and asset turnover. In the past, managers have tended to focus only on the profit margin earned and have ignored the turnover of assets. It is important to realize that excessive funds tied up in assets can be just as much of a drag on profitability as excessive expenses. The Du Pont Corporation was the first major company to recognize the importance of looking at both net profit margin and total asset turnover in assessing the performance of an organization. The ROI breakdown, known as the *Du Pont formula,* is expressed as a product of these two factors, as shown below.

$$\text{ROI} = \frac{\text{Net profit after taxes}}{\text{Total assets}} = \frac{\text{Net profit after taxes}}{\text{Sales}} \times \frac{\text{Sales}}{\text{Total assets}}$$

$$= \text{Net profit margin} \times \text{Total asset turnover}$$

The Du Pont formula combines the income statement and balance sheet into this otherwise static measure of performance. Net profit margin is a measure of profitability or operating efficiency. It is the percentage of profit earned on sales. This percentage shows how many cents attach to each dollar of sales. On the other hand, total asset turnover measures how well a company manages its assets. It is the number of times by which the investment in assets turns over each year to generate sales.

The breakdown of ROI is based on the thesis that the profitability of a firm is directly related to management's ability to manage assets efficiently and to control expenses effectively.

Example 2: Assume the same data as in Example 1. Also assume sales of $200,000.

Then,

$$\text{ROI} = \frac{\text{Net profit after taxes}}{\text{Total assets}} = \frac{\$18{,}000}{\$100{,}000} = 18\%$$

Alternatively,

$$\text{Net profit margin} = \frac{\text{Net profit after taxes}}{\text{Sales}} = \frac{\$18{,}000}{\$200{,}000} = 9\%$$

$$\text{Total asset turnover} = \frac{\text{Sales}}{\text{Total assets}} = \frac{\$200{,}000}{\$100{,}000} = 2 \text{ times}$$

Therefore,

ROI = Net profit margin × Total asset turnover = 9% × 2 times = 18%

The breakdown provides insight to financial managers on how to improve profitability of the company and investment strategy. (Note that net profit margin and total asset turnover are called hereafter margin and turnover, respectively, for short). Specifically, the Dupont formula has several advantages over the original formula (i.e., net profit after taxes/total assets) for profit planning. They are:

1. The importance of turnover as a key to overall return on investment is emphasized in the breakdown. In fact, turnover is just as important as profit margin in enhancing overall return.

2. The importance of sales is explicitly recognized, which is not in the original formula.

3. The breakdown stresses the possibility of trading one off for the other in an attempt to improve the overall performance of a company. The margin and turnover complement each other. In other words, a low turnover can be made up by a high margin and vice versa.

Example 3: The breakdown of ROI into its two components shows that a number of combinations of margin and turnover can yield the same rate of return, as shown below:

	Margin	×	*Turnover*	= *ROI*
(1)	9%	×	2 times	= 18%
(2)	6	×	3	= 18
(3)	3	×	6	= 18
(4)	2	×	9	= 18

The turnover-margin relationship and its resulting ROI is depicted in Exhibit 1.

Exhibit 1

Turnover-Margin Relationship

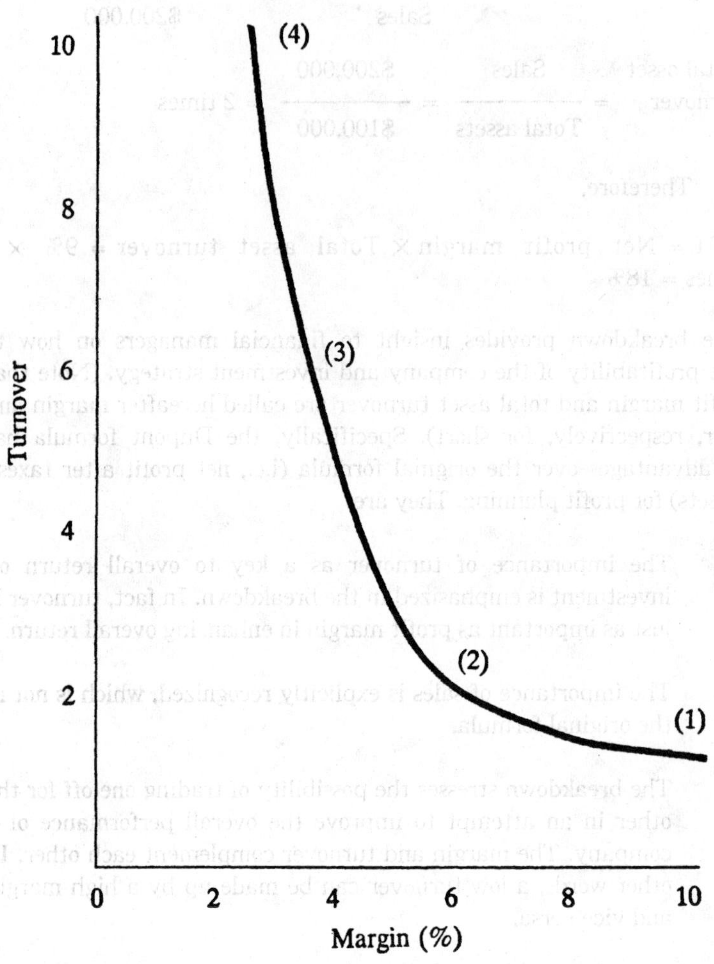

Is there an optimal combination? Exhibit 1 can also be looked at as showing four companies that performed equally well (in terms of ROI) but with varying income statements and balance sheets. There is no ROI that is satisfactory for all companies. Sound and successful operation must point toward the optimum combination of profits, sales, and capital employed. The combination will necessarily vary depending upon the nature of the business and the characteristics of the product. An industry with products tailor-made to customers' specifications will have different margins and turnover ratios, compared with industries that mass produce highly competitive consumer goods. For example, the combination (4) may describe a supermarket operation which inherently works with low margin and high turnover, while the combination (1) may be a jewelry store which typically has a low turnover and high margin.

How to use the Du Pont formula for profit improvement. The breakdown of ROI into margin and turnover gives management insight into planning for profit improvement by revealing where weaknesses exist: margin or turnover, or both. Various actions can be taken to enhance ROI. Generally, management can:

1. Improve margin.

2. Improve turnover.

3. Improve both.

Alternative 1 demonstrates a popular way of improving performance. Margins may be increased by reducing expenses, raising selling prices, or increasing sales faster than expenses. Some of the ways to reduce expenses are:

- Use less costly inputs of materials; although, this can be dangerous in today's quality-oriented environment.

- Automate processes as much as possible to increase labor productivity. But this will probably increase assets, thereby reducing turnover.

- Bring the discretionary fixed costs under scrutiny, with various programs either curtailed or eliminated. Discretionary fixed costs arise from annual budgeting decisions by management. Examples include advertising, research and development, and management development programs. The cost-benefit analysis is called for in order to justify the budgeted amount of each discretionary program.

A company with pricing power can raise selling prices and retain profitability without losing business. Pricing power is the ability to raise prices even in poor economic times when unit sales volume may be flat and capacity may not be fully utilized. It is also the ability to pass on cost increases to consumers without attracting domestic and import competition, political opposition, regulation, new entrants, or threats of product substitution. The company with pricing power must have a unique economic position. Companies that offer unique, high-quality goods and services (where the service is more important than the cost) have this economic position.

Alternative 2 may be achieved by increasing sales, while holding the investment in assets relatively constant, or by reducing assets. Some of the strategies to reduce assets are:

- Dispose of obsolete and redundant inventory. Computerized items make continuous monitoring of inventory more feasible for better control.
- Devise various methods of speeding up the collection of receivables and also evaluate credit terms and policies.
- Investigate the existence of unused fixed assets.
- Use the converted assets (primarily cash) obtained from the use of the previous methods to repay outstanding debts or repurchase outstanding issues of stock. In addition, the company may decide to use those funds elsewhere to increase profit which will improve margin as well as turnover.

Alternative 3 may be achieved by increasing sales or by any combination of alternatives 1 and 2.

Exhibit 2 shows complete details of the relationship of ROI to the underlying ratios, margin and turnover, and their components. This will help identify more detailed strategies to improve margin, turnover, or both.

Exhibit 2

Relationships of Factors Influencing ROI

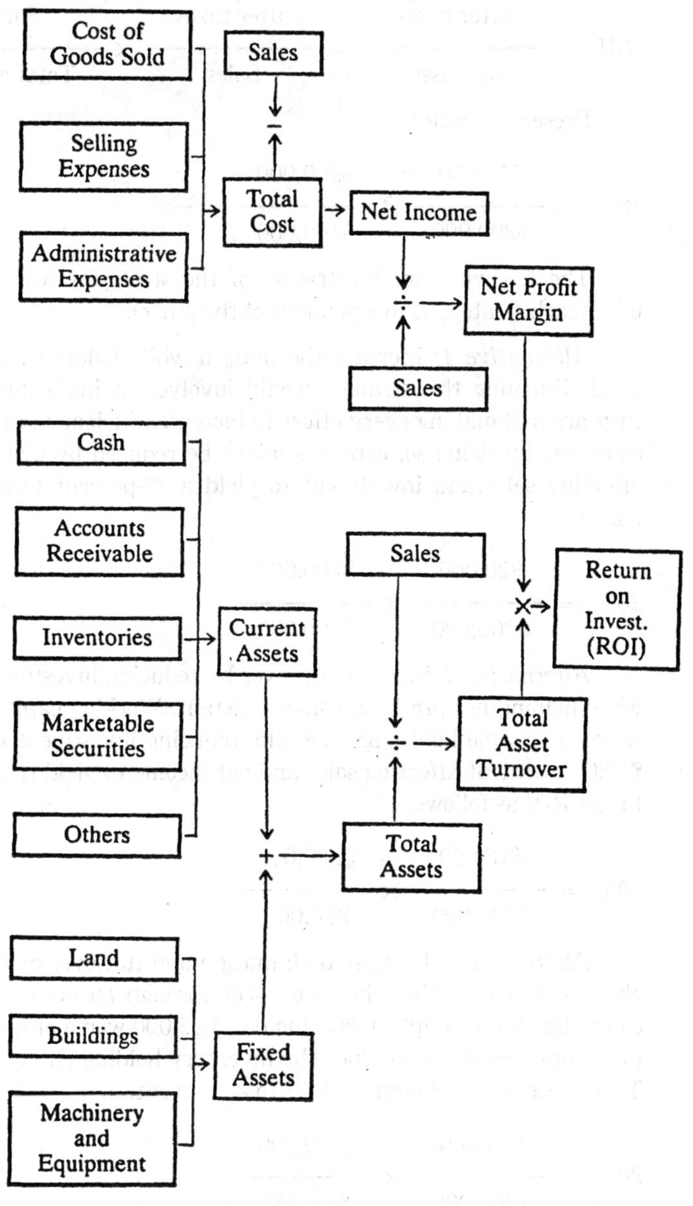

Example 4: Assume that management sets a 20-percent ROI as a profit target. It is currently making an 18-percent return on its investment.

$$\text{ROI} = \frac{\text{Net profit after taxes}}{\text{Total assets}} = \frac{\text{Net profit after taxes}}{\text{Sales}} \times \frac{\text{Sales}}{\text{Total assets}}$$

Present situation:

$$18\% = \frac{\$18{,}000}{\$200{,}000} \times \frac{\$200{,}000}{\$100{,}000}$$

The following are illustrative of the strategies which might be used (each strategy is independent of the other).

Alternative 1: Increase the margin while holding turnover constant. Pursuing this strategy would involve leaving selling prices as they are and making every effort to increase efficiency so as to reduce expenses. By doing so, expenses might be reduced by $2,000 without affecting sales and investment to yield a 20-percent target ROI, as follows:

$$20\% = \frac{\$20{,}000}{\$200{,}000} \times \frac{\$200{,}000}{\$100{,}000}$$

Alternative 2: Increase turnover by reducing investment in assets while holding net profit and sales constant. Working capital might be reduced or some land might be sold, reducing investment in assets by $10,000 without affecting sales and net income to yield the 20-percent target ROI as follows:

$$20\% = \frac{\$18{,}000}{\$200{,}000} \times \frac{\$200{,}000}{\$90{,}000}$$

Alternative 3: Increase both margin and turnover by disposing of obsolete and redundant inventories or through an active advertising campaign. For example, trimming down $5,000 worth of investment in inventories would also reduce the inventory holding charge by $1,000. This strategy would increase ROI to 20 percent.

$$20\% = \frac{\$19{,}000}{\$200{,}000} \times \frac{\$200{,}000}{\$95{,}000}$$

Excessive investment in assets is just as much of a drag on profitability as excessive expenses. In this case, cutting unnecessary inventories also helps cut down expenses of carrying those inventories, so that both margin and turnover are improved at the same time. In practice, alternative 3 is much more common than alternatives 1 or 2.

¶ 1510 How To Improve Return to Stockholders Through Financial Leverage

Generally, a better management performance (i.e., a high or above-average ROI) produces a higher return to equity holders. However, even a poorly managed company that suffers from a below-average performance can generate an above-average return on the stockholders' equity by increasing the return on equity (ROE) because borrowed funds can magnify the returns a company's profits represent to its stockholders.

Another version of the Du Pont formula, called the modified Du Pont formula, reflects this effect. The formula ties together the ROI and the degree of financial leverage (use of borrowed funds). The financial leverage is measured by the equity multiplier which is the ratio of a company's total asset base to its equity investment. The ratio is dollars of assets held per dollar of stockholders' equity calculated by dividing total assets by stockholders' equity. This measurement gives an indication of how much of a company's assets are financed by stockholders' equity and how much with borrowed funds.

The ROE is calculated as:

$$\text{ROE} = \frac{\text{Net profit after taxes}}{\text{Stockholders' equity}} = \frac{\text{Net profit after taxes}}{\text{Total assets}} \times \frac{\text{Total assets}}{\text{Stockholders' equity}}$$

$$= \text{ROI} \times \text{Equity multiplier}$$

ROE measures the returns earned on the owners' (both preferred and common stockholders) investment. The use of the equity multiplier to convert the ROI to the ROE reflects the impact of the leverage (use of debt) on the stockholders' return.

$$\text{Equity multiplier} = \frac{\text{Total assets}}{\text{Stockholders' equity}} = \frac{\text{Total assets}}{\text{Total assets} - \text{Total liabilities}}$$

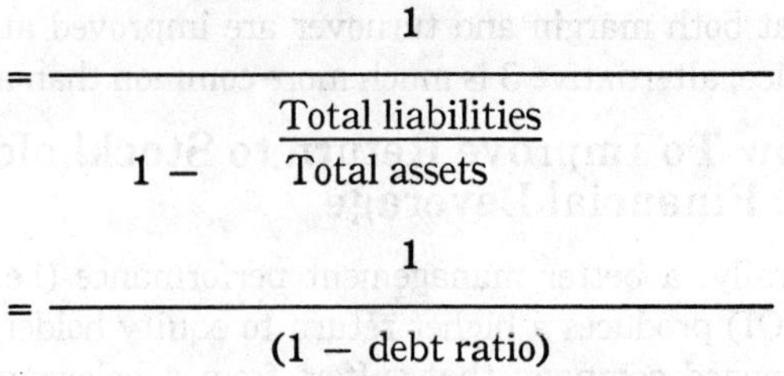

$$= \frac{1}{1 - \frac{\text{Total liabilities}}{\text{Total assets}}}$$

$$= \frac{1}{(1 - \text{debt ratio})}$$

Exhibit 3 shows the relationship among ROI, ROE, and financial leverage.

Exhibit 3

ROI, ROE, and Financial Leverage

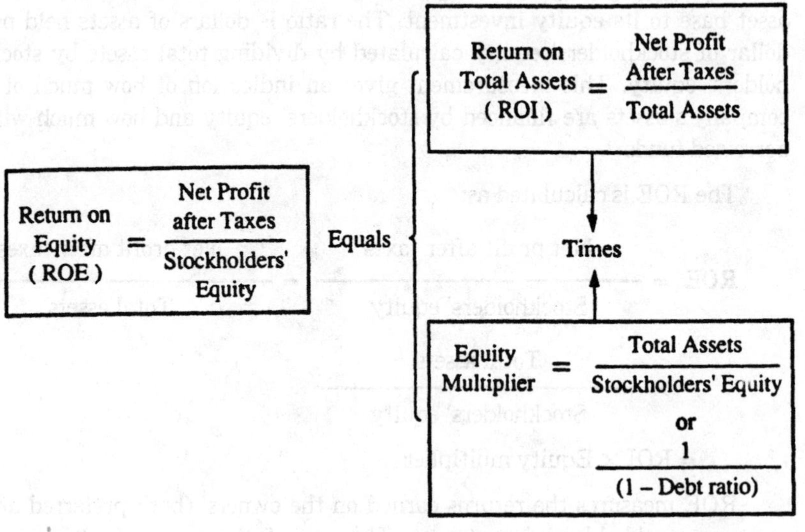

Example 5: In Example 1, assume stockholders' equity of $45,000.

Then,

$$\text{Equity multiplier} = \frac{\text{Total assets}}{\text{Stockholders' equity}} = \frac{\$100,000}{\$45,000} = 2.22$$

$$= \frac{1}{(1 - \text{debt ratio})} = \frac{1}{(1 - 0.55)} = \frac{1}{0.45} = 2.22$$

$$ROE = \frac{\text{Net profit after taxes}}{\text{Stockholders' equity}} = \frac{\$18{,}000}{\$45{,}000} = 40\%$$

$$ROI = \$18{,}000/\$100{,}000 = 18\%$$

$$ROE = ROI \times \text{Equity multiplier} = 18\% \times 2.22 = 40\%$$

If the company used only equity, the 18-percent ROI would equal ROE. However, 55 percent of the firm's capital is supplied by creditors ($45,000/$100,000 = 45% is the equity-to-asset ratio; $55,000/$100,000 = 55% is the debt ratio). Since the 18-percent ROI all goes to stockholders, who put up only 45 percent of the capital, the ROE is higher than 18 percent. This example indicates the company was using leverage (debt) favorably.

Example 6: To further demonstrate the interrelationship between a firm's financial structure and the return it generates on the stockholders' investments, let us compare two firms that generate $300,000 in operating income. Both firms employ $800,000 in total assets, but they have different capital structures. One firm employs no debt, whereas the other uses $400,000 in borrowed funds. The comparative capital structures are shown as:

	A	*B*
Total assets	$800,000	$800,000
Total liabilities	—	400,000
Stockholders' equity (a)	800,000	400,000
Total liabilities and stockholders' equity	$800,000	$800,000

Firm B pays 10-percent interest for borrowed funds. The comparative income statements and ROEs for firms A and B would look as follows:

Operating income	$300,000	$300,000
Interest expense	—	(40,000)
Profit before taxes	$300,000	$260,000
Taxes (30% assumed)	(90,000)	(78,000)
Net profit after taxes (b)	$210,000	$182,000
ROE [(b)/(a)]	26.25%	45.5%

The absence of debt allows firm A to register higher profits after taxes. Yet the owners in firm B enjoy a significantly higher return on their investments. This provides an important view of the positive contribution debt can make to a business, but within a certain limit. Too much debt can increase the firm's financial risk and, thus, the cost of financing.

If the assets in which the funds are invested are able to earn a return greater than the fixed rate of return required by the creditors, the leverage is positive and the common stockholders benefit. The advantage of this formula is that it enables the company to break its ROE into a profit margin portion (net profit margin), an efficiency-of-asset-utilization portion (total asset turnover), and a use-of-leverage portion (equity multiplier). It shows that the company can raise shareholder return by employing leverage—taking on larger amounts of debt to help finance growth.

Since financial leverage affects net profit margin through the added interest costs, management must look at the various pieces of this ROE equation, within the context of the whole, to earn the highest return for stockholders. Financial managers have the task of determining just what combination of asset return and leverage will work best in its competitive environment. Most companies try to keep at least a level equal to what is considered to be "normal" within the industry.

Caution: Unfortunately, leverage is a two-edged sword. It works two ways. If assets are unable to earn a high enough rate to cover fixed finance charges, then the stockholder suffers. The reason is that part of the profits from the assets that the stockholder has provided to the firm will have to go to make up the shortfall to the long-term creditors, and he/she will be left with a smaller return than otherwise would have been earned.

¶1515 The Sustainable Rate of Growth

The sustainable rate of growth (g*) represents the rate at which a firm's sales can grow if it wants to maintain its present financial ratios and does not want to resort to the sale of new equity shares. A simple formula can be derived for g* where we assume that a firm's assets and liabilities all grow at the same rate as its sales, that is:

$$\text{Sustainable rate of growth } (g^*) = \text{ROE } (1 - b)$$

Recall that ROE is the firm's return on equity:

$$\text{ROE} = \frac{\text{Net profit after taxes}}{\text{Stockholders' equity}} = \frac{\text{Net profit after taxes}}{\text{Total assets}} \times \frac{\text{Total assets}}{\text{Stockholders' equity}}$$

$$= \text{ROI} \times \text{Equity multiplier}$$

And, b is the firm's dividend payout ratio, that is:

$$\frac{\text{Dividends per share}}{\text{Earnings per share}}$$

The term (1 − b) is sometimes referred to as the *plowback ratio,* since it indicates the fraction of earnings that are reinvested or plowed back into the firm. Consequently, a firm's sustainable rate of growth is determined by its ROE (i.e., its anticipated net profit margin, asset turnover, and capital structure), as well as its dividend policy.

.01 *Calculating the Sustainable Rate of Growth*

Consider the three firms:

Firm	*ROI*	*Equity Multiplier*	*Plowback Ratio*	*g**
A	10%	3.33	50%	16.65%
B	10%	3.33	100%	33.30%
C	10%	2.00	100%	20.00%

Comparing Firms A and B, we see that the only difference is that Firm A pays out half its earnings in common dividends (i.e., plows back half its earnings), whereas Firm B retains or plows back all of its earnings. The net result is that Firm B, with its added source of internal equity financing, can grow at twice the rate of Firm A (33.30 percent compared to 16.65 percent). Likewise, comparing Firms B and C, we note that they differ only in that Firm B finances only 30 percent (1/3.33) of its assets with equity, whereas Firm C finances 50 percent (1/2.00) of its assets with equity. The result is that Firm C's sustainable rate of growth is 20 percent compared to 33.30 percent for Firm B. This example indicates Firm B was using leverage (debt) favorably.

For this equation to accurately depict a firm's sustainable rate of growth, the following assumptions must hold: First, the firm's assets must vary as a constant percent of sales (i.e., even fixed assets expand and contract directly with the level of firm sales). Second, the firm's liabilities must all vary directly with firm sales. This means that the firm's management will expand its borrowing (both spontaneous and discretionary) in direct proportion with sales to maintain its present ratio of debt to assets. Finally, the firm pays out a constant proportion of its earnings in common stock dividends regardless of the level of firm sales. Since all three of these assumptions are only rough approximations to the way that firms actually behave, the equation provides crude approximation of the firm's actual sustainable rate of growth. However, an estimate of g* using the equation can be a very useful first step in the firm's financial planning process.

¶ 1520 Economic Value Added (EVA®)

EVA is a concept similar to residual income but often applied at the overall firm level as well as at the departmental level. It is a registered trademark of Stern Stewart & Co. (www.sternstewart.com), which developed the concept.

EVA is a measure of economic profit but not the accounting profit we are accustomed to seeing in a corporate profit and loss statement. It is a measure of an operation's true profitability. The cost of debt capital (interest expense) is deducted when calculating net income, but no cost is deducted to account for the cost of common equity. Hence, in an economic sense, net income overstates "true" income. EVA overcomes this flaw in conventional accounting.

EVA is found by taking the net operating profit after taxes (NOPAT) for a particular period (such as a year) and subtracting the annual cost of *all* the capital a firm uses. EVA recognizes all capital costs, including the opportunity cost of the shareholder funds. It is a business's true economic profit. Such economic profits are the basis of shareholder value creation. *Note:* The calculation of EVA can be complex, because it makes various cost of capital and accounting principles adjustments.

The formula is:

EVA = NOPAT − After-tax cost of total capital

= Earnings before interest and taxes (EBIT) (1 − Tax rate)

− (Total capital) (After-tax cost of capital)

Total capital used here is total assets *minus* current liabilities. Hence, it is long-term liabilities *plus* equity (preferred stock and common equity). Thus, EVA is an estimate of a business's true economic profit for the year, and it differs sharply from accounting profit. EVA represents the residual income that remains after the cost of *all* capital, including equity capital, has been deducted, whereas accounting profit is determined without imposing a charge for equity capital. Equity capital has a cost because funds provided by shareholders could have been invested elsewhere where they would have earned a return. In other words, shareholders give up the opportunity to invest funds elsewhere when they provide capital to the firm. The return they could earn elsewhere in investments of equal risk represents the cost of equity capital. This cost is an *opportunity cost* rather than an *accounting cost,* but it is quite real nevertheless.

The following example illustrates how an operation's economic profit differs from its accounting profit.

Example 7: A company with $100,000 in equity capital (stated at fair value) and $100,000 in eight-percent debt (also at fair value) had $60,000 in EBIT. Assume also that $200,000 equals capital employed. The corporate tax rate is 40 percent. If that company's weighted-average after-tax cost of capital is 14 percent, the EVA is $8,000, calculated as follows:

EBIT	$60,000
Minus taxes (40% × $60,000)	(24,000)
NOPAT	$36,000
Capital charge (14% × $200,000)	(28,000)
EVA	$ 8,000

The company's traditional income statement reports income of $31,200, calculated as follows:

EBIT	$60,000
Minus interest (8% × $100,000)	(8,000)
Income before taxes	52,000
Income taxes (40% × $52,000)	(20,800)
Net income after taxes	$31,200

Initially, a 31.2-percent return on equity ($31,200 of net income/ $100,000 of equity capital) seems favorable, but what is the cost of that equity capital? Given equal amounts of debt and equity, the cost of the equity capital must be 23.2 percent because the after-tax weighted-average cost of capital was 14 percent, and the after-tax cost of debt capital was 4.8% (8% (1.0 – 40%)). *Note:* Since 14% = (4.8%)(1/2) + X (1/2), X = 23.2%.

Thus, $23,200 of the $31,200 of net income is nothing more than the opportunity cost of equity capital. The $8,000 of EVA is the only portion of earnings that has created value for the shareholders. Accordingly, if income after taxes had been only $20,000 (a 20-percent return on equity), shareholder value would have been reduced, because the cost of equity capital would have exceeded the return.

.01 EVA and Value Creation

In the previous example, the $8,000 of EVA is the only portion of earnings that has created value for the shareholders. EVA provides a good measure of whether the firm has added to shareholder value. Therefore, if managers focus on EVA, this will help to ensure that they operate in a manner that is consistent with maximizing shareholder value. Note also that EVA can be determined for divisions—it is more often called *residual income*—as well as for the company as a whole, so it provides a useful basis for determining managerial compensation at all levels.

Although most companies adopt EVA for purposes of internal reporting and for calculating bonuses, some are publishing the results in the corporate annual reports. For example, Eli Lilly reports EVA in the Financial Highlights section of the annual report. Companies like SPX made it clear in its 1998 annual report: "EVA is the foundation of everything we do . . . It is a common language, a mindset, and the way we do business."

.02 More on NOPAT

Before computing NOPAT, analysts routinely adjust the company's reported earnings figures. These adjustments fall into three broad categories:

1. Isolate a company's sustainable operating profits by removing nonoperating or nonrecurring items from reported income.

2. Eliminate after-tax interest expense from the profit calculation, so that profitability comparisons over time or across companies are not clouted by differences in financial structure.

3. Adjust for distortions related to as accounting quality concerns, which involve potential adjustments to both income and assets for items such as the off-balance sheet operating leases.

NOPAT is used to improve the comparability of EVA calculations. Otherwise, firms with different debt structures could have the same operating performance but different net incomes.

NOPAT = Net income after taxes + Charges and gains × (1 − Tax rate) + Interest × (1 − Tax rate)

The following example illustrates the NOPAT computation.

Example 8: Given the following income statement for years 20X1 and 20X2:

Comparative Income Statement

	20X2	*20X1*
Sales	$ 5,199.0	$5,954.0
Cost of sales	(2,807.5)	(3,294.4)
Gross margin	2,391.5	2,659.6
Selling, general and administrative expenses	(1,981.0)	(2,358.8)
Restructuring charges and gains	113.4	1,053.5
Interest expense	(106.8)	(131.6)
Other revenue and expenses	(1.5)	(2.2)
Before-tax income	415.6	1,220.5
Income taxes (40%)	(166.2)	(488.2)
Net income	$ 249.4	$ 732.3

NOPAT Calculations

	20X2	*20X1*
Net income as reported	$ 249.4	$ 732.3
Restructuring charges and gains after-tax	-68.04	-632.1
Interest expense after-tax	64.08	79.0
NOPAT	$ 245.4	$ 179.2

For example, for year 20X2:

NOPAT = Net income after taxes + Charges and gains × (1 − Tax rate) + Interest × (1 − Tax rate)

= $249.4 − $113.4 (1 − .4) + $106.8 (1 − .4) = $249.4 − $68.04 + $64.08 = $245.4

.03 Capital Charge

The capital charge is the most distinctive and important aspect of EVA. Under conventional accounting, most companies appear profitable but many in fact are not. The capital charge equals the after-tax weighted-average cost of capital (calculated based on fair values of debt and equity) times the investment base or total capital employed (total assets minus current liabilities or the sum of long-term debt, preferred stock, and common equity).

.04 Key Features of EVA

The main characteristics of EVA are summarized below.

1. For internal purposes, EVA is a better measure of profitability than ROI because a manager with a high ROI would be reluctant to invest in a new project with a lower ROI than is currently being earned, even though that return might be higher than the cost of capital. Thus, including a capital charge on departmental income statements helps managers to make decisions that will benefit the company.

2. There is an evidence of a direct correlation between EVA and increases in stock prices. For example, AT&T found an almost perfect correlation between its EVA and its stock price. In fact, many analysts have found that stock prices track EVA far more closely than other factors, such as earnings per share (EPS), operating margin, or ROE. The argument is that simply having a continuing stream of income is not enough; income must exceed the cost of capital for a stock to rise significantly in the stock market.

3. EVA uses dollars instead of percentages to measure changes. For example, it is much more appealing to report that the company generated $1 million in shareholder value than to say that the ROI increased from 10 to 15 percent.

4. EVA is the only financial management system that provides a common language for employees across all operating and staff functions and allows all management decisions to be modeled, monitored, communicated, and compensated in a single and consistent way—always in terms of the value added to shareholder investment.

.05 What Value-Driven Managers Can Do to Improve EVA

As a simplified form:

EVA = NOPAT – (After-tax weighted average cost of capital) (Net assets)

Another way to look at it is:

$$EVA = \frac{NOPAT}{\text{Net assets}} (\text{Net assets}) - (\text{After-tax weighted average cost of capital}) (\text{Net assets})$$

$$= \left(\frac{NOPAT}{\text{Net assets}} - \text{After-tax weighted average cost of capital} \right) (\text{Net assets})$$

$$= (\text{Return on net assets} - \text{After-tax weighted average cost of capital}) (\text{Net assets})$$

Assuming other variables stay constant, EVA increases when RONA (return on net assets) increases, WACC (after-tax weighted average cost of capital) decreases, net assets increase (assuming profitable growth), or net assets decrease (in the case of money-losing assets).

Evidence from EVA adopters shows several ways to achieve improvements:

1. Increase asset turnover.
2. Dispose of unprofitable businesses.
3. Refurbish assets.
4. Structure deals that require less capital.
5. Increase leverage and use less equity finance.
6. Invest in profitable growth.

Note that three of the above actions (increasing asset turnover, repairing assets, and structuring deals with less capital) increase EVA through improvement in RONA. Disposing of unprofitable businesses increases EVA, providing improvements in the spread between RONA and WACC are greater than the reduction in net assets. Increasing leverage increases EVA by reducing WACC, assuming that the company is underlevered when it begins taking on more debt. Investing is profitable, and increases EVA, as long as the RONA on the investment exceeds the WACC.

.06 EVA Compensation

EVA bonus plans don't just motivate managers to think about current EVA and future EVA. Otherwise, managers would focus entirely on short-term performance at the expense of the future. Value-creating investments might be avoided because their immediate effects on EVA are negative. The solution is to give managers a direct economic state in future EVA, not just the current period. The performance evaluation will be more meaningful if the current EVA is compared to EVAs from previous periods, target EVAs, and EVAs from other operating units or companies.

.07 A Caveat

EVA is no panacea, and it is no substitute for sound corporate strategies. But when EVA is at the center of a company's performance measurement system, and when bonus systems are linked, alignment between the interests of managers and shareholders improves. The effect is that when managers make important decisions, they are more likely to do so in ways that deliver superior returns for shareholders.

Chapter 16
Corporate Valuations

¶ 1601 What Is Corporate Valuation?

Corporate valuation, or broadly *business valuation,* involves estimating the worth or price of a company, one of its operating units, or its ownership shares. There are many reasons for the valuation. The reason for the valuation might be for the purchase or sale of the business, mergers and acquisitions, buy-back agreements, expanding the credit line, or tax matter (see Exhibit 1). The buying and selling of businesses is not the only reason for the demand for business valuations. Tough economic times result in increased litigation involving partner disputes and dissenting shareholder actions. Economies of scale encourage mergers and acquisitions to help maintain market share and ensure economic stability in a recessing economy.

For buying or selling a business, a valuation might be important for establishing an asking or offering price. But what is the value of the business? Is it the value of the company's assets? Is it the value of the company's earnings? Is it the value of the company's loyal customers and good reputation? Is it something else? The answer is that it might be any of the above or all of the above. Further, you must consider the type of business and its major activities, industry conditions, competition, marketing requirements, management possibilities, risk factors, earning potential, and financial health of the business.

Usually, *value* is determined by an interested party. Although there is usually no single value (or "worth") that can be associated with a business in all situations, there is usually a defendable value that can be assigned to a business in most situations. To be a proficient valuation analyst, a CFO requires analytical and writing skills. More specifically, one must be adept at financial analysis, economic forecasts, accounting and audit fundamentals, income taxes, and legal and economic research.

Exhibit 1

Business Valuation Opportunities

- Buy-sell agreements
- Mergers, acquisitions, and spinoffs
- Liquidation or reorganization of a business
- Initial public offering
- Minority shareholder interests
- Employee stock ownership plans
- Financing
- Return on investment analysis
- Government actions
- Allocation of acquisition price
- Adequacy of life insurance
- Litigation
- Divorce action
- Compensatory damage cases
- Insurance claims
- Estate and gift taxes
- Incentive stock options
- Charitable contributions

Source: National Association of Certified Valuation Analysts

The valuation process is an art and not a science because everyone's perception is slightly different. This chapter provides basic steps involved in valuation and various ways to determine what a business is worth. Further, various IRS Revenue Rulings are presented, recommending specific valuation measures especially with regard to income tax issues.

To determine a company's value, the purpose of the valuation and an appropriate perspective must be specified. The perspective might be that of a buyer, a seller, the IRS, or a court. When these are known, a business appraisal can be performed. Generally, the appraisal process determines the value of the business based on an asset, earnings (or cash flows), and/or market approach. In valuing the business, the following factors should be considered:

- History of the business
- Nature of the company
- Economic and political conditions
- Health of the industry
- Distribution channels and marketing factors
- Financial position
- Degree of risk
- Growth potential
- Trend and stability of earnings
- Competition
- Employee relationships
- Location
- Customer base
- Quality of management
- Ease of transferability of ownership

¶ 1605 Steps in Valuation

As an initial step in valuation, the key financial information must be accumulated and analyzed, including historical financial statements, projected financial statements, and tax returns. There must be familiarity with the business, including the company's strategic position in the industry. Further, the major assumptions of the valuation must be clearly spelled out. A variety of "what-if" scenarios must be investigated to reduce valuation errors. Exhibit 2 summarizes the basic steps in business valuations.

Exhibit 2

Steps in a Valuation

1. Analyze historical performance
   - Accumulate and analyze key financial information, such as earnings and invested capital.
   - Develop an integrated historical perspective.
   - Analyze financial health.
2. Project future performance
   - Understand strategic positon.
   - Develop performance scenarios.
   - Forecast financial statement line items.
   - Check overall forecast for reasonableness.
3. Estimate rate of capitalization
   - Develop target market value weights.
   - Estimate capitalization rate (cost of capital).
4. Estimate valuation
   - Select proper valuation method.
   - Choose forecast horizon.
   - Discount future value to present.
5. Compute and interpret results
   - Incorporate market and control discounts.
   - Compute and test results with major assumptions.
   - Interpret results within decision context.

.01 Definitions of "Value"

Various individuals will have different ideas of how much a business is worth and how its value should be determined. Various individuals and groups might define "value" differently.

Fair market value. Fair market value is generally defined as the price at which property would change hands between a willing buyer and a willing seller, when neither is compelled to act and both have a reasonable knowledge of the relevant facts. With the asset approach, assets are valued at fair (i.e., appraised) market value.

Fair market value is often an important valuation definition in estate, gift, and other federal tax related valuations. It is a well-accepted IRS and tax court concept. Generally, these groups will consider that a company's value is equivalent to its fair market value. Accordingly, a financial manager will need to consider this definition when performing valuations that may have the IRS as an interested party.

Replacement value. Replacement value is the cost of replacing something. The use of the definition might be applicable for establishing "damages" in antitrust suits, in condemnation proceedings, and in similar situations. At times, the definition could be used in a federal or state court. In some situations, replacement value might be determined to be a company's fair market value.

Liquidation value. The lowest value associated with a business is its liquidation value. Liquidation value is, in effect, the value of an item (a business) sold to the highest available bidder. Typically, the seller is compelled to sell, and the buyer knows of the seller's need to sell. Liquidation value is a depressed value. For a business, assets might be sold piecemeal. Usually, liquidation value is defined as the amount received by the seller after selling and administrative expenses are paid. At times, a company's liquidation value could be its fair market value.

"Going concern" value. "Going concern" value is the opposite of liquidation value. Going concern value is the value of a business based on the presumption that the business will continue as an operating entity. That is, the company will not be liquidated. A company's going concern value will usually be its fair market value.

.02 Matching Value Definitions and Valuation Reasons

An initial step in the business valuation process is to match the reason and perspective of the valuation with an appropriate definition of value. Note that each definition of "value" is not mutually exclusive. In a given situation, several definitions might concurrently apply. Exhibit 3 shows valuation reasons and value definitions that might be connected with them.

Exhibit 3

Definition of Value

Valuation Reason	*FMV*	*Liq. Value*	*Repl. Value*	*Going Concern Value*
Purchase of business	x		x	x
Sale of business	x			x
Shareholder litigation	x			x
Bankruptcy, dissolution		x		
Recapitalization	x			x

.03 General Approaches to Business Valuation

When a company is not publicly traded, willing buyers and willing sellers capable of establishing an independent and objective value for a business will not exist at most times when the valuation is needed. Accordingly, an estimate of the price at which the company might change hands between a willing buyer and a willing seller must be made. To do this, one or more of three approaches to valuation might be used.

Market comparison. Values of comparable companies in the industry may provide useful norms. The idea is to establish the company's value based on actual sales that are indicative of the company's current value.

A basic requirement for using prior sales of a firm's ownership interests in the appraisal of its current value is that each prior sale be indicative of the existing circumstances of the company. If prior sales were made in the too distant past, or were of a form or substance not indicative of the subject company's current situation, the use of the sale(s) may not be appropriate for establishing the company's current worth. In particular, small sales of noncontrolling interests and sales between related parties might not indicate the value of the company and its related ownership interests at the time of the sale. They would not be indicative of the company's current value either.

When comparable company sales are evaluated, the requirements are greater. Comparable company sales should only be used when the sales have occurred in the recent past and are of a sufficient size to appropriately establish a supportable value. They should be in the same industry. The companies should be similar in products and services offered, competitive positions, financial structures, and historical financial performance. Unfortunately, finding comparable companies is difficult because closely held company operating performance and sale information are frequently unavailable. Companies interested in comparative statistics might refer to *BIZCOMPS Business Sale Statistics* published by BIZCOMPS (P.O. Box 711777, San Diego, CA 92171, www.bizcomps.com). This is the annual report compiling information for 1,600 businesses in many industries.

Earnings (or cash flows). A second approach for business valuations is based on earnings. The earnings approach considers a company's value to be equivalent to its ability to create income (or cash flow). The concept is to associate the firm's income with a rate of return commensurate with the company's investment risk.

Assets. A third approach for establishing the value of a business is to consider the company's value to be equivalent to the value of its net tangible assets. For the dissolution of the business, the company's value might be based on the liquidated value of the company's assets. If the company is to be "duplicated," the company's value might be based on asset replacement values. If the company will continue as a going concern, the company's value might be based on the fair market value of the company's assets.

.04 *Performing a General Analysis of the Company being Valued*

For appraisal purposes, the determination of a company's value is usually based on a market, earnings, and/or assets approach to value. There are various business valuation methods associated with each. To understand and apply the methods, one needs to understand various attributes about the company being valued. Especially, an understanding is necessary of the company's:

- Industry.
- Customers and markets.
- Products and services.
- Employees and management.
- Assets.
- Historical and projected financial performance.

Each of these areas will significantly affect the valuation of the business and the use of various valuation methods.

Industry outlook. In assessing a company's industry, a CFO should evaluate the economic outlook for the industry, barriers to entry, government controls, and similar items. If the industry is expected to grow, firms in the industry might be perceived as being increasingly valuable. Further, you will need to consider competition. In a highly competitive industry, companies might be reduced in value because of competitive pressures, price discounting, etc.

Customers and markets. In assessing a company's customers and markets, you should evaluate the company's key customers and the strength of the customers. If the company has many customers, and none of the customers represent a significant percentage of the sales of the company, the company might be increasingly stable. The company may have a lower associated investment risk. If a company has only a few large customers, you will need to weigh carefully the implications and the likelihood of its losing the customers.

Products and services. In evaluating a company's products and services, you should look at their quality. You should compare the company's products and services with competitive products and services. Evaluate the company's investments in research and development and historical trends in sales and expenses of important products and services. Consider the number of products and services the company offers and the extent to which the company relies on one or several products or services for most of its sales and profits. When a company has only one or a few products or services, the competitive risks associated with the products and services become a factor. Generally, diverse and stable product lines might be associated with a stable company. Limited product lines might imply an increased investment risk.

Employees and management. Qualified management usually means that the company is stable. Qualified management might enhance the value of the company. To the extent that a firm has had significant turnover in its management (and/or employees), the company might be considered a risky investment. In general, inexperienced management and a high turnover rate are indicative of a high-risk company.

Assets. Typically, the value of a company's tangible assets is a minimum value associated with the business. For valuation purposes, judge a company's assets to ensure that the assets are indeed valuable. Scrutinize in detail such items as obsolete inventory, old fixed assets, bad debts in accounts receivable, and capitalized expenses. For some assets, specific evaluations may be necessary.

Historical and projected financial performance. Evaluating a company's historical and projected financial performance can be time consuming and complex. A CFO needs to establish the reliability of the company's historical financial statements and assess the implications of sales, expenses, and profits. Typically, for determining the value of a company, you evaluate the company's operating performance. Accordingly, you may have to remove the implications of non-typical and non-operating transactions included in the company's financial statements.

A company's historical financial statements might include excess compensation and significant perks to owners. Frequently, the CFO will need to add excess compensation paid to owners back to the company's income to fully understand the profitability of the company. Adjustments might also be made to the financial statements to convert cash basis statements to accrual basis statements. In particular, cash basis statements might not display accounts receivable, accounts payable, and accrued liabilities.

In evaluating a company's financial performance, the CFO will want to review various expense ratios as a percent of sales and various sales, income, and expense trends. In particular, the CFO would assess the financial statements for purposes of making assumptions about the future profitability of the company. Evaluate various company ratios and compare them with other companies in the industry. You might also develop projected financial statements for the company for three or more years.

.05 Business Valuation Methods

There are numerous ways of determining the value of the business. Further, there are many possible combinations of various methods. Nine popular valuation methods are illustrated below.

1. Adjusted net assets method. The adjusted net assets valuation method presumes the value of a company is equivalent to the value of its net tangible assets. Asset values are often based on fair market values when the company is expected to continue as a going concern, liquidated values when the company is not expected to continue as a going concern, and replacement values when the costs of duplicating the company are being assessed.

The fair market value of the net tangible assets of the company may be based on independent appraisal. An addition is made for goodwill. An investment banking firm who handles the purchase and sale of businesses may be hired to appraise the tangible property. Usually, the fair market value of the assets exceeds their book value.

An advantage of the adjusted net assets valuation method is that it is frequently easy to determine the value of a company's tangible net assets. A disadvantage of the method is that it ignores the important implications of company earnings. In many instances, an adjusted net assets valuation is a conservative valuation. It might be a minimum value associated with a business.

Example 1:

Net tangible assets (at fair market value)	$12,000,000
Plus goodwill	6,000,000
Valuation	$18,000,000

2. Gross revenue multiplier method. The value of the company may be determined based on the revenue generating capacity of the company. For example, many Internet stocks that lose money in the short run and yet have great future earnings potential tend to derive their value from their revenue generating capacity or registered member subscriptions. The formula for this method is as follows:

Value of the business = Revenue × Gross revenue multiplier

The gross revenue multiplier used is the one customary in the industry. The industry norm gross multiplier is based on the average ratio of market price to sales typical in the industry. *Note: Business Week* magazine of McGraw-Hill publishes every year a special weekly edition, *Corporate Scorecard,* containing average industry ratios.

If reported earnings are suspect, this method may also be advisable.

Example 2:

Gross revenue	$32,500,000
× Gross revenue multiplier	.4
Valuation	$13,000,000

3. Capitalization of earnings method. The capitalization of earnings valuation method is in many ways the opposite of the adjusted net assets valuation method. It uses income, as opposed to assets, to value the business. A variation of the method incorporates *cash flows* as opposed to earnings.

The capitalization of earnings valuation method is based on the notion that the investors will only acquire stock in a company if they can earn a rate of return that is high enough to offset the risks associated with the investment. The trade-off is the risk of the loss of the investment with the rate of return that might be realized. In general, high-risk companies need to yield high rates of return to stimulate equity investments. Low risk companies can produce lower rates of return and still attract equity investors.

The formula for the capitalization of earnings method follows:

Value of the business = Earnings (or cash flow)/Capitalization rate

Frequently, earnings or cash flow for this method is the current year's earnings (or cash flow), a simple average of two to five prior years, a weighted-average adjusted historical earnings, or the company's projected profit for the following year. The method presumes the earnings value used in the method is indicative of future earnings expectations on an ongoing basis. In this method, earnings can be any one of the following:

- Before-tax earnings.
- After-tax earnings.
- Earnings before interest and taxes (EBIT).

The capitalization rate is the rate of return an investor would expect to receive for investing in the company based on the company's perceived risk. It is typically a weighted cost of capital, weights being a target mix of different sources of financing, equity, or nonequity.

Two examples for this method are presented below.

Example 3:

Earnings (simple average)	$1,250,000
/Capitalization rate	10%
Valuation	$12,500,000

The following example uses weighted-average historical earnings, in which more weight is given to the most recent years. This is more representative than a simple average. Weighted-average makes sense, because current earnings reflect current prices and recent business activity. In the case of a five-year weighted average, the current year is assigned a weight of five, while the initial year is assigned a weight of one. The multiplier is then applied to the weighted-average five-year adjusted historical earnings to derive a valuation.

Example 4:

Year	*Historical Earnings*	*Weight*	*Total*
20X4	$2,780,000	5	$13,900,000
20X3	$1,670,000	4	$6,680,000
20X2	$1,350,000	3	$4,050,000
20X1	$1,780,000	2	$3,560,000
20X0	$2,100,000	1	$2,100,000
		15	$30,290,000

Weighted average five-year earnings:
$30,290,000/15 = $2,019,333

Weighted average five-year earnings	$2,019,333
/Capitalization rate (20%)	20%
Valuation	$10,096,667

Note:

1. In case where cash flow is used instead of earnings, we use *distributable* or *free cash flow*—a term gaining increasing popularity among financial analysts. *Free cash flow* is defined as the company's operating cash flows (before interests) *minus* cash outlays for the replacement of existing operating capacity, such as buildings, equipment, and furnishings. It is the amount available to finance planned expansion of operating capacity, to reduce debt, to pay dividends, or to repurchase stock.

2. Many analysts prefer to use accrual accounting earnings rather than cash flows, however, on the belief that *current* accrual accounting earnings are more useful than measures of *current* cash flows in predicting *future* cash flows.

4. Price-earnings ratio method. For publicly traded stocks, stock trading prices are often directly proportional to earnings. Often, within industries, there is a consistency between companies. The price-earnings ratio method is predicated on the notion that price-earnings ratios (P/Es) of publicly traded stocks might be indicative of a closely held company's value. The notion is this: if the closely held company were publicly traded, it would trade at a price similar to the price at which comparable companies trade.

The formula for this method is as follows:

Value of the business = Earnings per share (EPS)/Price-earnings multiplier

Typically, earnings for this method is the most recent year's earnings per share (EPS) or an average of two to five prior years. The P/E multiplier is usually a historical average based on comparable, actively traded stocks. Some use a P/E ratio based on the most current period rather than an average of prior years.

Example 5:

Earnings after taxes	$1,000,000
Outstanding shares	250,000
Earnings per share (EPS)	$4
P/E ratio	15
Estimated market price per share	$60
× Number of shares outstanding	250,000
Valuation	$15,000,000

5. Dividend payout (or dividend paying capacity) method. The dividend payout (or dividend paying capacity) valuation method presumes that the "compensation" for stock ownership is dividends. The method is based on the notion that a stock's value is related to the company's ability to pay dividends and the yield investors expect.

The dividend payout method involves the following steps:

1. Company's dividend paying capacity = Earnings × Dividend payout percentage
2. Value of business = Company's dividend paying capacity/ Dividend yield rate

Typically, earnings for this method is an average of two to five prior years. Some use before-tax profits; others use after tax profits. The dividend payout percentage and dividend yield rate are established with reference to comparable, publicly traded stocks. A variation of the method would establish the company's dividend paying capacity to be monies received by the owners of the closely held company as dividends, excess compensation, and perks.

Although the method is in infrequent use, the method incorporates some of the most defendable valuation principles of all methods.

Example 6:

Earnings after taxes	$1,000,000
Dividend payout percentage	40%
Dividend paying capacity	$400,000
/Dividend yield rate	4%
Valuation	$10,000,000

6. Excess earnings return on assets method. The excess earnings return on assets valuation method implies that within an industry, a given level of company assets will generate a particular level of earnings. To the extent a company has earnings above the expected level of earnings, the company is presumed to have an enhanced value. The enhanced value is attributed to goodwill (or intangible assets). The addition of the value of the goodwill and the fair market value of the net tangible assets equals the total valuation.

The excess earnings return on assets method involves the following steps:

1. Industry expected earnings = Company assets × Industry expected return on assets
2. Excess earnings = Company earnings − Industry expected earnings
3. Goodwill (intangible assets) = Excess earnings/Capitalization rate
4. Value of the business = Goodwill + Fair market value of net tangible assets

As per IRS Revenue Ruling 59-60 (to be discussed later), the IRS recommends this method to value a business for tax purposes.

Example 7:

Year	*Net Tangible Assets*	*Weight*	*Total*
20X0	$10,000,000	1	$10,000,000
20X1	$14,000,000	2	$28,000,000
20X2	$18,000,000	3	$54,000,000
20X3	$19,000,000	4	$76,000,000
20X4	$18,500,000	5	$92,500,000
		15	$260,500,000

Weighted average net tangible assets $260,500,000/15 = $17,366,667	
Weighted average earnings (5 years)—given	$1,800,000
Minus industry rate of return on weighted-average Net tangible assets ($17,366,667 × 10%)	1,736,667
Excess earnings	$63,333
/Capitalization factor (20%)	0.2
Plus goodwill (intangibles)	$316,667
Plus fair market value of net tangible assets	$16,000,000
Valuation	$16,316,667

7. Excess earnings return on sales method. The excess earnings return on sales valuation method values a company based on sales, earnings, and assets. Generally, the method implies that within an industry, a given level of sales will generate a given level of earnings. When a company has earnings above the industry's expected level of earnings, the company is considered to have goodwill (or intangible assets). The value of goodwill plus the fair market value of the net tangible assets is considered to be the value of the company.

The excess earnings return on sales method involves the following steps:

1. Industry expected earnings = Company sales × Industry expected return on sales
2. Excess earnings = Company earnings − Industry expected earnings
3. Goodwill (intangible assets) = Excess earnings/Capitalization rate
4. Value of the business = Goodwill + Fair market value of net tangible assets

Variations in this method include the use of the company's current year's sales or a two to five year average for computing the industry expected profits.

Example 8:

Year	*Sales*	*Weight*	*Total*
20X0	$11,100,000	1	$11,100,000
20X1	$12,500,000	2	$25,000,000
20X2	$20,000,000	3	$60,000,000
20X3	$21,000,000	4	$84,000,000
20X4	$24,200,000	5	$121,000,000
		15	$301,100,000

Weighted average sales $301,100,000/15 = $2,007,333	
Weighted average earnings (5 years)—given	$1,800,000
Minus industry rate of return on weighted-average sales ($20,073,333 × 4%)	802,933
Excess earnings	$997,067
/Capitalization factor (20%)	0.2
Valuation of goodwill (intangibles)	$4,985,335
Plus fair market value of net tangible assets	$16,000,000
Valuation	$20,985,335

8. Discounted cash flow method. The discounted cash flow (DCF) method equates the value of a business with the cash flows the business is expected to create.

The discounted cash flow method presumes that the purpose of a company is to generate cash flow (or earnings) and, therefore, assets, distribution channels, etc., have a value related to the cash flows they are able to create. Conceptually, the method is similar to the capitalization of earnings valuation method except that in the discounted cash flow method *projected* earnings (or cash flows) as opposed to historical earnings (or cash flows) are assessed. If the growth rate is used to project future earnings, the rate may be based on prior growth rate, future expectations, and the inflation rate. The discount rate may be based on the market interest rate of a low risk asset investment.

The formula for the discounted cash flow method follows:

Value of the business = Present value of the earnings (or cash flow) projection + Present value of terminal value (selling price)

Typically, cash flows are projected for at least five years, and a terminal value (or selling price) is established for the value of the business at the end of the term.

Example 9:

Year	*Cash Flows (7% growth rate)*	T_3 = *Present Value (PV) Factor at a 10% discount rate*	*Total PV*
20X0	$500,000	0.909	$ 454,500
20X1	$535,000	0.826	$ 441,910
20X2	$572,450	0.751	$ 429,910
20X3	$612,522	0.683	$ 418,352
20X4	$655,398	0.621	$ 407,002
Present value of future earnings			$ 2,151,674

If the anticipated selling price at the end of year 20X4 is $18,000,000, the valuation of the business equals:

Present value of future earnings	$ 2,151,674
Present value of selling price $18,000,000 × .621	$11,178,000
Valuation	$13,329,674

9. The abnormal earnings approach. The abnormal earnings approach is based on the notion that value is driven not by the level of earnings themselves but by the level of earnings *relative to some benchmark,* i.e., the cost of capital (or a minimum required rate of return). The rationale is that investors are willing to pay a premium for those firms that earn more than the cost of capital—implying firms that produce *positive abnormal earnings.* The formula is:

Value of the business = Book value of assets + Present value of expected future abnormal earnings (Actual earnings minus required earnings)

Example 10: Suppose a firm's book value of assets at the beginning of the year is $100 per share, and the cost of capital is 13 percent. Investors, therefore, require earnings of at least $13 per share ($100 × 13%). If the market expects the company to report earnings equal to the benchmark earnings and if it actually earns $23 per share for the year, thus exceeding the benchmark, the value of the company (stock price) will increase to reflect the firm's superior performance.

10. Combination valuation method. The combination valuation method is not really a method, but a combination of other methods. Often, the use of a combination method establishes a more reasonable value for a business than any single method. In particular, in a combination method, earnings, assets, comparable companies, prior sales of company stock, and other important valuation concepts might be accounted for.

Further, the valuation of the company may be estimated based on a weighted-average value of several methods. The most weight should typically be placed on the earnings method and the least on the asset approaches.

Example 11:

Method	*Valuation Amount*	*Weight*	*Total*
Adjusted net assets	$18,000,000	1	$18,000,000
Excess earnings on rate of return	$20,985,333	2	$41,970,666
		3	$59,970,666
Total/3 = $59,970,666/3 = $19,990,222			
Valuation			$19,990,222

Generally, before a combination method should be used, it should be established that the combination method results in a better valuation than any method individually and that the use of each method in the combination supports the final valuation.

.06 *Earnings Surprises*

Many valuation methods require estimates of future earnings. But estimates can (and usually do) prove to be off targets. When this transpires, an "earnings surprise" results. For example, a *positive* earnings surprise, i.e., reported earnings exceeding market expectations, tends to have an upward rift in stock value. Earnings estimates are reported by companies, *Zacks* (www.zacks.com), *First Call* (www.firstcall.com), and *Nelson's,* which are the leading trackers of analysis' earnings projections. These firms constantly poll brokerages for their earnings estimates. From that survey, these companies publish a compilation that includes the high, low, and mean prediction for a company's upcoming quarterly and fiscal year results.

.07 *Marketability Discounts*

Generally, a business ownership interest that can be sold quickly will be worth more than a similar ownership interest that cannot be sold quickly. In various business valuation methods, this implication may or may not be considered. When it is not, a marketability discount might be associated with the value of the ownership interest otherwise determined. A marketability discount is the reduction in the value of a company (or ownership interest) because the company (or ownership interest) might take considerable time to sell.

There are differences of opinion about marketability discounts. The IRS objects to them and will argue that the implications of marketability will have been accounted for elsewhere in the valuation process. Many believe that statistics prove there is in fact a depressed value for closely held company ownership interests, and they might assign discounts as high as 25 to 45 percent to account for this.

In assigning a marketability discount, some analysts compute the cost of taking the company public and deduct the amount from the value of the company otherwise determined. The presumption is that if the company is taken public, its ownership interests will be marketable.

.08 Control Premiums and Discounts

A business valuation does not have to be restricted to the valuation of an entire company. Frequently, partial ownership interests are valued for purchase or sale, divorce proceedings, estate planning, and other reasons.

When a partial ownership interest is appraised, it is not necessarily true that its value is equivalent to its ownership percentage times the value of the company. Generally, to the extent the ownership interest can control the activities of the business, the ownership interest may have an enhanced value. To the extent the ownership interest has little control over the operations of the company, the ownership interest might have a reduced value. Practitioners frequently account for this with control premiums and lack of control discounts.

For closely held companies, noncontrolling ownership interests can have a depressed value. The company might not be particularly marketable, and the noncontrolling interests might have an even greater lack of appeal because of their inability to influence the payment of dividends and the general operations of the company.

In developing control premiums and lack of control discounts, the circumstances of the ownership interests must be considered. Before a discount or premium is assigned, it should be determined that in fact an ownership interest has an increased or decreased value based on control/ lack of control implications. For example, in a company where the father is the controlling owner and two children are the noncontrolling owners, circumstances might indicate that the noncontrolling owners are in fact receiving dividends, etc., commensurate with the value of their ownership percentages. Accordingly, depending on the purpose of the valuation, the assignment of a discount to the noncontrolling interests might not be appropriate. Before assigning premiums or discounts, it is very important to ensure that the control/lack of control implications were not accounted for in some other way in the valuation process.

¶ 1610 Revenue Ruling 59-60

In valuing the stock of closely held corporations, or the stock of corporations where market quotations are not available, all other available financial data, as well as all relevant factors affecting the fair market value must be considered for estate tax and gift tax purposes. No general formula may be given that is applicable to the many different valuation situations arising in the valuation of such stock. However, the general approach, methods, and factors which must be considered in valuing such securities are outlined.

Section 1. Purpose.

The purpose of this Revenue Ruling is to outline and review the approach, methods and factors to be considered in valuing shares of the capital stock of closely held corporations for estate tax and gift tax purposes. The methods discussed herein will apply likewise to the valuation of corporate stocks on which market quotations are either unavailable or are of such scarcity that they do not reflect the fair market value.

Sec. 2. Background and Definitions.

01. All valuations must be made in accordance with the applicable provisions of the Internal Revenue Code of 1954 and the Federal Estate Tax & Gift Tax Regulations. Sections 2031(a), 2032 and 2512(a) of the 1954 Code (Sections 811 and 1005 of the 1939 Code) require that the property to be included in the gross estate, or made the subject of a gift, shall be taxed on the basis of the value of the property at the time of death of the decedent, the alternative date if so elected, or the date of gift.

02. Section 20.2031-1(b) of the Estate Tax Regulations (Section 81.10 of the Estate Tax Regulations 105) and Section 25.2512-1 of the Gift Tax Regulations (Section 86.19 of Gift Tax Regulations 108) define fair market value, in effect, as the price at which the property would change hands between a willing buyer and a willing seller when the former is not under any compulsion to buy and the latter is not under any compulsion to sell, both parties having reasonable knowledge of relevant facts. Court decisions frequently state in addition that the hypothetical buyer and seller are assumed to be able, as well as willing, to trade and to be well informed about the market for the property.

03. Closely held corporations are those company shares owned by a relatively limited number of stockholders. Often the entire stock issue is held by one family. The result of this situation is that little, if any, trading in the shares takes place. There is, therefore, no established market for the stock and such sales as occur at irregular intervals seldom reflect all of the elements of a representative transaction as defined by the term "fair market value."

Sec. 3. Approach To Valuation.

01. A determination of fair market value, being a question of fact, will depend upon the circumstances in each case. No formula can be devised that will be generally applicable to the multitude of different valuation issues arising in estate and gift tax cases. Often, an appraiser will find wide differences of opinion as to the fair market value of a particular stock. In resolving such differences, he or she should maintain a reasonable attitude in recognition of the fact that valuation is not an exact science. A sound valuation will be based upon all the relevant facts, but the elements of common sense, informed judgment, and reasonableness must enter into the process of weighing those facts and determining their aggregate significance.

02. The fair market value of specific shares of stock will vary as general economic conditions change from "normal" to "boom" or "depression," that is, according to the degree of optimism or pessimism with which the investing public regards the future at the required date of appraisal. Uncertainty as to the stability or continuity of the future income from a property decreases its value by increasing the risk of loss of earnings and value in the future. The value of shares of stock of a company with very uncertain future prospects is highly speculative. The appraiser must exercise his judgment as to the degree of risk attaching to the business of the corporation which issued the stock, but that judgment must be related to all of the other factors affecting value.

03. Valuation of securities is, in essence, a prophecy as to the future and must be based on facts available at the required date of appraisal. As a generalization, the prices of stocks which are traded in volume in a free and active market by informed persons best reflect the consensus of the investing public as to what the future holds for the corporations and industries represented. When a stock is closely held, is traded infrequently, or is traded in an erratic market, some other measure of value must be used. In many instances, the next best measure may be found in the prices at which the stocks of companies engaged in the same or a similar line of business are selling in a free and open market.

Sec. 4. Factors To Consider.

01. It is advisable to emphasize that in the valuation of the stock of closely held corporations or the stock of corporations where market quotations are either lacking or too scarce to be recognized, all available financial data, as well as all relevant factors affecting the fair market value, should be considered. The following factors, although not all inclusive are fundamental and require careful analysis in each case:

(a) Nature of the business and the history of the enterprise from its inception.

(b) Economic outlook in general and the condition and outlook of the specific industry in particular.

(c) Book value of the stock and the financial condition of the business.

(d) Earning capacity.

(e) Dividend-paying capacity.

(f) Whether or not the enterprise has goodwill or other intangible value.

(g) Sales of the stock and the size of the block of stock to be valued.

(h) Market price of stocks of corporations engaged in the same or a similar line of business having their stocks actively traded in a free and open market, either on an exchange or over-the-counter.

02. The following is a brief discussion of each of the foregoing factors.

(a) The history of a corporate enterprise will show its past stability or instability, its growth or lack of growth, the diversity or lack of diversity of its operations, and other facts to form an opinion of the degree of business risk. For an enterprise which changed its form of organization but carried on the same or closely similar operations of its predecessor, the history of the former enterprise should be considered. The detail considered should increase with the date of appraisal, since recent events are of greatest help in predicting the future, but a study of gross and net income, and of dividends covering a long prior period, is highly desirable. The history to be studied should include, but need not be limited to, the nature of the business, its products or services, its operating and investment assets, capital structure, plant facilities, sales records and management, all of which should be considered as of the date of the appraisal, with due regard for recent significant changes. Events of the past that are unlikely to recur in the future should be discounted, since value has a close relation to future expectancy.

(b) A sound appraisal of a closely held stock must consider current and prospective economic conditions as of the date of appraisal, both in the national economy and in the industry or industries with which the corporation is allied. It is important to know that the company is more or less successful than its competitors in the same industry, or that it is maintaining a stable position with respect to competitors. Equal or even greater significance may attach to the ability of the industry with which the company is allied to compete with other industries. Prospective competition which has not been a factor in prior years should be given careful attention. For example, high profits due to the novelty of its product and the lack of competition often lead to increasing competition. The public's appraisal of the future prospects of competitive industries or of competitors within an industry may be indicated by price trends in the markets for commodities and for securities. The loss of the manager of a so-called "one-man" business may have a depressing effect upon the value of the stock of such business, particularly if there is a lack of trained personnel capable of succeeding to the management of the enterprise. In valuing the stock of this type of business, therefore, the effect of the loss of the manager on the future expectancy of the business, and the absence of management-succession potentialities are pertinent factors to be taken into consideration. On the other hand, there may be factors which offset, in whole or in part, the loss of the manager's services. For instance, the nature of the business and of its assets may be such that, they will not be impaired by the loss of the manager. Furthermore, the loss may be adequately covered by life insurance, or competent management might be employed on the basis of the consideration paid for the former manager's services. These, or other offsetting factors, if found to exist, should be carefully weighed against the loss of the manager's services in valuing the stock of the enterprise.

(c) Balance sheets should be obtained, preferably in the form of comparative annual statements for two or more years immediately preceding the date of appraisal, together with a balance sheet at the end of the month preceding that date, if corporate accounting will permit. Any balance sheet descriptions that are not self-explanatory, and balance sheet items comprehending diverse assets or liabilities, should be clarified in essential detail by supporting supplemental schedules. These statements usually will disclose to the appraiser (1) liquid position (ratio of current assets to current liabilities); (2) gross and net book value of principal classes of fixed assets; (3) working capital; (4) long-term indebtedness; (5) capital structure; and (6) net worth. Consideration should be given to any assets not essential to the operation of the business, such as investments in securities, real estate, etc. In general, such nonoperating assets will command a lower rate of return than do the operating assets, although in exceptional cases the reverse may be true. In computing the book value per share of stock, assets of the investment type should be revalued on the basis of their market price and the book value adjusted accordingly. Comparison of the company's balance sheets over several years may reveal, among other facts, such developments as the acquisition of additional production facilities or subsidiary companies, improvement in financial position, and details as to recapitalizations and other changes in the capital structure of the corporation. If the corporation has more than one class of stock outstanding, the charter or certificate of incorporation should be examined to ascertain the explicit rights and privileges of the various stock issues including: (1) voting powers, (2) preference as to dividends, and (3) preference as to assets in the event of liquidation.

(d) Detailed profit-and-loss statements should be obtained and considered for a representative period immediately prior to the required date of appraisal, preferably five or more years. Such statements should show (1) gross income by principal items; (2) principal deductions from gross income including major prior items of operating expenses, interest and other expense on each item of long-term debt, depreciation and depletion if such deductions are made, officers' salaries, in total if they appear to be reasonable or in detail if they seem to be excessive, contributions (whether or not deductible for tax purposes) that the nature of its business and its community position require the corporation to make, and taxes by principal items, including income and excess profits taxes; (3) net income available for dividends; (4) rates and amounts of dividends paid on each class of stock; (5) remaining amount carried to surplus; and (6) adjustments to, and reconciliation with, surplus as stated on the balance sheet. With profit and loss statements of this character available, the appraiser should be able to separate recurrent from nonrecurrent items of income and expense, to distinguish between operating income and investment income, and to ascertain whether or not any line of business in which the company is engaged is operated consistently at a loss and might be abandoned with benefit to the company. The percentage of earnings retained for business expansion should be noted when dividend paying capacity is considered. Potential future income is a major factor in many valuations of closely-held stocks, and all information concerning past income which will be helpful in predicting the future should be secured. Prior earnings records usually are the most reliable guide as to the future expectancy, but resort to arbitrary five-or-ten-year averages without regard to current trends or future prospects will not produce a realistic valuation. If, for instance, a record of progressively increasing or decreasing net income is found, then greater weight may be accorded the most recent years' profits in estimating earning power. It will be helpful, in judging risk and the extent to which a business is a marginal operator, to consider deductions from income and net income in terms of percentage of sales. Major categories of cost and expense to be so analyzed include the consumption of raw materials and supplies in the case of manufacturers, processors and fabricators; the cost of purchased merchandise in the case of merchants; utility services; insurance; taxes; depletion or depreciation; and interest.

(e) Primary consideration should be given to the dividend-paying capacity of the company rather than to dividends actually paid in the past. Recognition must be given to the necessity of retaining a reasonable portion of profits in a company to meet competition. Dividend-paying capacity is a factor that must be considered in an appraisal, but dividends actually paid in the past may not have any relation to dividend paying capacity. Specifically, the dividends paid by a closely held family company may be measured by the income needs of the stockholders or by their desire to avoid taxes on dividend receipts, instead of by the ability of the company to pay dividends. Where an actual or effective controlling interest in a corporation is to be valued, the dividend factor is not a material element, since the payment of such dividends is discretionary with the controlling stockholders. The individual or group in control can substitute salaries and bonuses for dividends, thus reducing net income and understating the dividend-paying capacity of the company. It follows, therefore, that dividends are a less reliable criteria of fair market value than other applicable factors.

(f) In the final analysis, goodwill is based upon earning capacity. The presence of goodwill and its value, therefore, rests upon the excess of net earnings over and above a fair return on the net, tangible assets. While the element of goodwill may be based primarily on earnings, such factors as the prestige and renown of the business, the ownership of a trade or brand name, and a record of successful operation over a prolonged period in a particular locality, also may furnish support for the inclusion of intangible value. In some instances, it may not be possible to make a separate appraisal of the tangible and intangible assets of the business. The enterprise has a value as an entity. Whatever intangible value there is, which is supportable by the facts, may be measured by the amount by which the appraised value of the tangible assets exceeds the net book value of such assets.

(g) Sales of stock of a closely held corporation should be carefully investigated to determine whether they represent transactions at arm's length. Forced or distress sales do not ordinarily reflect fair market value nor do isolated sales in small amounts necessarily control as the measure of value. This is especially true in the valuation of a controlling interest in a corporation. Since, in the case of closely held stocks, no prevailing market prices are available, there is no basis for making an adjustment for blockage. It follows, therefore, that such stocks should be valued upon a consideration of all the evidence affecting fair market value. Although it is true that a minority interest in an unlisted corporation's stock is more difficult to sell than a similar block of listed stock, it is equally true that control of a corporation, either actual or in effect, representing as it does an added element of value, may justify a higher value for a specific block of stock.

(h) Section 2031(b) of the Code states, in effect, that in valuing unlisted securities the value of stock or securities of corporations engaged in the same or a similar line of business which are listed on an exchange should be taken into consideration along with all other factors. An important consideration is that the corporations to be used for comparisons have capital stocks which are actively traded by the public. In accordance with Section 2031(b) of the Code, stocks listed on an exchange are to be considered first. However, if sufficient comparable companies whose stocks are listed on an exchange cannot be found, other comparable companies which have stocks actively traded on the over-the-counter market also may be used. The essential factor is that whether the stocks are sold on an exchange or over-the-counter, there is evidence of an active, free public market for the stock as of the valuation date. In selecting corporations for comparative purposes, care should be taken to use only comparable companies (corporations specified in the statute have similar lines of business). However, consideration must be given to other relevant factors in order that the most valid comparison possible be obtained. For example, a corporation having one or more issues of preferred stock, bonds or debentures in addition to its common stock should not be considered to be directly comparable to one having only common stock outstanding. In like manner, a company with a declining business and decreasing markets is not comparable to one with a record of current progress and market expansion.

Sec. 5. Weight To Be Accorded Various Factors.

The valuation of closely held corporate stock entails the consideration of all relevant factors as stated in Section 4. Depending upon the circumstances in each case, certain factors may carry more weight than others because of the nature of the company's business. To illustrate:

(a) Earnings may be the most important criterion of value in some cases whereas asset value will receive primary consideration in others. In general, the appraiser will accord primary consideration to earnings when valuing stocks of companies which sell products or services to the public; conversely, in the investment or holding type of company, the appraiser may accord the greater weight to the assets underlying the security to be valued.

(b) The value of the stock of a closely held investment or real estate holding company, whether or not family owned, is closely related to the value of the assets underlying the stock. For companies of this type the appraiser should determine the fair market values of the assets of the company. Operating expenses of such a company and the cost of liquidating it, if any, merit consideration when appraising the relative values of the stock and the underlying assets. The market values of the underlying assets give due weight to potential earnings and dividends of the particular items of property underlying the stock, capitalized at rates deemed proper by the investing public at the date of appraisal. A current appraisal by the investing public should be superior to the retrospective opinion of an individual. For these reasons, adjusted net worth should be accorded greater weight in valuing the stock of a closely held investment or real estate holding company, whether or not family owned, than any of the other customary yardsticks of appraisal, such as earnings and dividend paying capacity.

Sec. 6. Capitalization Rates.

In the application of certain fundamental valuation factors, such as earnings and dividends, it is necessary to capitalize the average or current results at some appropriate rate. A determination of the proper capitalization rate presents one of the most difficult problems in valuation. That there is no ready or simple solution will become apparent by a cursory check of the rates of return and dividend yields in terms of the selling prices of corporate shares listed on the major exchanges of the country. Wide variations will be found even for companies in the same industry. Moreover, the ratio will fluctuate from year to year depending upon economic conditions.

Thus, no standard tables of capitalization rates applicable to closely held corporations can be formulated. Among the more important factors to be taken into consideration in deciding upon a capitalization rate in a particular case are: (1) the nature of the business; (2) the risk involved; and (3) the stability or irregularity of earnings.

Sec. 7. Average of Factors.

Because valuations cannot be made on the basis of a prescribed formula, there is no means whereby the various applicable factors in a particular case can be assigned mathematical weights in deriving the fair market value. For this reason, no useful purpose is served by taking an average of several factors (for example, book value, capitalized earnings, and capitalized dividends) and basing the valuation on the result. Such a process excludes active consideration of other pertinent factors, and the end result cannot be supported by a realistic application of the significant facts in the case except by mere chance.

Sec. 8. Restrictive Agreements.

Frequently, in the valuation of closely held stock for estate and gift tax purposes, it will be found that the stock is subject to an agreement restricting its sale or transfer. Where shares of stock were acquired by a decedent subject to an option reserved by the issuing corporation to repurchase at a certain price, the option price is usually accepted as the fair market value for estate tax purposes. See Rev. Rul. 54-76 C.B. 1954-1, 194. However, in such a case the option price is not determinative of fair market value for gift tax purposes. Where the option, or buy and sell agreement, is the result of voluntary action by the stockholders and is binding during the life as well as at the death of the stockholders, such agreement may or may not, depending upon the circumstances of each case, fix the value for estate tax purposes. However, such agreement is a factor to be considered, with other relevant factors, in determining fair market value. Where the stockholder is free to dispose of shares during life and the option is to become effective only upon death, the fair market value is not limited to the option price. It is always necessary to consider the relationship of the parties, the relative number of shares held by the decedent, and other material facts, to determine whether the agreement represents a bona fide business arrangement or is a device to pass the decedent's shares to the natural objects of his bounty for less than an adequate and full consideration in money or money's worth. In this connection see Rev. Rul. 157 C.B. 1953-2, 255, and Rev. Rul. 189, C.B. 1953-2, 294.

Sec. 9. Effect on Other Documents.

Revenue Ruling 54-77, C.B. 1954-1, 187, is hereby superseded.

¶ 1615 How To Market Valuation Services

1. Display openly your association affiliation and accreditation.
2. Get yourself published, either through your various association affiliations or in accounting journals and local publications.
3. Build relationships with local attorneys and other CPAs. Attorneys and CPAs are the primary source for valuation work.
4. Convince your financial planner why proper valuations are essential in preparing a meaningful financial plan.
5. Let the courts in your county know of your expertise and availability.
6. Present local seminars to attorneys, CPAs, financial planners, bankers, and business owners on the applications, complexities, and uses of a business valuation.

7. Encourage your tax and accounting clients to get a valuation for:
   - Estate planning
   - Buy/sell arrangements
   - As a measurement of management's performance
   - Use in obtaining business credit lines and loans

Source: National Association of Certified Valuation Analysts

¶ 1620 Summary

Performing a business valuation is not a simple task. Although a business valuation might seem overwhelming at first, valuation concepts are in fact very logical and intuitive. The major issue is to clearly understand the concepts of valuation and how the concepts are used by the interested party. The next step is to fully investigate the company being valued, its industry, and various implications that might affect its value. Financial forecasting, analytical reviews, sales forecasting, financial analysis, and various planning activities are an important part of the business valuation process.

Some additional readings are:

1. Copeland, T., T. Koller, and J. Murrin, *Valuation: Measuring and Managing the Value of Companies* (New York: Wiley, 1994).
2. Palepu, K., V. Bernard, and P. Healy, *Business Analysis and Valuation* (Cincinnati, OH: South-Western Publishing, 1996).
3. Sanders, John, *Biz-Comps Business Sale Statistics* (San Diego, CA: BizComps, www.bizcomps.com).
4. Yegge, Wilber, *Basic Guide for Buying and Selling a Company,* John Wiley & Sons, ISBN 0471149438.
5. Yegge, Wilber, *Basic Guide for Valuing a Company,* John Wiley & Sons, ISBN 0471149454.

Part 6

Financing Issues

Chapter 17

Short-Term Financing

¶ 1701 Overview

In this chapter, we provide a broad picture of short-term financing (financing that will be repaid in one year or less). Examples of short-term financing are trade credit, short-term bank loans, commercial paper, and financing for receivables and inventory.

We also discuss intermediate-term financing, instruments with a maturity in excess of one year, such as some bank loans and leases. In deciding on a particular source of financing, managers should consider cost, risk, liquidity, and flexibility.

¶ 1705 Why Short-Term Financing?

Short-term financing may be used to meet seasonal and temporary fluctuations in funds position as well as to meet long-term needs. For example, short-term financing may be used to provide additional working capital, finance current assets (such as receivables and inventory), or provide interim financing for a long-term project (such as the acquisition of plant and equipment) until long-term financing is arranged. (Long-term financing may not always be appropriate because of perceived long-term credit risk or excessively high cost.)

When compared to long-term financing (see Chapter 16), short-term financing has several advantages. It is usually easier to arrange and less expensive and has more flexibility. The drawbacks of short-term financing are that it is subject to greater fluctuations in interest rates and refinancing is frequently required. There is greater risk of default because the loan comes due sooner, and any delinquency may damage the company's credit rating.

¶ 1710 Sources of Short-Term Financing

The sources of short-term financing include trade credit, bank loans, bankers' acceptances, finance company loans, commercial paper, receivable financing, and inventory financing. One particular source may be more appropriate than another in a given circumstance; some are more desirable than others because of interest rates or collateral requirements.

You should consider the merits of the different sources of short-term financing, focusing on:

- Cost.
- Effect on financial ratios.
- Effect on credit rating. Some sources of short-term financing may negatively impact the company's credit rating, such as factoring accounts receivable.
- Risk (reliability of the source of funds for future borrowing). If your company is materially affected by outside forces, it will need more stable and reliable financing.
- Restrictions, such as requiring a minimum level of working capital.
- Flexibility.
- Expected money market conditions (e.g., future interest rates) and availability of future financing.
- Inflation rate.
- Company profitability and liquidity positions, both of which must be favorable if the company is to be able to pay its near term obligations.
- Stability and maturity of operations.
- Tax rate.

If the company can predict that it will be short of cash during certain times, the financial manager should arrange for financing (such as a line of credit) in advance instead of waiting for an emergency.

.01 Using Trade Credit

Trade credit (accounts payable) are balances owed by your company to suppliers. It is a spontaneous (recurring) financing source for creditworthy companies since it comes from normal operations. Trade credit is the least expensive form of financing inventory. Trade credit is readily available since suppliers want business. Trade credit requires no collateral. There is no interest charge or else a minimal one; it is convenient; and it is likely to be extended if the company gets into financial trouble. If the company has liquidity difficulties, it may be able to stretch (extend) accounts payable. However, the company will be required to give up any cash discount offered and accept a lower credit rating. The company should prepare a report analyzing accounts payable in terms of lost discounts, aged debit balances, aged unpaid invoices, and days to pay.

Example 1: The company purchases $500 worth of merchandise per day from suppliers. The terms of purchase are net/60, and the company pays on time. The accounts payable balance is:

$500 per day × 60 days = $30,000

The company should typically take advantage of a cash discount offered for early payment because failing to do so results in a high opportunity cost. The cost of not taking a discount equals:

$$\left[\frac{\text{Discount lost}}{\text{Dollar proceeds you have use of by not taking the discount}}\right] \times \left[\frac{360}{\text{Number of days you have use of the money by not taking the discount}}\right]$$

Example 2: The company buys $1,000 in merchandise on terms of 2/10, net/30. The company fails to take the discount and pays the bill on the 30th day. The cost of the discount is:

$$\frac{\$20}{\$980} \times \frac{360}{20} = 36.7\%$$

The company would be better off taking the discount even if it needed to borrow the money from the bank since the opportunity cost is 36.7 percent. The interest rate on a bank loan would be far less.

.02 Bank Loans

Even though other institutions, such as savings and loan associations and credit unions, provide banking services, most banking activities are conducted by commercial banks. Commercial banks allow the company to operate with minimal cash and still be confident of planning activities even in uncertain conditions.

Commercial banks favor short-term loans since they like to get their money back within one year. If the company is large, a group of banks may form a consortium to furnish the desired level of capital.

The prime interest rate is a benchmark for the short-term loan interest rate banks charge creditworthy corporate borrowers. Good companies with strong financial strength can get terms below prime. Your company's interest rate may be higher depending upon the risk the bank believes it is taking.

Types of loans. Bank financing may take the following forms:

- Unsecured loans
- Secured loans
- Lines of credit
- Letters of credit
- Revolving credit
- Installment loans

Unsecured loans. Most short-term unsecured (uncollateralized) loans are self-liquidating. This kind of loan is recommended if the company has an excellent credit rating. It is usually used to finance projects having quick cash flows and is appropriate if the company has immediate cash and can either repay the loan in the near future or quickly obtain longer-term financing. Seasonal cash shortfalls and desired inventory buildups are among the reasons to use an unsecured loan. The disadvantages of this kind of loan are that it carries a higher interest rate than a secured loan since there is no collateral and that a lump sum payment is required.

Secured loans. If the company's credit rating is deficient, the bank may lend money only on a secured basis. Collateral can take many forms, including inventory, marketable securities, or fixed assets. Even if the company is able to obtain an unsecured loan, it may be better off taking a collateralized loan at a lower interest rate.

Lines of credit. Under a line of credit, the bank agrees to lend money up to a specified amount on a recurring basis. The bank typically charges a commitment fee on the amount of the unused credit line. Credit lines are typically established for a one-year period and may be renewed annually. You can determine if the preferred line of credit is adequate for your company's present and immediate future needs by considering the current and expected cash requirements of the business.

The advantages of a line of credit are that it offers easy and immediate access to funds during tight money market conditions, and it enables the company to borrow only as much as it needs and to repay immediately when cash is available. You should use a line of credit if the company is working on large individual projects for a long time period and will obtain minimal or no payments until the job is completed. The disadvantages of lines of credit relate to the collateral requirements and the additional financial information that must be presented to the bank. Banks also may place restrictions on the company, such as setting a ceiling on capital expenditures or requiring a minimum level of working capital.

When the company borrows under a line of credit, it may be required to maintain a compensating balance (a noninterest-bearing account) with the bank. The compensating balance is stated as a percentage of the loan and effectively increases the cost of the loan. A compensating balance may also be placed on the unused portion of a line of credit, in which case, the interest rate is reduced.

> ***Example 3:*** The company borrows $200,000 and is required to keep a 12-percent compensating balance. It also has an unused line of credit of $100,000, for which a 10-percent compensating balance is required. The minimum balance that must be maintained is:

$$(\$200{,}000 \times .12) + (\$100{,}000 \times .10) = \$24{,}000 + \$10{,}000 = \$34{,}000$$

A line of credit is typically decided upon prior to the actual borrowing. In the days between the arrangement for the loan and the actual borrowing, interest rates may change. Therefore, the agreement will stipulate the loan is at the prime interest rate prevailing when the loan is extended plus a risk premium. (The prime interest rate will be unknown until the actual borrowing since market interest rates may change from the time you contract for a loan and the time you receive the funds.)

The bank may test the company's financial capability by requiring it to "clean up," that is, repay the loan for a brief time during the year (e.g., for one month). The payment shows the bank that the loan is actually seasonal rather than permanent. If the company is unable to repay a short-term loan, it should probably finance with long-term funds.

Letters of credit. A letter of credit is a document issued by a bank guaranteeing the payment of a customer's drafts up to a specified amount for a designated time period. In effect, the bank's credit is substituted for that of the buyer, minimizing the seller's risk. Payment may be made on submission of proof of shipment or other performance. Letters of credit are used primarily in international trade.

There are different types of letters of credit. A *commercial letter of credit* is typically drawn in favor of a third party. A *confirmed letter of credit* is provided by a correspondent bank and guaranteed by the issuing bank.

The advantages of letters of credit are that the company does not have to pay cash in advance of shipment, using funds that could be used elsewhere in the business.

Revolving credit. A revolving credit is an agreement between the bank and the borrower in which the bank contracts to make loans up to a specified ceiling within a prescribed time period. With revolving credit, notes are short term (typically 90 days). When part of the loan is paid, an amount equal to the repayment may again be borrowed under the terms of the agreement. Advantages are the readily available credit and few restrictions compared to line-of-credit agreements. A major disadvantage may be restrictions imposed by the bank.

Installment loans. An installment loan requires monthly payments of interest and principal. When the principal on the loan decreases sufficiently, you may be able to refinance at a lower interest rate. The advantage is that an installment loan may be tailored to satisfy seasonal financing needs.

Interest. Interest on a loan may be paid either at maturity (ordinary interest) or in advance (discounting the loan). When interest is paid in advance, the loan proceeds are reduced and the effective (true) interest rate is increased.

Example 4: The company borrows $30,000 at 16-percent interest per annum and repays the loan one year later. The interest is $30,000 × 0.16 = $4,800. The effective interest rate is 16 percent ($4,800/$30,000).

Example 5: Assume the same facts as in the prior example, except the note is discounted. The effective interest rate increases as follows:

Proceeds = Principal − Interest = $30,000 − $4,800 = $25,200

$$\text{Effective interest rate} = \frac{\text{Interest}}{\text{Proceeds}} = \frac{\$4{,}800}{\$25{,}200} = 19.2\%$$

A compensating balance will increase the effective interest rate.

Example 6: The effective interest rate for a one-year, $600,000 loan that has a nominal interest rate of 19 percent with interest due at maturity and requiring a 15-percent compensating balance is:

$$\text{Effective interest rate (with compensating balance)} = \frac{\text{Interest rate} \times \text{Principal}}{\text{Proceeds, \%} \times \text{Principal}}$$

$$\frac{0.19 \times \$600{,}000}{(1.00 - 0.15) \times \$600{,}000} = \frac{\$114{,}000}{\$510{,}000} = 22.4\%$$

Example 7: Assume the same facts as in the prior example, except that the loan is discounted. The effective interest rate is:

$$\text{Effective interest rate (with discount)} = \frac{\text{Interest rate} \times \text{Principal}}{(\text{Proceeds, \%} \times \text{Principal}) - \text{Interest}}$$

$$\frac{0.19 \times \$600{,}000}{(0.85 \times \$600{,}000) - \$114{,}000} = \frac{\$114{,}000}{\$396{,}000} = 28.8\%$$

Example 8: The company has a credit line of \$400,000, but it must maintain a compensating balance of 13 percent on outstanding loans and a compensating balance of 10 percent on the unused credit. The interest rate on the loan is 18 percent. The company borrows \$275,000. The effective interest rate on the loan is calculated as follows.

The required compensating balance is:

.13 × \$275,000	\$35,750
.10 × 125,000	12,500
	\$48,250

$$\text{Effective interest rate (with line of credit)} = \frac{\text{Interest rate (on loan)} \times \text{Principal}}{\text{Principal} - \text{Compensating balance}}$$

$$\frac{0.18 \times \$275{,}000}{\$275{,}000 - \$48{,}250} = \frac{\$49{,}500}{\$226{,}750} = 21.8\%$$

On an installment loan, the effective interest rate computation is illustrated below. Assuming a one-year loan payable in equal monthly installments, the effective rate is based on the average amount outstanding for the year. The interest is computed on the face amount of the loan.

Example 9: The company borrows \$40,000 at an interest rate of 10 percent to be paid in 12 monthly installments. The average loan balance is \$40,000/2 = \$20,000. Divide by 2 to obtain an average (the beginning balance is \$40,000 and the ending balance is 0, so the average is beginning plus ending divided by 2). The effective interest rate is:

$$\frac{\text{Interest}}{\text{Average loan balance}} = \frac{\$40{,}000 \times 10\%}{\$20{,}000} = \frac{\$4{,}000}{\$20{,}000} = 20\%$$

Example 10: Assume the same facts as in the prior example, except that the loan is discounted. The interest of \$4,000 is deducted in advance so the proceeds received are \$40,000 − \$4,000 = \$36,000. The average loan balance is \$36,000/2 = \$18,000. The effective interest rate is \$4,000/\$18,000 = 22.2%.

The effective interest cost computation may be more complicated when installment payments vary. The true interest cost of an installment loan is the *internal rate of return* of the applicable cash flows converted on an annual basis (if desired).

Example 11: The company borrows \$100,000 and will repay it in three monthly installments of \$25,000, \$25,000, and \$50,000. The interest rate is 12 percent.

Amount of borrowing equals:

Installment loan	\$100,000
Less: Interest on first installment (\$25,000 × .12)	3,000
Balance	\$ 97,000

We now compute the effective interest cost on the installment loan as follows:

$\$97{,}000 = \$25{,}000/(1 + \text{Cost}) + \$25{,}000/(1 + \text{Cost})^2 + \$50{,}000/(1 + \text{Cost})^3$

Solving for cost yields 1.37% on a monthly basis.

= 1.37% × 12 = 16.44% on annual basis

This shows that the effective annual interest rate on the installment loan is 16.44 percent.

Dealing with the banker. Banks are eager to lend money to meet self-liquidating, cyclical business needs. A short-term bank loan is an inexpensive way to obtain funds to satisfy working capital requirements during the business cycle. But the financial officer must be able to explain what the company's needs are in an intelligent manner.

.03 *Commercial Finance Loans*

When credit is unavailable from a bank, the company may have to go to a commercial finance company which typically charges a higher interest rate than the bank and requires collateral.

Typically, the value of the collateral is greater than the balance of the loan and may consist of accounts receivable, inventories, and fixed assets. Commercial finance companies also finance the installment purchases of industrial equipment. A portion of their financing is sometimes obtained through commercial bank borrowing at wholesale rates.

.04 *Commercial Paper*

Commercial paper is a short-term unsecured obligation with a maturity ranging from two to 270 days, issued by companies to investors with temporarily idle cash. Commercial paper can be issued only if the company possesses a very high credit rating; therefore, the interest rate is less than that of a bank loan, typically one-half percent below the prime interest rate. Commercial paper is sold at a discount (below face value), with the interest immediately deducted from the face of the note by the creditor; however, the company pays the full face value. Commercial paper may be issued through a dealer or directly placed to an institutional investor (a dealer is a company that buys securities and then sells them out of its own inventory, while an institutional investor is an entity that buys large volumes of securities, such as banks and insurance companies).

The benefits of commercial paper are that no security is required, the interest rate is typically less than that required by banks or finance companies, and the commercial paper dealer often offers financial advice. The drawbacks are that commercial paper can be issued only by large, financially sound companies and that commercial paper dealings are impersonal. Commercial paper is usually backed by a bank letter of credit.

We now look at an example that determines whether the amount of commercial paper issued by a company is excessive.

Example 12: A company's balance sheet appears below.

Assets:	
Current assets	$ 540,000
Fixed assets	800,000
Total assets	$1,340,000
Liabilities and stockholders' equity:	
Current liabilities—	
Notes payable to banks	$ 100,000
Commercial paper	650,000
Total current liabilities	$ 750,000
Long-term liabilities	260,000
Total liabilities	$1,010,000
Stockholders' equity	330,000
Total liabilities and stockholders' equity	$1,340,000

The amount of commercial paper issued by the company is a high percentage of both its current liabilities, 86.7 percent ($650,000/ $750,000), and its total liabilities, 64.4 percent ($650,000/$1,010,000). Because bank loans are minimal, the company may want to do more bank borrowing and less commercial paper financing. In the event of a money market squeeze, the company may find it advantageous to have a working relationship with a bank.

Example 13: The company issues $500,000 of commercial paper every two months at a 13-percent rate. There is a $1,000 placement cost each time. The percentage cost of the commercial paper is:

Interest ($500,000 × .13)	$65,000
Placement cost ($1,000 × 6)	6,000
Cost	$71,000

$$\text{Percentage cost of commercial paper} = \frac{\$71,000}{\$500,000} = 14.2\%$$

Example 14: Ajax Corporation issues $300,000 worth of 18-percent, 90-day commercial paper. However, the funds are needed for only 70 days. The excess funds can be invested in securities earning 17 percent. The brokerage fee associated with the commercial paper transaction is 1.5 percent. The dollar cost to the company in issuing the commercial paper is:

Interest expense [0.18 × $300,000 × (90/360)]	$13,500
Brokerage fee (0.015 × $300,000)	4,500
Total cost	$18,000
Less: Return on marketable securities [0.17 × $300,000 × (20/360)]	2,833
Net cost	$15,167

Example 15: The company needs $300,000 for the month of November. Its options are:

1. Obtaining a one-year line of credit for $300,000 with a bank. The commitment fee is 0.5 percent, and the interest charge on the used funds is 12 percent.

2. Issuing two-month commercial paper at 10-percent interest. Because the funds are needed only for one month, the excess funds ($300,000) can be invested in eight-percent marketable securities for December. The total transaction fee for the marketable securities is 0.3 percent.

The line of credit costs:

Commitment fee for unused period (0.005) (300,000) (11/12)	$1,375
Interest for one month (0.12) (300,000) (1/12)	3,000
Total cost	$4,375

The commercial paper costs:

Interest charge (0.10) (300,000) (2/12)	$5,000
Transaction fee (0.003) (300,000)	900
Less interest earned on marketable securities (0.08) (300,000) (1/12)	(2,000)
Total cost	$3,900

Since $3,900 is less than $4,375, the commercial paper arrangement is the better option.

.05 *Using Receivables for Financing*

In accounts receivable financing, the accounts receivable serve as security for the loan as well as the source of repayment.

Financing backed by accounts receivable generally takes place when:

- Receivables are at least $25,000.

- Sales are at least $250,000.
- Individual receivables are at least $100.
- Receivables apply to selling merchandise rather than rendering services.
- Customers are financially strong.
- Sales returns are low.
- The buyer receives title to the goods at shipment.

Receivable financing has several advantages. It eliminates the need to issue bonds or stock to obtain a recurring cash flow. Its drawback is the high administrative costs of monitoring many small accounts.

Accounts receivable may be financed under either a factoring agreement or an assignment (pledging) arrangement. *Factoring* is the outright sale of accounts receivable to a bank or finance company without recourse; the purchaser takes all credit and collection risks. The proceeds received by the seller are equal to the face value of the receivables less the commission charge, which is usually two to four percent higher than the prime interest rate. The cost of the factoring arrangement is the factor's commission for credit investigation, interest on the unpaid balance of advanced funds, and a discount from the face value of the receivables if there is high credit risk. Remissions by customers are made directly to the factor.

The advantages of factoring are that it offers immediate cash, reduces overhead because the credit examination function is no longer needed, provides financial advice, allows for receipt of advances as required on a seasonal basis, and strengthens the company's balance sheet position.

The disadvantages of factoring include both the high cost and the negative impression left with customers as a result of the change in ownership of the receivables. Factors may also antagonize customers by their demanding methods of collecting delinquent accounts.

In an *assignment* (pledging) arrangement, ownership of the accounts receivable is not transferred. Instead, receivables are given to a finance company with recourse. The finance company usually advances between 50 and 85 percent of the face value of the receivables in cash. Your company is responsible for a service charge, interest on the advance, and any resulting bad debt losses, and continues to receive customer remissions.

The assignment of accounts receivable has the advantages of providing immediate cash, making cash advances available on a seasonal basis, and avoiding negative customer feelings. The disadvantages include the high cost, the continuing of administrative costs, and the bearing of all credit risk.

Financial managers must be aware of the impact of a change in accounts receivable policy on the cost of financing receivables. When accounts receivable are financed, the cost of financing may rise or fall. For example, when credit standards are relaxed, costs rise; when recourse for defaults is given to the finance company, costs decrease; and when the minimum invoice amount of a credit sale is increased, costs decline.

The financial officer should compute the costs of accounts receivable financing and select the least expensive alternative.

Example 16: A factor will purchase the company's $120,000 per month accounts receivable. The factor will advance up to 80 percent of the receivables for an annual charge of 14 percent and a 1.5-percent fee on receivables purchased. The cost of this factoring arrangement is:

Factor fee [0.015 × ($120,000 × 12)]	$21,600
Cost of borrowing [0.14 × ($120,000 × 0.8)]	13,440
Total cost	$35,040

Example 17: A factor charges a three-percent fee per month. The factor lends the company up to 75 percent of receivables purchased for an additional one percent per month. Credit sales are $400,000 per month. As a result of the factoring arrangement, the company saves $6,500 per month in credit costs and a bad debt expense of three percent of credit sales. XYZ Bank has offered an arrangement to lend the company up to 75 percent of the receivables. The bank will charge two percent per month interest plus a four percent processing charge on receivable lending. The collection period is 30 days. If the company borrows the maximum per month, should it stay with the factor or switch to XYZ Bank?

Cost of factor:	
Purchased receivables (0.03 × $400,000)	$12,000
Lending fee (0.01 × .75 × $400,000)	3,000
Total cost	$15,000
Cost of bank financing:	
Interest (0.02 × .75 × $400,000)	$ 6,000
Processing charge (0.04 × $300,000)	12,000
Additional cost of not using the factor:	
Credit costs	6,500
Bad debts (0.02 × $400,000)	8,000
Total cost	$32,500

Since $15,000 is less than $32,500, the company should stay with the factor.

Example 18: A company needs $250,000 and is weighing the alternatives of arranging a bank loan or going to a factor. The bank loan terms are 18-percent interest, discounted, with a compensating balance of 20 percent. The factor will charge a four-percent commission on invoices purchased monthly; the interest rate on the purchased invoices is 12 percent, deducted in advance. By using a factor, the company will save $1,000 monthly credit department costs and avoid uncollectible accounts estimated at three percent of the factored accounts. Which is the better alternative for the company?

The bank loan which will net the company its desired $250,000 is:

$$\frac{\text{Proceeds}}{(100\% - \text{Proceeds deducted})} = \frac{\$250{,}000}{100\% - (18\% + 20\%)}$$

$$\frac{\$250{,}000}{1.0 - 0.38} = \frac{\$250{,}000}{0.62} = \$403{,}226$$

$$\text{Effective interest rate} = \frac{\text{Interest rate}}{\text{Proceeds, }\%} = \frac{0.18}{0.62} = 29.0\%$$

We must briefly switch to the factor arrangement in order to determine the $8,929 below as a bank cost.

The amount of accounts receivable that should be factored to net the firm $250,000 is:

$$\frac{\$250{,}000}{1.0 - 0.12 - 0.04} = \frac{\$250{,}000}{0.84} = \$297{,}619$$

The total annual cost of the bank arrangement is:

Interest ($250,000 × 0.29)	$72,500
Additional cost of not using a factor:	
Credit costs ($1,000 × 12)	12,000
Uncollectible accounts ($297,619 × 0.03)	8,929
Total cost	$93,429

The effective interest rate of factoring accounts receivable is:

$$\text{Effective interest rate} = \frac{\text{Interest rate}}{\text{Proceeds, }\%}$$

$$= \frac{12\%}{100\% - (12\% + 4\%)} = \frac{0.12}{0.84} = 14.3\%$$

The total annual cost of the factoring alternative is:

Interest ($250,000 × 0.143)	$35,750
Factoring ($297,619 × 0.04)	11,905
Total cost	$47,655

In Example 18, factoring should be used because costs are less than half that of the bank loan costs.

Before looking at the next example on factoring, we should discuss several items that were mentioned in that example. Reserve on accounts receivable is the amount retained by the factor against problem receivables, which reduces the proceeds received by the company. Average accounts receivable is the average balance held for the period and is the basis for the factor's commission at the time the receivables are purchased by the factor.

Example 19: A company is considering a factoring arrangement. The company's sales are $2,700,000, accounts receivable turnover is nine times, and a 17-percent reserve on accounts receivable is required. The factor's commission charge on average accounts receivable payable at the point of receivable purchase is two percent. The factor's interest charge is 16 percent of receivables after subtracting the commission charge and reserve. The interest charge reduces the advance. The annual effective cost under the factoring arrangement is computed below.

$$\text{Average accounts receivable} = \frac{\text{Credit sales}}{\text{Turnover}} = \frac{\$2{,}700{,}000}{9} = \$300{,}000$$

The company will receive the following amount by factoring its accounts receivable:

Average accounts receivable	$300,000
Less: Reserve ($300,000 × 0.17)	-51,000
Commission ($300,000 × 0.02)	-6,000
Net prior to interest	$243,000
Less: Interest ($243,000 × (16%/9)	4,320
Proceeds received	$238,680

The annual cost of the factoring arrangement is:

Commission ($300,000 × 0.02)	$ 6,000
Interest ($243,000 × (16%/9)	4,320
Cost each 40 days (360/9)	$ 10,320
Turnover	× 9
Total annual cost	$ 92,880

The annual effective cost under the factoring arrangement based on the amount received is:

$$\frac{\text{Annual cost}}{\text{Average amount received}} = \frac{\$92{,}880}{\$238{,}680} = 38.9\%$$

.06 *Using Inventories for Financing*

Financing inventory, which typically takes place when the company has completely used its borrowing capacity on receivables, requires the existence of marketable, nonperishable, and standardized goods that have quick turnover and that are not subject to rapid obsolescence. Good collateral inventory can be easily sold. However, consider the price stability of the merchandise and the costs of selling the inventory when deciding on a course of action.

The cash advance for financed inventory is high when there is marketable inventory. In general, the financing of raw materials and finished goods is about 75 percent of value; the interest rate is approximately three to five points over the prime interest rate.

The drawbacks of inventory financing include the high interest rate and the restrictions placed on inventory.

Types of inventory financing include floating (blanket) liens, warehouse receipts, and trust receipts. With a *floating lien,* the creditor's security lies in the aggregate inventory rather than in its components. Even though the company sells and restocks, the lender's security interest continues. With a *warehouse receipt,* the lender receives an interest in the inventory stored at a public warehouse; the fixed costs of this arrangement are high. There may be a field warehouse arrangement in which the warehouse sets up a secured area directly at the company's location; the company has access to the goods but must continually account for them. With a *trust receipt* loan, the creditor has title to the goods but releases them to the company to sell on the creditor's behalf. As goods are sold, the company remits the funds to the lender. The drawback of the trust receipt arrangement is that a trust receipt must be given for specific items.

A collateral certificate guaranteeing the existence of pledged inventory may be issued by a third party to the lender. The advantage of a collateral certificate is its flexibility; merchandise need not be segregated or possessed by the lender.

Example 20: The company wants to finance $500,000 of inventory. Funds are required for three months. A warehouse receipt loan may be taken at 16 percent with a 90-percent advance against the inventory's value. The warehousing cost is $4,000 for the three-month period. The cost of financing the inventory is:

Interest [0.16 × 0.90 × $500,000 × (3/12)]	$18,000
Warehousing cost	4,000
Total cost	$22,000

Example 21: The company shows growth in operations but is experiencing liquidity difficulties. Six large financially sound companies are customers and account for 75 percent of sales. On the basis of the following financial information for 20X1, should the financial manager borrow on receivables or inventory?

Balance sheet data follow:

Asset:		
Current assets		
Cash	$27,000	
Receivables	380,000	
Inventory (consisting of 55% of work-process)	320,000	
Total current assets		$727,000
Fixed assets		250,000
Total assets		$977,000
Liabilities and stockholders' equity:		
Current liabilities		
Accounts payable	$260,000	
Loans payable	200,000	
Accrued expenses	35,000	
Total current liabilities		$495,000
Noncurrent liabilities		
Bonds payable		110,000
Total liabilities		$605,000
Stockholders' equity		
Common stock	$250,000	
Retained earnings	122,000	
Total stockholders' equity		372,000
Total liabilities and stockholders' equity		$977,000

Selected income statement information follows:

Sales	$1,800,000
Net income	130,000

Receivable financing is the expected choice since a high percentage of sales are made to only six large and financially strong companies. Receivables thus are highly collectible. It is also easier to control a few large customer accounts.

Inventory financing is not likely because of the high percentage of partially completed items. Lenders are reluctant to finance inventory when a large work-in-process balance exists since it will be hard for them to process and sell the goods.

.07 *Financing with Other Assets*

Assets other than inventory and receivables may be used as security for short-term bank loans. Possibilities include real estate, plant and equipment, cash surrender value of life insurance policies, and securities. Lenders are also usually willing to advance a high percentage of the market value of bonds or to make loans based on a third-party guaranty.

Exhibit 1 presents a summary of the major features of short-term financing sources.

Exhibit 1

Summary of Short-Term Financing Sources

Secured sources			
Accounts receivable as collateral			
1. Pledging	Commercial banks and finance companies	Typically 2% to 5% above prime plus fees (usually 2% to 3%). Low administrative costs. Advances typically ranging from 60% to 85%.	Qualified accounts receivable accounts serve as collateral upon collection of the account, the borrower remits to the lender. Customers are not notified of the arrangement. With recourse means that the risk of nonpayment continues to be borne by the company.
2. Factoring	Factors, commercial banks, and commercial finance companies	Typically a 2% to 3% discount from the face value of factored receivables. Interest on advances of almost 3% over prime. Interest on surplus balances held by factor of about 1/2% per month. Costs with factoring are higher than with pledging.	Certain accounts receivable are sold on a discount basis without recourse. This means that the factor bears the risk of nonpayment. Customers are notified of the arrangement. The factor provides more services than is the case with pledging.
Inventory collateral			
1. Floating liens	Commercial banks and commercial finance companies	About 4% above prime. Advance is about 40% of collateral value.	Collateral is all the inventory. There should be a stable inventory with many inexpensive items.
2. Trust receipts (floor planning)	Commercial banks and commercial finance companies	About 3% above prime. Advances ranging from 80% to 100% of collateral value.	Collateral is specific inventory that is typically expensive. Borrower retains collateral. Borrower remits proceeds to lender upon sale of the inventory.
3. Warehouse receipts	Commercial banks and commercial finance companies	About 4% above prime plus about a 2% warehouse fee. Advance of about 80% of collateral value.	Collateralized inventory is controlled by lender. A warehousing company issues a warehouse receipt held by the lender. The warehousing company acts as the lender's agent.

Short-term financing is easier to arrange, has lower cost, and is more flexible than long-term financing. However, short-term financing leaves the borrower more vulnerable to interest-rate swings, requires more frequent refinancing, and requires earlier payment. As a rule, use short-term financing to provide additional working capital, to finance short-lived assets, or to serve as interim financing on long-term projects. Long-term financing is more appropriate for the financing of long-term assets or construction projects.

¶ 1715 Intermediate-Term Financing: Term Loans and Leasing

We now consider the use of intermediate-term loans, primarily through banks and leases, to meet corporate financing needs. Examples are bank loans, insurance company term loans, and equipment financing.

.01 Intermediate-Term Bank Loans

Intermediate-term loans are loans with a maturity of more than one year but less than five years. They are appropriate when short-term unsecured loans are not, such as when a business is acquired, new fixed assets are purchased, or long-term debt is retired. If a company wants to float long-term debt or issue common stock but market conditions are unfavorable, it may seek an intermediate loan to bridge the gap until conditions improve. A company may use extendable debt when it will have a continuing financing need, reducing the time and cost required for repeated debt issuance.

The interest rate on intermediate-term loans is typically higher than that for short-term loans because of the longer maturity period and varies with the amount of the loan and the company's financial strength. The interest rate may be either fixed or variable.

Ordinary intermediate-term loans are payable in periodic equal installments except for the last payment, which may be higher (a balloon payment). The schedule of loan payments should be based on the company's cash flow position to satisfy the debt. The periodic payment in a term loan equals:

$$\text{Periodic payment} = \frac{\text{Amount of loan}}{\text{Present value factor}}$$

Example 22: The company contracts to repay a term loan in five equal year-end installments. The amount of the loan is $150,000, and the interest rate is 10 percent. The payment each year is:

$$\frac{\$150{,}000}{3.791^{(a)}} = \$39{,}567{,}400$$

(a) Present value of annuity for five years at 10% = T_4 (10%,5) (see Table 4 in Appendix B)

The total interest on the loan is:

Total payments (5 × $39,567.40)	$197,837
Principal	150,000
Interest	$ 47,837

Example 23: The company takes out a term loan in 20 year-end annual installments of $2,000 each. The interest rate is 12 percent. The amount of the loan is:

$$\$2{,}000 = \frac{\text{Amount of loan}}{7.469^{(a)}}$$

Amount of loan = \$2,000 × 7.469 = \$14,938

(a) Present value of annuity for 20 years at 12% = T_4 (12%,20) (see Table 4 in Appendix B).

The amortization schedule for the first two years is:

Year	*Payment*	*Interest*[a]	*Principal*	*Balance*
0				\$14,938.00
1	\$2,000	\$1,792.56	\$ 207.44	14,730.56
2	2,000	1,767.67	232.33	14,498.23

(a) 12% times the balance of the loan at the beginning of the year.

Restrictions may be placed on the company by the lender in an intermediate-term loan agreement in order to protect the lender's interest. Typical restrictions include:

- Working capital requirements and cash dividend limitations, such as requiring a minimum amount of working capital or limiting dividend payment to no more than 20 percent of net income.
- Routine (uniform) provisions employed universally in most agreements, such as the payment of taxes and the maintenance of proper insurance to assure maximum lender protection.
- Specific provisions tailored to a particular situation, such as limiting future loans and requiring adequate life insurance for executives.

The advantages of intermediate-term loans are:

- Flexibility—terms may be altered as the company's financing requirements change.
- Confidentiality—no public issuance (offering to the investment public after registering with the Securities and Exchange Commission) is involved; so no information about the company's finances need be made public.
- Speed—the loan may be arranged quickly, compared to preparing a public offering.
- Security—avoids the possible nonrenewal of a short-term loan.
- Low cost—eliminates public flotation (issuance) costs.

The disadvantages of intermediate-term loans are these:

- Collateral and restrictive covenants are usually required.

- Budgets and financial statements may have to be submitted periodically to the lender.
- "Kickers" or "sweeteners," such as stock warrants or a share of the profits, are sometimes requested by the bank.

.02 Insurance Company Term Loans

Insurance companies and other institutional lenders, such as commercial finance companies, may be sources of intermediate-term loans. Insurance companies typically accept loan maturity dates exceeding 10 years, but their rate of interest is often higher than that of bank loans. Insurance companies do not require compensating balances but usually impose a prepayment penalty, which is typically not true with a bank loan. A company may opt for an insurance company loan when it desires a longer maturity range.

.03 Equipment-Backed Financing

Equipment may serve as collateral for a loan, with the advance based on the market value of the equipment. The more marketable the equipment and the lower the cost of selling it, the higher the advance will be. The repayment schedule is designed so that the market value of the equipment at any given time is in excess of the unpaid loan principal.

Equipment financing may be obtained from banks, finance companies, and manufacturers of equipment and is secured by a chattel mortgage or a conditional sales contract. A *chattel mortgage* serves as a lien on property, except for real estate. In a *conditional sales contract,* the seller of the equipment keeps title to it until the buyer has satisfied the terms; otherwise, the seller can repossess the equipment. Conditional sales contracts are generally used by small companies with low credit ratings.

Equipment trust certificates may be issued to finance the purchase of readily salable equipment, preferably equipment that is general purpose and easily movable. A trust is formed by the lessor to buy the equipment and lease it to the user. The trust issues the certificates to finance 75 to 85 percent of the purchase price and holds title to the equipment until *all* the certificates have been fully repaid, at which time the title passes to the lessee.

.04 Leasing

The parties in a lease are the *lessor,* who legally owns the property, and the *lessee,* who uses it in exchange for making rental payments. In our examples, your company is the *lessee.*

There are several types of leases:

1. *Operating (service) lease.* This type of lease includes both financing and maintenance services. The company leases property that is owned by the lessor, who may be the manufacturer

of the asset or a leasing company that buys assets from the manufacturer to lease to others. The lease payments under the contract are typically not adequate to recover the full cost of the property. Operating leases usually contain a cancellation clause that allows the lessee to return the property prior to the expiration date of the agreement. The life of the contract is less than the economic life of the property.

2. *Financial (capital) lease.* This type of lease usually does not provide for maintenance services. It is noncancellable, and the rental payments equal the full price of the leased property. The life of the contract approximates the life of the property.

3. *Sale and leaseback.* With this lease arrangement, the company sells an asset to another (usually a financial institution) and then leases it back. This allows the company to obtain cash from the sale and still have the use of the property.

4. *Leveraged lease.* In a leveraged lease, a third party serves as the lender. The lessor borrows a significant portion of the purchase price (usually up to 80 percent) to buy the asset and provides the balance of the purchase price as his equity investment. The property is then leased to the lessee. As security for the loan, the lessor grants the long-term lender a mortgage on the asset and assigns the lease contract to the lender. Leverage leasing is a cost-effective alternative to debt financing when the lessee cannot use the full tax benefits of asset ownership.

Leasing has a number of advantages:

- No immediate cash outlay is required.
- It is a satisfactory way to meet *temporary* equipment needs and provides flexibility in operations.
- Usually there is a purchase option that allows the company to obtain the property at a bargain price at the expiration of the lease. This allows the flexibility to make a purchase decision based on the value of the property at the termination date.
- The lessor's expert service is available.
- Leasing typically imposes fewer financing restrictions than are imposed by lenders.
- The company's obligation for future rental payment need not be reported on the balance sheet if the lease is considered an operating lease. However, capital leases must be stated in financial statements.

- Leasing allows the company, in effect, to depreciate land, which is not allowed if land is purchased.

- Lessors may claim a maximum of three years' lease payments in the event of bankruptcy or reorganization, whereas creditors have a claim for the total amount of the unpaid financing.

- Leasing eliminates equipment disposal.

Leasing may be more attractive than buying when a business cannot use all of the tax deductions and tax credits associated with purchasing the assets.

Drawbacks to leasing are these:

- It carries a higher cost in the long run than purchasing the asset; the lessee does not build equity.

- The interest cost of leasing is typically higher than the interest cost on debt.

- If the property reverts to the lessor at termination of the lease, the lessee must either sign a new lease or buy the property at higher current prices. Also, the salvage value of the property is realized by the lessor.

- The lessee may have to retain property it no longer needs or wants (i.e., obsolete equipment).

- The lessee cannot make improvements to the leased property without the permission of the lessor.

Examples 24 to 26 below require the use of the present value of annuity table (Table 4 in Appendix B).

Example 24: The company enters into a lease for a $100,000 machine. It is to make 10 equal annual payments at year-end. The interest rate on the lease is 14 percent. The periodic payment equals:

$$\frac{\$100{,}000}{5.216^{(a)}} = \$19{,}171.78$$

[a] The present value of an ordinary annuity factor for n=10, i=14% is 5.216 T_4 (14%,10) (see Table 4 in Appendix B).

Example 25: Assume the same facts as in Example 24, except that now the annual payments are to be made at the beginning of each year. The periodic payment equals:

Year	*Factor*
0	1.0
1-9	4.9464
	5.9464

$$\frac{\$100{,}000}{5.946} = \$16{,}818.03$$

The interest rate associated with a lease agreement can also be computed by dividing the value of the leased property by the annual payment to obtain the factor, which is then used to find the interest rate with the help of a present value of annuity table.

Example 26: The company leased $300,000 of property and is to make equal annual payments at year-end of $40,000 for 11 years. The interest rate associated with the lease agreement is:

$$\frac{\$300{,}000}{\$40{,}000} = 7.5$$

Going to the present value of annuity table and looking across 11 years to a factor nearest to 7.5, we find 7.499 at a seven-percent interest rate. Thus, the interest rate in the lease agreement is seven percent.

Lease-purchase decision. To decide whether to buy an asset or lease it, discounted cash flow (DCF) analysis may be used to determine the cheapest alternative (to be discussed in Chapter 20).

¶ 1720 Summary

When seeking short-term financing, you should select the best financing vehicle available to meet the company's objectives. The choice of a particular financing instrument depends on the company's particular circumstances and such factors as cost, risk, restrictions, stability of operations, and tax rate. Sources of short-term financing include trade credit, bank loans, bankers' acceptances, finance company loans, commercial paper, receivable financing, and inventory financing.

Intermediate-term financing has a maturity between one and five years and includes multi-year bank or insurance company loans and leases. Fixed assets may serve as collateral. Some advantages of intermediate-term financing are its flexibility and its lower flotation costs.

Example 26. Assume the same facts as in Example 24, except that now the annual payments are to be made at the beginning of each year. The periodic payment equals:

Year	Factor
0	1.0
1–9	[illegible]
	[illegible]

$$\frac{\$100{,}000}{[illegible]} = \$[illegible]$$

The interest rate associated with a lease agreement can also be computed by dividing the value of the leased property by the annual payment to obtain the factor, which is then used to find the interest rate with the help of a present value of annuity table.

Example 27. A company leased $300,000 of property and is to make equal annual payments at year-end of $40,000 for 11 years. The interest rate associated with the lease agreement is:

$$\frac{\$300{,}000}{\$40{,}000} = 7.5$$

Going to the present value of annuity table and looking across 11 years to a factor nearest to 7.5, we find 7.499 at a seven-percent interest rate. Thus, the interest rate in the lease agreement is seven percent.

Lease-purchase decision. To decide whether to buy an asset or lease it, discounted cash flow (DCF) analysis may be used to determine the cheapest alternative (to be discussed in Chapter 23).

¶1720 Summary

When seeking short-term financing, you should select the best financing vehicle available to meet the company's objectives. The choice of a particular financing instrument depends on the company's particular circumstances and such factors as cost, risk, restrictions, stability of operations, and taxes. The sources of short-term financing include trade credit, bank loans, bankers' acceptances, finance company loans, commercial paper, receivable financing, and inventory financing.

Intermediate-term financing has a maturity between one and five years and includes multiyear bank and insurance company loans and leases. The lease may have tax advantages. Some advantages of intermediate-term financing are its flexibility and its lower flotation costs.

Chapter 18

Debt and Equity Financing

¶ 1801 Overview

Long-term financing generally refers to financing with a maturity of more than five years. This chapter discusses the what, why, and how-to of long-term debt financing. Long-term debt financing consists primarily of bonds. Long-term financing is often used to finance long-lived assets, such as land or equipment, or construction projects. The more capital-intensive the business, the more it should rely on long-term debt and equity.

A company's mix of long-term funds is referred to as its *capital structure*. The ideal capital structure maximizes the total value of the company and minimizes the overall cost of capital. Managers charged with formulating an appropriate capital structure should take into account the nature of the business and industry, the company's strategic business plan, its current and historical capital structure, and its planned growth rate.

This chapter also discusses the advantages and disadvantages of the different kinds of stock and other equity securities a company can issue. We will discuss the role of the investment banker and the difference between a public and private placement of securities.

¶ 1805 Types of Long-Term Debt

Different types of debt instruments are appropriate in different circumstances. The amount of debt a company may have depends largely on its available collateral. Sources of long-term debt include mortgages and bonds.

.01 Mortgages

Mortgages are notes payable that are secured by real assets and that require periodic payments. Mortgages can be issued to finance the purchase of assets, the construction of a plant, or the modernization of facilities. Banks require that the value of the property exceed the mortgage on that property and usually lend up to between 70 percent and 90 percent of the value of the collateral. Mortgages may be obtained from a bank, life insurance company, or other financial institution. As a rule, it is easier to obtain mortgage loans for multiple-use real assets than for single-use real assets.

There are two types of mortgages: *senior* mortgages, which have first claim on assets and earnings, and *junior* mortgages, which have subordinate liens.

A mortgage may have a closed-end provision that prevents the company from issuing additional debt of the same priority against the specific property. If the mortgage is open-ended, the company can issue additional first-mortgage bonds against the property.

Mortgages have a number of advantages, including favorable interest rates, fewer financing restrictions than bonds, extended maturity dates for loan repayment, and easy availability.

.02 Bonds

Long-term corporate debt usually takes the form of bonds payable and loans payable. A *bond* is a certificate indicating that the company has borrowed money and agrees to repay it. A written agreement, called an *indenture*, describes the features of the bond issue (e.g., payment dates, call price should the issuer decide to reacquire the bonds, conversion privileges, and any restrictions).

The indenture is a contract between the company, the bondholder, and the trustee, who makes sure that the company meets the terms of the bond contract (in many instances, the trustee is the trust department of a commercial bank). Although the trustee is an agent for the bondholder, it is selected by the issuing company prior to the issuance of the bonds. If a provision of the indenture is violated, the bonds are in default. The indenture may also have a negative pledge clause which precludes the issuance of new debt that takes priority over existing debt in the event of liquidation. The clause can apply to assets currently held as well as to assets that may be purchased in the future.

The price of a bond depends on several factors, including its maturity date, interest rate, and collateral. In selecting a maturity period for long-term debt, structure the debt repayment schedule to spread out the payments to avoid the possibility that the cash flow will be inadequate to meet the debt payment.

Bond prices and market interest rates are inversely related. As market interest rates increase, the price of existing bonds falls because investors can invest in new bonds paying higher interest rates. The price of a bond on the open market depends on several factors, such as its maturity value, interest rate, and collateral.

Interest. Bonds are issued in $1,000 denominations; many have maturities of 10 to 30 years. The interest payment to the bondholder is called *nominal interest*, which is the interest on the face of the bond and which is equal to the coupon (nominal) interest rate times the face value of the bond. Although the interest rate is stated on an annual basis, interest on a bond is usually paid semiannually. Interest expense incurred by the issuer is tax deductible.

Example 1: A company issues a 20-percent, 20-year bond. The tax rate is 46 percent. The annual after-tax cost of the debt is:

$$20\% \times 54\% = 10.8\%$$

Example 2: A company issues a $100,000, 12-percent, 10-year bond. The semi-annual interest payment is:

$$\$100{,}000 \times 12\% \times 6/12 = \$6{,}000$$

Assuming a tax rate of 30 percent, the after-tax semiannual interest is:

$$\$6{,}000 \times 70\% = \$4{,}200$$

A bond sold at face value ($1,000) is said to be sold at 100. If a bond is sold below its face value, it is being sold at less than 100 and is issued at a discount. If a bond is sold above face value, it is being sold at more than 100, that is, at a premium. A bond is likely to be sold at a discount when the interest rate on the bond is below the prevailing market interest rate for that type of security, when the issuing company is risky or when it carries a long maturity period. A bond is sold at a premium when the opposite conditions exist.

Bond issue costs are also tax deductible.

Example 3: Travis Corporation issues a $100,000, 14-percent, 20-year bond at 94. The maturity value of the bond is $100,000. The annual interest payment is:

$$14\% \times \$100{,}000 = \$14{,}000$$

The proceeds from the issuance of the bond is:

$$94\% \times \$100{,}000 = \$94{,}000$$

The amount of the discount is:

$$\$100{,}000 - \$94{,}000 = \$6{,}000$$

Example 4: A bond having a face value of $100,000 with a 25-year life was sold at 102. The tax rate is 40 percent. The bond was sold at a premium since it was issued above face value. The total premium is $2,000 ($100,000 × 0.02).

Types of bonds. Companies may issue various types of bonds:

- *Debentures.* Because debentures are unsecured (have no collateral) debt, are usually issued only by large, financially strong companies with excellent credit ratings. Note, however, that most "junk bonds" are debentures of large companies that do *not* have good credit ratings.

- *Subordinated debentures.* The claims of the holders of these bonds are subordinated to those of senior creditors. Debt that has a prior claim over the subordinated debentures is set forth in the bond indenture. Typically, in the event a company is liquidated, subordinated debentures are paid off after short-term debt.

- *Mortgage bonds.* These are bonds secured by real assets. A first-mortgage claim must be met before a distribution is made to a second-mortgage claim. There may be several mortgages for the same property.

- *Collateral trust bonds.* The collateral for these bonds is the company's security investments in other companies (bonds or stocks) which are held by a trustee for safekeeping.

- *Convertible bonds.* These bonds may be converted to stock at a later date based on a specified conversion ratio. Convertible bonds are typically issued in the form of subordinated debentures. Convertible bonds are more marketable and are typically issued at a lower interest rate than are regular bonds because they offer the right to conversion to common stock. Of course if bonds are converted to stock, the debt is not repaid. A convertible bond is a quasi-equity security because its market value is tied to its value if converted to stock rather than as a bond.

- *Income bonds.* These bonds pay interest only if the company makes a profit. The interest may be cumulative, in which case it accumulates regardless of earnings and if bypassed must be paid in a later year when adequate earnings exist. Income bonds also may be noncumulative. Income bonds are appropriate for companies with large fixed capital investments and large fluctuations in earnings or for emerging companies that expect low earnings in the early years.

- *Guaranteed bonds.* These are debt issued by one party and guaranteed by another.

- *Serial bonds.* These bonds are issued with different maturities available. At the time serial bonds are issued, a schedule is prepared to show the yields, interest rates, and prices for each maturity. The interest rate on the shorter maturities is lower than the interest rate on the longer maturities because there is less uncertainty about the near future.

- *Deep discount bonds.* These bonds have very low interest rates and, thus, are issued at substantial discounts from face value. The return to the holder comes primarily from appreciation in price rather than from interest payments. The bonds are volatile in price.

- *Zero coupon bonds.* These bonds do not pay interest; the return to the holder is in the form of appreciation in price. Lower interest rates may be available for zero coupon bonds (and deep discount bonds) because they cannot be called.

- *Variable-rate bonds.* The interest rates on the bonds are adjusted periodically to reflect changes in money market conditions (e.g., prime interest rate). These bonds are popular when future interest rates and inflation are uncertain.

- *Eurobonds.* Eurobonds are issued outside the country in whose currency the bonds are denominated. Dollar-denominated Eurobonds cannot be sold by U.S. issuers to U.S. investors but may be sold only to foreign investors because they are not registered with the SEC. The bonds are typically in bearer form, meaning the securities are not registered on the books of the issuing corporation and, thus, are payable to whoever possesses them. A bearer bond has coupons attached which the bondholder sends in or presents on the interest date to receive payment. If you are considering a bond issue, check to see if the Eurodollar market will give the company a lower cost option than the U.S. market. Eurobonds typically can only be issued by high-quality borrowers.

Exhibit 1

Summary of Characteristics and Priority Claims of Bonds

Bond Type	*Characteristics*	*Priority of Lender's Claim*
Debentures	Available only to financially strong companies. Convertible bonds are typically debentures.	General creditor.

Subordinated debentures	Comes after senior debt holders.	General creditor.
Mortgage bonds	Collateral is real property or buildings.	Paid from the proceeds from the sale of mortgaged assets. If any deficiency exists, general creditor status applies.
Collateral trust bonds	Secured by stock and/or bonds owned by the issuer. Collateral value is usually 30 percent more than bond value.	Paid from the proceeds of stock and/or bond that is collateralized. If there is a deficiency, general creditor status applies.
Income bonds	Interest is only paid if there is net income. Often issued when a company is in reorganization because of financial problems.	General creditor.
Deep-discount (and zero coupon) bonds	Issued at very low or no (zero) coupon rates. Issued at prices significantly below face value. Usually callable at par value.	Unsecured or secured status may apply depending on the features of the issue.
Variable-rate bonds	Coupon rate changes within limits based on changes in money or capital market rates. Appropriate when uncertainty exists regarding inflation and future interest rates. Because of the automatic adjustment to changing market conditions, the bonds sell near face value.	Unsecured or secured status may apply depending on the features of the issue.

Small companies with unproven track records may have to issue what is commonly referred to as "junk bonds" (high-yielding risky bonds rated by Standard & Poor's as B+ or below or by Moody's Investors Service as B-1 or below). These are considered low-quality bonds. A summary of the characteristics and priority claims associated with bonds appears in Exhibit 1.

Bond ratings. Financial advisory services, such as Standard & Poor's and Moody's, rate publicly traded bonds according to their risk of default. An inverse relationship exists between the quality of a bond and its yield; low-quality bonds have a higher yield than high-quality bonds. Hence, a risk-return trade-off exists for the bondholder. Bond ratings are important because they influence marketability and the cost associated with the bond issue.

Advantages and disadvantages of debt refinancing. Among the advantages of long-term debt are these:

- Interest is tax-deductible, while dividends paid to stockholders are not.
- Bondholders do not participate in earnings growth of the company.
- Debt is repaid in cheaper dollars during inflationary periods.
- Company control remains undiluted.
- Financing flexibility can be achieved by including a call provision allowing the company to pay the debt before the expiration date of the bond in the bond indenture. However, the issuer pays a price for this advantage in the form of the higher interest rates that callable bonds require.
- It may safeguard the company's future financial stability if used in times of tight money markets when short-term loans are not available.

The disadvantages of issuing long-term debt are these:

- Interest charges must be met regardless of the company's earnings.
- Debt must be repaid at maturity.
- Higher debt implies greater financial risk which may increase the cost of financing.
- Indenture provisions may place stringent restrictions on the company.
- Overcommitments may arise from errors in forecasting future cash flow.

To investors, bonds have the following advantages:

- They pay a fixed interest payment each year.
- They are safer than equity securities.

However, investors should consider these disadvantages:

- Bonds carry interest rate risk, the chance that principal will be lost if interest rates rise and the bond drops in value.
- Bonds do not participate in corporate profitability.

- Bondholders have no voting rights and, therefore, no control of company management.

The proper mixture of long-term debt and equity depends on company organization, credit availability, and the after-tax cost of financing. If the company already has a high level of debt, it should take steps to minimize other corporate risks.

Long-term debt financing is appropriate when:

- The interest rate on debt is less than the rate of return that can be earned on the money borrowed. For example, a company may borrow at 10-percent interest but earn a return of 18 percent by investing that money in the business. Through the use of borrowed funds, the company can increase its after-tax profit. Stockholders make a profit with no additional investment.
- The company's revenue and earnings are stable, so that the company will be able to meet interest and principal in both good and bad years. Cyclical factors should not deter borrowing so long as the company accumulates no more interest and principal repayment obligations than can reasonably be satisfied in bad times as well as good.
- There is a satisfactory profit margin to provide earnings sufficient to meet debt obligations.
- The liquidity and cash flow positions are reasonable.
- The debt/equity ratio is low so that the company can handle additional obligations.
- The risk level of the firm is low.
- Stock prices are currently depressed, discouraging the issue of common stock at the present time.
- Control considerations are a primary factor (if common stock was issued, greater control might fall into the hands of a potential corporate raider).
- The firm is mature, meaning it has a long record of earnings and dividends.
- The inflation rate is expected to rise, so that debt may be paid back in cheaper dollars.
- There is a lack of competition (e.g., entry barriers exist in the industry, such as stringent governmental regulations).
- The markets for the company's products are expanding and the company is growing.

- The tax rate is high, so that the company will benefit by deducting interest payments from its taxes.
- Bond indenture restrictions are not burdensome.
- Money market trends are favorable, and any necessary financing is available.
- Project financing is tied to particular projects and may be suitable for large, self-contained undertakings, perhaps involving joint ventures.

If a company is experiencing financial difficulties, they may wish to refinance short-term debt on a long-term basis, perhaps by extending the maturity dates of existing loans. This may alleviate current liquidity and cash flow problems. As the default risk of a company becomes higher, so will the interest rate lenders demand to compensate for the greater risk.

When a high degree of debt (financial leverage) exists, one should try to reduce other risks (e.g., product risk), so that total corporate risk is controlled. The threat of financial distress or even bankruptcy is the ultimate limitation on leverage. If the company's debt is beyond a reasonable limit, the tax savings on interest expense will be offset by the increased interest rate demanded by creditors to compensate for the increased risk. Excessive debt also lowers the market price of stock because of the greater risk associated with the company.

Small companies with thinly traded stocks (little market activity) often issue debt and equity securities together in the form of *units*. A company may elect to issue units instead of convertible debt if it desires to increase its common equity immediately.

Bond refunding. Companies may refund bonds before maturity by either issuing a serial bond or exercising a call privilege on a straight bond. The issuance of serial bonds allows the company to refund the debt over the life of the issue; calling the bond enables the company to retire it before the expiration date.

When future interest rates are expected to drop, the prudent company may exercise the call provision. It can buy back the higher-interest bond and then issue one at lower interest. The timing for the refunding depends on expected future interest rates. The call price typically exceeds the face value of the bond; the resulting call *premium* equals the difference between the call price and the maturity value. The call premium is usually equal to one year's interest if the bond is called in the first year; it declines at a constant rate each year thereafter. Also involved in selling a new issue are flotation costs (e.g., brokerage commissions and printing costs).

A bond with a call provision typically has a lower offering price and is issued at an interest rate higher than one without the call provision.

Investors prefer not to have a situation in which the company can buy back the bond at its option prior to maturity; they would obviously prefer to hold onto a high-interest bond when prevailing interest rates are low.

Example 5: A $100,000 issue of eight-percent, 10-year bonds is priced at 94 percent. The call price is 103 percent. Three years after the issue, the bonds are called. The call premium is equal to:

Call price	$103,000
Face value of bond	100,000
Call premium	$ 3,000

Example 6: A company issues $40,000 of callable bonds. The call price is 104 percent. The tax rate is 35 percent. The after-tax cost of calling the issue is:

$$\$40{,}000 \times 0.04 \times 0.65 = \$1{,}040$$

Example 7: Your company has a $20 million, 10-percent bond issue outstanding that has 10 years to maturity. The call premium is seven percent of face value. New 10-year bonds in the amount of $20 million can be issued at an eight-percent interest rate. Flotation costs of the new issue are $600,000.

Refunding of the original bond issue should occur as shown below.

Old interest payments ($20,000,000 × 0.10)	$2,000,000
New interest payments ($20,000,000 × 0.08)	1,600,000
Annual savings	$400,000
Call premium ($20,000,000 × 0.07)	$1,400,000
Flotation cost	600,000
Total cost	$2,000,000

Year	*Calculation*	*Present Value*
0	-$2,000,000 × 1	-$2,000,000
1-10	$400,000 × 6.71[(a)]	2,684,000
	Net present value	$ 684,000

(a) Present value of annuity factor for i = 8%, n = 10 = T_4 (8%, 10)

Sinking fund. Bond issues may require a sinking fund into which the company puts aside money with which to buy and retire part of a bond issue each year. Usually, a mandatory fixed amount must be retired, but occasionally the amount is tied to the company's sales or profit for the year. If a sinking fund payment is not made, the bond issue may be in default.

In many instances, the company can handle the sinking fund in one of the following two ways:

- It can call a given percentage of the bonds at a specified price each year, for instance, 10 percent of the original amount at a price of $1,070.
- It can buy its own bonds on the open market.

The least costly of these alternatives should be selected. If interest rates have increased, the price of the bonds will have decreased and the open market option should be employed. If interest rates have decreased, bond prices will have increased; thus, calling the bonds is less costly.

Example 8: Your company has to reduce bonds payable by $300,000. The call price is 104 percent. The market price of the bonds is 103 percent. The company will opt to buy back the bonds on the open market because it is less expensive, as indicated below:

Call price ($300,000 × 104%)	$312,000
Purchase on open market ($300,000 × 103%)	309,000
Advantage of purchasing bonds on the open market	$3,000

¶ 1810 Equity Financing

All stock issued by a company is either preferred stock or common stock, regardless of what name the issue of stock may be given. Although some companies may describe several different types or classes, usually, there is only one class of common stock. All other classes of stock, regardless of name, are preferred in some way over the one class of common stock.

The sources of equity financing are preferred stock and common stock. There are advantages and disadvantages associated with issuing preferred and common, and each is the issue of choice in certain circumstances.

.01 *Preferred Stock*

Preferred stock is a hybrid of bonds and common stock. Preferred stock comes after debt but before common stock in the event of liquidation and in the distribution of earnings. The optimal time to issue preferred stock is when the company has excessive debt and an issue of common stock might encourage a corporate raider to try to take control of the company. Issuing preferred stock is a more expensive way to raise capital than issuing bonds, because dividend payments are not tax deductible

Preferred stock may be cumulative or noncumulative. If any prior year's dividend payments to holders of cumulative preferred stock have been missed, they must be made up before dividends can be paid to common stockholders. If preferred dividends are in arrears for a long time, the company may find it difficult to resume its dividend payments to common stockholders. The company need not pay missed preferred dividends to holders of noncumulative preferred stock. Most preferred stock is cumulative; dividends are limited to a specified rate, which is based on the total par value of the outstanding shares.

> ***Example 9:*** As of December 31, 20X6, Ace Company has 6,000 shares of $15 par value, 14 percent, cumulative preferred stock outstanding. Dividends have not been paid in 20X4 and 20X5. Assuming the company has been profitable in 20X6, the amount of the dividend to be distributed is:

Par value of stock = 6,000 shares × $15 = $90,000	
Dividends in arrears ($90,000 × 14% × 2 years)	$25,200
Current year dividend ($90,000 × 14%)	12,600
Total dividend	$37,800

If dividends exceed the amount typically given to preferred stockholders and common stockholders, the preferred and common stockholders will participate in the excess dividends. In such cases, the preferred stock is referred to as participating preferred stock. Unless stated otherwise, the distribution of the excess dividends will be based on the relative total par values. Nonparticipating preferred stock does *not* participate with common stock in excess dividends. Most preferred stock is nonparticipating.

Preferred stock may be callable. This provision is advantageous to the company when interest rates decline, since the company has the option of discontinuing payment of dividends at a rate that has become excessive by buying back outstanding preferred stock. Unlike bonds, preferred stock rarely has a maturity date; however, preferred stock that has a sinking fund associated with it in effect has a maturity date for repayment.

There are several forms of preferred stock issues. *Limited life preferred stock* has a specified maturity date or can be redeemed at the holder's option. *Perpetual preferred stock* automatically converts to common stock at a given date. There is also preferred stock with *"floating rate" dividends,* which keep the preferred stock at par by altering the dividend rate.

In the event of a corporate bankruptcy, preferred stockholders are paid after creditors and before common stockholders. In such a case, preferred stockholders receive the par value of their shares, dividends in arrears, and the current year's dividend. Any asset balance then goes to the common stockholders.

The cost of preferred stock usually follows changes in interest rates and is likely to be low when interest rates are low. When the cost of common stock is high, preferred stock may be issued at a lower cost.

A preferred stock issue has the following advantages:

- Preferred dividends do not have to be paid (important during periods of financial distress). Interest on debt must be paid.
- Preferred stockholders cannot force the company into bankruptcy.
- Preferred shareholders do not share in unusually high profits because the common stockholders are the real owners of the business.
- A growth company can generate better earnings for its original owners by issuing preferred stock having a fixed dividend rate than by issuing common stock.
- Preferred stock issuance does not dilute the ownership interest of common stockholders in terms of earnings participation and voting rights.
- No sinking fund is required.
- The company does not have to collateralize its assets as it may have to do if bonds are issued.
- The debt to equity ratio is improved.

A preferred stock issue does have some disadvantages:

- Preferred stock must offer a higher yield than corporate bonds because it carries greater risk (since preferred stock comes after bonds in corporate liquidation).
- Preferred dividends are not tax deductible.
- Preferred stock has higher flotation costs than bonds.

To an investor, a preferred stock offers the following:

- Preferred stock usually provides a constant return in the form of a fixed dividend payment.
- Preferred stockholders come before common stockholders in the event of corporate bankruptcy.

The disadvantages of preferred stock to an investor are:

- Return is limited because of the fixed dividend rate.
- Prices of preferred stock fluctuate more than those of bonds, because there is no maturity date on the stock.
- Preferred stockholders cannot require the company to pay dividends.

.02 Common Stock Issues

Common stock is the residual equity ownership in the business; it does not involve fixed charges, maturity dates, or sinking fund requirements. Holders of common stock have voting power but come after preferred stockholders in receiving dividends and in liquidation.

Common stockholders enjoy the following rights:

- The right to receive dividends.
- The right to receive assets if the business dissolves.
- The right to vote.
- The preemptive right to buy new shares of common stock prior to their sale to the general public, thus allowing them to maintain proportionate percentage ownership in the company.
- The right to a stock certificate which evidences ownership in the firm. The stock certificate may be sold by the holder to another investor in the secondary security market, exchanges, and over-the-counter markets in which securities are bought and sold after their original issuance. Proceeds of secondary market sales go to the dealers or investors, not to the company which originally issued the securities.
- The right to inspect the company's books.

Companies may occasionally issue different classes of common stock. Class A is stock issued to the public that has no dividends but does usually have voting rights (although these are insufficient to obtain control of the company). Class B stock, which is typically kept by the company's organizers, does not pay dividends until the company has generated adequate earnings; it provides majority voting rights in order for current management to maintain control.

Having two classes of stock enables the founders or management of the company to keep control by holding majority voting rights.

Authorized shares represent the maximum amount of stock the company can issue according to the corporate charter. *Issued shares* represent the number of authorized shares that have been sold by the firm. *Outstanding shares* are the issued shares actually being held by the investing public. *Treasury stock* is stock that has been reaquired by the company. Outstanding shares are, therefore, equal to the issued shares less the treasury shares; dividends are based on the outstanding shares.

The *par value* of a stock is a stated amount of value per share as specified in the corporate charter. The company usually cannot sell stock at a price below par value since stockholders would then be liable to creditors for the difference between par value and the amount received if the company were to fail.

The price of common stock moves in opposition to market interest rates. For example, if market interest rates increase, stock prices fall as investors transfer funds out of stock into higher-yielding money market instruments and bank accounts. Further, higher interest rates raise the cost of borrowing, lowering profits and thus stock prices.

Common stock is generally issued in one of the following ways:

- *Broad syndication.* In a broad syndication, many investment bankers distribute corporate securities. This method is most common, because it gives the issuer the greatest control over distribution and, thus, probably achieves the highest net price. It also provides the widest public exposure. Its drawbacks are that it may take longer and has high transaction costs.

- *Limited distribution.* In a limited distribution, a limited number of underwriters are involved in the issuance of the company's securities. As a result, the stock receives less public exposure. However, the issuing company may choose to work with only those investment bankers it believes are best qualified or who have the widest contacts.

- *Sole distribution.* In a sole distribution, only one underwriter is used, possibly resulting in unsold shares. The company has less control in this set-up than in a broad syndication but incurs lower transaction costs. Sole distribution is also fast.

- *Dribble-out.* In this method, the company periodically issues stock at different prices depending on market conditions. This approach is not recommended because of the high associated costs, and because it depresses stock price because of the constant issuance of shares.

In timing a public issuance of common stock, you should consider the following:

- Do not offer shares near the expiration date for options on the company's shares, since the option-related transaction may affect share price. (An option is the right to buy stock at a specified price within a given time period. If the right is not exercised within the specified time period, the option expires.)

- Offer higher yielding common stock just before the ex-dividend date to attract investors. Ex-dividend is a term used to indicate that a stock is selling without a recently declared dividend. The ex-dividend date is four business days before the date of record.

- Issue common stock when there is little competition from other recent issues in the industry.

- Issue shares in bull markets (a rising stock market) and refrain from issuing them in bear markets (declining markets).

You may need to determine the number of shares that must be issued to raise funds required to satisfy your capital budget.

Example 10: Your company currently has 650,000 shares of common stock outstanding. The capital budget for the upcoming year is \$1.8 million. Assuming new stock may be issued for \$16 a share, the number of shares that must be issued to provide the necessary funds to meet the capital budget are:

$$\frac{\text{Funds Needed}}{\text{Market Price Per Share}} = \frac{\$1{,}800{,}000}{\$16} = 112{,}500 \text{ shares}$$

Example 11: Your company wants to raise \$3 million in its first public issue of common stock. After its issuance, the total market value of stock is expected to be \$7 million. Currently, there are 140,000 outstanding shares that are closely held (that is, held by a few shareholders). The shares held by the controlling group are not considered likely to be available for purchase. We want to compute the number of new shares that must be issued to raise the \$3 million.

The new shares will constitute 3/7 (\$3 million/\$7 million) of the outstanding shares after the stock issuance, and current stockholders will be holding 4/7 of the shares.

$$140{,}000 \text{ shares} = 4/7 \text{ of the total shares}$$

$$\text{Total shares} = \frac{140{,}000}{4/7}$$

$$\text{Total shares} = 245{,}000$$

$$\text{New shares} = 3/7 \times 245{,}000 = 105{,}000 \text{ shares}$$

After the stock issuance, the expected price per share is:

$$\text{Price per share} = \frac{\text{Market Value}}{\text{Shares Outstanding}} = \frac{\$7{,}000{,}000}{245{,}000} = \$28.57$$

A company that is about to make its first public offering of stock is referred to as "going public." The estimated price per share to sell the securities is equal to:

$$\frac{\text{Anticipated market value of the company}}{\text{Total outstanding shares}}$$

The anticipated market value of the company is based on a valuation model.

For an established company, the market price per share can be determined as follows:

$$\frac{\text{Expected dividend}}{\text{Cost of capital} - \text{growth rate in dividends}}$$

Example 12: Your company expected the dividend for the year to be $10 a share. The cost of capital is 13 percent. The growth rate in dividends is expected to be constant at eight percent. The price per share is:

$$\text{Price per share} = \frac{\text{Expected dividend}}{\text{Cost of capital} - \text{growth rate in dividends}}$$

$$= \frac{\$10}{0.13 - 0.08} = \frac{\$10}{0.05} = \$200$$

Another approach to pricing the share of stock for an existing company is through the use of the price/earnings (P/E) ratio, which is equal to:

$$\frac{\text{Market price per share}}{\text{Earnings per share}}$$

Example 13: Your company's earnings per share is $7. It is expected that the company's stock should sell at eight times earnings. (This expectation is usually based on what the stock of similar companies sells for in the market.)

The market price per share is therefore:

$$\text{P/E} = \frac{\text{Market price per share}}{\text{Earnings per share}}$$

$$\text{Market price per share} = \text{P/E multiple} \times \text{earnings per share}$$
$$= 8 \times \$7 = \$56$$

You may want to determine the market value of your company's stock. There are a number of different ways to accomplish this.

Example 14: Assuming an indefinite stream of future dividends of $300,000 and a required return rate of 14 percent, the market value of the stock equals:

$$\text{Market value} = \frac{\text{expected dividends}}{\text{rate of return}} = \frac{\$300{,}000}{0.14} = \$2{,}142{,}857$$

If there are 200,000 shares, the market price per share is:

$$\text{Market value} = \frac{\$2{,}142{,}857}{200{,}000} = \$10.71$$

Example 15: Your company is considering a public issue of its securities. The average price/earnings multiple in the industry is 15. The company's earnings are $400,000. There will be 100,000 outstanding after the issue. The expected per share is:

$$\begin{aligned}\text{Total market value} &= \text{Net income} \times \text{Price earnings multiple}\\ &= \$400{,}000 \times 15 = \$6{,}000{,}000\end{aligned}$$

$$\text{Price per share} = \frac{\text{market value}}{\text{shares}} = \frac{\$6{,}000{,}000}{100{,}000} = \$60$$

If a company has significant debt, equity issues may lower overall financial risk.

Financing with common stock has the following advantages:

- The company is not required to pay fixed charges, such as interest of dividends.
- There is no repayment date or sinking fund requirement.
- A common stock issue improves the company's credit rating compared to a bond issue. For example, it improves the debt-equity ratio.

Financing with common stock also has disadvantages:

- Dividends are not tax deductible.
- Ownership interest is diluted. The additional voting rights might vote to remove the current ownership group from power.
- Earnings and dividends must spread over more shares outstanding.

- The flotation costs of a common stock issue are higher than those for preferred stock and debt financing.

Internally generated funds may best reduce overall costs because such financing involves no flotation costs. Retained earnings may be used as equity funding if the company believes its stock price is lower than the true value of its assets or if transaction costs for external financing are high.

The company may make use of dividend reinvestment plans, in which stockholders reinvest their dividends into the company by buying more shares, and employee stock option plans, which allow employees to buy company stock at an option price typically below what the market price of the stock will be when the option is exercised. Such plans allow the company to raise financing and avoid issuance costs and the market impact of a public offering.

A summary comparison of bonds and common stocks is presented in Exhibit 2.

Exhibit 2

Summary Comparison of Bonds and Common Stock

Bonds	*Common Stock*
Bondholders are creditors.	Stockholders are owners.
No voting rights exist.	Voting rights exist.
There is a maturity date.	There is no maturity date.
Bondholders have prior claims on profits and assets in bankruptcy.	Stockholders have residual claims.
Interest payments represent fixed charges.	Dividend payments do not continue fixed charges.
Interest payments are deductible on the tax return.	There is not tax deductibility for dividend payments.
The rate of return required by bondholders is typically lower than that by stockholders.	The required rate of return by stockholders is typically greater than that by bondholders.

Stock rights. Stock rights, options to buy securities at a specified price at a later date, provide a source of common stock financing. *Preemptive rights* provide existing stockholders with the first option to buy additional shares. Exercising this right permits investors to maintain voting control and protects against dilution in ownership and earnings.

Financial management decides on the life of the right (typically about two months), its price (typically below the current market price), and the number of rights needed to buy a share.

In a rights offering, a date of record indicates the last day that the receiver of the right must be the legal owner as reflected in the company's stock ledger. To compensate for bookkeeping lags, stocks are often sold *ex rights* (without rights) four business days before the record date. Prior to this point, the stock is sold *rights on,* which means the purchasers receive the rights and can exercise them, sell them, and let them expire.

Since stock rights are transferable, many are traded on the stock exchange and over-the-counter markets. They may be exercised for a given period of time at a *subscription price,* which is set somewhat below the prevailing market price. After the subscription price has been determined, financial management must ascertain the number of rights necessary to purchase a share of stock. The total number of shares that must be sold equals:

$$\text{Shares to be sold} = \frac{\text{Amount of funds to be obtained}}{\text{Subscription price}}$$

The number of rights needed to acquire one share equals:

$$\text{Rights per share} = \frac{\text{Total shares outstanding}}{\text{Shares to be sold}}$$

Example 16: Your company wants to obtain $800,000 by a rights offering. There are presently 100,000 shares outstanding. The subscription price is $40 per share. The shares to be sold equal:

$$\text{Shares to be sold} = \frac{\text{Amount of funds to be obtained}}{\text{Subscription price}}$$

$$= \frac{\$800{,}000}{\$40}$$

$$= 20{,}000 \text{ shares}$$

The number of rights to acquire one share equals:

$$\text{Rights per share} = \frac{\text{Total shares outstanding}}{\text{Shares to be sold}} = \frac{100{,}000}{20{,}000} = 5$$

Thus, five rights will buy one new share at $40. Each right enables the holder to buy 1/5 of a share of stock.

Value of a right. The value of a right should, theoretically, be the same whether the stock is selling with rights on or with ex rights.

When stock is selling with rights on, the value of a right equals:

$$\frac{\text{Market value of stock with rights on} - \text{subscription price}}{\text{Number of rights needed to buy one share} + 1}$$

Example 17: Your company's common stock sells for $55 a share with rights on. Each stockholder is given the right to buy one new share at $35 for every four shares held. The value of each right is:

$$\frac{\$55 - \$5}{4 + 1} = \frac{\$20}{5} = \$4$$

When stock is traded ex rights, the market price is expected to decline by the value of the right. The market value of stock trading ex rights should theoretically equal:

Market value of stocks with rights on –
Value of a right when stock is selling rights on

The value of a right when stock is selling ex rights equals:

$$\frac{\text{Market value of stock trading ex rights} - \text{subscription price}}{\text{Number of rights needed to buy one new share}}$$

Example 18: Assuming the same information as in Example 17, the value of the company's stock trading ex rights should equal:

Market value of stocks with rights on –
Value of a right when stock is selling rights on

or

$$\$55 - \$4 = \$51$$

The value of a right when stock is selling ex rights is:

$$\frac{\text{Market value of stock trading ex rights} - \text{subscription price}}{\text{Number of rights needed to buy one new share}}$$

$$\frac{\$51 - \$35}{4} = \frac{\$16}{4} = \$4$$

The theoretical value of the right is identical when the stock is selling rights on or ex rights.

¶ 1815 Governmental Regulation

When securities are issued publicly, they must conform to federal and state regulations. The major federal laws are the Securities Act of 1933 and the Securities Exchange Act of 1934. State rules are referred to as *blue sky laws*.

The financial manager must be familiar with these laws for several reasons. First, a violation of the laws makes the manager subject to personal legal liability. Second, governmental regulation impacts the availability and costs of financing. Third, regulations apply to the money and capital markets in which the company's shares are traded. Fourth, the laws serve as safeguards to investors.

The Securities Act of 1933 deals with the regulation of new security issues. Its purpose is to ensure full disclosure of financial information about the company's affairs and to furnish a record of representations. The Act applies to interstate offerings to the public in amounts exceeding $1.5 million. Securities must be registered with the Securities and Exchange Commission (SEC) at least 20 days before they are publicly offered. Prior to the issuance of a new security issue, the company must prepare a prospectus for investors which contains a condensed version of the registration statement filed with the SEC, including accounting, financial, and legal information about the company. The SEC may delay or cease a public offering if information contained in the registration statement is erroneous, misleading, or incomplete. If the SEC-approved registration statement or prospectus is later found to contain misrepresentations, an investor who suffers losses can sue the issuing company and its officers for damages.

The Securities Exchange Act of 1934 applies to existing securities transactions. It requires full and accurate disclosure of financial information. Companies whose securities are listed on securities exchanges must file registration statements and periodic financial reports with both the SEC and the listing stock exchange. "Insider transactions" are monitored; officers and major stockholders of the company must prepare monthly reports of their holdings in the company's stock and changes therein. (An insider is defined as an officer, director, or stockholder of the company who controls 10 percent or more of equity shares.) The SEC also monitors trading practices in the stock exchanges and is empowered to monitor and punish manipulative activities affecting the company's stock. The voting process for corporate elections, particularly proxy voting (power of attorney by which the holder of stock transfers the voting right to another party), is also subject to SEC scrutiny; margin requirements regulating the purchase of securities on credit are regulated by the Federal Reserve System.

State blue sky laws are designed to protect investors from being defrauded. Companies issuing securities must register their offerings with the state in which they are incorporated and furnish relevant financial information.

¶ 1820 Selecting a Financing Method

Some companies obtain most of their funds by issuing stock and from earnings retained in the business. Other companies borrow as much as possible and raise additional money from stockholders only when they can no longer borrow. Most companies are somewhere in the middle.

Financial managers are concerned with selecting the best possible source of financing based on the company's situation. They must consider the following:

- The cost and risk of alternative financing strategies.
- Future trends in market conditions and their impact on future fund availability and interest rates. For example, if interest rates are expected to go up, the company will be better off financing with long-term debt at the currently lower interest rates. If stock prices are high, equity issuance may be preferred over debt.
- The current debt-to-equity ratio. A very high ratio, for example, indicates financial risk, so additional funds should come from equity sources.
- The maturity dates of present debt instruments. For example, the company should avoid having all debt come due at the same time; in an economic downturn, it may not have adequate funds to meet required debt payments.
- The restrictions in loan agreements. For instance, a restriction may place a cap on the allowable debt-equity ratio.
- The type and amount of collateral required by long-term creditors.
- The company's ability to change financing strategy to adjust to changing economic conditions. For example, a company subject to large cyclical variations should have less debt, because it may not be able to meet principal and interest at the low point of the cycle. If earnings are unstable and/or there is a highly competitive environment, more emphasis should be given to equity financing.
- The amount, nature, and stability of internally generated funds. If earnings are stable, the company will be better able to meet debt obligations.
- The adequacy of present lines of credit to meet current and future needs.

- The inflation rate, since debt is repaid in cheaper dollars.
- The earning power and liquidity position of the company. For example, a liquid company is able to meet debt payments.
- The nature and risk of assets. High-quality assets in terms of cash realizability allow for greater debt.
- The nature of the product line. A company, for example, that faces obsolescence risk in its product line (e.g., computers) should refrain from overusing debt.
- The uncertainty of large expenditures. If huge cash outlays may be required (e.g., for a lawsuit or the acquisition of another company), additional debt capacity should be available.
- The tax rate. For example, a higher tax rate makes debt more attractive, because interest expense is tax deductible.

You have to select the best possible source of financing based on the facts.

Example 19: Your company is considering issuing either debt or preferred stock to finance the purchase of a plant costing $1.3 million. The debt position is currently very high. The interest rate on the debt is 15 percent. The dividend rate on the preferred stock is 10 percent. The tax rate is 34 percent.

The annual interest payment on the debt is:

$$15\% \times \$1{,}300{,}000 = \$195{,}000$$

The annual dividend on the preferred stock is:

$$10\% \times \$1{,}300{,}000 = \$130{,}000$$

The required earnings before interest and taxes to meet the dividend payment is:

$$\frac{\$130{,}000}{(1 - 0.34)} = \$196{,}970$$

If your company anticipates earning $196,970 or more, it should issue the preferred stock because of its currently excessive debt position.

Example 20: Your company has sales of $30 million a year. It needs $6 million in financing for capital expansion. The debt/equity ratio is 68 percent, which is considered quite high in the industry. Your company is in a risky industry, and net income is not stable. The common stock is selling at a high P/E ratio compared to competition. The company is considering either a common stock or a debt issue.

Because your company is in a high-risk industry and has a high debt/equity ratio and unstable earnings, issuing debt may be costly, restrictive, and potentially dangerous to the company's future financial health. A common stock issue is recommended.

Example 21: Your company is a mature one in its industry. It has limited ownership. The company has vacillating sales and earnings. The debt/equity ratio is 70 percent, compared to the industry standard of 55 percent. The after-tax rate of return is 16 percent. Since your company is in a seasonal business, there are certain times during the year when its liquidity position is inadequate. Your company is unsure of the best way to finance.

Preferred stock is one possible means of financing. Debt financing is not recommended because of the already high debt/equity ratio, the fluctuation in profit, the seasonal nature of the business, and the deficient liquidity posture. Because of the limited ownership, common stock financing may not be appropriate because it would dilute the ownership.

Example 22: A new company is established and plans to raise $15 million in funds. The company expects to obtain contracts that will provide $1,200,000 a year in before-tax profits. The company is considering whether to issue bonds only or an equal amount of bonds and preferred stock. The interest rate on AA corporate bonds is 12 percent. The tax rate is 50 percent.

The company will probably have difficulty issuing $15 million of AA bonds, because the interest cost of $1,800,000 (12% × $15,000,000) on these bonds is greater than estimated earnings before interest and taxes. The issuance of debt by a new company is a risky alternative.

Financing with $7.5 million in debt and $7.5 million in preferred stock is also not recommended. While some debt may be issued, it is not practical to finance the balance with preferred stock. If $7.5 million of AA bonds were issued at the 12-percent rate, the company would be required to pay $900,000 in interest. A forecasted income statement would look as follows:

Earnings before interest and taxes	$1,200,000
Interest	900,000
Taxable income	$ 300,000
Taxes	150,000
Net income	$ 150,000

The amount available for the payment of preferred dividends is only $150,000. Hence, the maximum rate of return that could be paid on $7.5 million of preferred stock is .02 ($150,000/$7,500,000), too low to attract investors.

The company should consider financing with common stock.

Example 23: Your company wants to construct a plant that will take about one and a half years to construct. The plant will be used to produce a new product line, for which your company expects a high demand. The new plant will materially increase corporate size. The following costs are expected:

1. The cost to build the plant, $800,000

2. Funds needed for contingencies, $100,000

3. Annual operating costs, $175,000

The asset, debt, and equity positions of your company are similar to industry standards. The market price of the company's stock is less than it should be, taking into account the future earning power of the new product line. What would be an appropriate means to finance the construction?

Since the market price of stock is less than it should be and considering the potential of the product line, convertible bonds and installment bank loans might be appropriate means of financing, since interest expense is tax deductible. Additionally, issuing convertible bonds might not require repayment, since the bonds are likely to be converted to common stock because of the company's profitability. Installment bank loans can be paid off gradually as the new product generates cash inflow. Funds needed for contingencies can be obtained through open bank lines of credit.

If the market price of the stock were not depressed, financing through equity would be an alternative financing strategy.

Example 24: Your company wants to acquire another business but has not determined an optimal means to finance the acquisition. The current debt/equity position is within the industry guideline. In prior years, financing has been achieved through the issuance of short-term debt.

Profit has shown vacillation; as a result, the market price of the stock has fluctuated. Currently, however, the market price of stock is strong. Your company's tax bracket is low.

The purchase should be financed through the issuance of equity securities for the following reasons:

- The market price of stock is currently at a high level.

- Issuing long-term debt will cause greater instability in earnings because of high fixed interest charges. Consequently, the stock price will become even more volatile.

- Issuing debt will result in a higher debt/equity ratio relative to the industry norm, negatively impacting the company's cost of capital and availability of financing.

- Short-term debt would have to be paid before the company receives a return from the acquired business and is, therefore, not advisable.

¶ 1825 Investment Banking

Investment banking is the underwriting of a securities issue by a firm that serves as an intermediary between the issuing company and the investing public.

The direct underwriting responsibilities of the investment banking firm may include preparing the SEC registration statement, assisting in pricing the issue, forming and managing a group of underwriters, and stabilizing the price of the issue during the offering and distribution period. When a client relationship exists, the underwriter provides counseling and may have a seat on the board of directors of the company.

Investment bankers conduct the following activities:

- *Underwriting.* The investment banker buys a new security issue, pays the issuer, and markets the securities. The underwriter's compensation is the difference between the price at which the securities are sold to the public and the price paid to the issuing company.

- *Distributing.* The investment banker markets the company's security issue.

- *Advice.* The investment banker advises the company on the best way to obtain funds. The investment banker is knowledgeable about alternative sources of long-term funds, debt and equity markets, and SEC regulations.

- *Providing funds.* The investment banker provides funds to the company during the distribution period.

A *syndicate* is a group of several investment bankers who have come together to market a particularly large or risky issue. One investment banker (originating house) in the group will be selected to manage the syndicate and underwrite the major amount of the issue. The syndicate makes one bid for the issue, but the terms and features of the issue are set by the company.

The distribution channels for a new security issue are illustrated in Exhibit 3.

In another approach to investment banking, the investment banker may agree to sell the company's securities on a best efforts basis or to an agent. Here, the investment banker does not act as underwriter but instead sells the stock and receives a sales commission. Depending on the agreement, the agent may exercise an option to buy enough shares to cover its sales to the public, or the agent may cancel the incompletely sold issue altogether. Investment bankers may insist on this type of arrangement if they have reservations about the likelihood of success of the offering, such as with speculative securities issued by new and financially weak companies. A best-efforts arrangement involves risks and delays to the issuing company.

Exhibit 3

Distribution Channels for a New Security Issue

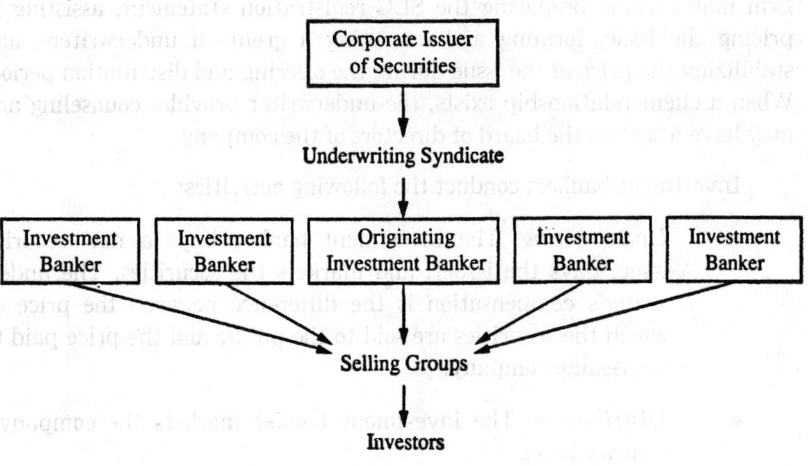

In selecting an investment banker for a new issue of securities, you should look for the following:

- Low spread. Spread is the difference between the price paid to the issuing company by the investment banker and the resale price to the investor.
- Good references, meaning other issuing companies were satisfied with the investment banker's performance.
- Ability to float many shares at a good price.
- Institutional (corporate) and retail (individual) clientele.

- Good after-market performance, meaning securities do well after issuance.
- Wide geographic distribution.
- Attractive secondary markets for resale.
- Knowledge of market, regulations, industry, and company.

¶ 1830 Public vs. Private Placement

Equity and debt securities may be issued either publicly or privately. In a public issuance, the shares are bought by the general public; in a private placement, the company issues securities directly to either one or a few large investors, usually financial institutions such as insurance companies, pension plans, and commercial banks.

Private placement has the following advantages compared to public issuance:

- The flotation cost is less. The flotation cost for common stock exceeds that for preferred stock and, expressed as a percentage of gross proceeds, is higher for smaller issues than for larger ones.
- It avoids SEC filing requirements.
- It avoids the need for disclosure of information to the public.
- It reduces the time lag for obtaining funds.
- It offers greater flexibility.
- It may be the only avenue available to small companies planning small issues that would not be sufficiently profitable to attract the interest of investment bankers.
- If the company's credit rating is low, private investors with limited funds may not be interested in purchasing the securities.

The drawbacks of private placement compared to public issuance are these:

- Private placement often requires a higher interest rate because of a reduced resale market.
- Private placements usually have a shorter maturity period than public issues.
- It is more difficult to obtain significant amounts of money in private placements than in public ones.

- Large private investors typically use stringent credit standards and require the company to be in strong financial condition. In addition, they impose more restrictive terms.
- Large institutional investors may watch the company's activities more closely than smaller investors in a public issue.
- Large institutional investors are more capable of obtaining voting control of the company, assuming they hold a large amount of stock.

Most private placements involve debt securities; in fact, only about two percent of common stock is placed privately. The private market is more receptive to smaller issues (e.g., those up to several million dollars). Small and medium-sized companies typically find it cheaper to place debt privately than publicly, especially when the issue is $5 million or less.

¶ 1835 Going Public—Initial Public Offering (IPO)

Going public, or often called an *initial public offering (IPO)*, refers to selling formerly privately held shares to new investors on the organized exchange (New York Stock Exchange) or the over-the-counter market for the first time. For the individual company, going public marks a historic moment. It often is the springboard for greater growth and success. There are the advantages and disadvantages of raising capital through a public offering. The market for stocks of companies that are going public is called the new issue market.

The public sale of ownership interests can generate funds for business expansion, working capital, repayment of debt, diversification, acquisitions, marketing, and other uses. In addition, a successful IPO increases the visibility and appeal of your company, thereby escalating the demand and value for shares. Investors can benefit from an IPO not only because of the potential increase in market value for their stock, but also because publicly-held stock is more liquid and can be readily sold if the business appears to falter or if the investor needs quick cash. The availability of a public market for shares will also help determine the taxable values of the shares and assist in estate transfers.

.01 How Does Going Public Work?

A company considering *going public* will typically work with an underwriter (an investment bank) who, either singly or as part of a group (syndicate), purchases the stock from the company (the issuer) at a discount from the public offering price. The underwriter or syndicate then sells the shares to the public through brokerage firms and other institutions. Creation of a syndicate pools the risk for underwriters and widens distribution channels for the new issue.

The underwriter advises the company on the marketability of, and demand for, its shares. Estimating the demand for the new stock issue is as much art as science. To estimate the demand, the underwriter and any dealers will collect *indications of interest* from their investors as to how many shares each would like to purchase.

Often, some IPOs may be oversubscribed, implying the demand for shares is larger than the number of shares to be issued. In the case of oversubscription, the underwriters determine who will get the shares at the public offering price. After the underwriter issues the shares, the shares begin trading on the open market. The laws of demand and supply take over. The price of IPO shares can increase or decrease substantially in a short time. For example, a company could have an IPO price of $15 per share, with the first trade in the open market executed at $80. Most of the players in the IPO market are fund managers from big institutions.

The pros of going public are:

- Going public raises money—if it is common stock, it does not have to be repaid. The typical IPO raises $20–$40 million, but offerings of $100 million are not unusual. This will vary widely by industry. Once public, companies can easily go back to the public market to raise more money. Typically, one third of all IPO issuers return to the public market within five years to issue a "seasoned equity offering." For example, in 1995 General Motors raised $1.14 billion by issuing new common stock. Since the shares sold were newly created, GM's issue was defined as a primary market offering, but since the firm was already publicly held, the offering was not an IPO. Firms generally prefer to obtain equity by retained earnings because of the flotation costs and market pressure involved with the sale of new common stock. However, if a firm needs more money than can be generated from retained earnings, a common stock offering may be necessary.

- As a company expands and becomes more valuable, its owners usually have most of their wealth tied up in the company. By selling some of their stock in a public offering, they can reduce the riskiness of their personal portfolios through this diversification of their holdings.

- Management often experiences an increase in prestige and reputation. Public firms have higher profiles than private firms. This is important in industries where success requires suppliers and consumers to make long-term investments. For example, software requires training, and no manager wants to buy software from a firm that may not be around for future improvements, upgrades, bug fixes, etc. The suppliers' and consumers' perception of company success is a self-fulfilling prophecy. However, public firms are usually bigger to begin with, and this may explain why public firms have a better image on average. Going public will not increase its sales. The important question is if going public improves the company's stockholders' perception of success.

- Publicly traded stock can make a business more attractive to prospective and existing employees if stock option and other stock compensation plans are offered. Employee stock-based programs are worth more if transfer restrictions, such as those normally accompanying private company stock, are not placed on the stock.
- Mergers and acquisitions. Many private companies do not just appear on the "radar screen" of potential acquirers. Being public makes it much easier for other firms to notice and analyze the company for synergy.
- The use of proceeds from the sale of the issue is generally unrestricted.
- Public companies can acquire other businesses with stock, without depleting cash reserves.
- Other financing alternatives may improve.

The cons of going public are:

- Much normally guarded information must be disclosed. The guarded items include management salaries, competitive position, transactions between the company and its management, and the identity of significant customers and suppliers. In addition to the required disclosure of results of operations and financial condition, public companies must be prepared to disclose information about the company, officers, directors, and certain shareholders. This information might include company sales and profits by product line, salaries and other compensation of officers and directors, data about major customers, competitive position, pending litigation, and related party transactions. By releasing the information, it will become available to competitors, customers, employees, and the general public. The information is required in the initial registration statement and is updated annually through annual reports, proxies, and other public disclosure documents. The company's IPO filings are with the Securities and Exchange Commission (www.sec.gov).

- In addition to the time and effort required to prepare for the filing and offering, a company must be prepared to incur the cost of going public. The principal costs include the underwriter's compensation, legal and accounting fees, printing charges, and transfer agent and filing fees. A company expecting to go public with a high-quality offering should anticipate spending approximately $200,000, excluding underwriter's commissions. The magnitude of these costs usually make public offerings grossing less than $5 million impractical. Furthermore, principals must remember that there is no guarantee that the offering will be a success. With the exception of underwriter's compensation, the costs are incurred regardless of the outcome. The cost of going public does not stop with the initial offering. Other costs associated with being a public company are ongoing. Management must devote time and money to such new areas as shareholder relations, public relations, public disclosures, periodic filings with the SEC, and reviewing stock activity. All of this time, and the time of the personnel hired to handle these functions, would be spent on other management tasks in a privately held company. There are other out-of-pocket expenses. Shareholder meetings, annual and quarterly reports, public relations efforts, and legal, accounting, and auditing fees must be paid. The total cost of these expenses vary from company to company, but in most cases, they range from $50,000 to $150,000 annually.

- Corporate decision making becomes more cumbersome as the company attempts to move from a tightly-controlled, entrepreneurially-oriented company to a professionally managed one where ownership and management are divorced. Any decision, long-term or short-term, may be manifested promptly in the company's stock price. The company may worry constantly about improving quarterly earnings (and stock prices) instead of trying to take a longer perspective in developing its strategy.

- All IPO participants in the coalition are jointly liable for each others' actions. In practice, they were routinely sued for various omissions in the IPO prospectus when the public market valuation fell below the IPO offering price. Congress recently passed The Private Securities Litigation Reform Act of 1995. This Act protects the disclosure of firm projections and forced the suing shareholders to have substantial participation in the suit. Although nothing can eliminate lawsuits, this Act reduces the likelihood of successful suits and, therefore, encourages settlement terms.

- Since the number of shares outstanding increases when the company goes public, greater earnings must be achieved to avoid reducing earnings per share.
- If the market price declines, many problems may result: management is usually personally blamed; the flexibility of issuing stock to make acquisitions may be hampered; if the decline occurs soon after the offering, litigation against everyone involved may take place; and other financing alternatives may evaporate.
- If the company is sitting on a gold mine, future earnings have to be shared with outsiders. After a typical IPO, about 40 percent of the company remains with insiders, but this can vary from one to 88 percent, with 20 to 60 percent being the comfortable norm.
- Outsiders can take control and even fire the entrepreneur. There is pressure on the managers to produce annual earnings gains, even when it may be in the shareholders' best long-term interests to adopt a strategy that reduces short term earnings but raises them in the future years. These factors have led a number of newly public firms to go private in leveraged buyout deals where the managers borrow the money to buy out the nonmanagement stockholders. The use of IPOs is limited primarily because:

    a. There is a very high cost and much complexity in complying with federal and state laws governing the sale of business securities. (The cost for a small business can run from $50,000 to $500,000.)
    b. Offering your business's ownership for public sale will have limited success unless your company has sufficient investor awareness and appeal to make the IPO worthwhile.
    c. Management must be ready to handle the administrative and legal demands of widespread public ownership. Of course, an IPO also means a dilution of the existing shareholders' interests, and the possibility of takeovers or adjustments in management control are present.

.02 *How to Avoid the Drawbacks of Going Public*

Here are some tips for avoiding the pitfalls of going public:

- Assemble the proper team. This involves selecting an underwriter, accountant, counsel, and perhaps some new directors.
- When choosing an underwriter, distribution capacity is important.

- An underwriter appropriate for one company or one industry may be inappropriate for another. In addition to technical ability, personalities and confidence should be considered.
- The selection of accountants and lawyers need careful examination.
- The registration process is complex, coupled with absolute liability for the company for material misstatements or omissions, regardless of good faith or motive. It is important to remember that malpractice insurance in the securities field is the most expensive of any specialty. Utilizing a nationally prominent accounting firm may enhance marketability and confidence. The use of a large accounting and legal firm may be viewed by the underwriter as "insurance" in the event of litigation.
- Securities laws are complicated. The sale of "securities" to the public is regulated by federal and state laws that have two primary objectives:
    a. Require businesses to disclose material information about the company to investors, and
    b. Prohibit misrepresentation and fraud in the sale of securities. Under federal law, a "security" is broadly defined and would include stocks, notes, bonds, evidence of indebtedness, and most ownership interests. The law defines a "public offering" of a security not by the number of investors to whom the stock is offered, but by the classification of whether the investors are considered "sophisticated" or not. However, state law definitions of a "security" and of a "public offering" can vary from the federal law.

.03 What is the Process of Going Public?

A company that is thinking of going public should start acting like a public company as much as two years in advance. Several "to do's" include developing a business plan and preparing detailed financial results on a regular basis. Once a company decides to go public, it needs to choose its IPO team consisting of a lead investment bank, accountant, lawyer, etc. The IPO process officially begins with an "all hands" meeting. This meeting usually takes place six to eight weeks before a company officially registers with the SEC. At this meeting, all members of the IPO team assign certain duties to each individual and plan a timetable for going public.

The most important and time consuming task facing the IPO team is the development of the prospectus, which is a business document that basically serves as a brochure for the company. Since the SEC requires a "quiet period" on firms once they file an IPO until 25 days after a stock starts trading, the prospectus will have to do most of the talking and selling for the team. The prospectus includes all financial data for a company for the past five years. It also includes information on the management team and a description of a company's target market, competitors, and growth strategy. With all the information in the prospectus, the underwriting team goes to great efforts to insure its accuracy.

Frequently, the next step in the IPO process is the management worldwide tour, also known as the "road show." The road show usually lasts a week, with company management going to a new city every day to meet with prospective investors and market their business plan. The typical stops generally include the larger cities such as Los Angeles, San Francisco, Boston, and Chicago. If necessary, international cities such as London and Hong Kong are included. The management team's performance is crucial during this time as it helps determine the success of the IPO. The team has to impress institutional investors and influence them to make significant long-term investments.

Once the road show ends and the final prospectus is distributed to investors, management officials meet with their investment bank to decide on the final offering size and price. Investment banks generally suggest an appropriate price based on expected demand for the deal and other market conditions. The pricing of an IPO is a delicate balancing act. Investment firms have to be concerned with two different sets of customers: the company going public, which wants to raise as much money as possible, and the investors buying the shares of stock, who expect to see immediate gains from their investment. If public interest appears to be slowing, it is common for the offering price and number of shares to decrease from expected ranges. Sometimes, a company even has to postpone an offering due to insufficient demand. If a deal is especially hot, the offering size and/ or price can be raised from initial projections.

Once the offering price has been agreed to, an IPO is declared effective. This is generally done after a market closes, with the trading of the new stock beginning the next day. In the meantime, the chief underwriter works to confirm its buy orders. The chief underwriter is responsible for ensuring smooth trading during the first crucial days. This underwriter is legally allowed to support the price of a newly issued stock through buying shares in the market or selling them short. They can also impose penalty bids on brokers to discourage "flipping," which is when investors sell shares of an IPO soon after the stock starts trading. An IPO is not declared final until seven days after the firm's initial market appearance. On rare occasions, an IPO can be canceled even after the stock begins trading.

.04 Alternatives to Going Public

Many businesses can sell stock to insiders or to a small group of investors without being subject to securities laws; in effect, they can take advantage of alternatives to going public. However, it's not always clear where the exemptions end, so you should always consult a knowledgeable attorney before selling any stock in your company. The process of soliciting money from the public through the issuance and sale of securities requires a working knowledge of the state and federal registration statements concerning the securities to be sold, complex disclosure documents about the company with detailed information for potential investors, and financial statements. Employing professionals (attorney, accountant, and sometimes a stock underwriter) to assist in the process is a practical necessity.

While many small businesses sell interests in their companies that are "securities," as defined by federal or state laws, the transactions are often exempt from registration regulations because the offerings are sufficiently small in dollar amount, and they are restricted to a limited number and/or type of investor. These exempt offers of securities are called "limited private offerings," and they can avoid much of the cost and delay of a public offering. Unfortunately, to qualify for any of the exemptions, you must fit the criteria for both federal and state security laws. Limited private offerings can be either debt or equity instruments, or a hybrid of both. For instance, a convertible debt warrant would be a debt instrument that allowed the holder to convert the debt into an equity interest at a certain time. These alternative offerings allow the business to tailor the amount of immediate equity (ownership and control) that it relinquishes and the amount of debt (cash outflow) that it can safely assume. In this module, discussion of the use of limited private offerings is largely confined to equity financing.

Federal exemptions. At the federal level, the most popular exemption from registration requirements for small businesses is Rule 504, commonly known as "Regulation D." Under this provision, private companies that are selling less than $1 million worth of securities to any number of investors within a 12-month period are exempt from federal registration requirements. Solicitations of investors by a private business may be made through almost any means, including advertisements and seminars, and no specific disclosure requirements regarding the stock or the company are required. Most startups and smaller businesses would fall within this exemption. Even if a securities offer is exempt from the registration requirements of federal or state law, the anti-fraud provisions of those laws may still apply. Therefore, you must take care to prevent misrepresentations or omissions in the offering that create an overly optimistic picture of the investment. The investor should be provided with sufficient information to make an informed decision regarding the investment.

Another exemption may be available to either private or publicly-held companies that sell less than $5 million within a 12-month period, if the sales are made only to "accredited investors" and no more than 35 such investors are involved. Accredited investors include institutional investors (e.g., banks, brokers and dealers, and insurance companies), company insiders (e.g., officers and directors), and wealthy investors ("wealthy" meaning they have more than $200,000 individual annual income or, individually or jointly with their spouse, have a net worth of over $1 million).

A lesser degree of exemption from regulation exists for a private or publicly-held company that sells an unlimited issuance of securities to an unlimited number of accredited investors or to no more than 35 nonaccredited but "sophisticated investors" (sophisticated investors have sufficient knowledge and experience so that they understand the risks of the sale, or the issuer reasonably believes the investors have these qualifications). Finally, an exemption exists for private offerings of stock that are sold only to persons living in the same state where the company is both incorporated and does significant business, although reliance upon this intra-state exemption is subject to continual policing because the securities must remain within the state.

State exemptions. Because each state has securities regulations, the local exemptions must be checked. Just because a sale may be exempt from federal registration does not mean state registration is not required. State securities laws are commonly referred to as "blue sky" laws, because the regulations were originally enacted to prevent unscrupulous issuers from selling "speculative schemes that have no more basis than so many feet of blue sky." The state laws need not match the federal regulatory exemptions, and even though a Uniform Securities Act exists for states to follow, that Act has not been adopted by each state nor is it consistently interpreted in those states which claim to follow it. The result is that consultation with a qualified professional is a practical necessity before soliciting investors for sales of securities. Forty-seven states currently have relaxed their securities regulations for small business by offering a Small Company Offering Registration (SCOR) procedure. Even if your business is not based in one of these states, you may still register and sell your securities in the states which have adopted SCOR. For a current list of eligible states, contact the North American Securities Administrators Association at 202-737-0900 or at www.nasaa.org.

¶ 1840 Venture Capital Financing

Venture capital firms supply funding from private sources for investing in select companies that have a high, rapid growth potential and a need for large amounts of capital. Venture capital (VC) firms speculate on certain high-risk businesses producing a very high rate of return in a very short time. The firms typically invest for periods of three to seven years and expect at least a 20-percent to 40-percent annual return on their investment.

When dealing with venture capital firms, keep in mind that they are under great pressure to identify and exploit fast growth opportunities before more conventional financing alternatives become available to the target companies. Venture capital firms have a reputation for negotiating tough financing terms and setting high demands on target companies. Three bottom-line suggestions

- Make sure to read the fine print
- Watch for delay maneuvers. (They may be waiting for your financial position to weaken further.)
- Guard your trade secrets and other proprietary information zealously.

Venture capital financing may not be available, nor a viable choice of financing for many businesses. Usually, venture capital firms favor existing businesses that have a minimal operating history of several years. Financing of startups is limited to situations where the high risk is tempered by special circumstances, such as a company with extremely experienced management and a very marketable product or service. In 1995, venture capital firms invested in less than 2000 companies. The target companies often have revenues in excess of two million dollars and a preexisting capital investment of at least one million.

VCs research target companies and markets more vigorously than conventional lenders, although the ultimate investment decision is often influenced by the market speculations of the particular venture capitalists. Due to the amount of money that venture capital firms spend in examining and researching businesses before they invest, they will usually want to invest at least a quarter of a million dollars to justify their costs.

Use caution in revealing any information you consider proprietary. Even with intellectual property protection (e.g., a patent, trademark, or copyright), avoid being forced to police your rights. Do your best to limit the details of your particular innovation and seek confidentiality arrangements for additional protection of any preexisting legal rights you may have. Practice disclosure avoidance as much as possible.

The price of financing through venture capital firms is high. Ownership demands for an equity interest in 30 percent to 50 percent of the company are not uncommon even for established businesses, and a startup or higher risk venture could easily require transfer of a greater interest. Although the investing company will not typically get involved in the ongoing management of the company, it will usually want at least one seat on the target company's board of directors and involvement, for better or worse, in the major decisions affecting the direction of the company.

The ownership interest of the VC firm is usually a straight equity interest or an ownership option in the target company through either a convertible debt (where the debt holder has the option to convert the loan instrument into stock of the borrower) or a debt with warrants to a straight equity investment (where the warrant holder has the right to buy shares of common stock at a fixed price within a specified time period). An arrangement that eventually calls for an initial public offering is also possible. Despite the high costs of financing through venture capital companies, they offer tremendous potential for obtaining a very large amount of equity financing, and they usually provide qualified business advice in addition to capital.

Venture capital firms are located nationwide, and a directory is available for $25 through the National Association of Venture Capital, 1655 N. Fort Meyer Dr., Arlington, VA 22209 (703-351-5269). In addition, other sources for venture capital can be found through bankers, insurance companies, and business associations. Visit the association on the web at www.nasaa.org.

Chapter 19

The Cost of Capital

¶ 1901 Overview

The cost of capital is defined as the rate of return that is necessary to maintain the market value of the firm (or price of the firm's stock). Financial managers must know the cost of capital (the minimum required rate of return) in (1) making capital budgeting decisions, (2) helping to establish the optimal capital structure, and (3) making decisions such as leasing, bond refunding, and working capital management. The cost of capital is used either as a discount rate under the NPV (Net Present Value) method or as a hurdle rate under the internal rate of return (IRR) method in Chapter 13. The cost of capital is computed as a weighted average of the various capital components, which are items on the right-hand side of the balance sheet such as debt, preferred stock, common stock, and retained earnings.

¶ 1905 Computing Individual Costs of Capital

Each element of capital has a component cost that is identified by the following:

k_i = before-tax cost of debt

$k_d = k_i(1 - t)$ = after-tax cost of debt, where t = tax rate

k_p = cost of preferred stock

k_s = cost of retained earnings (or internal equity)

k_e = cost of external equity, or cost of issuing new common stock

k_o = firm's overall cost of capital, or a weighted average cost of capital

.01 Cost of Debt

The before-tax cost of debt can be found by determining the internal rate of return (or yield to maturity) on the bond cash flows.

However, the following short-cut formula may be used for approximating the yield to maturity on a bond:

$$k_i = \frac{I + (M - V)/n}{(M + V)/2}$$

Where:

I	=	annual interest payments in dollars
M	=	par or face value, usually $1,000 per bond
V	=	market value or net proceeds from the sale of a bond
n	=	term of the bond in years

Since the interest payments are tax-deductible, the cost of debt must be stated on an after-tax basis. The after-tax cost of debt is:

$$k_d = k_i(1 - t)$$

Where t = the tax rate

Example 1: Assume that the Carter Company issues a $1,000, eight-percent, 20-year bond whose net proceeds are $940. The tax rate is 40 percent. Then, the before-tax cost of debt, ki, is:

$$k_i = \frac{I + (M - V)/n}{(M + V)/2}$$

$$= \frac{\$80 + (\$1{,}000 - \$940)/20}{(\$1{,}000 + \$940)/2} = \frac{\$83}{\$970} = 8.56\%$$

Therefore, the after-tax cost of debt is:

$$k_d = k_i(1 - t)$$
$$= 8.56\% \ (1 - 0.4) = 5.14\%$$

.02 Cost of Preferred Stock

The cost of preferred stock, kp, is found by dividing the annual preferred stock dividend, dp, by the net proceeds from the sale of the preferred stock, p, as follows:

$$k_p = \frac{d_p}{p}$$

Since preferred stock dividends are not a tax-deductible expense, these dividends are paid out after taxes. Consequently, no tax adjustment is required.

Example 2: Suppose that the Carter company has preferred stock that pays a $13 dividend per share and sells for $100 per share in the market. The flotation (or underwriting) cost is three percent, or $3 per share. Then the cost of preferred stock is:

$$k_p = \frac{d_p}{p}$$

$$= \frac{\$13}{\$97} = 13.4\%$$

.03 *Cost of Equity Capital*

The cost of common stock, ke, is generally viewed as the rate of return investors require on a firm's common stock. Two techniques for measuring the cost of common stock equity capital are widely used: (1) the Gordon's growth model and (2) the capital asset pricing model (CAPM) approach.

The Gordon's growth model. The Gordon's model is:

$$P_0 = \frac{D_1}{r - g}$$

Where:
P_0 = value (or market price) of common stock
D_1 = dividend to be received in one year
r = investor's required rate of return
g = rate of growth (assumed to be constant over time)

Solving the model for r results in the formula for the cost of common stock:

$$r = \frac{D_1}{P_0} + g \quad \text{or} \quad k_e = \frac{D_1}{P_0} + g$$

Note: That the symbol r is changed to k_e to show that it is used for the computation of cost of capital.

Example 3: Assume that the market price of the Carter Company's stock is $40. The dividend to be paid at the end of the coming year is $4 per share and is expected to grow at a constant annual rate of six percent. Then, the cost of this common stock is:

$$k_e = \frac{D_1}{P_0} + g = \frac{\$4}{\$40} + 6\% = 16\%$$

The cost of new common stock, or external equity capital, is higher than the cost of existing common stock because of the flotation costs involved in selling the new common stock. Flotation costs, sometimes called issuance costs, are the total costs of issuing and selling a security that include printing and engraving, legal fees, and accounting fees.

If f is the flotation cost shown as a percentage of market price, the formula for the cost of new common stock is:

$$k_e = \frac{D_1}{P_0(1 - f)} + g$$

Example 4: Assume the same data as in Example 3, except the firm is trying to sell new issues of stock A and its flotation cost is 10 percent.

Then:

$$k_e = \frac{D_1}{P_0(1 - f)} + g$$

$$= \frac{\$4}{\$40(1 - 0.1)} + 6\% = \frac{\$4}{\$36} + 6\% = 11.11\% + 6\% = 17.11\%$$

The capital asset pricing model (CAPM) approach. An alternative approach to measuring the cost of common stock is to use the CAPM which involves the following steps:

1. Estimate the risk-free rate, r_f, generally taken to be the U.S. Treasury bill rate.

2. Estimate the stock's beta coefficient, b, which is an index of systematic (or nondiversifiable market) risk.

3. Estimate the rate of return on the market portfolio, rm, such as the Standard & Poor's 500 Stock Composite Index or Dow Jones 30 Industrials.

4. Estimate the required rate of return on the firm's stock using the CAPM equation:

   $$k_e = r_f + b(r_m - r_f)$$

Example 5: Assuming that r_f is seven percent, b is 1.5, and r_m is 13 percent, then:

$k_e = r_f + b(r_m - r_f) = 7\% + 1.5(13\% - 7\%) = 16\%$. This 16 percent cost of common stock can be viewed as consisting of a seven-percent risk-free rate plus a nine-percent risk premium, which reflects that the firm's stock price is 1.5 times more volatile than the market portfolio to the factors affecting nondiversifiable, or systematic, risk.

.04 Cost of Retained Earnings

The cost of retained earnings, k_s, is closely related to the cost of existing common stock since the cost of equity obtained by retained earnings is the same as the rate of return investors require on the firm's common stock. Therefore:

$$k_e = k_s$$

.05 Measuring the Overall Cost of Capital

The firm's overall cost of capital is the weighted average of the individual capital costs, with the weights being the proportions of each type of capital used. Let k_o be the overall cost of capital.

k_o = Σ (percentage of the total capital structure supplied by each source of capital × cost of capital for each source)

$$= w_d k_d + w_p k_p + w_e k_e + w_s k_s$$

Where:

w_d = % of total capital supplied by debts
w_p = % of total capital supplied by preferred stock
w_e = % of total capital supplied by external equity
w_s = % of total capital supplied by retained earnings (or internal equity)

The weights can be *historical, target,* or *marginal.*

Historical weights. Historical weights are based on a firm's existing capital structure. The use of these weights is based on the assumption that the firm's existing capital structure is optimal and therefore should be maintained in the future. Two types of historical weights can be used-book value weights and market value weights.

Book value weights. The use of book value weights in calculating the firm's weighted cost of capital assumes that new financing will be raised using the same method the firm used for its present capital structure. The weights are determined by dividing the book value of each capital component by the sum of the book values of all the long-term capital sources. The computation of overall cost of capital is illustrated in the following example.

Example 6: Assume the following capital structure and cost of each source of financing for the Carter Company:

		Cost
Bonds ($1,000 par)	$20,000,000	5.14% (from Example 1)
Preferred stock ($100 par)	5,000,000	13.40% (from Example 2)
Common stock ($40 par)	20,000,000	17.11% (from Example 4)
Retained earnings	5,000,000	16.00% (from Example 3)
Total	$50,000,000	

The book value weights and the overall cost of capital are computed as follows:

Source	*Book Value*	*Weights*	*Cost*	*Weighted Cost*
Debt	$20,000,000	40%[(a)]	5.14%	2.06%[(b)]
Preferred stock	5,000,000	10	13.40%	1.34
Common stock	20,000,000	40	17.11%	6.84
Retained earnings	5,000,000	10	16.00%	1.60
	$50,000,000	100%		11.84%

Overall cost of capital = k_o = 11.84%

(a) $20,000,000/$50,000,000 = .40 = 40%

(b) 5.14% × 40% = 2.06%

Market value weights. Market value weights are determined by dividing the market value of each source by the sum of the market values of all sources. The use of market value weights for computing a firm's weighted average cost of capital is theoretically more appealing than the use of book value weights, because the market values of the securities closely approximate the actual dollars to be received from their sale.

Example 7: In addition to the data from Example 6, assume that the security market prices are as follows:

Mortgage bonds = $1,100 per bond

Preferred stock = $90 per share

Common stock = $80 per share

The firm's number of securities in each category is:

$$\text{Mortgage bonds} = \frac{\$20{,}000{,}000}{\$1{,}000} = 20{,}000$$

$$\text{Preferred stock} = \frac{\$5{,}000{,}000}{\$100} = 50{,}000$$

$$\text{Common stock} = \frac{\$20{,}000{,}000}{\$40} = 500{,}000$$

Therefore, the market value weights are:

Source	*Number of Securities*	*Price*	*Market Value*
Debt	20,000	$1,100	$22,000,000
Preferred stock	50,000	$ 90	4,500,000
Common stock	500,000	$ 80	40,000,000
			$66,500,000

The $40 million common stock value must be split in the ratio of 4 to 1 (the $20 million common stock versus the $5 million retained earnings in the original capital structure), since the market value of the retained earnings has been impounded into the common stock.

The firm's cost of capital is as follows:

Source	*Market Value*	*Weights*	*Cost*	*Weighted Average*
Debt	$22,000,000	33.08%	5.14%	1.70%
Preferred stock	4,500,000	6.77	13.40%	0.91
Common stock	32,000,000	48.12	17.11%	8.23
Retained earnings	8,000,000	12.03	16.00%	1.92
	$66,500,000	100.00%		12.76%

Overall cost of capital = k_o = 12.76%

Target weights. If the firm has a target capital structure (desired debt-equity mix) which is maintained over the long term, then the use of that capital structure and associated weights can be used in calculating the firm's weighted cost of capital.

Marginal weights. Marginal weights involve the use of actual financial mix used in financing the proposed investments. In using target weights, the firm is concerned with what it believes to be the optimal capital structure or target percentage. In using marginal weights, the firm is concerned with the actual dollar amounts of each type of financing to be needed for a given investment project. This approach, while attractive, presents a problem. The cost of capital for the individual sources depends on the firm's financial risk which is affected by the firm's financial mix. If the company alters its present capital structure, the individual costs will change which makes it more difficult to compute the weighted cost of capital. The important assumption needed is that the firm's financial mix is relatively stable and that these weights will closely approximate future financing practice.

Example 8: The Carter Company is considering raising $8 million for plant expansion. Management estimates using the following mix for financing this project:

Debt	$4,000,000	50%
Common stock	2,000,000	25%
Retained earnings	2,000,000	25%
	$8,000,000	100%

The company's cost of capital is computed as follows:

Source	*Marginal Weights*	*Cost*	*Weighted Cost*
Debt	50%	5.14%	2.57%
Common stock	25	17.11%	4.28
Retained earnings	25	16.00%	4.00
	100%		10.85%

Overall cost of capital = k_o = 10.85%

.06 *Level of Financing and the Marginal Cost of Capital (MCC)*

In the previous illustration, the weighted cost of capital was determined under the assumption that no new common stock was issued. If new common stock is issued, the firm's weighted cost of capital will increase for each dollar of new financing, because external equity capital has a higher cost than retained earnings due to flotation costs. Therefore, the lower-cost capital sources are used first. In fact, the firm's cost of capital is a function of the size of its total investment outlay.

A schedule or graph relating the firm's cost of capital to the level of new financing is called the *weighted marginal cost of capital* (MCC). Such a schedule is used to determine the discount rate to be used in the firm's capital budgeting process. The steps to be followed in calculating the firm's marginal cost of capital are summarized below.

1. Determine the cost and the percentage of financing to be used for each source of capital (debt, preferred stock, and common stock equity).

2. Compute the break points on the MCC curve where the weighted cost will increase. The formula for computing the break points is:

$$\text{Break point} = \frac{\text{Maximum amount of the lower} - \text{Cost source of capital}}{\text{Percentage financing provided by the source}}$$

3. Calculate the weighted cost of capital over the range of total financing between break points.

4. Construct an MCC schedule or graph that shows the weighted cost of capital for each level of total new financing. This

schedule will be used in conjunction with the firm's available investment opportunities schedule (IOS) in order to select the investments. As long as a project's IRR is greater than the marginal cost of new financing, the project should be accepted. Also, the point at which the IRR intersects the MCC gives the optimal capital budget.

Example 9: A firm is contemplating three investment projects, A, B, and C, whose initial cash outlays and expected IRR are shown below. IOS for these projects is:

Project	*Cash Outlay*	*IRR*
A	$2,000,000	13%
B	$2,000,000	15%
C	$1,000,000	10%

If these projects are accepted, the financing will consist of 50 percent debt and 50 percent common stock. The firm should have $1.8 million in earnings available for reinvestment (internal common). The firm will consider only the effects of increases in the cost of common stock on its marginal cost of capital.

1. The costs of capital for each source of financing have been computed and are given below:

Source	*Cost*
Debt	5%
Common stock ($1.8 million)	15%
New common stock	19%

If the firm uses only internally generated common stock, the weighted cost of capital is:

k_o = E percentage of the total capital structure supplied by each source of capital × cost of capital for each source.

In this case, the capital structure is composed of 50 percent debt and 50 percent internally generated common stock. Thus:

$$k_o = (0.5)5\% + (0.5)15\% = 10\%$$

If the firm uses only new common stock, the weighted cost of capital is:

$$k_o = (0.5)5\% + (0.5)19\% = 12\%$$

Range of Total New Financing (In Millions of Dollars)	Type of Capital	Proportion	Cost	Weighted Cost
$0–$3.6	Debt	0.5	5%	2.5%
	Internal common	0.5	15%	7.5
				10.0%
$3.6 and up	Debt	0.5	5%	2.5%
	New common	0.5	19%	9.5
				12.0%

2. Next compute the break point, which is the level of financing at which the weighted cost of capital increases.

$$\text{Break point} = \frac{\text{Maximum amount of source of the lower cost source of capital}}{\text{Percentage of financing provided by the source}}$$

$$= \frac{\$1{,}800{,}000}{0.5} = \$3{,}600{,}000$$

3. That is, the firm may be able to finance $3.6 million in new investments with internal common stock and debt without having to change the current mix of 50 percent debt and 50 percent common stock. Therefore, if the total financing is $3.6 million or less, the firm's cost of capital is 10 percent.

4. Construct the MCC schedule on the IOS graph to determine the discount rate to be used in order to decide in which project to invest and to show the firm's optimal capital budget. See Exhibit 1.

The firm should continue to invest up to the point where the IRR equals the MCC. From the graph in Exhibit 1, note that the firm should invest in projects B and A, since each IRR exceeds the marginal cost of capital. The firm should reject project C, since its cost of capital is greater than the IRR. The optimal capital budget is $4 million since this is the sum of the cash outlay required for projects A and B.

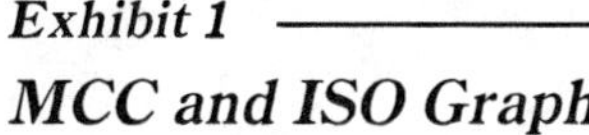

Exhibit 1

MCC and ISO Graph

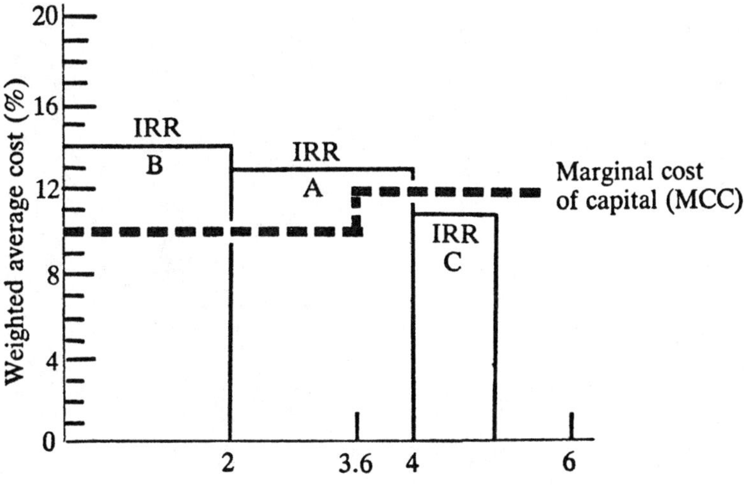

¶ 1910 Summary

Cost of capital is an important concept within financial management. It is the rate of return that must be achieved in order for the price of the stock to remain unchanged. Therefore, the cost of capital is the minimum acceptable rate of return for the company's new investments. The chapter discussed how to calculate the individual costs of financing sources, various ways to calculate the overall cost of capital, and how the optimal budget for capital spending can be constructed. Financial officers should be thoroughly familiar with the ways to compute the costs of various sources of financing for financial, capital budgeting, and capital structure decisions.

Chapter 20

Capital Structure Decisions

¶ 2001 Overview

In the previous chapters we developed an understanding of how securities are valued in the marketplace. Drawing on the tenets of valuation theory, we then presented various approaches to measuring the cost of funds to the company. The concepts to be covered in this chapter relate closely to those discussions of the valuation process and the cost of capital, and they also extend to the crucial problem of determining the firm's optimal capital structure.

Capital structure management is closely related to the firm's cost of capital. Capital structure is the mix of the long-term sources of funds used by the firm. The primary objective of capital structure decisions is to maximize the market value of the firm through an appropriate mix of long-term sources of funds. This mix, called the *optimal capital structure*, will minimize the firm's overall cost of capital. However, there are arguments about whether an optimal capital structure actually exists. The arguments center on whether a firm can, in reality, affect its valuation and its cost of capital by varying the mixture of the funds used.

The decision to use debt and/or preferred stock in the firm's capitalization causes two types of financial leverage effects. The first effect is the increased risk in earnings per share (EPS) due to the use of fixed financial obligations. As was discussed in Chapter 10, this was measured by the *degree of financial leverage* (DFL). The second effect relates to the level of EPS at a given earnings before interest and taxes (EBIT) under a specific capital structure. We rely upon *EBIT-EPS analysis* to measure this second effect.

¶ 2005 EBIT-EPS Approach To Capital Structure Decisions

This analysis is a practical tool that enables the financial manager to evaluate alternative financing plans by investigating their effect on EPS over a range of EBIT levels. Its primary objective is to determine the EBIT break-even, or indifference points between the various alternative financing plans. The indifference point identifies the EBIT level at which the EPS will be the same regardless of the financing plan chosen by the financial manager.

This indifference point has major implications for capital structure decisions. At EBIT amounts in excess of the EBIT indifference level, the more heavily levered financing plan will generate a higher EPS. At EBIT amounts below the EBIT indifference level, the financing plan involving less leverage will generate a higher EPS. Therefore, it is of critical importance for the financial manager to know the EBIT indifference level. The indifference points between any two methods of financing can be determined by solving for EBIT in the following equation:

$$\frac{(EBIT - I)(1 - t) - PD}{S1} = \frac{(EBIT - I)(1 - t) - PD}{S2}$$

Where:

t = tax rate
PD = preferred stock dividends
S1 and S2 = number of shares of common stock outstanding after financing for plan 1 and plan 2, respectively
I = interest expense

Example 1: Assume that ABC Company, with long-term capitalization consisting entirely of $5 million in stock, wants to raise $2 million for the acquisition of special equipment by (1) selling 40,000 shares of common stock at $50 each, (2) selling bonds at 10-percent interest, or (3) issuing preferred stock with an eight-percent dividend. The present EBIT is $800,000, the income tax rate is 50 percent, and 100,000 shares of common stock are now outstanding. To compute the indifference points, we begin by calculating EPS at a projected EBIT level of $1 million.

	All Common	*All Debt*	*All Preferred*
EBIT	$1,000,000	$1,000,000	$1,000,000
Interest		200,000	
Earnings before taxes (EBT)	$1,000,000	$ 800,000	$1,000,000
Taxes	500,000	400,000	500,000
Earnings after taxes (EAT)	$ 500,000	$ 400,000	$ 500,000
Preferred stock dividend			160,000
Earnings available to common stockholders	$ 500,000	$ 400,000	$ 340,000
Number of shares	140,000	$ 4.00	$ 3.40

Now connect the EPSs at the level of EBIT of $1 million with the EBITs for each financing alternative on the horizontal axis to obtain the EPS-EBIT graphs. We plot the EBIT necessary to cover all fixed financial costs for each financing alternative on the horizontal axis.

For the common stock plan, there are no fixed costs, so the intercept on the horizontal axis is zero. For the debt plan, there must be an EBIT of $200,000 to cover interest charges. For the preferred stock plan, there must be an EBIT of $320,000 [$160,000/(1—0.5)] to cover $160,000 in preferred stock dividends at a 50-percent income tax rate; so $320,000 becomes the horizontal axis intercept. See Exhibit 1.

In this example, the indifference point between all common and all debt is:

$$\frac{(\text{EBIT} - \text{I})(1 - \text{t}) - \text{PD}}{\text{S1}} = \frac{(\text{EBIT} - \text{I})(1 - \text{t}) - \text{PD}}{\text{S2}}$$

$$\frac{(\text{EBIT} - 0)(1 - 0.5) - 0}{140{,}000} = \frac{(\text{EBIT} - 200{,}000)(1 - 0.5) - 0}{100{,}000}$$

Rearranging yields:

$$\begin{aligned} 0.5(\text{EBIT})(100{,}000) &= 0.5(\text{EBIT})(140{,}000) - 0.5(200{,}000)(140{,}000) \\ 20{,}000\ \text{EBIT} &= 14{,}000{,}000{,}000 \\ \text{EBIT} &= \$700{,}000 \end{aligned}$$

Similarly, the indifference point between all common and all preferred would be:

$$\frac{(\text{EBIT} - \text{I})(1 - \text{t}) - \text{PD}}{\text{S1}} = \frac{(\text{EBIT} - \text{I})(1 - \text{t}) - \text{PD}}{\text{S2}}$$

$$\frac{(\text{EBIT} - 0)(1 - 0.5) - 0}{140{,}000} = \frac{(\text{EBIT} - 160{,}000)(1 - 0.5) - 0}{100{,}000}$$

Rearranging yields:

$$\begin{aligned} 0.5(\text{EBIT})(100{,}000) &= 0.5(\text{EBIT})(140{,}000) - 160{,}000(140{,}000) \\ 20{,}000\ \text{EBIT} &= 22{,}400{,}000{,}000 \\ \text{EBIT} &= \$1{,}120{,}000 \end{aligned}$$

Based on the above computations and observing Exhibit 1, we can draw the following conclusions:

1. At any level of EBIT, debt is better than preferred stock since it gives a higher EPS.
2. At a level of EBIT above $700,000, debt is better than common stock. If EBIT is below $700,000, the reverse is true.
3. At a level of EBIT above $1,120,000, preferred stock is better than common. At or below that point, the reverse is true.

Exhibit 1

The EPS-EBIT Graph

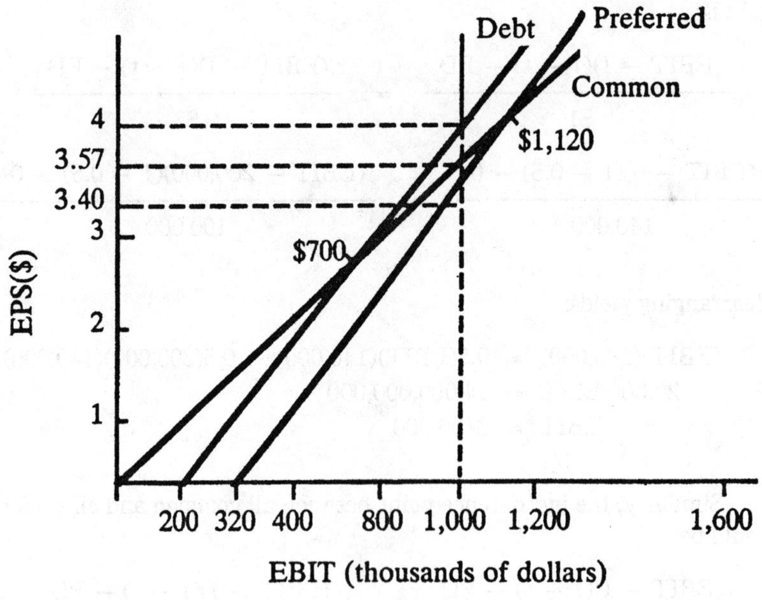

Caution: It is important to realize that financial leverage is a two-edged sword. It can magnify profits, but it can also increase losses. The EBIT-EPS approach helps financial managers examine the impact of financial leverage as a financing method. Investment performance is crucial to the successful application of any leveraging strategy.

¶ 2010 Analysis of Corporate Cash Flows

A second tool of capital structure management involves the *analysis of cash flows.* When considering the appropriate capital structure, among other things, it is important to analyze the cash-flow ability of the firm to service fixed charges. The greater the dollar amount of debt and/or preferred stock the firm issues and the shorter their maturity, the greater the fixed charges of the firm. These charges include principal and interest payments on debt, lease payments, and preferred stock dividends. Before assuming additional fixed charges, the firm should analyze its expected future cash flows because for fixed charges must be met with cash. The inability to meet these charges, with the exception of preferred stock dividends, may result in insolvency. The greater and more stable the expected future cash flows of the firm, the greater the debt capacity of the company.

¶ 2015 Coverage Ratios

A third tool is the calculation of *comparative coverage ratios.* Among the ways we can gain insight into the debt capacity of a firm is through the use of coverage ratios, which were introduced in Chapter 12. In the computation of these ratios, a corporate financial officer typically uses EBIT as a rough measure of the cash flow available to cover debt-servicing obligations. Perhaps the most widely used coverage ratio is *times interest earned,* which is simply:

$$\text{Times interest earned} = \frac{\text{EBIT}}{\text{Interest on debt}}$$

Assume that the most recent annual EBIT for a company was $4 million and that interest payments on all debt obligations were $1 million. Therefore, times interest earned would be four times. This tells us that EBIT can drop by as much as 75 percent and the firm still will be able to cover its interest payments out of earnings.

However, a coverage ratio of only 1:0 indicates that earnings are just sufficient to satisfy the interest burden. While it is difficult to generalize as to what is an appropriate interest coverage ratio, a financial officer usually is concerned when the ratio gets much below 3:1. However, it all depends. In a highly stable industry, a relatively low times-interest-earned ratio may be appropriate, whereas it is not appropriate in a highly cyclical one.

Unfortunately, the times-interest-earned ratio tells us nothing about the ability of the firm to meet principal payments on its debt. The inability to meet a principal payment constitutes the same legal default as failure to meet an interest payment. Therefore, it is useful to compute the coverage ratio for the full debt-service burden. This ratio is:

$$\text{Debt-service brokerage} = \frac{\text{EBIT}}{\text{Interest} + \dfrac{\text{Principal payments}}{1 - \text{Tax Rate}}}$$

Here principal payments are adjusted upward for the tax effect. The reason is that EBIT represents earnings before taxes. Because principal payments are not tax deductible, they must be paid out of after-tax earnings. Therefore, we must adjust principal payments so that they are consistent with EBIT. If principal payments in our previous example were $1.5 million per annum and the tax rate were 34 percent, the debt-service coverage ratio would be:

$$\text{Debt-service brokerage} = \frac{\$4 \text{ million}}{\$1 \text{ million} + \dfrac{\$1.5 \text{ million}}{1 - 0.34}} = 1{:}22$$

A coverage ratio of 1:22 means that EBIT can fall by only 22 percent before earnings coverage is insufficient to service the debt. Obviously, the closer the ratio is to 1:0, the worse things are, all other things being equal. However, even with a coverage ratio of less than 1:0, a company may still meet its obligations if it can renew some of its debt when it comes due.

The financial risk associated with leverage should be analyzed on the basis of the firm's ability to service total fixed charges. While lease financing is not debt per se, its impact on cash flows is exactly the same as the payment of interest and principal on a debt obligation. Therefore, annual lease payments should be added to the denominator of the formula in order to properly reflect the total cash-flow burden associated with financing.

Two types of comparison should be undertaken with a coverage ratio. First, it should be compared with past and expected future ratios of the same company. The idea behind *trend analysis* is to determine if there has been an improvement or a deterioration in coverage over time. Another method of analyzing the appropriate capital structure for a company is to evaluate the capital structure of other companies having similar business risk. Companies used in this comparison may be those in the same industry. If the firm is contemplating a capital structure significantly out of line with that of similar companies, it is conspicuous to the marketplace. This is not to say, however, that the firm is wrong; other companies in the industry may be too conservative with respect to the use of debt. The optimal capital structure for all companies in the industry might call for a higher proportion of debt to equity than the industry average. As a result, the firm may well be able to justify more debt than the industry average. Because investment analysts and creditors tend to evaluate companies by industry, however, the firm should be able to justify its position if its capital structure is noticeably out of line in either direction.

Ultimately, a financial officer wants to make generalizations about the appropriate amount of debt (and leases) for a firm to have in its capital structure. It is clear that over the long run, the source to service debt for a going concern is earnings. Therefore, coverage ratios are an important analytical tool. However, coverage ratios are but only one tool by which a financial manager is able to reach conclusions with respect to the company's best capital structure. Coverage ratios are subject to certain limitations and, consequently, cannot be used as a sole means for determining the capital structure. For one thing, the fact that EBIT falls below the debt-service burden does not spell immediate doom for the company. Often alternative sources of funds, including renewal of a loan, are available, and these sources must be considered.

¶ 2020 Capital Structure Decisions in Practice

How do companies decide in practice which route to go in raising capital? It is a complex decision, related to a company's balance sheet, market conditions, outstanding obligations, and a host of other factors.

Many financial managers believe that the following factors influence capital structure:

1. Growth rate and stability of future sales.
2. Competitive structure in the industry.
3. Asset makeup of the individual firm.
4. The business risk to which the firm is exposed.
5. Control status of owners and management.
6. Lenders' attitudes toward the industry and the company.

Surveys indicate that the majority of financial managers of large firms believe in the concept of an optimal capital structure. The optimal capital structure is approximated by the identification of target debt ratios. The most frequently mentioned factor that affects the level of the target debt ratio was the company's ability to service fixed financing costs. Other factors identified as affecting the target were (1) maintaining a desired bond rating, (2) providing an adequate borrowing reserve, and (3) exploiting the advantages of financial leverage.

¶ 2025 Summary

The chapter discussed the process of arriving at an appropriate capital structure for the firm. Tools that can assist financial officers in this task were examined. In deciding upon an appropriate capital structure, the financial manager should take into account a number of factors. One important method of gaining insight into the question of the optimal capital structure involves analyzing the relationship between EBIT and EPS for alternative methods of financing. In addition, the financial manager can learn much from a comparison of capital structure ratios and coverage ratios (such as times interest earned and debt-service coverage) for similar companies and over time.

Part 7

Securities and Other Investments

Chapter 21
Survey of Investment Instruments

¶ 2101 Types of Investments

Investments can be classified into two forms: *fixed income* and *variable income.* Simply stated, fixed-income investments promise a stated amount of income periodically. These include corporate bonds, preferred stocks, U.S. government securities (Treasury bills), municipal bonds, and other savings instruments (savings account and certificate of deposit). On the other hand, variable-dollar investments are those where neither the principal nor the income is contractually set in advance in terms of dollars. That is, both the value and income of variable-income investments can change in dollar amount, either up or down, with changes in internal or external economic conditions. These include common stocks, mutual funds, real estate, and variable annuities.

Investments can be viewed as *financial* or *real assets.* Financial assets refer to intangible investments—things you cannot touch, wear, or walk on. They are your equity interest in a company, evidence of money owed to you, or a right to buy or sell your ownership interest. Real assets have tangible, physical substance. Exhibit 1 lists the various forms of financial and real assets.

Exhibit 1

Overview of Investment Vehicles

Financial Assets	*Real Assets*
1. Equity claims—direct	1. Real estate
Common stock	
Options, rights, and warrants	
2. Equity claims—indirect	2. Precious metals and gems
Mutual funds	
3. Creditor claims	3. Collectibles
Savings accounts and certificates of deposits (CDs)	
Treasury bills	
Money market funds	
Commercial paper	
Corporate and government bonds	
4. Preferred stock	
5. Commodities and financial futures	
6. Annuities—variable and fixed	

.01 Direct and Indirect Investments

When you make a *direct* investment, you acquire a claim on a particular investment vehicle. When you choose an *indirect* investment, you have a portfolio of stocks, bonds, or properties. What is a popular indirect investment? It is a share of a mutual fund, which holds a portfolio of securities issued by mutual fund investment companies, or a share of Real Estate Investment Trusts (REITs). You can have a portfolio of securities representing diversified investment types. This variety of investments minimizes risk while bringing in a satisfactory return.

.02 Long-Term and Short-Term Investments

An investment may be *short term* or *long term*. Short-term investments last for one year or less. Long-term investments last more than one year. A short-term investment might be a three-month Treasury bill. A long-term investment might be a five-year Treasury note. Some long-term investments do not mature, such as equity securities. However, you can buy a long-term investment and consider it as a short-term one by disposing of it within one year. How many of your investments are short term? How many are long term? Is that the combination you consider best for you?

Short-term securities involve little risk and offer liquidity. They include the liquid investments listed earlier in this chapter: savings accounts, certificates of deposit, money market certificates, mutual funds, U.S. Treasury bills, and commercial paper.

Long-term securities are debt or equity instruments with a maturity of more than one year. A debt instrument is a certificate or security showing that you loaned funds to a company or to a government in return for future interest and repayment of principal. Equity securities are ones you have ownership interests in.

¶ 2105 Features of Bonds

Bonds are one type of debt instrument—a certificate of corporate or government obligation to you in return for your loan (investment). Bonds are usually sold in $1,000 denominations. You can purchase or sell a bond before maturity at a price other than face value. The bond indenture specifies the terms of the borrowing arrangement. Many bonds are callable at the command of the issuing company. This means that the issuing firm can buy back the debt prior to maturity.

The interest you receive on a bond equals the nominal interest rate times the face value. Suppose, for example, that you buy a ten-year $40,000 bond at eight-percent interest. You pay 94 percent of face value. Interest is payable semiannually, which is typical. The purchase price is $37,600 (94% × $40,000). You receive a semiannual interest payment of $1,600 (4% × $40,000). At maturity, you will receive the full maturity value of $40,000.

Corporate bonds are riskier than government bonds, because companies can fail. Most individuals in high tax brackets do not find corporate bonds attractive because interest received is fully taxable.

U.S. government obligations include Treasury notes and Treasury bonds. Treasury notes are U.S. obligations having a maturity from two to ten years. The yield is slightly higher than on Treasury bills. Treasury bonds are long-term obligations for over ten years. They usually pay a higher interest rate than do Treasury notes. The default risk is nonexistent.

The interest on local (state and city) bonds is exempt from federal and local taxes. However, to be free from state tax, you must buy bonds issued by your home state. For example, interest on California State bonds is exempt from California state tax, but interest on New York bonds is not exempt from California State. Municipal bonds appeal to high-tax-bracket investors, because the interest received is tax free. If you are in a high tax bracket, you should consider buying municipal bonds.

Zero-coupon bonds are a relatively recent innovation. They pay no interest and are issued at a discount and redeemed at face value at maturity. They can be risky but of some interest to longer-term investors.

¶ 2110 Features of Stock

An equity investment is ownership in a business (evidenced by a security) or property (evidenced by title). You obtain an equity interest by buying stock. Equity securities have no maturity date. You purchase them in order to receive income (dividends) and capital gain. Two types of stock are common and preferred.

Common stock is an equity investment reflecting ownership in a company. If you hold 1,000 shares of common stock in a firm that has 100,000 shares outstanding, you own a one-percent ownership interest in that company. Thus, you can control the company. In many instances, an investor can gain control by owning a considerably smaller percentage than this.

Here are some of the advantages of owning common stock:

- Inflation hedge.
- You can vote.
- If the company does well, your stock price will appreciate and your dividends will increase.

Owning common stock also carries disadvantages, however. These disadvantages include the following:

- When the firm is not thriving, your earnings will drop and price stability will suffer, meaning that the stocks' resale value will decrease.
- You may not receive sizable dividends.
- Common stock is riskier than debt securities and preferred stock, since you will be the last to receive money if the company fails. (Debt holders come before equity holders in liquidation, and in this instance, you are an equity holder.)

Common stock owners have the preemptive right, which allows them to maintain their proportionate share in the company. Thus, they can buy new shares issued before they go on sale to the general public. This way they can maintain their percentage of ownership.

Preferred stock holders have no voting rights, but they do receive a fixed dividend rate. They also take precedence over common stock holders in the receipt of dividends and in the event of liquidation. Preferred stock may be callable at the company's option, and it generally provides only dividend income, with no capital gain potential. See Exhibit 2 for a comparison of debt instruments, preferred stock, and common stock.

Exhibit 2

Comparison of Securities

	Debt	*Preferred Stock*	*Common Stock*
Voting rights	No	No	Yes
Risk	Low	Medium	High
Appreciation in value of company	No	Yes	Yes
Fixed annual return	Yes	Yes	No
Partial tax exclusion for interest or dividends	No	Yes	Yes

.01 Types of Dividends

There are three types of dividends: cash, stock, and property. Cash dividends are taxable. They are usually paid quarterly. If a stock dividend differs from the security receiving the dividend (in other words, if you own common stock but get a preferred stock dividend), you must pay taxes on the dividends you receive. If they are the same (in other words, if you own common stock and get common stock dividends), you do not pay taxes on those dividends. You can look up the dividend records and ratings of companies in *Standard and Poor's Stock Guide.*

¶ 2115 Convertible Securities

Convertible securities can be converted into common stock at a later date. Two examples of these securities are convertible bonds and convertible preferred stock. These securities give you fixed income in the form of interest (convertible bonds) or dividends (convertible preferred stocks). They also let you benefit from the appreciation value of the common stock.

¶ 2120 Derivative Products

Options and futures are derivative instruments. Their value is derived from the underlying security. Options and futures are also leverage-inherent investments that can be used to increase potential return or to reduce risk. An option is the right to buy a security or property at a given price during a specified time period. An option is neither a debt nor equity; it is an opportunity to acquire securities. You might buy options in order to take advantage of an anticipated change in the price of common stocks. As an option holder, you have no guaranteed return; the option may not be attractive to exercise because the market price of the underlying common stock has not increased, for example, or the option time period may elapse. If this happens, you will lose your entire investment. Hence, options involve considerable risk.

Commodity and financial futures are seller commitments to deliver a specific commodity or financial instrument at a set price by a given date. The profitability of these investments depends on many uncontrollable factors linked to the world economy. Therefore, futures are high-risk investments.

.01 Leveraged Investments

Warrants, stock rights, options, and futures are called leveraged investments, since you will be able to participate in these investment vehicles with a small sum of money. The value of these instruments are derived from the value of their underlying securities.

¶ 2125 Other Types of Investments

There are many other forms of investments. Some are real assets such as real estate, precious metals and gems, and collectibles. Some are tax-advantaged investments whose income grows tax-deferred. They include Individual Retirement Accounts (IRAs), Keoghs, and annuities. Limited partnerships provide tax shelters with passive participation and limited liabilities.

¶ 2130 Common Stock

Common stock is a security that represents an ownership interest in a corporation. This ownership interest is evidenced by a transferable stock certificate. For example, if you hold 5,000 shares of ABC Corporation, which has 100,000 shares outstanding, your ownership interest is five percent. Each share is a fractional ownership interest in a corporation. You acquire an equity interest in the corporation by buying its stock. As a stockholder, you can vote for the board of directors of the corporation. The equity investment has no maturity date. Common stock return comes in the form of dividend income and appreciation in the market price of stock.

The corporation's stockholders have certain rights and privileges including:

1. *Control of the firm.* The stockholders elect the firm's directors who in turn select officers to manage the business.

2. *Preemptive rights.* This is the right to purchase new stock.

   A preemptive right entitles a common stockholder to maintain his or her proportional ownership by offering the stockholder an opportunity to purchase, on a pro rata basis, any new stock being offered or any securities convertible into common stock.

   (a) Value of right "cum rights"

$$\text{Value of right} = \frac{\text{Market price (M)} - \text{Subscription price (S)}}{\text{\# of rights required (N)} + 1}$$

(b) Value of right "ex-rights"

$$\frac{\text{Adjusted M} - \text{S}}{\text{N}}$$

Example 1. If a stock is selling for \$60 and two rights are required to purchase a single share at the subscription price of \$51, the value of a single right would be (\$60 − \$51)/(2 + 1) = \$3. If the stock is now "ex-rights," its market value should reflect that and be \$60 − \$3 or \$57. Thus we have (\$57 − \$51)/2 = \$3.

3. *Voting rights.* Shareholders have rights to vote on all important matters affecting them:

    - Alterations to the corporate charter
    - Mergers and acquisitions
    - Recapitalization (e.g., an exchange of bond for stock)
    - Financial reorganization
    - Election of the board of directors

.01 Characteristics of Common Stock

The characteristics that make common stock an attractive investment alternative can be summarized as follows:

1. Common stocks provide an ownership feature, as compared with fixed income securities, such as bonds, which do not.

2. Common stocks provide an income potential not only in terms of current income in the form of dividends but also future capital gain (or loss).

3. Common shareholders can participate in the firm's earnings and lay claim to all the residual profits of the entity.

4. Common stock can be an effective inflation hedge if the total return from investment in common stock exceeds the rate of inflation.

5. Because there are a variety of stocks available, as discussed above, the investor may choose from a broad spectrum of risk-return combinations from common stock investment.

Exhibit 3 summarizes characteristics of common stock.

Exhibit 3

Characteristics of Common Stock

Voting rights	One vote per share
Income	Dividends; not fixed
Capital gain/loss potential	Yes
Price stability	No
Inflation hedge	Yes
Preemptive right	Yes
Priority of claim	Residual after all other claims paid
Unit of purchase	Often in units of 100 shares

Some key terms regarding common stock are as follows:

1. *Par value.* Traditionally set at a low price partly for tax purposes; a corporation may also issue no-par stock.
2. *Book value.* The net worth (assets minus liabilities) of the corporation divided by the number of shares outstanding.

$$\text{Book value} = \frac{\text{Assets} - \text{Liabilities}}{\text{Number of shares outstanding}}$$

3. *Market value.* Currently quoted price of a share of stock in the market. The market value or capitalization of a firm is its stock price times the number of shares outstanding. The ratio of a stock's market price to its book value (price/book ratio) gives an indication of how investors regard the company. Dividing the share price by the book value gives a market/book ratio, and thus the higher the ratio, the more expensive the stock price (compared with its book value).
4. *Cash dividends.* Cash dividends are paid to investors if and when declared by the board of directors. Important dates to remember:

(a) Declared date—the date on which the board declares the dividend.

(b) Record Date—investors registered on the corporate books on the record date (set by the board) will receive the dividend.

(c) Ex-dividend date—the date that a stock will begin trading without the value of the pending dividend factored into its market value; the ex-dividend date is *two business days before the record date. Note:* The general sequence of the dividend process should never change: There always should be first a declaration, then an ex-dividend date, followed by a date of record, and finally, the date when investors receive the payment. Today, settlement of stocks is T+3, which means that when one first buys or sells a stock, it takes three days for the change to be entered into the company's record books. If one is not in the company's record books on the date of record, he/she won't receive the dividend payment. To ensure that one is in the record books, he/she needs to buy the stock at least *three* days before the date of record.

Example 2. Assume the date of record is Thursday the 11th.

	Ex-dividend date ↓		*Record date* ↓	
Mon 8th	*Tues 9th*	*Wed 10th*	*Thurs 11th*	*Fri 12th*

If one buys it on the ex-dividend date (9th), he/she will not receive the dividend because his/her name will not appear in the company's record books until Friday (12th). If one wants to buy the stock and receive the dividend, he/she needs to buy it on the 8th. If one wants to sell the stock and still receive the dividend, he/she needs to sell on the 9th.

(d) Payable date—the date on which investors on record will receive dividends.

5. *Stock dividends.* For example, if XYZ Corp. declares a five-percent stock dividend, a holder of 200 shares would receive a stock certificate for 10 additional shares. Most often, firms redeem fractional shares for cash.

6. *Stock splits.* Each old share is equal to some number of new shares. Stock splits do not change the value of the underlying corporation, and so the other values are changed proportionately.

7. *Reverse splits.* Each old share is equal to some fraction of a new share.

Example 3. A stock with a par value of $1 and a market value of $20 which had a two-for-one stock split would now have twice as many authorized shares. But both the par and market values would be halved. In a one-for-two reverse split, 200 shares of old stock would be 100 shares of the new stock. Both the par and market values would be doubled.

.02 Types of Stocks

The stock you buy should be best for your particular circumstances and goals. The types of stock include:

1. *Income stocks.* These stocks are issued by companies having high dividends and a fairly stable stream of earnings. They are desirable if you seek high current income, instead of capital growth, and desire less risk. An example is utility companies. Income stocks give you the highest stable income to satisfy your present living needs.

2. *Cyclical stocks.* They are stocks whose price movements follow the business cycle. Firms' prices increase in expansion and decline in recession. These stocks are thus somewhat risky. Examples include construction and airlines.

3. *Defensive stocks.* Often called countercyclical stocks, they are stocks that remain stable during periods of contraction. They are safe and consistent but have a lower return. However, the return earned is lower. An example is consumer goods stocks.

4. *Growth stocks.* Growth stocks are companies evidencing higher rates of growth in operations and earnings than other firms. An example is high-technology firms. These stocks normally pay little or no dividends. Growth stocks usually increase in price faster than others, but they may fluctuate more. They appeal to investors seeking capital appreciation rather than dividend income.

5. *Blue chips.* Blue chips are common stocks that provide uninterrupted streams of dividends and strong long-term growth prospects, such as General Electric. These stocks have low risk but are less susceptible to cyclical market changes than other stocks.

6. *Penny stocks.* Penny stocks are stocks which usually have market prices below $1 a share. Penny stocks are issued by financially weak and risky companies.

7. *Speculative stocks.* These stocks are ones for which there is an opportunity for large profits, with uncertainty in earnings. You buy a speculative stock if you are willing to take a high risk for a very high return. Speculative stocks have high price fluctuations and price-earnings ratios. Examples of speculative stocks include mining and biotechnology company stocks.

.03 The Difference Between Common Stocks and Mutual Funds

A mutual fund is a diversified group of stocks, bonds, or other assets contributed by investors and managed by professional money managers. The primary appeal of mutual funds is that they are professionally managed and provide diversification.

Exhibit 4

Difference Between Stocks and Mutual Funds

	Stocks	*Mutual Funds*
Ownership	Shares of a single company	Shares in the fund; fractional ownership of a group of assets
Voting rights	Yes	No
Value	Per share price	Net asset value (NAV)
Professional management	No	Yes
Diversification	No	Yes
Liquidity	3 business days	Almost immediate
Dividends and capital gains	Direct	Can be reinvested
Investment decision by	Yourself	Fund manager
Choice of investment goals	No	Yes
Accessibility	Via broker	Yes, via a toll-free phone
Flexibility	No	Yes, exchange privileges and check-writing services
Commission	Full or discount	Load or no-load

¶ 2135 Preferred Stock

Preferred stock is paid quarterly and carries a fixed dividend. The dividend is stated as a percentage of par value of the stock, or in dollar terms per share. Preferred stock is viewed as a hybrid security, because it possesses features of both corporate bonds and common stocks. It is similar to common stock in that:

- It pays dividends.
- It represents owners' equity.
- It is issued without stated maturity dates.

Preferred stock is also similar to a corporate bond in that:

- Its dividends are fixed for the life of the issue.
- It provides for prior claims on assets and earnings.
- It can carry convertible and call characteristics and sinking fund provisions.

Preferred stocks are traded on the basis of the yield offered to investors. They are viewed as fixed income securities and, as a result, are in direct competition with bonds in the marketplace. *Note:* Corporate bonds, however, occupy a position senior to preferred stocks.

Advantages of owning preferred stocks are:

- Relatively higher yields than comparably rated fixed-income securities.
- Quarterly dividend payments. Bonds pay interest every six months.
- Safety. Preferred stocks take precedence over common stocks. The preferred stock dividend must be paid before *any* dividends on common stock can be paid. *Note:* Most preferreds are cumulative.
- Lower per share cost, which even small investors can afford.
- Call protection for the first five to ten years of issuance.
- Active—both listed and OTC—and fairly liquid.

Disadvantages include:

- Their vulnerability to interest rates and price level changes.
- They have restricted capital gains, except for convertible preferreds.

Note: Convertible preferreds allow the holder to exchange your preferred shares for a fixed number of common shares.

Exhibit 5 presents major features of preferred stock.

Exhibit 5

Characteristics of Preferred Stock

Voting rights	No, unless dividend not paid
Income	Fixed as long as dividend paid
Capital gain/loss potential	Only if interest rates change or company's preferred stock rating changes
Inflation hedge	No, except for adjustable
Preemptive right	No
Priority of claim	Prior to common stock
Unit of purchase	Usually 100 shares

.01 Types of Preferred Stock

There are many types of preferred stock. They are:

- *Perpetual preferreds.* The most common type of preferred stock. Its dividend can be either fixed or floating and is paid quarterly. It has no maturity date. Most issues, however, are callable at the option of the issuer after a specified period of time. Perpetual preferreds typically offer the highest current yields.
- *Convertible preferreds.* Convertible into common shares and thus offering growth potential plus fixed income. It tends to behave differently in the marketplace than straight preferred. The market price of a convertible preferred should equal the common stock price times the conversion rate.
- *Cumulative preferreds.* Any dividend due that is not declared accumulates and must be paid before any common stock dividend can be declared. Most preferreds are cumulative.
- *Non-cumulative preferreds.* Left over from the heyday of the railroads and is rare today. Dividends, if unpaid, do not accumulate.
- *Participating preferreds.* Usually and typically issued by firms desperate for capital. Preferred shareholders share in profits with common holders by way of extra dividends declared after regular dividends are paid. This type may have voting rights.
- *Prior preferred stock (or preference shares).* This type has a priority claim on assets and earnings over other preferred shares.
- *Callable preferreds.* This type carries a provision that permits the company to call in the issue and pay it off at full value, plus a premium of perhaps five percent.
- *Adjustable-rate preferreds (ARPs).* Also called floating or variable-rate preferreds, these are perpetual preferreds with a floating dividend rate that resets each quarter. The rate is determined by using the highest of the three benchmark rates: the three-month T-bill, 10-year T-note, and 20- or 30-year T-bond. Thus, you are assured of a favorable dividend regardless of the shape of the yield curve.
- *Foreign bank preferreds, American depository receipt (ADR).* Shares issued by foreign banks. They are SEC-registered, U.S.-dollar-denominated perpetual preferreds. They offer the following advantages:

  a. Higher fixed dividend rates than domestic preferreds.

  b. A special tax advantage on a portion of the dividend income in the form of a tax credit for foreign taxes paid. This may mean a higher after-tax yield than many comparable tax exempt municipal bonds. *Note:* Tax-deferred retirement accounts such as IRAs do not qualify, however.

c. Opportunity to diversify globally without foreign currency exposure.

.02 Investing in Money Market Preferred Stock

Money market preferred stock (MMPS), also known as auction-rate preferred stock, is the newest and most popular member of the preferred stock group attractive to many investors since it offers the following advantages:

- Low market risk in the event of price decline.
- Competitive yield.
- Liquidity.

MMPS pays dividends and adjusts rates up or down, depending on the current market, every seven weeks. Unlike other adjustable-rate preferreds, the market, not the issuer, sets the rate at the auction. If no bids are placed for a stock, MMPS' dividend rate is automatically set at the 60-day AA commercial paper rate quoted by the Federal Reserve Bank. There is a possibility, however, of a failed auction if no buyers show up at the auction. You must take into account the credit quality of an MMPS. Money market preferreds include:

- Short-Term Auction-Rate Stock (STARS)
- Dutch-Auction-Rate Transferable Securities (DARTS)
- Market-Auction Preferred Stock (MAPS)
- Auction-Market Preferred Stock (AMPS)
- Cumulative Auction-Market Preferred Stock (CAMPS)

¶ 2140 Fixed Income Securities

Fixed income securities generally emphasize current fixed income with minimal capital appreciation potential. They are typically marketable with low risk. They do better during low inflation and economic stability. As interest rates drop, the price of fixed income investments increase. Examples of fixed income securities include: corporate bonds, convertible bonds, government bonds, tax-exempt bonds, and short-term debt securities. Bonds have interest rate and default risk.

¶ 2145 Bonds

A bond is a certificate evidencing a loan by you to a business or to the government. You will receive for your investment a principle repayment. Advantages of bonds include:

- Periodic annual interest income.

- Bonds are safer than stock because bondholders come before common stockholders in profit distribution and in bankruptcy.

Disadvantages of bonds include:

- They do not share in incremental income.
- No voting rights.

The terms and features of bonds include:

1. *Indenture.* A legal document of the issuer's duties related to the bond issue. It includes the terms of the bond issue and the *restrictive provisions* referred to as restrictive covenants. An independent trustee is assigned. A restrictive covenant includes maintenance of minimum ratio percentages and working capital amounts.

2. *Trustee.* A third party responsible for insuring the indenture provisions are satisfied.

3. *Maturity date.* The date the last principle payment is due.

4. *Par value.* The face value of a bond is typically $1,000.

5. *Coupon rate.* The periodic payment coupon rate you will receive. It is based on the interest rate multiplied by face value.

6. *Yield.* Yield differs from the coupon interest rate (see Example 1). It is the effective interest rate you earn on the bond investment. If a bond is purchased below its face value (discount), the yield is higher than the coupon rate. If a bond is bought above face value (premium), the yield is below the coupon rate. Computations of alternative yield measures on a bond are presented later in this chapter.

Example 4.

A bond with an 8% coupon rate	*Annual interest*	*Yield*
If you buy it at par—$1,000	$ 80.00	8%
If you buy it at a discount price of $800	80.00	10%
If you buy it at a premium price of $1,200	80.00	6 2/3%

7. *Call feature.* Most bonds may be redeemed early by the issuing company, at face or at a premium. An issuer may opt to call a bond early if market interest rates decline. The issuer can issue bonds to replace the old bonds at a lower interest rate. Investors are insulated from calls for a specified time, subsequent to the bonds' issuance (usually 10 years).

8. *Sinking fund provision.* The issuing company may have to put money aside periodically (e.g., annually) into a "sinking fund." The funds will be used to retire the bonds at maturity or to retire part of the issue each year after a particular date. Such a stipulation may exist to protect investors.

.01 Types of Bonds

Exhibit 6 summarizes the various features of bonds.

Exhibit 6

The World of Bonds

	Maturity	*Denomination*	*Pricing*	*Call Provision*
Corporate bonds	20-30 years	$1,000	% of par	Often callable
Municipal bonds	1 mo.–30 yrs.	$5,000–$10,000 (usually $5,000)	Quoted on yield-to-maturity basis	Often callable
Agency bonds	30 days–20 yrs.	$1,000–$25,000 and up	Quoted on yield-to-maturity basis	No
Marketable government securities				
Treasury bills	13, 26, or 52 wks.	$10,000–$1 m in increments of $5,000	Issued at discount; priced in basis points	No
Treasury notes	2–10 yrs.	$1,000–$1 m	Issued at par; priced at % of par	Usually not callable
Treasury bonds	Over 10 yrs.	$1,000–$1 m (usually $10,000)	Priced at % of par	Usually not callable
Non-marketable government securities				
Series EE	Adjustable	$50–$10,000	Issued at 50% discount	No
Series HH	10 yrs.	$500–$10,000	Issued at par	No

*Government securities are priced in 1/32 of a percentage point, corporate bonds in 1/8.

Bonds may be categorized as follows:

1. *Secured bonds.* Specific collateral is pledged to back the bond issue.

   a. *Mortgage bonds.* Mortgage bonds are backed by collateralized property which may be sold if the bonds are defaulted on. In case of default, the bondholders may foreclose on the secured property and sell it to satisfy their claims. They take various forms: first mortgage bonds (senior lien bonds) that have claim against the corporation's fixed assets and second mortgage bonds (junior liens), backed by real property, but second in priority.

b. *Collateral trust bonds,* backed by marketable securities deposited with the trustees.

c. *Equipment trust certificates,* issued generally by transportation corporations (railroads or airlines). The trustee holds title to the equipment until the certificate is paid.

2. *Unsecured bonds.*

a. *Debentures.* They are backed by the issuing corporation's good faith and credit. The issuing company must be financially sound. High credit ratings are essential. Government bonds are examples.

b. *Subordinated debentures,* honored after debentures in the case of liquidation or reorganization (though still before stocks). Junior debentures are sometimes issued by finance companies.

3. *Income bonds.* The bonds pay interest only if there is profit.

4. *Convertible bonds.* These bonds may be converted to common stock at a later date at a specified conversion price. They have features of both bonds and common stock in that they generate constant interest income and capital appreciation through related common stock. Relevant formulas are:

Conversion ratio = Par value of a bond/Conversion price

Parity = equality

Parity price = price pegged to another price

Parity price of a bond = Common stock price × conversion ratio

Parity price of a stock = Price of the bond/conversion ratio

***Example** 5.* If a $1,000 par value bond had a conversion price of $40, this would imply a conversion ratio of 25:1 ($1,000/$40 = 25 or $40 × 25 = $1,000). If the bond was selling at $1,150, then the parity price of the stock would be $1,150/25 = $46.

5. *Zero-coupon bonds.* Zeros are purchased at a discount and mature at par. Each year, the portion of the discount that is earned is taken as interest income on the tax return. Tax must be paid on the "earned" portion of the discount every year even though no payment is made by the issuer. Zero coupon bonds involve a lower initial investment. *Note:* Many corporations, municipalities, federal agencies such as Fannie Mae and Fred-

die Mac, and the U.S. Treasury issue zero coupon bonds. Zero coupon Treasury bonds are also called *Treasury STRIPs.*

6. *Tax-exempt bonds.* Municipal bonds are free of tax on interest. They have a lower interest rate than comparable corporate bonds. The after tax yield is usually higher than an equivalent taxable bond.

7. *U.S. government securities.* These include bills, notes, bonds, and mortgages (e.g., "Ginnie Maes"). Treasury bills are used for near-term government financing and have a maturity of 12 months or less. U.S. Treasury notes mature in one to 10 years. Treasury bonds mature in 10 to 25 years. They can be bought in denominations of $1,000. Interest earned on U.S. government securities is tax free for state and local returns. "Ginnie Maes" are guaranteed pools of 25- to 30-year Federal Housing Administration (FHA) or Veterans Administration (VA) mortgages.

8. *Deep discount bonds.* They are bought at a substantial discount from face value. The bonds may be risky and/or have a long maturity date.

9. *Junk bonds.* They are bonds with low credit ratings from Moody's and Standard & Poor's. They are issued by financially unsound companies. They offer high return but have high risk.

10. *Serial bonds.* They are bonds that mature in installments over time rather than at one maturity date. Some serial bonds have balloon maturity where most mature in one year.

11. *Series bonds.* They are issued over a period but with the same maturity date.

.02 Municipal Bonds

Municipal bonds (munis) are issued by state or local governments or by any political subdivision or public agency that is not federal. *Interest income from municipal bonds is exempt from federal tax.* Bonds issued by a state and purchased by residents of that state are exempt from state income taxes. For this reason, munis will pay the lowest rate of interest compared to other taxable bond issues. The minimum investment in munis is $5,000 principal. Any capital gain realized in the purchase and sale of a municipal bond is subject to capital gain tax. (When municipals are issued at a discount, however, the difference between the discount and par is considered interest income).

Munis may be categorized either as *general obligation (G.O.) bonds* or *revenue bonds.*

1. G.O. bonds are backed by the full faith and credit (and by the taxing power) of the issuer. Local governments have the ability

to collect property taxes, known as "ad valorem" taxes, while most state governments collect income and sales taxes. In the event of a default, G.O. bondholders have the right to compel a tax levy or legislative appropriation to make payment on the debt.

2. Revenue bonds are backed by revenues from the facilities built with the proceeds of the bond issue. Sewer bonds, stadium bonds, solid waste disposal, or toll bridge bonds are examples of revenue bonds. Since only the specified revenues back a revenue bond, this is a self-supporting debt. *Note:* Because revenue bonds are backed by a single source of funds, they have greater credit risk than G.O. bonds. Because of this, most revenue bonds are issued under a "Trust Indenture."

Trading in municipal bonds. Municipal bonds are *not* traded on national exchanges but in the over-the-counter market. Generally, this confines investor interest in municipal issues to residents of the state of issuance. Note: Be sure to ask your broker if he or she has access to any online services such as J.J. Kennedy Information Systems, which provides a comprehensive data basis of most munis outstanding and is necessary for accurate portfolio analysis and the prompt answering of credit questions. Another factor that limits municipal trading is that most issues are "serial" maturities. Within a bond offering are multiple maturities, each having a relatively small principal amount. The small amount of each maturity available limits trading.

.03 Government Bonds

Government bonds are the most liquid issues traded on any market, are extremely safe, have some tax advantages (returns are not usually subject to state and local taxes), and can be used as loan collateral.

Treasury bills. Treasury bills (T-bills) have a maximum maturity of one year and common maturities of three months (91 days, or 13 weeks), six months (182 days, or 26 weeks), or one year (52 weeks). They trade in minimum units of $10,000. They do not pay interest in the traditional sense; they are sold at a discount and redeemed, when the maturity date comes around, at face value. T-bills are extremely liquid in that there is an active secondary or resale market for these securities. T-bills have an extremely low risk because they are backed by the U.S. government. Another reason for the popularity of Treasuries is that the interest income that they produce is exempt from state and local income taxes.

The price is quoted in terms of the discount yield. "March 4, bid 4.30%, asked 4.20%"; offering to buy the bill at 95.70 percent of par (an offer to pay $9,570 for the bill since par value of T-bills is usually $10,000) and offering to sell at 95.80 percent of par.

The yield on discount securities such as T-bills, called the discount yield (d), is calculated using the formula:

$$d = \frac{\$10{,}000 - P}{P} \times \frac{365}{\text{days-to-maturity}}$$

Where P = purchase price. The formula simply states that the yield on the discount security is equal to the gain on the bill relative to its face of $10,000, ($10,000 – P)/$10,000, *times* a factor which annualizes this gain, 365/days-to-maturity.

Example 6. Assume that P = $9,800. The T-bill yield is:

$$\frac{\$10{,}000 - \$9{,}800}{\$9{,}800} \times \frac{365}{90} = \frac{\$200}{\$9{,}800} \times 4.06 = 0.0829 = 8.29\%$$

The so-called *equivalent bond yield* (EBY) allows you to compare the yields on discount securities with other kinds of bonds. It makes discount instruments comparable to bonds. The idea is to compute a yield that reflects the opportunity that bond market investors have to receive and reinvest semiannual coupon payments. The formula is:

$$\text{EBY} = \frac{365 \times d}{360 - (d \times \text{days-to-maturity})}$$

Example 7. For the 90-day instrument used in the previous example, the EBY would be:

$$\text{EBY} = \frac{365 \times 0.0829}{360 - (0.0829 \times 90)} = 0.0858 = 8.58\%$$

Auctions for 3- and 6-month T-bills take place weekly and 12-month bills are auctioned monthly.

Treasury notes. Treasury notes have maturities of two to 10 years, available either in registered form or without coupons. They are not callable. They are quoted in 1/32 of a percentage point; "Maturing 11/10/90—Bid: 99.16; Ask: 99.24" means bid at 99 16/32 or $995; ask at 99 24/32 or $997.50.

Treasury bonds. Treasury bonds have maturities ranging from 10 to 30 years. Some have *optional call dates,* as "Due 6/30 1992/97" where the first date shown is the call date, the second the maturity date. They are quoted like Treasury notes.

Treasury STRIPS (Separate Trading of Registered Interest and Principle of Securities). Also called zero coupon Treasuries, Treasury STRIPS are designated Treasury notes and bonds that can be stripped directly by dealers in order to create zero-coupon securities. The bonds are "stripped" of their coupons, and units are sold representing only the repayment of principal at the maturity date. Each of the interest payments on the bonds is grouped into a unit and sold as a separate "zero-coupon" issue. All new Treasury notes and bonds of 10 years or longer are eligible for the STRIP program. Investors are attracted to STRIPS because of their predictability, fixed rate of interest, and maturity at a known value. One chief drawback: Although they do not pay interest until maturity, the IRS requires you to pay taxes on each year's accrued value as though you had received a check in the mail. Note: They typically outperform straight Treasuries by 15 to 50 basis points.

How do you buy treasuries? You can buy Treasuries for as little as $1,000 to $10,000 (depending on the type of security), with no commission cost, through a program called Treasury Direct. Or, you can pay $50 or $60 per transaction and buy through a broker. Each of these purchasing methods has its pros and cons.

Treasury securities are sold in a variety of maturities at regularly scheduled auctions. The dates for non-weekly auctions are announced about a week in advance. Exhibit 7 compares Treasuries. To learn the exact dates, call the nearest Federal Reserve Bank. *Note:* Treasury securities carry the lowest markup, and you can even buy them without commission directly from Federal Reserve branches (for information, go to www.publicdebt.treas.gov). Treasury yields are published daily in the larger newspapers and are available on numerous websites.

Exhibit 7

U.S. Treasury Securities

Treasury Bills

What: 13-week and 26-week.

When: Every Monday, except holidays.

How much: $10,000 minimum, then $1,000 increments.

What: 52-week.

When: Every four weeks, generally on a Thursday.

How much: $10,000 minimum, then $1,000 increments.

Treasury Notes

What: 2-year.

When: Monthly, generally on a Tuesday late in the month.

How much: $5,000 minimum, then $1,000 increments.

What: 3-year.

When: Quarterly, in early February, May, August, and November.

How much: $5,000 minimum, then $1,000 increments.

What: 5-year.

When: Monthly, generally on a Wednesday late in the month.

How much: $1,000 minimum, then $1,000 increments.

What: 10-year.

When: Quarterly, in early February, May, August, and November.

How much: $1,000 minimum, then $1,000 increments.

Treasury Bonds

What: 30-year.

When: Twice a year, in February and in August.

How much: $1,000 minimum, then $1,000 increments.

Zero Coupon Treasuries—Treasury Strips

What: Three months to 30-year.

When: Quarterly, in early February, May, August, and November.

How much: $1,000 minimum, then $1,000 increments.

.04 Government Agency Bonds

The next area of fixed-income bonds is that of government agency bonds. The U.S. government promotes home ownership through the activities of the Federal Home Loan Banks, the Federal National Mortgage Association (FNMA or "Fannie Mae"), the Government National Mortgage Association (GNMA or "Ginnie Mae"), and the Federal Home Loan Mortgage Corporation (FHLMC or "Freddie Mac"). These agencies make a secondary market in home mortgages. Their function is to add liquidity and safety to investing in the mortgage market. They purchase the mortgages from the local banks that originated the loans. The agencies obtain the funds to buy the mortgages by selling bonds to the public. The U.S. government does not directly back these issues with the exception of the Government National Mortgage Association.

The Government National Mortgage Association (GNMA) is described as a mortgage pass-through agency. It buys pools, or groups, of a large number of home mortgages insured by the VA and FHA from conventional lenders and then reissues new certificates of these mortgage pools to GNMA investors *("pass through" certificates).* GNMA is offered with a minimum $25,000 face amount and $5,000 increments thereafter. They pay interest and part principal monthly. In this sense, you, as a GNMA investor, are in a similar position to that of a mortgage lender. *Note:* There are many mutual funds available which invest primarily, or exclusively, in GNMAs. GNMA funds enjoy the same advantages as regular mutual funds, diversification and professional management.

Fannie Mae also issues mortgage backed pass-through certificates, but they are not limited to FHA or VA approved loans. FHLMAC, or "Freddie Mac," offers collateralized mortgage obligations (CMOs). Note that Fannie Mae and Freddie Mac are not truly government agencies but "privatized" companies, whose stocks are listed on the NYSE and are legally owned by the shareholders.

Pass-through certificates have problems because mortgage pools have a long fixed life and mortgage prepayment risk is high. CMOs were developed to eliminate or minimize these risks.

On the basis of expected cash flows to be received over the life of the pool, separate classes of securities called "tranches" are created. For example, a 15-year mortgage pool may be broken up into five tranches as follows:

Tranch 1	1-3 years
Tranch 2	4-6 years
Tranch 3	7-9 years
Tranch 4	10-12 years
Tranch 5	13-15 years

As mortgages are prepaid, the payments are applied to Tranch 1 securities. After Tranch 1 is retired, prepayments then are used to retire

Tranch 2 starting in the fourth year, etc. Thus, *prepayment risk is reduced.* Investors can buy a mortgage backed security with a wide range of maturities. Even though prepayment risk is reduced, CMO pricing can be volatile. The most volatile are so-called "zero-Tranch" portions of CMOs, which receive no interest payments until the preceding tranches are retired.

.05 Investing in U.S. Savings Bonds

U.S. Savings Bonds are non-transferable instruments. They can only be redeemed by the purchaser and can neither be marketed nor used as collateral for loans. There are two types of U.S. savings bonds: Series EE and Series HH.

Series EE is a bond purchased for 50 percent of its face value. It pays no periodic interest, since the interest accumulates between the purchase price and the bond's maturity value. For example, a Series EE bond can be purchased for $100 and redeemed at maturity for $200. Series EE bonds can be purchased in denominations from $50 to $10,000, with a maximum purchase limit of $30,000 annually. EE bonds will earn interest for 30 years from issue date. There is a three-month penalty for cashing in an EE bond before it is five years old.

For Series EE bonds issued on or after May 1, 1997, the interest rate is 90 percent of the average of prevailing market yields on five-year Treasury marketable securities. A new rate is announced each May and November. *Note:* Since yields are adjusted every six months, the bonds offer unique opportunities in times of rising interest rates.

Series HH, also called a *current income bond,* is a bond issued only in exchange for Series E and EE savings bonds. It is purchased at face value and pays interest semiannually until maturity. Early redemption will lose interest as of the end of the interest period preceeding the date of redemption. It can be redeemed after six months and has a maturity period of 20 years. Maximum purchase in one year is $20,000 face value, but it can be purchased only by trading EE bonds. Interest on HH Series bonds is taxable in the year in which it is received. Interest is exempt from state and local taxes.

Example 8. George Lee decided to invest $5,000 in a Series EE savings bond for his retirement. If the interest averages eight percent after 10 years, how much will he have after 10 years? (Assume a semi-annual interest accrual.)

The future value of $1 (Table 1 in Appendix B) for 20 periods at a semi-annual rate of four percent, i.e., T1 (2%, 20 periods), is 2.191 calculated to $10,955 or ($5,000 × 2.191).

.06 Investing in Series I Savings Bonds

The Series I savings bond (I-bond) protects the purchasing power of your principal and guarantees a real fixed rate of return above *inflation* for the life of the bond (up to 30 years). The current I-bond guarantees three percent above inflation. You can purchase up to $30,000 worth of the bonds each year, you can never lose principal, earnings are free from state and local taxes, and federal taxes are deferred until you redeem the bond. Plus, there are no fees when you buy or sell these bonds. Although you can cash an I-bond six months after the issue date, there is a three-month earnings penalty if you redeem them in less than five years. I-bonds are sold in denominations of $50 to $10,000 at most banks and also online at www.savingsbonds.com.

Some advantages are:

- The interest earned on them is free from state and local taxes. Federal income taxes can be deferred on Series EE bonds until they are redeemed. It can be deferred even beyond this point by rolling over the EE bonds into Series HH bonds. Parents who sell EE bonds to pay for their children's college tuition don't have to pay federal income taxes on the interest earned if their income is under a certain amount. The full interest exclusion is only available for married couples filing joint returns with modified adjusted gross incomes of up to and including $83,650 and for single filers with modified adjusted gross incomes of up to and including $55,750 if the bonds are in the parents' names. These are the limits currently in effect in 2001. The taxpayer must be at least 24 years old before the issue date of the bond.

- There are no service charges when one purchases or redeems savings bonds, unlike many other investments.

- Safety and complete security backed by the U.S. government.

Some disadvantages are:

- Lack of liquidity. You are barred from cashing them in for at least six months.

- Relatively lower yield. *Note:* Instead of exchanging all the bonds, you might be better off selling the EE bonds paying the low rates and putting the proceeds in a high-yielding investment vehicle. Hold onto the higher-yielding EE bonds.

- Once EE Bonds are converted to higher yielding HH Bonds, the interest is no longer exempt when used for educational purposes.

U.S. savings bonds can be purchased without fees at most banks and other financial institutions or through payroll thrift plans. They can be replaced if lost, stolen, or destroyed. Both series must be held at least six months before redeeming. U.S. savings bonds may also be purchased online at www.savingsbonds.com.

Note: (1) To find out what a particular savings bond is worth, go to any bank that sells the bonds or the Treasury to obtain a redemption value table. Send request to *Savings Bond Marketing Office,* 800 K St. NW, Suite 800, Washington, D.C. 20226; and (2) for details involving mistakes and anxieties regarding U.S. Savings and Bonds, refer to a new book by Daniel Pederson, *U.S. Savings Bonds: A Comprehensive Guide for Bond Owners and Financial Professions,* TSBI, Detroit, Michigan. (800) 927-1901.

U.S. savings bond interest rates. U.S. savings bond interest rates effective November 1, 2002 are as follows.

Bond Series	*Current rate if purchased between Nov. 1, 2002 and April 30, 2003*	*Rate of prior period (From May 1, 2002 to Oct. 31, 2002)*
Series EE bonds ..	3.25%	3.96%
Series HH bonds ..	4.00%	4.00%
Series I bonds	4.08%	2.57%
Series I bond fixed rate	1.60%	2.00%

Source: Adapted from www.savingsbonds.com/rates.cfm

.07 Should You Invest in a Bond Fund?

It is possible that an investor may decide to invest in a bond fund. There are the following three key facts about the bonds in any portfolio:

1. *Quality.* Check the credit rating of the typical bond in the fund. Ratings by Standard & Poor's and Moody's show the relative danger that an issuer will default on interest or principal payments. AAA is the best grade. A rating of BB or lower signifies a junk bond.

2. *Maturity.* The average maturity of your fund's bonds indicates how much you stand to lose if interest rates rise. The longer the term of the bonds, the more volatile is the price. For example, a 20-year bond may fluctuate in price four times as much as a four-year issue.

3. *Premium or discount.* Some funds with high current yields hold bonds that trade for more than their face value, or at a premium. Such funds are less vulnerable to losses if rates go up. Funds that hold bonds trading at a discount to face value can lose the most.

You must keep in mind the following guidelines:

- Rising interest rates drive down the value of all bond funds. For this reason, rather than focusing only on current yield, you should look primarily at total return (yield plus capital gains from falling interest rates or minus capital losses if rates climb).

- All bond funds do not benefit equally from tumbling interest rates. If you think interest rates will decline and you want to increase total return, you should buy funds that invest in U.S. Treasuries or top-rated corporate bonds. You should consider high-yield corporate bonds (junk bonds) if you believe interest rates are stabilizing.

- Unlike bonds, bond funds do not allow the investor to lock in a yield. A mutual fund with a constantly changing portfolio is not like an individual bond, which can be kept to maturity. If you want steady, secure income over several years or more, you should consider, as alternatives to funds, buying individual top-quality bonds or investing in a municipal bond *unit trust,* which maintains a fixed portfolio.

.08 Investing in Municipal Bonds: Three Approaches

As discussed earlier, you may consider municipal bonds for tax or income reasons. If you do, you may face three investment choices for diversification: (1) buying them on your own, (2) muni unit investment trust (UIT), and (3) muni mutual funds. If the preservation of capital is of primary importance, the UIT may be a better investment than a mutual fund. Exhibit 8 compares aspects of the three approaches.

Exhibit 8

Investing in Municipal Bonds: Three Choices

	Direct Purchase	*UIT*	*Mutual Fund*
Portfolio policy and management	Your own selection	Passive; no management	Active management
Payments	Twice a year	Monthly	Monthly or automatic reinvestment
Commissions	Usually some percent buy-sell spread	Some percent buy-sell spread plus front-end load	Load or no-load
Investor profile	Experienced with sizable funds	Long-term (10 years)	Smaller and short-term
Interest rate risk	High	Low	Medium
Capital gain/loss potential	High	Low	Medium

.09 Investing in Mortgage-Backed Securities

A mortgage-backed security is a share in an organized pool of residential mortgages. Some are pass-through securities where the principal and interest payments on them are passed through to shareholders, usually monthly. There are several kinds of mortgage-backed securities. They include:

- *Government National Mortgage Association (GNMA—Ginnie Mae)* securities. GNMA primarily issues pass-through securities. These securities pass through all payments of interest and principal received on a pool of federally insured mortgage loans. GNMA guarantees that all payments of principal and interest will be made on the mortgages on a timely basis. Since many mortgages are repaid before maturity, investors in GNMA pools usually recover most of their principal investment well ahead of schedule. Ginnie Mae is considered an excellent investment. The higher yields, coupled with the U.S. government guarantee, provide a competitive edge over other intermediate-term to long-term securities issued by the U.S. government and other agencies.

- *Federal Home Loan Mortgage Corporation (FHLMC—Freddie Mac)* securities. Freddie Mac was established to provide a secondary market for conventional mortgages. It can purchase conventional mortgages for its own portfolio. Freddie Mac also issues pass-through securities, called participation certificates (PCs), and guaranteed mortgage certificates (GMCs) that resemble bonds. Freddie Mac securities do not carry direct government guarantees and are subject to state and federal income tax.

- *Federal National Mortgage Association (FNMA—Fannie Mae)* securities. The FNMA is a publicly held corporation whose goal is to provide a secondary market for government-guaranteed mortgages. It does so by financing its purchase by selling debentures with maturities of several years and short-term discount notes from 30 to 360 days to private investors. The FNMA securities are not government guaranteed and are an unsecured obligation of the issuer. For this reason, they often provide considerably higher yields than Treasury securities.

- *Collaterized mortgage obligations (CMOs).* CMOs are mortgage-backed securities that separate mortgage pools into short-, medium-, and long-term portions. You can choose between short-term pools (such as five-year pools) and long-term pools (such as 20-year pools). CMOs offer high current income from a mortgage security that gets around the problem of uncertainty regarding the timing of principal return. They offer, however, a slightly lower yield than other pass-through securities in exchange for easing that uncertainty. CMOs typically sell in minimum denominations ranging between $1,000 and $12,000.

Note: In general, mortgage-backed securities enjoy liquidity and a high degree of safety since they are either government-sponsored or otherwise insured.

¶ 2150 Other Fixed Income Securities

Other fixed income securities are available with very secure debt obligations whose maturities are less than one year, characterized by their short-term, high quality, and marketability. They may be held temporarily and include:

- *Certificates of deposit (CDs).* High quality instruments of banks usually from $1,000 and up. The maturity period is usually three months or more. A penalty is assessed for early redemption. However, the penalty on early withdrawal is treated for tax purposes as a deduction of gross income.

- *Banker's acceptances (BAs).* A banker's acceptance is a time draft (an order to pay a specified amount to the holder on a specified date), drawn on and "accepted" by a bank. By accepting the draft, a bank assumes the responsibility to make payment at maturity of the draft, thereby making the draft more readily marketable. It is usually used in foreign trade. BAs are bearer securities and can be held to maturity or can be traded. The maturity is nine months or less, and the security trades at a discount to face value. Only the highest quality BAs are eligible for Fed trading, known as "prime BAs."

- *Eurodollars.* These are deposit liabilities, denominated in U.S. dollars, of banks located outside the United States. Since the Eurodollar market is relatively free of regulation, banks in the Eurodollar market can operate on narrower margins or spreads between dollar borrowing and lending rates than banks in the United States.

- *Commercial paper.* A short-term financial instrument issued by high quality large companies on an unsecured discount basis. It is typically for $100,000 or more.

- *Money market fund.* A safe class of mutual fund type investing in high quality, near-term, liquid securities (e.g., Treasury Bills). It is a conservative investment usually stated on a $1 per share basis.

Exhibit 9 ranks various short-term investment vehicles in terms of their default risk.

Exhibit 9

Default Risk Among Short-Term Investment Vehicles

Degree of Risk	
Higher ↑	Eurodollar time deposits and CDs
	Commercial paper (top quality)
	Bankers' acceptance (BAs)
	U.S. Treasury repurchase agreements
↓	U.S. government agency obligations
Lower	U.S. Treasury obligations

¶ 2155 Unit Investment Trusts

Like a mutual fund, a unit investment trust offers to investors the advantages of a large, professionally selected and diversified portfolio. Unlike a mutual fund, however, its portfolio is fixed; once structured, it is not actively managed. Unit investment trusts are available with tax-exempt bonds, money market securities, corporate bonds of different grades, mortgage-backed securities, preferred stocks, utility common stocks, and other investments. Unit trusts are most suitable for investors who need a fixed income and a guaranteed return of capital. They disband and pay off investors after the majority of their investments have been redeemed.

Chapter 22

Tax-Advantaged Investments

¶ 2201 Overview

Many investments are designed specifically for tax benefits. Therefore, they can be excellent investment vehicles for retirement planning. They include limited partnerships, various retirement plans, such as Individual Retirement Accounts (IRAs), and annuities. You will learn the pros and cons of each in this chapter.

Some important tax rules are:

1. Portfolio income is divided into "investment income" (and loss) and capital gain (and loss). The expenses associated with earning investment income are generally deductible only to the extent of investment income. Capital losses are generally deductible only to the extent of capital gains.
2. Dividend income is fully taxed.
3. A long term capital gain is the excess of net proceeds on sale over the initial cost for stock owned more than one year. A capital loss is the opposite. Most long-term capital gains are taxed at 20 percent.
4. Net capital losses are tax deductible up to $3,000 ($1,500 for married individuals filing separately). The balance over $3,000 is carried forward to future years.
5. Capital losses reduce ordinary income. An ordinary gain or loss is for stock owned less than one year. The tax rate for ordinary and capital gains is the same under present law.
6. Gains and losses from the sale of securities is reported on the trade date (date you sell the stock) not the settlement date

(three business days later, when the broker pays you). The settlement date may go into the next year.

7. A way to delay the tax on the gain from the sale of stock, while assuring that gain, is to sell short. You may sell short close to year-end and then deliver the security to the brokerage firm and report the gain next year.

8. Passive income is defined as income received from real estate investments and limited partnership interests. Expenses associated with managing real estate or the limited partnership are deductible only against passive income.

9. Wash sale rule: The IRS disallows the loss if a position is sold at a loss and is repurchased within 30 days of the sale date. Furthermore, the IRS considers a transaction to be a wash sale if an equivalent security, such as a convertible, is purchased; if a call option, warrants, or rights are purchased; or if the customer sells a "deep in the money" put.

¶ 2205 Tax Advantages of Real Estate

Tax relief comes with real estate because the investor can deduct expenses, mortgage interest, and depreciation. Two major types of real estate investments are: limited partnerships and real estate investment trusts (REITs).

.01 Limited Partnerships

Limited partnerships, now usually referred to as direct investments or private investments, are an investment strategy used for tax benefits. They include real estate partnerships, oil and gas partnerships, equipment leasing partnerships, cable partnerships, etc. For example, real estate partnerships is a form of investing in real estate that enables investors to buy into real estate projects too costly for one investor. A group of investors is set up, each investing money to buy a large project like a shopping mall or an apartment house. There are both general and limited partners. The *general manager* typically originates and manages the property for compensation. The *limited partners* invest money and are liable just for that investment. Limited partnerships offer the following benefits:

- Tax deductible expenses.
- Professional management.
- Exemption from the double taxation of distributions faced by a corporate structure. A limited partnership functions as a pass-through agency, so it does not have to pay taxes on the income it receives.

The disadvantages are:

- IRS rulings disallow certain real estate losses.
- High management charges and costs (typically, 15 to 30 percent).
- High risk.
- Illiquidity from a lack of secondary market, unlike, for example, REITs. This means you would be likely to lose money if you wish to sell your interest before it liquidates its assets. *Note:* In recent years, a new securities market has emerged—the limited partnership secondary market. This new market offers a long-term benefit to limited partnership investors. Secondary market liquidity softens what has perhaps been the principal negative of limited partnership investing—the long-term illiquid nature of the security.

Information on the limited partnership secondary market includes:

1. *Partnership Profiles* (P.O. Box 7938, Dallas, TX 75209; (817) 488-6115) provides quarterly research reports on actively traded partnerships. In addition, The Perspective, a newsletter, carries news and analysis of the partnership market including secondary market trading prices.

2. *The Stanger Report: A Guide to Partnership Investing* (Robert A. Stanger & Company, 1129 Broad Street, Shrewsbury, NJ 07702-4790; (908) 389-3600) provides review articles on the partnership market, listings of partnerships traded in the secondary market, as well as listings of new issue partnerships currently being marketed.

Oil and gas programs. Limited partnerships exist for oil and gas. They include:

1. Drilling programs—exploratory (wildcatting) drilling in an unproven area and development drilling in or near proven fields.

2. Income programs—acquiring producing properties.

Oil and gas programs have the chance to deduct "intangible drilling costs" and a "depletion allowance" reflecting the using up of estimated reserves.

- *Recapture rules.* The tax breaks are "recaptured" by the IRS when the asset is sold. For example, if tangible property is sold, all depreciation is recaptured and taxed upon sale.
- *Alternative minimum tax (AMT).* If an investor relies on "tax preference" items to reduce his regular tax liability excessively,

the alternative computation adds back the preference items to the investor's taxable income, and a flat 24-percent tax rate is applied to the "alternative income."

.02 Real Estate Investment Trusts (REITs)

REITs is another form of real estate investing. REITs are companies similar to *closed-end mutual funds.* REITs invest investor's money in diversified real estate or mortgage portfolios rather than stocks or bonds. REITs are traded on the stock exchanges and over-the-counter market.

To continue their tax exempt status, REITs must distribute 95 percent of their profit to shareholders, and in turn they are exempt from corporate taxes on income or gains.

Are REIT yields attractive? Yields might be high because there is no corporate tax on earnings, so it all flows to shareholders.

Kinds of REITs. Three types of REITs exist: Equity REITs concentrate on income producing properties; mortgage REITs lend to developers and builders; hybrid REITs do both. Equity REITs are the safest; but, their total returns are the lower than the others.

Are REITs for you? You may determine the suitability of REITs for your investment objectives by considering the following factors.

- How to purchase: Contact a stockbroker.
- Advantages:
  - — Capital appreciation potential.
  - — Liquid investment relative to other real estate investments.
  - — Diversification in real estate projects with smaller cash investment.
  - — Portfolio diversification effects since REITs generally behave differently from stocks and bonds.
- Disadvantages: Risk of loss in declining real estate market.
- Liquidity: Because shares are traded on the stock exchange, it may be sold.
- Taxes: Tax on capital gains and dividends.

Note: Low correlation with the stock and bond markets make REITs a compelling opportunity for investors seeking portfolio diversification, as shown in Exhibit 1. Adding REITs to a diversified portfolio may provide better risk-adjusted returns.

Exhibit 1

REITs Correlation with Indexes for 10 Years Ended 6/30/2002

Russell 2000 Index	0.46
S&P 500 Index	0.25
Merrill Lynch Government/Corporate Bond Index	0.05

Choosing an REIT. Before investing in an REIT, review the current annual report, *SNL Real Estate Securities Weekly* (www.snl.com/real_estate) or *Realty Stock Review* (www.realtystock.com). Consider:

- Profitability, measured by net income before gains or losses on real estate.
- Dividend per share and history.
- Cash available for distribution (CAD) per share.
- Annual cash flow measured by *funds from operations (FFO) per share.*
- Condition of properties.
- Location of properties, good or bad areas.
- Nature of property (e.g., residential or commercial).
- Degree of leverage.
- Years REIT has been in existence.

Note: Earnings estimates on REITs are posted to *Thompson/First Call* based on the basis of net income before gains or losses on real estate and also in FFOs.

Sources of information for REITs. Since REITs are traded on the national exchanges, contact information and financial data can be obtained through many of the same sources you would use for listed stocks, such as *S&P's Stock Guide* and *Value Line Investment Surveys. Moody's Bank and Finance Manual,* published annually with twice weekly supplement by Moody's Investment Service and also available on CD-ROM, covers 109 REITs, giving detailed financial information. For a list of current REITs, contact *National Association of Real Estate Investment Trusts* at (202) 785-8717.

Also, visit SNL Financial's website (www.snl.com/real_estate) for detailed information on the nation's REITs and real estate operating companies (REOCs).

.03 Real Estate Operating Company (REOC)

Real estate operating companies (REOCs) are publicly traded real estate companies that have chosen not to be taxed as REITs. The three primary reasons for such a choice are (1) the availability of tax-loss carry-forwards, (2) operation in non-REIT-qualifying lines of business, and (3) the ability to retain earnings. In the first instance, an REOC may be indistinguishable from an REIT in all except tax status. In the second, an REOC may be involved, for example, in the operation of hotels, a line of business that generates taxable revenue. In the third case, a real estate company may decide that greater growth is available through reinvestment of earnings rather than by paying out dividends and hoping that its stock price remains high enough to use as acquisition currency.

¶ 2210 Tax Implications of Retirement Plans

Retirement plans are either "tax qualified" or "non-tax qualified." Tax qualified plan contributions are deductible against the contributor's taxable income. Earnings in the plan build up tax deferred. When distributions are taken from the plan, the entire distribution is taxable at that time.

Non-tax qualified plan contributions are not deductible against the contributor's taxable income. Earnings in the plan build up tax deferred. When distributions are taken from the plan, the portion of the distribution that represents that "build-up" is taxable.

Tax-deferred investments are important parts of any retirement planning effort. A key to this is that earnings, including dividends and capital gains, will compound tax deferred until they are distributed. To see how tax-deferred growth can make a significant difference over the years, consider the following example.

> ***Example 1.*** Assume that you will earn an eight-percent return on your investment annually and that your current income tax rate is 15 percent, while you will be taxed at a 31-percent rate 30 years from now when you retire. If you make annual tax-deferred contributions of $2,000 for 30 years (such as to an IRA account), you could build a nest egg of $226,566, while the same investment in a taxable account may produce $145,376.

¶ 2215 Keeping Your Eye on Retirement

When you retire, how much you will have depends on such factors as interest rates and switching funds around for the best return. The following example illustrates the power of tax-deferred compounding.

> ***Example 2.*** Assume a $2,000 annual investment at the beginning of each year, an eight-percent fixed return, and a 39.6 percent tax bracket. Then, the after-tax dollar amount of the tax-deferred investment upon withdrawal at retirement (assuming that contributions

were not deductible) would be $226,566, while taxable investment would grow only to $129,107, as shown in Exhibit 2.

Exhibit 2

The Power of Tax-Deferred Growth

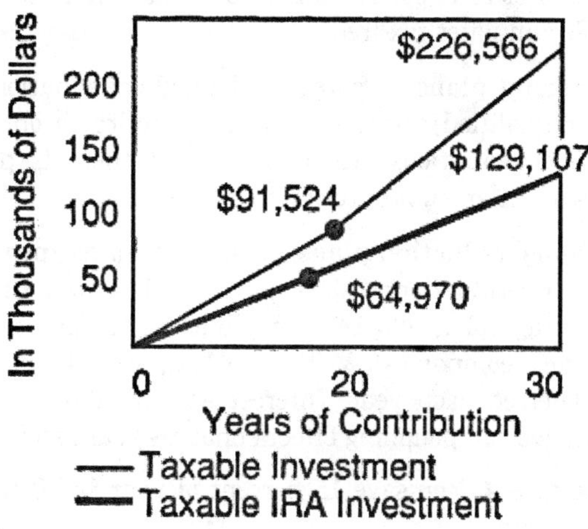

A couple of percentage points mean a lot. Assume a $50,000 tax-free pension fund earning six percent. It will be $287,150 after 30 years. The same amount invested at nine percent will give you $663,400 after 30 years.

Example 3. $10,000 invested at 10, 12, or 14 percent after 30 years:

	10%	*12%*	*14%*
Amount invested	$10,000	$10,000	$10,000
Future value of $1 (Table 1, Appendix B) = T1	17.450	29.960	50.950
Compound amount after 30 years	$174,500	$299,600	$509,500

Even if your pension is professionally managed, you may select different investments based on return rate and risk. You may apportion your savings, with the privilege of periodic switching from stocks to bonds, for example.

What interest rate are you earning? The interest rate should exceed the inflation rate. Compound tax-free interest will make your pension grow.

¶ 2220 Types of Pension Funds

.01 Company-Sponsored Pension Plans

Qualified company retirement plans. The IRS allows a company to contribute to a pension plan that is qualified. Qualified is defined as satisfying certain criteria so that contributions are tax deductible. Investment income accumulates tax-free.

Profit-sharing plans. A category defined contribution plan. Different from other qualified plans, you need not retire to obtain payments. *Note:* Because contributions are made only if there is profit, there is uncertainty as to the amount of retirement benefit.

401(k) salary reduction plans. A 401(k) plan postpones part of your salary until you retire. Each salary payment is lower. Employers often match a percentage of employee's contributions (50-percent matches are common at many companies). With a 401(k), you can put away up to $10,500 tax deferred each year. Interest accumulates tax-free until you retire. The untaxed compounding effect enhances your retirement savings.

Example 4. You save 15 percent of your $60,000 annual salary in a 401(k) plan.

	With 401(k) Plan	*Without 401(k) Plan*
Base pay	$60,000	$60,000
Salary reduction	9,000	None
Taxable income	$51,000	$60,000
Federal taxes	10,000	12,000
Savings after taxes	None	9,000
Take-home pay	$41,000	$39,000

Incremental take-home pay under plan = $2,000.

Tax-sheltered annuities (TSA). This applies if you work for a nonprofit entity. It is like a 401(k), but you may take out money at any age and not incur a tax penalty. The withdrawals are subject to ordinary tax rates.

Employee stock ownership plans (ESOP). A stock-bonus plan in which employer contributions are tax deductible.

Simplified employee pension (SEP). SEP, sometimes referred to as "super IRA," is a plan whereby an employer who could not afford nor want the administrative burden of establishing a Keogh plan makes annual payments for the employee to an IRA established by the employee.

Once a contribution is made to an SEP, it is nonforfeitable. The money contributed belongs to the employee and cannot be returned to the employer. If employment is terminated, the entire balance in the SEP account belongs to the former employee. As in the case with most qualified plans, employers receive a deduction for contributions made to an SEP plan. SEPs have higher contribution limits. The contribution limits are the lesser of 25 percent of an eligible employee's compensation or $40,000 (subject to cost-of-living adjustments after contributions in 2002).

.02 *Individual Retirement Plans*

Types of individual retirement plans are:

- Individual retirement accounts (IRAs).
- Roth IRAs.
- Keoghs.
- Annuities.

¶ 2225 Retirement Plans: The Basic Rules

An easy way to start narrowing the field when choosing between retirement plans is to consider the restrictions. IRAs, 401(k)s, and Roth IRAs, though ubiquitous, are not available to everyone. Your ability to contribute to a Roth IRA is restricted by income; your ability to deduct contributions to a traditional IRA depends on whether you're covered by another qualified retirement plan; your ability to contribute to a 401(k) plan depends on your employer.

Here's a rundown of who can and can't contribute to each type of plan.

.01 *Traditional IRA*

If you are offered a qualified plan at work—that's a "defined-benefit" pension, a 401(k), an SEP-IRA, or a public employee pension—your ability to deduct contributions to a traditional IRA depends on your income. Single filers who earn less than $34,000 and married couples with a joint income of less than $54,000 can fully deduct contributions to a traditional IRA in 2002. The income restrictions are adjusted annually. Once your annual income exceeds those thresholds, your ability to deduct contributions phases out until it disappears completely at $44,000 for singles and $64,000 for married couples in 2002. If you are not covered by a qualified pension at work, you can deduct contributions to a traditional IRA no matter how much you earn. Any wage earner can make a nondeductible contribution to a traditional IRA. However, if your contribution is not deductible, it's smarter to invest in a Roth IRA instead.

.02 *Roth IRAs*

If you earn less than $95,000 as a single person or $150,000 as a married couple, you can contribute up to $3,000 annually to a Roth IRA in 2002. Currently, the amounts allowed to be contributed to a Roth IRA are due to be increased to $4,000 in 2005 and $5,000 in 2008. Your contribution is not tax deductible, but assuming that you follow the rules, when your money comes out of the account at retirement, the distributions are tax-free. For someone who is young and has lots of time to let compound interest work, that can be exceptionally valuable.

However, if *you* earn more than those income thresholds, your ability to contribute to a Roth begins to phase out and is eliminated once you earn more than $110,000 for single filers or $160,000 for married couples filing a joint tax return.

.03 401(k) Plans

Your ability to contribute to a 401(k) is up to your employer. If your employer offers a plan for which you qualify, you can contribute up to $11,000 annually, or about 15 percent of your income, whichever is less.

.04 Keogh Plan

A Keogh pension plan, also called HR 10 plan, is tax deferred for self-employed people satisfying specified criteria. It can take three forms: a profit sharing plan, a money purchase pension plan, or a combination of both. The maximum contribution rate is 25 percent of "after Keogh deduction" earnings or $40,000, whichever is less. Thus, the effective contribution rate is 20 percent.

Example 5.

Net earnings	$100,000
Keogh contribution	20,000 (effective 20%)
After Keogh earnings	80,000

The Keogh contribution of $20,000 is 25 percent of the "after Keogh deduction" earnings of $80,000.

.05 Higher Limits of Contribution to Various Retirement Accounts

The Economic Growth and Tax Relief Reconciliation Act of 2001 gradually raises the amount employees can contribute via salary reduction to employer-sponsored retirement plans. The current annual limit for contributions to employer-sponsored retirement plans is $11,000 for 403(b) and 401(k) plans, and $11,000 for government 457 plans (see Exhibit 3). Contributions to these plans will increase each year until they reach $15,000 for the 2006 tax year. The law includes "catch-up" provisions that enable people age 50 and over to make additional contributions.

IRA contribution limits will also increase and, as with employer-sponsored plans, will include catch-up provisions. The law also increases contribution limits for Keogh plans, which are tax-deferred retirement plans for self-employed individuals and their employees. Starting in 2002, people with self-employment income can contribute up to $40,000 per year, or 100 percent of eligible compensation, to a Keogh account. Previously, the limits were $35,000 per year, or 25 percent of eligible compensation.

Exhibit 3

Higher Limits of Contribution

Year	*IRA limits*[*]	*IRA catch-up provisions*	*401(k), 403(b), & 457 plan limits*[***]	*401(k), 403(b) & 457 plan limits catch-up provisions*
2002	*$ 3,000*	*$ 3,500*	*$ 11,000*	*$ 12,000*
2003	*3,000*	*3,500*	*12,000*	*14,000*
2004	*3,000*	*3,500*	*13,000*	*16,000*
2005	*4,000*	*4,500*	*14,000*	*18,000*
2006	*4,000*	*5,000*	*15,000*	*20,000*
2007	*4,000*	*5,000*	*15,000*[**]	*20,000*
2008	*5,000*	*6,000*	*15,000*[**]	*20,000*

[*]Includes Roth and regular IRAs.
[**]Contribution limits are adjusted annually for inflation, rising in increments of $500.
[***]In the last three years before retirement, workers age 50 and over in 457 plans can save double the limit for those who are under age 50.

¶ 2230 Annuities

Annuities are insurance contracts. You can pay a single large premium, annual premiums, or flexible premiums to the company, and at retirement, you can obtain periodic payments for a stated time period (the maximum being lifetime) or take periodic withdrawals. The periodic withdrawals have limits set by the insurance company. The payments accumulate tax-free and are subject to tax only when withdrawn when you retire. Hopefully, your tax rate will be lower at that time. Annuity payments begin at retirement. The two types are fixed and variable.

.01 Fixed (Guaranteed) Annuities

Your principal plus a minimum interest is guaranteed for a year or more. There is *no* capital gains (or appreciation) potential with fixed annuities. There is low risk with this policy. You get both a "minimum" interest rate plus an "extra" interest rate based on prevailing rates in the market. The following is a summary of information on fixed annuities.

Tax-deferred income	Yes
Price stability	Yes
Capital gain (or loss) potential	No
Different payout options	Yes
Different payment options	No (except due to age)
Contribution limits	Not restricted to earned income
Source of funds	No
Choice of underlying investments	No
Federal deposit insurance	No
Surrender change	Yes
IRS early withdrawal penalty	Yes
Mandatory withdrawals	Typically by age 85
Rate-guaranteed periods	For 1, 3, 5, 7, or 10 years

Like a bond or a bond fund, a fixed annuity may fail to provide a satisfactory inflation hedge, thereby subjecting the investor to purchasing-power risk.

.02 Variable Annuities

In a variable annuity, there are no guarantees like fixed annuities. The policy value, variable rates, changes with the performance of an underlying investment fund, much like a mutual fund within a family of funds. Investment risk lies with the investor. Many insurance companies permit you to change to a different fund of a variable type and to change the percentage mix of the funds as frequently as the annuity contract allows. You pay taxes on the amount distributed from the capital appreciation of the annuity value.

Tax-deferred income	Yes
Price stability	No
Capital gain (or loss) potential	Yes
Different payout options	Yes
Different payment options	Yes
Contribution limits	No (except due to age)
Source of funds	Not restricted to earned income
Choice of underlying investments	Yes
Federal deposit insurance	No
Grace period	Yes
Surrender charge	Yes
IRS early withdrawal penalty	Yes
Mandatory withdrawals	Typically by age 85
Rate-guaranteed periods	No

.03 Advantages of Annuities

Annuities offer three main advantages:

- Tax-deferred compounding of interest.
- Unlike retirement plans, annual contributions are not restricted.
- Another form of savings plan.

.04 Disadvantages of Annuities

The disadvantages of annuities are:

- Commission (usually 7 or 8 percent) is often high.
- You cannot withdraw funds before age 59 1/2. Otherwise, a tax penalty will be assessed (10-percent charge). Also, there are penalties called *surrender charges* imposed by the insurance carrier if you cash in the policy early. However, no penalty would apply if you become disabled or die. (One way to avoid

the early withdrawal penalty is to annuitize, taking regular payments for the remainder of your life). Such charges may start around seven percent for withdrawals in the first year and phase down by one percentage point each year after that.

- The interest earned may not keep up with and/or be less than the return on alternative investment opportunities.
- Annuity income is taxed as income, not as capital gains, which can be stiff if you are in a high tax bracket.
- They are *non-qualified* annuities, meaning annuities having a tax-deferral benefit but paid in after-tax dollars.

.05 Qualified Annuities

Qualified annuities, on the other hand, fund pension plans. The contributions accumulate tax-free and are either tax deductible or exempt from your income. If you qualify, always take advantage of IRAs and Keoghs, because contributions are in before-tax dollars.

.06 Some Types of Annuities

Annuities may include:

- *Life annuity.* The annuity continues for the life of the annuitant. This usually results in the highest periodic payment.
- *Life annuity with period certain.* The annuity covers the life of the annuitant, but if that person dies early, the annuity continues for a specified minimum period.
- *Joint and last survivor annuity.* If the annuitant dies, the annuity continues for the life of another person (usually the spouse).

.07 What Sales Charges Apply?

You can invest in variable annuity contracts by making lump-sum investments or by signing a long-term investment contract (contractual plans). The plan custodian is required to send investors a statement of total charges within 60 days after the plan certificate is issued and inform you of the right to withdraw within 45 days from the date the notice is mailed. Sales charges vary.

Front-end load. Up to 50 percent of the sales charges may be deducted from the first 12 monthly payments (in equal amounts). If the plan is liquidated within 18 months, you receive a refund of sales charges paid in excess of 15 percent of the total invested.

Spread-load plan. Up to 64 percent of all sales charges over the first four years can be deducted, but no more than 20 percent in any one year.

.08 *How Do You Purchase Annuities?*

Advice in purchasing annuities follows:

- Be wary of unusually high "teaser" rates offered, which are a sign of a financially weak company. Deal with a firm that is financially sound and strong. There was an instance where Baldwin-United, a leading annuity seller, filed for bankruptcy.
- Just purchase annuities from highly rated insurance companies by referring to A.M. Best's publication, *Best's Insurance Reports.* Also refer to *Standard & Poor's, Moody's,* and *Duff & Phelps* rating publications.
- Diversify among insurance companies to get a blending of rates and maturities. In fact, dozens of mutual fund families manage variable annuity portfolios.
- Evaluate the insurance companies investment performance.
- Diversify the variable annuities.
- Consider all service charges as well as contract features and terms.
- Closely review the prospectus.
- Compare insurance companies.

Note: For comparison shopping, refer to the monthly *Morningstar Variable Annuity/Life Performance Report* ((800) 876-5005) and *Lipper Mutual Fund Quarterly on Variable Annuities and Life Accounts* that appear in *Barron's.*

.09 *Is an Annuity Right for You?*

Consider an annuity if you:

- Do not have other tax-free pension plan Keoghs.
- Want to save for retirement or otherwise at a good price.
- Want the assurance of a guaranteed check when you retire.
- You are uncomfortable with selecting your own investments, such as stocks.

You may not consider annuities if you:

- Can use alternative tax-deferred savings plans.
- Anticipate adequate income and savings from other sources.

Chapter 23

Hybrids and Derivatives

¶ 2301 Overview

Warrants, stock rights, options, and futures are called leveraged investments since you will be able to participate in these investment vehicles with a small sum of money. The value of these instruments are derived from the value of their underlying securities. In this chapter, we discuss the following:

- The different types of options.
- The advantages of receiving stock rights from a company already owned.
- The use of stock warrants in connection with debt issuances.
- How to determine the value of an option and the rate of return on investment.
- How to use stock options by hedgers and speculators.
- The investment approaches of straddles and spreads.
- The functions of an option writer.

¶ 2305 Options

Options give you the right to purchase a security at a specified price for a stated period of time. Options possess their own inherent value and are traded in secondary markets. You may want to acquire an option so that you can take advantage of an expected rise in the price of the underlying stock. Option prices are directly related to the prices of the common stock to which they apply. The types of options include stock rights, warrants, and calls and puts. Investing in options is very risky and requires specialized knowledge.

.01 Stock Rights

In a stock rights offering, current stockholders have the first right to buy new shares and thus to maintain their present ownership interest. This is known as a preemptive right.

> ***Example 1.*** Assume that you own three percent of XYZ Company. If the company issues 5,000 additional shares, you may receive a stock rights offering—a chance to buy three percent or 150 shares of the new issue.

This right enables you to purchase new common stock at a subscription price (sometimes called an exercise price) for a short time, usually no more than several weeks. This subscription price, or exercise price, is lower than the current market price of the stock.

> ***Example 2.*** If a company has two million shares outstanding and wants to issue another 100,000 shares, each existing stockholder will receive one right per share owned. Thus, a stockholder needs 20 rights in order to buy one new share. One advantage of the stock rights option is of course the lower exercise price. Another is that stockholders do not have to pay a brokerage fee when they buy the additional stock. *Note:* Stockholders who do not want to buy additional stock can sell their rights in the secondary market. (Of course, if a right is not used before the expiration date, it no longer has value.)

The value of a right. The value of a right depends on whether the stock is traded "rights-on" or "rights-off." In a rights-on trade, the stock is traded with rights attached, so the investor who purchases a share receives the attached stock right. In a rights-off or ex-rights trade, the stock and its rights are separate from each other and are traded in different markets. Regardless of the form of the rights, the value of the right equals:

$$\frac{\text{Market price of current stock} - \text{subscription price of new stock}}{\text{Number of rights to purchase one share}}$$

> ***Example 3.*** Assume the current market price of stock is \$30 a share. The new share has an exercise price of \$26. An investor needs two rights to obtain one new share. The right equals:

$$\frac{\$30 - \$26}{2} = \frac{\$4}{2} = \$2$$

Provided the stock price holds at around \$30 a share, the right has a value of \$2.

.02 Stock Warrants

A warrant is an option to purchase a certain number of shares at a stated price for a specified time period at a subscription price that is higher than the current market price. A warrant may or may not come in a one-to-one ratio with stock already owned. Unlike an option, a warrant is usually good for several years; some, in fact, have no maturity date.

Warrants are often given as sweeteners for a bond issue. This allows the firm to float the debt or issue the bond at a lower interest rate. Warrants included with a bond may also occur in a merger when the acquiring company offers cash plus warrants in exchange for the voting common stock of the acquired business.

Generally, warrants are detachable from the bond, once it has been issued. Detachable warrants have their own market price. So even though warrants are exercised, the debt with which they were first issued still exists. Also stock warrants may be issued with preferred stock. Most warrants are traded on the AMEX, and some are traded on the NYSE.

Warrants are not frequently issued and are not available for all securities. They pay no dividends and carry no voting privileges. The warrant enables the holder to take part indirectly in price appreciation of common stock and to obtain a capital gain. One warrant usually equals one share, but in some cases, more than one warrant is needed to get one share.

Warrants can be bought from a broker. The price of a warrant is listed along with that of the common stock of the company. Brokerage fees for warrants are the same as those for stocks and depend on the market price of the security.

When the price per common share goes up, the holder of the warrant may either sell it (since the warrant also increases in value) or exercise the warrant and get the stock. Trading in warrants is speculative; there is potential for high return, but high risk exists because of the possibility of variability in return.

> ***Example 4.*** Assume a warrant of XYZ Company stock enables you to purchase one share at $25. If the stock increases past $25 before the expiration date, the warrant increases in value. If the stock goes below $25, the warrant loses its value.

The exercise price for a warrant is usually constant over the warrant's life. However, the price of some warrants may rise as the expiration date approaches. Exercise price is adjusted for stock splits and large stock dividends.

Return on a warrant. The return on a warrant for a holding period of no more than one year equals:

$$\frac{\text{Selling price} - \text{acquisition price}}{\text{Acquisition price}}$$

Example 5. Assume that you sell a warrant at $21. That same warrant costs you only $12. The return is:

$$\frac{\$21 - \$12}{\$12} = \frac{\$9}{\$12} = 75\%$$

The return on a warrant for a holding period in excess on one year equals:

$$\frac{\frac{\text{Selling price} - \text{acquisition price}}{\text{Years}}}{\text{Average investment}}$$

Note: Warrants are speculative, because their value depends on the price of the common stock for which they can be exchanged. If stock prices fluctuate widely, the value of warrants will sharply vacillate.

Value of a warrant. The value of a warrant is greatest when the market price of the related stock is equal to or greater than the exercise price of the warrant. The value of a warrant thus equals:

(Market price of common stock − exercise price of warrant) × number of common stock shares bought for one warrant

Example 6. Suppose that a warrant has an exercise price of $25. Two warrants equal one share. The market price of the stock is $30. The warrant has a value of:

($30 − $25) × .5 = $2.50

Usually the market value of a warrant is greater than its intrinsic value because of the speculative nature of warrants. Typically, as the value of a warrant goes up, the premium goes down. Premium equals the market price of the warrant minus its intrinsic value.

Example 7. If the warrant in Example 6 has a market price of $4.00, the premium is $1.50. Assume that $100,000 in bonds are issued. There are, therefore, 100 bonds. Each bond has eight warrants attached. Each warrant permits the investor to purchase one share of stock at $12 until one year from the date of the bond. The warrant will have no value at the issue date if the stock is selling below $12. If the stock increases in value to $25 a share, the warrant will be worth about $13. The eight warrants will thus be worth approximately $104.

Example 8. Assume XYZ common stock is $40 per share. One warrant can be used to buy one share at $34 in the next three years. The intrinsic (minimum) value per warrant is $6 = ($40 − $34) × 1. Because the warrant has three years left and can be used for speculation, it may be traded at an amount higher than $6. Assuming the warrant was selling at $8, it has a premium of $2. The premium is the $2 difference between the warrant price and intrinsic value.

Even when the stock is selling for less than $34 a share, there might be a market value for the warrant because speculators may wish to buy it on the expectation of an attractive increase in common stock price in the future.

Example 9. If the common stock was at $30, the warrant has a negative intrinsic (minimum) value of $4, but the warrant might have a dollar value of $1 because of an expected rise in common stock value.

Leverage effect of a warrant. You may use the leveraging effect to boost your dollar returns.

Example 10. Let's say that you have $7,000 to invest. If you purchase common stock when the market price is $35 a share, you can buy 200 shares. If the price increases to $41 a share, you will have a capital gain of $1,200. But if you invest the $7000 in warrants priced at only $7 a share, you can acquire 1,000 of them. (One warrant equals one share.)

If the price of the warrants increases by $6, your profit will be $6,000. In this instance you earn a return of only 17.1 percent on the common stock investment whereas on the warrants, you get a return of 85.7 percent.

On the other hand, assume the price of the stock drops by $6. If you invest in the common stock you will lose $1,200 for a remaining equity of $5,800. However, if you invest in the warrant you will lose everything (assuming no warrant premium exists).

Note: If an investor is to get maximum price potential from a warrant, the market price of the common stock must equal or exceed the warrant's exercise price. Also, lower-priced issues offer greater leverage opportunity. Furthermore, a warrant with a low unit price generates higher price volatility and less downside risk and, thus, is preferable to a warrant with a high unit price.

Warrants can be used to protect a speculative transaction. For example, assume an investor sells a stock short and the price rises. The speculator cannot keep the short position continually open, and it may be too costly to wait till the stock goes down. To protect the short sale the investor may purchase a warrant, fixing the purchase price and limiting the potential loss on the trade.

Example 11. Assume that you sell short 100 shares at $15 each. Then you buy warrants for 100 shares at $13 a share. The cost of the option is $3, or 3 points a share, a total of $300. In effect, you are buying the stock at $16 a share. Thus, if the stock rises above $15, your loss is limited to $1 a share.

Here are some of the advantages of warrants:

- The price change in a warrant follows that of the related common stock, making a capital gain possible.
- The low unit cost allows the investor to obtain a leverage opportunity in the form of lowering the capital investment without damaging the investment's capital appreciation. This increases the potential return.
- Lower downside risk potential exists because of the lower unit price.

These are the disadvantages of warrants:

- If no price appreciation occurs before the expiration date, the warrant loses its value.
- The warrant holder receives no dividends.
- Investment in warrants requires extensive study and experience.

.03 Calls and Puts

Calls and puts are another type of stock option. You can buy or sell them in round lots, usually 100 shares. When you purchase a call, you are buying the right to purchase stock at a fixed price. You do this when you expect the price of that stock to rise. In buying a call, you stand a chance of making a significant gain from a small investment, but you also risk losing your full investment if the stock does not rise in price. Calls come in bearer negotiable form and have a life of one month to nine months.

Purchasing a put gives you the right to sell stock at a fixed price. You might buy a put when you expect a stock price to fall. By purchasing a put you get an opportunity to make a considerable gain from a small investment, but you will lose the entire investment if the stock price does not fall. Like calls, puts come in bearer negotiable form and have a life of one month to nine months. With calls there are no voting privileges, ownership interest, or dividend income. However, option contracts are adjusted for stock splits and stock dividends.

Note: The life of calls and puts is shorter than that of warrants but longer than that of rights. They are similar to warrants in that they are an alternative investment to common stock, leverage opportunity, and speculative investment.

Calls and puts are not issued by the company with the common stock but rather by option makers or option writers. The maker of the option receives the price paid for the call or put minus commission costs. The option trades on the open market. Calls and puts are written and can be acquired through brokers and dealers. The writer is required to purchase or deliver the stock when requested.

Holders of calls and puts do not necessarily have to exercise them to earn a return. They can trade them in the secondary market for whatever their value is. The value of a call increases as the underlying common stock goes up in price. The call can be sold on the market before its expiration date. Calls and puts are traded on listed option exchanges, which are secondary markets like the Chicago Board Options Exchange, American Stock Exchange, Philadelphia Stock Exchange, and Pacific Stock Exchange. They are also traded in the OTC markets. Option exchanges deal only in the purchase and sale of call and put options. Listed options are options traded on organized exchanges. Conventional options are those options traded in the OTC market.

The Options Clearing Corporation issues calls listed on the options exchanges. Orders are placed with this corporation, which then issues the calls or closes the position. No certificates are issued for options, so the investor must have a brokerage account. When a holder exercises a call, he goes through the Clearing Corporation, which picks at random a writer from member accounts. A call writer would be required to sell 100 shares of the common stock at the exercise price.

Exchanges permit general order (i.e., limit) and orders applicable only to option (i.e., spread order).

The price per share for 100 shares, which the purchaser may buy at (call), is referred to as the striking price (exercise price). For a put, it is the price at which the stock may be sold. The purchase or sale of the stock is to the writer of the option. The striking price is set for the life of the option on the options exchange. When stock price changes, new exercise prices are introduced for trading purposes reflecting the new value.

In case of conventional calls, restrictions do not exist on what the striking price should be. However, it is usually close to the market price of the stock to which it relates. But in the case of listed calls, stocks having a price lower than $50 a share must have striking prices in $5 increments. Stocks between $50 and $100 have striking prices in $20 increments. Striking prices are adjusted for material stock splits and stock dividends.

The expiration date of an option is the last day it can be exercised. For conventional options, the expiration date can be any business day; for a listed option, there is a standardized expiration date.

The cost of an option is referred to as a premium. It is the price the purchaser of the call or put has to pay the writer. (With other securities, the premium is the excess of the purchase price over a determined theoretical value.)

The premium for a call depends on:

- The dividend trend of the related security.
- The volume of trading in the option.

- The exchange on which the option is listed.
- The variability in price of the related security. (A higher variability means a higher premium because of the greater speculative appeal of the option.)
- Prevailing interest rates.
- The market price of the stock to which it relates.
- The width of the spread in price of the stock relative to the option's exercise price. (A wider spread means a higher price.)
- The amount of time remaining before the option's expiration date. (The longer the period, the greater the premium's value.)

In-the-money and out-of-the-money call options. When the market price exceeds the strike price, the call is said to be "in-the-money." But when the market price is less than the strike price, the call is "out-of-the-money."

Call options in-the-money have an intrinsic value equal to the difference between the market price and the strike price.

Value of call = (market price of stock − exercise price of call) × 100

Example 12. Assume that the market price of a stock is $45 with a strike price of $40. The call has a value of $500.

Note: Out-of-the-money call options have no intrinsic value.

If the total premium (option price) of an option is $7 and the intrinsic value is $3, there is an additional premium of $4 arising from other considerations. In effect, the total premium consists of the intrinsic value plus speculative premium (time value) based on factors such as risk, variability, forecasted future prices, expiration date, leverage, and dividend.

Total premium = intrinsic value + speculative premium

In-the-money and out-of-the-money put options. The definition of in-the-money and out-of-the-money are different for puts, because puts permit the owner to sell stock at the strike price. When the strike price exceeds the market price of stock, we have an in-the-money put option. Its value is determined as follows:

Value of put = (exercise price of put − market price of stock) × 100

Example 13. Assume the market price of a stock is $53, and the strike price of the put is $60. The value of the put is $700.

When the market price of a stock exceeds the strike price, there is an out-of-the-money put. Because a stock owner can sell it for a greater amount in the market than he could get by exercising the put, there is no intrinsic value of the out-of-the-money put.

Exhibit 1

Call and Put Premium Chart

	XYZ Calls at 50 Strike Price & Stock Price	*XYZ Puts at 50 Strike Price & Stock Price*
In-the-money:	Over 50	Under 50
At-the-money:	50	50
Out-of-the-money:	Under 50	Over 50

The theoretical value for calls and puts indicate the price at which the options should be traded. But typically they are traded at prices higher than true value when options have a long period to go.

This difference is referred to as investment premium.

$$\text{Investment premium} = \frac{\text{option premium} - \text{option value}}{\text{option value}}$$

Example 14. Assume that a put has a theoretical value of $1,500 and a price of $1,750. It is, therefore, traded at an investment premium of 16.67 percent [($1,750 – $1,500)/$1,500 = $250/$1,500].

Calls. The call purchaser takes the risk of losing the entire price he or she paid for the option if a price increase does not incur. For example, assume a two-month call option allows you to acquire 500 shares of XYZ Company at $20 per share. Within that time period, you exercise the option when the market price is $38. You make a gain of $9,000 before paying the brokerage commission. If the market price had declined from $20 you would not have exercised the call option, and you would have lost the cost of the option.

By buying a call, you can own common stock for a fraction of the cost of purchasing regular shares. Calls cost significantly less than common stock. Leverage is obtained because a little change in common stock price can result in a major change in the call option's price. An element of the percentage gain in the price of the call is the speculative premium attributable to the remaining time left on the call. Calls can also be viewed as a means of controlling 100 shares of stock without a large dollar investment.

Significant percentage gains on call options are possible from the low investment compared to the price of the related common stock.

Example 15. Assume that a stock has a present market price of $35. A call can be purchased for $300 allowing an acquisition of 100 shares at $35 each. If the price of the stock increases, the call will also be worth more. Assume that the stock is at $55 at the call's expiration date. The profit is $20 on each of the 100 shares of stock in the call, or a total of $2,000 on an investment of $300. A return of 667 percent is thus earned. In effect, when the holder exercises the call for 100 shares at $35 each, he or she can immediately sell them at $55 per share.

Note: The investor could have earned the same amount by investing directly in the common stock, but the investment would have been $3,500, so the rate of return would have been significantly lower.

You can buy ABC Company stock at $30 a share, or $3,000 for 100 shares. You can acquire a $33 three-month call for $400. Thus, you could invest $2,600 cash and have the opportunity to buy 100 shares at $33. Assume, however, that you decide to invest your $2,600 in a three-month CD earning 14-percent interest. The CD will return $91 (14% × $2,600 × 3/12). If the ABC Company stock goes to $16, the option will be worthless but the significant loss on the stock of $14 a share did not occur. Rather, the loss is limited to $309 ($400 − $91). However, note that by not buying a stock you may have foregone a dividend.

If the stock went up to $43, the call would be exercised at $33 resulting in a sizable gain with little investment.

Here is another example of call trading. Assume that a call gives you the right to acquire 100 shares of $30 stock at $27. The call will trade at a price of about $3 a share. Call options may also be used when you believe the stock price will increase in the future but you have a cash flow problem and are unable to buy the stock. However, you will have sufficient cash to do so later. In this situation, you can buy a call so as not to lose a good investment opportunity.

Example 16. On February 6, you purchase a $32 June call option for $3 a share. If the stock has a market price of $34 1/2, the speculative premium is $0.50. In June, you exercise the call option when the stock price is $37. The cost of the 100 shares of stock for tax reporting is the strike price ($32) plus the option premium ($3), or $35.

Puts. The put holder may sell 100 shares at the strike price for a given period to a put writer. A put is purchased when there is an anticipation of a price decline. The maximum loss is the premium cost (investment), which will be lost if the price of the stock does not drop.

Let's suppose that a stock has a market price of $35. You acquire a put to sell 100 shares of stock at $35 per share. The cost of the put is $300. At the exercise date of the put, the price of the stock goes to $15 a share. You, therefore, realize a profit of $20 per share, or $2,000. As the holder of the put, you simply buy on the market 100 shares at $15 each and then sell them to the writer of the put for $35 each. The net gain is $1,700.

Example 17. Assume that the stock's price was $55 on March 2. You buy a $56 June put for $4. The speculative premium is therefore $3. On June 7, the stock price falls to $47 and the price of the June $56 put to $10. The intrinsic value is $9, and the speculative premium is $1. As the put holder, you now have a gain of $6.

Call and put investment strategies. The investment approaches one can take with calls and puts include (1) hedging speculation, (2) straddles, and (3) spreads.

Owners of call and put options can hedge by holding on to two or more securities to lower risk and at the same time make some profit. It may involve buying a stock and later purchasing an option on it.

For example, a stock may be bought along with writing a call on it. Also, a holder of stock that has risen in price may buy a put to furnish downside risk protection.

Example 18. As an example of hedging, let's say that you buy 100 shares of XYZ at $26 each and a put for $200 on the 100 shares at an exercise price of $26. If the stock remains static, you will lose $200 on the put. If the price decreases, your loss on the stock will be offset by your gain on the put. If stock price rises, you'll earn a capital gain on the stock and lose your investment in the put. In other words, to get the benefit of a hedge, you have to incur a loss on the put. (Also, note that at expiration of the put, you incur a loss with no further hedge.)

You can also buy a put to hedge your position after making a profit on the stock. For example, let's say you hold 100 shares of XYZ stock purchased at $60 a share. That stock increased to $80, earning a profit of $20 a share. To guarantee your profit you buy a put with an $80 exercise price at a cost of $300. No matter what happens later, you will have a minimum gain of $1,700. If the stock falls, your minimum profit will be $1,700, but if the stock price rises, you'll realize an additional profit. Some other time you might buy a call to protect a short sale from the risk of increasing stock price.

Calls and puts may also be used for speculation as an alternative to investment in the related stocks. The idea is buy low and sell high. You would acquire options when you think you will earn a higher return than you would by investing in the underlying stock. In general, you can obtain a higher return rate at lower risk with out-of-the-money options. The problem with out-of-the-money options is that price consists only of the investment premium, which you can lose if the stock does not rise.

Here is an example of this kind of speculation.

Example 19. A speculator purchases an option contract to buy 100 shares at $25 a share. The option costs $150. Assume a rise in stock price to $33 a share. The speculator exercises the option and sells the shares in the market, realizing a gain of $650 ($33 − $25 − $1.50 = $6.50 × 100 shares). Or the speculator can sell the option in the market and make a profit because of its increased value. However, if there is a decline in stock price, the loss to the holder is limited to $150 (the option's cost). Of course, brokerage fees are also involved. In effect, this call option permitted the speculator to purchase 100 shares worth $2,500 for $150 for a short period.

"Straddling" integrates a put and call on the same stock with the identical strike price and exercise date. It is used by a speculator trading on both sides of the market. This speculator hopes for significant movement in stock price in one direction so as to make a gain that exceeds the cost of both options. If the price movement does not go as expected, however, the loss will equal the cost of the options. The straddle holder may widen risk and profit potential by closing one option before closing the other.

Example 20. You buy a call and put for $4 each on September 30 when the stock price is $42. The expiration period is four months. The investment is $8, or $800 in total. Assume the stock increases to $60 at expiration of the options. The call earns a profit of $14 ($18 − $4), and the loss on the put is $4. Your net gain is $10, or $1,000 all together.

A "spread" is the purchase of an option (long position) and the writing of an option (short position) in the same security, using call options. Sophisticated investors may write many spreads to gain from the differences in option premiums. Return potential is significant, but the risk is very high. There are different types of spreads:

- A vertical spread is the purchase and writing of two contracts at different striking prices with the same expiration date.
- A horizontal spread is the purchase and writing of two options with the same strike price but for different periods.
- A diagonal spread combines the horizontal and vertical.

Spreads require the investor to buy one call and sell another call. The gain or loss from a spread position depends on the change between two option prices as the price of the stock increases or decreases. The difference between two option prices is the price spread.

The speculator who uses a vertical bull spread anticipates an increase in price of stock, but this strategy reduces the risk. Here there is a ceiling on the gain or loss.

A speculator using a vertical bear spread expects the stock price to decline. This investor sells short the call with the lower strike price and places a cap on upside risk by buying a call with a higher strike price.

Puts, straddles, and spreads may be bought either to maximize return or to minimize risk. They are not traded on listed exchanges but rather must be acquired through brokerage houses and members of the Put and Call Brokers and Dealers Association.

Those who employ straddles, spreads, and other similar strategies often use extensive computer analysis. These investment approaches should be left to very sophisticated investors.

Option writing. The writer of a call agrees to sell shares at the strike price for the price paid for the call option. Call option writers do the opposite of what buyers do. Investors write options because they believe that a price increase in the stock will be less than what the call purchaser expects. They may even expect the price of the stock to remain static or to decrease. Option writers receive the option premium minus related transaction costs. So if the option is not exercised, the writer earns the price paid for it. However, when an option is exercised, the writer suffers a loss, sometimes quite a significant one.

When the writer of an option decides to sell, he/she must come up with the stock at the agreed-upon price if the option is exercised. In either case, the option writer receives income from the premium. (Shares are sold in denominations of 100.) An investor usually sells an option when he or she expects it not to be exercised. The risk of option writing is that the writer, if uncovered, must buy stock or, if covered, loses the gain. As the writer, you can buy back an option to terminate your exposure.

> ***Example 21.*** Assume the strike price is $40, and the premium for the call option is $5. If the stock is at less than $40, the call would not be exercised, and you would earn the premium of $5. If the stock exceeds $40, the call may be exercised, and you must provide 100 shares at $40. However, the call writer would lose money only if the stock price exceeded $45.

Naked or covered options. Options may be "naked" (uncovered) or "covered." Naked options are options on stock that the writer does not own. The investor writes the call or put for the premium and will keep it if the price change is in his favor or immaterial in amount. However, the writer's loss exposure is unlimited.

Covered options are written against stocks the writer owns and are not quite as risky. For example, a call can be written for stock the writer owns, or a put can be written for stock sold short. This is a conservative mechanism to obtain positive returns. The goal is to write an out-of-the-money option, keep the premium paid, and have the market price of the stock equal but not exceed the option exercise price. The writing of a covered call option is similar to hedging a position, since if stock price falls, the writer's loss on the stock is partly netted against the option premium.

¶ 2310 Black-Scholes Option Pricing Model (OPM)

The Black-Scholes option pricing model is an option pricing equation developed in 1973 by Fischer Black and Myron Scholes. The model provides the relationship between call option value and the five factors that determine the premium of an option's market value over its expiration value:

1. *Time to maturity.* The longer the option period, the greater the value of the option.
2. *Stock price volatility.* The greater the volatility of the underlying stock's price, the greater its value.
3. *Exercise price.* The lower the exercise price, the greater the value.
4. *Stock price.* The higher the price of the underlying stock, the greater the value.
5. *Risk-free rate.* The higher the risk-free rate, the higher the value.

The formula is:

$V = P[N(d_1)] - PV(E)\,[N(d_2)]$

Where V = current value of a call option

P = current stock price

PV(E) = present value of exercise or strike price of the option, E

$= E / e^{rt}$

r = risk-free rate of return, continuously compounded for t time periods

e = 2.71828

t = number of time periods until the expiration date (For example, 3 months means t = 3/12 = 1/4 = 0.25)

N(d) = probability that the normally distributed random variable Z is less than or equal to d

σ = standard deviation per period of (continuously compounded) rate of return on the stock

$d_1 = \ln[P/PV(E)] / \sigma\sqrt{t} + \sigma\sqrt{t}/2$

ln() = natural logarithm of the argument

$d_2 = d_1 - \sigma\sqrt{t}$

The formula requires readily available input data, with the exception of σ^2, or volatility. P, X, r, and t are easily obtained. The implications of the option model are as follows:

1. The value of the option increases with the level of stock price relative to the exercise price [P/PV(E)], the time to expiration, and the time to expiration times the stock's variability ($\sigma\sqrt{t}$).

2. Other properties:

   a) The option price is always less than the stock price.

   b) The option price never falls below the payoff to immediate exercise (P − E or zero, whichever is larger).

   c) If the stock is worthless, the option is worthless.

   d) As the stock price becomes very large, the option price approaches the stock price less the present value of the exercise price.

Example 22. The current price of Sigma Corporation's common stock is \$59.375 per share. A call option on this stock has a \$55 exercise price. It has three months to expiration. If the standard deviation of continuously compounded rate of return on the stock is 0.2968 and the risk free rate is five percent per year, the value of this call option is determined as follows.

First, calculate the time until the option expires in years:

t in years = 30 days/365 days = 0.0822

Second, calculate the values of the other variables:

$$PV(E) = E/e^{rt} = \$55/e^{0.05 \times 0.0822} = \$54.774$$

$$d_1 = \ln[P/PV(E)] / \sigma\sqrt{t} + \sigma\sqrt{t} / 2$$

$$= \ln[\$59.375/\$54.774]/(0.2968 \times \sqrt{0.0822}) + (0.2968 \times \sqrt{0.0822})/2$$
$$= 0.9904$$

$$d_2 = d_1 - \sigma\sqrt{t} = 0.9904 - 0.2968 \times \sqrt{0.0822} = 0.9053$$

Next, use a table for the standard normal distribution (see Table 5 in Appendix B) to determine $N(d_1)$ and $N(d_2)$:

$N(d_1) = N(0.9904) = 0.8389$

$N(d_2) = N(0.9053) = 0.8173$

Finally, use those values to find the option's value:

$V = P[N(d_1)] - PV(E)\,[N(d_2)]$

$= \$59.375[0.8389] - \$54.774[0.8173]$

$= \$5.05$

This call option is worth \$5.05, a little more than its value if it is exercised immediately, \$4.375 (\$59.375 − \$55), as one should expect.

Example 23. You want to determine the value of another option on the same stock that has an exercise price of $50 and expires in 45 days. The time until the option expires in years is:

t in years = 45 days/365 days = 0.1233

The values of the other variables are:

$$PV(E) = E / e^{rt} = \$50/e^{0.05 \times 0.1233} = \$49.6927$$

$$d_1 = \ln[P/PV(E)] / \sigma\sqrt{t} + \sigma\sqrt{t} / 2$$

$$= \ln[\$59.375/\$49.6927] / (0.2968 \times \sqrt{0.1233}) + (0.2968 \times \sqrt{0.1233})/2$$
$$= 1.7602$$

$$d_2 = d_1 - \sigma\sqrt{t} = 1.7602 - 0.2968 \times \sqrt{0.1233} = 1.6560$$

Next, use a table for the standard normal distribution (see Table 5 in Appendix B) to determine $N(d_1)$ and $N(d_2)$:

$N(d_1) = N(1.7603) = 0.9608$

$N(d_2) = N(1.6561) = 0.9511$

Finally, use those values to find the option's value:

$V = P\,[N(d_1)] - PV(E)\,[N(d_2)]$

$= \$59.375\ [0.9608] - \$49.6927\ [0.9511]$

$= \$9.78$

The call option is worth more than the other option ($9.78 versus $5.05), since it has a lower exercise price and a longer time until expiration.

Note: The cfo.com/toolbox has *Stock Options Calculator* that allows us to calculate equity put and call values using the Black-Scholes model, as shown below.

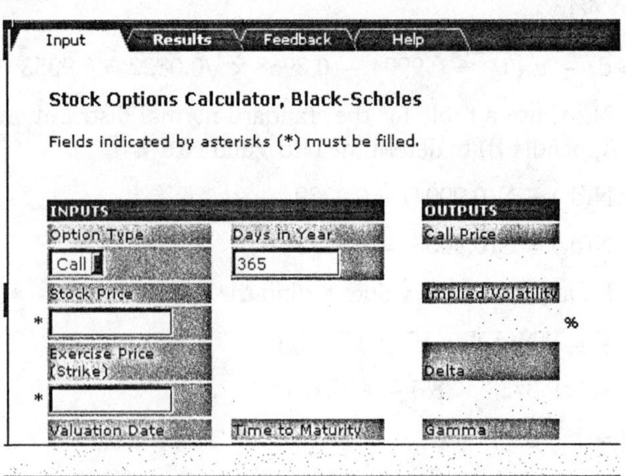

Source: CFO.com.

¶ 2315 Futures Contracts

Futures is another derivative instrument. In the futures market, you trade in commodities and financial instruments. A futures is a contract to purchase or sell a given amount of an item for a given price by a certain date (in the future—thus the name "futures market"). The seller of a futures contract agrees to deliver the item to the buyer of the contract, who agrees to purchase the item. The contract specifies the amount, valuation, method, quality, month, means of delivery, and exchange to be traded in. The month of delivery is the expiration date, in other words, the date on which the commodity or financial instrument must be delivered.

A futures contract is somewhat like a home sale, in which the buyer and seller agree on:

1. The quantity of the commodity,
2. The price to be paid, and
3. A future date for delivery.

Commodity contracts are guarantees by a seller to deliver a commodity (e.g., cocoa or cotton). Financial contracts are a commitment by the seller to deliver a financial instrument (e.g., a Treasury bill) or a specific amount of foreign currency. Exhibits 2 and 3 show the types of commodity and financial futures available.

Exhibit 2

Commodities Futures

Grains & Oilseeds	*Livestock & Meat*	*Food, Fibre, & Wood*	*Metals & Petroleum*
Barley	Broilers	Butter	Copper
Canola	Beef—Boneless	Cheddar Cheese	Gold
Corn	Cattle—Feeder	Cocoa	Palladium
Flaxseed	Cattle—Live	Coffee	Silver
Oats	Cattle—Stocker	Cotton #2	Silver—1000 oz.
Peas—Feed	Hogs—Lean	Lumber	Light Sweet Crude
Rice—Rough	Pork Bellies—Fresh	Milk Bfp	Heating Oil
Rye	Pork Bellies—Frozen	Milk—Non-Fat Dry	Natural Gas
Soybeans	Turkeys	Orange Juice	Platinum
Soybean Meal		Oriented Strand Board	High-Grade Copper
Soybean Oil		Potatoes	Mercury
Wheat—Duram		Rice	Propane
Wheat		Shrimp—Black Tiger	Unleaded Gasoline
Wheat—Feed		Shrimp White	Palo Verde Electricity
Wheat—Spring		Sugar	Twin City Electricity
Wheat—White		Sugar—World	
Wheat—Winter			

Exhibit 3

Financial Futures

Currencies	*Interest Rates*	*Securities*	*Indexes*
Australian Dollar	Eurodollars	Bank CDs	Dow Jones Industrials
Brazilian Real	Federal Funds—30 Days	GNMA Passthrough	Eurotop 100 Index
British Pound	Libor—1-Month	Stripped Treasuries	Goldman Sachs
Canadian Dollar	Treasury Bills		Major Market
Euro	Treasury Bonds—30-Year		Municipal Bond Index
French Franc	Treasury Notes—10-Year		NASDAQ 100
German Mark	Treasury Notes—2-Year		Nikkei 225
Japanese Yen	Treasury Notes—5-Year		NYSE Composite
Mexican Peso			PSE 100 Tech
Russian Ruble			Russell 1000
S. African Rand			Russell 2000
Swiss Franc			S&P 400 MidCap
Thai Baht			S&P 500
U.S. Dollar			S&P 500—Mini
			S&P Barra—Growth
			S&P Barra—Value
			Value Line
			Value Line—Mini

.01 What Is the Difference Between a Long and Short Position?

A long position is the purchase of a contract, expecting the price to increase. A short position is selling, expecting price to decrease. The position may be terminated by reversing the transaction. For example, the long buyer can subsequently engage in a short position of the commodity or financial instrument. Mostly all futures are offset (canceled out) prior to delivery. It is unusual for delivery to settle the futures contract.

.02 How Are Futures Contracts Traded?

A futures contract is traded in the futures market. Trading is performed by specialized brokers. Some commodity firms deal exclusively in futures. The fee for a futures contract is tied to the amount of the contract and the item's price. Commissions vary depending on the amount and nature of the contract. The trading in futures is basically the same as with stocks, except the investor needs a commodity trading account. However, the margin buying and the types of orders are the same. You buy or sell contracts with desired terms.

.03 Is Futures Trading Very Risky?

Futures trading may assist an investor handling inflation but is specialized with much risk. Your loss may be magnified due to *leverage.* Leverage (using of other people's money) means with minimal down payment you control something of much greater value. For instance, you can put down $2,000 to control a futures contract valued at $40,000. Each time the price of a commodity increases $1, you could earn or lose $20. With an *option,* you just lose money invested. With a futures, you lose a lot more. Further, futures contract prices may be very unstable. However, many exchanges place per day price limits on each contract trading to insulate traders from huge losses.

.04 What Are Commodities Futures?

A commodity contract involves a seller who contracts to deliver a commodity by a specified date at a set price. The contract stipulates the item, price, expiration date, and standardized unit to be traded (e.g., 100,000 pounds). Commodity contracts may last up to one year. You must always appraise the impact of market activity on the contract's value.

Assume that you purchase a futures contract for the delivery of 2,000 units of a commodity six months from now at $5 per unit. The seller of the contract does not have to have physical custody of the item, and the contract buyer does not have to take possession of the commodity at the "deliver" date. Commodity contracts are typically reversed, or terminated, before consummation. For example, as the initial buyer of 5,000 bushels of wheat, you may engage in a similar contract to sell the same amount, in effect closing your position.

You may enter into commodity trading to achieve high return rates and hedge inflation. In times of increasing prices, commodities react favorably because they are tied to economic trends. However, there is high risk, and uncertainty exists since commodity prices fluctuate and there is a lot of low-margin investing. You need a lot of cash in case of a margin call to cover losses. To minimize risk, hold a diversified portfolio. Futures contracts are only for knowledgeable and experienced investors.

The buyer of a commodity can opt to terminate the contract or continue holding on expectation of higher profits. Conversely, the investor may use the earnings to furnish margin on another futures contract (called an inverse pyramid in a futures contract).

Commodity futures enable buyers and sellers to negotiate cash (spot) prices. Cash is paid to immediately obtain custody of a commodity. Prices in the cash market depend partly upon prices in the futures market. There may be higher prices for the commodity over time, taking into account carrying costs and expected inflation.

Commodity futures are traded in the Chicago Board of Trade (CBOT), the largest exchange. There are other exchanges specializing in particular commodities, such as the New York Cotton Exchange (NYCE), Chicago Mercantile Exchange (CME), and Kansas City Board of Trade (KCBT). Because of the possibility of substantial gains and losses in commodities, exchanges have caps on the highest daily price changes for a commodity. The Commodity Futures Trading Commission is a federal agency that regulates commodities exchanges. Commodity futures trading is accomplished through open outcry auction.

.05 *What Returns and Risks Are There for Futures Contracts?*

The return on a futures contract stems from capital appreciation (selling price less acquisition cost), because no current income is earned. Significant capital gain may arise from price fluctuation in the commodity and the impact of leverage due to low margin. If the opposite occurs, much of your investment may be lost. The return on investment in commodities (a long or short position) equals:

$$\text{Return on investment} = \frac{\text{Selling price} - \text{purchase price}}{\text{Margin deposit}}$$

Example 24. Assume you buy a contract on a commodity for $80,000, with a deposit of $10,000. Subsequently, you sell the contract for $85,000. The return is:

$$\frac{\$85{,}000 - \$80{,}000}{\$10{,}000} = 50\%$$

The margin requirement for commodity contracts is small, typically from three to six percent of the contract's value. (For stocks, the margin requirement is currently 50 percent, although some brokerage firms require a deposit of more than 50 percent). Because in commodities trading there is no loan involved, there is no interest.

An *initial margin* deposit must be made on a futures contract so as to cover a drop in market price on the contract. Such deposit varies with the type of contract and the particular commodity exchange.

A *maintenance deposit* may also be required, which is lower than the initial deposit. It furnishes the minimum margin that must be kept in the account. It is typically about 80 percent of the initial margin.

Example 25. On September 1, you contract to purchase 50,000 pounds of sugar at $2 a pound to be delivered by December 31. The value of the total contract is $100,000. The initial margin requirement is 15 percent, or $15,000. The margin maintenance requirement is 80 percent, or $12,000. Assuming a contract loss of $2,500, you must pay $2,500 to cover the margin position. If not, the contract will be terminated with the ensuing loss.

.06 Who Employs Futures?

Trading in futures is performed by hedgers and speculators. Investors employ hedging to protect their position in a commodity. For instance, a farmer (the seller) may hedge to obtain a higher price for his goods while a processor (or buyer) of the product will hedge to get a lower price. By hedging, you reduce the risk of loss but forego earning a sizable profit.

Example 26. A commodity is presently selling at $160 a pound. The potential buyer (assume a manufacturer) anticipates the price to increase. To protect against higher prices, the purchaser buys a futures contract selling at $175 a pound. Five months later, the commodity price is $225. The futures contract price will similarly increase to $250. The buyer's profit is $75 a pound. If 10,000 pounds are involved, the total profit is $750,000. However, the cost on the market rose by only $65 a pound, or $650,000. The producer has hedged his position, deriving a profit of $100,000, and has put a tip on the rising commodity costs.

Commodities may also be used for speculation in the market. Speculators engage in futures contracts to obtain capital gain on price increases of the commodity, currency, or financial instrument.

Example 27. You buy a September futures contract for 20,000 pounds of wheat at $2 a pound. If the price rises to $2.20, you'll gain $.20 a pound for a total gain of $4,000. The percent gain, assuming an initial margin requirement of five percent, is 200 percent ($.2/$.1). Assuming transactions occur over a three-month period, the annual gain would be 800 percent (200% × 12 months/3 months). This resulted from a mere 10-percent ($.2/$2.00) gain in the price of a pound of wheat.

.07 What Ways Are Available to Minimize Risks?

Spreading capitalizes on wide swings in price and at the same time limits loss exposure. Spreading is like stock option trading. You engage in at least two contracts to earn some profit while capping loss potential. You buy one contract and sell the other, expecting to achieve a reasonable profit. If the worst occurs, the spread aids in minimizing the investor's loss.

Example 28. You buy Contract A for 20,000 pounds of commodity T at $300 a pound. Simultaneously, you sell short Contract B for 20,000 pounds of the identical commodity at $325 per pound. Later, you sell Contract A for $325 a pound and buy Contract B for $345 a pound. Contract A earns a profit of $25 a pound while Contract B has a loss of $20 a pound. The net effect is a profit of $5 a pound, or a total gain of $100,000.

.08 What Are Financial Futures?

Financial futures include: (1) interest rate, (2) foreign currency, and (3) stock-index. Financial futures trading is similar to commodity trading. It represents about 70 percent of all contracts. Due to fluctuation in interest and exchange rates, financial futures can be used as a hedge. They may also be used to speculate having potential for a wide price swing. Financial futures have a *lower* margin requirement than commodities do. For instance, the margin on a U.S. Treasury bill might be as low as two percent.

Financial futures are traded in the New York Futures Exchange, AMEX Commodities Exchange, International Monetary Market (part of Chicago Mercantile Exchange), and the Chicago Board of Trade.

.09 How Do Interest Rate Futures Work?

An interest rate futures contract gives the holder the right to a specified amount of the underlying debt security at a later date (typically not exceeding three years). They may be in such forms as Treasury bills, notes, and bonds, paper, "Ginnie Mae (GNMA)" certificates, CRB Index, Eurodollars, and U.S. Dollar Index.

Interest rate futures are expressed as a percentage of the face value of the applicable debt security. The value of interest rate futures contracts is linked to interest rates. For instance, as interest rates drop, the contract's value rises. If the price or quote of the contract increases, the buyer gains but the seller loses. A change of one basis point in interest rates causes a price change. A basis point equals 1/100 of one percent.

Those trading in interest rate futures do not typically take custody of the financial instrument. The contract is employed either to hedge or to speculate on future interest rates and security prices.

.10 How Do Currency Futures Work?

A *currency futures contract* provides the right to a stipulated amount of foreign currency at a later date. The contracts are standardized, and secondary markets exist. Currency futures are stated in dollars per unit of the underlying foreign currency. They usually have a delivery not exceeding one year.

Currency futures may be used to either hedge or speculate. Hedging in a currency may lock you into the best possible money exchange.

.11 What Is a Stock-Index Futures?

A *stock-index futures contract* is linked to a stock market index (e.g., the S & P 500 Stock Index and New York Stock Exchange Composite Stock

Index). But smaller investors can use the S & P 100 futures contract, which has a lower margin deposit. Stock-index futures allows you to participate in the overall stock market. You can buy and sell the "market as a whole" instead of one security. If you expect a bull market but are not certain which stock will increase, you should purchase (long position) a stock-index future. Since there is a lot of risk, trade in stock-index futures only to hedge.

.12 How Do You Transact in Futures?

You may invest directly in a commodity or indirectly through a *mutual fund.* A third way is to buy a *limited partnership* involved with commodity investments. The mutual fund and partnership approaches are more conservative because risk is spread and there is professional management.

Futures may be directly invested as follows:

1. *Commodity pools.* Professional traders manage a pool. A filing is made with the Commodity Futures Trading Commission (CFTC). Check out www.cftc.gov.
2. *Full service brokers.* They may recommend something when attractive.
3. *Discount brokers.* You must decide on your own when and if.
4. *Managed futures.* You deposit funds in an individual managed account and choose a commodity trading advisor (CTA) to trade it.

To obtain information on managed futures:

1. *Barclay Trading Group* publishes quarterly reports on trading advisers (www.barclaygrp.com).
2. *CMA Reports* monitors the performance of trading advisers and private pools (www.cyberfutures.com).
3. *Management Account Reports,* monthly newsletters, tracks the funds and furnishes information on their fees and track records (www.solomonsmithbarney.com).
4. *Trading Advisor* follows more than 100 trading advisers (www.impulsiveprofits.com).

There are several drawbacks to managed futures, including:

1. High cost of a futures program, ranging from 15 to 20 percent of the funds invested.
2. Substantial risk and inconsistent performance of fund advisors. *Note:* Despite its recent popularity, managed futures is still a risky choice and should not be done apart from a well-diversified portfolio.

Chapter 24

Mutual Funds

¶ 2401 Mutual Fund Basics

.01 *Mutual Funds Defined*

Investors who want professional money management and diversification can get both by investing in a mutual fund, even with just a small amount of money. A mutual fund is an investment company that is managed by professionals who are trained in investing and managing other people's money. Those professional money managers buy, sell, and monitor a diversified group of securities to support the fund's investment goals. Each share of a mutual fund actually owns a proportional share of the fund's current portfolio of securities.

Example 1: Gary Nelson bought 120 shares of A-1 Mutual Fund, which currently owns the following stocks:

A-1 Mutual Fund Portfolio	*Number of Shares*
Upriver Utility......	200
Total Technology	300
Fine Foods	500
Total	1,000

The 120 shares that Nelson owns represent three percent of the 4,000 total ownership shares issued by A-1 Mutual Fund. Thus, Nelson actually owns a three percent proportional share of the fund's portfolio, that is, six shares of Upriver Utility, nine shares of Total Technology, and 15 shares of Fine Foods.

.02 Advantages of Mutual Fund Investing

The key reasons that make mutual fund investing so popular include:

- *Diversification.* An investor's money is proportionally diversified among the fund's entire portfolio of equity, debt, or other securities. Such diversification reduces the investor's risk.
- *Professional money management.* Professionals monitor the marketplace as well as the fund's performance and mix on a day-to-day basis to best meet the fund's investment goals.
- *Small minimum investment.* Many mutual funds accept initial investments of less than $1,000.
- *Liquidity.* Shares may be redeemed at any time (however, it may take up to a week to receive the proceeds from the fund).

.03 Account Services Provided by Mutual Funds

Mutual funds are also attractive because of the many convenient services they offer their shareholders. Common services include:

- *Automatic investments.* An investor may set up periodic deductions from their checking account to be invested in the mutual fund. Such investments, which may be as small as $50 a month, can help keep savings goals on track.
- *Automatic reinvestments.* Dividends, interest, and capital gains may be reinvested into the mutual fund, usually at no charge.
- *Automatic withdrawals.* Funds may be withdrawn from the mutual fund on a set schedule, usually at no charge. Such periodic withdrawals may be for a set dollar value or number of shares.
- *Switching funds.* Investments may be moved from one fund type to another in a family of funds. Such exchange privileges are usually provided at no charge.
- *Tax and accounting records.* Monthly and year-end statements from the mutual fund record all of an account's investment activity as well as other information needed for tax purposes.
- *Safekeeping of securities and custodian services.* Certificates of mutual fund ownership are recorded and kept safe by the fund's designated custodian.
- *Tax-deferred accounts.* Mutual fund accounts may be set up as IRA, Roth IRA, and Keogh plans.

- *Guardianship for children's accounts.* Mutual funds may be set up to recognize account guardians under the Uniform Gift to Minor Act.
- *Check-writing privileges.*

.04 Net Asset Value of Mutual Fund Shares

The price of a mutual fund share is stated as net asset value (NAV). It is computed as follows:

NAV Formula

$$\frac{\text{Fund's total assets} - \text{Debt}}{\text{Number of shares outstanding in the fund}}$$

Example: 2 At the end of 20X1, the market values of securities owned by EZ Mutual Fund are as follows. The fund also has liabilities of $4,500. The NAV of the fund is calculated below:

a.	Diet Drugs ($100 per share × 200 shares)	$20,000
b.	Earth Energy ($50 per share × 300 shares)	15,000
c.	Impact Insurance ($75 per share × 100 shares)	7,500
	Total assets = (a + b + c)	$42,500
d.	Less liabilities	4,500
e.	Net asset value of fund's portfolio = (a + b + c) − (d) .	$38,000
f.	Number of shares outstanding in the fund	1,000
g.	Net asset value (NAV) per share = (e) ÷ (f)	$ 38

Using the NAV per share, Jane Brown, who owns 30 shares of EZ Mutual Fund, calculated her investment to be worth the following: 30 shares × $38 = $1,140. (Brown's 30 shares represent a three-percent ownership of the 1,000 total ownership shares issued by EZ Mutual Fund.)

.05 Total Return of Mutual Fund Shares

Money is made in a mutual fund by a gain in its net asset value, as well as its payment of dividends and its distribution of capital gains.

Net asset value. An investor should look at the difference between their shares' *ending (or current) net asset value* and *beginning (or average) net asset value* to determine the price appreciation or depreciation of the shares. However, to look at the *total return* of those shares, the dividends and capital gains must also be considered. The more dividends and capital gains there were to reinvest into more shares, the greater the number of shares that were purchased over time.

Dividends. Mutual funds typically pay out a large percentage of their income. Dividends are fully taxed.

Capital gains distributions. Capital gains are distributed each year to fund holders. Capital gains are taxed at the maximum capital gains rate of 28 percent.

Dollar Return Formula

$$\text{Dividends} + \text{Capital gains distributed} + \text{Change in NAV}$$

Where:

Change in NAV = (Ending NAV − Beginning NAV)

Percentage Return Formula / Rate of Return Formula

$$\frac{\text{Dividends} + \text{Capital gain distributions} + (\text{Ending NAV} - \text{Beginning NAV})}{\text{Beginning NAV}}$$

Example 3. XY Mutual Fund paid dividends of $1 per share and distributed capital gains of $.40 per share in 20X1. NAV at the beginning of 20X1 was $10; year-end was $12. The percentage return for 20X1 equals:

$$\frac{\$1 + \$.40 + (\$12 - \$10)}{\$10} = \frac{\$3.40}{\$10} = 34\%$$

.06 *Loads and Fees Charged by Mutual Funds*

Mutual funds charge for their services through various kinds of loads and fees. When researching funds, note that some funds ave higher charges than others. The charges, described below, are classified as follows: loads, management fees, 12b-1 fees, back-end loads, deferred loads, and reinvestment loads.

Loads. A load is a sales fee charged an investor when buying shares in a fund. Such a charge may range from one percent to 8.5 percent (maximum legal limit) of the amount invested. That means that of a $1,000 invested in a fund with an 8.5 percent load, only $915 goes into the fund. Mutual fund prices are stated in "bid" and "ask" form. The bid is the price the fund will buy back its shares (at the NAV). The ask or "offer" is the price the investor must pay to buy shares. The difference between the offer and bid is the load. "No-load" mutual funds have no sales fees so they have the same bid and ask prices. Also, just because a fund has a sales fee does not mean the fund will perform better than a no-load fund. The fee, however, *will* reduce the net return rate.

Management and expenses fees. All funds ("no load" or "load") charge a fee to pay a portfolio manager. It typically ranges from 0.5 percent to one percent of the fund's assets.

12b-1 fees. These charges are for advertising and promotion. They typically range from 0.25 percent to 0.30 percent, but some run as high as 1.25 percent.

Back-end loads, or redemption fees. These are charged when shares are sold. They are based on a percentage of the shares' net asset value, so steep back-end loads can reduce profits or increase losses.

Deferred loads, or contingent deferred sales fees. These are deducted from the original investment if shares are sold before a specified period.

Reinvestment loads. These fees are taken out of reinvested interest, dividends, and capital gains. For example, if a capital-gains distribution of $150 has a reinvestment fee of seven percent, the fund will keep $10.50 and only reinvest $139.50.

¶ 2405 Types of Mutual Funds

Mutual funds are categorized according to their purpose, structure, fees, switching privileges, return potential, and risk. Investments in any type of fund should be based on investment goals.

.01 Open-End Funds (Mutual Funds)

Open-end funds, commonly called mutual funds, can sell an unlimited number of ownership shares. Shares may be purchased from and sold back to the fund when desired. Shares are bought at their net asset value (NAV) plus a service fee, and redeemed at NAV less a commission.

Exhibit 1 summarizes the differences between open-end funds, known just as mutual funds, and closed-end funds (described in ¶ 2405.02).

Exhibit 1

Differences Between Open-End Funds (Mutual Funds) and Closed-End Funds

Differences	*Open-End Funds (Mutual Funds)*	*Closed-End Funds*
Number of shares . . .	Fluctuates	Fixed
Traded at net asset value (NAV)	Yes	No—traded at a discount or premium from NAV
Liquidity	Almost immediate	Three business days
Dividends and capital gain	Can be reinvested	Some offer automatic reinvestment
Accessibility	Yes; via a toll-free phone; check-writing privileges	Limited
Method of purchase .	Direct from fund or fund salesperson	Stock exchange or OTC
Flexibility	Yes, exchange privileges	No
Commission	Load or no-load	Yes

.02 Closed-End Funds

Closed-end funds can issue only a limited (fixed) number of shares. The shares are traded on the stock exchange or over-the-counter market. Share price is determined independently of NAV by factors of supply and demand. Management fees are assessed by all funds.

Closed-end funds have features similar to both mutual funds and common stocks. They do differ from open-end funds in two ways. First, they operate with a fixed number of shares outstanding, which trade among individuals in secondary markets like common stocks. That is, an investor in a closed-end fund must purchase shares from someone willing to sell them the shares. In the same manner, an investor selling closed-end funds shares must locate a buyer. Transactions involving closed-end mutual funds are easy to arrange, however, since most of these funds are traded on the New York Stock Exchange, American Stock Exchange, or the over-the-counter market. Second, the price of a closed-end fund is based on a demand/supply relationship because the shares are traded on the stock exchange. New shares are not issued. Therefore, the net asset value of the fund may be more or less than its current market price of stock. A major point of closed-end funds is the size of discount or premium. Many funds of this type sell at discounts, which enhances their investment appeal.

When the market price is above its NAV, it is said to be selling at a premium; when market price is below the NAV, it is selling at a discount. A number of publications such as the *Wall Street Journal* and *Barron's* report the share premiums or discounts of closed-end funds. *Barron's* also publishes the trends in *Herzfeld Closed-End Average,* which tracks 20 closed-end mutual funds accounting for about 50 percent of the value of all the funds traded on the exchanges. An upward trend is a positive sign in a bullish market. In addition to the *Wall Street Journal* and *Barron's,* current and historical data are provided in the following publications: *Morningstar Closed-End Funds, Standard & Poor's Stock Reports,* and *Standard & Poor's Stock Guide.* Current and historical quotes are also available on the Internet through various online services and websites.

Advantages of closed-end funds. Closed-end funds are well suited for income investors and those seeking international diversification.

- Diversification
- Professional management
- Discount purchase prices

Disadvantages of closed-end funds.

- High management fees range from 1/2 percent to 1 1/2 percent.
- Brokerage commissions vary widely. A negotiated commission or the use of a discount broker can help lower commissions.

.03 Money Market Funds

Money market funds are a special form of mutual fund. Money market funds invest solely in short-term debt securities that provide high interest income with safe principal. Money market funds are considered very conservative because most of the securities purchased by the funds are quite safe.

In a money market fund, an investor may actually own a diversified portfolio of high-yielding CDs, T-bills, and other similar securities of short-term nature, while only investing a small amount of money. In addition, there is a great deal of liquidity and flexibility in withdrawing funds through check-writing privileges. Money market funds are therefore called "cash equivalents."

The price of a money market fund is constant—shares are bought and sold at $1. The yield, however, fluctuates daily. Despite the myth that all money funds perform about the same, some regularly offer significantly higher yields than others, chiefly because they keep their expenses low.

Advantages of money market funds.

- Interest income
- No load charges
- Possible small initial deposit
- Possible check-writing privileges

Disadvantage of money market funds.

- Funds are not federally insured
- Conservative investments have lower yields

Selection criteria. The following issues should be considered when selecting a money market fund.

- *Average investment maturity.* The shorter the average maturity, the safer the fund is likely to be, and the faster the fund will begin offering competitive yields if interest rates rise.
- *Check-writing privileges.* Does the fund allow check-writing? Does the fund charge for check-writing? What is the minimum required when writing a check—$200, $250, $500? The smaller the minimum, the more often the fund can be used as a parking place for future investment or for emergency.
- *Initial investment.* What is the minimum required to open an account?
- *Expense ratios.* The expense ratios of money-market funds range from about 0.3 percent a year to two percent. Investor yields will be higher when expenses are kept low.

.04 Funds Categorized by Investment Objective

Growth funds. Growth funds want high return via capital gains. They usually invest in companies with growth exceeding the inflation rate. The stocks have constant long-term, current income. Like other growth investments, the aim of these funds is to increase share value, not pay dividends.

Aggressive growth (capital appreciation) funds. These funds take greater risk for high capital appreciation. Dividend income is secondary. They concentrate on new high-technology businesses. They offer the greatest potential for growth, but also the greater risk. These funds are appropriate for investors who are not especially worried about the near-term variability of return, but are instead focused on long-term appreciation. Aggressive strategies taken may consist of leveraged purchases, short selling, call options, put options, and buying stock.

Income funds. Income funds generate current income through investments in securities that pay interest or a cash dividend. These securities include dividend-paying stocks, corporate bonds, and a variety of government securities. Generally, the higher the income sought, the riskier the underlying investments. They offer current income with low to high risk.[1]

Growth and income funds. Growth and income funds emphasize current dividends, or interest and capital appreciation. They offer moderate growth potential and moderate risk. The objective is long-term growth. Share value should be stable.

Balanced funds. Balanced funds seek preservation of capital while seeking growth and income. The aim of these funds is to "balance" the portfolio with the best ratio of stocks and bonds within the funds' investment objective guidelines. This is done to adjust to prevailing market conditions. Balanced funds tend to underperform all-stock funds in strong bull markets.

.05 *Funds Categorized by Sector*

Sector (specialized) funds invest by industry(ies). High-risk exists because the fortunes of the fund depend of the performance of the specific industry. If an industry, such as pharmaceuticals, takes a "hit," huge losses will ensue.

.06 *International Funds*

International funds invest in securities of overseas (foreign) companies. Some international funds, such as Fidelity Canada Fund, invest in just one geographic area. Fund value increases if the dollar decreases due to exchange rates.

.07 *Index Funds*

To achieve the returns of the stock or bond market (without the risk of picking an underachieving mutual fund), some experts suggest index funds. It is a sensible, no-brainer method for investors who are not interested in the ongoing process of evaluating funds and who wish to obtain the market's return with absolutely no effort and minimal expense. Some index funds, such as the Vanguard Index Trust Fund, match the entire stock index. Others invest in the Standard & Poor's (S&P) 500 index, which represents approximately 70 percent of the market value of all outstanding U.S. common stocks. Still others are now emulating the broader Wilshire 5,000 stock index. There are also index funds that track foreign securities markets, typically emulating the Europe, Australia, and Far East (EAFE) index. These foreign index funds are excellent vehicles for obtaining the risk reduction and profit opportunities from international diversification. Vanguard offers the widest selection of index funds—funds that follow a great

---

[1] See Bond Funds at ¶ 2405.08 and Tax-Exempt Municipal Bond Funds at ¶ 2405.09.

variety of stock, bond, and EAFE indexes. Other investment companies offering index funds include DFA and Wells Fargo.

According to a study by Lipper Analytical Services of New York, 83 percent of the basic stock mutual funds did *not* beat the S&P 500 index for the year 1994. Furthermore, stock fund managers have been beaten by the S&P 500 in 10 of the past 15 years.

Advantages of index funds.

- *Guaranteed market index return.* After making an initial investment, no further decisions are necessary to make the same annual return as the fund's particular market index.
- *Lower management costs.* Index funds are cheap to run since there is no need for any research staff. These lower costs are typically passed to the fund owner. The average index fund charges about 0.3 percent, or $3 for every $1,000 invested.
- *Holdings include more investments, less cash.* Index funds usually have all their money in stocks or bonds with no cash cushion needed. In contrast, the typical actively managed mutual fund keeps a cash cushion of three to 10 percent of the portfolio to handle investor withdrawals and to seek new opportunities. Cash, being the worst performing asset, has been a drag on long-term performance.
- *Tax savings from less capital gains.* Since index funds rarely trade the securities they hold, there exists significantly less capital gains and thus fewer taxes.

.08 Bond Funds

Considerations for selecting a bond fund. The following are important criteria when selecting a bond fund (income fund):

- *Quality and ratings.* Bond funds are rated by Standard & Poor's and Moody's, as well as on the basis of the Securities and Exchange Commission (SEC) standardized yield. Bond funds vary greatly. Some are aggressively managed and contain high risks; others buy only government issues and are best suited for conservative investors. The fund's prospectus will list its holdings.
- *Maturity.* Because interest rates change over time, bond funds with longer maturities will have wider price fluctuations. For example, a 10-year bond will vary more in price than a five-year bond. Some bond funds manage to produce top returns without undue volatility. For example, Harbor Bond Fund has returned a respectable return—an annualized 11.5 percent over the past five years, yet its average duration is a middle-of-road 5.3 years.

- *Premium or discount.* Funds with high-return rates have bonds with prices more than their par value (premium). Such funds are less susceptible to losses if interest rates increase. Funds selling at a discount are below face value. Bonds trading at a discount to face value can lose the most.

- *Total return.* Bonds generate more than interest payouts. There is also the question of capital gains or losses, which can make a huge difference in performance. Total return reflects both interest and price changes.

- *Commissions, loads, or fees.* The difference between yields on the best and worst bond funds is often slight. Instead, the expense ratio will show how loads and fees can be more important to total return than the money manager.

- *Prepayment risk.* Prepayment risk exists with funds that invest in mortgage-backed securities, such as Ginnie Maes. Mortgage prepayments accelerate when interest rates decline, and can appreciably shorten the expected long-term string of high payments.

- *Currency risk.* Currency risk exists with international bond funds. For example some international funds frequently generate handsome returns, not because of higher interest abroad, but because of a fall in the U.S. dollar value.

Interest rate trends when investing in a bond fund.

- *Increasing interest rates.* Increasing interest rates means lower net asset values for bond funds. Therefore, instead of concentrating just on current yield, consider the total return (yield + capital gains from declining interest rates) or (yield − capital losses from increasing interest rates). Consider high-yield junk bonds if interest rates will be stable or going up.

- *Decreasing interest rates.* All bond funds do not react the same way when interest rates decline. If interest rates are likely to drop, purchase funds that invest in U.S. Treasuries or high-quality corporate bonds. Also consider how long the maturities are in the fund when measuring interest rate risk.

.09 Tax-Exempt Municipal Bond Funds

Tax-free mutual funds seek current, tax-free income by investing for the most part in tax-exempt bonds issued by municipalities to build schools, highways, and public projects. They offer current tax-exempt income with low to high risk depending on the yield sought and individual investments.

Increases in tax rates have brought tax-free income more attention lately. Interest payments on municipal bonds are generally free from federal income tax and from some state taxes if issued within that state, which is particularly important for investors living in states with high tax rates. But an investor doesn't need to be in the top brackets to benefit from municipal bonds. Even those with a federal tax rate of 28 percent should give serious consideration to municipal bond funds. When trying to decide how much better (or worse) a tax-exempt bond fund is than a taxable bond fund, it's useful to examine the investor's taxable equivalent yield, which was discussed earlier.

If a *taxable* bond fund has an equivialent yield that is less than a *similar tax-exempt* bond fund, then the investor is better off in the tax-exempt fund. However, if the taxable fund's equivalent yield is more, then the investor would be better off in the taxable fund. What is meant by "similar"? It is important to compare bond funds with a similar average maturity and credit quality. Comparing, for example, the taxable equivalent yield of a short-term muni portfolio with a long-term, high-yield corporate fund is not meaningful. Muni-bond funds have call risk, which refers to the danger that a bond carrying a relatively high coupon will be called in for early redemption by its issuer. Nearly all municipal bonds have some sort of call provision.

In picking a municipal bond fund, the following factors should be considered?

- *Portfolio composition.* What sectors does the fund invest in? Is this diversified enough?
- *Credit quality.* Look at the breakdown of the fund in terms of credit rating. The larger the proportion of investment grade bonds, the lower the credit risk.
- *Duration.* The longer the duration of the bonds in the fund, the greater the interest rate risk.
- *Standard deviation.* The most common statistical indicator of an asset's risk.
- *Yield and total return.* Good comparisons can be made based on the Securities and Exchange Commission (SEC) standardized 30-day yield and total return.
- *Expense ratio.*

.10 Unit Investment Trusts

Similar to a mutual fund, a unit investment trust gives investors the benefits of a professionally managed diversified portfolio. But, unlike a mutual fund, the portfolio is constant. After the initial selections are done, there is no active management. Unit investment trusts include tax-free municipals, corporate bonds, preferred stock, and common stock. Unit trusts are good for those who want a fixed income and a guaranteed return of capital. After the fund ceases, investors' shares are redeemed.

¶ 2411 Evaluating a Mutual Fund's Performance

Mutual funds, like other investments, are evaluated on the basis of return and risk.

.01 Measuring the Return of a Mutual Fund

The dollar return of a mutual fund equals the sum of its (1) dividend (interest) income, (2) capital gains, and (3) change in net asset value (NAV).[2] Using a hypothetical fund's statement (US Mutual Fund) in Exhibit 3, Exhibit 2 shows the calculation steps for arriving at the fund's rate of return. These are the same steps behind the scenes in most professional software.

[2] See Dollar Return and Percentage Return Formulas at ¶ 2401.05.

Exhibit 2

Figuring the Rate of Return of a Mutual Fund

Step		*US Mutual Fund (See Exhibit 3)*	*Another Fund*
1.	The number of months for which the fund's performance is being measured.	5	____
2.	The investment at the beginning of the period. (Multiply the total number of shares owned by the NAV.) [(0 + 246.063) × $10.16]	$2,500.00	____
3.	The ending value of the investment. (Multiply the number of shares currently owned by the current NAV.) (578.537 × $11.91)	$6,890.38	____
4.	Total dividends and capital gains received in cash—not reinvested. ($0)	$ 0.00	____
5.	All additional investments (any redemptions subtracted). ($2,500 + $1,000)	$3,500.00	____
6.	Computation of gain or loss:		
6a.	Add line 2 to ½ of the total on line 5. [$2,500 + (.5 × $3500)]	$4,250.00	____
6b.	Add line 3 and line 4, then subtract ½ of the total on line 5. [($6,890.38 + $0) − (.5 × $3,500)]	$5,140.38	____
6c.	Divide line 6b by line 6a. ($5,140.38 ÷ $4,250)	1.2095	____
6d.	Subtract the numeral 1 from the result of line 6c, then multiply by 100. [(1.2095 − 1) × 100]	20.95%	____
7.	Compute the annualized return. (Divide the number of months on line 1 into 12; multiply the result by line 6d.) [(12 ÷ 5) × 20.95]	50.28%	____

Exhibit 3

U.S. Mutual Fund Statement

(Figures from this hypothetical fund statement are used in Exhibit 2 calculations)

Date (20X1)	*Transaction*	*Dollar Amount*	*Share Price (NAV)*	*Shares*	*Total Shares Owned*
	Beginning balance				0.000
07/19	Purchase	$2,500.00	$10.16	246.063	246.063
08/17	Purchase	2,500.00	10.87	229.991	476.054
11/30	Purchase	1,000.00	11.27	88.731	564.785
12/22	Dividend reinvest (.09)	50.83	11.91	4.268	569.053
12/22	Short-term capital gain reinvest (.07)	39.53	11.91	3.319	572.372
12/22	Long-term capital gain reinvest (.13)	73.42	11.91	6.165	578.537
12/22	Ending balance	$6,890.38	$11.91		578.537

.02 *Measuring the Risk or Volatility of a Mutual Fund*

In evaluating how a mutual fund did, consider the published measures of risk or volatility of the funds to ascertain the amount of risk. There are three popular measures of risk: beta, R-squared, and standard deviation.

Beta. Beta shows how volatile a mutual fund is compared with the market as a whole, as measured by the Standard & Poor's 500 index on the equity side and the Lehman Brothers Aggregate Index on the bond side.

Beta	*Meaning*
1.0	A fund goes up in price the same as the market.
>1.0	The fund goes higher in bull markets and lower in bear markets than the market.
<1.0	The fund is risky relative to the market.

Thus, a fund with a 1.10 beta is expected to perform 10 percent better than the market in up markets, and 10 percent worse in down markets. By the same token, a fund with a beta of 0.75 should capture 75 percent of the market gains in a rally and lose only 75 percent as much in a decline.

R-squared. Some analysts prefer to use R-squared, shown as "R^2" in mutual fund tables such as Morningstar's Mutual Fund Values. R-squared, ranging from 0 to 100, gives a percentage comparison of a fund's performance to its benchmark index (such as the S&P 500). The higher the R-squared, the higher the relationship between the fund and the benchmark and, thus, the more relevant is the beta figure.

Standard deviation. Some analysts prefer to use standard deviation, shown as "Std.Dev" in mutual fund tables such as Morningstar's Mutual Fund Values. Standard deviation says that in 95 cases out of 100, the fund's period-ending price will be plus or minus a certain percentage of its price at the beginning of the period, usually a month. In general, the higher the standard deviation, the greater the volatility or risk.

Risk measurement. If beta, R^2, and/or standard deviation are used to help pick a fund, these measures should cover at least three years to give the most accurate picture about the risk and instability of the fund. All these numbers, of course, should be weighed against other indicators, including total return over at least five years, performance in an up and down market, and the experience of the fund manager.

Risk measures such as beta, R^2, and standard deviation for mutual funds are published in many investment publications, such as *Value Line Mutual Fund Survey* and *Morningstar Mutual Funds.* See Exhibit 4, below, for a sample mutual fund report by Morningstar.

Alpha value. In addition to the three risk measures discussed above, mutual fund reports (as shown in Figure 1 below) will also evaluate the performance of a fund by giving its alpha value, or *average differential return.* The alpha value is the difference between the fund's actual return and the return predicted by the overall mutual fund *beta.* Generally, a positive alpha (excess return) indicates superior performance, while a negative value leads to the opposite conclusion.

Example 4. In 20X1, the entire market had a rate of return (r_m) of eight percent and a risk-free rate (r_f) of five percent. The IQ Mutual Fund, with a beta of 1.5, returned 7.5 percent. IQ Mutual Fund's expected return would have been 9.5 percent [5% + (1.5 × (8% − 5%))]. Thus, the fund has a negative alpha of 1.5 percent (9.5% − 8%).

"Keep your alpha high and your beta low" is a basic strategy for those who wish to generate good investment performance. However, investors continue to grapple with whether funds can consistently perform at positive alpha levels.

Exhibit 4

Rankings of a Mutual Fund's Alpha, Beta, R^2, and Standard Deviation

		Alpha	Beta	R^2	Std.Dev
		-1.7	0.83	96	4.85
Pct. Rank	All Funds	49	59	8	50
	Objective	22	22	9	23

Percentile Ranks: 1=Highest 100=Lowest
Except MFV RISK: 1=Lowest 100=Highest

Source: Morningstar Reports

¶ 2415 Criteria for Selecting a Mutual Fund

.01 Considerations When Selecting a Mutual Fund

Selecting the "right" mutual fund involves the following considerations:

- *What type of fund is needed?* Prepare a fund listing to check what type of fund is appropriate for the investor's risk tolerance and financial needs and objectives.

- *How does the fund prospectus describe the fund.* Read the prospectus to choose a fund satisfying the desired risk level and investment requirements. The prospectus includes the fund's purpose, selection criteria, performance, fees, and financial condition. Read the statement of objectives as well as risk considerations and investment constraints. Look at the statement of additional information showing the fund's charges and investment portfolio. Review for annual and quarterly financial information.

- *How has the fund performed?* Check the performance in both good and bad times over the past 10 years. Compare this fund to similar funds and market averages of the same type. Examine its standard deviation in financial publications. What is the trend in per-share and dollar values? Many magazines such as *Business Week, Worth, Consumer Reports, Forbes,* and *U.S. News and World Report* publish mutual fund performance statistics. Investment newsletters, such as *Morningstar* and

Lipper Analytical, publish fund rankings that provide a benchmark to objectively measure a fund's performance.

- *How good is the fund management?* The *Value Line Mutual Fund Survey* has a manager ratings box on its one-page fund reviews to give investors an idea of how that fund manager's performance ranks against those of his or her peers. Keep in mind that a fund is only going to do as well as the person or people who run it.

- *What is the quality of the stock portfolio?* How diversified is it? *Morningstar Mutual Funds* has a special securities section on its fund-data page to show what percentage of a fund's assets were invested in derivatives, which are regarded as risky securities.

- *What are the fund's expenses?* Check out a fund's expense ratio, which is the percentage of a fund's net assets going annually to cover management fees, transaction costs, administrative overhead, legal and auditing fees, and marketing costs (12b-1 fees). This information is listed in the prospectus under the heading "Annual Fund Operating Expenses." Compare expense ratios in similar funds since expenses can affect a fund's overall performance (see the table below for average expense ratios). For example, a $10,000 investment in two no-load funds, each earning nine percent over 20 years, would grow to $30,475 in the fund with a three-percent expense ratio and $45,840 in the fund with a one-percent expense ratio.

Type of Funds	*Average Expense Ratio*
Stock funds	1.5 %
Taxable bond funds	1.0
Tax-exempt municipal bond funds	0.75

- *What are the fund's transaction fees and services?* Compare sales and redemption fees, and shareholder services.

- *What funds are offered in specific plans?* Consider the mutual funds that are available to an investor if they are participating in any of the following plans.
    - — *401(k) payroll deduction plans.* Amounts are withheld from salaries and used to buy fund shares. Typically, there is no load.
    - — *Individual retirement accounts (IRAs).* Investors may contribute $2,000 of before-tax income each year to such ac-

counts. When money is eventually withdrawn at retirement, the investor may have a lower tax rate, thus saving on taxes.

— *403(b) plans.* This is a form of a payroll deduction plan for employees working at nonprofit entities.

— *Life insurance mutual fund plans.* There is a combination of life insurance with shares of a mutual fund. If the fund performs well, it pays the life insurance premiums. If not, the insured must pay the premiums.

.02 Market Indexes as Performance Benchmarks

One way to objectively measure a fund's performance is to compare it to similar groups of investments by using market indexes. Each fund's prospectus describes its strategy and objective and also lists relevant market indexes (see Exhibit 5). These market indexes are also found in the *Wall Street Journal, Barron's,* and *Investor's Business Daily.* First find the total average annual return for the 1-, 5-, and 10-year periods for the benchmark and compare those figures with the fund's returns for the exact same periods. Compare bid positive and negative differences between the two before making a decision about buying or staying in a fund.

Exhibit 5

Typical Market Indexes Used as Performance Benchmarks

Type of Mutual Fund	*Index for Benchmarking*
Domestic	
Growth stocks	S&P 500
Aggressive growth stocks	Value Line
Small company stocks . .	Russell 2000
Government bonds	Various Lehman Bros. Government/ Corporate Bond Indexes
Municipal bonds	Lehman Bros. Municipal Bond Index
International	
Global stocks.	Morgan Stanley International World Index, Morgan Stanley Europe, Australia, and the Europe, Australia, and Far East (EAFE) Indexes
Foreign bonds	Salomon Bros. Non-U.S. Dollar World Bond Index
Global bonds	Shearson World Bond Index

.03 Peer Group Rankings

Mutual fund peer group rankings compare the performance of funds with similar asset classes, strategies, objectives, and risk levels. A peer group is one objective source of information that can assist in picking a good fund. Typically, funds are first sliced into various categories based on their investment goals. Then each fund is ranked according to a chosen criteria (such as a five-year total return, risk, or risk-adjusted return) by where it falls among all funds in its category. For example, funds in the top 20 percent get a "1" ranking and the bottom 20 percent get a "5."

Morningstar rankings. Morningstar uses a proprietary system that measures a mutual fund's price and dividend performance as well as the risks taken by the fund management to get those results. The rankings are then made from comparing a fund against both its own category and the industry as a whole. Their system rates stock and bond funds from five stars (the best) to no stars (the worst or unrated). Thus, the best performing fund in a category that is in a weak market sector might get only two or three stars.

When choosing among mutual funds, investors can use Morningstar rankings to find potentially better-performing investments. Many brokerages and financial planning firms limit their clients' investments to five-star and four-star funds. But choosing a five-star fund over a three-star fund is not always the correct choice. Since Morningstar's rankings reflect past performance, that often slants the reviews toward funds with recently successful investment styles.

In addition, within each category—especially containing a poorly performing sector—the highest rated fund may have succeeded by limiting its exposure to certain risks. If an investor believes that an out-of-favor market sector is ready to return, he or she might want to buy a fund with a lower rating that is more fully invested in that sector.

Other fund rankings. Before buying or selling a fund, an investor should consult other fund-watching sources. *Lipper Mutual Fund Rankings* and *Value Line Mutual Fund Survey* are two important sources. Magazines, such as *Business Week, Fortune, Forbes,* and *Money,* all print periodic analyses of individual funds and their rankings, as do many newsletters and newspapers.

.04 Risk-Reducing Strategies

In a bearish market, minimizing or spreading risks is particularly important. Below are five proven risk-reducing strategies for making money in mutual funds.

1. *Shoot for low-cost funds.* Especially in difficult times, fees and expenses will loom larger, deepening losses and prolonging subsequent recoveries.

2. *Build a well-balanced, diversified portfolio.* Sensible diversification will spread (or minimize) risks.

3. *Divide money among fund managers with different styles and philosophies.* Funds with differing styles will take turns outperforming, and being outperformed by, those with other styles. In a nutshell, diversify across mutual funds or a family of funds.

4. *Concentrate on short- or intermediate-term bond funds.* Typically, the longer the maturity of the bonds in a fund's portfolio, the greater the fund's return—but also the deeper its losses as interest rates rise.

5. *Use the dollar-cost averaging method.* Investing a fixed amount of money at regular intervals keeps an investor from committing their whole savings at a market peak. When a fund's NAV drops, the next automatic investment picks up more of the low-prices shares, cutting the total average cost per share and raising the ultimate gain.

Dollar-cost averaging. Dollar-cost averaging is an investment strategy designed to take advantage of the market's long-term upward bias while reducing risk over time. It simply means that one invests the same amount of money on a regular schedule, whatever the market price. It eliminates the need to predict share-price movements and to figure out the right time to buy, and it protects an investor from putting too much money into the market at just the wrong time. Under this strategy, an investor buys more shares when the share price of a fund is down, and fewer shares when the price of the fund is high, which can potentially lower the average cost per share. While lowering one's cost reduces an investment's downside risk, it also ensures that the entire portfolio will not be purchased at temporarily inflated prices.

Dollar-cost averaging has been most effective for mutual fund investing, whose typically small investment minimums make it easy to implement this strategy in a cost-effective way. Many funds and brokerages allow such purchases through direct deductions from investors' checking accounts or paychecks.

An investor may unknowingly be using this strategy as part of their employer-sponsored savings plan, such as a 401(k) retirement program. Many of these benefit plans routinely make equal purchases of assets at set periods, quietly accomplishing dollar-cost averaging.

Dollar-cost averaging will work as long as prices of the fund targeted by the strategy rise over the long haul. Exhibit 6 shows how dollar cost-averaging works for a no-load mutual fund. Exhibits 7 and 8 then compare the results of that same dollar investment using two other strategies: a lump-sum, up-front investment and a lump-sum investment after waiting to save.

Exhibit 6

Dollar-Cost Averaging Investment

Investment Period	*Amount Invested*	*Share Price*	*Shares Purchased*	*Total Shares Purchased*	*Current Market Value*
1	$ 100	$ 12.50	8	8	$ 100.00
2	100	8.00	12.5	20.5	$ 164.00
3	100	10.00	10	30.5	$ 305.00
4	100	8.00	12.5	43	$ 344.00
5	100	10.00	10	53	$ 530.00
6	100	12.50	8	61	$ 762.50
7	100	14.28	7	68	$ 971.04
8	100	12.50	8	76	$ 950.00
9	100	16.67	6	82	$1,366.94
10	100	20.00	5	87	$1,740.00
Total	$1,000	$ 124.45	87.0		

Where:

Average Share Price =
Total Share Price ÷ Total Investment Periods =
$124.45 ÷ 10 = $12.45

Average Share Cost =
Total Amount Invested ÷ Total Shares Purchased =
$1,000 ÷ 87 = $11.49

Current Market Value =
Total Shares Purchased × Current Share Price =
87 × $20 = $1,740

Exhibit 7

Lump-Sum, Up-Front Investment

Investment Period	*Amount Invested*	*Share Price*	*Shares Purchased*	*Total Shares Purchased*	*Current Market Value*
1	$1,000	$ 12.50	80	80	$1,000.00
2–9	0	11.49 (Avg.)	0	80	$ 919.20
10	0	20.00	0	80	$1,600.00
Total	$1,000	$ 124.45	80		

Where:

Average Share Price =
Total Share Price ÷ Total Investment Periods =
$124.45 ÷ 10 = $12.45

Average Share Cost =
Total Amount Invested ÷ Total Shares Purchased =
$1,000 ÷ 80 = $12.50

Current Market Value =
Total Shares Purchased × Current Share Price =
80 × $20 = $1,600

Exhibit 8

Lump-Sum Investment After Waiting to Save $1,000

Investment Period	*Amount Invested*	*Share Price*	*Shares Purchased*	*Total Shares Purchased*	*Current Market Value*
10	$1,000	$ 20.00	50	50	$1,000

Where:

Average Share Price =
Total Share Price ÷ Total Investment Periods =
$20.00 ÷ 1 = $20.00

Average Share Cost =
Total Amount Invested ÷ Total Shares Purchased =
$1,000 ÷ 50 = $20.00

Current Market Value =
Total Shares Purchased × Current Share Price =
50 × $20 = $1,000

Note that by the process of dollar-cost averaging shown in Exhibit 6, the investor in this scenario has purchased 87 shares, now worth $20 apiece, for a total market value of $1,740 ($20 × 87 shares). Yet only $1,000 was invested over the period. In other words, the average share cost of $11.49 is lower than the average market price ($12.45) of the fund's shares during the periods in which they were accumulated. So money was made through this process because more shares were purchased when they were cheap and fewer shares were purchased when they were dear.

In some circumstances, however, dollar-cost averaging can result in high transaction costs that can lower returns over time. That is why mutual funds, which often charge either no sales fee or a flat commission, are a popular way to implement this strategy.

.05 Tax Considerations

Unless an investor is in a tax-deferred IRA or a tax-free bond fund, the capital gains from mutual fund investing are taxable. Capital gains distributions usually come once during the year, typically in December. Also, if shares are purchased right before a distribution, the investor can be caught in a tax bind. A portion of the price paid will be returned as a taxable gain.

In general, a fund that turns over securities frequently in pursuit of a high return may generate more taxable gains than one that holds onto securities that are climbing in value. For this reason, *Consumer Reports* includes in their ratings a column ranking "tax efficiency." Below are some common tax tips for mutual fund investing.

- Never buy shares of a mutual fund late in the year without going over its distribution, or "ex-dividend," date.
- Try to sell the shares with the highest original cost.
- Check out tax consequences when moving money from one fund to another. Such switches are viewed as a taxable event by the IRS.
- Use tax efficiency as an added screening device. Try to pick funds that rate high in tax efficiency.

¶ 2421 Sources of Information on Mutual Funds

With 6,000-plus mutual funds in existence today, there is not one source that will satisfy all information needs completely. The following are important sources of mutual fund information—many libraries have them available.

.01 Books

While there are many entire books devoted just to listing sources of information on investments such as mutual funds, some of the most frequently used are the following:

- *Mutual Fund Fact Book.* Washington, D.C.: The Investment Company Institute. Lists most mutual funds broken down by investment objective, statistics on specific funds, background on trends in the mutual fund industry, and brief mutual fund term definitions.
- *A Guide to Mutual Funds* by Wiesenberger Investment Companies Service. Boston: Warren, Gorham & Lamont. Lists most mutual funds broken down by investment objective, statistics on specific funds, background on trends in the mutual fund industry, and brief mutual fund term definitions.
- *The Individual Investor's Guide to No-Load Mutual Funds.* Chicago: The American Association of Individual Investors. This classic guide provides investment objective, operating statistics, and various performance measures, covering 436 mutual funds.
- *Investor's Directory and No-Load Mutual Fund Resource List.* New York: No-Load Mutual Fund Association.

- *The Investor's Guide to Closed-End Funds.* Miami: Thomas J. Herzfeld Advisors, Inc. Excellent publication providing a description of various fund characteristics, covering over 160 traded closed-end funds on the NYSE, AMEX, and OTC markets.
- *The Complete Guide to Closed-End Funds.* Chicago: International Publishing Corporation. Excellent publication providing a description of various fund characteristics, covering over 160 traded closed-end funds on the NYSE, AMEX, and OTC markets.
- *Value Line Investment Survey.* New York: Value Line Publishing, Inc. This loose-leaf book revises each fund's information quarterly.

.02 Periodicals

While mutual funds will provide their own detailed publications, such as the fund prospectus, there are many definitive newspapers, magazines, and newsletters that are full of mutual fund information. Some of the more popular and useful include the following:

Newspapers. The *Wall Street Journal* and *Barron's* are subscribed to by most libraries.

Magazines. Readily available on most newsstands are *Money, Forbes,* and *Kiplinger's Personal Finance.* Special mutual fund editions are often published by these magazines once or twice a year, rating mutual funds on performance and risk.

Internet. Many financial and investment websites offer ways for investors to quickly screen for mutual funds that mirror their investment philosophy. Current and historical quotes are also available at many sites. The best way to find specific information is to use a search engine, such as google.com. A list of popular websites for mutual funds is available in Chapter 30.

Chapter 25
International Investing

¶ 2501 Overview

As an investor learns more about portfolio management and mutual funds, it becomes increasingly clear that there are advantages to holding a broad range of investment vehicles. In this chapter, you will see that risk can further be reduced by holding securities issued in foreign markets.

Global investing involves the direct or indirect acquisition of foreign securities by individuals or institutions without any control over or participation in the management of the foreign companies. Interest in overseas equities has increased notably in the recent years, spurred by the strong performance of markets abroad and relatively easy availability of overseas investment vehicles for U.S. investors.

¶ 2505 Advantages of Global Investing

An investor can derive a number of important benefits from expanding the horizon of his portfolio beyond his home country: a far greater universe for stock selection, potentially greater returns, and an opportunity to reduce risk exposure. In addition, changes in currency relationships, while a double-edged sword, can enhance appreciation and offset part of the impact of price declines in foreign equity positions.

.01 Broader Stock Selection

Global investment provides you with a much bigger pool of investment opportunities from which to choose. U.S. stocks accounted for only 36.2 percent of the world's total stock market capitalization. Consequently, an investor who focuses solely on domestic issues will miss nearly two-thirds of the investment opportunities in the world.

.02 Higher Prospective Returns

Global investing offers more opportunities for achieving higher returns. Non-U.S. stocks now account for more than half the value of all global equity securities. Recent financial studies show that investors who hold a blend of foreign and U.S. stocks receive higher returns—at lower risk—than those who are fully invested in U.S. stocks.

.03 Reduction of Risk

Adding international investments to a portfolio of U.S. securities diversifies and reduces your risk. This reduction of risk will be enhanced because international investments are much less influenced by the U.S. economy, and the correlation to U.S. investments is much less. Foreign markets sometimes follow different cycles than the U.S. market, and from each other.

Although foreign stocks can be riskier than domestic issues, supplementing a domestic portfolio with a foreign component can actually reduce your portfolio's overall volatility. The reason is that by being diversified across many different economies, which are at different points in the economic cycle, downturns in some markets may be offset by superior performance in others. There is considerable evidence that global diversification reduces systematic risk (beta) because of the relatively low correlations between returns on U.S. and foreign securities.

Exhibit 1 illustrates this, comparing the risk reduction through diversification within the United States to that obtainable through global diversification. A fully diversified U.S. portfolio is only 27 percent as risky as a typical individual stock, while a globally diversified portfolio appears to be about 12 percent as risky as a typical individual stock. This represents about 44 percent less than the U.S. figure.

Exhibit 1

Risk Reduction Through National and International Diversification

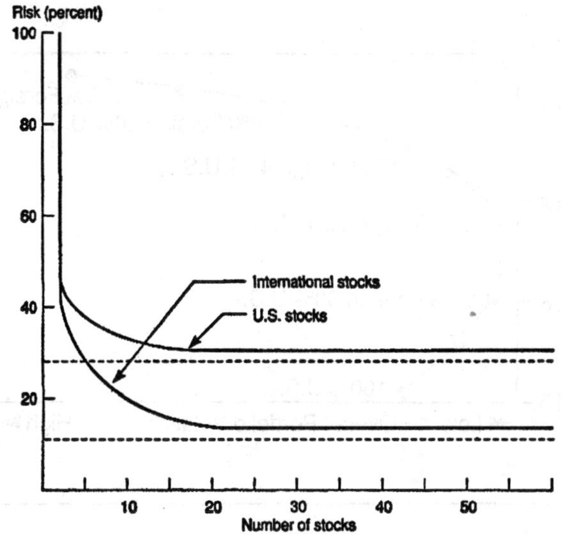

Exhibit 2 demonstrates the effect over the past 10 years. Notice how adding a small percentage of foreign stocks to a domestic portfolio actually decreased its overall risk while increasing the overall return. The lowest level of volatility came from a portfolio with about 30 percent foreign stocks and 70 percent U.S. stocks. And, in fact, a portfolio with 60 percent foreign holdings and only 40 percent U.S. holdings actually approximated the risk of a 100 percent domestic portfolio, yet the average annual return was over two percentage points greater.

Exhibit 2

How Foreign Stocks Have Benefited a Domestic Portfolio

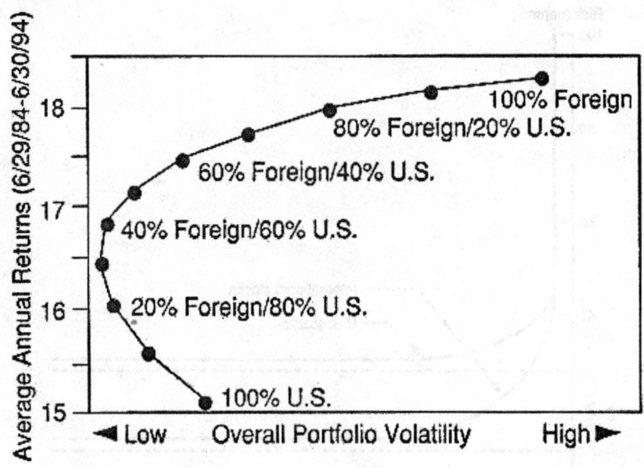

¶ 2510 Risks in Investing Globally

The advantages of lower risk must be balanced against other risks associated with foreign securities. Risks that are inherent in international investing are: currency and political risks in addition to the risks of emerging markets, economies, and companies.

.01 *Currency (or Foreign Exchange) Risk*

When you invest in a foreign market, the return on the foreign investment in terms of the U.S. dollar depends not only on the return on the foreign market in terms of local currency but also on the change in the exchange rate between the local currency and U.S. dollar. Since the exchange rates among major currencies have been volatile in recent years, exchange rate uncertainty has often been mentioned as one of the potential barriers to international investment.

For example, a strong dollar, meaning that foreign currency buys less dollars, would push down foreign returns of the U.S. investor. The following example illustrates how a change in the dollar affects the return on a foreign investment.

Example 1. You purchased bonds of a German firm paying 12-percent interest. You will earn that rate, assuming interest is paid and in marks. What if you are paid in dollars? As Exhibit 3 shows, you must then convert marks to dollars before the payout has any value to you. Suppose that the dollar appreciated 10 percent against the mark during the year after purchase. (A currency appreciates when acquiring one of its units requires more units of a foreign currency.) In this example, one mark acquired .616 dollars, and later, one mark acquired only .554 dollars; at the new exchange rate, it would take 1.112 (.616/.554) marks to acquire .616 dollars. Thus, the dollar has appreciated while the mark has depreciated. Now, your return realized in dollars is only 10.91 percent. The adverse movement in the foreign exchange rate—the dollar's appreciation—reduced your actual yield.

Exhibit 3

Exchange Risk and Foreign Investment Yield

Transaction	*Marks*	*Exchange Rate: No. of Dollars per 1 Mark*	*Dollars*
On 1/1/20X2, purchased one German bond with a 12% coupon rate	500	$.6051	$302.55
On 12/31/20X2, expected interest received	60	.6051	36.31
Expected yield	12%		12%
On 12/31/20X2, actual interest received	60	.5501*	33.01
Realized yield	12%		10.91%**

*$.6051/(1 + .1) = $.6051/1.1 = $.5501
**$33.01/$302.55 = .1091 = 10.91%

Currency risks can be hedged by borrowing in the local currency or selling it forward. However, this type of tool is too costly and impractical for individual investors. *Note:* Choosing countries with strong currencies and investing in international mutual funds could be an answer to minimizing currency risk.

Note, however, that currency swings work both ways. A weak dollar would boost foreign returns of U.S. investors. Exhibit 4 is a quick reference to judge how currency swings affect your foreign returns.

Exhibit 4

Currency Changes vs. Foreign Returns in U.S. Dollars

Foreign Return	*Change in Foreign Currency against the Dollar* 20%	10%	0%	-10%	-20%
20%	44%	32%	20%	8%	-4%
10	32	21	10	-1	-12
0	20	10	0	-10	-20
-10	8	-1	-10	-19	-28
-20	-4	-12	-20	-28	-36

.02 Political (or Sovereign) Risk

Political or sovereign risk is viewed by many as a major obstacle to international investment. Clearly, political factors are a major determinant of the attractiveness for investment in any country. Countries viewed as likely candidates for internal political upheaval or with a pronounced trend toward elimination of the private sector will be unattractive to all investors, foreign and domestic alike. There is no reason to believe that local investors will be systematically optimistic regarding their country's future. When political risks increase significantly, such investors will attempt to diversify from the home market as rapidly as will foreigners. As a result, prices will fall until someone will be satisfied to hold the securities of a risky country.

In light of political risk, how risky are investments in foreign markets? There is, of course, no easy answer. Political instability, limited track records, and poor statistics all make gauging risk extremely difficult. Several companies try to evaluate the risk in some of the countries that are receiving the most attention from foreign investors. Listed at the end of this chapter are sources of country risk information.

However, if domestic investors are prevented from liquidating their domestic holdings or from purchasing foreign assets by national regulations or moral suasion, the market prices may not reflect generally shared views of the political situation. Of course, if foreign investors are constrained by the same regulations, then all investors lose. A careful evaluation of the relative flexibility of domestic and foreign investment, therefore, is a key element in determining whether political risks jeopardize cross-border holdings. The risk of currency controls is one of the few political risks that is borne primarily by foreign investors.

In some cases, political risks might even favor foreign investors relative to domestic investors because risks are domestic phenomena that can be diversified away globally. As a result, they will have a greater impact on the risk of a domestic investor whose portfolio is concentrated in home assets than on a globally diversified investor. Accordingly, domestic shares might well be more attractive to foreign than domestic investors in periods of perceived high political uncertainty.

.03 Institutional Obstacles

A recurrent objection to global diversification is that the practical scope for foreign investing is limited. Many markets are perceived to be small, less liquid, and less efficient than those of the United States. Undoubtedly, there are many foreign stocks whose total capitalization and turnover are too limited for them to be of interest to most U.S. institutional investors. Further, in many markets—particularly the Japanese and West German—market capitalizations are often misleading indicators of an issue's marketability because a large proportion of the shares might be owned by banks, holding companies, or other concerns.

However, these considerations do not necessarily imply that these markets are less attractive to foreign institutional investors than to local investors. In fact, just the opposite might be the case. Domestic investors who depend primarily on their own market for liquidity and diversification are likely to be more constrained by these limitations than international investors who, through diversification, can virtually eliminate the nonmarket risk unique to individual companies, even if they hold only a small number of shares in each market. International investors also do not have to rely on any single market for liquidity and, as a result, can take a longer view in regard to each market and security, even though they wish to realize profits within a reasonable period in each market and currency.

Another concern is related to the market efficiency of foreign markets. An efficient market is one where new information is quickly reflected in securities' prices, and hence it is unlikely that any single investor will beat the market. Although less efficiency can be desirable from an active investment manager's perspective because it implies that superior performance is possible, it also puts the international investor at a disadvantage relative to the domestic investor, who has greater knowledge and better information. Studies of foreign markets suggest that they generally can be considered to be efficient in the sense that prices adjust rapidly to new information and that most professional managers are unable to consistently outperform the market.

There are several institutional obstacles that can make international investing costly, undesirable, or, in some cases, impossible. They include formal barriers to international transactions, such as exchange controls, double taxation of portfolio income for certain investors in particular countries, and restrictions on ownership of securities according to the nationality of the investor. These obstacles also include informal barriers, such as the difficulty of obtaining information about a market, differences in reporting practices that make international comparisons difficult, and subtle impediments to foreign investment based on traditional practice.

A major implication of the existence of such obstacles is that even if one assumes an integrated, efficient world capital market, investors with different legal domiciles or tax situations might want to hold different investments. However, it is difficult to determine by how much such portfolios should differ from the world optimal market portfolio in the absence of such obstacles. This would depend on the balancing of the effect of the obstacles against the gains from more complete diversification.

¶ 2515 Ways to Invest Globally

The advantages of international investing can be reaped from participation in international money and capital markets, direct or indirect.

.01 Purchasing Foreign Stock Directly

A U.S. investor can place an order to purchase foreign securities through a U.S. brokerage firm, which will instruct its respective branch office or a local broker to buy the stock. One advantage of owning ordinary shares is a much larger selection of foreign stocks from which to choose. Also, trading is usually more active, resulting in greater liquidity.

The direct purchase of foreign securities suffers from the following difficulties:

1. It involves high transaction costs in terms of brokerage commissions and additional costs associated with the international clearing process.
2. It involves a lot of information and research costs. Further, the information is often difficult to obtain and its reliability is questionable.
3. An investor must be familiar with the financial reporting and disclosure standards of the country in which the stock is issued.
4. When owning foreign shares, U.S. investors are subject to the rules and regulations of the foreign stock exchanges. Moreover, delays in settlement can occur.

How may your account be handled? Like domestic stock purchases, the foreign stock purchased may be registered in your name or it may be registered in "Street" name—the name of the broker who initiates the transaction. In the former case, you must arrange to open custodian accounts at banks in the countries in which you plan to buy securities. This process can be simplified by opening a global custody account with a multinational commercial bank. This type of account enables you to utilize the foreign subsidiaries of a single institution for the safekeeping of all securities rather than having to establish accounts at separate banks around the world. Many U.S. brokers also establish their own global custody accounts overseas to act as receiving and delivery agents.

Many foreign nations impose a withholding tax on dividends, though these taxes vary from country to country. U.S. investors can file for a refund on this tax if tax treaties exist between the United States and the other nation involved. Most foreign shares can be held in either registered or bearer form, though in some countries foreign investors may only own stock in bearer form. If the shares are registered, the investor will receive dividends in local currency (less withholding taxes) and notices from the company in the local language. If the securities are held in bearer form, the investor can receive dividends (after deduction of withholding taxes) in U.S. dollars through the agent bank.

The following example illustrates how to determine a rough price for foreign securities in U.S. dollars. This illustration is based on hypothetical numbers.

> ***Example 2.*** The foreign exchange rates quoted in newspapers are interbank rates. To determine the rate for stock transactions, as a rule of thumb, add two percent to the interbank rate. To determine a rough price for foreign securities in U.S. dollars, you must multiply the price by the applicable exchange rate. For example, in Exhibit 5, in the case of Ajinomodo closing at 1,020 yen, for the Japanese yen, the exchange rate is \$.011204 (given). Two percent added to this gives you an estimated exchange rate of \$.011428 (\$.011204 + .000224).
>
> If you multiply the price of the stock in foreign currency by the approximate U.S. equivalent of yen, you obtain a rough per-share price of the stock in U.S. dollars.

1,020	Yen (price of stock)
× \$.011428	U.S.\$ (rough exchange value of \$1)
\$11.6566	U.S.\$ (price of stock in U.S. dollars)

Exhibit 5

Foreign Securities Quotations

Closing Prices
JAPAN (Japanese Yen)

	Cur.	*Prev.*
Ajinomto	1020	1040
Alps	971	1000
Amada	855	900
Anitsu	1030	1030
Asahi Chem	600	614
Asahi Glas	1050	1050
Bank of Tokyo	1300	1340
Banyu	920	949
Bridgestone	1300	1310
Brother	472	504

American Depositary Receipts (ADRS). In recent years, there has been an increasing trend of the shares of many firms being listed on foreign exchanges. This cross-listing is usually accomplished by depositary receipts. American Depository Receipts, or ADRs, are certificates that represent stock in foreign companies. The process of ADRs works as follows: a foreign company places shares in trust with a U.S. bank, which in turn issues depository receipts to U.S. investors. The ADRs, then, are claims to shares of stock and are essentially the same as shares. The depository bank performs all clerical functions—issuing annual reports, keeping a shareholder ledger, paying and maintaining dividend records, etc.—allowing the ADRs to trade in markets just like domestic securities trade. ADRs are traded on the NYSE, AMEX, and OTC markets as a share in stock, minus the voting rights. Examples of ADRs are Hanson, Cannon, and Smithkline Beecham.

ADRs have become an increasingly convenient and popular vehicle for investing internationally. Investors do not have to go through foreign brokers, and information on company operations is usually available in English. Therefore, ADRs are good substitutes for direct foreign investment. They are bought and sold with U.S. dollars and pay their dividends in dollars. Further, the trading and settlement costs are waived that apply in some foreign markets. The certificates are issued by depository banks (for example, the Bank of New York). To purchase ADRs, contact your stockbroker or call Bank of New York, which is the largest seller of ADRs, at (212) 815-2000.

ADRs, however, are not for everyone. Disadvantages are the following:

1. ADRs carry an element of currency risk. For example, an ADR based on the stock of a British company would tend to lose in value when the dollar strengthens against the British pound, if other factors were held constant. This is because as the pound weakens, less U.S. dollars are required to buy the same shares of a U.K. company.

2. Some thinly traded ADRs can be harder to buy and sell. This could make them more expensive to purchase than the quoted price.

3. You may face problems obtaining reliable information on the foreign companies. It may be difficult to do your own research in selecting foreign stocks. For one thing, there is a shortage of data: the annual report may be all that is available, and its reliability is questionable. Furthermore, in many instances, foreign financial reporting and accounting standards are substantially different from those accepted in the United States.

4. ADRs can be either sponsored or unsponsored. Many ADRS are not sponsored by the underlying companies. Non-sponsored ADRs oblige you to pay certain fees to the depository bank. The return is reduced accordingly.

5. There are a limited number of issues available, for only a small fraction of the foreign stocks traded internationally. As of December 2002, over 2200 ADRs were available in the United States. Many interesting and rewarding investment opportunities exist in shares with no ADRs.

.02 Buying Foreign Bonds

All international bonds fall within two generic classifications, Eurobonds and foreign bonds. The distinction between categories is based on whether the borrower is a domestic or a foreign resident, and whether the issue is denominated in the local currency or a foreign currency.

What is the difference between a eurobond and foreign bond? A *Eurobond* is underwritten by an international syndicate of banks and other securities firms and is sold exclusively in countries other than the country in whose currency the issue is denominated. For example, a bond issued by a U.S. corporation, denominated in U.S. dollars, but sold to investors in Europe and Japan (not to investors in the United States), would be a Eurobond. Eurobonds are issued by multinational corporations, large domestic corporations, sovereign governments, governmental enterprises, and international institutions. They are offered simultaneously in a number of different national capital markets but not in the capital market of the country, nor to residents of the country, in whose currency the bond is denominated. Almost all Eurobonds are in bearer form with call provisions and sinking funds.

A *foreign bond* is underwritten by a syndicate composed of members from a single country, sold principally within that country, and denominated in the currency of that country. The issuer, however, is from another country. A bond issued by a Swedish corporation, denominated in dollars, and sold in the United States to U.S. investors by U.S. investment bankers, would be a foreign bond. Foreign bonds have nicknames: foreign bonds sold in the United States are "Yankee bonds"; those sold in Japan are "Samurai bonds"; foreign bonds sold in the United Kingdom are "Bulldogs."

Exhibit 6 specifically reclassifies foreign bonds from a U.S. investor's perspective.

Exhibit 6

Foreign Bonds to U.S. Investors

		Sales In the United States	*Sales* In Foreign Countries
Issuer	→ Domestic	Domestic bonds	Eurodollar bonds
	→ Foreign	Yankee bonds	Foreign currency bonds; Eurodollar bonds

Foreign currency bonds are issued by foreign governments and foreign corporations, denominated in their own currency. As with domestic bonds, such bonds are priced inversely to movements in the interest rate of the country in whose currency the issue is denominated. For example, the values of German bonds fall if German interest rates rise. In addition, values of bonds denominated in foreign currencies will fall (or rise) if the dollar appreciates (or depreciates) relative to the denominated currency. Indeed, investing in foreign currency bonds is really a play on the dollar. If the dollar and foreign interest rates fall, investors in foreign currency bonds could make a nice return. It should be pointed out, however, that if both the dollar and foreign interest rates rise, the investors will be hit with a very significant loss.

What are the advantages of foreign convertibles? In addition to participation in the appreciation of overseas stocks, foreign convertibles enable investors to earn greater current returns while incurring less risk compared with the underlying common stocks. Their yields are usually higher than those provided by the dividends of the underlying common stocks. Moreover, the conversion premium (the difference between the cost of acquiring the underlying stock through the conversion provisions of the bond and the current share price) on these bonds is normally quite low, allowing an investor to pick up this yield advantage at a relatively low cost. Most Japanese convertibles are issued with five percent premiums, for example.

Because of their hybrid nature, convertible bonds have less downside risk than the underlying common, i.e., the fixed coupon provides a price floor determined by the yields available on comparable straight debt issues. Also, convertible securities are senior to common stocks. In the event of bankruptcy, holders of convertible securities have priority over stockholders in claiming the assets of a firm. In addition, coupon payments on Euroconvertibles are not subject to withholding taxes, while the dividend payments on the common stocks usually are.

What does the yield depend on? The yield on a foreign bond, for a U.S. investor, will depend on both the local bond market of the issuing company and how the currency in which the bond is denominated appreciates (depreciates) against the U.S. dollar. International bond funds would be an excellent route. It provides diversification benefits since it has a low correlation between the returns of U.S. government bonds and those of most major foreign bond markets.

.03 Investing in International Money Markets

A market for short-term financial claims performs the essential service of enabling financial investment to be transformed into real investment. A well-developed money market is able to attract savings and channel them to their most efficient uses, making funds more cheaply and freely available to the business sector. Every country that has banks which accept short-term deposits (time deposits) has a money market of sorts. As the economy grows, a demand appears for a wider range of financial instruments, such as commercial paper, acceptances, and government securities, and these would be traded in a secondary market where financial claims could be freely bought and sold. As the economy becomes open through international transactions, the national money market becomes linked to international money markets just as the national capital market has its linkages with international capital markets.

Ways of investing in international money markets. There are three major ways of investing in international money markets. The first approach is to purchase foreign short-term money market instruments directly. By investing in foreign money market assets denominated in the foreign currency, the full impact of currency variation is reflected in returns along with the yield of the money market investments. If, for example, interest rates are higher in England and a U.S. investor thinks sterling will strengthen or remain on the same exchange rate with the dollar, then an investment denominated in the sterling currency would make sense.

The second approach would be through the Eurocurrency market where funds are intermediated outside the country of the currency in which the funds are denominated. Thus, the Eurocurrency market comprises financial institutions that compete for dollar time deposits and make dollar loans outside the United States, for example. An example of Eurocurrency markets would be that a U.S. investor purchases Eurodollar CDs from a bank in London.

Eurocurrency banking is not subject to domestic banking regulation, such as reserve requirements and interest-rate restrictions. This enables Eurobanks to operate more efficiently, cheaply, and competitively than their domestic counterparts and to offer slightly better terms to both borrowers and lenders. Therefore Eurodollar deposit rates are somewhat higher, and effective lending rates a little lower, than they are in the U.S. money market.

The third approach is to place foreign currency deposits with U.S. banks in the United States. This enables U.S. investors to conveniently take advantage of the expected weakness of the dollar relative to the currency in which the deposit is denominated.

.04 Buying Shares of U.S.-Based Multinational Corporations

Many investors achieve a reasonable degree of global diversification when investing in multinational corporations (MNCs). Companies such as IBM, Coca Cola, and General Motors do a considerable portion of their business outside the United States. Further, buying shares of MNCs not only achieve global diversification but also avoid high transaction costs and information problems faced by investors directly purchasing foreign securities.

An MNC owns, controls, and manages income, generating assets in a variety of countries. Thus an MNC can be viewed as representing a portfolio of globally diversified cash flows originating in different countries and currencies. Since the cash flows of an MNC are likely to be strongly influenced by foreign factors, it has been suggested that you may be able to achieve global diversification in income indirectly in the shares of MNCs.

However, several studies have found that the share price behavior of MNCs is nearly indistinguishable from that of purely domestic firms. The share prices of MNCs show far more sensitivity to the index of their home markets than to foreign market indices. Thus, investing in domestic MNCs would not be an effective means of global diversification of share/price behavior.

.05 *Investing in International Mutual Funds*

You may find mutual funds attractive because they offer the services of full-time professional managers, safekeeping of securities, the chance to invest in terms of dollar amounts (as funds offer both full and fractional shares), and the ability to reduce the amount invested without reducing diversity. Coupled with such benefits, there has been a significant increase in international mutual funds as more investors are diversifying globally.

Global portfolio diversification via mutual funds. International mutual funds are probably the best way for you to achieve global diversification, either on a broad basis or by targeting specific countries or geographical regions. It is a relatively easy, low cost way and takes a lot of different factors out of investing in foreign securities.

In general, mutual funds are classified as stock funds, bond funds, and money market funds, based on the securities invested. Thus, global and international funds are made up of all of the above three, though international money market funds are a relatively recent development.

Features of the various types of international funds.

Global and international stock funds. In terms of geographical diversity, international stock funds can be divided into four groups, ranging from highly diversified to highly focused: global, international, regional, and single-country funds.

- *Global funds* can invest anywhere in the world, including the United States. However, most global funds keep the majority of their assets in foreign markets. Global funds are worth considering if you are unsure about how much to allocate to foreign markets. The fund's foreign allocation is not based on the specific circumstances of any single investor.

- *International (or foreign) funds* invest only in foreign stocks. Because these funds focus only on foreign markets, they allow investors to control what portion of their personal portfolio they want to allocate to non-U.S. stocks.

- International funds with a *regional focus* allow investors to narrow their sights on a particular region. There are a number of European funds, Asian-Pacific, and Latin American funds. Most regional funds are closed-end funds, although there are some open-end regional funds. International index funds are being introduced, such as Vanguard's European Stock Index Fund.

- *Single-country funds* are the most focused and therefore by far the most aggressive foreign stock funds. Almost all single-country funds are closed-end funds (exceptions are the Japan Fund and French Fund). This exaggerates their aggressiveness because single-country (and regional) closed-end funds have been known to sell at both large discounts and premiums to their net asset value. Thus, closed-end single-country funds are well suited for only the most sophisticated investors who are confident in their ability to assess the potential for a specific market as well as the trends in the fund's stock price versus its net asset value. *Note:* Because of their broad focus, global and international funds are less risky and therefore a better choice for the average investor than a single country or a regional fund.

International bond funds. Compared with international stock funds, international bond funds are limited in the number of available funds as well as in the performance history. In selecting international bond funds, consider the following factors: open-end vs. closed-end, average maturity, country focus, and currency risk. It is often suggested that you should stay short-term (typically, four years or less) and locate a fund that *hedges* some of the foreign exchange risk and invests in countries with currencies that move with the U.S. dollar.

International money market funds. International money market funds are a relatively recent phenomenon. Many funds invest only in dollar-denominated foreign money market instruments, thereby eliminating the currency risk. If you are a currency risk-averse investor, you should put your money in international money market funds.

Hedged funds. In order to minimize an exposure to currency risk, many funds try to hedge. It is a matter of degree. In general, international short-term bond funds usually hedge most of the currency risk while longer-term funds have substantial exposure. Funds use currency options, futures, and elaborate cross currency hedges, but the most effective hedges are expensive.

How do you select mutual funds? In evaluating a mutual fund, domestic or foreign, you should look at the objectives of the fund, the fund's management and track record, the fund's expense ratio, and so on. It is important to note that when considering any mutual fund, you should realize that a big part of what you are buying is management. Therefore, continuity of management is important, as evidenced by consistent track records for at least five years.

The performance of foreign mutual funds must be measured against their peers and the correct market benchmarks. For example, a broadly diversified international fund should be compared with the EAFE index. On the other hand, the Japanese funds should be judged against each other as well as with the Nikkei average.

With closed-end funds, a well-diversified, multi-country fund that sells at a discount should be sought. But if you buy at a premium, make sure that it is at least the low-end of its range. Another fact to consider is: the fund's expense ratio relative to other comparable funds and relative to its premium or discount level.

¶ 2520 Sources of Information

.01 Country Risk

Various sources dealing with country risk (such as were *Euromoney* magazine's annual *Country Risk Rating*) are listed in Chapter 23.

.02 Foreign Firms

The following is a list of sources that provides addresses, phone numbers, area of business, officers, directors, and financial data:

- *Moody's International Manual,* published by Moody's Investment Service annually in two volumes with weekly updating.
- *International Directory of Corporate Affiliations,* published twice a year by National Register Publishing Co.
- *The International Corporate 1000,* published by Monitor Publishing Co. with annual updating.

.03 Some Useful Websites

The following Internet sites discuss global investing:

Web Address	*Primary Focus*
adr.com	ADR quotations.
cbs.marketwatch.com	General financial market information. Includes extensive list of global market, sector and bond indexes.
www.bankofny.com/adr	Educational material on the definition and trading of ADRs, along with a listing of all ADRs in the U.S. markets.
www.bloomberg.com	General financial market information, includes a listing of world indexes.
www.msci.com	Global investment information and index listings.
www.spglobal.com	Listing of S&P global indexes.

Part 8

Special Topics

Chapter 26

Risk Management, Financial Engineering, and Computer Software

¶ 2601 Overview

As businesses become increasingly complex, it is becoming more and more difficult for CEOs and directors to know what problems might lie in wait. Therefore, companies need to have someone systematically look for potential problems and design safeguards to minimize potential damage. With this in mind, most larger firms have designated "risk managers" who report to the chief financial officer, while the CFOs of smaller firms personally assume risk management responsibilities. In any event, risk management is becoming increasingly important. This chapter covers the basics of risk management, with particular emphasis on how derivatives can be used to hedge financial risks.

¶ 2605 Risk Management and Analysis

Risk management involves identifying risk exposure, analyzing risk, measuring potential loss, determining the best insurance strategy (or whether to self-insure), cost projections and control, volatility of operations, timing of adverse events, claims adjustment, proper cost allocation, and the use of risk management software.

Risks facing a business may negatively affect its reputation, bottom line, cost and availability of financing, credit rating, market price of stock, regulatory or legislative changes, and elimination of barriers to entry. An evaluation must be made of the trade-off between risk and return. A higher risk mandates a higher rate of return to justify taking the extra risk.

A risk program must be in place. The program must have built-in flexibility to adjust, as conditions require. The program must conform to the goals, objectives, and policies of the business.

The company must have a workable contingency plan, such as a recovery plan. Employees must be instructed what to do in such eventualities. Test runs should be practiced. Contingency plans must be updated periodically to incorporate new technologies, changing staff, and new areas of business activity. Areas of risk must be identified and corrective action taken to reduce those risks. Unusually high risk will not only have negative effects on earnings but might also place in question the continuity of the operation.

Models and quantitative approaches including actuarial techniques may be used to appraise potential catastrophic losses, product/service liability, intellectual property losses, and business interruption. Probability distributions should be arrived at of expected losses based on the model or quantitative technique used.

.01 Appraisal of Risk

The "red flags" of undue risk must be identified and controlled. "Red flags" include poor employee training and performance, inadequate planning, fragmentation, poor communication, lateness, improper focus, failure to observe government regulations or laws (e.g., the federal Comprehensive Environmental Response and Compensation and Liability Act covering the release and disposal of hazardous substances and wastes), overconfidence, and "hostile" attitudes.

When appraising a particular situation, evaluate the risk profile, financial status, and acceptable risk exposure. What is the entity's risk tolerance level? To what extent does the risk of a situation exceed predetermined maximum risk levels? Has management received proper approval to undertake the high-risk level? Has proper planning been performed to take into account the adverse effects on the business if things do not work out? For example, if losses are incurred that significantly exceed the entity's traditional insurance program, the company might be permanently crippled. Examples include a business interruption resulting from a terrorist bombing, loss of a major vendor, misinterpretation of law, or a product recall.

In appraising risk, consideration must be given to the company's liquidity and solvency position to withstand loss. A determination must be made of the costs associated with various risks. Risk should be evaluated and minimized. Risk may be reduced through the following means:

- Vertically integrate to reduce the price and supply risk of raw materials.
- Take out sufficient insurance coverage for possible asset and operating losses (including foreign risk protection). A lower trend in insurance expense to the asset insured may indicate inadequate coverage.

- Diversify activities, product/service line, market segments, customer bases, geographic areas, and investments.
- Sell to diversified industries to protect against cyclical turns in the economy.
- Sign a forward contract to take delivery of raw materials at fixed prices at a specified future date so the entity insulates itself from price increases.
- Enter into foreign currency futures contracts to lock in a fixed rate.
- Participate in joint ventures and partnerships with other companies. In so doing, obligations of the parties must be taken into account. For example, questions to be asked are: Which company is to absorb most of the losses? What are our company's duties and exposure under the agreement?
- Sell low-priced products as well as more expensive ones to protect against inflationary and recessionary periods.
- Change suppliers who prove unreliable.
- Take steps so the company is less susceptible to business cycles (e.g., inelastic demand products and negatively correlated products/services).
- Add products/services having different seasonal attractiveness and demand.
- Emphasize a piggyback product base (similar merchandise associated with the basic business).
- Balance the company's financing mix.

In analyzing the company's product/service line, determine:

- Extent of correlation between products. Positive correlation means high risk because the demand for all the products goes in the same direction. Negative correlation minimizes the risk. No correlation means indifference between products.
- Product demand elasticity equal to the percentage change in quantity relative to the percentage change in price. Elastic demand means that a minor change in price has a significant impact on quantity demanded. This indicates higher risk. Inelastic product demand minimizes risk because a change in price will have little effect on quantity demanded.

In analyzing the risk associated with multinational companies, compute:

- Total assets in high-risk foreign countries to total assets.
- High-risk foreign revenue to total revenue. High-risk revenue is based on risk ratings of companies in published sources (e.g., International Country Risk Guide).
- High-risk foreign revenue to net income.
- Percentage of earnings associated with foreign government contracts.
- Fluctuation in foreign exchange rates.

When evaluating risk, a number of questions must be answered:

- What is the internal process in place to reduce risk?
- What appraisal is being made of control aspects?
- Are controls effective?
- Do controls function as planned?
- Who is responsible for risk management?
- Is risk being managed properly to prevent fraud?
- What are the specific areas of risk vulnerability?
- Is financial and operational information being reported correctly?

.02 Fundamentals of Risk Management

The corporate financial manager needs to take into account the various types of risk the entity faces. For example, corporate risk may be in the form of overrelying on a few key executives or the underinsurance of assets. Industry risk may be the high technological environment, an industry scrutinized under the "public eye," or a capital-intensive business. Moving toward a variable cost-oriented business may minimize industry risk. Economic risk includes susceptibility to the business cycle. This risk may be reduced by having a low-priced substitute for a high-priced one.

Social risk occurs when a company experiences customer boycott or discrimination cases. A way to reduce this risk is to be engaged in community involvement and sensitivity training.

A company must properly instruct its personnel not to intrude with electronic mail, slander others, or commit libel. The company must carefully train and monitor staff to guard against possible infractions causing employee lawsuits or federal/local government investigation.

Political risk applies to relations with U.S. and local government agencies, and with foreign governments when operations are carried out overseas. This risk may be reduced through lobbying efforts and by avoiding activities or placing assets in high-risk foreign areas.

Environmental risk includes product lines and services susceptible to changes in the weather. Having counterseasonal goods and services or moving to another geographic location may reduce this risk. Multinational entities are susceptible to environmental risk, particularly in the former Iron Curtain countries. There are often problems with land and resource use, including pollution and hazardous waste. The acquiring company must be cautious of not only the cleanup costs but also associated penalties and fines. Prior to acquisition, the acquirer must be assured that there is a contract under which the seller will be responsible for all or part of the environmental obligations. A high-risk premium applies to corporate investments in countries with environmental problems. Insurance companies, for example, should reject potential clients that are not environmentally certified or fail to meet particular environmental norms. Banks need to be concerned with the collectibility of loans to companies with major environmental exposure. If a company is "dirty," it may have difficulty obtaining adequate insurance or loans. Further, the effect of impending government environmental laws on the business must be considered. Environmental problems and disasters may significantly reduce earnings.

Terrorism is also of concern to certain types of businesses. Security measures must be in place to guard against bombing. A determination must be made as to how the risks facing a business interact. A model must consider alternative scenarios.

There are some commonly used terms that describe different risks. Some of these risks can be mitigated or managed, and that is what risk management is all about.

1. *Pure risks* are risks that offer only the prospect of a loss. Examples include the risk that a plant will be destroyed by fire or that a product liability suit will result in a large judgment against the firm.

2. *Speculative risks* are situations that offer the chance of a gain but might result in a loss. Thus, investments in new projects and marketable securities involve speculative risks.

3. *Demand risks* are associated with the demand for a firm's products or services. Because sales are essential to all businesses, demand risk is one of the most significant risks that firms face.

4. *Input risks* are risks associated with input costs, including both labor and materials. Thus, a company that uses copper as a raw material in its manufacturing process faces the risk that the

cost of copper will increase and that it will not be able to pass this increase on to its customers.

5. *Financial risks* are risks that result from financial transactions. As we have seen, if a firm plans to issue new bonds, it faces the risk that interest rates will rise before the bonds can be brought to market. Similarly, if the firm enters into contracts with foreign customers or suppliers, it faces the risk that fluctuations in exchange rates will result in unanticipated losses.

6. *Property risks* are associated with destruction of productive assets. Thus, the threat of fire, floods, and riots imposes property risks on a firm.

7. *Personnel risks* are risks that result from employees' actions. Examples include the risks associated with employee fraud or embezzlement, or suits based on charges of age or sex discrimination.

8. *Environmental risks* include risks associated with polluting the environment. Public awareness in recent years, coupled with the huge costs of environmental cleanup, has increased the importance of this risk.

9. *Liability risks* are associated with product, service, or employee actions. Examples include the very large judgments assessed against asbestos manufacturers and some health care providers, as well as costs incurred as a result of improper actions of employees, such as driving corporate vehicles in a reckless manner.

10. *Insurable risks* are risks that can be covered by insurance. In general, property, personnel, environmental, and liability risks can be transferred to insurance companies. Note, though, that the *ability* to insure a risk does not necessarily mean that the risk *should be* insured. Indeed, a major function of risk management involves evaluating all alternatives for managing a particular risk, including self-insurance, and then choosing the optimal alternative.

Note that the risk classifications we used are somewhat arbitrary, and different classifications are commonly used in different industries. However, the list does give an idea of the wide variety of risks to which a firm can be exposed.

.03 An Approach To Risk Management

Firms often use the following process for managing risks.

1. *Identify the risks faced by the firm.* Here the risk manager identifies the potential risks faced by his or her firm.

2. *Measure the potential impact of each risk.* Some risks are so small as to be immaterial, whereas others have the potential for dooming the company. It is useful to segregate risks by potential impact and then to focus on the most serious threats.

3. *Decide how each relevant risk should be handled.* In most situations, risk exposure can be reduced through one of the following techniques:

   - Transfer the risk to an insurance company. Often, it is advantageous to insure against, hence transfer, a risk. However, insurability does not necessarily mean that a risk should be covered by insurance. In many instances, it might be better for the company to *self-insure,* which means bearing the risk directly rather than paying another party to bear it.

   - Transfer the function that produces the risk to a third party. For example, suppose a furniture manufacturer is concerned about potential liabilities arising from its ownership of a fleet of trucks used to transfer products from its manufacturing plant to various points across the country. One way to eliminate this risk would be to contract with a trucking company to do the shipping, thus passing the risks to a third party.

   - Purchase derivative contracts to reduce risk. As we indicated earlier, firms use derivatives to hedge risks. Commodity derivatives can be used to reduce input risks. For example, a cereal company may use corn or wheat futures to hedge against increases in grain prices. Similarly, financial derivatives can be used to reduce risks that arise from changes in interest rates and exchange rates.

   - Reduce the probability of occurrence of an adverse event. The expected loss arising from any risk is a function of both the probability of occurrence and the dollar loss if the adverse event occurs. In some instances, it is possible to reduce the probability that an adverse event will occur. For example, the probability that a fire will occur can be reduced by instituting a fire prevention program, by replacing old electrical wiring, and by using fire-resistant materials in areas with the greatest fire potential.

   - Reduce the magnitude of the loss associated with an adverse event. Continuing with the fire risk example, the dollar cost associated with a fire can be reduced by such actions as installing sprinkler systems, designing facilities with self-contained fire zones, and locating facilities close to a fire station.

- Totally avoid the activity that gives rise to the risk. For example, a company might discontinue a product or service line because the risks outweigh the rewards, as with the recent decision by Dow-Corning to discontinue its manufacture of silicon breast implants.

Note that risk management decisions, like all corporate decisions, should be based on a cost/benefit analysis for each feasible alternative. For example, suppose it would cost $50,000 per year to conduct a comprehensive fire safety-training program for all personnel in a high-risk plant. Presumably, this program would reduce the expected value of future fire losses. An alternative to the training program would be to place $50,000 annually in a reserve fund set aside to cover future fire losses. Both alternatives involve expected cash flows, and from an economic standpoint, the choice should be made on the basis of the lowest present value of future costs.

Thus, the same financial management techniques applied to other corporate decisions can also be applied to risk management decisions. Note, though, that if a fire occurs and a life is lost, the trade-off between fire prevention and expected losses may not sit well with a jury. The same thing holds true for product liability.

¶ 2610 Using Derivatives to Reduce Risks

Derivatives and their skillful use in risk management, broadly known as *financial engineering*, are a rapidly growing and important area of the financial landscape. This section discusses what derivatives are and how they can be used to help manage risk.

Companies are exposed to numerous risks related to interest rate, stock price, and exchange rate fluctuations in the financial markets. For an investor, one of the most obvious ways to reduce financial risks is to hold a broadly diversified portfolio of stocks and debt securities, including foreign securities and debt of varying maturities. However, derivatives can also be used to reduce the risks associated with financial and commodity markets.

.01 Security Price Exposure

Firms are obviously exposed to losses due to changes in security prices when securities are held in investment portfolios, and they are also exposed during times when securities are being issued. In addition, firms are exposed to risk *if* they use floating rate debt to finance an investment that produces a fixed income stream. Often, these risks can be mitigated by using derivatives. As we discussed earlier, derivatives are securities whose value stems, or is derived, from the values of other assets. Thus, options and futures contracts are derivatives, because their values depend on the prices of some underlying asset. Now we will explore further the use of two types of derivatives, futures and swaps, to help manage certain types of risk.

Futures. Futures are used for both speculation and hedging. Speculation involves betting on future price movements, and futures are used because of the leverage inherent in the contract. Hedging, on the other hand, is done by a firm or individual to protect against a price change that would otherwise negatively affect profits. For example, rising interest rates and commodity (raw material) prices can significantly reduce profits, as can adverse currency fluctuations. If two parties have mirror-image risks, then they can enter into a transaction that eliminates, as opposed to transfers, risks. This is a "natural hedge." Of course, one party to a futures contract could be a speculator, the other a hedger. Thus, to the extent that speculators broaden the market and make hedging possible, they help decrease risk to those who seek to avoid it.

There are two basic types of hedges: (1) long hedges, in which futures contracts are bought in anticipation of (or to guard against) price increases, and (2) short hedges, where a firm or individual sells futures contracts to guard against price declines. Recall that rising interest rates lower bond prices and thus decrease the value of bond futures contracts. Therefore, if a firm or individual needs to guard against an *increase* in interest rates, a futures contract that makes money if rates rise should be used. That means selling, or going short, on a futures contract. To illustrate, assume that in January, Carson Foods is considering a plan to issue $10,000,000 of 20-year bonds in June to finance a capital expenditure program. The interest rate would be 10 percent if the bonds were issued today, and at that rate, the project would have a positive NPV (Net Present Value). However, interest rates may rise over the next five months, and when the issue is actually sold, the interest rate might be substantially above 10 percent, which would make the project a poor investment. Carson can protect itself against a rise in rates by hedging in the futures market.

In this situation, an increase in interest rates would be detrimental, so Carson should use a short hedge. It would choose a futures contract on that security most similar to the one it plans to issue, long-term bonds. In this case, Carson would probably hedge with Treasury bond futures. Consider the Chicago Board of Trade's contract on Treasury bonds whose basic contract is for $100,000 of a hypothetical eight-percent coupon, semiannual payment Treasury bond with 20 years to maturity. Assume that each June futures contract has a value of 110 plus 11/32 percent. Since Carson plans to issue $10,000,000 of bonds, it would sell $10,000,000/$100,000 = 100 Treasury bond contracts for delivery in June. Carson would have to put up 100($3,000) = $300,000 in margin money and also pay brokerage commissions. Note that each June contract has a value of 110 plus 11/32 percent, so the total value of the 100 contracts is 1.1034375($100,000)(100) = $11,034,375. Now suppose renewed fears of inflation push the interest rate on Carson's debt up by 100 basis points, to 11 percent, over the next five months. If Carson issued 10-percent coupon bonds, they would bring only $920 per bond, because investors now require an 11-percent return. Thus, Carson would lose $80 per bond times 10,000 bonds, or $800,000, as a result of delaying the financing. However, the increase in interest rates would also bring about a change in the value of Carson's short position in the futures market. Since interest rates have increased, the value of the futures contract would fall, and if the interest rate on the futures contract also increased by the same full percentage point, from 7.029 to 8.029 percent, the contract value would fall to $9,971,288. Carson would then close its position in the futures market by repurchasing for $9,971,288 the contracts that it earlier sold short for $11,034,375, giving it a profit of $1,063,087, less commissions. *Note:* 7.029 percent is the implied rate inherent in the futures contracts, computed as follows: Setting up the equation, $1,103.4375 = $40 T4(r, 40 periods) + $1,040 T3(r, 40th period) and solving for r, using a financial calculator or an Excel function IRR, yields 3.5145 percent semiannually, which is equivalent to a rate of 7.029 percent.

Thus, Carson would, if we ignore commissions and the opportunity cost of the margin money, offset the loss on the bond issue. In fact, in our example, Carson more than offsets the loss, pocketing an additional $263,087. Of course, if interest rates had fallen, Carson would have lost on its futures position, but this loss would have been offset by the fact that Carson could now sell its bonds with a lower coupon.

If futures contracts existed on Carson's own debt, and interest rates moved identically in the spot and futures markets, then the firm could construct a *perfect hedge*, in which gains on the futures contract would exactly offset losses on the bonds. In reality, it is virtually impossible to construct perfect hedges, because in most cases the underlying asset is not identical to the futures asset, and even when they are, prices (and interest rates) may not move exactly together in the spot and futures markets.

Note too that if Carson had been planning an equity offering, and if its stock tended to move fairly closely with one of the stock indexes, the company could have hedged against falling stock prices by selling short the index future. Even better, if options on Carson's stock were traded in the option market, then it could use options rather than futures to hedge against falling stock prices.

The futures and options markets permit flexibility in the timing of financial transactions, because the firm can be protected, at least partially, against changes that occur between the time a decision is reached and the time when the transaction will be completed. However, this protection has a cost—the firm must pay commissions. Whether or not the protection is worth the cost is a matter of judgment. The decision to hedge also depends on management's risk aversion as well as the company's strength and ability to assume the risk in question. In theory, the reduction in risk resulting from a hedge transaction should have a value exactly equal to the cost of the hedge. Thus, a firm should be indifferent to hedging. However, many firms believe that hedging is worthwhile. Trammell Crow, a large Texas real estate developer, recently used T-bill futures to lock in interest costs on floating rate construction loans, while Dart & Kraft used Eurodollar futures to protect its marketable securities portfolio. Merrill Lynch, Salomon Brothers, and the other investment banking houses hedge in the futures and options markets to protect themselves when they are engaged in major underwritings.

Swaps. A *swap* is another method for reducing financial risks. As we noted earlier, a swap is an exchange. In finance, it is an exchange of cash payment obligations, in which each party to the swap prefers the payment type or pattern of the other party. In other words, swaps occur because the counterparties prefer the terms of the other's debt contract, and the swap enables each party to obtain a preferred payment obligation. Generally, one party has a fixed rate obligation and the other a floating rate obligation, or one has an obligation denominated in one currency and the other in another currency.

Major changes have occurred over time in the swaps market. First, standardized contracts have been developed for the most common types of swaps, and this has had two effects: (1) standardized contracts lower the time and effort involved in arranging swaps, and thus lower transactions costs; (2) the development of standardized contracts has led to a secondary market for swaps, which has increased the liquidity and efficiency of the swaps market. A number of international banks now make markets in swaps and offer quotes on several standard types. Also, as noted above, the banks now take counterparty positions in swaps, so it is not necessary to find another firm with mirror-image needs before a swap transaction can be completed. The bank would generally find a final counterparty for the swap at a later date, so its positioning helps make the swap market more operationally efficient.

To further illustrate a swap transaction, consider the following situation. An electric utility currently has outstanding a five-year floating rate note tied to the prime rate. The prime rate could rise significantly over the period. In this case, the note carries a high degree of interest rate risk. The utility could, however, enter into a swap with a counterparty, say, Citibank, wherein the utility would pay Citibank a fixed series of interest payments over the five-year period, and Citibank would make the company's required floating rate payments. As a result, the utility would have converted a floating rate loan to a fixed rate loan, and the risk of rising interest rates would have been passed from the utility to Citibank. Such a transaction can lower both parties' risks—because banks' revenues rise as interest rates rise, Citibank's risk would actually be lower if it had floating rate obligations.

Longer-term swaps can also be made. Recently, Citibank entered into a 17-year swap in an electricity cogeneration project financing deal. The project's sponsors were unable to obtain fixed rate financing on reasonable terms, and they were afraid that interest rates would increase and make the project unprofitable. The project's sponsors were, however, able to borrow from local banks on a floating rate basis and then arrange a simultaneous swap with Citibank for a fixed rate obligation.

.02 Commodity Price Exposure

As we noted earlier, futures markets were established for many commodities long before they began to be used for financial instruments. We can use Porter Electronics, which uses large quantities of copper as well as several precious metals, to illustrate inventory hedging. Suppose that in May 2002, Porter foresaw a need for 100,000 pounds of copper in March 2003 for use in fulfilling a fixed price contract to supply solar power cells to the U.S. government. Porter's managers are concerned that a strike by Chilean copper miners will occur, which could raise the price of copper in world markets and possibly turn the expected profit on the solar cells into a loss.

Porter could, of course, go ahead and buy the copper that it will need to fulfill the contract, but if it does, it will incur substantial carrying costs. As an alternative, the company could hedge against increasing copper prices in the futures market. The New York Commodity Exchange trades standard copper futures contracts of 25,000 pounds each. Thus, Porter could buy four contracts (go long) for delivery in March 2002. Assume that these contracts were trading in May for about $1.00 per pound, and that the spot price at that date was about $1.02 per pound. If copper prices do rise appreciably over the next 10 months, the value of Porter's long position in copper futures would increase, thus offsetting some of the price increase in the commodity itself. Of course, if copper prices fall, Porter would lose money on its futures contract, but the company would be buying the copper on the spot market at a cheaper price, so it would make a higher-than-anticipated profit on its sale of solar cells. Thus, hedging in the copper futures market locks in the cost of raw materials and removes some risk to which the firm would otherwise be exposed.

Eastman Kodak uses silver futures to hedge against short-term increases in the price of silver, which is the primary ingredient in black-and-white film. Many other manufacturers, such as Alcoa with aluminum and Archer Daniels Midland with grains, routinely use the futures markets to reduce the risks associated with input price volatility.

¶ 2615 The Use and Misuse of Financial Engineering

Most of the news stories about derivatives are related to financial disasters. Much less is heard about the benefits of derivatives. However, because of these benefits, more than 90 percent of large U.S. companies use derivatives on a regular basis, and sophisticated investors and analysts are demanding that firms use derivatives to hedge certain risks. For example, Compaq Computer was recently sued by a shareholder group for failing to properly hedge its foreign exchange exposure. The shareholders lost the suit, but Compaq got the message and now uses currency futures to hedge its international operations. In another example, Prudential Securities reduced its earnings estimate for Cone Mills, a North Carolina textile company, because Cone did not sufficiently hedge its exposure to changing cotton prices. These examples lead to one conclusion: if a company can safely and inexpensively hedge its risks, it should do so.

There can, however, be a downside to the use of derivatives. Hedging is invariably cited by authorities as a "good" use of derivatives, whereas speculating with derivatives is often cited as a "bad" use. Some people and organizations can afford to bear the risks involved in speculating with derivatives, but others are either not sufficiently knowledgeable about the risks they are taking or else should not be taking those risks in the first place. Most would agree that the typical corporation should use derivatives only to hedge risks, not to speculate in an effort to increase profits. Hedging allows managers to concentrate on running their core businesses without having to worry about interest rate, currency, and commodity price variability. However, problems can arise quickly when hedges are improperly constructed or when a corporate treasurer, eager to report relatively high returns, uses derivatives for speculative purposes.

One interesting example of a derivatives debacle involved Kashima Oil, a Japanese firm that imports oil. It pays with U.S. dollars but then sells oil in the Japanese market for yen. Kashima began by using currency futures to hedge, but then it started to speculate on dollar-yen price movements, hoping to increase profits. When the currency markets moved against Kashima's speculative position, lax accounting rules permitted it to avoid reporting the losses by simply rolling over the contract. By the time Kashima bit the bullet and closed its position, it had lost $1.5 billion. Other companies have experienced similar problems.

Our position is that derivatives can and should be used to hedge against certain risks, but that the leverage inherent in derivatives contracts makes them potentially dangerous instruments. Also, CFOs, CEOs, and board members should be reasonably knowledgeable about the derivatives their firms use, should establish policies regarding when they can and cannot be used, and should establish audit procedures to ensure that the policies are actually carried out. Moreover, a firm's derivatives position should be reported to stockholders, because stockholders have a right to know when situations such as that involving Kashima might arise.

¶ 2620 Risk Control

Risk control includes environmental compliance, periodic inspections, and alarm systems. Loss prevention and control must consider physical and human aspects. For example, "safer" machines may be used to prevent worker injury. Appropriate sprinklers may be installed to prevent fires. Consultants may be retained in specialized areas, such as industrial hygiene. Product labeling should be appraised as to appropriateness and representation. Any consumer complaints should be immediately investigated to avoid possible government action or litigation.

The financial manager must determine the best kind, term, and amount of insurance to carry to guard against losses. Insurance coverage may be taken out for losses to plant, property, and equipment, product/service deficiencies, and employee conduct. The financial manager should consider insuring areas not typically insured against, such as industrial espionage, loss of intellectual property, or employee theft. An example of the latter is employment practice liability insurance (EPLI). This policy is available from many insurance companies, such as Chubb and Lexington. Unfortunately even this type of policy often excludes coverage for bodily injury, workers' compensation, and infractions under ERISA. It is not unusual for an employee to sue because of an employer's promotion and hiring policies. The insurance premium may be lowered by increasing the deductible or changing to less expensive insurance carriers.

The financial manager must carefully monitor the entity's fiduciary responsibilities, working conditions, contractual commitments, and employment practices. Systems such as fire alarm devices must be checked on an ongoing basis for defects in functioning. The company must be certain that its employee policies are fair and in conformity with federal and local laws.

Risk control includes provisions against terrorist acts related to loss of life, product losses, and property damage. Security procedures including access controls must be strong in high-risk areas, such as in a foreign country with extremist groups. Employees must be instructed to use safety precautions.

¶ 2625 Risk Analysis and Management Software

Software is available to assess, evaluate, and control the risks facing a company. A risk management information system (RMIS) includes hardware and software components. However, we consider here software availability, implications, benefits, and applications. The software selected should be that which offers a proper "fit" with the environment and circumstances of the company.

In deciding on the "right" software, the financial manager should consider the company's requirements and expectations, corporate culture, report preparation needs, regulatory reporting mandates, product/service line, nature of operations, claims processing and administration, government compliance laws, business policies and procedures, insurance coverage, technological resources, employee background and experience, levels of communication, legal liability aspects, organizational structure, and work flow. The risk management and analysis software should include the ability to manipulate data into risk patterns.

Are the "right" managers being provided with the appropriate information on a timely basis? A determination must also be made of the communication and distribution features of the software.

The software should be flexible so that reports may be customized depending on the data needed and for whom. For example, a factory supervisor or manager wants to know how many employee injuries occurred and of what nature. On the other hand, the accounting department manager wants to know the negative financial effects the accidents have on the company's financial position and operating performance.

Software may be used to evaluate safety statistical data by division, department, responsibility unit, geographic location, and manager. Potential difficulties may be highlighted. An example of a risk management software application is providing a report on how many employee injuries took place by department, operation, and activity. Is the client's incidence rate above or below expected ranges? How does the client injury rate compare to competitors and industry averages? There should be a software feature, such as an expert system, on how to correct the problem of a high rate of employee accidents and offer other relevant recommendations.

If a company is exchanging risk information with others (e.g., insurance company, investment banker, and government agencies), then software compatibility is needed. Further, there should exist appropriate operating systems and network support. A company may use its intranet to expand risk management throughout the company. Proper user interfaces are important.

.01 Risk Software Packages and Products

There are many risk management software packages available to financial managers. Some useful packages are described below.

- Strohl Systems offers business continuity planning software and services to plan for unexpected disruptions in the company's operations. It is better to anticipate interruptions before they turn into major problems. BIA Professional is a business impact analysis tool allowing the company to quickly and easily define the effects of disaster and help target critical functions for contingency planning. Living Disaster Recovery Planning Systems (LDRPS) 9.0 is continuity (recovery) planning software including a question-and-answer feature, sample documents and diagrams, graphics, report writer, recovery strategies and contingency planning, and presentation of recovery activities in the form of Program Evaluation and Review Technique (PERT) and Gantt charts. Plans and procedures cover emergency response, crisis management, notification, facilities relocation, security, asset management and retrieval, vital records, contamination, safety, and health. (For information, write: Strohl Systems, 631 Park Avenue, King of Prussia, PA 19406, telephone: (800) 634-2016, fax: (610) 768-4135, or website: www.strohlsystems.com.)

- Alert's OpsCenter software helps quickly assess the situation, activate pre-tested emergency plans and monitor response progress. It assists in managing incidents across organizational boundaries and to transparently track resource requests, allocations, and utilization. (Website: www.alerttech.com).

- Corporate Systems' ClaimSuite series offers a risk-management information system providing claim processing and evaluation, accident analysis, management of fixed assets, and risk reporting and appraisal. (For information, telephone: (800) 858-4351, or website: www.csedge.com.)

- CARDdecisions Inc. offers CARD®map, a software package capable of providing a broad and insightful view of the state of risk, control, assurance, and performance. It incorporates and integrates the results of all risk management and assurance providers, including senior management and work units, and auditors of all types. CARD®map assists clients who wish to meet and/or exceed rapidly emerging risk management and control governance expectations. Information technology is a critical component of Collaborative Assurance & Risk Design™. CARD®map is the only product that has been developed specifically to support an integrated enterprise approach to risk and assurance management and to show, at a glance, the linkage between risk and control design choices and actual performance. (For information, write: 2655 North Sheridan Way, Suite 510, Mississauga, Ontario, Canada L5K 2P8, telephone: (905) 823-5518, or website: www.carddecisions.com.)

- Decisioneering develops and markets software for modeling and risk analysis. Crystal Ball® is a Monte Carlo simulation add-in for Microsoft Excel and Lotus 1-2-3. Crystal Ball Pro is a suite of risk analysis programs that includes Crystal Ball, OptQuest (global optimizer that works with uncertainty analysis), and the Developer's Kit (VBA macros that allow users to customize the user interface). CB Predictor is an automated, time-series forecasting program that adds in to Excel for Windows. (For information contact Eric Wainwright, Vice President of R&D, at 1515 Arapahoe St., Suite 1311, Denver, CO 80202, telephone: (303) 534-1515, fax: (303) 534-4818, or website: www.decisioneering.com.)

- International Security Technology, Inc.'s CORA® (Cost-of-Risk Analysis) is a powerful risk management decision support system that helps risk managers to optimize strategies for mitigation and transfer of, and recovery from, operational risks of all kinds. CORA risk management projects are two-step processes. First, it provides a convenient context for risk analysts to organize, collect, store, validate, and collate the data that describe the risks and loss exposures of an organization. It then uses sophisticated algorithms to contruct a quantitative risk model using these data. (For information, write: International Security Technology, Inc., 99 Park Ave., 11th Floor, New York, NY 10016-1501, telephone: (888) 478-2672, fax: (212) 808-5206, or website: www.ist-usa.com).

- Kiodex Inc. provides risk management and trading expertise through cost-effective, easily accessible, web-based risk management tools that enable commodity market participants such as traders, managers, and corporate officers to easily and accurately understand, quantify, and manage their risks. Kiodex Risk Workbench℠ provides pricing tools, market data, and financial reports to assist corporations in managing their exposure to market volatility and in complying with U.S. GAAP—particularly Financial Accounting Standards Board (FASB) Statement 133. The real-time, Internet-based order-matching Kiodex Trade Engine™ powers major electronic exchanges. (For information, telephone: (877) 6-KIODEX, fax: (646) 437-3910, or website: www.kiodex.com.)

- Palisade Corporation offers a variety of Risk and Decision Analysis software such as the DecisionTools® Suite: @RISK (Monte Carlo simulation), BestFit® (distribution fitting), PrecisionTree® (decision analysis), TopRank® (what-if analysis), and RISKview™ (distribution previewing), as well as @RISK for Project (Monte Carlo simulation in Microsoft Project), the @RISK Developer's Kit (Monte Carlo development environment), and Evolver™ (optimization). (For more information, write: 31 Decker Rd., Newfield, NY 14867, phone: (800) 432-7475 or (607) 277-8000, fax: (607) 277-8001, or website: www.palisade.com.)

- Virtual Research Associates, Inc. (VRA) addresses the need to monitor global situations of terrorism and political risk. VRA's web-based software tool, VRA Knowledge Manager, supports interactive analysis and intuitive display of global news reports. VRA's Knowledge Manager is a real-time data development and interactive analysis software system designed to process large volumes of text-based reports. The system can illuminate countries' vulnerabilities to political instability, social turmoil, and violence by automatically monitoring global news wire service reports, assessing them, and presenting up-to-the-minute intelligence in graphs, maps and tables. By spotting areas where instability or violence are likely to occur, VRA's Knowledge Manager is currently providing early warnings about potential "hot spots" to government agencies, academic and humanitarian organizations, and the intelligence community. (For more information, call (781) 647-5952 or website: www.vranet.com.)

- QA Systems QASYS is innovative, flexible risk-management software for insurance companies. (For information, telephone: (800) 946-1717 or (212) 599-1717, write: QA Systems, 220 E. 42nd St., New York, NY 10017, or website: www.qasys.com.)

.02 Risk Modeling Software Applications

Risk modeling is a decision-making aid to the financial manager. Models may be used in analyzing risks while financial models can evaluate the financial consequences arising from accidents or other adverse developments. Risk models may be developed for measuring the financial impact due to catastrophes (fire, flood, earthquake, and nuclear). The probable loss arising from the accident, disaster, or other event may be estimated. The model may also determine the probable effects on business activities as well as possible competitive reactions. A contingency model may help in planning an appropriate strategy and response.

A "what-if" scenario analysis may be formulated to see the end-result effects of changing input variables and factors. An example of a scenario modeling analysis is to simulate the possible operating and financial consequences to the company from various possibilities arising from a hurricane. The company's risk vulnerability from such an event may be "mapped" and appraised. The "best-case," "worst-case," and "likely" scenarios may be depicted and reviewed. The model simulation has the benefit of aiding the company in determining beforehand how to best minimize the damage operationally and financially and how to provide proper protective measures.

The software enables the company to determine the areas, types, and degrees of risk facing the business. A minimum-maximum range of loss figures may be derived.

Risk modeling may be used to identify and define the type and amount of risks related to various exposures. A priority ranking based on risk and uncertainty may also be prepared and studied. Risk problem areas may be analyzed along with a set of appropriate alternative responses.

.03 Risk Management Information Systems (RMIS) Testing Laboratory

Deloitte and Touche, CPAs has started the first independent risk management systems testing laboratory that tests software, develops systems solutions, evaluates software usefulness, provides benchmarking information, and customizes applications. Deloitte and Touche, CPAs will compare software products, compare reporting and application features, and appraise their effectiveness in meeting your needs. (For information, contact David Duden, RMISILab Director at telephone: (860) 543-7341, e-mail: dduden@ dttus.com, or website: www.rmislab.com.)

.04 Online Risk-Management Database Services

There are many online services available providing important risk-management information. For example, the National Council on Compensation Insurance Inc. (NCCI) provides an online InsNet Workers' Compensation Characteristic Series containing claims data useful in having a cost-effective workers' compensation system. The service aids in evaluating risks, determining and appraising workers' compensation costs, including frequency data, specifying injury claim characteristics, providing demographic and body claim characteristics, and specifying benefit type information. (For information about NCCI's InsNet online service, website: www.ncci.com, write to: National Council on Compensation Insurance, Corporate Headquarters, 901 Peninsula Corporate Circle, Boca Raton, FL 33487, telephone: (561) 893-1000, or fax: (561) 893-1191.)

Chapter 27

Mergers, Acquisitions, and Divestitures

¶ 2701 Overview

This chapter discusses all facets of mergers, acquisitions, and divestitures, including deciding on terms, key factors to consider, pros and cons of mergers, types of arrangements, evaluative criteria, valuation methods, financial effects of the merger, holding companies, takeover bids, SEC filing requirements, accounting and reporting requirements for business combinations, and financial analysis of combinations.

External growth occurs when a business purchases the existing assets of another entity through a merger. Decision-makers are often required to appraise the suitability of a potential merger as well as participate in negotiations. Besides the growth aspect, a merger may reduce risk through diversification. The three common ways of joining two or more companies are a merger, consolidation, or a holding company.

In a *merger,* two or more companies are combined into one, where only the acquiring company retains its identity. Generally, the larger of the two companies is the acquirer. With a *consolidation,* two or more companies combine to create a new company. None of the consolidation firms legally survive. For example, companies A and B give all their assets, liabilities, and stock to the new company, C, in return for C's stock, bonds, or cash. A holding company possesses voting control of one or more other companies. The *holding company* comprises a group of businesses, each operating as a separate entity. By possessing more than 50 percent of the voting rights through common stock, the holding company has effective control of another company with a smaller percent of ownership.

Depending on the intent of the combination, there are three common ways in which businesses get together so as to obtain advantages in their markets. They are:

- *Vertical merger.* This occurs when a company combines with a supplier or customer. An example is when a wholesaler combines with retailers.
- *Horizontal merger.* This occurs when two companies in a similar business combine. An example is the combining of two airlines.
- *Conglomerate merger.* This occurs when two companies in unrelated industries combine, such as where an electronics company joins with an insurance company.

¶ 2705 Mergers

A merger may be accomplished in one of two ways. The acquirer may negotiate with the management of the prospective acquired company, which is preferred. If negotiations fail, the acquirer may make a tender offer directly to the stockholders of the targeted company. A tender offer represents a cash offering (but can be a stock offering) for the common shares held by stockholders. A good takeover candidate includes a cash-rich business, a company with significant growth potential, and a company with a low debt-to-equity ratio.

In discussions with management, the acquirer typically makes a stock offer at a specified exchange ratio. The merger may take place if the acquired company receives an offer at an acceptable premium over the current market price of stock. Sometimes contingent payments are also given, such as stock warrants.

There are several financing packages that buyers may use for mergers, such as common stock, preferred stock, convertible bonds, debt, cash, and warrants. A key factor in selecting the final package is its impact on current earnings per share (EPS).

If common stock is exchanged, the seller's stock is given in exchange for the buyer's stock, resulting in a tax-free exchange. The drawback is that the stock issuance lowers earnings per share because the buyer's outstanding shares are increased. When there is an exchange of cash for common stock, the selling company's stockholders receive cash, resulting in a taxable transaction. This type of exchange may increase EPS since the buying company is obtaining new earnings without increasing outstanding shares.

There are many reasons why your company may prefer external growth through mergers instead of internal growth.

The following are advantages of a merger:

- Increases corporate power and improves market share and product lines.
- Aids in diversification, such as reducing cyclical and operational effects.
- Helps the company's ability to raise financing when it merges with another entity having significant liquid assets and low debt.
- Provides a good return on investment when the market value of the acquired business is significantly less than its replacement cost.
- Improves the market price of stock in some cases, resulting in a higher P/E ratio. For example, the stock of a larger company may be viewed as more marketable, secure, and stable.
- Provides a missed attribute; that is, a company gains something it lacked. For instance, superior management quality or research capability may be obtained.
- Aids the company in financing an acquisition that would not otherwise be possible to obtain, such as where acquiring a company by exchanging stock is less costly than building new capital facilities, which would require an enormous cash outlay. For instance, a company may be unable to finance significant internal expansion but can achieve it by purchasing a business already possessing such capital facilities.
- Achieves a synergistic effect, which means that the results of the combination are greater than the sum of the parts. For instance, greater profit may result from the combined entity

that would occur from each individual company due to increased efficiency (e.g., economies of scale) and cost savings (e.g., eliminating overlapping administrative functions, and volume discounts on purchases). There is better use of people and resources. A greater probability of synergy exists with a horizontal merger since duplicate facilities are eliminated.

- Obtains a tax loss carryforward benefit if the acquired company has been losing money. The acquirer may utilize the tax loss carryforward benefit to offset its own profitability, thus reducing its taxes. The tax loss may be carried forward 15 years to reduce the acquiring company's future earnings for losses incurred for tax years ended prior to 8/5/97 and 20 years for losses incurred thereafter. In effect, the government is financing part of the acquisition.

Example 1. H Company is deciding whether to buy S Company. S has a tax loss of $500,000. H Company anticipates pretax earnings of $400,000 and $300,000 for the next two years. The tax rate is 34 percent. The taxes to be paid by H Company follow:

Year 1: $400,000 – $400,000 = 0

Year 2: $300,000 – $100,000 = $200,000 × 34% = $68,000

The following are disadvantages of a merger:

- Reverse synergies, which reduce the net value of the combined entity (e.g., adjustments of pay scales, costs of servicing acquisition debt, and defections of key acquired company staff).
- Adverse financial effects because the anticipated benefits did not materialize; for example, expected cost reductions were not forthcoming.
- Antitrust action delaying or preventing the proposed merger.
- Problems caused by dissenting minority stockholders.

In evaluating a potential merger, you have to consider its possible effect upon the financial performance of the company, including:

- *Earnings per share.* The merger should result in higher earnings or improved stability.
- *Dividends per share.* The dividends before and after the merger should be maintained to stabilize the market price of the stock.
- *Market price of stock.* The market price of the stock should be higher or at least the same after the merger.
- *Risk.* The merged business should have less financial and operating risk than before.

¶ 2710 Due Diligence—Information to Consider Before "Doing a Deal"

Financial:

1. Latest audited financial statements.

2. Last unaudited financial statements.

3. Ten-year summary financial statements. (Product P&L (profit & loss statement) is essential if more than one product.)

4. Protected operating and financial statements.

5. Full description of securities, indebtedness, investments, and other assets and liabilities other than normal day-to-day accounts.

6. Trial balance and chart of accounts and/or description of accounting practices relative to inventories, fixed assets, reserve accounts, etc.

7. List of bank accounts and average balances.

8. Credit reports from banks and Dun & Bradstreet.

9. Federal income tax status; i.e., tax credits, loss or unused carry forwards, any deficiency claims, etc.

10. Summary of state and local tax situation; i.e., applicable taxes, unemployment tax rate, deficiency claims, etc.

11. Tax status of proposed transaction; recommendation of best method of acquisition.

12. Complete list of insurance policies, including description of coverage and cost: workmen's compensation rate.

13. Statement of responsible officer of business as to unrecorded or contingency liabilities.

14. Statement of inventories.

15. Compare last two physical inventories of sizable money items to reflect slow-moving and obsolete materials. Note finished products particularly. Determine how physical compared with book at last physical inventory.

16. Aged list of accounts receivable, credit and collection policies, and trial balance of accounts payable.

17. Detailed statement of general and administrative expenses, selling expenses, and factory overhead on a comparative basis for three years.

18. Status of re-negotiation and price re-determination.

19. Bonus and pension plans; salary and commission contracts.

20. Statement of unfilled orders—present and past.

21. Statistics regarding industry group (trends, return on investment, margin on sales, etc.)

22. If any defense contracts in backlog, check margin of profit. Also, if any existing equipment is government-owned.

23. Statements regarding company's break-even point, including details of product mix, costs, and fixed and variable expenses.

24. Status of production or other contracts requiring company performance for a fixed amount where work is yet to be accomplished.

25. List of outstanding capital-asset items.

26. Status of patents, copyrights, royalty agreements, etc.

27. Details of corporate equity accounts.

Operations:

Production

1. Review Estimating Department Procedure and formula used for computing cost to establish sales prices. Also review record of performance versus existing sales prices to determine if all items show a profit. Determine if sales prices are actually based on costs or fixed and influenced by competition without regard to cost.

2. Appraise key production personnel, and constructions and age of buildings, noting those with special fixtures such as those equipped with overhead cranes.

3. Determine if any improvements are planned and authorized, or if any were recently presented and disapproved.

4. Review planning and scheduling procedures.

5. Make casual inspection of property, plant, and equipment and note their condition. Determine age of machinery and if of reputable make.

6. Determine if production employees paid day work exclusively, or both day work and piece work, or if some other means of incentive is employed. If other than day-work pay is employed, obtain procedure and any formulas used in establishing the incentive.

7. Determine method of inspection employed.

8. Determine if all power is purchased, manufactured, or combinations of both.

9. Obtain general history of plant growth and rearrangements as far back as possible.

10. Check intrinsic value of patents (if any) and royalty paid on any products or parts produced.

11. Review past overhead charges and obtain explanation of the larger charges.

12. Obtain copies of the following:
    a. Plant plans and flow-charts
    b. Produce list, catalogues, or circulars
    c. Production schedules and forecasts
    d. Labor contracts
    e. Commitments
    f. List of machinery, equipment, fixtures and furniture
    g. Organization chart
    h. Labor utilization reports
    i. Equipment utilization reports
    j. Production reports
    k. Minutes of meetings
    l. Standard cost data

13. Examine union contracts, paying attention to any prior negotiations that are apt to reoccur.

14. Labor supply in various geographical areas impacted by company.

Industrial relations

1. Number of employees—trend with prior years.

2. Labor turnover—trend with prior years.

3. Absentee rate.

4. Is the company unionized? How long? Contracts?

5. What is the labor dispute history?

6. Is the relationship between the company and employees friendly? Between the company and union?

7. Scope of industrial relations department responsibilities.

8. What executives participate in negotiations?

9. What procedures exist for:

   a. Hiring

   b. Firing

   c. Promotion

10. What percentage of promotions comes from within?

11. What types of training programs exist? Is there a training department? Training Director?

12. Is there an active safety program?

13. How are pay rates determined?

14. How are fringe benefits determined?

Engineering and research

1. Description and condition of facilities.

2. To whom does the head of the engineering department report?

3. Is there a policy manual?

4. What are the short-range and long-range objectives?

5. Obtain department budget.

6. Determine employee turnover.

7. What is the source of engineering employees?

8. Who owns product designs, patents, copyrights, etc.?

Purchasing

1. Make complete analysis of inventory supply.

2. Determine existence of contracts and/or agreements for materials or outside services which are obligations that would have to be assumed.

3. Determine existence of a supplier's equipment or facilities on company property for which responsibility would have to be assumed.

4. Review the details of inventory including the following:

   a. Method, accuracy, and date of prices used.

   b. Compare with current prices.

c. Evaluate inventory on basis of what material would bring on an open market.

d. Determine if material is used currently. Make certain that it is not obsolete and/or actually not usable.

5. Review the present employees in the purchasing department as to:

   a. Number of employees

   b. Experience

   c. Ability

6. Review the functions of the purchasing department including:

   a. Policies

   b. Procedures

   c. Records

   d. Internal control

Legal

1. Does the seller have power to do the acts the deal requires?

   a. Legal power: SEC, state corporate laws, "Blue Sky" laws, etc.

   b. Corporate power: charter, bylaws, etc.

   c. Contractual power: restriction in bank loan agreements, etc.

2. Does risk exist that seller's shareholders will resist a merger, etc.?

3. Does risk of attack by creditors exist? Review need for compliance with Bulk Sales Act in an asset deal.

4. Is seller's corporation in good standing and qualified in all states in which its business requires same?

5. Is a voting trust needed?

6. If seller was organized within five years, determine names of promoters, nature and amount of anything of value (including money, property, options, etc.) received or to be received by each promoter directly and indirectly.

7. Is there a material relationship between buyer (or any of its officers and directors) and seller (or any of its officers and directors)?

8. Will the seller indemnify the buyer against business brokers' and finders' fee?

9. Would the acquisition invite antitrust investigation or prosecution?

10. Are seller's beneficial contracts assignable?
    a. Licenses and royalty agreements
    b. Employment agreements
    c. Leases
    d. Suppliers' contracts
    e. Customers' contracts, particularly U.S. government
    f. Collective-bargaining agreements

11. Are any of its beneficial contracts already subject to prior assignments, e.g., to lending institutions?

12. Are there customs or contracts which would place an obligation or duty on the buyer in either a stock or an asset deal?
    a. Profit sharing plans
    b. Contributory employee stock-purchase or savings plans
    c. Restricted stock-option plans
    d. Pension and bonus plans
    e. Pattern of traditionally high salaries and fringe benefits
    f. Group insurance and similar employee benefit plans
    g. Other beneficial contracts listed above

13. Obtain brief description of location and general character of principal plants and officers. If any such property is not owned or is held subject to a major encumbrance, so state and briefly describe how held (consider lease termination dates and powers to renew). Check:
    a. Liens for tax assessments
    b. Restrictions, such as zoning, on use of real property and easements

14. Are all required federal and state tax returns filed, examined, and settled?
    a. Income and excess-profits taxes
    b. Franchise and capital stock taxes
    c. Sales and use taxes
    d. Real- and personal-property taxes
    e. Other excise taxes

15. Determine adequacy of all established reserves.

16. Examine re-negotiation procedures, settlements, and reserves.
17. Determine whether contracts with customers have any re-determination clauses and determine the minimum net exposure thereunder.
18. Determine whether contracts with suppliers and customers have escalation clauses and maximum net exposure thereunder.
19. How secure are seller's property rights in its:
    a. Patents
    b. Trademarks, trade names, and copyrights
    c. Goodwill
20. Is seller party to any unusual "confidential treatment" or "secret" agreements?
21. Does seller maintain adequate insurance on all insurable property and all reasonable risk? If not, has any significant event occurred with respect to an uninsured property or risk?
22. Review warranties to customers, particularly warranties of design. Determine whether reserves have been established and review history.
23. Does selling company presently have requisite amount of general and specialized legal counsel? Can or should they be continued or changed?
24. Will goodwill or other intangibles result from the transaction? Will the transaction produce the anticipated accounting result? Are any appraisers required?
25. Does seller have benefits under any contracts or other arrangements which would terminate or increase in cost following acquisition?
26. Will transaction result in any minority stockholders, or provide dissenting stockholders with any appraisal rights?

Marketing

1. Description of product line and brief company history.
2. Does the product line of subject company have anything in common with the lines produced by existing divisions of the buyer?
3. Ten-year record of the company's product sales performance and methods of distribution.
4. What reputation does the company enjoy among its customers?

5. Check the consistency of production covering the last three to five years for seasonal trends or diminishing demand for any products.
6. Long-range forecast of growth or contraction trends for this industry. What are the prospects of substitute materials, processes, or products?
7. Who are the customers? What is the long-range outlook for the future business of these customers?
8. Three- to five-year forecast of demand for the product, and estimate of industry's ability to supply.
9. An evaluation of the company's three- to five-year forecast of sales expectations (share of market).
10. Present competitors:
    a. Description of competitive products
    b. Location and size of plants
    c. Share of market
    d. Pricing policies
    e. Methods of distribution
    f. Reputation and financial details
11. Analysis of past price trends and policies and present or future pricing policies for the production lien, considering:
    a. Competitive pricing
    b. Cost pricing
12. Analysis of present and potential customers:
    a. Major types of customers and percentage of sales to each
    b. Geographical location
    c. Buying habits
13. Analysis—location of plant:
    a. Competitive accessibility to major markets
    b. Distribution costs
14. Review and evaluate sales department:
    a. Sales management
    b. Organization and operating procedures
    c. Field sales force—compensation, turnover rate, and sales training

d. Sales policies

15. Review and evaluate advertising and promotion programs and policies:

a. Objectives and techniques of the advertising program

b. Analysis of principal elements of advertising budget

c. Appraisal of advertising organization, personnel, and agency relationships

d. Comparison of techniques and programs with those of major competitors

Organization

1. Does the company have an organization chart?

a. Is it maintained currently?

b. Does it properly reflect the assigned functions?

2. Does the company have an organization manual which maintains organization charts and job descriptions?

a. Is it maintained up to date?

b. Do the job specifications properly reflect the jurisdiction, authority, and responsibility of the job?

3. Does the company have a policy manual containing the president's policy statements and the written interpretations of policy issued by the officers, executives, and general management?

4. Is there a program which is actively pursued to train and develop outstanding employees for management and executive positions?

5. Is there a program of individual executive ratings on an annual basis? If so, review the ratings pertaining to key personnel.

6. Does the company maintain an education program for its employees?

a. What are the annual costs?

b. What percentage of the employees participate in the program?

7. Does the company maintain a scholarship program? What are the annual costs?

8. Review the salary rates of key personnel.

Public relations

1. Does the company have a public relations department? Is it properly staffed? To whom does the public relations director, or the person responsible for the function, report?
2. Does the company have a planned public relations program? Does the program encompass the major public, including:
   a. Press
   b. Stockholders
   c. Financial community
   d. Plant communities
   e. Employees
   f. Customers
3. How does the above-mentioned public consider the company?
4. Does the company have an institutional advertising campaign?
5. Does the company employ outside public relations consultants?
6. Will the acquisition of the company be a public relations asset to the buyer?

¶ 2715 Antitrust Guidelines

In an effort to provide guidelines as to what type of business combinations would and would not be challenged in antitrust actions, the Justice Department developed the Herfindahl-Hirshman Index. It essentially breaks all business combinations into the three broad types: horizontal integration, vertical integration, and conglomeration (Exhibits 2, 3, and 4).

Market Share Squared	*Likelihood of Challenge*
Less than 1,000	Unlikely
1,000 - 1,800	Possible
More than 1,800	Likely

Consider this hypothetical market share breakdown in the widget industry in Exhibit 1.

Exhibit 1

Widget Industry Market Share Data

	Market Share	*Market Share Squared*
Company A	41%	1,681
Company B	26%	676
Company C	18%	324
Company D	8%	64
Company E	5%	25
Company F	2%	4

.01 What does this mean?

It is obvious that Company A cannot combine with either Company B or C, but how about Company E or even F? Company A would actually be prohibited from combining with any other company listed above. Combining the market shares of Company A and any other company and then squaring them would produce a number higher than 1,800 as shown below.

Wrong Calculation

	Market Share	*Market Share Squared*
Company A	41%	1,681
Company F	2%	4
		1,685

Note: Do not make this mistake unless you are hungry for attention by the antitrust division of the Justice Department.

Correct Calculation

	Market Share	*Market Share Squared*
Company A	41%	
Company F	2%	
	43%	1,849

Exhibit 2

Conglomerate Mergers

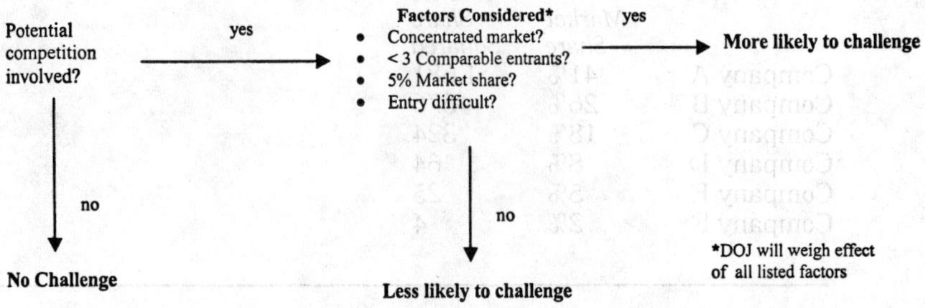

Exhibit 3

Vertical Mergers

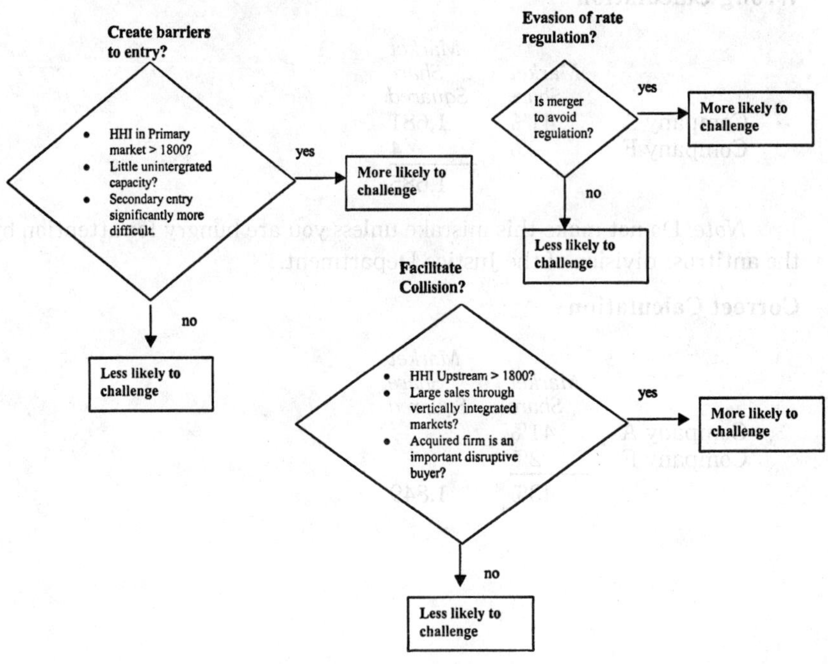

Exhibit 4

Horizontal Mergers

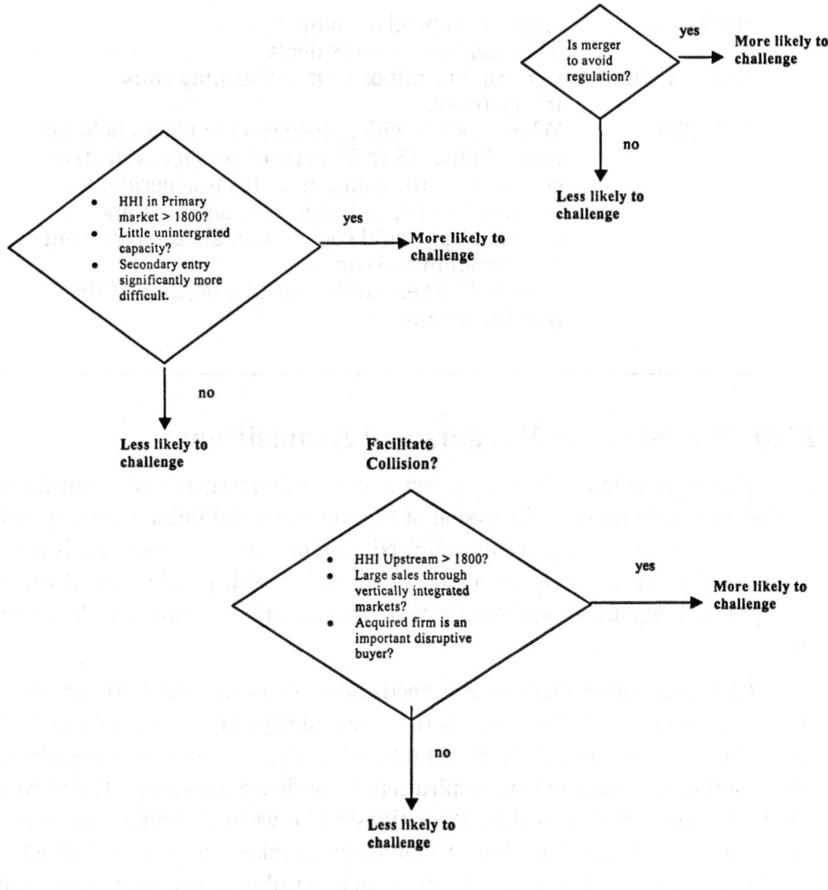

Exhibit 5 summarizes the merger and acquisition percent rules.

Exhibit 5

Merger and Acquisition Percent Rules

100%	Absolute control of company.
80%	Threshold for tax-free deals.
50% + 1 share	Control, but minority interests may cause interference.
15%–25%	When stock is widely-held (no big blocks held by individuals), 15 to 25 percent provides effective control over the company. This is generally true because in a proxy battle, management and stockholders would each obtain about 50 percent of the uncommitted shares.
5%	Threshold when public must be notified of the purchaser's intent.

¶ 2720 Planning for Mergers and Acquisitions

Perhaps the most striking aspect of corporate mergers and acquisitions is the seemingly random dispersion of the successes and failures among such combinations. For every well-publicized case of "one plus one equals more than two" there seems to be another (albeit less well publicized) in which one plus one equals, if not exactly zero, at any rate substantially less than two.

Obviously some mergers are good, and others are fatal. It would be naive to assert that the good mergers are always the result of effective planning and the careful study of facts, while the fatal ones are invariably the result of management by inspiration. Experience does suggest, however, that there is more than a chance relationship between planning and success in cooperate combinations. Smart management takes the time and effort to study each prospective combination in such detail as is necessary to permit a well-thought out decision. Such a study invariably begins with a clear understanding of what the company hopes to achieve through the combination in question.

.01 Defining Objectives

Why are there corporate mergers and acquisitions? At the risk of oversimplification, it might be helpful if we arranged some of the more common reasons for business combinations into a few broad categories:

1. *Market considerations.* One frequent merger objective is to capture a greater share of the market which the company serves. A merger may make it possible for the company to offer a complete product line for the first time, or it may expand the geographic area in which the company sells its goods. Foreign acquisitions are frequently made for this latter reason.

2. *Distribution economies.* Often a single distribution system (including salesmen, jobbers, dealers, retail outlets, and, of course, transportation facilities) can handle two products having common, or at least similar, markets *and* distribution methods at a lower unit cost than it can a single product.

3. *Diversification.* Many companies embark on merger programs to avoid the cyclical effect of a single industry, to minimize the impact of adverse conditions in a particular market, and/or to be able to participate in new growth areas.

4. *Manufacturing advantages.* By combining two manufacturing units, weaknesses can often be strengthened, overcapacity eliminated, and overhead reduced. Seasonal problems, particularly, can often be solved in this way.

5. *Research and development (R&D) needs.* R&D cost is becoming an increasingly important element of overhead in almost every field of business and industry. Common laboratories and other R&D facilities frequently result in a reduction in research cost per unit of production.

6. *Financial considerations.* The purpose of a merger is often to secure higher earnings per share and an improved image in the marketplace and consequently a higher price/earnings ratio or to achieve greater financial security and stability.

7. *Redeployment of excess capital.* Many insurance companies have millions of dollars in low-yield securities in excess of their reserve requirements.

8. *Personnel considerations.* This is most commonly a motive of service organizations. Frequently a merger is undertaken to provide key personnel for an organization weakened through death or through failure to plan ahead for orderly management succession.

9. *Complexity and automation.* The business world is becoming increasingly complex. A small enterprise unable to support a staff of specialists or to afford the cost savings available to larger entities through automation may seek refuge in a merger with a larger operation. Similarly, two small companies, neither of which is able to afford these necessities, may join to create an organization of sufficient size to cope with the growing complexity of business life and to compete with larger operations.

A review of these considerations will at least serve to start management thinking in an orderly, logical way about the possibility of merger. Could your company benefit in any of the areas outlined above? If so, you have the beginning of a merger plan. This plan must be carefully developed by top management until the specific objectives of your merger program are clearly defined and understood.

.02 Defining Criteria

A major product of the acquisition planning process is the definition of detailed acquisition criteria for each area where acquisition appears to be a viable alternative to internal growth. A list of criteria should resemble a purchase order, describing the most desirable candidate imaginable. A typical list would include such factors as the following:

- Industry or industry segment.
- Method of distribution.
- Size.
- Geographic constraints.
- Particular strengths.
- Importance of management continuation.
- Preferred consideration (cash or stock).
- Maximum price.

Admittedly, it is unlikely that a willing and available dream candidate will be identified, but it is important to create a benchmark against which to evaluate candidates. Weighting the importance of each characteristic, either formally or informally, also aids in the candidate-screening process and in ranking candidates in order of attractiveness.

.03 Finding and Screening Candidates

The next step is to find what companies that would fit your plan are available. Do you feel that the secrecy of your plan is important? If so, the problem of finding available companies becomes considerably more difficult. Most managements under these circumstances have found that secrecy is a relative term. The old cynic's saying that two can keep a secret if one of them is dead, has a great deal of support among those who have been involved in mergers. In most cases the best approach is to throw open your doors and cry in the marketplace that you are interested in a purchase or merger. In practice this can be accomplished simply by passing the word, either personally or by advertisement, to your business friends, your lawyers, your brokers, your bankers, and your CPAs.

It is generally desirable to establish two or three benchmarks against which to measure prospective acquisitions to decide whether they are worth pursuing further. Since this is a first rough screening, the criteria should be as objective as possible, and capable of simple application on the basis of readily available data. Some illustrative benchmarks are:

- In the auto parts replacement market,

- A price/earnings ratio not more than 10 percent higher than ours, or
- A growth rate for the last five years of 12 percent per annum, compounded annually.

Your first screening will, of course, let through some bad deals. More seriously, the application of any arbitrary criteria is likely to eliminate some desirable deals. But where there is a large number of a choice, an arbitrary method of elimination is better than none at all.

The process of identifying prospective acquisition candidates begins with building a list of all companies that appear to meet the criteria. Multiple sources should be consulted. Easily accessible electronic databases generally can provide 80 percent to 90 percent of the names with some amount of additional information. Other sources of candidate information include the following:

- Trade association membership lists.
- Trade publications.
- Industry experts.
- Government publications.
- Acquirer's employees—purchasing, sales, and so on.
- Public library.

Naturally, the law of diminishing returns applies to the last few names, but more than 95 percent of the qualified candidates that exist can be identified easily.

Screening a universe of several hundred companies to identify the most attractive candidates sounds like a difficult and time-consuming task. Actually, applying unequivocal knockout criteria such as size or location quickly reduces the universe to a manageable number. Comparing the remainder against the other criteria should produce 10 or 15 priority candidates. The task of gathering comprehensive information regarding that smaller number of candidates is not nearly as formidable.

The prospect identification process also gives the acquirer a feel for the dynamics of the targeted industry. Competitive conditions, industry growth trends, profit margins, and other important data can easily be gathered at the same time. Analyzing the characteristics that distinguish high-performing industry participants is also a useful exercise.

Once the internal universe-building process is complete, it is important to turn to external sources of prospective candidates—financial intermediaries. Typically, an investment banker or broker is present in about two thirds of all merger transactions. Contact with intermediaries should be established to get an early look at as many opportunities as possible—to be plugged into the "deal flow."

.04 Deciding on Acquisition Terms

In deciding on acquisition terms, consideration should be given to the following:

- Earnings in terms of absolute dollars and percentage change.
- Dividends.
- Market price of stock.
- Book value per share.
- Net working capital per share.

The weight assigned to each of the above varies with the circumstances involved.

Earnings. In determining the value of earnings in a merger, you should take into account anticipated future earnings and projected Price-Earnings (P/E) ratio. A rapidly growing company is expected to have a higher P/E multiple.

Dividends. Dividends are attractive to stockholders. However, the more a company's growth rate and earnings, the less is the impact of dividends on market price of stock. On the other hand, if earnings are falling, the effect of dividends on per share is greater.

Market price of stock. The price of a security considers projected earnings and dividends. The value assigned to the company in the acquisition will most likely be greater than the present market price in the following instances:

- The business is in a depressed industry.
- The acquired company is of greater value to the acquirer than to the stock market in general.
- A higher market price than the current one is offered to induce existing stockholders to give up their shares.

Book value per share. Since book value is based on historical cost rather than current value, it is not a key factor to consider. However, when book value exceeds market value, there may be an expectation that market price will increase subsequent to the merger due to improved circumstances (e.g., superior management).

Net working capital per share. If the acquired company has very low debt or very liquid assets, the acquirer may borrow the funds for the acquisition by using the acquired company's strong liquidity position.

.05 Factors in Determining a Price

There are many factors to be considered in determining the price to be paid for a business including:

- Financial health of the acquired company (e.g., quality of earnings, growth rate, and realizability of assets).
- Type and stability of operations.
- Maturity of business.
- Degree of competition.
- Tax consequences, such as unused tax credits.
- Expected return on assets and sales.
- Employee relations, such as the absence of unionization.
- Risk level, such as having adequate insurance.
- Corporate characteristics, including having negatively correlated product lines and favorable lease terms.
- Management quality, such as experienced executives.
- Marketing position, such as quality product line, market share, distribution channels, and customer base.
- Economic environment, including recession-resistant business.
- Political environment, such as the absence of strict governmental regulation and operations in politically unstable areas.
- Structure of the arrangement, including debt or equity, cash or stock, costs of the transaction, and time period.
- Improvement in diversification and/or integration.
- Ease of transferability of ownership.
- Exchange rate fluctuations.
- Legal issues, such as the possibility of stockholder liability suits.
- Industry characteristics, such as being in a growing industry instead of a declining one. For example, in 1981, Sohio's acquisition of Kennecott Copper for $1.77 billion resulted in financial disaster due to downside trends in the industry.
- Impact of the acquisition on the acquiring company's financial strength and operation performance. For instance, Baldwin United's acquisition of Mortgage Guaranty Insurance ultimately forced both companies into bankruptcy. There was an

evident failure to appraise appropriately the effect of the acquisition on financial posture.

- Possible violation of antitrust laws. These laws are administered by the Department of Justice's Antitrust Division and the Federal Trade Commission.

When looking at the targeted company, see what the positive and negative effects of the acquisition would be on your company. By examining what the overall picture after the merger would be, you can properly assess what to pay for the candidate. If your analysis includes many uncertain factors, sensitivity analysis may be used to look at the effect of changes in outcome.

Be careful: Detailed financial planning and analysis are required in the acquisition process. An example of an acquisition that did not work out well is the 1980 acquisition by Pan American of National Airlines for $400 million. A major reason for the acquisition was to enable Pan Am to use National's routes to feed its overseas routes. However, management did not make progress in rescheduling for almost two years.

Warning: If an acquiring company overpays for a target company, this negatively affects its financial position. For example, was it worth it to J. Ray McDermott to fight off United Technologies to obtain control of Babcock and Wilcox, even though it pushed the stock price up from about $35 to $65?

.06 Grading Criteria

In acquisition strategy, document what you want to accomplish by the acquisition and how the acquisition will complement your overall strategy. Industries and companies are then screened by employing various quantitative measures and considering qualitative factors. The broad industry sectors should be narrowed down by comparing each industry to your specified industry criteria. The industry best satisfying your goals is then selected. After you have identified the target industry, companies in that industry are then screened. Make sure to compare the target's trend to industry averages to determine the company's relative position.

In identifying an acquisition target, clearly defined criteria should be established for acceptable candidates, all companies within the category should be reviewed, suitable companies should be listed in priority order, and a short list of targets (generally no more than 10) coming closest to the ideal profile should be prepared. This short list can either consist of the highest-scoring companies regardless of score or all companies. The profile criteria include what is important to your company, such as industry classification, size, profitability, leverage, market share, and geographic area. The company's first choice may not be possible so flexibility is needed.

Different criteria should have different weights depending upon importance to your company. For example, the weight may go from 1 (least important) to 10 (most important). For example, you may decide to assign a 1 to dividend history and a 10 to industry. Most criteria will fall between 1 and 10 (e.g., leverage may be assigned a weight of 2 because all candidates have already been screened to have a debt-to-equity ratio below 25 percent). Intermediate attributes within a range may also be scored. For example, revenues under $100 million or above $300 million may be given a score of 4. Exhibit 6 shows an illustrative grading guide.

Exhibit 6

Illustrative Grading Guide

Industry Classification

1 = specialty shops, diversified companies in which food products retailing is only minor

10 = convenience store chain

Size

1 = revenues under $10 million or over $40 million

10 = revenues of $30 million

Fixed Assets (book value)

1 = $2 million

10 = over $5 million

Net Income

1 = profit margin below 2%

5 = profit margin above 10%

Leverage

1 = over 40% debt-to-equity ratio

10 = below 5% debt-to-equity ratio

Geographics

1 = West

5 = South

10 = Northeast

You can save time by using a computer database to find possible target companies. The database enables you to select ranges for size, profitability, leverage, and so on and then screen out candidates fulfilling your requirements. Information on publicly held companies is much more available than for closely held businesses.

¶ 2725 Acquisition Strategy and Process

The buyer should prepare a brochure of itself so the target company may be acquainted with the buyer's objectives, philosophy, and background. A proposal should also be prepared explaining the financial and operating benefits of a merger to the target company.

Planning to integrate the acquired company into the buyer should take place early in the acquisition process. Areas requiring planning include policies and procedures, data processing, organizational and management structure, personnel, operations, financial reporting, customer base, and supplier relationships.

After discussions become serious, the investigation of the target company should involve reviewing available financial information and audit work papers, reviewing tax returns, visiting the target's facilities, and interviewing management (e.g., research and development programs, and manufacturing and distribution methods). There should be a purchase audit, particularly to "key" accounts and exposure areas, to uncover problems and issues not fully disclosed in the financial statements. For example, inventory should be observed and counted and a determination made whether their valuation in the financial records is appropriate. The purchase audit must consider financial, accounting, and operating matters. Outside consultants may need to be retained in specialized areas (e.g., technology and product capability).

The areas of investigation include:

- Industry (e.g., competition, growth rate, governmental regulation, and barriers to entry).
- Target company background and history (e.g., nature of business, locations and facilities, lawsuits, and environmental considerations).
- Financial and accounting information (e.g., ratios by major business segment, effect of inflation or recession on the company, and current values). The financial statements for the last three years should be reviewed.
- Taxes (e.g., tax attributes of target and tax-planning strategies). Tax returns should be reviewed and analyzed for the last three years. Financial income and taxable income should be reconciled. Does the state penalize multi-state enterprises? Will foreign countries impose significant tax burdens? What tax benefits will the purchase accomplish (e.g., available tax credits)? Are there any questionable items or limitations that may be challenged by the tax authorities?

- Management quality (particularly important when moving into an unrelated industry).
- Pension and health care obligations.
- Marketing (e.g., backlog, new product developments, and obsolescence problems).
- Manufacturing (e.g., production facilities and manufacturing processes and efficiencies).
- Distribution network, facilities, and methods.
- R&D (Research & development) experience.

¶ 2730 Financing of the Merger

The range of possible transaction structures is infinite, but the following are some of the basic alternatives:

- All cash transaction—financed from existing cash resources.
- All cash transaction—financed by issuing stock.
- Stock transaction—merger through exchange of stock.
- Mixed stock/cash.
- Leveraged cash transaction—financed through debt issue.
- Leveraged buyout—majority of equity replaced by debt.
- Debt transaction—debt offered to selling company shareholders.
- Mixed cash/debt.
- Preferred stock.

.01 Stock or Assets

Should stock or assets (generally cash) be given in the acquisition?

The following are advantages of giving stock:

- No cash or financing requirement for acquirer.
- Quick and simple in terms of document preparation. There is a transfer of stock certificates in exchange for immediate or deferred payment.
- In certain cases, stock transactions can be exempt from taxation to shareholders, thus potentially raising the value of the transaction.
- A stock acquisition can maintain the equity-to-assets ratio and even provide additional capital for further growth strategies.

- Target shareholders share risk of acquisition.
- Minority stockholders may not have appraisal rights.
- Typically, stockholder votes authorizing the purchase or sale are not required.
- May take advantage of acquirer's high stock price.
- Target management has incentive to maintain commitment.

The following are disadvantages of giving stock:

- Can be less attractive to target shareholders.
- The acquirer, in buying stock of the target company, assumes its liabilities, whether disclosed or not.
- Dilution of acquirer shareholder earnings.
- Dilution of ownership/control.
- Risk of conflict after merger.
- If the target is liquidated subsequent to the acquisition, considerable effort is required in conveying the target company's assets as part of the liquidation.

The following are advantages of giving assets:

- Acquirer has complete control over the assets it buys and the liabilities it assumes.
- Attractive to shareholders because they have value immediately and have no risk.
- Typically, no acquiring company stockholder vote is needed.
- Easier to understand.

The following are disadvantages of giving assets:

- Dilution of earnings.
- Difficult to determine the fair value of each asset.
- Current target management may have little incentive to facilitate transaction or maintain commitment after transaction.
- Target company's stockholders must approve.
- State transfer taxes must be paid.
- A cash acquisition can materially lower the equity to assets ratio of the surviving company.
- Creation of goodwill is not tax deductible. Further, income depressed by significant goodwill amortization costs may result

in a lower stock price, potentially making the buyer in turn vulnerable to takeover.

- Creditor agreement may be needed for certain transfers and assignments.
- Must conform to bulk sales laws.

.02 Leverage

If the decision is made to give cash to the targeted company shareholders, some form of equity and/or debt will have to be issued because it is unusual for the acquiring company to have sufficient cash or liquid assets to finance the entire transaction. Debt financing may range from an intermediate-term loan for part of the purchase price to structural debt financing of 90 percent or more of the price (leveraged buyout). There are many considerations in deciding whether to use leverage and in determining the appropriate amount of leverage.

The following are advantages of leverage:

- Interest expense is tax deductible.
- Increased return to shareholders.
- Since shareholders' ownership is maintained, there is a lack of dilution.

The following are disadvantages of leverage:

- Creditors have priority claim on merged company.
- The greater financing risk may lower the company's stock and bond prices as well as result in increasing costs of financing.
- Possible lowering in credit standing and bond ratings.
- A cash problem may result in default.
- Interest payments lower earnings.
- Interest and principal payments reduce cash flow.

Leveraged buyouts are quite popular. A leveraged buyout occurs when an entity primarily borrows money (sometimes 90 percent or more) in order to buy another company. Typically, the acquiring company uses as collateral the assets of the acquired business. Generally, repayments of the debt will be made from the yearly operating funds flow of the acquired company. A leveraged buyout may also be made when the acquiring company uses its own assets as security for the loan. It may also be used if a firm wishes to go private. In most cases, the stockholders of the acquired company will receive an amount greater than the current price of the stock. A leveraged buyout involves more risk than an acquisition done through the issuance of equity securities.

The high debt service requirement drains cash flow during the period that the debt is outstanding. However, once debt is retired, shareholders enjoy ownership of the remaining enterprise. The debt may be reduced rapidly by selling some assets or divisions of the acquired company, if warranted.

The characteristics conducive to a leveraged buyout are:

- The earnings and cash flow of the company must be predictable so they may cover interest and principal payments on the debt financing.
- The growth rate of the firm should exceed the inflation rate.
- There must be a good market share and product line, otherwise the firm is vulnerable to an economic decline or competitive actions.
- There should be a good asset base to serve as collateral.
- The assets should not be presently encumbered, and the debt-equity ratio should currently be low.
- There are minimal capital expenditure requirements.
- The company should be liquid in order to meet its debt obligations.
- There is future salability of the company, if desired.
- Technological change is not a problem.
- Management is highly qualified and is given a significant equity stake.
- The business is selling at a low P/E ratio.

.03 Preferred Stock Financing

One important development in year 2001 is the disappearance of the pooling-of-interests merger-accounting method, which required the use of common stock. Now, companies must employ purchase accounting, regardless of payment terms, and stock offers no advantage in purchase accounting.

Preferred stock is one tool companies may now employ more frequently in financing their acquisitions. Like corporate bonds, preferred shares offer investors a predictable income stream in the form of dividends that must be paid before any distributions to common shareholders. While those preferred dividends allow for no deduction for tax purposes, as interest payments on debt are, preferred shares offer the same equity relief for stressed corporate balance sheets that common stock does.

A big advantage of equity is its ability to preserve a transaction's tax-free status for selling shareholders. For an acquisition to qualify as a tax-free reorganization, sellers must maintain a "continuity of interest" in the new business. Continuity is usually accomplished by a common share swap, but preferred shares may also accomplish the same result.

¶ 2735 The Use of Capital Budgeting Techniques in Appraising the Acquisition

In deciding whether to buy another business, capital budgeting may be used. Also, the effect of the new capital structure on the firm's overall cost of capital has to be projected.

> ***Example 2.*** W Company is contemplating purchasing P Company for $95,000. W's current cost of capital is 12 percent. P's estimated overall cost of capital after the acquisition is 10 percent. Projected cash inflows from years one through eight are $13,000. (Assume no residual value.)

The net present value is:

Year	*Present Value*
0 (-$95,000 × 1)	($95,000)
1–8 ($13,000 × 5.3349)	+ 69,354*
Net present value	($25,646)

*Using 10 percent as the discount rate, from Table 4 (present value of an annuity of $1) = T4 (10%, 8 years).

The acquisition is not feasible since there is a negative net present value.

> ***Example 3.*** C Company wants to buy some fixed assets of B Company. However, the latter wants to sell out its business. The balance sheet of B Company follows:

Assets	
Cash	$ 4,000
Accounts receivable	8,000
Inventory	10,000
Equipment 1	16,000
Equipment 2	28,000
Equipment 3	42,000
Building	110,000
Total assets	$218,000
Liabilities and Stockholders' Equity	
Total liabilities	80,000
Total equity	138,000
Total liabilities and equity	$218,000

C wants only equipment 1 and 2 and the building. The other assets, excluding cash, can be sold for $24,000. The total cash received is thus $28,000 ($24,000 + $4,000 initial cash balance). B desired $50,000 for the whole business. C will thus have to pay a total of $130,000 which is $80,000 in total liabilities and $50,000 for its owners. The actual net cash outlay is therefore $102,000 ($130,000 - $28,000). It is expected that the after-tax cash inflows from the new equipment will be $27,000 per year for the next five years. The cost of capital is eight percent. (Assume no residual value.)

The net present value of the acquisition is:

Year	*Present Value*
0 (-$102,000 × 1)	($102,000)
1–8 ($27,000 × 3.9927)	107,803
Net present value	$5,803

Since there is a positive net present value the acquisition should me made.

.01 *Exchange Ratio*

The exchange ratio is the number of shares of the aquiring company that a shareholder will receive for one share of the aquired company.

Example 4. T Company buys B Company. T Company's stock sells for $75 per share while B's stock sells for $45. As per the merger terms, T offers $50 per share. The exchange ratio is 0.667 ($50/$75). Thus, T exchanges 0.667 shares of its stock for one share of B.

¶ 2740 Effect of Merger on Earnings Per Share and Market Price Per Share

A merger can have a positive or negative impact on net income and market price per share of common stock.

Example 5. Relevant information follows:

	Company A	*Company B*
Net income	$50,000	$84,000
Outstanding shares	5,000	12,000
EPS	$10	$7
P/E ratio	7	10
Market price	$70	$70

Company B acquires Company A and exchanges its shares for A's shares on a one-for-one basis. The effect on EPS follows:

	B Shares Owned After Merger	*EPS Before Merger*	*EPS After Merger*
A stockholders	5,000	$10	$7.88*
B stockholders	12,000	7	7.88*
Total	$17,000		

*Total net income is determined as:

5,000 shares × \$10	\$50,000
12,000 shares × \$7	84,000
	\$134,000

$$\text{EPS} = \frac{\text{Net income}}{\text{Total shares}} = \frac{\$134{,}000}{17{,}000} = \$7.88$$

EPS decreases by \$2.12 for A stockholders and increases by \$0.88 for B stockholders.

The effect on market price is not clear. Assuming the combined entity has the same P/E ratio as Company B, the market price per share will be \$78.80 (10 × \$7.88). The stockholders experience a higher market value per share. The increased market value occurs because net income of the combined entity is valued at a P/E ratio of 10, the same as Company B, while before the merger Company A had a lower P/E multiplier of seven. However, if the combined entity is valued at the lower P/E multiplier of seven, the same as Company A, the market value would be \$55.16 (7 x \$7.88). In this case, the stockholders in each firm experience a reduction in market value of \$14.84 (\$70.00 – \$55.16).

Since the effect of the merger on market value per share is not clear, the crucial consideration is EPS.

Example 6. The following situation exists:

Market price per share of acquiring company	\$100
Market price per share of acquired company	\$20
Price per share offered	\$24
The exchange ratio equals:	
Shares \$24/\$100	0.24
Market price \$24/\$20	1.2

Example 7. M Company wants to buy J Company by issuing its shares. Relevant information follows:

	M Company	*J Company*
Net income	\$40,000	\$26,000
Outstanding shares	20,000	8,000

The exchange ratio is 2 to 1. The EPS based on the original shares of each company follows:

EPS of combined equity = Combined net income/Total shares

$$\frac{66{,}000}{20{,}000 + (8{,}000 \times 2)} = \frac{66{,}000}{36{,}000 \text{ shares}} = 1.83 \text{ EPS}$$

EPS of M = \$1.83

EPS of J = \$1.83 × 2 = \$3.66

Example 8. O Company wants to buy P Company by exchanging 1.8 shares of its stock for each share of P. O expects to have the same P/E ratio after the merger as before. Applicable data follows:

	O Company	*P Company*
Net income	$500,000	$150,000
Shares	225,000	30,000
Market price per share	$50	$60

The exchange ratio of market price equals:

$$\frac{\text{Offer price}}{\text{Market price of P}} = \frac{\$50 \times 1.8}{\$60} = \frac{90}{\$60} = 1.5$$

EPS and P/E ratios for each company follow.

	O Company		*P Company*	
EPS	$500,000/225,000	= $2.22	$150,000/30,000	= $5
P/E Ratio	$50/$2.22	= 22.5	$60/$5	= 12

The P/E ratio used in obtaining P is:

$$\frac{1.8 \times \$50}{\$5} = \frac{\$90}{\$5} = 18 \text{ times}$$

The EPS of O after the acquisition is:

$$\frac{650{,}000}{225{,}000 + (30{,}000 \times 1.8)} = \frac{\$650{,}000}{279{,}000} = \$2.33$$

The expected market price per share of the combined entity is:

$2.33 × 22.5 times = $52.43

¶ 2745 Risk of the Acquisition

In appraising the risk associated with an acquisition, a scenario analysis may be used, looking at the best case, worst case, and most likely case. Operating scenarios consider assumptions as to variables, including sales, volume, cost, competitive reaction, governmental interference, and customer perception. The probability for each scenario is on the basis of experience. Sensitivity analysis may be used to indicate how sensitive the project's returns are to variances from expected values of essential variables. For example, you may undertake a sensitivity analysis on selling prices assuming they are, for example, 10 to 15 percent higher or lower than expected. The theory behind sensitivity analysis is to adjust key variables from their expected values in the most likely case. The analysis can be performed to show their expected values in the most likely case. The analysis can be performed assuming one purchase price or all possible purchase prices. What is the effect, for example, of a four-percent change in the gross profit rate on projected returns?

Based on sensitivity analysis, you should pay an amount for a target company resulting in cutoff return given the most likely operating scenario.

Warning: It is difficult to accomplish successful unrelated diversification. An example is General Electric's acquisition of Utah International. The firm eventually divested of its acquisition.

Recommendation: Acquisition of companies operating in related fields usually has a higher success rate.

¶ 2750 Holding Company

A holding company is one whose sole purpose is to own the stock of other companies. To obtain voting control of a business, the holding company may make a direct market purchase or tender offer. A company may elect to become a holding company if its basic business is declining, and it decides to liquidate its assets and uses the funds to invest in growth companies.

Since the operating companies owned by the holding company are separate legal entities, the obligations of one are isolated from the others.

Recommendation: A loan officer lending to one company should attempt to obtain a guarantee by the other companies.

The following are advantages of a holding company:

- Risk protection—in that the failure of one company does not cause the failure of another or of the holding company. If the owned company fails, the loss of the holding company is restricted to its investment in it.
- Ability to obtain a significant amount of assets with a small investment. The holding company can control more assets than it could acquire through a merger.
- Ease of obtaining control of another company; all that is needed is to purchase enough stock in the marketplace. Unlike a merger which requires stockholder or management approval, no approval is needed for a holding company.

The following are disadvantages of a holding company:

- More costly to administer than a single company resulting from a merger because economies of scale are not achieved.
- Incurrence of increased debt because the acquisition may magnify variability in earnings, thus subjecting the holding company to more risk.

- The chance that the U.S. Department of Justice will deem the holding company a monopoly and force dissolution of some of the owned companies.
- Multiple taxes because the income the holding company receives is in the form of cash. Before paying dividends, the subsidiary must pay taxes on the earnings. When profit is distributed to the holding company as dividends, it must pay tax on the dividends received unless an 80 percent or more of the subsidiary's shares or a 100 percent dividend exemption exists. No multiple tax exists for a subsidiary that is part of a merged company.

Example 9. A holding company owns 70 percent of another firm. Dividends received are $20,000. The tax rate is 34 percent. The tax paid on the dividend follows:

Dividend	$20,000
Dividend exclusion (80%)	16,000
Dividend subject to tax	4,000
Tax rate	× 34%
Tax	$1,360

The effective tax rate is 6.8 percent ($1,360/$20,000).

¶ 2755 Hostile Takeover Bids

If a negotiated takeover of another company is impossible, a hostile bid may be needed. In a hostile bid, management of the targeted company is bypassed, and the stockholders are approached directly. The acquirer argues that management is not maximizing the potential of the company and is not protecting the interest of the shareholders.

In a tender offer, the buyer goes directly to the stockholders of the target business to tender (sell) their shares, typically for cash. The tender in some cases may be shares in the acquiring company rather than cash. If the buyer obtains enough stock, it can gain control of the target company and force the merger. Cash, rather than securities, is usually used because a stock offering requires a prospectus thereby losing the advantages of timeliness and surprise. Stockholders are induced to sell when the tender price substantially exceeds the current market price of the target company stock. Typically, there is an expiration date to tender.

Hostile takeovers are typically quite costly because they usually involve a significant price incentive and antitakeover measures. They can be disruptive to both buyer and seller because of "slur" campaigns. It is rare that smooth transitions of management take place.

The typical features of a hostile takeover candidate may include:

1. A multidivisional organization has diverse business activities.

2. Asset values of component divisions are not reflected in the market price of the company's stock.

3. Financial performance of the individual business lines could be better.

4. Existing management is unable to realize the true value of the company.

The usual initial step in launching a hostile bid is to buy stock of the target company in the open market. The SEC requires that any investor who buys more than a five-percent interest in a public company should register his or her holding and provide the intent (e.g., passive or to gain eventual control) through a Schedule 13-D filing. Beyond five-percent ownership, it becomes difficult to make open-market purchases of stock without revealing the intention to acquire control. A greater percentage of holding within the five days allowed for the 13-D filing may be difficult. A company may elect to make a passive investment for a limited period before reassessing the intention to acquire control. The acquiring business must furnish to the management of the potential acquired company and to the SEC 30 days notice of its intent to acquire. Once the intention to acquire control is made public, the stock price of the target company generally rises in expectation of a tender offer at a higher price.

The direct appeal to shareholders, which often follows, is frequently made through a public tender offer. Management of the target company will typically recommend that shareholders reject the offer and possibly propose an alternative restructuring arrangement.

The management of a targeted company can fight the takeover attempt in the following ways:

1. Purchase treasury stock to make fewer shares available for tendering.

2. Initiate legal action to prevent the takeover, such as by applying antitrust laws.

3. Postpone the tender offer (some states have laws to delay the tender offer).

4. Declare an attractive dividend to keep stockholders happy.

The following are advantages of a hostile bid:

- Direct communication with stockholders to bypass management intransigency.
- Flexibility to alter terms.
- Increased value of existing stake.
- Improved profitability of the target.

The following are disadvantages of a hostile bid:

- Price: hostile bidders may pay a high premium especially if competition arises in the takeover attempt.
- Cost: high transaction and advisory costs.
- Risk: hostile bids often fail.
- Creation of ill will and problems with integrating the target after merger.
- Possible adverse litigation or regulatory action.
- Possible retaliatory action by target.

The targeted company may have in place preventive measures against being taken over including:

1. *Golden Parachute.* Management compensation arrangements that are triggered when there is a purchase of the business, such as lump-sum benefits, employment agreements, and stock options. Recent examples are Greyhound and Hughes Tool.
2. *Poison Pill.* When a hostile bid is eminent, the targeted company takes out significant debt (or issues preferred stock) that makes the company unattractive to the hostile acquirer because of the high debt position. Recent examples are Union Carbide and CBS, Inc.
3. *Self-Tender.* After a hostile bid, the target company itself makes a counteroffer for its own shares. A recent example is Newmont Mining.
4. *Greenmail.* The target company buys back the stock accumulated by the raider, at a premium. Recent examples are Texaco, Walt Disney, and Goodyear.
5. *PAC-MAN.* The defending company makes a counteroffer for the stock of the raiding company. Recent examples are American Brands and Bendix Corporation.
6. *White Knight.* The defending company finds a third party who is willing to pay a higher premium, typically with "friendlier" intentions than the raider. Recent examples are Gulf Oil Corp. (Chevron) and Sterling Drugs (Eastman Kodak).
7. *Asset Spinoff.* The defending party identifies the assets most desirable to the raider. It then spins off the assets to one of its separate companies or sells them to a third party. Recent examples are Union Carbide and Marathon Oil.

¶ 2760 The Valuation of a Targeted Company

In a merger, we have to value the targeted company. As a starting point in valuation, the key financial data must be accumulated and analyzed including historical financial statement, forecasted financial statements, and tax returns. The assumption of the valuation must be clearly spelled out.

The valuation approaches may be profit- or asset-oriented. Adjusted earnings may be capitalized at an appropriate multiple. Future adjusted cash earnings may be discounted by the rate of return that may be earned. Assets may be valued at fair market value, such as through appraisal. These methods were discussed in Chapters 8 and 14. Comparative software programs are available for merger analysis.

.01 Comparison with Industry Averages

Valid comparisons can be made between the entity being valued and others in the same industry. Industry norms should be noted. General sources of comparative industry data found financial advisory services include Standard and Poor's, Moody's, Value Line, Dun and Bradstreet, and Robert Morris Associates. Trade publications may also be consulted. Reference may be made to the *Almanac of Business and Industrial Financial Ratios* (based on corporate tax returns to the IRS) written by Leo Troy and published by Prentice Hall. If a small company is being acquired, reference may be made to *Financial Studies of the Small Business* published annually by Financial Research Associates (Washington, D.C.: Financial Research Associates, 1984).

Publicly available information on the targeted company include the annual report; SEC Forms 10-K, 10-Q, and 8-K; interim shareholder reports; proxy statements; press releases; and offering prospectuses.

¶ 2765 Divestiture

The divestiture of business segments by corporations has become an accepted strategy for growth rather than diversification. Divestiture involves the partial or complete conversion, disposition, and reallocation of people, money, inventories, plants, equipment, and products. It is the process of eliminating a portion of the enterprise for subsequent use of the freed resources for some other purpose. A divestment may involve a manufacturing, marketing, research, or other business function.

A business segment may be subject to divestiture if:

1. They do not produce an acceptable return on invested capital.
2. They do not generate sufficient cash flow.
3. They fit in with the overall corporate strategy.
4. They are unrelated to their primary lines of business.

5. They fail to meet management goals for growth in profits, sales, or in other respects.

6. The worth of the pieces is greater than that of the whole.

.01 *Objectives and Types of Divestitures*

Sooner or later a corporation will find itself in the position of needing to divest some of its assets. This may be for a variety of reasons. The usual objectives behind divestiture are to reposition the company in a market, raise cash, and to reduce losses. The other alternatives to divestiture are liquidation and bankruptcy; however, in this time of acquisitions and buyouts usually a buyer can be found. There are four primary types of divestitures:

1. Sale of an operating unit to another firm.

2. Sale to the managers of the unit being divested.

3. Setting up the business to be divested as a separate corporation and then giving (or "spinning off") its stock to the divesting firm's stockholders on a pro rata basis.

4. Outright liquidation of assets.

When the divestiture is in the form of a sale to another firm, it usually involves an entire division or unit and is generally for cash but sometimes for stock of the acquiring firm. In a managerial buyout, the division managers themselves purchase the division, often through a leverage buyout, and reorganize it as a closely held firm. In a spin-off, the firm's existing stockholders are given new stock representing separate ownership in the company that was divested. The new company establishes its own board of directors and officers and operates as a separate entity. In liquidation, the assets of the divested unit are sold off separately instead of as a whole.

.02 *Determining What Areas/Units Should Be Sold*

When trying to determine which areas or units of the company could be sold off, there are some simple guidelines that management should follow:

- The sum of a division's parts may be greater in value than the whole division.

- Simple components of a division may be sold more easily than the whole division itself.

- The disposal of a corporate division is a major marketing operation.

- Planning should include an evaluation from the viewpoint of the potential buyer.

- A spin-off should be considered if the division is large enough and may be potentially publicly traded.

In addition, management must review existing operations and identify those divisions that do not relate to the primary focus of the company or do not meet internal financial and performance standards. Special strength of each division must also be considered. Does a division provide a unique service or have a special marketing, distribution system, or production facilities that may be of more value to another company? Also, the financial aspects must be considered. The historical and projected return on investment needs to be calculated and tabulated for each division.

Using these guidelines and the information determined above, management can focus on three topics. First, the attractiveness and value to others versus the arguments for keeping the division. Secondly, what corrective action would need to be taken to make the division viable. Thirdly, the current value of the division to the company. Only after considering all of these factors can a divestiture decision be made for a division.

¶ 2770 Divestiture or Restructuring Planning

Planning for divestitures, as for acquisitions, should be related to the company's overall objectives and long-range plans. Typically, this process requires that management:

- *Review existing operations.* Identify those lines that either do not relate to primary product areas or do not meet internal financial and operating goals. Special strengths and weaknesses should be inventoried. These might include, for example, the existence (or absence) of special marketing, distribution, or product facilities that might be more valuable to another company.

- *Calculate historical and projected return.* Calculate each operating unit's historical and projected return on investment (historical and current value) and profit contributions.

- *Determine what units are to be divested.* Using the information obtained in the steps above, study high-priority divestiture possibilities. Focus on (1) the attractiveness and value to others versus the arguments for retention, (2) corrective action that might be taken, and (3) the current value to the company. Only then should a decision be made about which units, if any, to divest.

- *Identify logical acquirers.* Identify companies, groups, or individuals for whom the particular strengths of a unit to be divested would be of most value as well as the weaknesses that would be of least concern. Consideration should also be given to selling a unit to management through a leveraged buyout or to employees through an Employee Stock Ownership Plan (ESOP).

The use of these techniques allows employees to become owners of the divested unit and thereby helps ensure their continued employment.

¶ 2775 Sale Planning

Selling a business is one of the most difficult decisions that management and stockholders face. In the case of publicly owned companies, the decision process is similar to that noted above for acquisition and divestiture planning. In particular the following considerations need to be addressed:

- The company's present position and outlook compared with its long-term goals and objectives.
- Its capabilities for overcoming likely obstacles or threats, and its ability to capitalize on expected opportunities and accomplish long-term goals and objectives.
- Its market value in relation to underlying intrinsic or expected value.
- Its value to others (likely to be realized only through merger) in relation to present market value.
- Alternative approaches to realizing intrinsic value if it is higher than current market value.
- The outlook for the business and reinvestment opportunities compared with the stock market's perception of these factors.

In evaluating the company's present position, outlook, and capabilities, the following questions need to be asked:

- Is the company and/or its products nearing *maturity,* thereby indicating that stockholder value might be maximized by sale in the near future? (*Note:* Studies show that maximum value is achieved through sale while revenues and *profits* are still growing at, or above, their historical rates.)
- Is the company's industry nearing a mature stage?
- Will some form of corporate development activity (e.g., acquisition, new product development, joint venture, and marketing arrangements) be required to penetrate the company's markets beyond current levels?
- Are the company's products likely to lose their uniqueness in the near future, and/or is the company unable to make the commitment necessary to maintain the uniqueness of its products?

- Is the company's market stable or declining? Are capital requirements likely to be a drain on the company in the future due to aging facilities, rapidly growing sales and/or industry, changing technology, or increasing competition?
- Is the company finding it difficult to obtain raw materials or labor at competitive prices?
- Is the company's performance (based on key financial ratios) behind the industry norm, or is it declining relative to the rest of the industry?
- Is competition likely to increase in the near future?
- Is management lacking in depth, experience, or capability when compared with the rest of the industry?
- Does the company have excess capacity that is unlikely to be filled in the near future?
- Is the company lacking a well-defined strategy for future growth and profitability?
- Is management/employee morale waning for any reason?
- Is the company worth more to others than to current stockholders (i.e., are there potential buyers that can maximize potential quicker than the current stockholders can)? How saleable is the business?
- Will a sale really accomplish the business objectives of the company? Are there better alternatives?

Needless to say, making the decision requires complete objectivity on the part of both privately owned and publicly owned companies. Privately owned companies, however, must also consider the personal objectives of stockholders, whether or not they are active in the business. The questions below are designed to help those stockholders weigh various personal considerations that generally enter into a decision to sell or not sell. These personal considerations, of course, must be evaluated together with the business considerations already noted above:

- Are stockholders who are active in the business also approaching retirement age?
- Does the company have a competent manager to assume leadership of the business upon retirement or death of active stockholders?
- Do the stockholders need to create personal liquidity (for retirement, estate taxes, and lifestyle or other reasons) or to diversify investment risk?

- Are there other personal considerations (e.g., personal or family health problems, marital difficulties, family disagreements, disagreements with other stockholders or with management, age, boredom, and commitments to philanthropic, civic, leisure, and other business activities) that would cause stockholders to consider a sale or that might make them less effective in running the business?

- Will a sale really accomplish the personal objectives of the stockholders? Are there better alternatives?

- What is the value of the business to current stockholders if intangible personal considerations are included compared with its value to others?

Once a decision to sell has been made, in-depth planning should begin. Answers to the following questions should help management and/or stockholders with that planning:

- Have you exploited the strengths of the business and done all you can to minimize the weaknesses?

- Have you estimated the worth of the business versus its worth in the future?

- Is the timing right for achieving maximum value?

- Do you know the tax ramifications of the sale?

- What form of transaction best satisfies the business objectives and, in the case of privately held companies, the personal objectives of stockholders?

- Has adequate information been assembled to present to potential buyers?

- Who are the logical buyers?

- Have you developed an effective plan to identify and approach those buyers?

- Should you involve an investment banker or merger and acquisition consultant? How should he be chosen and compensated? (*Note:* Generally, such an adviser should be engaged).

- Do you have a plan to deal with interested buyers, employees, customers, and others during the sale process?

- Are there other details that need to be nailed down?

It is particularly important to do everything that can be done to increase the attractiveness of the business prior to sale, such as divesting undesirable assets or improving profitability. It is also important to anticipate the information potential buyers will want and the questions they will ask. A few final questions should also be answered before marketing of the company begins:

- Have all possible buyers been identified, not just the most probable ones?
- How will marketing of the company to possible buyers and inquiries be handled?
- Have pricing strategies been developed?
- Have negotiating strategies been developed?
- Has consideration been given on how to structure the transaction from a financial viewpoint (and a tax and accounting viewpoint as well)?
- Have acceptable forms of financing the transaction by the buyer been considered?
- Have alternative selling strategies been considered?

In summary, management should design an acquisition, divestiture, or sale program that identifies major issues and opportunities, analyzes alternatives, fixes responsibility for performance and monitors progress. This overview is intended only to suggest the basic steps involved in acquisition, divestiture, and sale planning; each company embarking on such a program should develop a planning system that meets its own special requirements.

¶ 2780 Valuation and Appraisal in Divestiture

When the time comes to sell a division, an asking price needs to be determined. Valuation of a division is not an exact science, and in the final analysis, the value of a division is in the eye of the purchaser. While the expertise of an investment banker or business broker can and should be enlisted in setting the price of the division, there are some standard accounting methods that can be used to estimate a division's value. A business broker will usually be very willing to help in the initial estimate phase in hopes that they will get the opportunity to act as your agent in selling the division. These valuation methods will be broken down into asset valuation methods, those based on sales and income, and those based on market comparisons. Although these methods vary in their applicability and depend on certain facts and circumstances, they can be used to determine a range of values for a division.

There are basically four groups of methods of valuation or appraisal: (1) asset valuation methods, (2) sales and income methods, (3) market comparison methods, and (4) discounted cash flow methods.

.01 Asset Valuation Methods

Asset valuation methods are based on the asset value of a business segment. Four popular methods are described below.

Adjusted net book value. One of the most conservative methods of valuation is the adjusted net book value, because it determines the value based on historical (book) value and not on market value. To adjust for conservatism, add in such items as favorable lease arrangements and other intangible items, such as customer lists, patents, and goodwill.

Replacement cost. Another method is the replacement cost technique. It asks, "What would it cost to purchase the division's assets new?" This method will give a higher division value than the adjusted net book value method and is therefore adequate for adjusting the book value to account for new costs. This figure can also be used as a basis for determining the liquidation value of the division's assets. The most reasonable value comes from adjusting the replacement value for depreciation and obsolescence of equipment.

Liquidation value. The liquidation value is also a conservative estimate of a division's value, since it does not consider the division's ongoing earning power. The liquidation value does provide the seller with the lowest that the price can be. The liquidation value is determined by estimating the cash value of assets assuming that they are to be sold in a short period of time. All the liabilities, real and estimated, are then deducted from the cash that was raised to determine the net liquidation value. Liquidation value can be determined based on fire sale prices or on a longer-term sales price. Obviously, the fire sale value would be lower.

Secured loan value. The secured loan value technique is based on the borrowing power of the division's assets. Banks will usually lend up to 90 percent of the value of accounts receivable and anywhere from 10 to 60 percent on the value of inventory depending on the quantity of the inventory in the conversion process.

.02 Sales and Income Factors

Using sales and/or income figures as the basis for valuation can be made in two different ways.

Price-Earnings (P/E) ratios. The P/E ratio for publicly held companies is known and therefore valuation is made easy. The division's value can be determined by multiplying the P/E ratio by the expected earnings for the division. This will give a derived price that all potential buyers can readily understand. The earnings can be estimated from quarterly or annual reports published by the company.

For privately held companies, however, it is difficult to determine a P/E ratio as the stock of the company is not traded and the earnings are rarely disclosed. However, the earnings can be estimated and an industry average P/E ratio can be used in the calculation to estimate the private company's sales value.

Sales or earnings multiples. There are many rules of thumb that can be used when estimating a division's value based on a multiple of sales or earnings. For example, insurance agencies sell for 200 percent of annual commissions, or liquor stores sell for 10 times monthly sales. Another example would be radio stations selling for eight times earnings or cash flow. These rules provide only a very rough estimate and may result in a completely erroneous estimate of a division's value. Most business brokers will know these rule of thumb values to assist management in estimating the value of a division.

.03 *Market Based Comparisons*

Every day that a public company is traded on the stock market, a new value is assigned to it by the traders. Thus, the stock price can be compared to equivalent companies, in terms of products, size of operations, and average P/E ratios. From these P/E ratios, an estimated sales price can be estimated as described earlier.

In the case of private companies, it is difficult for the buyer to determine the earnings of the company. However, they can compare the company to other companies that are publicly traded. Comparison to publicly traded companies is necessary as the sales price is typically disclosed in the sale or acquisition announcement.

.04 *Discounted Cash Flow Analysis*

Another method of determining value of a business segment is to use discounted cash flow (DCF) analysis. This bases the value of the segment on the current value of its projected cash flow. In theory, this method should result in a division's value being equal to that determined by one of the P/E ratio calculations, since both reflect the current worth of the company's earnings. In actuality, discounted cash flow is basing the value of the company on actual forecasted cash flows, whereas the stock market is basing the stock price on other relevant factors including the markets perception of the company and its potential cash flow.

The DCF method requires information on:

- Forecasted actual cash flows.
- Assumed terminal (residual) value of the division at the end of the forecast period (book value, zero, or a multiple of earnings are frequently used).
- Discount rate. Choosing the right discount rate is the key to the successful use of the DCF technique. It must take into account the following factors:
  - — Purchaser's expected return on investment (ROI)

— Purchaser's assessment of risk

— Cost of capital

— Projected inflation rates

— Current interest rates

In general, whichever method of evaluation is chosen, it is wise to check that resulting value with at least one other method to see if it is a reasonable figure. We have to be careful of excessively high or low figures. Determining the liquidation value of the company or division should set a *floor* for negotiations.

An illustration: discounted cash flow analysis. Management will choose to divest a segment of their business if they perceive that the action will increase the wealth of the stockholders, as reflected in the price of the firm's stock. It can be further said that the price of the firm's stock will react favorably to a divestiture if the new present value of the transaction is perceived by the market to be positive.

Should a profitable business segment be retained and not divested, it would generate annual cash inflows for a particular or infinite number of years. Discounted cash flow analysis involves a comparison of initial incoming cash flows resulting from the sale of a business unit with the present value of the foregone future cash inflows given up by the firm. Foregone future cash flows refer to the cash flows that the business unit is anticipated to generate and will do so for the acquiring firm. The divesting firm gives up these cash inflows in exchange for the selling price of the business segment. For divestiture analysis to be of any value, the foregone future cash flow must be accurately estimated. The present value of these future inflows are found by discounting them at the firm's weighted average cost of capital, k.

Example 10. Exhibit 1 shows estimated cash inflows and outflows for a fictitious divestment candidate (FDC) over the next five years. The cash flows represent the best estimates by the managers of FDC's parent company, and they further believe that FDC will be able to be sold at its residual value of $58.7 million in five years.

The firm's cost of capital is assumed to be known and is 15 percent.

The net present value of the future cash inflows of FDC is $47.26 million. If FDC were to be divested, the managers of its parent company should only consider selling prices greater than this amount. This logic also assumes that the $47.3 million can be reinvested at a 15-percent rate of return.

Another way of looking at this valuing task makes use of the following equation for divestiture net present value (DNPV):

$$DNPV = I - \sum \frac{NCF_t}{(1+k)^t} \quad (1)$$

Where I = the selling price of the business unit, and NCF_t = net cash flow in period t. If a $50 million offer was made by a firm for FDC, the DNPV from equation 1 will equal $2.7 million, as shown below.

$$DNPV = 50 - \sum \frac{9.8}{1.15} + \sum \frac{3.4}{1.15^2} + \sum \frac{2.4}{1.15^3} + \sum \frac{5.8}{1.15^4} + \sum \frac{62.9}{1.15^5}$$

DNPV = $50 − $47.26 = $2.74 million.

Exhibit 7

FDC's Cash Flow Projections (In Millions)

Cash Inflows	*1*	*2*	*3*	*4*	*5*
Net Operating Profit	$3.10	$3.60	$4.00	$5.10	$6.00
Depreciation	2.1	2.4	1.8	2.3	2.1
Residual Value					58.7
Total	$5.20	$6.00	$5.80	$7.40	$66.80
Cash Outflows					
Capital Expenditure	$1.70	$1.30	$0.80	$2.10	$1.70
Increase (Decrease) in Working Capital	-6.3	1.3	2.6	-0.5	2.2
Total	-$4.60	$2.60	$3.40	$1.60	$3.90
Net Cash Inflow	$9.80	$3.40	$2.40	$5.80	$62.90
Present Value of $1* = T3	0.8696	0.7561	0.6575	0.5718	0.4972
Present Value	$8.52	$2.57	$1.58	$3.32	$31.27
Total Present Value	$47.26				

**Note:* Table 3 in Appendix B = Present value interest factor for the cost of capital of 15 percent.

From a financial point of view, this divestment is acceptable. If the divestment candidate has an unlimited life, such as a division in a healthy industry, then cash flows must be forecasted to infinity. This task is made simple by treating the cash flows similarly to a constant growth stock and value accordingly. If the cash inflows are expected to remain constant (zero growth) to infinity, then the present value of the NCF (net cash flows) can be determined in the same manner as for a preferred stock, or perpetuity. In this case, the DNPV will be:

$$DNPV = I - \frac{NCF}{k} \quad (2)$$

For future cash flows that are expected to grow at an after tax rate of g, the present value of those flows can be found using the constant growth valuation model. In this case, the DNPV will be:

$$DNPV = I - \frac{NCF_1}{k - g} \quad (3)$$

Where NCF_1 = the expected NCF in the next period.

A final situation encountered often when evaluating divestiture candidates is the case where the NCFs are expected to be uneven for a number of years followed by even growth. In this case, the DNPV can be found as:

$$DNPV = I - \Sigma \frac{NCF_1}{(1+k)^1} + \Sigma \frac{NCF_2}{(1+k)^2} + \ldots + \Sigma \frac{NCF_{c-1}}{(k-g)} \times \frac{1}{(1+k)}$$

Where NCF_1 and NCF_2 represent foregone cash flows in periods 1 and 2 and c = the first year in which constant growth applies.

Firms should only divest of assets with positive DNPVs. To do so will increase the value of the firm and, subsequently, the price of its stock. If two different candidates are mutually exclusive, the one with the highest DNPV should be chosen since this will increase the value of the firm the most. If divestiture is forced by the government, for example, and the firm finds it has a choice of candidates, all with negative DNPVs, it should divest the one whose DNPV is closest to zero, since this will reduce the value of the firm the least.

¶ 2785 Divestiture with Uncertainty

Due to the difficulty in predicting the NCFs and also in knowing what kinds of prices will be offered for the divestment candidate, the divestment's net present value is normally uncertain.

For situations involving an unknown selling price (due to a lack of offers), the parent firm can either elect not to divest of the candidate or set its asking price such that the DNPV will equal zero. This should be the minimum they are willing to accept. They can also look for other divestment candidates that offer promising DNPVs.

Adjusting for uncertain NCFs is much more difficult, and while there is no generally accepted method for accounting for this risk, there are a number of useful techniques similar to those used in capital budgeting which can be used here.

.01 Risk-Adjusted Discount Rate

Employing a risk-adjusted discount rate is one technique that can be used to account for the uncertainty of the expected NCFs. In the previous examples, the firm's weighted average cost of capital was used to discount the NCFs to their present value. This is an appropriate choice when the divestiture candidate is as risky as the firm itself. When it is more risky, the use of a higher discount rate can be used for adjustment. This will reduce the present values of the cash flows and increase the DNPV. This is logical since a relatively risky divestment candidate with uncertain cash flows will be of less value to the firm, in present dollars. The added benefit of divesting such a candidate will be reflected in the increased DNPV. On the other hand, when the NCFs are more certain than those of the rest of the firm, the discount rate should be lowered. This lowers the DNPV and makes the divestiture less attractive. Equation 1 in Example 10 can be rewritten as shown below:

$$DNPV = I - \Sigma \frac{NCF_t}{(1 + k')^t}$$

Where all terms are the same except for k' which now is the adjusted rate to be used for discounting the cash flows. Using data from Exhibit 1 and assuming that the divestment candidate is less risky than the firm as a whole (lowering k from .15 to .14) shows:

$$DNPV = 50 - \Sigma \frac{9.8}{1.14} + \Sigma \frac{3.4}{1.14^2} + \Sigma \frac{2.4}{1.14^3} + \Sigma \frac{5.8}{1.14^4} + \Sigma \frac{62.9}{1.14^5}$$

DNPV = \$50 − \$48.94 = \$1.06 million.

	1	*2*	*3*	*4*	*5*
Net Cash Inflow (NCF)	\$9.80	\$3.40	\$2.40	\$5.80	\$62.90
PV of \$1* = T3	0.8772	0.7695	0.675	0.5921	0.5194
Present Value	\$8.60	\$2.62	\$1.62	\$3.43	\$32.67
Total PV:	\$48.94				

**Note:* Table 3 = Present value interest factor for the cost of capital of 14 percent.

Using a lower discount rate lessened the DNPV by \$1.68 million (\$2.74 million − \$1.06 million). This is reasonable in that the attractiveness of a divestment candidate at a certain selling price will be lessened as the candidate is found to be less risky.

.02 Sensitivity Analysis

Sensitivity analysis is another technique that can be used in making divestiture decisions. In sensitivity analysis, the parent company evaluates the effect that certain factors have on the NCFs. For example, a divestment candidate's NCFs might be largely influenced by the price of copper, the U.S. Navy Defense budget, and upcoming union contract talks. For these three influencing factors, a number of different scenarios or forecasts can be projected, each with their expected NCFs. For instance, the expected NCFs would be highest in the scenario where all three influencing factors are favorable. Having evaluated the NCFs and DNPVs for different scenarios, the parent firm has a better understanding of the range that the NCFs might fall in and also what factors influence them the most. Further, if the probability of the scenarios can be forecasted, statistical techniques can be used to give the probability of realizing a negative DNPV, the expected DNPV and the standard deviation, and coefficient of variation of DNPVs. This information would be very useful in making divestment decisions. Using sensitivity analysis, the NCFs are discounted at the firm's weighted average cost of capital.

.03 Simulation

Simulation is a third technique used to account for the uncertainty of future cash flows. It is similar to but more sophisticated than the sensitivity analysis previously discussed. In simulation, the parent firm's managers first identify key factors that they believe are likely to influence the NCFs of a divestment candidate. Next, they create a probability distribution describing the future outcome of each key factor. The managers finally must specify the impact of each key variable on the NCFs and ultimately the DNPVs. The firm's cost of capital is again used to discount the NCFs.

Computer programs are available to assist managers in the simulation analysis. After the data has been input and the program run, the computer will estimate NCFs and corresponding DNPVs over the whole range of probabilities. From this distribution, the analyst can determine the expected DNPV and the probability that the actual DNPV will be above or below some critical level. The uncertainty associated with the DNPV can also be determined, as measured by the dispersion of possible DNPV value. This technique provides a comprehensive evaluation of the divestiture proposal.

¶ 2790 Closing the Form of the Transaction

Various considerations have an important impact on the form of the transaction.

.01 Cash Versus "Paper"

The seller's willingness to accept notes or stock of the buyer is determined partially by the personal need for current cash and more importantly by the quality and liquidity of the buyer's "paper." The seller who is not in need of immediate liquidity may, therefore, be somewhat flexible in this respect. The principal advantages of accepting the buyer's "paper" versus accepting cash are:

- It may increase the number of potential purchasers and the selling price.
- It may make it possible to structure the deal as a nontaxable transaction.
- If the interest and/or dividend rate is set at an attractively high level, it may present the seller with a better-yielding investment otherwise obtainable. The seller may be in a better position to follow and understand this investment as well.
- If attractively yielding preferred stock is taken back, the seller will hold a preferential position over common equity holders and the risk of a decline in value may, therefore, be lessened. Conversion, participation, or other equity features may permit the seller to benefit from future appreciation of the underlying common stock.
- When marketable stock is received in a nontaxable transaction, the seller has substantial freedom in deciding when to sell stock at a gain. Future tax planning may be easier, and the shareholder may avoid bunching and alternative minimum tax problems.
- Installment sales reporting (matching the tax liability with collection of the principal on notes received) may allow for the deferral of tax payment to when the cash is received.
- Elderly stockholders may permanently escape the payment of tax by allowing the "paper" to be stepped-up to current fair value in their estate upon death.

The advantages of cash are:

- The risk of nonpayment does not exist.
- "Paper," particularly common stock, usually has considerable downside investment risk.
- The ability of successor management is not as important.

.02 *Installment Sales*

Changes in the installment sales provisions have expanded their application to sales of businesses. The general purpose of these rules is to achieve a matching of the tax liability with the collection of cash. Thus, when one-tenth of the purchase price has been collected, one-tenth of the gain will be taxed. The principal changes are as follows:

- There is no longer a 30-percent limit on the amount that can be received in the year of the sale. Thus, the installment method can be utilized even when 90 percent of the sales price is collected in the year of the sale.

- Special rules have been added to make the installment method available when the purchase price is contingent in amount.

- Tax is no longer triggered when installment notes received during the course of a 12-month liquidation are distributed in the liquidation.

.03 Contingent Earnout Arrangements

In both taxable and nontaxable transactions, the seller and the buyer may disagree on the growth potential for the business and, therefore, on its value. Such disagreements can be remedied by structuring an earnout contingency whereby the amount of stock issued or cash paid is increased if earnings exceed agreed levels. In nontaxable transactions, care must be exercised when incorporating such features. The IRS has published guidelines that can be followed to produce the desired results. In taxable transactions, in which an allocation of the purchase price must be made, the rules regarding the allocation of contingent payments are unsettled. The IRS may assert that contingencies based upon future earnings should be treated as nondeductible goodwill.

.04 Leveraged Buyouts (LBO)

The term "leveraged buyout" refers to a very popular form of taxable transaction in which the purchase price is funded primarily by lenders rather than by the buyer. *From the seller's perspective, it is a cash sale, but from the perspective of the purchaser, it is largely a "paper" transaction.* In a management leveraged buyout, key members of the management join or organize the buyer's equity group and must contribute their own funds or shares held in the seller's name to the transaction. These transactions are more complex than most because they involve additional participants (lenders, management, and the equity investors), each of which must be satisfied with the transaction.

The tax consequences of the transaction are generally no different than those of any taxable transaction. Thus, the buyer must decide whether to take advantage of the step-up opportunities. Similarly, the sale of assets versus stock must also be analyzed by the participants.

Expanding concept. The LBO is an evolving and expanding concept. The lenders are increasingly basing financing on cash flow rather than on the collateral value of assets, thereby making this a viable option for businesses with high cash flow but nominal physical assets. Because of the large profits that can be reaped by the equity participants, numerous leveraged buyout firms have been established, some of which specialize in smaller transactions. These firms have established relationships with interested lenders.

The LBO technique also permits the seller the choice of retaining a portion of his equity interest, thereby providing considerable flexibility to the seller in selling an entire interest versus sharing the future appreciation in the business' value.

What makes a good LBO candidate? The principal qualifications for a good LBO candidate are:

- Stable cash flow.
- Moderate growth prospects.
- Sound management.
- Ability to cover pro forma debt service and repay all debt in 10–20 years.

.05 Regulated Investment Company Technique

If the selling shareholder(s) in a taxable transaction is not in need of cash but does have an interest in developing a diversified investment portfolio, an asset sale may be used advantageously. Instead of distributing the sales proceeds to the shareholder(s) and liquidating the corporation, which may result in substantial capital gains tax, the sale's proceeds could be left in the corporation and used to build the desired diversified investment portfolio. This technique is most popular when the tax basis of the corporation's assets is much greater than the shareholder's stock basis. In such a situation, a corporate sale of assets may produce a relatively low gain, or maybe even a loss, while the sale of the shareholder's stock may produce a much larger gain. In order to avoid or minimize the imposition of a duplicate tax on portfolio earnings, once to the corporation and a second time to the shareholder(s), this tactic requires either that the corporation invest in securities eligible for the 85-percent dividends-received deduction so that any double taxation is minimized, or that it qualify as a regulated investment company (more commonly known as a mutual fund), which means that there are at least 100 remaining stockholders. Regulated investment companies are not generally subject to corporate tax if they distribute the income earned to their shareholders. Of course, those stockholders who do desire cash may redeem their shares.

.06 Recapitalizations

The "recapitalization" is a nontaxable exchange that is typically used to pass control of a corporation to new owners, frequently the younger generation. The recapitalization leaves the former owners with a nonappreciating but safer income-producing equity interest. Appreciation that accrues after the recapitalization is for the benefit of the new common stockholders.

This transaction does not provide current liquidity and generally does not require the involvement of investment bankers, except possibly to evaluate the worth of the business at the time of the recapitalization. This is a relatively old and well-established technique.

.07 ESOP Techniques

Employee Stock Ownership Plans (ESOPs) are frequently used where broad-based employee ownership is appropriate. They are also used occasionally to provide more equity in an LBO. In these transactions the ESOP borrowings are used to purchase stock, thereby providing working capital to the employer corporation. The corporation makes an annual contribution to the plan to cover the ESOP's debt service. The contributions are fully tax deductible even though they are comprised of interest and principal components.

.08 Partial Sale Transactions

If the owner desires to maintain a substantial continuing equity position, he may wish to consider a transaction in which he sells only a portion of his interest in the business. The following transactions might accomplish this objective:

- Public offering of a minority position.
- Private placement of a minority position.
- Syndication of business real estate.

¶ 2795 Summary

The price to be paid for a business depends upon many factors including the seller's strengths, weaknesses, and prospects. The buyer's objectives and requirements are also relevant. A total cash transaction justifies a lower price than an installment sale, because with an installment sale, there are the uncertainties of cash collection and the time value of money.

When valuing a company, more weight should be placed on the earnings approaches and less on the asset approaches. Valuation may be based on a combined approach of methods including earnings and asset valuation. In deriving a value, industry standards may be quite helpful. Consideration should be given to adjusted cash earnings, gross revenue, fair value of net assets, and recent sales of similar businesses. A proper valuation is needed so as to come up with a realistic price that is fair to all concerned parties.

The present business environment has made both divestiture and diversification an acceptable strategy for businesses to pursue. The requirement for public disclosure of business segment operating results has forced management to take action when a segment is not performing to company standards. Their action has been divestiture of the undesirable divisions. However, there are other alternatives for underperforming divisions. Divestiture has become an accepted method of dealing with problem business segments.

When developing the strategies involved with divestiture, management must consider the interrelationships between that division and the rest of the company and the costs of discontinuing that operation. The carrying out of a divestiture has an effect across the whole company, including the production, distribution, and marketing areas. Divestiture may also greatly affect the public's image of the company.

When considering divestiture as an alternative, all of these factors must be evaluated. The divestiture decision must be closely thought out.

Chapter 28

Multinational Finance

¶ 2801 Financial Management of a Multinational Corporation (MNC)

Many companies are multinational corporations (MNCs) that have significant foreign operations deriving a high percentage of their sales overseas. The controllers of MNCs require an understanding of the complexities of international finance to make sound financial and investment decisions. International finance involves consideration of managing working capital, financing the business, control of foreign exchange and political risks, and foreign direct investments. Most importantly, the controller has to continuously consider the value of the U.S. dollar relative to the value of the currency of the foreign country in which business activities are being conducted. Currency exchange rates may materially affect receivables and payables, and imports and exports of the U.S. company in its multinational operations. The effect is more pronounced with increasing activities abroad.

The following are some problems facing management of an MNC:

- *Multiple-currency problem.* Sales revenues may be collected in one currency, assets denominated in another, and profits measured in a third.

- *Various legal, institutional, and economic constraints.* There are variations in such things as tax laws, labor practices, balance of payment policies, and government controls with respect to the types and sizes of investments, types and amount of capital raised, and repatriation of profits.

- *Internal control problem.* When the parent office of an MNC and its affiliates are widely located, internal organizational difficulties arise.

A survey made of controllers of MNCs lists the financial goals of MNCs in the following order of importance:

1. Maximize growth in corporate earnings, whether total earnings, earnings before interest and taxes (EBIT), or earnings per share (EPS).
2. Maximize return on equity.
3. Guarantee that funds are always available when needed.

¶ 2805 The Types of Foreign Operations

When strong competition exists in the United States, a company may look to enter or expand its foreign base. However, if a company is unsuccessful in the domestic market, it is likely to have problems overseas as well. Further, the controller must be cognizant of local customs and risks in the international markets.

A large, well-established company with much international experience may eventually have wholly-owned subsidiaries. However, a small company with limited foreign experience operating in "risky areas" may be restricted to export and import activity.

If the company's sales force has minimal experience in export sales, it is advisable to use foreign brokers when specialized knowledge of foreign markets is needed. When sufficient volume exists, the company may establish a foreign branch sales office including sales people and technical service staff. As the operation matures, production facilities may be located in the foreign market. However, some foreign countries require licensing before foreign sales and production can take place. In this case, a foreign licensee sells and produces the product. A problem with this arrangement is that confidential information and knowledge are passed on to the licensees who can then become competitors at the expiration of the agreement.

A joint venture with a foreign company is another way to proceed internationally and share the risk. To operate in their countries, some foreign governments require that companies follow this path. The foreign company may have local goodwill to assure success. A drawback is less control over activities and a conflict of interest.

In evaluating the impact that foreign operations have on the entity's financial health, the controller should consider the extent of intercountry transactions, foreign restrictions and laws, tax structure of the foreign country, and the economic and political stability of the country. If a subsidiary is operating in a high-tax country with a double-tax agreement, dividend payments are not subject to further U.S. taxes. One way to transfer income from high tax areas to low tax areas is to levy royalties or management fees on the subsidiaries.

¶ 2810 The Foreign Exchange Market

Except in a few European centers, there is no central marketplace for the foreign exchange market. Rather, business is carried out over telephone or telex. The major dealers are large banks. A company that wants to buy or sell currency typically uses a commercial bank. International transactions and investments involve more than one currency. For example, when a U.S. company sells merchandise to a Japanese firm, the former wants to be paid in dollars but the Japanese company typically expects to receive yen. Due to the foreign exchange market, the buyer may pay in one currency while the seller can receive payment in another currency.

.01 Spot and Forward Foreign Exchange Rates

An exchange rate is the ratio of one unit of currency to another. An exchange rate is established between the different currencies. The conversion rate between currencies depends on the demand/supply relationship. Because of the change in exchange rates, companies are susceptible to exchange rate fluctuation risks because of a net asset or net liability position in a foreign currency.

Exchange rates may be in terms of dollars per foreign currency unit (called a *direct quote*) or units of foreign currency per dollar (called an *indirect quote*). Therefore, an indirect quote is the reciprocal of a direct quote and vice versa.

An indirect quote = 1/direct quote

Pound/$ = 1/($/pound)

Example 1. Exhibit 1 presents a sample of indirect and direct quotes for selected currencies. A rate of 1.617/British pound means each pound costs the U.S. company $1.617. In other words, the U.S. company gets 1/1.617 = .6184 pounds for each dollar.

The spot rate is the exchange rate for immediate delivery of currencies exchanged, while the forward rate is the exchange rate for later delivery of currencies exchanged. For example, there may be a 90-day exchange rate. The forward exchange rate of a currency will be slightly different from the spot rate at the current date because of future expectations and uncertainties.

Exhibit 1

Foreign Exchange Rates (A Sample)

May 30, 20X2

Country	*Contract*	*U.S. Dollar Equivalent*	*Currency per U.S. $*
Britain	Spot	1.6170	.6184
(Pound)	30-day future	1.6153	.6191
	90-day future	1.6130	.6200
	180-day future	1.6089	.6215
Germany	Spot	.7282	1.3733
(Mark)	30-day future	.7290	1.3716
	90-day future	.7311	1.3677
	180-day future	.7342	1.3620
Japan	Spot	.011955	83.65
(Yen)	30-day future	.012003	83.31
	90-day future	.012100	82.64
	180-day future	.012247	81.65

Forward rates may be greater than the current spot rate (premium) or less than the current spot rate (discount).

.02 Cross Rates

A cross rate is the indirect calculation of the exchange rate of one currency from the exchange rates of two other currencies.

Example 2. The dollar per pound and the yen per dollar rates are given in Exhibit 2. From this information, you could determine the yen per pound (or pound per yen) exchanges rates. For example, you see that:

($/pound) × (yen/$) = (yen/pound)

1.6170 × 83.65 = 135.26 yen/pound

Thus, the pound per yen exchange rate is:

1/135.26 = .00739 pound per yen

Note: The Wall Street Journal routinely publishes key currency cross rates, as shown in Exhibit 2.

Exhibit 2

Key Currency Cross Rates (A Sample)

	British	Germany	Japan	U.S.
British	—	.45032	.00739	.61843
Germany	2.2206	—	.01642	1.3733
Japan	135.26	60.912	—	83.65
U.S.	1.6170	.72817	.01195	—

Example 3. On February 1, 20X2, forward rates on the British pound were at a premium in relation to the spot rate, while the forward rates for the Japanese yen were at a discount from the spot rate. This means that participants in the foreign exchange market anticipated that the British pound would appreciate relative to the U.S. dollar in the future but the Japanese yen would depreciate against the dollar.

The percentage premium (P) or discount (D) is computed as follows.

$$\text{P (or D)} = \frac{F - S}{S} \times \frac{12 \text{ months}}{n} \times 100$$

Where F, S = the forward and spot rates and n = length of the forward contract in months.

If F>S, the result is the annualized premium in percent; otherwise, it is the annualized discount in percent.

Example 4. On May 3, 20X2, a 30-day forward contract in Japanese yens was selling at a 4.8 percent discount (see Exhibit 1):

$$\frac{.012003 - .011955}{.011955} \times \frac{12 \text{ months}}{1 \text{ month}} \times 100 = 4.82\%$$

¶ 2815 The Control of Foreign Exchange Risk

Foreign exchange rate risk exists when the contract is written in terms of the foreign currency or denominated in foreign currency. The exchange rate fluctuations increase the riskiness of the investment and incur cash losses. The controllers must not only seek the highest return on temporary investments but must also be concerned about changing values of the currencies invested. Foreign exchange risk may only be contained but not completely eliminated.

.01 Financial Strategies

In countries where currency values are likely to drop, controllers of the subsidiaries should:

- Avoid paying advances on purchase orders unless the seller pays interest on the advances sufficient to cover the loss of purchasing power.

- Not have excess idle cash. Excess cash can be used to buy inventory or other real assets.

- Buy materials and supplies on credit in the country in which the foreign subsidiary is operating, extending the final payment date as long as possible.
- Avoid giving excessive trade credit. If accounts receivable balances are outstanding for an extended time period, interest should be charged to absorb the loss in purchasing power.
- Borrow local currency funds when the interest rate charged does not exceed U.S. rates after taking into account expected devaluation in the foreign country.

.02 Different Types of Foreign Exchange Exposure

MNCs' controllers are faced with the dilemma of three different types of foreign exchange risk.

Translation exposure. Translation exposure, often called *accounting exposure,* measures the impact of an exchange rate change on the firm's financial statements. An example would be the impact of French Franc devaluation on a U.S. firm's reported income statement and balance sheet.

A major purpose of translation is to provide data of expected impacts of rate changes on cash flow and equity. In the translation of the foreign subsidiaries' financial statements into the U.S. parent's financial statements, the following steps are involved:

1. The foreign financial statements are put into U.S. generally accepted accounting principles.
2. The foreign currency is translated into U.S. dollars.

Current FASB rules require translation by the current rate method. Under the current rate method:

- All balance sheet assets and liabilities are translated at the current rate of exchange in effect on the balance sheet date. If a current exchange rate is not available at the balance sheet date, use the first exchange rate available after that date.
- Income statement items are usually translated at an average exchange rate for the reporting period.
- All equity accounts are translated at the historical exchange rates that were in effect at the time the accounts first entered the balance sheet.
- Translation gains and losses are reported as a separate item in the stockholders' equity section of the balance sheet. Translation gains and losses are only included in net income when there is a sale or liquidation of the entire investment in a foreign entity.

Transaction exposure. Transaction exposure measures potential gains or losses on the future settlement of outstanding obligations that are denominated in a foreign currency. An example would be a U.S. dollar loss after the Franc devalues on payment received for an export invoiced in Francs before that devaluation.

Foreign currency transactions may result in receivables or payables fixed in terms of the amount of foreign currency to be received or paid. Transaction gains and losses are reported in the income statement.

Foreign currency transactions are those transactions whose terms are denominated in a currency other than the entity's functional currency. Foreign currency transactions take place when a business:

- Buys or sells on credit goods or services the prices of which are denominated in foreign currencies.
- Borrows or lends funds, and the amounts payable or receivable are denominated in a foreign currency.
- Is a party to an unperformed forward exchange contract.
- Acquires or disposes of assets, or incurs or settles liabilities denominated in foreign currencies.

Note: Transaction losses differ from translation losses, which do not influence taxable income.

Operating exposure. Operating (economic) exposure is the possibility that an unexpected change in exchange rates will cause a change in the future cash flows of a firm and its market value. It differs from translation and transaction exposures in that it is subjective and thus not easily quantified. *Note:* The best strategy to control operation exposure is to diversify operations and financing internationally.

.03 *Long Versus Short Position*

When there is a devaluation of the dollar, foreign assets and income in strong currency countries are worth more dollars as long as foreign liabilities do not offset this beneficial effect.

Foreign exchange risk may be analyzed by examining expected receipts or obligations in foreign currency units. A company expecting receipts in foreign currency units ("long" position in the foreign currency units) has the risk that the value of the foreign currency units will drop. This results in devaluing the foreign currency relative to the dollar. If a company is expecting to have obligations in foreign currency units ("short" position in the foreign currency units), there is risk that the value of the foreign currency will rise and it will need to buy the currency at a higher price.

If net claims are greater than liabilities in a foreign currency, the company has a "long" position since it will benefit if the value of the foreign currency rises. If net liabilities exceed claims with respect to foreign currencies, the company is in a "short" position because it will gain if the foreign currency drops in value.

.04 Monetary Position

Monetary balance is avoiding either a net receivable or a net payable position. Monetary assets and liabilities do not change in value with devaluation or revaluation in foreign currencies.

A company with a long position in a foreign currency will be receiving more funds in the foreign currency. It will have a net monetary asset position (monetary assets exceed monetary liabilities) in that currency.

A company with net receipts is a net monetary creditor. Its foreign exchange rate risk exposure has a net receipts position in a foreign currency that is susceptible to a drop in value.

A company with a future net obligation in foreign currency has a net monetary debtor position. It faces a foreign exchange risk of the possibility of an increase in the value of the foreign currency.

.05 Ways To Neutralize Foreign Exchange Risk

Foreign exchange risk can be neutralized or hedged by a change in the asset and liability position in the foreign currency. Here are some ways to control exchange risk.

Entering a money-market hedge. Borrowing or lending in the money market offsets the exposed position in a foreign currency.

Example 5. XYZ, an American importer, enters into a contract with a British supplier to buy merchandise of 4,000 pounds. The amount is payable on the delivery of the goods, 30 days from today. The company knows the exact amount of its pound liability in 30 days. However, it does not know the payable in dollars. Assume that the 30-day money market rates for both lending and borrowing in the United States and United Kingdom are .5 percent and one percent, respectively. Assume further that today's foreign exchange rate is $1.7350 per pound.

In a money-market hedge, XYZ can take the following steps:

- *Step 1.* Buy a one-month U.K. money market security, worth 4,000/(1 + .005) = 3,980 pounds. This investment will compound to exactly 4,000 pounds in one month.

- *Step 2.* Exchange dollars on today's spot (cash) market to obtain the 3,980 pounds. The dollar amount needed today is 3,980 pounds × $1.7350 per pound = $6,905.30.

- *Step 3.* If XYZ does not have this amount, it can borrow it from the U.S. money market at the going rate of one percent. In 30 days XYZ will need to repay $6,905.30 × (1 + .1) = $7,595.83.

Note: XYZ need not wait for the future exchange rate to be available. On today's date, the future dollar amount of the contract is known with certainty. The British supplier will receive 4,000 pounds, and the cost of XYZ to make the payment is $7,595.83.

Hedging by purchasing forward (or futures) exchange contracts. Forward exchange contracts are a commitment to buy or sell, at a specified future date, one currency for a specified amount of another currency (at a specified exchange rate). This can be a hedge against changes in exchange rates during a period of contract or exposure to risk from such changes. More specifically, you do the following: (1) Buy foreign exchange forward contracts to cover payables denominated in a foreign currency, and (2) sell foreign exchange forward contracts to cover receivables denominated in a foreign currency. This way, any gain or loss on the foreign receivables or payables due to changes in exchange rates is offset by the gain or loss on the forward exchange contract.

Example 6. In the previous example, assume that the 30-day forward exchange rate is $1.7272. XYZ may take the following steps to cover its payable.

- *Step 1.* Buy a forward contract today to purchase 4,000 pounds in 30 days.

- *Step 2.* On the 30th day pay the foreign exchange dealer 4,000 pounds × $1.7272 per pound = $6,908.80 and collect 4,000 pounds. Pay this amount to the British supplier.

Note: Using the forward contract, XYZ knows the exact worth of the future payment in dollars ($6,908.80).

Note: The basic difference between futures contracts and forward contracts is that futures contracts are for specified amounts and maturities, whereas forward contracts are for any size and maturity desired.

Hedging by foreign currency options. Foreign currency options can be purchased or sold in three different types of markets: (a) Options on the physical currency, purchased on the over-the-counter (interbank) market, (b) options on the physical currency, on organized exchanges such as the Philadelphia Stock Exchange and the Chicago Mercantile Exchange, and (c) options on futures contracts, purchased on the International Monetary Market (IMM) of the Chicago Mercantile Exchange. *Note:* The difference between using a futures contract and using an option on a futures contract is that with a futures contract, the company must deliver one currency against another or reverse the contract on the exchange, while with an option, the company may abandon the option and use the spot (cash) market if that is more advantageous.

Repositioning cash by leading and lagging the time at which an MNC makes operational or financial payments. Often, money- and forward-market hedges are not available to eliminate exchange risk. Under such circumstances, leading (accelerating) and lagging (decelerating) may be used to reduce risk. *Note:* A net asset position (i.e., assets minus liabilities) is not desirable in a weak or potentially depreciating currency. In this case, you should expedite the disposal of the asset. By the same token, you should lag or delay the collection against a net asset position in a strong currency.

Maintaining balance between receivables and payables denominated in a foreign currency. MNCs typically set up "multilateral netting centers" as a special department to settle the outstanding balances of affiliates of an MNC with each other on a net basis. It is the development of a "clearing house" for payments by the firm's affiliates. If there are amounts due among affiliates, they are offset insofar as possible. The net amount would be paid in the currency of the transaction. The total amounts owed need not be paid in the currency of the transaction; thus, a much lower quantity of the currency must be acquired. *Note:* The major advantage of the system is a reduction of the costs associated with a large number of separate foreign exchange transactions.

Positioning of funds through transfer pricing. A transfer price is the price at which an MNC sells goods and services to its foreign affiliates or, alternatively, the price at which an affiliate sells to the parent. For example, a parent that wishes to transfer funds from an affiliate in a depreciating-currency country may charge a higher price on the goods and services sold to this affiliate by the parent or by affiliates from strong-currency countries. Transfer pricing affects not only transfer of funds from one entity to another but also the income taxes paid by both entities.

.06 Key Questions to Ask that Help to Identify Foreign Exchange Risk

A systematic approach to identifying an MNC's exposure to foreign exchange risk is to ask a series of questions regarding the net effects on profits of changes in foreign currency revenues and costs.

The questions are:

- Where is the MNC selling? (Domestic vs. foreign sales share)
- Who are the firm's major competitors? (Domestic vs. foreign)
- Where is the firm producing? (Domestic vs. foreign)
- Where are the firm's inputs coming from? (Domestic vs. foreign)

- How sensitive is quantity demanded to price? (Elastic vs. inelastic)
- How are the firm's inputs or outputs priced? (Priced in a domestic market or a global market, the currency of denomination)

Exhibit 3 summarizes the impacts of changes in foreign exchange rates on the company's products and financial transactions.

Exhibit 3

The Impacts of Changes in Foreign Exchange Rates

	Weak Currency (Depreciation)	*Strong Currency (Appreciation)*
Imports	More expensive	Cheaper
Exports	Cheaper	More expensive
Payables	More expensive	Cheaper
Receivables	Cheaper	More expensive

¶ 2820 Forecasting Foreign Exchange Rates

The forecasting of foreign exchange rates is a formidable task. Most MNCs rely primarily on bank and bank services for assistance and information in preparing exchange rate projections. The following economic indicators are considered to be the most important for the forecasting process:

- Recent rate movements.
- Relative inflation rates.
- Balance of payments and trade.
- Money supply growth.
- Interest rate differentials.

.01 Interest Rates

Interest rates have an important influence on exchange rates. In fact, there is an important economic relationship between any two nations' spot rates, forward rates, and interest rates. This relationship is called the *interest rate parity theorem* (IRPT). The IRPT states that the ratio of the forward and spot rates is directly related to the two interest rates.

Specifically, the premium or discount should be:

$$P \text{ (or D)} = -\frac{r_f - r_d}{1 + r_f}$$

Where r_f and r_d = foreign and domestic interest rates.

(When interest rates are relatively low, this equation can be approximated by: P (or D) = $-(r_f - r_d)$).

The IRPT implies that the P (or D) calculated by the equation should be the same as the P (or D) calculated by:

$$P \text{ (or D)} = \frac{F - S}{S} \times \frac{12 \text{ months}}{n} \times 100$$

Example 7. On May 3, 20X2, a 30-day forward contract in Japanese yens was selling at a 4.82 percent premium:

$$\frac{.012003 - .011955}{.011955} \times \frac{12 \text{ months}}{1 \text{ month}} \times 100 = 4.82\%$$

The 30-day U.S. T-bill rate is eight percent annualized. What is the 30-day Japanese rate?

Using the equation:

$$P \text{ (or D)} = -\frac{r_f - r_d}{1 + r_f}$$

$$.0482 = \frac{.08 - r_f}{1 + r_f}$$

$$-0.0318 = -1.0482\, r_f$$

$$r_f = 0.0303 = 3.03\%$$

The 30-day Japanese rate should be 3.03 percent.

.02 Inflation

Inflation, which is a change in price levels, also affects future exchange rates. The mathematical relationship that links changes in exchange rates and changes in price level is called the *purchasing power parity theorem* (PPPT). The PPPT states that the ratio of the forward and spot rates is directly related to the two inflation rates:

$$\frac{F}{S} = \frac{1 + P_d}{1 + P_f}$$

Where F = forward exchange rate (e.g., \$/foreign currency)

S = spot exchange rate (e.g., \$/foreign currency)

P_d = domestic inflation rate

P_f = foreign inflation rate

Example 8. Assume the following data for the United States and France:

Expected U.S. inflation rate = 5%

Expected French inflation rate = 10%

S = \$0.220/FR

Then,

$$\frac{F}{0.220} = \frac{1.05}{1.10}$$

F = \$0.210/FR

Note: If France has the higher inflation rate, then the purchasing power of the franc is declining faster than that of the dollar. This will lead to a forward discount on the franc relative to the dollar.

¶ 2825 Analysis of Foreign Investments

Foreign investment decisions are basically capital budgeting decisions at the international level. The decision requires two major components:

- *The estimation of the relevant future cash flows.* Cash flows are the dividends and possible future sales price of the investment. The estimation depends on the sales forecast, the effects on exchange rate changes, the risk in cash flows, and the actions of foreign governments.
- *The choice of the proper discount rate (cost of capital).* The cost of capital in foreign investment projects is higher due to the increased risks of:
  - — Currency risk (or foreign exchange risk)—changes in exchange rates. This risk may adversely affect sales by making competing imported goods cheaper.
  - — Political risk (or sovereignty risk)—possibility of nationalization or other restrictions with net losses to the parent company.

Some examples associated with political risks are:

- Expropriation of plants and equipment without compensation or with minimal compensation that is below actual market value.
- Nonconvertibility of the affiliate's foreign earnings into the parent's currency—the problem of "blocked funds."
- Substantial changes in the laws governing taxation.

- Government controls in the host country regarding wages, compensation to the personnel, hiring of personnel, the sales price of the product, making of transfer payments to the parent, and local borrowing.

.01 *How To Measure Political Risk*

Many MNCs and banks have attempted to measure political risks in their businesses. They even hire or maintain a group of political risk analysts. Several independent services provide political risk and country risk ratings.

- *Euromoney* magazine's annual *Country Risk Rating,* which is based on a measure of different countries' access to international credit, trade finance, political risk, and a country's payment record. The rankings are generally confirmed by political risk insurers and top syndicate managers in the Euromarkets.
- Rating by *Economist Intelligence Unit,* a New York-based subsidiary of the *Economist Group,* London, which is based on such factors as external debt and trends in the current account, the consistency of the government policy, foreign-exchange reserves, and the quality of economic management.
- *International Country Risk Guide,* published by the PRS Group (www.prsgroup.com/icrg/icrg-html), which offers a composite risk rating, as well as individual ratings for political, financial, and economic risk for 140 countries. The political variable, which makes up half of the composite index, includes factors such as government corruption and how economic expectations diverge from reality. The financial rating looks at such things as the likelihood of losses from exchange controls and loan defaults. Finally, economic ratings consider such factors as inflation and debt-service costs.

.02 *Methods for Dealing with Political Risk*

To the extent that forecasting political risks is a formidable task, what can an MNC do to cope with them? There are several methods suggested. They are:

- *Avoidance.* Try to avoid political risk by minimizing activities in or with countries that are considered to be of high risk. Use higher discount rates for projects in riskier countries.
- *Adaptation.* Try to reduce risk by adapting the activities (for example, by using hedging techniques discussed previously).
- *Diversification.* Diversify across national borders, so that problems in one country do not severely damage the company.
- *Risk transfer.* Buy insurance policies for political risks.

Example 9. Most developed nations offer insurance for political risk to their exporters. Examples are:

- In the United States, the *Eximbank* offers policies to exporters that cover such political risks as war, currency inconvertibility, and civil unrest. (See www.exim.gov/index.html.) Furthermore, the *Overseas Private Investment Corporation (OPIC)* offers policies to U.S. foreign investors to cover such risks as currency inconvertibility, civil or foreign war damages, or expropriation. (See www.opic.gov.)

- In the United Kingdom, similar policies are offered by the *Export Credit Guarantee Department (ECGD);* in Canada, by the *Export Development Council (EDC);* and in Germany, by an agency called *Hermes.*

¶ 2830 International Sources of Financing

A company may finance its activities abroad, especially in countries it is operating in. A successful company in domestic markets is more likely to be able to attract financing for international expansion.

The most important international sources of funds are the Eurocurrency market and the Eurobond market. Also, MNCs have access to national capital markets in which their subsidiaries are located. Exhibit 4 presents an overview of international financial markets.

The Eurocurrency market is a largely short-term (usually less than one year of maturity) market for bank deposits and loans denominated in any currency except the currency of the country where the market is located. For example, in London, the Eurocurrency market is a market for bank deposits and loans denominated in dollars, yen, franc, marks, and any other currency except British pounds. The main instruments used in this market are CDs and time deposits, and bank loans. *Note:* The term "market" in this context is not a physical market place but a set of bank deposits and loans.

The Eurobond market is a long-term market for bonds denominated in any currency except the currency of the country where the market is located. Eurobonds may be of different types such as straight, convertible, and with warrants. While most Eurobonds are fixed rate, variable rate bonds also exist. Maturities vary but 10 to 12 years is typical.

Although Eurobonds are issued in many currencies, select a stable, fully convertible, and actively traded currency. In some cases, if a Eurobond is denominated in a weak currency, the holder has the option of requesting payment in another currency.

Sometimes, large MNCs establish wholly owned offshore finance subsidiaries. These subsidiaries issue Eurobond debt, and the proceeds are given to the parent or to overseas operating subsidiaries. Debt service goes back to bondholders through the finance subsidiaries.

If the Eurobond was issued by the parent directly, the United States would require a withholding tax on interest. There may also be an estate tax when the bondholder dies. These tax problems do not arise when a bond is issued by a finance subsidiary incorporated in a tax haven. Hence, the subsidiary may borrow at less cost than the parent.

In summary, the Euromarkets offers borrowers and investors in one country the opportunity to deal with borrowers and investors from many other countries, buying and selling bank deposits, bonds, and loans denominated in many currencies.

Exhibit 5 provides a list of funding sources available to a foreign affiliate of an MNC (debt and equity).

Exhibit 4

International Financial Markets

Market	*Instruments*	*Participants*	*Regulator*
International monetary system	Special drawing rights, gold, foreign exchange	Central banks, International Monetary Fund	International Monetary Fund
Foreign exchange markets	Bank deposits, currency, futures and forward contracts	Commercial and central banks, firms, individuals	Central banks in each country
National money markets (short term)	Bank deposits and loans, short-term government securities, commercial paper	Banks, firms, individuals, government agencies	Central bank, other government agencies
National capital markets	Bonds, long-term bank deposits and loans, stocks, long-term government securities	Banks, firms, individuals, government agencies	Central bank, other government agencies
Eurocurrency markets (short-term)	Bank deposits, bank loans, short-term and rolled-over credit lines, revolving commitment	Commercial banks, firms, government agencies	Substantially unregulated
Euro-commercial paper markets (short-term)	Commercial paper issues and programs, note-issuing facility, revolving underwritten facilities	Commercial banks, firms, government agencies	Substantially unregulated
Eurobond market (medium and long-term)	Fixed coupon bonds, floating-rate notes, higher-bound bonds, lower-bound bonds	Banks, firms, individuals, government agencies	Substantially unregulated
Euroloan market (medium and long-term)	Fixed-rate loans, revolving loans, revolving loans with cap, revolving loans with floor	Banks, firms, individuals, government agencies	Substantially unregulated

Exhibit 5

International Sources of Credit

Borrowing	*Domestic Inside the Firm*	*Domestic Market*	*Foreign Inside the Firm*	*Foreign Market*	*Euromarket*
Direct, short-term	Intrafirm loans, transfer pricing, royalties, fees, service charges	Commercial paper	International intrafirm loans, international transfer pricing, dividends, royalties, fees		Euro-commercial paper
Intermediated short-term		Short-term bank loans, discounted receivables	Internal back-to-back loans	Short-term bank loans, discounted receivables	Euro short-term loans
Direct, long-term	Intrafirm loans, invested in affiliates	Stock issue, Bond issue	International intrafirm long-term loans, foreign direct investment	Stock issue, Bond issue	Eurobonds
Intermediated long-term		Long-term bank loans	Internal back-to-back loans	Long-term bank loans	Euro long-term loans

Chapter 29

Personal Financial Planning

¶ 2901 Personal Financial Planning—An Overview

Financial planning is the process of meeting your life goals through the proper management of your finances. Life goals can include buying a home, saving for your child's education, or planning for retirement. Financial planning is the way to arrive at solutions to your financial concerns and problems and to take advantage of your earning years to become financially independent. It involves implementation of total, coordinated plans for the achievement of overall personal objectives. Financial planning can start at any age, but the sooner the better. You may want to have substantial assets during midlife to buy a business or just to enjoy yourself.

Personal financial planning helps you to:

- Obtain what you really want through each life cycle.
- Preserve assets.
- Use credit prudently.
- Exercise good risk management including establishing risk tolerance for investing.
- Provide adequate insurance protection. Protection against personal risk is needed for death, disability, income loss, medical care, property and liability, and unemployment.
- Increase your wealth.
- Control costs.

.01 Key Areas in Personal Financial Planning

The major areas of personal financial planning include:

- *Proper insurance coverage to protect against personal risk such as death, disability, and losses.* For example, adequate life insurance is needed for dependents. Insurance coverage should be modified periodically, as necessary.

- *Capital accumulation.* There should be a regular savings and investment program. A balanced investment portfolio should exist (for example, certificates of deposit, equity securities, fixed-income securities) taking into account financial goals and risk tolerance.
- *Investment and property management.* You should manage your assets for high return without undue risk.
- *Tax planning.* Tax saving techniques should be employed.
- *Debt and credit management.* You should not be overextended.
- *Planning for retirement.* You should provide for adequate retirement income.
- *Estate planning.* Proper estate planning is needed to assure assets are transferred to beneficiaries, as desired. Some assets may be arranged in such a way as to provide your heirs protection from creditors' claims in bankruptcy. Examples are spendthrift provisions in life insurance settlement options and personal trust agreements.

.02 Steps in Personal Financial Planning

As Exhibit 1 shows, personal financial planning process involves the following steps.

Step 1: Determine your current financial situation. In this first step of the financial planning process, you must determine your current financial situation with regard to income, savings, living expenses, and debts. You need to obtain needed information (for example, current investments, provisions in insurance policies, retirement benefits, and tax law provisions). The personal financial statements discussed in Chapter 2 will provide the information you need to match your goals with your current income and your potential earning power.

Step 2: Set goals. Specific financial goals are vital to financial planning. Your financial goals can range from spending all of your current income to developing an extensive savings and investment program for your future financial security. The goals you choose should be based on your current situation, your values, and your financial situation. Further, you should determine desired risk level. The best way to consider risk is to gather information based on your own and others' experiences and to use financial planning sources. The goals can be short, intermediate, and long term. *Short-term goals* are goals to be achieved within the next year or so, such as saving for a vacation or paying off small debts. *Intermediate goals* have a time frame of two to five years. *Long-term goals* involve financial plans that are more than five years away, such as retirement savings, money for children's college education, or the purchase of a vacation home.

Goal frequency is another ingredient in the financial planning process. Some goals, such as vacations or money for gifts, may be set annually. Other goals, such as a college education, a car, or a house, occur less frequently. Your financial goals should have the following characteristics:

- *Goals should be realistic.* Goals should be based on your income and life situation. For example, it may not be realistic to buy a house if you are a full-time student.
- *Financial goals should be stated in specific, measurable terms.* Defining exactly what your goals are will allow you to create a plan that is designed to achieve them. For example, the goal of "putting $20,000 in an investment account within four years" is a less ambiguous guide to planning than the goal of "putting money into an investment account."
- *Financial goals should have a time frame.* A time frame helps you measure your progress toward your financial goals. In the previous example, the goal is to be achieved in four years. Dividing your clear goal into manageable pieces will allow you to better achieve your financial objective.

Step 3: Identify alternative courses of action. Identifying alternatives is critical for making good decisions. Although many external factors will influence the available alternatives, your possible courses of action will usually fall into these categories:

- *Keep on the same course of action.* For example, you may determine that the amount you have saved each month is still appropriate.
- *Enhance the current situation.* You may choose to save a larger amount each month.
- *Alter the current situation.* You may decide to buy a money market fund instead of using a regular savings account.
- *Undertake a new course of action.* You may decide to use your monthly budget to pay off credit card debts.

Step 4: Evaluate alternatives, including appraising current financial status. You need to assess possible courses of action, taking into consideration your life situation and current economic conditions. In the assessment process, you should also look at the consequences and risks associated with each alternative. Every option in life can have positive or negative effects. Various information sources are available to help you assess these possible outcomes. Every decision has a trade-off. For example, a decision to invest in stock may mean that you cannot take a vacation.

You must understand the effect of each financial decision. Each financial decision you make can affect several other areas of your life. For example, an investment decision may have tax consequences that are harmful to your estate plans. Or a decision about your child's education may affect when and how you meet your retirement goals. Remember that all of your financial decisions are interrelated.

Step 5: Formulate an action plan to meet goals. The fifth step of the financial planning process is to develop a plan of action—a blueprint. This requires choosing ways to achieve your goals. For example, you can increase your savings by reducing your spending or by increasing your income through extra time on the job. Don't delay your financial planning, and implement your plan in accordance with your blueprint.

Step 6: Review your plan periodically and make necessary revisions. Financial planning is a dynamic and on-going process that does not end when you take a particular action. You need to regularly assess your financial decisions. You should do a complete review of your finances at least once a year. Your goals may change over the years due to changes in your lifestyle or circumstances, such as an inheritance, marriage, birth, house purchase, or change of job status. Revisit and revise your financial blueprint as time goes by to reflect these changes so that you stay on track with your long-term goals. *Note:* External events beyond your control, such as inflation or changes in the stock market or interest rates, can affect your financial planning results.

Exhibit 1

Personal Financial Planning Process

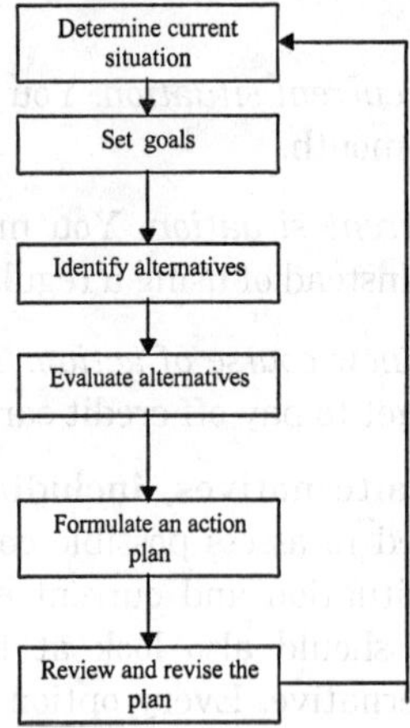

.03 Personal Financial Planning Aids

Various journals and periodicals may be read to aid you in personal financial planning including:

- *Money Magazine* (www.money.com)
- *Kiplinger's Personal Finance* (www.kiplinger.com)
- MSN (www.moneyinsider.msn.com)
- *Smartmoney* (www.smartmoney.com)
- *Institute of Certified Financial Planners Journal*
- U.S. Government Consumer Information Center (www.pueblo.gsa.gov)

Software packages exist to aid you in planning. Many packages can conduct detailed analyses of financial data and formulate suitable recommendations. Some software can evaluate "what-if" scenarios to see the effect of alternative courses of action. The two most popular software packages are *Quicken* (www.quicken.com) and Microsoft's *Money*.

There are also numerous useful websites to aid you in financial planning. They include: www.Gefn.com, www.latimes.com/money, www.quicken.com. For example, GEFN and latimes provide free numerous planning tools on line.

¶ 2910 Strategies for Funding College Tuition

Some financial planning ways to meet college costs are to use long-term savings plans, take advantage of financial assistance programs, and shift income to your lower-tax-bracket child.

Clearly, it helps to begin saving early, preferably as soon as the child is born. The idea is to save or invest as much money as you can and pay taxes on as little as possible. Like buying a house, the more you have saved ahead of time, the less you will need to borrow. Set aside or invest as much as you can, even if it is just a small amount from every paycheck.

Increase your contributions to the fund as your salary increases. Add extra cash from raises or yearly bonuses, as well as some of the money your child receives as gifts. Money that comes unexpectedly and has not been budgeted will not be missed. Also, if your older child has a part-time job, encourage him or her to put some of those earnings aside for college.

.01 Growth Stocks and Growth Mutual Funds

Good investments in the stock market have the potential to provide better returns than insured, fixed-rate investments (such as savings accounts and CDs, which are generally FDIC insured) if you have time to let the money ride the ups and downs of the market. This is a long-term approach to investing. Just remember: What the stock market did in the past is no guarantee of how it will perform in the future.

The word to look for here is growth. When assessing the growth potential of a particular stock, consider looking for long-term appreciation rather than dividends. Growth stocks also allow you to postpone paying taxes on the capital appreciation realized until you withdraw funds.

Investing in just one or two stocks is always risky. If you'd like to participate in the growth potential of the stock market with less risk, consider a growth mutual fund. Money invested in such a fund is professionally managed and is usually diversified over many stocks, which helps reduce risk. Also, you can start investing in mutual funds with a relatively small amount of money.

.02 U.S. Savings Bonds (Series EE)

You need only go as far as your local bank to invest in Series EE U.S. Government Savings Bonds. The face values of these bonds range from $50 to $10,000, but you buy them at only half their face value. For example, when you buy a $50 bond, you pay $25 for it. The interest rate paid on these bonds varies, and EE bonds reach face value in a maximum of 17 years.

These bonds can offer substantial tax savings if they're used to pay qualified higher education expenses. If all requirements are met, no federal income tax is due on the interest. To get this important advantage, you'll need to follow certain guidelines. Among them: The savings bonds must be issued in 1990 or later and be purchased in one or both parents' name(s)—not the child's. Married taxpayers must file a joint return. The owner must be at least 24 years old before the bond's issue date. The bonds must be redeemed by the owner in the year used to pay for qualified higher educational expenses. Qualified higher educational expenses generally include tuition and fees and exclude room and board. Talk to your tax advisor and the person selling you the bond to be sure you have set up the purchase properly. Also, there are income restrictions on who can take advantage of this benefit. You'll need to call the IRS or your tax advisor to verify your eligibility.

.03 Life Insurance

You should purchase life insurance only if you need protection. If you have a permanent life insurance policy paid with fixed annual premiums, you generally have the option of borrowing against its cash value. Of course, the amount of cash value available to borrow against varies, depending on the specific policy. The death benefit will be decreased by the amount of the outstanding loan. The interest rate charged on such loans is often reasonable, and in many cases you can pay back the loan on a flexible schedule. Talk to your insurance representative about the advantages of life insurance when planning your child's college education.

.04 Prepaid Tuition Plans

Certain states, such as Alabama, Alaska, Colorado, Florida, Massachusetts, Michigan, Ohio, Oklahoma, Pennsylvania, Tennessee, and West Virginia, offer various types of prepaid tuition plans, generally for students attending state schools. Residents of these states can buy a contract or bonds at a fixed price, based on the rates of college tuition today. Payments can be made in lump sums or monthly installments. The state, in turn, invests the money to earn the difference between the amount you are paying and the projected cost of tuition at the time your child reaches college age. Those who sign up are fully protected, as the state assumes all the risk of the investments. Check with your state's commission on higher education to see if a prepaid tuition plan is available where you live.

Prepaid tuition plans are not for everyone. They mostly attract middle-income families who tend to be more conservative in their investments. Lower-income families using this option may jeopardize their chances for state aid and forfeit money needed for immediate essentials. If you're interested and a plan is offered in your state, you'll want to know if it covers only the cost of tuition, or room and board too. Also, check to see if it applies to other than state schools. Finally, confirm that your original deposit will be returned if your child attends a private or out-of-state college, is not accepted at a state school, or chooses not to attend college at all.

.05 Savings Plan Trusts

Certain states, such as Connecticut, Iowa, Kentucky, Louisiana, Massachusetts, New Hampshire, and New York, offer special college savings accounts known as savings plan trusts. These accounts allow the contributor to save as little or as much as they like on behalf of a designated beneficiary's qualified education expenses. Contributions may be as little as $25. These accounts may guarantee a minimum rate of return and generally provide favorable tax treatment. The monies from the account may be used at any qualified institution of higher learning within the United States. If you move to another state, the money in the trust goes with you. Some savings plan trusts allow monies to be used for other family members' qualified education expenses. Check with your state's commission on higher education to see if a savings plan trust is available where you live.

.06 Hope Scholarship Credit

Generally, for tax years after 1997, this credit will reimburse $1,500 per year of the cost of tuition and fees paid during the first two years of secondary education for joint filers with adjusted gross incomes of up to $82,000 and single filers up to $41,000. This credit phases out as your adjusted gross income increases and you are not eligible for this credit if your joint income is above $102,000 and single income is above $51,000.

.07 Lifetime Learning Credit (LLC)

Effective July 1, 1998, this credit will reimburse up to $1,000 of college tuition and fees per year through the year 2002 and $2,000 each year afterward. To qualify for the full credit, a taxpayer would need to spend $5,000 on qualifying expenses through 2002 and $10,000 each year after. Parents with more than one child may claim an LLC for one child and a Hope credit for a different child in the same year. The two credits, however, may not be claimed in the same year for one child.

.08 CDs and Bank Accounts

Bank Certificates of Deposit (CDs) and bank savings accounts are two other places to put college savings. Although CDs and bank savings accounts are generally FDIC insured, they generally offer a lower return potential than other investment vehicles and are most appropriate for those with short-term goals.

.09 Other Avenues for Revenue

Even if you start early, it may be impossible to save enough for your child's college education. That doesn't mean, however, that college is out of the question. You have other cost-saving options available.

Student strategies. While they may not be options you should rely on, there are some strategies students can follow to help reduce their expenses prior to entering college and once they're in college. For example, many college students, particularly those who commute to a local school, are able to work part-time and summer jobs to help subsidize their tuition or simply to earn spending money. Be aware, however, that money earned by the child prior to college may reduce his or her eligibility for financial aid. Some colleges offer cooperative education programs where students rotate study with periods of career-related work, allowing them to earn money and credits at the same time. However, it may take more than four years to complete a degree through a cooperative education program. Ask the college admissions office about the specifics of their program.

Depending on a child's scholastic ability, he or she may be able to earn college credits by taking college courses or advance placement exams while still in high school. First- and second-year college students can also take College Level Examination Program tests for course credit. These options can represent a significant savings over the cost of a full-semester course in the classroom. Check with your child's high school guidance counselor or with the college admissions office for eligibility requirements and program specifics.

Another cost-savings possibility is to attend a community college for the first year or two, then transfer to a four-year college to complete a degree. This can be a more affordable approach to receiving a degree from a prestigious institution that you may have been unable to afford for four years or which may have been more competitive to gain entrance as a freshman.

Financial aid. Think of financial aid in broad terms. You need not be the sole source of funding for your child's higher education. For example, when your child receives a gift of money, put it into a college fund. When grandparents ask what to give for birthdays, suggest college fund contributions.

And remember, the traditional sources of financial aid: scholarships, grants, work-study programs, and government loans. Your child's scholastic record, course of study, athletic ability, and choice of college are just a few of the variables that may affect the availability of these options.

If your family meets certain financial criteria, the federal government has a program of low-interest loans with extended payment terms. Relying too heavily on loans, however, is costly and can burden graduates with large debts just when they are working to establish their financial independence. Also, you should be aware that government financial aid programs are subject to change.

Home equity. If you bought your home when your child was small, you're likely to have built up a significant amount of equity by the time college is in the picture. You can tap that resource for your child's education with a home-equity line of credit. Interest payments may be tax deductible.

.10 Determining Need—Future Value Calculations Can Help

How much money will you need to have accumulated when your child is ready for college? Exhibit 2 illustrates how to develop a college education cost analysis/savings plan.

Exhibit 2

College Education Cost Analysis/Savings Plan

1	**Estimated cost of college education**	
	a. Current cost of college education (including tuition, fees, room and board, books, travel, and other expenses)	$18,000
2	b. Future value for six years until starting college at an expected inflation rate of six percent (Future value of current cost at six percent for six years = 1.419 from Table 1 in Appendix B)	$25,542
3	**Projected future cost of college education adjusted for inflation**	$25,542
4	Future value of a series of deposits for six years until starting college and expected annual return on saving and investments of eight percent (use Table 2) (Future value of eight percent for six years = 7.336 from Table 2 in Appendix B)	7.336
	Estimated annual deposit to achieve needed education fund (3 divided by 4)	$3,482

.11 Sources of Financial Aid

It is important to know sources that are available for financial aid. In examining financial aid, do the following:

- Check out federal and state government programs first, since they represent the most funding available. *Note:* You can use one form to apply for various federal, state, and college programs.

- Consider specialized programs directed toward certain types of people (for example, based on race or religion).

- Find out about funds available from the college itself.

You may obtain assistance to determine the sources of financial aid by contacting Scholarship Search, 1775 Broadway, New York, NY 10019. You also may obtain information on scholarships and student college aid by contacting Student College Aid, 3641 Deal Street, Houston, TX 77025. A publication discussing college aid offerings is *Don't Miss Out: The Ambitious Student's Guide to Financial Aid,* published by Octameron Associates, P.O. Box 3437, Alexandria, VA 22302. The Early Financial Aid Planning Service provides a computerized estimate of your eligibility for financial aid from various sources, in addition to a comprehensive analysis of your family's financial status relative to college costs and potential aid. Information can be obtained from Early Financial Aid Planning, Box 2843, Princeton, NJ 08541.

Grants and scholarships. Grants and scholarships are the best because the money is usually tax-free and never has to be repaid. These include federal Pell Grants, primarily for low-income families, which offer a maximum of $3,800 annually, based on need for the 2002-2003 school year.

The federal Supplemental Educational Opportunity Grant, which is administered by colleges, offers awards ranging from $100 to $4,000 a student per year. Most students who receive need-based grants also are expected to participate in the federal Work-Study program, whereby students work part-time jobs to meet the family's remaining financial need. Eligibility for scholarships may be based on merit (academic or athletic) or financial need. Scholarships may be based on religion, nationality, race, and occupation.

Loans. Loans come in two basic varieties: *need-based,* which help families who can't afford college costs; and *non-need-based,* designed to fill a gap when the family doesn't have available cash but may have illiquid assets. Loans represent 59 percent of all financial aid for college.

The two most common and attractive need-based loans are the *Perkins* and the *Stafford,* both federally funded. The Perkins loan is made directly to students; parents need not co-sign this loan. Repayment begins only after students graduate, leave college, or fall below half-time student status, and they have 10 years to repay the loan. With a Perkins, one pays a low interest rate (five percent), and interest doesn't accrue until repayment begins. A school's financial aid office determines how much a student gets, but the cap on borrowing is $4,000 per year for a lifetime total up to $20,000.

Interest rates for Stafford loans are variable, but the lifetime cap is 8.25 percent. With the subsidized Stafford, interest does not accrue until six months after a student graduates, leaves, or falls below half-time status. Students can borrow up to maximums that rise the longer a student remains in school, between $2,625 freshman year and $5,500 senior year. The unsubsidized Stafford is a non-need-based loan for which most students who apply for aid are eligible. Interest accrues immediately, but payment may be postponed until after graduation. Students can borrow up to maximums that rise the longer a student remains in school, between $4,000 freshman year and $5,000 senior year above any subsidized Stafford loans they may receive.

Another common, non-need-based loan is the *PLUS (Parent Loans for Undergraduate Students).* This loan is made to parents, not students. Parents can borrow up to the annual cost of attending college, minus any financial aid received. This loan is dependent on your credit rating, although the requirements are not as stringent as those for a mortgage. If you have a bad credit rating, such as that resulting from judgments or liens against you, you may still be eligible for a PLUS if you can find a co-signer willing to take responsibility to pay the loan if you can't. The drawback of PLUS loans is that repayment begins 60 days after you receive the money, although the repayment period can last 10 years. The interest rate is variable, tied to the short-term Treasury bill rate, with a maximum of nine percent.

There are also private loan options such as bank lines of credit; home-equity loans; Signature Student loans, which are offered by Sallie Mae; and Excel loans, which are offered by Nellie Mae. Private loans such as these are less appealing than the unsubsidized Stafford, however, because the interest rate is usually at a premium to the prime rate, and repayment may start immediately, rather than being postponed until the student graduates. *Note:* In 2002, the interest rate for Stafford Loans is 4.06 percent, down from 5.99 percent. (The in-school interest rate is 3.46 percent.) The interest rate for PLUS loans is 4.86 percent, down from 6.79 percent. Students who will be graduating or who have already graduated but not yet consolidated their loans should consider consolidating their loans in order to lock in the new low rates.

Top strategies to maximize aid eligibility:

1. Save money in the parent's name, not the child's name.
2. Spend down student assets and income first.
3. Pay off consumer debt, such as credit cards and car loans.
4. Maximize contributions to your retirement fund.
5. Accelerate necessary expenses, to reduce available cash.

Source: www.FinAid.org

.12 New Opportunities for Education Savings

The new law, the Economic Growth and Tax Relief Reconciliation Act of 2001, offers significant tax advantages for education investing. These changes will affect Section 529 qualified state tuition savings programs and Education Savings Accounts (ESAs, formerly, Education IRAs). One noteworthy change: You can now invest in a Section 529 college savings program and in an ESA in the same year for the same beneficiary without penalty.

Section 529 college savings plans. These state-sponsored plans got a big boost from the new tax law, which makes their earnings tax-free, instead of merely tax-deferred. After 2001, no federal income tax is owed on funds withdrawn to pay for qualified educational expenses, regardless of your income. Most plans allow you to contribute even if you don't live in the state that sponsors the plan, and there are no income limitations. Also, because you own the account, you can always get the money back, minus income taxes and a penalty, or roll the assets over to the account of another eligible family member with no tax consequences.

Contribution limits are as high as a lifetime total of $250,000 in some states, and special gift-tax provisions make Section 529 plans useful estate-planning tools. You can give as much as $55,000 in a single year to a beneficiary, but for tax purposes, treat the gift as five annual tax-free gifts of $11,000. A husband and wife could combine their exemptions to remove $110,000 from their estate with a single tax-free gift.

The main drawback of Section 529 plans is a lack of investment flexibility. The sponsoring state selects the investment manager and investment options. Costs can be another concern. The Section 529 plan may charge administrative expenses in addition to those charged by the underlying mutual funds, which can make plans more expensive than mutual funds in which you invest directly. Even so, a number of low-cost plans exist.

Note:

1. You can take a federal income tax deduction of up to $3,000 for college tuition, whether or not you itemize. The deduction increases to $4,000 in 2004 and 2005 and phases out in 2006.

2. 529 plans are offered by at least 45 states.

Education Savings Accounts (ESAs). The annual contribution limit for Coverdell Education Savings Accounts (ESA, formerly, an Education IRA) is $2,000 for each beneficiary. The AGI requirements for eligibility to make contributions to an ESA by married couples filing jointly will also increase. Allowed contributions will phase out for couples with AGIs from $190,000 to $220,000. (The AGI phase out range for single filers remains at $95,000 to $110,000.) Additionally, starting in 2002, corporations, tax-exempt organizations, and other entities will be eligible to make contributions to ESAs. (Contributions to ESAs are still not tax deductible, though earnings grow tax deferred and are generally not taxed when taken out for qualified education expenses.)

An ESA gives you complete control over where and how you invest, but it's not for everyone. If the prospective scholar hasn't used the funds by age 30, he or she can take the money, minus taxes and penalties, unless the assets are rolled over to the account of an eligible family member. Finally, these accounts are off-limits to high-income investors. The level of eligible contributions falls to $0 for single filers earning more than $110,000 and for married couples earning more than $220,000.

Also beginning in 2002, funds in an ESA can be used to pay for qualified public, private, or religious elementary or secondary school expenses. Previously, ESA funds could only be used for qualified higher education expenses.

.13 *Information Sources*

The following sources provide valuable information on college financial planning:

- *Getting Into College: A Quick Guide to Everything You Need to Know* by Pat Ordovensky, Peterson's.
- *Financial Aid for College: A Quick Guide to Everything You Need to Know* by Pat Ordovensky, Peterson's.
- *College Check Mate: Innovative Tuition Plans That Make You a Winner* by Debra Wexler, Octameron Press.
- The federal government is a major source of financial aid. Start by filling out the free Application for Federal Student Aid (FAFSA), available from your child's high school counselor or by calling 1-800-4-FEDAID.

The following websites provide a good deal of information on the various education investment options:

- www.sensible-investor.com/529_plans.html and www.kiplinger.com—Great sites for Section 529 information and comparions.
- www.finaid.org—The Financial Aid Information page on the World Wide Web. You'll find a variety of free information including a database of 180,000 private sector scholarships, fellowships, grants, and loans.
- www.collegesavings.org—The College Savings Plans Network (1-877-CSPN4YOU)
- www.Savingforcollege.com—A website that provides information about 529 plans and other college savings options.
- www.nelliemae.com—Compare the features of various types of student loans.
- www.Ed.gov—The U.S. Department of Education website, which contains the *Student Guide to Financial Aid* and *Funding Your Education.* Use their step-by-step instructions for learning about financial aid and for completing the Free Application for Federal Student Aid (FAFSA).

¶ 2920 How to Take On and Manage Debt

Virtually everybody uses credit everyday. We live in an era of what seems to be abundant credit, which in turn allows people to spend more than ever before. Credit becomes a vicious cycle for many people. If you do not exercise caution, you can run into serious financial trouble, including the possibility of bankruptcy.

.01 How Does Fair Credit Reporting Affect Your Credit?

If you've ever applied for a charge account, a personal loan, insurance, or a job, there's a file about you. This file contains information on where you work and live, how you pay your bills, and whether you've filed for bankruptcy, been sued, or arrested. Companies that gather and sell this information are called Consumer Reporting Agencies (CRAs). The most common type of CRA is the credit bureau. The information CRAs sell about you to creditors, employers, insurers, and other businesses is called a consumer report. The Fair Credit Reporting Act (FCRA), enforced by the Federal Trade Commission, is designed to promote accuracy and ensure the privacy of the information used in consumer reports. Recent amendments to the Act expand your rights and place additional requirements on CRAs. Businesses that supply information about you to CRAs and those that use consumer reports also have new responsibilities under the law.

Here are some questions consumers commonly ask about consumer reports and CRAs—and the answers. Note that you may have additional rights under state laws. Contact your state Attorney General or local consumer protection agency for more information.

How do I find the CRA that has my report? Contact the CRAs listed in the Yellow Pages under "credit" or "credit rating and reporting." Because more than one CRA may have a file on you, call each until you locate all the agencies maintaining your file. The three major national credit bureaus are:

- Equifax, P.O. Box 740241, Atlanta, GA 30374-0241; (800) 685-1111.
- Experian (formerly TRW), P.O. Box 949, Allen, TX 75013; (888) EXPERIAN (397-3742).
- Trans Union, 760 West Sproul Road, P.O. Box 390, Springfield, PA 19064-0390; (800) 916-8800.

In addition, anyone who takes action against you in response to a report supplied by a CRA—such as denying your application for credit, insurance, or employment—must give you the name, address, and telephone number of the CRA that provided the report. The CRA must tell you everything in your report, including medical information, and in most cases, the sources of the information. The CRA must also give you a list of everyone who has requested your report within the past year—two years for employment related requests.

There's no charge if a company takes adverse action against you, such as denying your application for credit, insurance or employment, and you request your report within 60 days of receiving the notice of the action. The notice will give you the name, address, and phone number of the CRA. In addition, you're entitled to one free report a year if (1) you're unemployed and plan to look for a job within 60 days, (2) you're on welfare, or (3) your report is inaccurate because of fraud. Otherwise, a CRA may charge you up to $8 for a copy of your report.

What can I do about inaccurate or incomplete information? Under the new law, both the CRA and the information provider have responsibilities for correcting inaccurate or incomplete information in your report. To protect all your rights under this law, contact both the CRA and the information provider.

First, tell the CRA in writing what information you believe to be inaccurate. CRAs must reinvestigate the items in question, usually within 30 days, unless they consider your dispute frivolous. They must also forward all relevant data that you provide about the dispute to the information provider. After the information provider receives notice of a dispute from the CRA, it must investigate, review all relevant information provided by the CRA, and report the results to the CRA. If the information provider finds the disputed information to be in fact inaccurate, it must notify all nationwide CRAs so that they can correct this information in your file.

When the reinvestigation is complete, the CRA must give you the written results and a free copy of your report if the dispute results in a change. If an item is changed or removed, the CRA cannot put the disputed information back in your file unless the information provider verifies its accuracy and completeness, and the CRA gives you a written notice that includes the name, address, and phone number of the provider.

Second, tell the creditor or other information provider in writing that you dispute an item. Many providers specify an address for disputes. If the provider then reports the item to any CRA, it must include a notice of your dispute. In addition, if you are correct—that is, if the information is in fact inaccurate—the information provider may not use it again.

How long can a CRA report negative information? Seven years. There are certain exceptions:

- Information about criminal convictions may be reported without any time limitation.
- Bankruptcy information may be reported for 10 years.
- Information reported in response to an application for a job with a salary of more than $75,000 has no time limit.
- Information reported because of an application for more than $150,000 worth of credit or life insurance has no time limit.
- Information about a lawsuit or an unpaid judgment against you can be reported for seven years or until the statute of limitations runs out, whichever is longer.

.02 *What is a FICO Score?*

A FICO (an acronym for Fair, Isaac & Company) or credit score is a computer-generated numerical grade that predicts a lender's risk in doing business with a borrower. Any company or individual that issues mortgage loans, home-equity loans, car loans, insurance policies, or healthcare services (even the IRS) bases much of its lending decisions and terms on the applicant's FICO score. FICO scores are determined by computers and released through the three credit bureaus to their subscribing members. At Experian, the scores are called *Experian/Fair, Isaac;* at Equifax, they are called *Beacon* scores; at Trans Union, they are called *Empirica* scores.

Scoring is based on things like time on the job, the time you've lived at your current address, plus about 30 other factors, none of which are your income or assets:

1. *Payment history.* Do you make your payments on time? Have you had accounts turned over to collection? FICO deducts points for bad payment history, and it gives points for maintaining a good payment relationship.

2. *Outstanding debt.* FICO is very interested in the number of balances you have currently, the average of all balances, and the relationship between the total balance and total credit limit. Carrying too much credit lowers your score even if some of your accounts have zero balances, but FICO doesn't like to see you close to or at your limits, either.

3. *Credit history.* FICO looks at how long you've had those accounts, the total number of inquiries, and if you have opened new accounts. It is highly concerned about inquiries and accounts less than 12 months old.

4. *The types of credit you use.* FICO is very interested in the diversity of the credit you use. It looks to see if you use department store or bankcards, debit or credit cards, travel and entertainment cards, personal finance companies, and installment loans.

5. *Negative information.* Bankruptcies, late payments, collections, late fees, too many credit lines with maximum available funds borrowed, too little credit history (less than five credit lines in the past two years), and too many credit report inquiries are considered negatives.

What constitutes a good score varies from lender to lender. FICO scores range from 375 to 900 points, and a score of 650 to 675 is generally considered excellent. However, to qualify for the most favorable terms, a lender might require a score in excess of 700. *Note:*

1. Rate shopping can hurt credit scores, since shopping leisurely for rates over an extended period can be interpreted as a sign that you're applying for vast amounts of credit.
2. For a detailed view of how credit scores are tabulated, go to www.Myfico.com.

How to improve your credit scores. Here are tips for boosting your credit score:

- Apply for credit only when necessary. New credit applications can lower your score.
- Pay your bills on time, every time.
- Check your credit report for errors. If there are erroneous items, write to the credit reporting company and have those items removed.
- Close unused credit card accounts, but only if they were opened recently.
- Leave old credit accounts open, even if you're not using them, because part of your score is based on how long you've had credit.

.03 Is It a Good Idea to Obtain a Home Equity Loan?

Interest incurred on your first and second homes are deductible for tax purposes. However, limitations exist on the deductibility of other types of interest—especially, interest on consumer loans. As a result, you should convert your consumer loan interest to interest on a home equity loan in order to take the full tax-deductibility of your interest expenses. The home equity loan comes in two forms: a second trust deed (mortgage) and a line of credit.

Second trust deed. A second trust deed is similar to a first trust deed (mortgage), except that in the event of foreclosure, the holder of the first mortgage has priority in payment over the holder of the second mortgage.

Line of credit. Under the line of credit provision for an equity loan, you may write a check when you need funds. You are charged with interest only on the amount borrowed. However, before you join the rush to a home equity loan, you should consider the pluses and minuses of the home equity loan.

Advantages of a home equity loan.

- *Low interest rates,* because (a) the loan is secured by your house, and (b) the loan usually bears variable rates.
- *No loan processing fees.* You do not have to go through a loan application and incur fees each time you borrow money.

- *Convenience.* You may write a check only when you need money. You are charged interest only on the amount borrowed.

Pitfalls of a home equity loan.

- *High points.* Points imposed on an equity loan are based on the amount of the credit line, not on the amount actually borrowed. Many home equity loans have no caps on interest rates.
- *Long payback period.* It is convenient to have to pay a small minimum amount each month, but stretching out the loan payback period usually means higher interest rates over the period.
- *High balloon payments.* Some loans require a large balloon payment of the principal at the end of the loan period.
- *Risk of home loss.* Unlike other loans, you risk losing your home. You may not be so lucky to sell your home fast enough and at fair market price to be able to meet the balloon.
- *Frivolous spending habit.* You may get into the habit of spending on unnecessary things. Use home equity loans very conservatively. You may easily end up borrowing up to the limit and struggling through each month with heavy repayment burden. Don't forget: Your home, and the equity it represents, is probably your biggest investment. Anything borrowed against it must be repaid upon its sale. You could lose your home if your equity line becomes greater than your ability to pay it back.

Recommendation: You should shop around and carefully compare the various equity loan alternatives in terms of each of the above pitfalls. You could obtain a traditional second trust deed.

.04 Debt Management Websites

Here are popular websites for debt management. Use the Web to get confidential advice on debt management or bankruptcy. You can even arrange for a service to negotiate with creditors and set up a payment plan.

About.com Credit/Debt Management (Credit.about.com/money/credit). The credit-and-debt-management channel run by financial consultant Michael Killian provides advice on how to deal with creditors. There are discussion boards and links to articles like "What to do if your husband leaves you with a mound of debt?" Find out about budgeting and credit repair. There is also information on consolidating your debts; moving debt from one credit card to another with a lower interest rate doesn't necessarily lower your total payments.

Auriton Solutions (www.auriton.org). Auriton's debt management program costs $25 to sign up plus up to $35 per month. It will consolidate your debts, reduce the interest rates you pay, and process your payments. Go online to see which bills have been paid. Check on the Learning Center for five signs that you're on the road to financial crisis. A sure sign: taking cash advantages to pay your bills.

MyVesta.org (www.myvesta.org). This is an information-packed site that runs a debt management program for $60 per month. For that price, MyVesta will consolidate your debt and negotiate lower interest rates with your creditors. For a $495 set-up fee plus a monthly fee, MyVesta will also process your monthly bills and payments and provide counseling. The site provides free articles on topics like how to respond if you are sued. Suggestion: Answer the complaint so the judge knows you intend to resolve the issue. Debt bytes, a free e-mail service, keeps you posted on your rights when a creditor comes after you. There's even a call-in Internet radio show where debt experts answer questions.

National Foundation for Credit Counseling (www.nfcc.org). This nonprofit organization is associated with 1,450 counseling centers nationwide. The site provides a search engine to find the center nearest you. Contact them by phone or online and a licensed representative will set up a plan and will negotiate with creditors. The site offers lots of tips, for example: When choosing a credit counseling agency, find out whether the counselors are certified and how your funds are protected.

Nolo.com (www.nolo.com). Need to improve your credit rating? Nolo suggests making purchases with a credit card and then paying off the bill. The Debt & Bankruptcy channel of this authoritative legal site also offers advice on which bills you should pay (mortgage payments) and which can wait (legal bills). Click on Debt & Bankruptcy to discover how to get out of debt, deal with annoying bill collectors, and whether to file for Chapter 7 and 13.

Profina Debt Solutions (www.profina.org). Profina's debt management program costs $50 to set up and then up to $50 per month. It will consolidate your unsecured debt, negotiate lower interest rates, and process payments. Get a breakdown of payments made and contact counselors by e-mail. Listen to Profina's Internet radio call-in show and take the debt quiz to see if you are heading toward financial ruin.

¶ 2930 Life, Health, and Property and Liability Insurance

An integral part of any financial plan is insurance protection. Insurance provides a vital means of meeting your financial objectives. The type and amount of insurance depends on your age, assets, income, and needs. Insurance is basically "replacement": life insurance provides income lost at the death of the wage earner, disability insurance assures income when you are not able to work full time, health insurance covers medical bills, and property/casualty policies pay most of the costs of theft, fire, or accident.

With the variety of insurance products on the market, you are faced with a number of decisions.

.01 Types of Risk

The most common risks are classified as personal risks, property risks, and liability risks.

Personal risks. The uncertainties surrounding loss of income or life due to premature death, illness, disability, old age, or unemployment.

Property risks. The uncertainties of direct or indirect losses to personal or real property due to fire, windstorms, accidents, theft, and other hazards.

Liability risks. Possible losses due to negligence resulting in bodily harm or property damage to others. Such harm or damage could be caused by an automobile, professional misconduct, injury suffered on one's property, and so on.

Personal risks, property risks, and liability risks are types of *pure risk* (see Exhibit 3), or insurable risk, since there would only be a chance of loss if the specified events occurred. Pure risks are accidental and unintentional risks for which the nature and financial cost of the loss can be predicted. A *speculative risk* is a risk in which there is a chance of either loss or gain. Starting a small business that may or may not succeed or gambling are examples of speculative risk. Speculative risks are legally defined as uninsurable.

Exhibit 3

Types of Insurance Available for Certain Risks

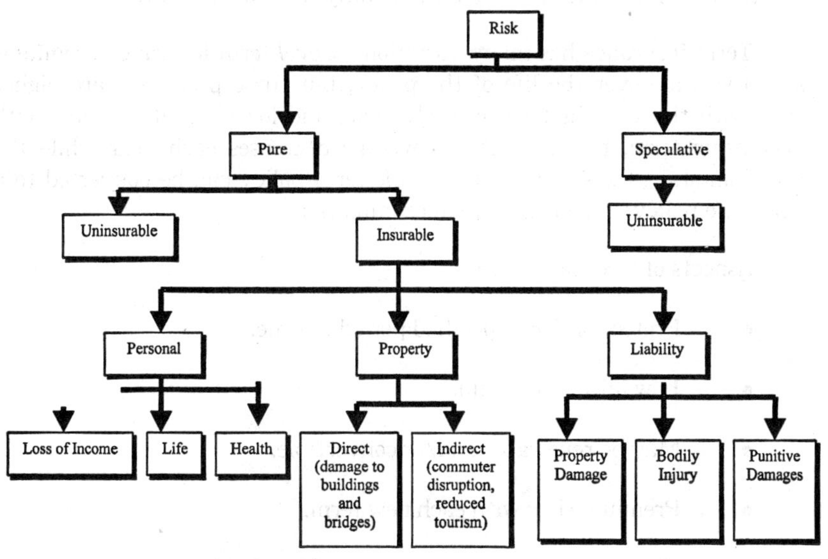

.02 Which Life Insurance Policy Is Right for You?

Life insurance is the most important tool of estate planning and one of the most valuable aids to financial planning. The main purpose of life insurance is to provide cash to your family after you die. The money your dependents will receive (the "death benefit") is an important financial resource: It can help pay the mortgage, run the household, and ensure that your dependents aren't burdened with debt. The proceeds from a life insurance policy could mean that they won't have to sell assets to pay outstanding bills or taxes. What's more, there is no federal income tax on life insurance benefits.

There are two basic types of life insurance policies—term insurance and permanent insurance. All other kinds of policies are variations on one or more of the two basic types.

Term insurance. Term insurance is death protection for a specified period of time and provides no cash value or savings element. It pays a benefit only if the insured dies during the period covered by the policy. It provides for a level premium rate for the set period after which the policy ceases and becomes void, except when renewed or changed to some other form of policy. It is the cheapest form of life insurance because it provides the most coverage for the least money. It is appropriate for young people who need large amounts of insurance, those who desire only death protection, and those whose insurance need will decrease over time. The premium rates increase at each renewal date. Many policies require that you present evidence of insurability at renewal to qualify for the lower rates.

Term insurance has many variations. *Level* term insurance premiums stay the same over the life of the policy, but these premiums are higher than with the straight term in early years and lower in later years. With *decreasing* term, the amount of coverage decreases each year while the premium stays the same. A *convertible* term policy can be converted to a whole life policy without a medical examination.

Aspects of term insurance:

- Protection for a specified period of time.
- Low initial premium.
- May be renewable and/or convertible.
- Premium rises with each new term.
- You or your dependents get nothing back if you survive the term.

The term rates increase as the insured ages. Many people, in fact, discontinue needed coverage because of the increasing cost. When evaluating term policies, compare (1) initial premiums as well as those charged in later years and (2) renewal provisions.

Permanent insurance. Permanent insurance, also called *cash value, straight, whole, universal, adjustable, variable,* or *ordinary life* insurance, provides insurance protection by the payment of a fixed premium throughout the lifetime of the insured. However, in addition to death protection, whole life insurance has a savings element called "cash value" or "cash surrender value." As the policies mature, they develop cash values representing the early surplus plus investment earnings.

This feature, not found in most term insurance policies, provides you with some options.

- You can cancel or "surrender" the policy, in total or in part, and receive the cash value as a lump sum. If you surrender your policy in the early years, there may be little or no cash value.
- If you need to stop paying premiums, you can use the cash value to continue your current insurance protection for a specified time or to provide a lesser amount of protection covering you for your lifetime.
- You can usually borrow from the insurance company, using the cash value in your life insurance as collateral. Unlike loans from most financial institutions, the loan is not dependent on credit checks or other restrictions. You ultimately must repay any loan with interest or your beneficiaries will receive a reduced death benefit.

The most common type of permanent insurance is *whole life* or *ordinary life.* The premiums generally remain constant over the life of the policy and must be paid periodically in the amount indicated in the policy.

Advantages of whole-life insurance:

- Future uninsurability, old age, or other contingencies cannot terminate the policy.
- When you are older and no longer need a large face amount of insurance protection, you can cash in the policy and use the cash as a source of retirement income.
- Interest earned on cash value is tax-deferred until you surrender the policy, or tax free if you hold it for life.

Disadvantages of whole-life insurance:

- More death protection can be purchased with term insurance.

- The interest rate on cash value is generally below prevailing market rates. Therefore, high yields can be obtained on other investment or savings plans.
- Cash values grow slowly in early years because of large up-front commissions and start-up expenses.

Aspects of whole-life insurance:

- Protection for life.
- Fixed premium.
- Growing cash value.
- Higher initial premium than term.
- You or your dependents always receive benefits.
- Available in several different forms such as universal, variable, or single-premium life.
- Should be purchased with the intention of keeping for life or for a long period of time.

Whole-life policies are most appropriate for those who want lifetime coverage and desire a structured savings plan.

There are many variations of whole life insurance: universal life, variable life, and single-premium whole life.

Universal life. Universal life is a combination of term insurance and a tax-deferred savings plan that pays a flexible interest, either indexed to a particular investment, such as the 90-day Treasury bill, or formulated by the company. The guaranteed minimum rate typically is four or five percent. *Tip:* It is most appropriate for those who desire flexibility and wish to vary premiums to reflect changing life situations and needs.

Variable life. Variable life offers lifetime protection with level premiums. The cash value is invested, at your choosing, in any combination of stocks, bonds, or money-market funds. The investment risk is yours. There is no guaranteed minimum rate. The death benefit can grow if the cash value increases. *Tip:* It is best suited for those who are investment oriented, desire high yields on policy premiums, and are willing to accept investment risk.

Single-premium life is explained later.

Note: Insurance experts say you should make sure you can buy enough coverage before you consider a cash-value policy. You can get quotes for term policies at several websites, including www.quotesmith.com or www.insweb.com.

.03 How Much Life Insurance Is Enough?

Unfortunately, there is no fixed formula in assessing the amount of life insurance a family should have. There are basically two approaches to use in determining the amount of insurance you need: the multiple-of-income approach and the needs approach.

Multiple-of-income approach. Under this method, you simply multiply your gross annual income by some selected number. The American Council of Life Insurance (ACLI) suggest that life insurance should equal five to seven times your annual gross income.

This rule of thumb, however, may not always be appropriate because no two families are exactly the same. The amount will vary with family needs, goals, net worth, future expenses and income, and life style requirements. *Note:* You can find worksheets and articles at www.latimes.com/money and calculators at www.insure.com.

Needs approach. This approach determines the financial needs of your family and other dependents in the event of your death. The needs approach emphasizes meeting financial objectives and obligations while the multiple-of-income approach stresses replacement of your future earnings. The idea is to first add up the total financial needs and then to deduct accumulated assets. If you decide to use the needs approach, consider the following funds:

1. *Emergency and administrative fund.* Funds for the costs of final illness, funeral and burial bills, probate costs, uninsured medical costs, debts, and estate taxes.
2. *Special fund.* Fund needed for other specific needs, such as educational expenses and paying mortgages.
3. *Retirement fund.* Additional money set aside to support your spouse and dependents.
4. *Family income fund.* Fund to support surviving dependents until they are self-supporting.

Example. Exhibit 4 illustrates the use of the needs approach to help estimate the amount of life insurance to buy.

Exhibit 4

How Much Life Insurance?

		Sample Entries
(1)	Funding needs	
	1. Emergency and Administrative Fund	$15,000
	2. Special Fund	125,000
	3. Family Income Fund	80,000
	4. Retirement Fund	60,000
	Total Needs	$280,000
(2)	Available Resources	
	1. Savings	$30,000
	2. Investments	60,000
	3. Life Insurance	
	a. Group Insurance	50,000
	b. Social Security	1,000
	Total Resources	$141,000
	Life Insurance Gap	$139,000

Keep in mind that life insurance is not a static product. Family needs may change; family income might vary; family size may alter. Therefore, basic insurance needs can vary over time. It is wise to reassess your coverage periodically in keeping with the changes that occur in your life.

.04 How Do You Evaluate Whole-Life Policies?

When shopping for whole-life insurance policies, here are some tips for evaluation:

- Load charges.
- Investment return.
- Death benefits and net annual premium amounts.
- Guaranteed cash-value growth.
- Insurance costs. What is the charge for the term coverage?
- Policy loan rates, in case you borrow money against the cash value.
- Cost-index numbers. The smaller the number, the lower the policy's net cost.
- Cash surrender values and charges, if any.
- How projected annual dividends, if any, would offset premium payments.
- Medical requirements, for increasing the policy's face amount.

.05 *What Is Single Premium Whole Life (SPWL) Insurance?*

Single premium whole life insurance is a policy with a low risk investment flavor. For a minimum amount of $5,000, paid once, you get a paid-up insurance policy. Your money is invested at a guaranteed rate of interest for one year or longer. SPWL has the following features:

- Its cash value earns interest immediately at competitive rates.
- It allows you to borrow interest earned annually after the first year.
- It allows you to take out a loan for up to 90 percent of principal at lower rates.
- It allows you to receive permanent life insurance coverage.
- Withdrawals and loans are not subject to tax.
- It provides tax-deferred accumulation of cash values.
- It provides tax-free death benefits to named beneficiaries.

Minuses of SPWL include:

- There are usually surrender charges if you withdraw your money.
- Interest rate is generally guaranteed for only one year and could drop.

If you consider SPWL, get answers to the following questions:

- What is the "net interest" rate at which your cash value will grow? The net interest rate is the yield after subtracting costs of the insurance and administrative expenses.
- What is the surrender charge?
- Are there any loan-processing fees? What is the loan interest rate?
- Is there a bailout plan, which enables you to cash in the policy without penalty if interest rates drop below the initial rate?

Select only a company with an A or A+ rating by A.M. Best Company (Best's Insurance Reports are available from a broker, company, or library) that has been in business at least five to ten years. Note that rate comparison can be very confusing and difficult because of the existence of many variations.

Try to deal with a most consistent and reputable agent instead of shopping around for better rates. You might want to use various services offered by SelectQuote Insurance Services (140 Second Street, San Francisco, CA 94105, (800)-343-1985). It is an insurance brokerage agency that (1) provides rate comparisons, (2) searches the rates of 1,600 companies to find the 16 that have a reputation for low rates on the type of coverage you want and have maintained an A or A+ rating from A.M. Best, and (3) sells one of the policies via its toll free number. *Note:* Also, check websites such as www.bestquote.com and www.masterquote.com. Exhibit 5 presents A.M. Best's ratings.

Exhibit 5

A.M. Best Company's Ratings

Ratings	*Description*
A+	**Superior.** Negligible risk.
A+c, A, Ac, A−	**Excellent.** Small, slightly variable risk.
A−c, B+, B+c	**Good.** High claims-paying ability for now.
B, Bc−, B−	**Adequate.** But less protection against risk.
B−c, C+, C+c	**Below average** quality, higher risk factor.
C, Cc, C−	**Financially weak,** high risk factor.
CCC, CC, D	**Nonviable,** or about to be.

¶ 2940 Estate Planning: Preserving Your Estate

A primary purpose of estate planning is to distribute your assets according to your wishes after your death. Successful estate planning transfers your assets to your beneficiaries quickly and with minimal tax consequences. The process of estate planning includes inventorying your assets and making a will or establishing a trust, with an emphasis on minimizing taxes. This paragraph provides only a general overview of estate planning. *Note:* Estate planning is complex, so this paragraph should not be viewed as tax advice. Consult with your attorney before changing your plan.

The objectives of your estate plan will typically include the following:

- Simplifying the probate process for your estate.
- Providing your surviving family members with sufficient assets to maintain their lifestyle and pay for necessary expenses while your estate is in probate.

- Having a competent person, who is familiar with your family, manage the transfer of your property.
- Ensuring important financial and/or healthcare decisions are handled according to your wishes, if you become unable to do so.
- Providing input as to who will raise your children should you become unable to do so.
- Minimizing estate taxes.

Note: Probate is a legal process that usually involves filing a deceased person's will with the local probate court, taking an inventory and getting appraisals of the deceased's property, paying all legal debts, and eventually distributing the remaining assets and property.

First, you have to ask yourself: Do you and your family members know the answers to the questions in the following checklist?

1. Can you locate your copies of last year's income tax returns?
2. Where is your safe deposit box located? Where is the key to it kept?
3. Do you know what kinds and amounts of life insurance protection you have?
4. Can you locate your insurance policies—life, health, property, casualty, and auto?
5. Do you know the names of the beneficiaries and contingent beneficiaries of your life insurance policies?
6. Do you know what type of health insurance protection you have and what the provisions of your health insurance policy are?
7. Do you and your spouse have current wills? Can you locate those wills, along with the name and address of the attorney who drafted them?
8. Do you have a separate record of the important papers you keep in your safe deposit box? Where is this record located?
9. Do you have a record of your spouse's Social Security number?
10. Can you locate your marriage certificate and the birth certificates of all the members of your family?
11. Do you know the name and address of your life insurance agent?
12. Do you have a clear understanding of what the principal financial resources and liabilities of your estate are?

13. Are you knowledgeable about simple, daily, and compound interest rates and about retirement funds and property ownership?

14. Have you given any thought to funerals and burial arrangements?

15. Do you know what papers and records will be important in the event of your death?

16. Can you explain the functions of a bank trust department, the meaning of joint ownership, and so forth?

Exhibit 6 presents data needed for estate planning.

Exhibit 6

Factual Data Required in Estate Planning

Personal data:	Names, addresses, phone numbers, family consultants, family birth dates, occupations, health problems, support needs, citizenship, marital status, marital agreements, wills, trusts, custodianships, trust beneficiary, gifts or inheritances, social security numbers, education, and military service.
Property (except life insurance or business):	Classification, title, indebtedness, basis, date and manner of acquisition, value of marketable securities, and location.
Life insurance:	Insured, kind of policies, amounts, insurance company, agents' names and addresses.
Health insurance:	Medical expense insurance: insurance company, policy benefits, and disability income.
Business interest:	Name, address, and ownership.
	Valuation factors: desired survivorship control; name, address, and phone number of business attorney and accountant.
Employee benefits:	Insurance, 401(k).
Family income:	Income of client, spouse, and dependent children and income tax information.
Family finances:	Budget information, investment preferences, ranking of economic objectives, capital needs, and other objectives.
Income and capital needs:	Retirement: age, required amount, potential sources.
	Disability: Required amount and sources.
	Death: Expected sources of income.

Liabilities:	Classification of liabilities, creditors, amounts, and whether insured or secured.
Factors affecting plan:	Gift propensity charitable inclinations, emotional maturity of children, and basic desires for estate distribution.
Authorization for information:	Life insurance.
Receipt for documents:	Personal and business.
Observations from interview:	

Once you know the value of your estate, you're ready to do some planning. Keep in mind that estate planning is not a one-time job. There are a number of changes that may call for a review of your plan. Take a fresh look at your estate plan if:

- The value of your assets changes significantly.
- You marry, divorce, or remarry.
- You have a child.
- You move to a different state.
- The executor of your will or the administrator of your trust dies or becomes incapacitated, or your relationship with that person changes significantly.
- One of your heirs dies or has a permanent change in health.
- The laws affecting your estate change.

.01 Wills

The simplest way to ensure that your funds, property, and personal effects will be distributed after your death according to your wishes is to prepare a will. A will is a legal document designating the transfer of your property and assets after you die. Usually, wills can be written by any person over the age of 18 who is mentally capable, commonly stated as "being of sound mind and memory." Your state may impose additional requirements.

Without a will to indicate your wishes, the court steps in and distributes your property according to the laws of your state. Wills are not just for the rich; the amount of property you have is irrelevant. A will ensures that what assets you do have will be given to family members or other beneficiaries you designate. If you have no apparent heirs and die without a will, it's even possible the state may claim your estate.

Elements of a will. Here are the basic elements generally included in a will:

- Your name and place of residence.
- A brief description of your assets.
- Names of spouse, children, and other beneficiaries, such as charities or friends.
- Alternate beneficiaries, in the event a beneficiary dies before you do.
- Specific gifts, such as an auto or residence.
- Establishment of trusts, if desired.
- Cancellation of debts owed to you, if desired.
- Name of an executor to manage the estate.
- Name of a guardian for minor children.
- Name of an alternative guardian, in the event your first choice is unable or unwilling to act.
- Your signature.
- Witnesses' signatures.

Two of the most important items included in your will are naming a guardian for minor children and naming an executor.

Naming a guardian. In most cases, a surviving parent assumes the role of sole guardian. However, it's important to name a guardian for minor children in your will in case neither you nor your spouse is able and willing to act. The guardian you choose should be over 18 and willing to assume the responsibility. If you do not name a guardian to care for your children, a judge will appoint one, and it may not be someone you would have chosen.

Naming an executor. An executor is the person who oversees the distribution of your assets in accordance with your will. Most people choose their spouse, an adult child, a relative, a friend, a trust company, or an attorney to fulfill this duty. You should expect your estate to pay an independent executor for this service.

If no executor is named in a will, a probate judge will appoint one. The executor files the will in probate court, where a judge decides if the will is valid. If it is found to be valid, assets are distributed according to the will. If the will is found to be invalid, assets are distributed in accordance with state laws.

Responsibilities usually undertaken by an executor include:

- Paying valid creditors.

- Paying taxes.
- Notifying Social Security and other agencies and companies of the death.
- Canceling credit cards, magazine subscriptions, etc.
- Distributing assets according to the will.

Preparing a will. Start by organizing what you need: outline your objectives, inventory your assets, estimate your outstanding debts, and prepare a list of family members and other beneficiaries. Use this information to carefully consider how you want to distribute your assets. Ask yourself lots of questions: Is it important to pass my property to my heirs in the most tax-efficient manner? Do I need to establish a trust to provide for my spouse or other beneficiaries? How much money will my grandchild need for college? Do I need to provide for a child who has a disability?

Taking inventory of the assets may be the key to making a will. Assets should be mentioned in your will. Any items not specifically mentioned may be addressed in a catchall clause of your will called a residuary clause, which generally states, "I give the remainder of my estate to . . ." Without this clause, items not specifically mentioned will be distributed in accordance with state law.

Outstanding debts usually will be paid by your estate before your beneficiaries receive their shares. You may want to clear up debts that you know will be a problem, or make specific provisions for payment of those debts in your will.

States require that you sign the will in front of witnesses; the number of witnesses varies by state. A witness should not be a beneficiary under the will. Only one copy should be signed.

Updating a will. You'll probably need to update your will several times during the course of your life. For example, a change in marital status, the birth of a child, or a move to a new state should all prompt a review of your will. You can update your will by amending it by way of a codicil or by drawing up a new one. Generally, people choose to issue a new will that supersedes the old document. Be sure to sign the new will and have it witnessed; then destroy the old one.

Where to keep your will. Once your will is written, store it in a safe place that is accessible to others after your death. If you name a trust company as executor, it will hold your will in safekeeping. You can keep it in your safe deposit box, but be aware that some states will seal your safe deposit box upon your death, so this may not always be the safest place to store your will. Make sure a close friend or relative knows where to find your will. If you had an attorney prepare your will, have him or her retain a copy with a note stating where the original can be found.

A living will. A living will is not a part of your will. It is a separate document that lets your family members know what type of care you do or don't want to receive should you become terminally ill or permanently unconscious. It becomes effective only when you cannot express your wishes yourself. If your state recognizes a power of attorney for health care, have one executed to authorize someone to act in accordance with your present intentions.

.02 Living Trusts

The probate process can be costly and time-consuming. Many states have simplified probate for estates below a certain amount, but that amount varies among states. If an estate meets the state's requirements for "expedited" or "unsupervised" probate, the process is faster and less costly.

A living trust, created while you're alive, lets you control the distribution of your estate. You transfer ownership of your property and your assets into the trust. You can serve as the trustee or you can select a person or an institution to be the trustee. If you're the trustee, you will have to name a successor trustee to distribute the assets at your death.

The advantage of a living trust is that, if properly drafted and executed, it can avoid probate because the trust owns the assets, not the deceased. Only property in the deceased's name must go through probate. The downside is that poorly drawn or unfunded trusts can cost you money and endanger your best intentions.

Note: A living trust is different from a *living will.* A living will expresses your wishes about being kept alive if you're terminally ill or seriously injured.

Chapter 30

Financial Information on the Internet

¶ 3001 Overview

The popularity that the Internet enjoys today is based, in part, on the information available to the public as they "surf the Net." Companies have established websites that offer information to the public. Governmental and nonprofit organizations often provide free information as a service to the public. Although private websites often charge for information, a number of sites offer free information in order to generate site traffic.

In order to obtain information on large companies, many businesses, investors, and creditors no longer need to subscribe to traditional business publications and brokerage house services. The following can all be found on the Internet at no cost: financial statements, SEC filings, brokerage house recommendations and future earnings forecasts, company specific news accounts, bond and stock quotations, financial indexes, and company and pension plan profiles. The instantaneous nature of the Internet also makes a great deal of this information much more timely than is the case with similar information from traditional sources.

¶ 3005 Financial Statements

As a public service, the SEC makes a number of SEC filings, the EDGAR archives, available to the public through the Internet. Within the EDGAR archives, the public may obtain such filings as a company's Form 10-K. The Form 10-K contains the business's annual report to shareholders, along with additional information on the company's products, competitors, marketing activities, product development, major contracts and leases (including employment contracts) and legal proceedings. The Form 10-K also includes schedules that are more detailed than those that appear in the annual report on inventories, bad debts, warranties, and advertising.

Form 10-Q filings are also part of the EDGAR archives. The Form 10-Q contains the quarterly report to shareholders. Along with the unaudited balance sheet and income statement found in most quarterly reports, the Form 10-Q contains information not normally found in quarterly reports. For example, the Form 10-Q contains unaudited cash flow statements, shareholders' equity or retained earnings statements, footnotes, and management discussion of the company. The EDGAR archives also contain Form 8-Q filings, which inform the SEC of material events that have developed since the previous Form 10-K and 10-Q filings.

A number of websites that retrieve the EDGAR archived filings are shown in Exhibit 1. The SEC's site retrieves these filings, but it operates through the use of key words, and it may be difficult to locate the filings of a particular company. Other sites allow viewers to search the archives using ticker symbols. FreeEDGAR allows viewers to download the filings as spreadsheet files. 10K Wizard will e-mail filings to viewers as word processing files. Moreover, with 10K Wizard, financial statements within the filings can be received as spreadsheet files. EDGARScan allows viewers to download tables from the filings as spreadsheet files. Filings that occur within the last 24 hours are not available through EDGAR ONLINE.

Exhibit 1

Edgar Websites

Site	Ticker Symbol Search	Spread-sheet Files	Word Processing Files	All Filings Available	Subscrip-tion Only
EDGARScan .... (edgarscan.pwcglobal.com)	✓	✓	✓	✓	
FreeEDGAR .... (www.freeedgar.com)	✓	✓	✓	✓	
10K Wizard .... (www.tenkwizard.com)	✓	✓	✓	✓	✓
EDGAR ONLINE ... (www.edgar-online.com)	✓	✓	✓	✓	✓
SEC.............. (www.sec.gov/cgi-bin/ srch-edgar)			✓	✓	

Some company annual reports to shareholders are also available to the public through the Internet (see Exhibit 2). A number of companies have placed their annual report on their websites, and Report Gallery and Online Annual Reports Service contain links to these annual reports. Both of these services will also mail hard copies of these annual reports to visitors upon request. Report Gallery also has links to the annual reports of Japanese, Korean, United Kingdom, and South African companies.

In addition to online annual reports, Annual Reports Service and Investor Communications Business Inc. will mail copies of the annual reports of selected companies to visitors upon request. A number of major companies do not participate in these services. For example, neither service carries the Microsoft annual report. Moreover, Investor Communications Business Inc. does not carry the IBM annual report. Investor Communications Business Inc. also makes available to the public the annual reports of Canadian and United Kingdom companies.

Exhibit 2

Annual Report Websites

Site	Online	Hard Copy/ PDF Sales	Number of Companies
Report Gallery (www.reportgallery.com)	✓	✓	Over 2,000
Online Annual Report Service (www.annualreportservice.com)	✓	✓	2,114
Annual Report Service (www.prars.com)	✓	✓	3,600

¶ 3011 Brokerage Recommendations and Future Earnings Forecasts

Besides information on companies that can be obtained from SEC filings and financial statements, information on the future operations of a company can be gleaned from future earnings forecasts by brokers/analysts, as well as their recommendations to investors regarding investments in the company. Generally, broker/analyst recommendations and future earnings forecasts are provided free on a consensus (composite) basis. The information contained in the consensus recommendations and future earnings forecasts include the following:

- Future earnings forecast.
- Recent history of changes in earnings forecasts.
- Recommendations on investing in a company.
- Recent history of changes in recommendations.
- Names of brokers/analysts surveyed for consensus.

Some of the companies that provide broker/analyst forecasts and recommendations provide more information on other websites (see Exhibit 3) than they do on their own site (e.g., Zacks (my.zacks.com) and First Call (www1.firstcall.com)). The following websites provide the most information for a given source.

Exhibit 3

Consensus Recommendation and Earnings Forecast Websites

Site	*Fore-cast*	*Forecast History*	*Rec.*	*Recomd. History*	*Names*
Multex Investor Network .... (www.multexinvestor.com)	✓	✓	✓	✓	✓
Yahoo Finance (Zacks Investment Research)... (finance.yahoo.com)	✓	✓	✓	✓	✓
Standard & Poor's Personal Wealth (www.businessweek.com/investor/index.html)	✓		✓		
Nordby International .... (www.nordby.com)			✓		✓
ABC News.................... (abcnews.go.com)			✓		
123Jump Network (Financial Web) (www.123jump.com/reg.htm)	✓				
EarningsWhispers.com .... (www.earningswhispers.com)	✓				

Besides providing consensus broker/analyst recommendations and forecasts, 123Jump Network (Financial Web) (www.123jump.com/reg.htm) and Nordby International (www.nordby.com) provide a short summary of the recommendations and future earnings forecasts of individual, named broker/analysts.

VectorVest provides an in-house recommendation and future earnings forecast. The VectorVest website (www.vectorvest.com) limits the number of reports that can be accessed by non-subscribers. An unlimited number of VectorVest reports, however, can be accessed from Investor Guide (www.investorguide.com).

¶ 3015 Corporate News Stories

Another source of information on a company is news stories involving that company. The Internet abounds with the sites of news organizations, and these sites contain business news stories. For example, the CNN Money (money.cnn.com) and Bloomberg (www.bloomberg.com) websites offer extensive general business news. Apart from these news sites, a number of websites specialize in corporation specific news stories.

These corporation specific news sites (see Exhibit 4) are valuable in researching a particular company. All of these websites are searchable by ticker symbol, plus they provide press releases via Business Wire and PR Newswire, in-house news stories and company press releases, and news stories from various news sources such as CBS and CNN.

Exhibit 4

Websites with Corporate News Stories

Site
Yahoo Finance (finance.yahoo.com)
News Alert (www.newsalert.com)
Companylink (www.companylink.com)
123Jump Network (Financial Web) (www.123jump.com/reg.htm)
CBS Market Watch (cbs.marketwatch.com)
Northern Light (www.northernlight.com/news.html)
SmartMoney.com (www.smartmoney.com)
MSN Money (moneycentral.msn.com)
The Motley Fool (www.fool.com)
Lycos Finance (Quote.com) (finance.lycos.com)
CNET News.com (www.news.com/investor)
Standard &Poor's Personal Wealth (www.businessweek.com/investor/index.html)

¶ 3021 Macroeconomic Information

Macroeconomic information is readily available from many government sources (see Exhibit 5) including the Bureau of Labor Statistics, the Census Bureau, the Federal Reserve Board of Governors, the individual Federal Reserve Banks, and the White House. In addition, macroeconomic information can be obtained from the Conference Board and the National Federation of Independent Business.

Exhibit 5

Macroeconomic Information Websites

Atlanta Federal Reserve Bank	www.frbatlanta.org
Boston Federal Reserve Bank	www.bos.frb.org
Bureau of Labor Statistics	stat.bls.gov
Census Bureau	www.census.gov/econ/www
Chicago Federal Reserve Bank	www.chicagofed.org
Cleveland Federal Reserve Bank	www.clev.frb.org
Conference Board	www.conference-board.org
Dallas Federal Reserve Bank	www.dallasfed.org
Fed Stats	www.fedstats.gov
Federal Reserve Board of Governors....	www.federalreserve.gov
Kansas City Federal Reserve Bank	www.kc.frb.org
Minneapolis Federal Reserve Bank	woodrow.mpls.frb.fed.us
National Federation of Independent Business	www.nfibonline.com
New York Federal Reserve Bank	www.ny.frb.org
Philadelphia Federal Reserve Bank	www.phil.frb.org
Richmond Federal Reserve Bank	www.rich.frb.org
San Francisco Federal Reserve Bank ...	www.frbsf.org
St. Louis Federal Reserve Bank	www.stls.frb.org
White House Economic Briefing Room ..	www.whitehouse.gov/fsbr/esbr.html

¶ 3025 Bond Quotations and Ratings

Two of the three major bond rating services, Moody's and Fitch, make their ratings available to the public through their websites (see Exhibit 6). The ratings of the third service (Standard & Poor's) can be obtained from Bonds Online, which also offers bond quotations.

Exhibit 6

Bond Ratings Websites

Bonds Online . .	www.bondsonline.com
Fitch Ratings .	www.fitchibca.com
Moody's	www.moodys.com

¶ 3031 Mutual Fund Ratings and Rankings

A number of websites related to magazines and newsletters provide rankings and/or ratings of mutual funds. A number of sites also offer mutual fund profiles with information provided by Lipper, Morningstar, Value Line, and Wiesenberger. (See Exhibit 7.)

Exhibit 7

Mutual Fund Rankings or Ratings Websites

Proprietary Rankings	
Business Week	www.businessweek.com
Forbes	www.forbes.com
Morningstar	www.morningstar.com
Smart Money	www.smartmoney.com
Standard & Poor's	www.businessweek.com/investor/index.html
Lipper Rankings	
CBS MarketWatch	cbs.marketwatch.com
CNN Money	money.cnn.com
Morningstar Rankings	
Yahoo Finance	finance.yahoo.com
Wall Street Research Net	www.wsrn.com
MSN Money (Microsoft Corp.)	moneycentral.msn.com
Quicken	quicken.com
Excite	www.excite.com
AOL	www.aol.com
Value Line Rankings	
Pinnacor	www.pinnacor.com
Wiesenberger Rankings	
Wiesenberger (Thomson Financial)	www.wiesenberger.com

¶ 3035 American Depository Receipts (ADRs)

J.P. Morgan's website maintains extensive foreign stock indexes along with ADR price quotations. Bank of New York maintains leading ADR indexes that are available on its website. (See Exhibit 8.)

Exhibit 8

ADR Websites

JP Morgan	adr.com
Bank of New York	www.bankofny.com
ADR City	www.stockcity.com/adr

¶ 3041 Options and Futures

Exhibit 9 lists websites to educate the investor on the rewards and risks associated with investing options, futures, and financial derivatives.

Exhibit 9

Options and Futures Websites

Web Address	*Primary Focus*
tfc-charts.w2d.com	Futures quotations
www.cboe.com	Home page for the Chicago Board Options Exchange (CBOE)
www.cbot.com	Home page for the Chicago Board of Trade
www.kcbt.com	Home page for the Kansas City Board of Trade
www.schaeffersresearch.com	Excellent comprehensive site for learning about options
www.futuresmag.com	Covers various aspects of derivatives trading such as strategies and market analyses
www.ino.com	The latest information and prices of options and financial futures as well as the corresponding historic price charts
www.adtrading.com	Applied derivatives trading magazine has articles on options and other derivatives; its beginners corner is for new investors
www.pacificex.com	Good information on specific options, such as LEAPS and index options
www.optionscentral.com	Both education and trading material, as well as links to other option sites
www.worldlinkfutures.com/trad.htm	Provides an electronic course on futures and options for beginners
www.cftc.gov	The Commodity Futures Trading Commission site has information on the regulation and trading of futures

¶ 3045 Indexes

A number of websites report the performance of major indexes. These indexes are located throughout the news media. The following websites (see Exhibit 10) report the performance of indexes other than the commonly reported ones. The CBS MarketWatch website provides the most extensive listing of domestic and foreign indexes (including bond and equity indexes).

Exhibit 10

Stock and Equity Index Websites

Website	*Stock*	*Bond*	*Foreign Stock*	*Foreign Bond*
CBS MarketWatch (cbs.marketwatch.com)	✓	✓	✓	✓
MSN Money (Microsoft Corp.) (moneycentral.msn.com/investor/home.asp)	✓	✓		
JP Morgan (www.jpmorgan.com)			✓	✓
Merrill Lynch (www.ml.com)		✓		✓
Morgan Stanley Capital International (www.mscidata.com)			✓	✓
NASDAQ (nasdaq.com)	✓	✓		
Solomon Smith Barney (www.salomonsmithbarney.com)	✓	✓		
Standard & Poor's (www.spglobal.com)	✓		✓	
Red Herring (StockMaster) (www.stockmaster.com)	✓		✓	
American Stock Exchange (www.amex.com)	✓			
J.P.Morgan (adr.com)			✓	
U.S. Bancorp Piper Jaffray (www.pjc.com)		✓		

¶ 3051 Industry Groups

Wall Street City (www.wallstreetcity.com), Clearstation (E-Trade) (clearstation.etrade.com), and MSN Money (Microsoft Corp.) (moneycentral.msn.com/investor/home.asp) provide extensive information comparing companies that operate within the same industry/sector. Yahoo (finance.yahoo.com) and Multex Investor (www.multexinvestor.com) also provides a listing of companies within the same industry/sector.

¶ 3055 Investment Suites

A growing number of websites have attempted to offer "one-stop shopping" to investors. These investment "suites" offer some or all of the above services, along with general business news, investment advice and other information (see Exhibit 11). This additional information can be useful to investors, creditors, competitors, and other businesses. For example, the Standard and Poor's Personal Wealth site grades the credit worthiness of companies. The information available on these sites include:

Exhibit 11 **Investment Suite Websites and Services Offered**

(Column keys are at the end of this exhibit)

Site	*A*	*B*	*C*	*IT*	*M*	*MF*	*N*	*P*	*PR*	*Q*	*S*	*SEC*	*SH*
ICLUBcental (old.iclub.com/investorama.html)	✓	✓		✓	✓		✓	✓	✓	✓	✓	✓	✓
Nawed Usmani (www.nrmcapital.com)	✓	✓		✓	✓	✓	✓	✓	✓	✓		✓	✓
CBS Market Watch (cbs.marketwatch.com)	✓	✓		✓		✓	✓	✓	✓	✓	✓	✓	
Excite (excite.com)		✓		✓	✓	✓	✓	✓	✓	✓	✓	✓	
Quicken (quicken.com)		✓		✓	✓	✓	✓	✓	✓	✓	✓	✓	
AOL (aol.com)		✓		✓	✓	✓	✓	✓	✓	✓	✓	✓	
CNN Money (money.cnn.com)		✓		✓	✓	✓	✓	✓	✓	✓	✓	✓	
Yahoo Finance (finance.yahoo.com)		✓			✓	✓	✓	✓	✓	✓	✓	✓	
MSN Money (Microsoft Corp.) (moneycentral.msn.com)		✓		✓		✓	✓	✓	✓	✓	✓	✓	

Exhibit 11 ***Investment Suite Websites and Services Offered (Continued)***

(Column keys are at the end of this exhibit)

Site	*A*	*B*	*C*	*IT*	*M*	*MF*	*N*	*P*	*PR*	*Q*	*S*	*SEC*	*SH*
Company Sleuth .... (www.companysleuth.com)		✓		✓	✓		✓		✓	✓		✓	✓
123Jump Network (Financial Web) .... (www.123jump.com/reg.htm)		✓				✓	✓	✓	✓	✓	✓	✓	
Clearstation (E-Trade)............. (clearstation.etrade.com)		✓		✓	✓		✓	✓	✓	✓			
Multex Investor.................... (www.multexinvestor.com)	✓		✓	✓		✓	✓	✓	✓				
Wall Street Research Net .... (www.wsrn.com)	✓		✓	✓		✓	✓	✓	✓			✓	
Standard & Poor's Personal Wealth (www.businessweek.com/investor/index.html)		✓	✓	✓		✓	✓	✓			✓	✓	
Morningstar .... (www.morningstar.net)	✓	✓	✓	✓		✓	✓	✓				✓	
Zacks Investment Research........ (my.zacks.com)			✓	✓		✓	✓	✓				✓	✓

Exhibit 11 Investment Suite Websites and Services Offered (Continued)

(Column keys are at the end of this exhibit)

Site	*A*	*B*	*C*	*IT*	*M*	*MF*	*N*	*P*	*PR*	*Q*	*S*	*SEC*	*SH*
Lycos Finance (Quote.com) .... (finance.lycos.com)		✓	✓	✓		✓	✓	✓					
Wall Street City .... (www.wallstreetcity.com)		✓	✓	✓		✓	✓		✓				
Pinnacor .... (www.pinnacor.com)		✓	✓	✓		✓	✓	✓				✓	
Thomson Investors Network .... (www.thomsoninvest.net)		✓	✓	✓		✓				✓		✓	
PC Quote .... (www.pcquote.com)	✓		✓	✓	✓	✓	✓	✓					

Column Keys to All of Exhibit 11 (above)

A	Annual Reports to Shareholders	P	Portfolio Tracking
B	Broker Recommendations and Earnings Forecasts	PR	Company Profiles
C	Credit Ratings	Q	Stock Price Quotes (Real Time or Delayed)
IT	Insider Trading Information	S	Stock Screens
M	Message Board Information	SEC	SEC Filings
MF	Mutual Fund Profiles	SH	Short Sale Information
N	Corporation Specific News Stories		

¶ 3061 Money Sources

.01 Entrepreneurial Money

Entrepreneurs in search of money for their new enterprises should check out these websites:

- "Money Hunt" (www.moneyhunter.com). This public-television program to help entrepreneurs turn their ideas into reality. The site provides business plan templates to write that all-important plan for investors, a directory of relevant contacts, and advice from experts.

- The Angel Capital Electronic Network (ACE-Net) (ace-net.sr.unh.edu/pub). Developed in consultation with the U.S. Small Business Administration. It is an Internet securities listing service to help entrepreneurs and investors find each other. The site is hosted by the University of New Hampshire.

- America's Business Funding Directory (www.businessfinance.com). This portal helps locate venture capitalists, commercial lenders, equipment leasers, investment funds, government funds, real estate financing, and more. A panel of experts answer questions posted on the site's bulletin board. Some parts of the site are for members only.

.02 Business Loans

Among the most useful sites for business borrowers are:

- Lendingtree (www.lendingtree.com) provides small business loans in the following types: line of credit, term or installment loans, and receivable financing.

- AmericaOneUnsecured.com (www.americanunsecured.com) offers an online application for all kinds of unsecured business loans.

- Lenders Interactive Services (www.lendersinteractive.com) is a Web-based loan broker for all types of financing: commercial real estate, equipment leasing, factoring, U.S. Small Business Administration (SBA) loans, construction loans, rental property, franchises, and many more.

- BuyZone.com (www.buyerzone.com) helps get free business loans and leasing quotes from multiple lenders.

There is also no end of sites offering advice to the business borrower. Netscape, for example, offers one highly useful site (netbusiness.netscape.com/finance) with a link ("Getting Financing for Your Business") to pages outlining:

- The financing options open at different points in the business life cycle.
- The advantages and disadvantages of debt versus equity financing.
- Sources of debt and equity financing.
- Sources of government-backed financing.

The web pages of Entrepreneur magazine (www.entrepreneurmag.com), Intuit (www.quicken.com), and Inc. magazine (www.inc.com) are also useful.

.03 Equity and Venture Capital

It is not possible to do an equity deal by remote control on the Internet. However, the Internet can help simplify the first step in a search for equity or venture capital by getting a business plan in front of potential investors. A number of good websites seek to help make such connections, among them:

- The Adventure Capital Register (www.adventurecapital.com). A good place to start searching for capital to launch a new business venture, invention, or idea. Gives tips on how to find funding and links to funding sources.
- The Venture Capital Resource Library (www.vfinance.com). A place to post a synopsis of a business idea along with basic information about the business.
- The National Venture Capital Assn. (www.nvca.org). This site lists over 300 venture capital and private equity firms along with links to many of their websites, allowing one to gauge the firms' likes and dislikes.
- The National Financial Services Network (www.nfsn.com). Identify specific banks, investment banks, venture capital firms, insurers, and other sources of finance by state.
- Commercial Finance Online (www.cfol.com). Search through a large database for financing sources likely to have an interest in a business and its capital needs.
- The Capital Network (www.thecapitalnetwork.com). Search a database of financing sources or, as an alternative, profile a business's capital needs, matching them to potential sources.
- The Angel Capital Electronic Network (ACE-Net) (ace-net.sr.unh.edu/pub). Developed in consultation with the U.S. Small Business Administration. It is an Internet securities list-

ing service to help entrepreneurs and investors find each other. The site is hosted by the University of New Hampshire.

- Garage Technology Ventures (www.garage.com). A site that matches entrepreneurs and investors through a rigorous and detailed "vetting" process probing business plans, management expertise, and the like.

Appendices and Index

Glossary, Financial Tables, and Other Practice Tools

Appendix A

Glossary of Financial Terms

AAII. American Association of Individual Investors.

Absorption (full) costing. The cost of a product that is the full unit manufacturing cost, consisting of direct materials, direct labor, and factory overhead.

Accelerated depreciation method. A depreciation method that allows the owner of an asset to take greater amounts of depreciation during the early years of its life, thereby deferring some of the taxes until later years. *See also* Straight-line depreciation method.

Acceleration clause. A clause in a credit contract or mortgage that states that if the borrower does not meet the payment schedule, all remaining payments may become immediately due.

Accountability. The liability of a board of directors to shareholders and stakeholders for corporate performance and actions of the corporation.

Accounting exposure. The effect of changes in exchange rates on balance sheet and income statement accounts; also called translation exposure.

Accounting life. The number of years over which an asset is depreciated. *See* Economic life.

Accounting principles. Rules governing the systematic collection, organization, and presentation of financial information; also called accounting standards.

Accounting rate of return. A capital-budgeting criterion that relates the returns generated by a project, as measured by average accounting profits after tax, to the average dollar size of the investment required; also called simple rate of return or unadjusted rate of return.

Accounting standards. *See* Accounting principles.

Accounts payable. Cash owed by a firm to its suppliers for purchases made on credit and not yet paid; reported in the firm's balance sheet as a current liability.

Accounts receivable. Cash owed to a firm by its customers for sales made on credit and not yet paid; reported in the firm's balance sheet as a current asset.

Accrual basis of accounting. A method of accounting whereby income is recorded when earned, whether or not the income has been received at that time, and expenses are recorded when incurred, whether or not any money has actually been paid out.

Accrued expenses. Liabilities other than accounts payable that arise from the lag between the date at which these expenses have been incurred and the date at which they are paid.

Accumulated depreciation. The sum of the periodic depreciation expenses deducted from the gross value of a fixed asset in order to obtain its net book value.

Acid test ratio. Currents assets minus inventories, divided by current liabilities. This ratio is a more stringent measure of liquidity than the current ratio in that it subtracts inventories (the least liquid current asset) from current assets; also called quick ratio.

Acquisition. A combination of two or more businesses into a single operational entity.

Actively managed funds. Funds managed by managers who can use their discretion to buy and sell stocks, bonds, or other investments within the fund. These funds stand in contrast to passively managed funds.

Actual cash value (ACV). Replacement cost less depreciation.

Actuarial method. A method that uses one-twelfth of the annual percentage rate (APR) to figure the interest to be credited to a borrower when a loan is retired early.

Add-on method. A method for calculating loan payments in which the interest is figured on and then added to the amount to be financed.

Adjustable rate mortgage (ARM). A mortgage on which the interest rate can change prior to maturity, depending on the changes of a particular fund cost index.

Adjusted book value. Asset values from a company's balance sheet restated to fair market values, minus the fair market value of liabilities.

Adjusted earnings. A company's earnings "adjusted" for unusual income or expense items, distributions to owners in the form of excessive compensation and perks, and similar items. (Also referred to as normalized earnings.)

Adjusted net assets valuation method. A valuation method that establishes the value of a company by restating its assets and liabilities from book values to fair market values. For cash-basis companies, accounts receivable, accounts payable, and accrued liabilities are established. The value of the company is the value of the company's assets minus the value of its liabilities.

Adjusted present value (APV). A valuation method that values a firm's assets as equal to the sum of (1) their value, assuming that they are financed only with equity capital (unlevered value), and (2) the present value of the tax savings provided by the portion of the assets financed with debt.

Adjustment period. In an adjustable rate mortgage, the period of time between one rate or payment change and the next.

Administrative budget. A formal and comprehensive financial plan through which management of an organization may control day-to-day business affairs and activities.

Administrator. The individual appointed by a court to handle an estate.

Advance. (1) Money given to an employee before it is earned, such as an advance against salary. (2) Payment received from customers in advance for work, goods, or services. (3) Money given by a banker to a borrower in advance, usually short term, and in the form of an overdraft.

Advisory letters. Specialized newsletters on various investment media.

Affiliated group. A group of firms related by affiliation, expressed in terms of one firm's owning, either directly or indirectly, 80 percent of the firm paying the dividend.

After-tax cash flow. Net cash flow (cash revenue less cash expenses) after taxes have been subtracted. It is the cash flow generated from operations.

Agency costs. The costs, such as a reduced stock price, associated with potential conflict between managers and investors when these two groups are not the same.

Agency problem. A problem arising from the separation of ownership and control of a firm.

Aggressive growth fund. A mutual fund that aims for a greater return or maximum appreciation (instead of current dividend income) by accepting greater investment risk, either by investing in new or small companies or by using speculative techniques in its investment strategy. Return can be great but so can risk. Also know as a maximum capital gain fund or capital appreciation fund.

AGM. Annual general meeting—this company gathering, usually held at the end of each fiscal year, brings shareholders and management together to discuss the previous year and the outlook for the future. Directors are elected and other shareholder concerns are addressed.

Allotment. A part of an appropriation that may be encumbered or expended during an allotment period, which is usually a period of time less than one fiscal year. Bimonthly and quarterly allotment periods are most common.

American depository receipts (ADRs). Foreign stocks that are traded in the U.S. markets. They are like common stock, as each one represents a specific number of shares in a specific foreign firm.

American option. An option that can be exercised at any time before the option's maturity date. *See* European option.

American Stock Exchange (AMEX). The second-largest stock exchange in the U.S., after the New York Stock Exchange (NYSE). Stocks and bonds traded on the AMEX tend to be those of smaller companies than on the NYSE. Some index options and interest rate options are also traded on the AMEX; also called the Curb Exchange.

Amortization. The process of converting the cost of an intangible asset, such as goodwill, into periodic expenses reported in the firm's income statement. When the asset is tangible, the same process is called depreciation.

Analysis of variances. The analysis and investigation of causes for variances between standard costs and actual costs; also called variance analysis. A variance is considered favorable if actual costs are less than standard costs; it is unfavorable if actual costs exceed standard costs. Unfavorable variances are the ones that need further investigation for their causes. Analysis of variances reveal the causes of these deviations. This feedback aids in planning future goals, controlling costs, evaluating performance, and taking corrective action. Management by exception is based on the analysis of variances, and attention is given to only the variances that require remedial actions.

Analytical information. Available current data in conjunction with projections and recommendations about potential investments.

Annual budget. A budget prepared for a calendar or fiscal year. *See also* Long-range budget.

Annualized returns. The total return the investment would have had to have earned each year to produce the actual change in value for that investment between the start and end of the period. Returns for periods greater than one year are usually annualized. These returns include the effects of compounding, so the numbers are lower than those arrived at by simply dividing the total return for a period by the number of years.

Annual percentage rate (APR). A measure of the total cost of the loan, expressed as a yearly percentage rate. This method of calculating interest rates is required by the Federal Consumer Credit Protection Act (Truth in Lending Act); also called effective annual yield.

Annual report. A formal audited financial statement issued yearly by all publicly listed corporations to their shareholders in accordance with SEC regulations. It contains information on financial results and overall performance of the previous fiscal year and comments on future outlook. The document consists of the president's letter, management's discussion of operations, balance sheet, income statement, statement of cash flows, footnotes, and the audit report.

Annuitant. A person who receives regular annuity benefits.

Annuity. (1) A contract that guarantees a fixed income to the annuitant and other beneficiaries of the annuity for life, or for a specified period of years. (2) A cash-flow stream that is composed of a sequence of equal and uninterrupted periodic cash flows.

Antidilution provision. An agreement that protects an investor from a reduction in fractional ownership in a company in the event of a stock split, issuance of additional stock, or other such measure.

Antitakeover defense. A device designed to prevent a hostile takeover by increasing the takeover cost usually through the issuance of new preferred shares that carry severe redemption provisions.

Appraisal. The process of establishing an estimate of the value of something; also called valuation. A general way to determine value using one or more specific appraisal methods, i.e., asset-based methods, income-based methods, or market methods.

Appraisal date. The date at which the property is being valued. As distinguished from the report date.

Appraisal method. Assumptions and mathematical computations used to estimate the value of a business or ownership holding. Within "approaches" to value, a specific way of determining value.

Appraisal value. The value of a company or a piece of property as stated by an independent appraisal firm.

Appreciation (currency). The increase in the value of one currency expressed in terms of another currency.

Approaches to value. A variety of methods to determine the value of an asset. Three common "approaches" to value are the "assets" approach, the "income" approach, and the "market" approach.

Arbitrage pricing model (APM). A theory that relates stock returns and risk. The theory maintains that security returns vary from their expected amounts when there are unanticipated changes in basic economic forces. Such forces would include unexpected changes in industrial production, inflation rates, term structure of interest rates, and the difference between interest rates of high- and low-risk bonds.

Arbitrage transaction. A transaction that attempts to take advantage of discrepancies between asset prices.

Arbitrageur. A person involved in the process of buying and selling in more than one market to make a riskless profit.

Arrearage. An overdue payment, generally referring to omitted preferred stock dividends.

Ask price. The lowest price at which a trader or dealer in the market is willing to sell a security. Thus, the price at which one can purchase a security. Also called offer price. *See* Bid price.

Assessed value. The value assigned property for tax purposes, generally a percentage of the appraised value. Assets are the items of value that a person owns, such as cash, autos, and stocks.

Asset allocation. A plan for dividing a portfolio among different classes of securities in order to preserve capital by protecting the portfolio against negative market development. The asset allocation determines what percentage of a portfolio is held in stocks versus bonds versus cash, and within each of those asset classes, what percentage is held in different types of stocks and bonds.

Asset beta. The beta of a firm's stock if the firm is all equity financed; also called unlevered beta.

Asset management account (AMA). A comprehensive deposit account, offered primarily by brokerage houses and mutual funds, that combines checking, investing, and borrowing activities, and automatically sweeps excess funds into short-term investments and provides loans when shortages exist.

Assets approach to value. A valuation approach that presumes the value of a company or ownership interest is worth the value of its identifiable assets less the value of its liabilities.

Asset turnover. Sales divided by assets. A measure of the efficiency of asset management.

Assumption. The ability of a new buyer to take over the seller's old mortgage, typically at the original rate.

Asymmetric information. A situation that arises when managers (as insiders to the firm) know more about the firm's current performance and future prospects than do outsiders.

Audit report. The statement of an accounting firm's assessment of the validity and accuracy of a company's financial information and conformity with accepted accounting principles.

Automated teller machine (ATM). A type of remote computer terminal at which customers of a bank or other depository institution can make basic transactions 24 hours a day, seven days a week.

Automatic reinvestment plan. A plan frequently offered by mutual funds that allows share owners to elect to have dividends and capital gains distributions reinvested in additional fund shares.

Automobile insurance. Insurance purchased to pay for the loss to individuals or to property, resulting from an automobile accident, theft, or other perils specified in the insurance contract.

Average age of accounts receivable. *See* Average collection period.

Average collection period. Accounts receivable at the end of the period divided by the average daily sales during that period. A ratio that expresses how rapidly the firm is collecting its credit accounts.

Average daily balance (ADB). A method for determining the balance on which interest is to be paid. The figure is calculated by averaging the daily balance throughout the month.

Averages. Numbers used to measure the general behavior of stock prices by reflecting the arithmetic average price behavior of a representative group of stocks at a given point in time.

Average tax rate. The rate is calculated by dividing the total tax liability by the entity's taxable income.

Back-end load. A fee or commission charged for redeeming mutual fund shares. These charges are intended to discourage frequent trading in the fund. Also know as deferred sales charges.

Balance sheet. A basic accounting statement that represents the financial position of a firm on a given date. The condensed financial statement shows the nature and amount of a company's assets and liabilities, and the stockholders' equity that finances the assets. In short, it shows what the company owns, what it owes, and the ownership interest.

Balanced (mutual) fund. A mutual fund that stresses income over growth by combining investments in common stock and bonds and often preferred stock, attempting to provide income and some capital appreciation. Balanced funds tend to underperform all-stock funds in strong bull markets.

Balloon clause. A final payment specified in a loan agreement.

Balloon note mortgage. A mortgage that carries a fixed rate of interest and is written like a conventional mortgage but for a short period of time, for example, three to five years.

Balloon payment. *See* Balloon clause.

Bank credit card. A credit card issued by a bank or other financial lending institution that allows the holder to charge purchases at any establishment that accepts it; can also be used to obtain cash advances.

Banker's acceptance. Time draft drawn by a business firm whose payment is guaranteed by the bank's "acceptance" of it. It is especially important in foreign trade, because it allows the seller of goods to be certain that the buyer's draft will actually have funds behind it.

Bankruptcy. (1) A legal procedure or court action through which the ownership of a firm's assets is transferred to debtholders. It involves taking some of a debtor's assets, selling them, and dividing the proceeds among the creditors. (2) The inability to pay debts when due. A business is insolvent in a legal sense when its financial condition is such that total liabilities exceed the fair market value of the assets.

Bank wire. A private wire service used and supported by approximately 250 banks in the United States for transferring funds, exchanging credit information, or effecting securities transactions.

Barron's. A weekly publication by Dow Jones covering finance and investment news.

Base-period earn-out. An agreement by which the stockholders of an acquired company receive additional stock in future years provided the firm improves its earnings above those of the base period. Base-period earnings are those in the last year prior to the acquisition.

Basic disability. A definition in a disability insurance policy that describes the insured as unable to perform the duties of his or her regular occupation.

Basis point. A unit of measure for the change in interest rates for bonds and notes equal to one hundredth of one percent, so one basis point is equal to one percent of one percent, that is, 0.01 percent. Thus, 100 basis points = 1 percent, and 14 basis points = 0.14 percent .

Bear. Someone who believes the market will decline. *See* Bull.

Bearer bonds/securities. Bonds/securities that do not indicate the holder's name. *See* Registered bonds/securities.

Bearer (coupon) certificate. A certificate that does not have the name of the owner on it. Payment of interest is made to whomever presents the coupon.

Bearish. The expectation of a decline in the price of a stock or the market in general.

Bear market. A period of declining prices; the bear's claws point down.

Benchmark. An appropriate stock or bond index used to gauge the performance of an investment such as a mutual fund. An example is the Russell 2000, an index of 2,000 small stocks, which is often used to evaluate the performance of small-cap funds.

Benchmark rate. Rate to which the coupon rate of a floating rate bond is linked.

Beneficiaries. Those who are to receive the proceeds from a policy or estate at the time of an individual's death.

Best efforts basis. A method of distributing securities whereby an investment bank undertakes to do its best to sell on behalf of the firm the securities the firm has issued.

Beta (coefficient). A measure of risk based on the sensitivity of an individual stock's returns to changes in the returns of a broad stock market index; also called systematic, market, nondiversifiable, and relative risk. It provides a reflection of how the price of a share of stock responds to market forces. In general, the higher the beta, the riskier the security. A beta less than 1 means that the company's stock is less risky than the market.

Better Business Bureau (BBB). A local agency supported by business organizations that helps to resolve problems between businesses and customers.

Bid and asked. Often referred to as a quotation or quote. The bid is the highest price anyone has declared that they want to pay for a security at a given time; the asked is the lowest price anyone will take at the same time.

Bid-ask spread. The difference between the bid price and the ask price.

Bidder. In a takeover, the firm that wants to acquire all or a portion of another firm's shares.

Bid price. The price at which a trader in a market is willing to buy. Thus, the price at which one can sell a security. *See* Ask price.

Big Board. A popular term for the New York Stock Exchange (NYSE).

Billing cycle. The time period between periodic billings for merchandise or services rendered, typically one month.

Blank endorsement. The signature of only the payee's name on the back of a check.

Blue-chip stocks. Stocks of major companies that are leaders in their industry and have a proven track record of earnings and dividend payments; blue chips in poker are worth more than red or white chips.

Blue Cross Blue Shield plans. Prepaid hospital and medical expense plans under which health care services are provided to plan participants by member hospitals and physicians.

Bodily injury liability losses. A clause in an auto insurance policy that protects individuals against losses from bodily injury; may specify coverage as a combination of per-individual and per-accident limits.

Boiler room. A firm that uses high-pressure sales tactics to push questionable investments over the phone.

Bond. Basically an IOU or promissory note of a corporate, municipal, or government debt, expressed in a stipulated face value, a stipulated rate of interest, and a date at which the issuer will pay the holder the face value of the bond.

Bond funds. Mutual funds that invest primarily in bonds in order to emphasize current income.

Bond market. Market where bonds are issued and traded.

Bond par value. The face value appearing on the bond, which is to be returned to the bondholder at maturity.

Bond rating. Letter grades signify the rating assigned by an agency (such as Standard and Poor's or Moody's Investors Service), providing an assessment of the bond's credit risk or investment quality.

Bond yield. The summary measure of the return an investor would receive on a bond if it were held to maturity; reported as an annual rate of return.

Book. A notebook the specialist in a stock uses to keep a record of the buy and sell orders at specified prices, in strict sequence of receipt, which are left with him or her by other brokers. *See* Specialist.

Book value. The stated sum of all of a company's assets, minus its liabilities, divided by the number of common shares outstanding, is the book value per common share. Book value of the assets of a company or a security may have little or no significant relationship to market value.

Book-value weights. The percentage of financing provided by different capital sources as measured by their book values from the company's balance sheet.

Bottom line. *See* Earnings after tax.

Bounced check. A check that has been returned for not sufficient funds (NSF).

Break-even analysis. An analytical technique used to determine the quantity of output or sales that results in a zero level of earnings before interest and taxes (EBIT). Relationships among the firm's cost structure, volume of output, and EBIT are studied.

Bridge loan. Short-term loan that is made in expectation of intermediate- or long-term loans. The interest rate on a bridge loan is generally higher than that on longer-term loans. An example is a temporary loan made to permit a closing on a building purchase prior to a closing on long-term mortgage financing.

Broker. An agent who handles the public's orders to buy and sell securities or commodities. For this service a commission is charged.

Budget. (1) Detailed guideline for spending over a short period of time. (2) A quantitative plan of activities and programs expressed in terms of the assets, equities, revenues, and expenses that will be involved in carrying out the plans, or in other quantitative terms such as units of product or service. The budget expresses the organizational goals in terms of specific financial and operating objectives. Advantages of budget preparation are planning, communicating company-wide goals to subunits, fostering cooperation between departments, control by evaluating actual figures to budget figures, and revealing the interrelationship of one function to another. *See also* Master (comprehensive) budget.

Budget control. Budgetary actions carried out according to a budget plan. Through the use of a budget as a standard, an organization ensures that managers are implementing its plans and objectives, and their activities are appraised by comparing their actual performance against budgeted performance. Budgets are used as a basis for rewarding or punishing them, or perhaps for modifying future budgets and plans.

Budgeted balance sheet. A schedule for expected assets, liabilities, and stockholders' equity. It projects a company's financial position as of the end of the budgeting year. Reasons for preparing a budgeted balance sheet include: (1) discloses unfavorable financial condition that management may want to avoid; (2) serves as a final check on the mathematical accuracy of all other budgets; and (3) highlights future resources and obligations.

Budgeted income statement. A summary of various component projections of revenues and expenses for the budget period. It indicates the expected net income for the period.

Build-up capitalization rate. Well-accepted method for establishing the rate of return an investor should expect to earn from an investment in a security (closely held company).

Bull. One who believes the market will rise.

Bulletin Board. More appropriately known as the OTC Bulletin Board, an electronic quotation service that lists the prices of stocks that do not meet the minimal requirements for listing on a stock exchange or the NASDAQ stock-listing system.

Bullish. The expectation of a rise in the price of a stock or the market in general.

Bull market. A period of rising prices; the bull's horns thrust upward.

Business cycle. An indication of the current state of the economy. It is the variability in economic activity.

Business risk. The relative dispersion or variability in the firm's expected earnings before interest and taxes (EBIT). The nature of the firm's operations causes its business risk. This type of risk is affected by the firm's cost structure, product demand characteristics, and intra-industry competitive position. In capital-structure theory, business risk is distinguished from financial risk. *See* Financial risk.

Business valuation. The act or process of establishing an opinion or estimate of value for a business or ownership interest.

Buy-back program. *See* Share buy-back program.

Call. The right to buy 100 shares (usually) of a specified stock at a fixed price per share (the striking price) for a limited length of time (until expiration).

Callable. A bond issue, all or part of which may be redeemed by the issuing corporation under definite conditions before maturity. The term also applies to preferred shares, which may be retired by the issuing corporation.

Callable bond. A bond that gives the issuer the option to redeem (repay) the bond before it reaches its maturity date.

Call option. The right to buy a fixed number of shares of a stock at a predetermined price during the life of the option (American option) or on its expiration date (European option). *See also* Put option.

Call premium. The difference between the call price and the security's par value.

Call provision. A provision that entitles the corporation to repurchase its bonds or preferred stock from their holders at stated prices over specified periods. This provision can be immediate or deferred.

Call value. The price at which the issuer can buy a callable bond from its holder.

Capital appreciation fund. *See* Aggressive growth fund.

Capital asset. All property used in conducting a business, other than assets held primarily for sale in the ordinary course of business, or depreciable and real property used in conducting a business.

Capital asset pricing model (CAPM). A formula according to which a security's expected return is equal to the risk-free rate plus a risk premium. The model shows the relationship between an investment's expected (or required) return and its beta. It can be used to estimate the cost of equity of a firm or a project.

Capital budget. A budget or plan of proposed acquisitions and replacements of long-term assets and their financing. A capital budget is developed using a variety of capital budgeting techniques such as the payback period method, the net present value (NPV) method, or the internal rate of return (IRR) method. *See also* Capital budgeting.

Capital budgeting. The process of making long-term planning decisions for capital investments. There are typically two types of investment decisions: (1) Selecting new facilities or expanding existing facilities. Examples include: (a) investments in long-term assets such as property, plant, and equipment; and (b) resource commitments in the form of new product development, market research, refunding of long-term debt, information technology (IT), etc. (2) Replacing existing facilities with new facilities. An example is replacing an inefficient lathe with one that is numerically controlled.

Capital employed. The sum of owners' equity and all borrowed funds (short-term and long-term); also called invested capital.

Capital expenditure budget. A budget plan prepared for individual capital expenditure projects. The time span of this budget depends upon the project. Capital expenditures to be budgeted include replacement, acquisition, or construction of plants and major equipment. *See also* Capital budgeting.

Capital gain or capital loss. The profit or loss resulting from the sale of a capital asset. A capital gain may be either short term (one year or less) or long term (more than one year).

Capital gains distribution. The income distributed to investors resulting from net long-term profits of a mutual fund, realized when portfolio securities are sold at a gain. These profits from sales of securities are passed on by fund managers to shareholders at least once a year.

Capitalization. (1) The capital structure of a business; the total amount of various securities issued by a corporation. Capitalization may include bonds, debentures, and preferred and common stock. Bonds and debentures are usually carried on the books of the issuing company in terms of their par or face value. Preferred and common shares may be carried in terms of par or stated value. (2) The conversion of income into value. (3) The determination of an asset value based on expenditures.

Capitalization factor. The inverse of a capitalization rate. For example, a capitalization rate of 20 percent is a capitalization factor of 5.0 (1.0/20%). Capitalization factors and capitalization rates are used interchangeably by appraisers.

Capitalization of earnings valuation method. A valuation methodology that presumes the value of a business is generally determined by dividing its earnings by the investment rate of return the business should yield for investors.

Capitalization rate. A divisor used to convert an income amount into a value equivalent. The rate used in the denominator of the capitalization of earnings method. Generally determined to be the rate of return expected for an investment, reduced by the growth expected for the investment. A key component of many valuations is the determination of this rate.

Capitalized cost. The price of a car that is being leased.

Capital market. The long-term financial market in which long-term securities such as stocks and bonds are bought and sold.

Capital rationing. The problem of selecting the mix of acceptable projects that provides the highest overall net present value (NPV) when a company has a limit on the budget for capital spending. The profitability index is used widely in ranking projects competing for limited funds.

Capital stock. All shares, common and preferred, representing ownership of a business.

Capital structure. The mix of long-term sources of funds used by the firm; also called capitalization. The relative total (percentage) of each source of fund is emphasized.

Capital structure decision. A decision on the amount of debt relative to equity capital that a firm should take on; also called financial structure decision.

Cash advances. A loan that can be obtained by a bank credit cardholder at any participating bank or financial institution; it begins to accrue interest immediately and requires no formal application.

Cash and cash equivalent. Cash in hand, cash on deposit with banks, and short-term liquid investments with less than a year's maturity (marketable securities).

Cash budget. A budget for cash planning and control, presenting expected cash inflow and outflow for a designated time period. The cash budget helps management keep cash balances in reasonable relationship to its needs. It aids in avoiding idle cash and possible cash shortages.

Cash dividend. The portion of a firm's net profit distributed to shareholders in cash. *See also* Dividend.

Cash flow. (1) Net income plus noncash expenses (e.g., depreciation) minus noncash revenue (e.g., amortization of deferred revenue) yields cash flow from operations. (2) Cash receipts minus cash payments.

Cash flow forecasting. Forecasts of cash flow, including cash collections from customers, investment income, and cash disbursements.

Cash flow statement. The compilation of cash receipts and disbursements used to develop the monthly budget.

Cashier's check. A check from a depository institution made out to a specified person for a specified amount.

Cash value insurance. The accumulated portion of life insurance premiums as a savings feature that can be borrowed against or obtained as cash if the policy is canceled.

CBOE. Chicago Board Options Exchange.

CBT or CBOT. Chicago Board of Trade.

Certainty equivalents. The amount of cash a person would require with certainty to make him indifferent between this certain sum and a particular risky or uncertain sum.

Certificate of deposit (CD). A term account paying a slightly higher rate of interest than passbook or other savings, with a penalty for early withdrawal.

Certification role. The role played by underwriters in guaranteeing the quality of underwritten securities.

Certified check. A check from an individual's own checking account that has been completely filled out and certified by the depository institution. The certification guarantees the validity of the signature and the amount of the check.

CFTC. Commodity Futures Trading Commission.

Chapter 7. *See* Straight bankruptcy.

Chapter 13. A court approved and coordinated plan that pays off an individual's debts over a period of three years; also known as the wage earner plan.

Chartered property and casualty underwriter (CPCU). An agent who has met various experiential and educational requirements and passed a series of written examinations in the fields of property and liability insurance.

Chattel mortgage agreement. A loan agreement in which the lender can increase their security interest by having specific items of inventory identified in the loan agreement. The borrower retains title to the inventory but cannot sell the items without the lender's consent.

Checking account. An account that allows the depositor to transfer funds to another party through a written order, a demand deposit, or a check.

Check truncation. The procedure whereby depository institutions keep the canceled checks and send only a listing of the month's activities to the account holder, thus saving on processing and mailing of checks.

Chop-shop value. A valuation approach that values a firm based on its various business segments. It is an attempt to identify multi-industry companies that are undervalued and would be worth more if separated into their parts.

Claims adjustor. An insurance specialist, employed by an insurance company, an adjustment bureau, or self-employed, who investigates claims.

Cleaning deposit. A nonrefundable fee paid to cover the painting and cleaning of a rental unit after a tenant moves out.

Clientele effect. The belief that individuals and institutions that need current income will invest in companies that have high dividend payouts. Other investors prefer to avoid taxes by holding securities that offer only small dividend income, but large capital gains. Thus, there is a "clientele" of investors.

Closed-end account. A credit account that allows a customer to use its extended credit feature only once, usually to make a specific purchase.

Closed-end investment company. An investment company that issues a limited number of shares.

Closed-end lease. A lease that entails monthly payments over a specified period of time. At the end of the leasing period, the lessor sells the leased item and bears any gain or loss from the entire transaction.

Closed-end mutual fund. A mutual fund that operates with a fixed number of shares outstanding.

Closely held business. Typically, a company that is owned by relatively few individuals and is not publicly traded.

Closing costs. Costs resulting from the financing and transfer of property ownership in a real estate sale.

CME. Chicago Mercantile Exchange.

Codicil. A document amending a will.

Coefficient of variation. A measure of the relative dispersion of a probability distribution—that is, the risk per unit of return. Mathematically it is defined as the standard deviation divided by the expected value.

Coinsurance effect. A term used to describe a situation in which merged firms are perceived by their creditors to be less likely to fail as a combination than as separate entities.

Coinsurance factor. The percentage of medical expenses covered by the insured over and above the deductible amount.

Cold calling. Brokers' practice of making unsolicited phone calls to potential investors to urge them to buy a stock.

Collateral. An asset that is used to secure a loan.

Collectible. An item collected for its value or enjoyment.

Collision insurance. Insurance purchased to pay for damages to the insured's own car in case of an accident.

COMEX. Commodity Exchange, Inc. of New York.

Commercial bank. A depository institution commonly referred to as a bank, with stockholders as owners and an elected board of directors.

Commercial paper. Short-term unsecured note issued by financially strong businesses. Unlike most other money market instruments, commercial paper has no developed secondary market.

Commission. A broker's fee for buying or selling securities.

Common stock. Securities that represent an ownership interest in a corporation. If the company has also issued preferred stock, both common and preferred have ownership rights, but the preferred normally has prior claim on dividends and in the event of liquidation, assets. Claims of both common and preferred stockholders are junior to claims of bondholders or other creditors of the company.

Community property. Property held jointly by husband and wife. If acquired after the marriage, it is considered to be owned equally by both spouses, no matter who contributes the earnings to pay for the property.

Compensating balance. A deposit that a bank can use to offset an unpaid loan. No interest is earned on the compensating balance, which is stated as a percentage of the loan. It increases the effective interest rate on the loan.

Compounded value. The situation in which interest paid on the investment during the first period is added to the principal, and during the second period, interest is earned on the original principal as well as on the interest earned during the first period.

Compounding. The process of earning interest on the interest already earned on an investment. Compound interest is earned when the interest is left to accumulate.

Comprehensive budget. *See* Master (comprehensive) budget.

Comprehensive auto insurance. Insurance purchased to cover losses resulting from a stolen car, or from repairs if the car is hit by a falling object or damaged by fire, flood, or vandals.

Comprehensive major medical insurance. A health care insurance plan that combines into a single policy the coverage for basic hospital, surgical, and physician expense with major medical protection.

Concentration banking. Acceleration of cash collections from customers by having funds sent to several regional banks and transferred to a main concentration account in another bank. The transfer of funds can be accomplished electronically.

Condominium. A form of home ownership in which each individual owns the interior living space in a planned community.

Conference call. A valuable opportunity to hear senior management's take on the company's prospects for future earnings and new products in the pipeline. Institutional investors and financial analysts of brokerage firms call into a special number to listen and ask questions. The Yahoo Finance Web site (http://biz.yahoo.com/cc) maintains a calendar of upcoming conference calls. Enter a company's ticker symbol to listen in on a current meeting or access an archive of a recent call.

Conforming loans. Loans that adhere to national guidelines by Fannie Mae and Freddie Mac, government-sponsored corporations that buy the loans on the secondary market.

Conglomerate. A multifaceted corporation involved in a variety of products and services.

Conglomerate merger. The combination of unrelated businesses for which there are no obvious synergies.

Consolidated balance sheet. A balance sheet showing the financial condition of a parent and its subsidiaries.

Consolidated liability plan. Liability coverage in automobile insurance that sets a specific dollar amount as the maximum that would be paid for all losses resulting from a liability claim.

Constant dividend payout ratio. A dividend payment policy in which the percentage of earnings paid out in dividends is held constant. The dollar amount fluctuates from year to year as profits vary.

Consumer credit counseling service. A nonprofit organization that provides several inexpensive services to assist consumers with financial difficulties in getting back on their feet.

Consumer Credit Protection Act. A federal act that includes the Fair Credit Billing, Equal Credit Opportunity, Fair Credit Reporting, and Consumer Leasing Acts, and the Truth in Lending Act.

Consumer price index (CPI). A price index that measures the changes in the cost of a specific "market basket" of goods and services. A CPI measures the cost of living. The U.S. Consumer Price Index is issued monthly by the Bureau of Labor Statistics.

Continuous budget. An annual budget that continues from the earliest one month or period and adds the most recent one month or period, so that a 12-month or other periodic forecast is always available.

Control. Usually, the implication of a partial holding in a business that enables the holding to have higher than proportional influence over the operations of the business. Often equated with the majority holding, but not necessarily so. The power to direct the management and policies of the business. A valuation issue that is often important but measured by appraisers in significantly different ways.

Control concept. A concept that ensures that actions are carried out or implemented according to a plan or goal. *See also* Control.

Control premium. The enhanced value associated with a controlling ownership interest. Usually, a percentage increase in the value of a holding made solely because the holding has enhanced value due to its ability to control the operations of the business. Valuation studies often imply the percentage should be 35 percent or more.

Conventional mortgage. A mortgage that requires a large down payment, is typically only available to good credit risks, and has fixed monthly payments of principal and interest for the life of the loan.

Conversion price. Price at which the holder of a convertible bond has the right to buy one share of the firm's common stock.

Conversion ratio. The number of shares of common stock for which a convertible security can be exchanged.

Conversion value. The current price of the stock multiplied by the number of shares to which the convertible bond can be converted.

Convertible. A bond, debenture, or preferred share that may be exchanged by the owner for common stock or another security, usually of the same company, in accordance with the terms of the issue.

Convertible bonds. Bonds that may be converted into a predesignated number of shares of common stock.

Convertible stock. Preferred stock that may be converted into common stock.

Cooling off ruling. A federal rule that provides a buyer with three business days in which to cancel a door-to-door sales contract.

Cooperative. A form of home ownership that entails issuing stock and then leasing dwelling units to each stockholder.

Corporate bond. A debt instrument of a corporation. It is a corporate IOU. It represents an agreement that the face value of a loan will be repaid at maturity and that interest will be paid at regular intervals.

Corporate bylaws. Regulations that govern the internal affairs of the corporation, designating such items as the time and place of the shareholders' meetings, voting rights, the election process for selecting members of the board of directors, the procedures for issuing and transferring stock certificates, and the policies relating to the corporate records.

Correlation. The degree of relationship between variables, such as cost and volume. Correlation analysis evaluates cause-effect relationships. It looks consistently at how the value of one variable changes when the value of the other is changed. An example is the effect of advertising on sales.

Cost behavior patterns. The way a cost will react or respond to changes in the level of activity. Costs may be viewed as variable, fixed, or mixed (semivariable). A mixed cost is one that contains both variable and fixed elements. For planning, control, and decision-making purposes, mixed costs need to be separated into their variable and fixed components, using such methods as the high-low method and the least-squares method. An application of the variable-fixed breakdown is a break-even and cost-volume-profit (CVP) analysis.

Cost control. The steps taken by management to assure that the cost objectives set down in the planning stage are attained, and to assure that all segments of the organization function in a manner consistent with its policies. For effective cost control, most organizations use standard cost systems, in which the actual costs are compared against standard costs for performance evaluation, and the deviations are investigated for remedial actions. Cost control is also concerned with feedback that might change any future plans, the production method, or both.

Cost effective. Among decision alternatives, the one whose cost is lower than its benefit. The most cost-effective program would be the one whose cost-benefit ratio is the lowest among various programs competing for a given amount of funds.

Cost of capital. The rate that must be earned in order to satisfy the required rate of return of the firm's investors; also called minimum required rate of return. It may also be defined as the rate of return on investments at which the price of the firm's common stock will remain unchanged. The cost of capital is based on the opportunity cost of funds as determined in the capital markets.

Cost synergies. Cost reductions resulting from combining the operations of two or more firms. *See also* Market synergies.

Cost-volume formula. A cost function in the form of Y = a + bX. Where: Y = the semivariable (or mixed) costs to be broken up; X = any given measure of activity such as volume and labor hours; a = the fixed cost component; b = the variable rate per unit of X. Financial managers use the formula for cost prediction and flexible budgeting purposes.

Country risk. The risk that the cash flows from a project may be affected by changes in local regulations governing foreign investments; also called political risk.

Coupon bond. A bearer bond, so called because the annual or semiannual interest payments are made when the coupons attached to the bond are presented to the paying agent.

Coupon (interest) rate. The interest to be paid annually on a bond as a percent of par value, which is specified in the contractual agreement.

Covenants (restrictive). Conditions imposed by lenders and stipulated in a bond indenture that require managers to achieve certain financial targets or refrain from certain actions that may be detrimental to lenders' interests.

Coverage ratios. A group of ratios that measure a firm's ability to meet its recurring fixed charge obligations, such as interest on long-term debt, lease payments, and/or preferred stock dividends.

Covered options. Options written against stock owned.

Credit bureau. An organization that supplies credit information to creditors and to others who demonstrate an acceptable need for the information.

Credit counselor. A professional financial advisor who assists overextended consumers in repairing budgets for both spending and debt repayment.

Credit health and accident insurance. Insurance purchased as payment protection for a loan in case the borrower is unable to meet the payments due to a disability or illness.

Credit life insurance. Insurance that will retire a loan if the borrower dies.

Credit limit. A specified amount beyond which a customer may not borrow or purchase on credit.

Credit line. A specified amount of money available to a borrower from a bank, usually for one year. A credit line is a moral, not a contractual, commitment, and no commitment fee is charged.

Credit loans. Extended to businesses, individuals, or the government.

Creditor. The person or institution to whom money is owed.

Credit or consumer report. A report from a credit bureau describing an individual's credit history and providing other information such as name, address, length of time at an address, occupation (past and present), public record, and similar background material.

Credit property insurance. Insurance purchased to compensate the tender if property placed as security for a loan is destroyed.

Credit rating. A rating to help the business determine if a credit applicant should be granted credit. It is based on factors such as the applicant's job history, income, assets owned, and credit history.

Credit record. An individual's credit history.

Credit risk. The risk that a borrower will be unable to service their debt.

Credit scoring. An objective method for evaluating whether an individual should be extended credit.

Credit statement. A monthly statement that summarizes the transactions in a consumer credit account; includes a record of new charges, credits, and payments, any interest charges, and the minimum monthly payment required on the account.

Credit union. A depository institution formed as a cooperative. Individuals interested in membership may have to meet specific credit union requirements.

Cross rates. Foreign exchange rates between two currencies computed from their exchange rate with a third currency.

Cumulative dividends. Preferred dividends that if not paid as scheduled must be paid before any common stock dividends can be paid.

Cumulative preferred (stock). A stock having a provision that if one or more dividends are omitted, the omitted dividends must be paid before dividends may be paid on the company's common stock.

Curb Exchange. Former name of the American Stock Exchange, second largest exchange in the country. The term comes from the market's origin on the streets of downtown New York.

Currency forward contract. An agreement between two parties specifying the fixed price at which two currencies will be exchanged at a specified future date (settlement date).

Currency futures (contract). A currency forward contract that has a standardized contract size and a standardized delivery date; traded on futures markets.

Currency market. *See* Foreign exchange market.

Currency option hedge. Hedging with currency options.

Currency options. Put and call options written on foreign currencies.

Currency rate. *See* Foreign exchange rate.

Currency risk. Risk arising from unexpected changes in the exchange rate between two currencies; also called foreign exchange risk.

Currency swap (contract). An agreement with a bank to exchange a set of future cash flows denominated in one currency for another set denominated in another currency.

Current income. Income received on a periodic basis, including interest, dividends, and rent.

Current ratio. Current assets divided by current liabilities. A measure of liquidity.

Current (translation) method. A method of translating the financial statements of a foreign business unit. Balance sheets accounts are translated at the exchange rate prevailing

Current yield. The measurement of return that relates investment income to the market price.

Custodian. The individual who retains control of and manages property.

CV. *See* Convertible.

Cyber investing. Investing on the Internet; also called online trading.

Cyberspace. Originally used in *Neuromancer,* William Gibson's novel of direct brain-computer networking, refers to the collective realms of computer-aided communication.

Cyclical stock. Stock that fluctuates with changes in business conditions, improving its position when the economy is on an upswing and failing during times of decline.

Damage deposit. A fee paid to cover any physical damage beyond normal wear and tear, or any economic damage beyond normal wear and tear, or any economic damage such as failure to pay rent, caused by a tenant or a tenant's guests.

Database. A file containing information on a particular subject or subjects. For example, in a database system there are many such files, each devoted to a particular kind of data element, so that one database may hold all the shareholder names, another all their addresses, another all their social security numbers, etc.

Date of record. Date at which the stock transfer books are to be closed for determining which investors receive the next dividend payments. *See also* Ex-dividend date.

Day-of-deposit-to-day-of-withdrawal (DDDW). A method of calculating the account balance on which interest is earned. Interest is calculated on the actual number of days the money is deposited in the account.

Days of sales outstanding (DSO). *See* Average collection period.

Dead days. Days appearing at the end of an interest period during which the bank will allow funds to earn interest even though they are not actually on deposit (typically a maximum of 10 days).

Dealer. A buyer and seller of securities who maintains an inventory of the issues in which he trades, as distinguished from the broker who acts as the buyer's or seller's agent for a fee.

Debenture. A promissory note secured only by the general credit and assets of a company and usually not backed by a mortgage or lien on any specific assets.

Debit card. A card issued for making electronic transfers of funds in stores, depository institutions, and other businesses.

Debt capacity. The maximum proportion of debt that a firm can include in its capital structure and still maintain its lowest composite cost of capital.

Debt consolidation loans. Loans that combine all of a person's debts into one loan with small monthly payments. The tremendously high rate of interest for the new loan greatly increases the total cost of the credit although the monthly payment may be lower than the sum of all the former payments.

Debt ratio. Total liabilities divided by total assets. A ratio that measures the extent to which a firm has been financed with debt. It is a measure of financial leverage.

Debt safety ratio. The proportion of total monthly consumer credit obligations to monthly take-home pay.

Debt service. The timely and full payment of interest on borrowed funds as well as the repayment of the borrowed funds.

Debt-to-equity ratio. Total interest-bearing debt divided by owners' equity. It is a measure of financial leverage.

Declaration date. The date upon which a dividend is formally declared by the board of directors.

Decreasing term insurance. Term insurance that provides decreasing death benefits while maintaining a stable premium.

Deductible. The amount that an individual must pay on any insured loss before payment by the insurance company begins.

Deduction. An expenditure listed on the federal tax return that reduces adjusted gross income in order to arrive at taxable income.

Deed. A detailed description of a piece of property that formally transfers the title of the property over to the buyer.

Default. Failure to meet the conditions of a loan contract. It generally refers to the failure to meet interest and/or principal payments.

Default risk. *See* Credit risk.

Defensive stock. A stock that has relatively stable prices during business downturns and market declines.

Deferred sales charge. *See* Back-end load.

Deferred tax (liability). Taxes owed to the tax authority originating from the difference between the amount of tax due on a firm's reported pretax profit and the amount of tax claimed by the tax authorities.

Defined benefits plan. A pension plan in which the formula for computing benefits is stipulated in its provisions, thus allowing an employee to determine prior to retirement how much his or her retirement income will be.

Defined contribution plan. A pension plan that specifies a certain plan contribution but not future benefits.

Degree of combined leverage. The percentage change in earnings per share caused by a percentage change in sales. It is the product of the degree of operating leverage and the degree of financial leverage; also called degree of total leverage.

Delivery. Transfer of stocks from seller to buyer. The certificate representing shares bought "regular way" on the New York Stock Exchange normally is delivered to the purchaser's broker on the fourth business day after the transaction.

Demand deposit. Deposit from which funds may be drawn on demand and from which funds may be transferred to another party by means of a check.

Dental insurance. Insurance to pay for dental care, typically including preventive expense.

Deposit insurance. Insurance on certain depository institution accounts provided by either a federal or a state agency.

Depository transfer checks. A means for moving funds from local bank accounts to concentration accounts. The depository transfer check itself is an unsigned, nonnegotiable instrument. It is payable only to the bank of deposit for credit to the firm's specific account.

Depreciation. (1) In real estate appraisal, the decrease in value of property due to use, deterioration, or the passing of time. The cost of wear and tear. (2) The means by which an asset's value is expensed over its useful life for federal income tax purposes.

Depreciation (currency). Reduction in the value of one currency expressed in terms of another currency.

Derivative securities. Securities, such as futures and options, whose value is derived from (or linked to) the price behavior of an underlying real or financial asset.

Descriptive information. Factual data on the past behavior of the economy, the stock market, the industry, or a given investment vehicle.

Diamonds (DIAs). Shares in a trust representing all 30 stocks in the Dow Jones Industrial Average. They are traded on the American Stock Exchange.

Dilution. Reduction in the fraction of a firm's equity held by its existing shareholders after the firm sells common stock to new investors.

Direct labor budget. A schedule for expected labor cost. Expected labor cost is dependent upon expected production volume (production budget). Labor requirements are based on production volume multiplied by direct labor hours per unit. Direct labor hours needed for production are then multiplied by direct labor cost per hour to derive budgeted direct labor costs.

Direct materials budget. A budget that shows how much material will be required for production and how much material must be bought to meet this production requirement. The purchase depends on both expected usage of materials and inventory levels.

Direct quotes. The exchange rate that indicates the number of units of the home currency required to buy one unit of foreign currency.

Disability insurance. Insurance to provide income to the insured in the event of disability.

Disbursing float. Funds available in the company's bank account until its payment check has cleared through the banking system.

Discharge of bankruptcy. An order in which the bankrupt debtor is relieved of responsibility to pay his or her obligations.

Discount. (1) A reduction in the amount paid for an item. As for investments, it is a security that sells for less than its face value. (2) Value reduction for specific reasons. For business valuation purposes, values otherwise determined are often decreased by lack of marketability discounts, minority discounts, illiquidity discounts, lack of control discounts, key person discounts, and others.

Discount broker. A broker with low overhead who charges low commissions and offers little or no services to investors.

Discounted cash flow (DCF) techniques. Methods of selecting and ranking investment proposals, such as the net present value (NPV) and internal rate of return (IRR) methods, where time value of money is taken into account.

Discounted earnings valuation method. A valuation methodology that presumes the value of a business or ownership holding is equivalent to the expected earnings anticipated for the company in future years. A conceptually sound methodology often dismissed as being too speculative to be valuable for fair market value appraisals.

Discounted payback period. Capital budgeting method that measures a project's payback period with cash flows that have been discounted to the present at the project's cost of capital.

Discounting. The inverse of compounding. This process is used to convert future cash flows into their equivalent value today.

Discount interest. A method for calculating the interest charged on a loan wherein the lender subtracts the interest from the principal amount and lends the borrower the difference, to be repaid in installments.

Discount loan. A loan in which the whole interest charge is deducted in advance from the face value of a loan reducing the proceeds received. This increases the effective interest cost of the loan.

Discount rate. (1) A rate of return used to convert a value in the future into a present value. The rate of return used to discount future values to present values in the discounted earnings valuation method. (2) The interest rate charged to financial institutions for loans by the Federal Reserve Bank.

Discretionary account. An account in which a customer gives a broker or someone else discretion (which may be complete or within specific limits) as to the purchase and sale of securities or commodities, including their selection, timing, and price to be paid or received.

Discretionary cash flow. Cash flow available to the firm for strategic investment and financing decisions after all of the firm's financial obligations are met; also called free cash flow.

Disposable income. Income left after deducting taxes from gross income.

Distribution. Selling, over a period of time, of a large block of stock without unduly depressing the market price.

Diversifiable risk. Risk that can be eliminated through portfolio diversification; also called unsystematic risk or company-specific risk.

Diversification. The spreading of investment money among many investment vehicles in order to reduce overall risk.

Divestitures. The removal of a division or subsidiary from a company. Typically, the part of the firm being separated is viewed as not contributing to the company's basic purposes.

Dividend. The portion of a corporation's profits paid to stockholders.

Dividend payout ratio. The amount of dividends relative to a company's net income or earnings per share.

Dividend policy. The decision regarding the portion of a year's profit that should be paid out in the form of cash dividends to a firm's shareholders.

Dividend reinvestment. Dividends that an investor reinvests in a company or mutual fund through the purchase of additional shares. A mutual fund does not charge a sales commission on reinvested dividends.

Dividend reinvestment plan (DRIP). A program offered by over 1,000 major corporations whereby stockholders can choose to take their dividends in the form of more shares of the company's stock, rather than cash; it provides a relatively painless way of earning a fully compounded rate of return.

Dividend yield. The percentage return provided by the dividends paid on common stock; calculated by dividing the cash dividends paid during the year by the stock's market price.

Dollar cost averaging. A system of buying stocks or mutual funds at regular intervals. A fixed amount regularly invested buys more shares in a low market and fewer in a high market. When averaged over a long term, a relatively low price per share results.

Double or triple indemnity. A life insurance rider that pays the beneficiary two or three times the policy's face value if the death of the insured is due to an accident.

Dow Jones Bond Averages. Mathematical averages of closing prices for groups of utility, industrial, and corporate bonds.

Dow Jones Industrial Average (DJIA). A benchmark stock average made of 30 blue chip industrial stocks selected for total market value and broad public ownership and believed to reflect overall market activity.

Dow theory. A method of analyzing market trends by observing the movement of the Dow Jones industrial and transportation averages. A bull market is supposed to continue as long as one average continues to make new highs that are "confirmed" by the other. A reversal is signaled when one average refuses to confirm the other; a bear market is supposed to continue as long as one average makes new lows that are confirmed by the other.

Down payment. The cash a borrower puts toward a purchase, with the remainder of the purchase price borrowed from a creditor.

Downtick. A transaction of securities executed at a price below that in the preceding transaction; also know as a minus tick. For example, if a stock has been selling at $23 per share, the next transaction is a downtick if it is at $22⅛.

Dread disease insurance. A health insurance policy that provides protection against medical expenses resulting from a certain dreaded disease such as cancer.

Due-on-sale clause. A clause permitting a lender to raise the interest rate or require full payment of the mortgage at the time of assumption.

Dunning letter. Notices that insistently demand repayment of debts from customers.

Duplexes. Two living units placed side by side in one building.

Durable power of attorney. A legal device that allows individuals to grant to other persons general or specific powers for managing their finances.

EAFE Index. The Europe, Australia, and Far East Index.

Earnest money deposit. Money pledged by a buyer to show good faith when making an offer to buy a home.

Earnings. Another word for income. It also refer to net income, pretax income, or other variations of "income."

Earnings after tax (EAT). Revenues minus all expenses, including interest and tax expenses. Same as net income, net profit, and bottom line.

Earnings before depreciation, interest, and tax (EBDIT). Revenues minus all operating expenses, excluding depreciation expenses and amortization. Same as earnings before interest, tax, depreciation, and amortization (EBITDA).

Earnings before interest and tax (EBIT). Difference between the firm's operating profit and any extraordinary items reported in its income statement.

Earnings before interest, tax, depreciation, and amortization (EBITDA). Revenues minus all operating expenses, excluding depreciation and amortization. Same as earnings before depreciation, interest, and tax (EBDIT).

Earnings before taxes (EBT). (1) An earnings value used for valuation purposes, because the presumption is the use of such an earnings value will eliminate distortions created by companies having different income tax rates. (2) Income before federal income taxes; may also refer to income before federal and state income taxes.

Earnings multiple. Share price divided by the firm's earnings per share, also called price-to-earnings ratio. It is used to value a firm.

Earnings per share (EPS). The amount of annual earnings available to common stockholders, as stated on a per-share basis.

Earn-out. A deferred payment plan, under which an acquiring firm agrees to make a specified initial payment of cash or stock and additional compensation if the acquired company can maintain or increase earnings.

Easy money. An increase in money available for business and individual spending as a result of economic conditions.

EBIT-EPS indifference point. The level of earnings before interest and taxes (EBIT) that will equate earnings per share (EPS) between two different financing plans.

Economic exposure. The effect of changes in exchange rates on the value of a firm's future cash flows generated either by past and known transactions (contractual or transaction exposure) or by future and uncertain transactions (operating exposure).

Economic life. The useful life of an asset.

Economic risk. The chance of loss due to economic conditions.

Economic value added (EVA). Net operating profit after tax (NOPAT) for a particular period (such as a year) minus the annual cost of all the capital a firm uses. EVA is a measure of economic profit, but not the accounting profit we are accustomed to seeing in a corporate profit and loss statement.

Effective annual yield. *See* Annual percentage rate (APR).

Efficient market. A market in which the values of all assets and securities at any instant in time fully reflect all available information.

Electronic funds transfer (EFT). A number of systems that are electronically linked via a communications network. Funds may be automatically transferred by telephone, telex, terminal, or microcomputer.

Elimination period. The period of time before insurance begins.

Emergency fund. Money kept at maximum liquidity in order to have access to cash for unexpected situations.

Employee Retirement Income Security Act (ERISA). A law passed in 1974 to ensure that workers eligible for pensions actually receive such benefits; also permits uncovered workers to establish individual tax-sheltered retirement plans. Also known as the Pension Reform Act.

Endowment policy. A cash value life insurance policy that assesses premiums over a specified period of time. At the end of that time, the cash value equals the face value, the policy endows, and is redeemed.

Energy labels. Labels attached to certain appliances that give operation costs and energy information.

Enterprise value. The value of a business in total. This generally presumes the business is owned by a single individual. Usually, a value without respect to a control premium or minority discount.

EPS. Earnings per (common) share.

Equal Credit Opportunity Act. A federal law making it illegal to discriminate when giving credit.

Equipment financing loan. A medium- to long-term loan backed by a piece of machinery.

Equipment trust certificate. A type of security, generally issued by a railroad, to pay for new equipment. Title to the equipment, such as a locomotive, is held by a trustee until the notes are paid off. An equipment trust certificate is usually secured by a first lien of the equipment.

Equity. (1) The ownership value of a business. In reference to real estate, the portion of a property owned by an individual, that is, the market value of the property less any amount owed on the property. (2) Owner investments in a company. An important implication is whether the value is expressed as a book value or a fair market value.

Equity beta. The beta of a firm's common stock; also called levered beta or market beta.

Equity capital. Funds contributed by shareholders that are equal to the difference, at a particular date, between what a firm's shareholders collectively own, called assets, and what they owe, called liabilities; also called equity funds, owners' equity, shareholders' equity or funds, or net asset value.

Equity funds. *See* Equity capital.

Equity multiplier. Invested capital divided by owners' equity. It is a measure of financial leverage.

Equity REIT. A type of real estate investment trust (REIT) whose investment money is directed toward the purchase of a portfolio of identified properties to be managed for the purpose of producing investment return through current income as well as capital gains.

Escrow account. An account to which payment is made for a specified expense to ensure that funds will be available.

Estate planning. The creation of wealth and conservation of assets so that an individual will reap the greatest benefit from their use.

Estate tax. A tax levied by federal and/or state governments on the value of certain types of gifts (or an estate) made upon the giver's death.

Eurocommercial paper (EuroCP). Commercial paper issued in the Euromarket.

Eurocurrency. The currency in which securities issued outside the jurisdiction of a particular country are denominated.

Eurodollar bonds. Bonds denominated in U.S. dollars that are sold simultaneously to investors in several countries via the Euromarket.

Eurodollar market. A banking market in U.S. dollars outside the U.S. Large sums of U.S. dollars can be borrowed or invested in this unregulated financial market. Similar external markets exist in Europe and Asia and for other major currencies.

Euroequity. Equity issued in the Euromarket.

Euromarket. A market that is outside the direct control and jurisdiction of the issuer's country of origin.

European option. An option that can be only exercised on the maturity date of the option. *See also* American option.

Europe, Australia, and Far East Index. The EAFE Index, for short. Compiled by Morgan Stanley Capital International, a value-weighted index of the equity performance of major foreign markets. It is, in effect, a non-American world index.

Eviction. The action taken by a landlord to remove a tenant from leased property.

Excess earnings valuation method. A valuation method that presumes a company should be able to earn a predictable level of income based on its tangible assets. To the extent the company earns more than the predictable level of income, the company is deemed to have intangible assets that are then capitalized to estimate their value; also referred to as the formula method, the IRS method, and the Treasury method.

Excess major medical policy. Medical insurance that provides coverage over and above the benefits of a major medical policy.

Exchange rate. The price paid in one country's currency to buy one unit of another country's currency; also called foreign exchange rate or currency rate.

Exchange rate risk. The variability in future cash flows borne by firms with foreign operations that originates from unexpected changes in the exchange rate between two currencies; also called currency risk.

Exchange-traded fund (ETF). A security that tracks an index but has the flexibility of trading like a stock. Just like an index fund, an ETF represents a basket of stocks that reflect an index. The difference is that an ETF isn't a mutual fund—it trades just like any other company on a stock exchange. Unlike a mutual fund that has its net asset value (NAV) calculated at the end of each trading day, an ETF's price changes throughout the day from buying and selling.

Excise taxes. Taxes levied at the point of sale of certain items and services, such as automobiles, gasoline, telephone services, tobacco products, and liquor.

Exclusive listing. An agreement with a real estate agent that pays commission to the agent even if the property is sold to a buyer found by the owner.

Exclusive provider organization (EPO). A health plan that reimburses members only if they use affiliated providers.

Ex-dividend. A synonym for "without dividend." Stocks and registered bonds have record dates for the payment of dividends and interest. The New York Stock Exchange sets ex-dividend dates a few days ahead of record dates to allow for the physical transfer of the securities. Investors who buy stocks before the ex-dividend date receive dividends; investors who buy after it do not.

Ex-dividend date. The date upon which stock brokerage companies have uniformly decided to terminate the right of ownership to the dividend, which is four days prior to the record date.

Executor. A person appointed in a will to handle the disposition of an estate according to the will's directives.

Exemption. When filing a tax return, the amount deductible from income that each taxpayer is allowed for oneself, a spouse, and each dependent, plus an additional deduction for each person who is blind and over 65.

Exercise. The actual fulfillment of the terms of an option contract. The specified number of shares of the underlying stock are bought or sold at the price predetermined in the option contract.

Exercise price (currency option). The fixed exchange rate at which a currency can be bought or sold in an option contract; also called strike price.

Exercise price (warrant). The fixed price at which the holder of a warrant has the right to buy shares.

Exit fees. Charges assessed upon redemption of mutual fund shares regardless of the length of time the investor has owned the shares; also know as redemption fees.

Exit strategy. The way leveraged buyout (LBO) investors cash in on their investment by selling some (or all) of their shares after a period of time (to other investors or through an initial public offering (IPO)).

Expected return. The arithmetic mean or average of all possible outcomes where those outcomes are weighted by the probability that each will occur.

Expiration. The date an option contract becomes void unless previously exercised. All option contracts expire on the Saturday following the third Friday of the expiration month.

Ex-rights. Without the rights.

Ex-rights date. The date on or after which a stock sells without rights.

External common equity. A new issue of common stock.

External funds need. Internally generated funds less funding needs.

Extra. The short form for "extra dividend." A dividend in the form of stock or cash in addition to the regular or usual dividend the company has been paying.

Extraordinary items. Nonrecurrent losses or gains.

Face value. (1) A security's value at maturity. (2) The maximum coverage available on an insurance policy. (3) The fixed amount that has to be paid back to bondholders at the maturity date of a bond; also called principal, par value, or redemption value.

Factoring. The outright sale of a firm's accounts to another party (the factor) without recourse. The factor, in turn, bears the risk of collection.

Factory overhead budget. A schedule of all expected manufacturing costs except for direct material and direct labor. Factory overhead items include indirect material, indirect labor, factory rent, and factory insurance. Factory overhead may be variable, fixed, or a combination of both.

Fair Credit Billing Act. A federal law providing credit cardholders certain rights in case of billing errors.

Fair Credit Reporting Act (FCRA). A federal law passed to control the use of credit and investigative reports.

Fair Debt Collection Practices Act. A federal act regulating professional bill collectors and their actions.

Fair market value. The price at which property would change hands between a willing buyer and a willing seller, in an arm's-length transaction, when both parties have relevant knowledge of the facts, and neither is compelled to buy or sell. The definition of value for tax valuations and many others.

Fair program. An insurance program sponsored by the federal government for individuals who are unable to obtain insurance through the marketplace.

Fair value. (1) A definition of value used in litigation situations in particular. Generally, what is "fair" is based on either the circumstances of the situation or in terms of statutory or case law. (2) The mathematically calculated value of an option. It is determined by (a) the striking price of the option, (b) the current price of the underlying stock, (c) the time left until expiration, and (d) the volatility of the underlying stock.

Fallen angels. Securities (stocks or bonds) of once-promising companies that have fallen on difficult financial times.

Family of funds. A group of mutual funds, all with different investment objectives, that are under the same management company. A shareholder can switch between the funds, sometimes at no charge, as his or her investment objectives and perceptions change.

Fannie Mae. *See* Federal National Mortgage Association (FNMA).

Farmers Home Administration. A federal agency that offers home financing to qualified individuals in low-income rural areas.

Favorable variance. The excess of standard (or budgeted) costs over actual costs. *See also* Standard cost system; Variance.

Federal agency securities. Debt investments issued by federal government agencies that are backed either by the full faith and credit of the agency or by the federal government itself.

Federal Deposit Insurance Corporation (FDIC). The federal agency that insures depository institution accounts.

Federal estate tax. The federal tax that must be paid by a decedent's estate.

Federal Home Loan Mortgage Corporaton (FHLMC). Also known as Freddie Mac.

Federal Housing Administration (FHA). A federal agency that provides financing opportunities for home buyers, especially those with little down payment funds or with a need for smaller monthly payments.

Federal Insurance Administration. A federal agency that sponsors crime insurance for families living in high crime areas.

Federal Insurance Contributions Act (FICA) tax. The law establishing the combined old-age, survivors, disability, and hospital insurance tax levied on both employer and employee, also called Social Security tax.

Federal National Mortgage Association (FNMA). Also known as Fannie Mae. A government-sponsored corporation engaged in the buying and selling of FHA or VA mortgages (Federal Housing Administration and Veterans Administration mortgages).

Federal Reserve System (FRS). The central bank of the United States. Its primary function is to control the money supply and financial markets.

Federal Savings and Loan Insurance Corporation (FSLIC). The federal agency that provides deposit insurance to savings and loan associations.

Federal Trade Commission (FTC). A federal agency responsible for policing unfair trade practices.

FICO. Short for Fair, Isaac and Company, which develops the mathematical formulas used to produce credit scores. Every score is calculated by using a mathematical formula that evaluates many types of information on an individual's credit report, compared to information patterns in millions of past credit files. The score can then identify that person's level of future credit risk. Credit scores range from 300 to 850. Scores provide an extremely valuable guide to future risk based solely on credit report data. The higher a consumer's score, the lower the risk to lenders when extending new credit to that consumer.

Field warehouse financing agreement. A security agreement in which inventories are used as collateral, physically separated from a firm's other inventories, and placed under the control of a third-party field warehousing firm.

Filing status. Indicated on a tax return, showing whether a taxpayer is filing a return as a single, married (filing jointly or separately), or head of household taxpayer.

Finance charge. The total dollar amount paid when obtaining a loan or charging a purchase.

Finance companies. Companies that primarily make smaller loans at higher interest rates than competitive institutions because they will accept individuals with lower-than-average credit ratings.

Financial advisor. A businessperson who sells a particular product and financial advice, or one who sells only financial advice.

Financial assets. Intangible assets, such as savings accounts and securities, that are acquired for some promised future return.

Financial budget. A budget that embraces the impacts of the financial decisions of the firm. It is a plan including a budgeted balance sheet, which shows the effects of planned operations and capital investments on assets, liabilities, and equities. It also includes a cash budget, which forecasts the flow of cash and other funds in the business.

Financial futures. A type of futures contracts in which the underlying commodities are financial assets such as debt securities, foreign currencies, or market baskets of common stocks.

Financial goals. Short- and long-term results that an individual wants to attain, such as controlling living expenses, managing one's tax burden, establishing savings and investment programs, and meeting retirement needs.

Financial information services. Services providing historical, financial, market and economic information, and current stock market prices and financial news. Information is generally obtained on an online database.

Financial intermediaries. Institutions that act as "middlemen" between the ultimate recipients of capital (firms) and the ultimate suppliers of capital (household sector). They include commercial banks, savings and loan associations, credit unions, life insurance companies, and mutual funds that assist the transfer of savings from economic units with excess savings to those with a shortage of savings.

Financial lease. A noncancelable contractual commitment on the part of the firm leasing the asset (the lessee) to make a series of payments to the firm that actually owns the asset (the lessor) for the use of the asset.

Financial leverage. The use of debt financing to complement equity financing. It is a measure of financial risk that arises from fixed financial costs. The use of financial leverage exposes the firm to financial risk.

Financial markets. Institutions and procedures that facilitate transactions in all types of financial claims (securities).

Financial model. A system of mathematical equations, logic, and data that describes the relationship among financial and operating variables.

Financial needs approach. A method for calculating life insurance needs, which bases the amount of insurance protection on the goals, net worth, and projected income and expense figures of the insured.

Financial planner. One who is engaged in providing personal financial planning services to individuals. He or she may be an independent professional or may be affiliated with a large investment, insurance, accounting, or other institution.

Financial planning software. Personal finance computer programs that keep track of income and expenses by budget category, reconcile accounts, store tax records, figure net worth, track stocks and bonds, and print checks and financial reports. Some programs are sophisticated enough to generate a detailed, long-term personal financial plan covering planning for college education, investment planning, and retirement planning. Examples of financial planning software are Quicken® and Microsoft® Money.

Financial projection. An essential element of planning that is the basis for budgeting activities and estimating future financing needs of a firm. Financial projections (forecasts) begin with forecasting sales and their related expenses.

Financial responsibility laws. Laws that attempt to force motorists to be financially responsible for the damages they cause, and are legally obligated to pay, as a result of automobile accidents.

Financial risk. The added variability in earnings available to a firm's common shareholders, and the added chance of insolvency caused by the use of securities bearing a limited rate of return in the firm's financial structure. The use of financial leverage gives rise to financial risk.

Financial slack. Cash surplus that firms may build up during good times.

Financial structure. The mix of all funds sources that appear on the right-hand side of the balance sheet.

Financial structure decision. *See* Capital structure decision.

Financial structure effect. The positive effect of an increase in debt financing on return on equity (ROE). More debt means less equity capital and thus higher ROE.

Financial tables. Tables found in most daily newspapers that provide price, yield, and volume information on secondary markets. Extensive listings appear in the *Wall Street Journal.*

First-in, first-out (FIFO). A method for calculating the account balance on which interest is earned. In this case, interest is earned on any balance remaining after deducting all withdrawals from the deposits available at the beginning of the interest period.

Fiscal policies. An economic policy that employs government spending and taxation programs.

Fiscal year. A corporation's accounting year. It may not coincide with a calendar year, either by chance or because of some peculiarity of the company's business; e.g., the meatpacker's February-through-January year, which ends with the most money in hand and the least meat in storage.

Fisher effect. The theory that states that the nominal interest rate is the sum of the real interest rate and the expected inflation rate.

Fixed asset turnover. Sales divided by fixed assets. It is a measure of the efficiency of fixed assets management.

Fixed budget. *See* Static (fixed) budget.

Fixed charges. Expenses, such as bond interest, taxes, and royalties, that a company must meet whether it has earnings or not.

Fixed costs. Charges that do not vary in total amount even when there are changes in sales volume or the quantity of output.

Fixed-income investment. An investment that promises to pay a specified amount of income on a periodic basis, such as a bond.

Fixed-income securities. Investment vehicles that provide a fixed periodic return. Examples are debt securities such as bonds.

Fixed-rate annuity. An annuity in which an insurance company safeguards an investor's principal and agrees to pay a guaranteed rate of interest on that money. The (minimum) monthly benefit is set by the contract.

Fixed-rate certificate. Certificates of deposit (CDs) issued for periods ranging from three months to eight years or more. These CDs have minimum deposit requirements that are established by each institution, and interest rate ceilings that are set by the federal government's Regulation Q.

Fixed-rate mortgage. The traditional type of mortgage in which both the rate of interest and the monthly mortgage payment are fixed over the full term of the loan.

Flash report. A report that provides the highlights of key information promptly to the responsible managers. An example is an exception report (such as performance reports) that highlight favorable or unfavorable variances. A flash report allows managers to take a corrective action for an unfavorable variance.

Flexible budget. A listing of budgeted figures at different capacity levels.

Flexible budget formula. *See* Cost-volume formula.

Flexible budgeting. *See* Flexible budget.

Flexible (variable) budget. A budget based on different levels of activity. It is an extremely useful tool for comparing the actual cost incurred to the cost allowable for the activity level achieved. It is dynamic in nature rather than static.

Float. (1) The amount of funds represented by checks that have been issued but not yet collected. (2) The time between the deposit of checks in a bank and payment. Due to the time difference, many firms are able to "play the float"; that is, to write checks against money not presently in the firm's bank account.

Floater endorsement. An addition to a policy that itemizes specific item(s) for insurance protection under the endorsement.

Floating rate bond or floater. A bond whose rate is linked to another rate that is revised periodically.

Flotation costs. The underwriter's spread and issuing costs associated with the issuance and marketing of new securities; also called issuance or issue costs.

Foreign bonds. Bonds issued in the domestic bond market of another country.

Foreign exchange market. Market in which currencies are bought and sold; also called currency market or exchange rate market.

Foreign exchange rate. *See* Exchange rate.

Foreign exchange risk. Risk arising from unexpected changes in the exchange rate between two currencies; also called exchange risk or currency risk.

Form 10-K. A statement filed with the Securities Exchange Commission (SEC) by all firms listed on an exchange.

Formula valuation method. Another name for the excess earnings valuation method. *See* Excess earnings valuation method.

Forward exchange contract. A contract that requires delivery of one currency at a specified future date for a specified amount of another currency.

Forward hedge. Hedging with forward contracts.

Forward rate. The fixed rate at which a forward contract is settled.

Freddie Macs. Nickname for Federal Home Loan Mortgage Corporation (FHLMC) securities. The FHLMC buys mortgages, pools them, and then sells the packages to individual investors.

Free cash flow. Operating cash flows less any incremental investments made to support a firm's future growth. The value of these flows is equal to their present value.

Fringe benefits. Legislated or employer-provided benefits that exceed wages.

Front-end load. Initial sales commission at the time a mutual fund is purchased. Administration and management fees continue to be charged annually regardless of a fund being a front-end load, back-end load (12b-1), or no load.

Full replacement policy. A homeowner's policy that will replace, rebuild, or repair damaged property for up to the maximum of the policy, which is set at a value equal to what is estimated as the cost of replacing the property.

Full service brokerage house. A brokerage house that provides research reports, investment advice, and a broker to act as a sounding board for ideas.

Full warranty. The term used to describe warranties that meet certain requirements of the Magnusson-Moss Warranty Act and offer the best warranty protection available.

Fundamental analysis. The process of gathering basic financial, accounting, and economic data on a company and determining whether that company is fairly priced by market standards.

Funded pension plan. A pension plan that formally establishes charges against current income to allow for pension liabilities as they accrue in order to minimize the risk that benefits will be unavailable to an eligible employee upon retirement.

Funding risk. Risk arising from the unwillingness of a lender to renew loans made to finance assets, thus forcing a firm to sell part or all of those assets to repay the loan. *See also* Interest rate risk.

Future value. The value at a future date of an amount deposited today that grows at a given compound, or growth, rate.

Futures contract. A forward contract that has a standardized contract size and delivery date. It is a contract to buy or sell a stated commodity (such as soybeans or corn) or financial claim (such as U.S. Treasury bonds) at a specified price at some future, specified time.

Futures hedge. Hedging with a futures contract.

Futures market. The commodity market that trades futures contracts; also know as futures exchange. It is a self-regulating body whose aim is to decide the conditions for acceptance of members, their trading terms, and their behavior in trading. Examples are the Commodity Exchange, Inc. (COMEX), the New York Mercantile Exchange, the Chicago Board of Trade, and the Chicago Mercantile Exchange.

Garnishment. Court-ordered payment of a portion of a defaulting borrower's wages to a lender.

Gearing. *See* Financial leverage.

General mortgage bond. A bond secured by a blanket mortgage on a corporation's property, often subordinated to specific pledges against certain properties.

General obligation bond. A municipal bond that has the payment of the bond interest and principal backed up by the full faith and credit of the issuing government.

Gift splitting. A method of reducing gift taxes whereby a gift given by one spouse, with the consent of his or her spouse, can be treated as if each had given one-half of it.

Gift tax. A tax levied by the federal government on the value of certain types of gifts made during a giver's lifetime.

Ginnie Maes. Nickname for Government National Mortgage Association (GNMA) securities, which are issued by approved organizations that pool their FHA- or VA-backed mortgages and then sell them as a package to investors.

Goals. Specific objectives for which a person aims and that are based on the person's values.

Going concern value. The value of a company presuming it remains in operation, as opposed to liquidation value.

Good-till-canceled order (GTC). A type of order for the purchase or sale of stock or options that remains in effect until filled or canceled.

Goodwill. The intangible value of a company's trade name, customer base, and similar items. Sometimes referred to as "blue sky," sometimes as intangible assets.

Government bills. Short-term marketable securities issued by governments.

Government bonds. Obligations of the U.S. government, regarded as the highest grade issues in existence.

Government National Mortgage Association (GNMA). Government-owned corporation, nicknamed Ginnie Mae. GNMA primarily issues pass-through securities. These pass through all payments of interest and principal received on a pool of federally insured mortgage loans. GNMA guarantees that all payments of principal and interest will be made on the mortgages on a timely basis.

Grace days. Days appearing at the beginning of an interest period during which a depository institution will allow its funds to earn interest even though the funds are not actually on deposit.

Grace period. The 30-day period allowed on life and health insurance policies, which maintains the policy coverage although the premium has not yet been paid.

Graduated payment mortgage. A mortgage that carries a fixed rate of interest for the life of the mortgage; however, the payments are not fixed but instead slowly increase to a fixed amount that is maintained until the end of the loan period.

Grantor. The person setting up a trust.

Gross estate. All property—both probate and nonprobate—subject to federal estate taxes at a person's death.

Gross profit margin. Gross profit divided by net sales. A ratio denoting the gross profit of the firm as a percentage of net sales.

Ground floor financing. Equity capital financing in a leveraged buyout (LBO).

Group health care insurance. A type of health car insurance consisting of contracts written between a group (employer, union, and so forth) and either a private insurance company, Blue Cross Blue Shield, or managed care organization.

Group life insurance. A type of life insurance that provides a master policy for a group and a certificate of insurance for each eligible member.

Growth. An investment objective that aims at producing a capital gain at the time of sale.

Growth and income fund. A mutual fund that attempts to provide regular dividends along with capital gains by investing in bonds and quality stocks.

Growth fund. A mutual fund whose primary objective is long-term capital appreciation and that generally invests in companies' common stocks that are expected to show increased earnings.

Growth stock. A stock whose earnings and market price have increased over time at a rate that is well above average.

GTC order. "Good-till-canceled" order. A customer's order to his or her broker to buy or sell securities at a specified price; the order remains in effect until it is either executed or canceled.

Guaranteed insurability. A cash value life insurance feature that allows a policyholder to purchase additional cash value insurance at predesignated intervals and standard rates without passing a medical examination.

Guaranteed investment contract (GIC). An investment product, offered mostly by life insurance companies, that promises to pay a set rate of interest to investors over the life of the contract; found mostly in 401(k) and other company-sponsored retirement plans. The only guarantee they carry is that of the company that sold the contract.

Guaranteed purchase option. An option in a life insurance contract that allows a policyholder the right to purchase additional coverage, at stipulated intervals, without having to provide evidence of insurability.

Guaranteed renewable policy. A policy that is always renewable as long as the premiums are paid, although the company can raise the policy's rates.

Guardian. An individual appointed to take care of minors.

Guideline company. Company similar to a company being valued that is used to value the company. A guideline company might be a publicly traded company or another closely held company.

Hardware. The mechanical components of a computer system, such as input and output devices and a central processing unit (CPU).

Hazard. A condition that affects the probability of loss.

Health maintenance organizations (HMOs). Health insurance agencies that offer group health insurance for a fixed, prepaid premium and stress preventive health care.

Hedge (currency). The process of protecting the value of an asset or a liability from currency fluctuations. It is a means to neutralize exchange risk on an exposed asset position, whereby a liability of the same amount and maturity is created in a foreign currency.

Hedging. Protecting against wide market swings by taking both buy and sell positions in a security or commodity.

High-yield bonds. *See* Junk bonds.

Holding company. A corporation that owns the securities of another, in most cases with voting control.

Holding period. The time period over which an investment is held.

Holding period return (HPR). The total return earned from holding an investment for a stated time period.

Holographic will. A will that does not meet all the formal requirements of a valid will.

Home equity credit line (line of credit). A line of credit issued against the existing equity in a home.

Homeowners insurance. An insurance policy designed for a variety of risks of homeowners.

Homeowners warranty (HOW) program. A program in which builders guarantee their workmanship, materials, and construction defects.

Horizontal merger. Two firms in the same sector pooling their resources.

House poor. Purchasing more house than one can afford.

Hurdle rate. An investment's cost of capital (*see* Weighted average cost of capital) when used in comparison with the investment's internal rate of return; also called cost of capital or minimum required rate of return.

Illiquid. (1) Lacking enough liquid assets, such as cash and marketable securities, to cover short-term obligations. (2) Having current liabilities exceed current assets.

Implied warranty. Warranty stating that a product is capable of doing what it is supposed to do.

Income approach to value. Valuation methodology that establishes the value of a company or ownership holding based on the company's earnings. Sometimes overlaps with the concept of the "market approach" to value.

Income bond. A bond that requires interest payments only if earned. Failure to meet these interest payments will not result in bankruptcy.

Income stocks. Stocks of companies with relatively large and stable dividends.

Incontestable clause. A clause in life insurance policies providing that the insurer cannot question the validity of the information provided by the insured after the policy has been in force for two years.

Increasing-stream hypothesis of dividend policy. A smoothing of the dividend stream in order to minimize the effect of company reversals. Corporate managers make every effort to avoid a dividend cut, attempting instead to develop a gradually increasing dividend series over the long-term future.

Incremental cash flows. The difference between a firm's expected cash flows if an investment is made and its expected cash flows if the investment is not undertaken; also called differential cash flows.

Indemnity (fee-for-service) plan. Health care insurance plan in which the person or organization providing the health care services is separate from the insurer, who pays the provider or reimburses the patient for a percentage of expenses after a deductible. These plans provide unlimited choices of doctors and hospitals.

Indemnity. A legal principle that determines the amount of economic loss to be reimbursed when property is destroyed.

Indenture. A written agreement under which bonds or debentures are issued, setting forth maturity date, interest rate, security, and other terms.

Independent agent. An insurance agent who may place coverage with any company with which he or she has an agency relationship as long as the insured meets that company's underwriting standards.

Index. An index differs from an average in that it weighs changes in prices by the size for the companies affected. The Standard & Poor's Index of 400 stocks calculates changes in prices as if all the shares of each company were sold each day, thus giving a giant like General Motors its due influence.

Index fund. A mutual fund that has as its primary objective the matching of the performance of a particular stock index such as the Standard & Poor's 500 Composite Stock Price Index. An example is Vanguard's Index 500 Fund.

Index options. While stock indexes are a measure of the value of a group of stocks, index options are option contracts on these stock indexes. Since there is no single underlying asset, covered writing is not possible with stock indexes.

Index rate. An interest rate index that is meant to capture the movement of interest rates; used by mortgage lenders as a base rate for determining the rate of interest charged on adjustable rate mortgages (ARMs).

Indirect quote. The price of a unit of a home currency, expressed in terms of a foreign currency. For example, in the United States, a quotation of 110 yens per dollar is an indirect quote for the Japanese yen. Indirect and *direct* quotations are reciprocals.

$$\text{Indirect quote} = \frac{1}{\text{Direct quote}} = \frac{1}{\$0.00909} = 110 \text{ yens}$$

Individual investor. An individual whose principal concerns in the purchase of a security are regular dividend income, safety of the original investment, and, if possible, capital appreciation.

Individual practice association (IPA). A form of HMO in which subscribers receive services from physicians operating out of their own offices and from community hospitals rather than from a central facility.

Individual retirement account (IRA). A retirement plan for an individual.

Inflation. A general rise in the prices of goods and services.

Inflation risk. The risk that the value of investments do not rise due to inflation.

Information asymmetry. The difference in accessibility to information between managers and investors, which may result in a lower stock price than would be true if there were conditions of certainty.

Inheritance tax. A state tax levied on individuals who inherit property.

Initial margin. A requirement to deposit a portion of an initial investment when trading in a securities or futures market

Initial public offering (IPO). When a firm sells equity to the public for the first time.

Insolvency. A company's inability to pay debt. An analysis of insolvency concentrates on the operating and capital structure of a business. The proportion of long-term debt in the capital structure must also be considered.

Installment credit. A type of consumer credit in which the consumer pays the amount in equal payments, usually monthly.

Installment loan. A loan that is repaid in a series of periodic, fixed scheduled payments instead of in a lump sum.

Installment sales. The sale of property on installment terms.

Institutional investor. An institution, such as a mutual fund, bank, insurance company, or pension fund, operating on behalf of a broad client base that trades large blocks of securities.

Intangible assets. Assets such as goodwill, patents, trademarks, and copyrights.

Interbank (currency) market. The foreign exchange market whose major participants are large banks.

Interest-adjusted cost index. A method of determining the cost of life insurance that takes into account the cost to a policyholder of the lost interest on premiums paid for coverage.

Interest coverage ratio. *See* Times-interest-earned ratio.

Interest rate cap. A feature of an adjustable-rate mortgage loan that places a limit on the amount that the interest rate can increase each adjustment period (periodic cap) as well as over the life of the loan (overall cap).

Interest rate futures. Futures contracts on fixed income securities.

Interest rate options. Put and call options written on fixed-income securities.

Interest rate parity theory. States that (except for the effect of small transaction costs) the forward premium or discount should be equal and opposite in size to the difference in the national interest rates for securities of the same maturity.

Interest rate risk. The changes in the value of fixed-income securities, such as bonds and preferred stocks, due to changes in market interest rates.

Interest tax shield. The annual and recurrent tax saving resulting from debt financing.

Internal common equity. Profits retained within a business for investment purposes.

Internal equity financing. Refers to retained earnings, the part of a firm's profit that the firm's owners decide to invest back into their company.

Internal growth. A firm's growth rate in earnings resulting from reinvesting company profits rather than distributing the earnings in the form of dividends. The growth rate is a function of the amount retained and the return earned on the retained funds.

Internally generated funds. The sum of retained earnings and depreciation expenses.

Internal rate of return (IRR). A capital-budgeting technique that reflects the rate of return a project earns. Mathematically it is the discount rate that equates the present value of the inflows with the present value of the outflows.

International Fisher effect. States that the difference in interest rates between two countries reflects the difference in their expected inflation rates.

International fund. A mutual fund that does all or most of its investing in foreign securities; also includes global funds, a special type of international fund that invests in both international and domestic securities.

Intestacy. The situation created when an individual dies without leaving a valid will.

In-the-money. A call option with a striking price less than the market price of the underlying security; a put option with a striking price greater than the market price of the underlying security.

Intrinsic value. (1) The present value of an investment's expected future cash flows, discounted at the investor's required rate of return. (2) The intrinsic value of an option is what its premium would be if the price of the underlying stock would remain at its current level until expiration.

Inventory turnover. Cost of goods sold divided by ending inventories. It is a measure of the efficiency of inventory management.

Invested capital. Usually, the value of a company's equity and long-term debt at book values. Possibly, equity and interest-bearing debt or another variation. Possibly, values at fair market values.

Investment. The use of money for the purpose of making more money, to gain income or increase capital, or both. Safety of principal is an important consideration.

Investment banker. Also known as an underwriter. The middleman between the corporation that wants to raise money and the public. When an investment banker or syndicate underwrites a new issue, he, she, or it stands ready to buy the new securities if they cannot be sold to the public.

Investment banks. Financial intermediaries that act as "middlemen" between firms wanting to issue securities to raise funds and the suppliers of capital.

Investment club. A club of members who pool their funds to buy and sell securities.

Investment company. *See* Investment trust.

Investment counselor. One who is professionally engaged in rendering investment advisory and supervisory services.

Investment grade bonds. Highly rated bonds (BBB and above) that can be purchased by pension funds and other institutional investors.

Investment letters. Newsletters that provide on a subscription basis analyses and recommendations from various experts of different aspects of investment vehicles.

Investment trust. A company that invests in other companies after which it sells its own shares to the public. If it is a closed-end company, it sells its shares once and for all. If it is an open-end company, or a mutual fund, it continuously buys and sells its shares.

Investor's required rate of return. The minimum rate of return necessary to attract an investor to purchase or hold a security.

Irrevocable living trust. A trust in which the grantor relinquishes title to the property placed in it as well as the right to revoke or terminate it.

IRS valuation method. *See* Excess earnings valuation method.

Issuance or issue costs. Costs incurred when issuing securities; also called flotation costs.

Issue. Any of a company's securities, or the act of distributing such securities.

Joint account. A bank account in the names of two or more persons.

Joint tenancy. A form of ownership of property in which more than one person shares an undivided interest in the property.

Joint tenancy with right of survivorship. A special form of joint tenancy where if one person dies, the surviving owner automatically becomes the sole owner of the property.

Jumbo loans. Loans that differ from conforming loans in that they are above the maximum conforming amount and reflect each lender's own guidelines.

Junior bonds. Bonds whose priority of claims are lower than that of senior bonds.

Junk bond. A bond with a speculative credit rating of BB or lower by the major rating agencies such as Standard & Poor's or Moody's.

Just-in-time (JIT). An inventory management system in which a company buys and manufactures in small quantities "just-in-time" for use, resulting in a minimization of inventory costs.

Kelley Blue Book. A source that lists the wholesale and retail value of used cars. Available at depository institutions and libraries.

Keogh plan. A plan that allows self-employed persons to establish tax-sheltered retirement programs themselves.

Krugerrand. Gold bullion coin from the Republic of South Africa.

Lack of marketability. A phrase used to describe the lack of a market for the sale of ownership holdings in closely held businesses, particularly when such businesses are compared to publicly traded businesses.

Lack of marketability discount. A value reduction in dollars or as a percentage of the value of a company or ownership holding without regard to the discount. Often, a percentage reduction of 15 percent to 45 percent. Might be referred to as a "marketability discount" or an "illiquidity discount."

Law of one price (LOP). States that any traded good should sell for the same price (when expressed in the same currency) regardless of the country where it is sold.

Lead and lag strategies. Techniques used to reduce exchange risk when a firm maximizes its asset position in the stronger currency and its liability position in the weaker currency.

Lease agreement. A rental contract intended to protect the lessor from nonpayment or some adverse action of the lessee.

Ledger. A financial record book that should contain separate sections for assets, liabilities, sources of income, and expenditure items.

Letter of last instructions. An informal memorandum containing suggestions or recommendations for carrying out the provisions of a will.

Leverage. The use of borrowed funds or other people's money (OPM) to magnify returns.

Leveraged buyout (LBO). A corporate restructuring where the existing shareholders sell their shares to a small group of investors. The purchasers of the stock use the firm's unused debt capacity to borrow the funds to pay for the stock.

Leveraged lease. A financial lease in which the leasing company finances the purchase of an asset with a substantial level of debt, using the lease contract as collateral.

Levered assets. Assets financed with some debt capital.

Levered beta. The beta of a stock when the firm is indebted; also called equity or market beta.

Liabilities. A person's debts. Examples are department store or bank card charges, installment loans, and mortgages on real estate.

Liability exposures. Risk incurred by an individual who might negligently cause property damage or bodily injury to someone else.

Liability insurance. A type of insurance coverage that pays for damages an insured has accidentally caused another and for the insureds defense against another who is seeking compensation arising out of a covered occurrence.

Licensing fees. The means by which state and local governments obtain revenue by licensing certain professions and from the sale of automobile licenses.

Lien. A legal claim that permits a lender to liquidate the items that serve as collateral in the event of a default.

Life annuity, period certain. A type of guaranteed minimum annuity in which an annuitant is guaranteed a stated amount of monthly income for life and the insurer agrees to pay for at least a minimum number of years, regardless of whether the annuitant survives.

Life annuity with no refund (straight life). Annuitant receives a specified amount of income for life, regardless of whether the period over which income is distributed is one year or 50 years.

Life expectancy. The age that half the people in an age group are expected to live to; also called the average lifespan. It is used primarily by insurance companies to determine premiums.

Life goals. Goals, not necessarily financial, which most individuals wish to achieve during their lives. The ability to achieve them often depends on realizing a certain level of financial success.

Limited liability. The concept under which an investor in a business cannot lose more than his or her investment.

Limited partnership (syndicate). A type of partnership in which a limited partner is legally liable only for his or her initial investment. The general partner (usually the organizer) who operates the syndicate has unlimited financial liability.

Limited payment whole life. Whole life insurance policy that offers coverage for the entire life of the insured but schedules the premium payments to end after a limited period.

Limit order. An order to either buy a security at a specified price or lower or sell a security at or above a specified price.

Line of credit. An arrangement by which a credit customer can borrow up to a specified maximum amount of funds.

Liquid. The state of having sufficient cash and near-cash assets to meet current debt.

Liquid asset. Cash asset (e.g., cash or an unrestricted bank account) or readily marketable security. A liquid asset can be converted into cash in a short time without a material concession in price. Excluded from this definition are accounts receivable and inventory.

Liquidation. (1) The process of converting securities or other property into cash. (2) The dissolution of a company, with cash remaining after the sale of its assets and payment of all indebtedness being distributed to the shareholders.

Liquidation value. The value of a business not as a going concern. Often, the accumulated value of a company's assets (less liabilities) presuming the assets are sold separately.

Liquidity. The ability of a firm to meet short-term recurrent cash obligations. *See* Solvency.

Liquidity ratio. Ratio of liquid assets divided by total current debt.

Listed securities. Securities that trade on organized markets.

Listed stock. The stock of a company that is traded on a national securities exchange and for which a listing application and a registration statement (giving detailed information about the company and its operations) have been filed with the SEC and the exchange itself.

Living (inter vivos) trust. Trust created while the grantor is still alive.

Living will. A document that states, in very precise terms, the treatments that a person wants and to what degree he or she wishes them continued if he or she becomes terminally ill.

Load (mutual) fund. A mutual fund sold to the public that charges sales commissions, usually called a front-end load when purchased.

Load (sales charge). A sales commission charged to purchase shares in many mutual funds sold by brokers or other members of a sales force. Typically, the charge ranges from 2 percent to 8.5 percent of the initial investment. The charge is added to the net asset value (NAV) per share when determining the offer price. Not all mutual funds have a load.

Loan amortization. The systematic repayment of a loan's principal and interest.

Loan application. An application that provides a lender with information about the purpose of the requested loan, whether it will be secured or unsecured, and the applicant's financial condition.

Loan disclosure statement. A document that lenders are required to supply borrowers that states both the dollar finance charges and the annual percentage rate (APR) applicable to a loan.

Loan-to-value (LTV) ratio. The percentage of a property's value that a lender is willing to make a loan on.

Lockbox. A box in a U.S. Postal Service facility, used to facilitate collection of customer remittances. The use of a lockbox reduces processing float. The recipient's local bank collects from these boxes periodically during the day and deposits the funds in the appropriate corporate account.

London interbank offered rate (LIBOR). The interest rate at which international banks charge each other for large loans.

Long. Signifies ownership of securities. "I am long 100 General Electric" means the speaker owns 100 shares in that company. This term is used as the opposite of being "short" on an investment.

Long-range budget. Projections that cover more than one fiscal year; also called strategic budgeting. The five-year budget plan is the most commonly used in practice. *See also* Annual budget.

Long-term care. The delivery of medical and personal care, other than hospital care, to persons with chronic medical conditions resulting from either illness or frailty.

Long-term financing. Equity plus long-term debt.

Long-term gains (losses). The sale of a capital asset held for more than one year at a higher (lower) price than the original cost.

Long-term residual dividend policy. A dividend plan by which residual capital is distributed smoothly to investors over the planning period.

Low-load fund. A mutual fund that charges a small commission.

Lump-sum payments. Payments under workers' compensation of a specific amount for specific types of losses.

M. Abbreviation for 1,000. It is used to specify the face value of a bond.

Magnetic Ink Character Recognition (MICR). A magnetic coding imprinted on checks and deposit slips to speed up the check- and deposit-clearing process.

Mail float. The float, or lag in time, from when a customer mails his or her remittance check until the firm begins to process it.

Maintenance margin. The minimum percentage equity an investor must maintain in a stock that was purchased using borrowed funds.

Majority holding. Ownership holding in a business of more than 50 percent.

Major medical plan. An insurance plan designed to supplement the basic coverages of hospital, surgical, and physician expenses, coverages which are designed to cover smaller health care costs. Major medical is used to finance medical costs of a more catastrophic or long-term nature.

Managed care plan. Health care plan in which subscribers/users contract directly with a provider organization, which furnishes comprehensive health care services for a fixed fee from a designated group of providers who meet stringent selection criteria. These plans emphasize cost control and preventive treatment.

Management. The board of directors, elected by the stockholders, and the officers of the corporation, appointed by the board of directors.

Management by exception. A management concept or policy by which management devotes its time to investigating only those situations in which actual results differ significantly from planned results. The idea is that management should spend its valuable time concentrating on the more important items (such as the shaping of the company's future strategic course).

Management by objective (MBO). A system of performance appraisals having the following characteristics: (1) It is a formal system in that each manager is required to take certain prescribed actions and to complete certain written documents; and (2) The manager and subordinates discuss the subordinate's job description, agree to short-term performance targets, discuss the progress made toward meeting these targets, and periodically evaluate the performance and provide the feedback.

Management control system. A system under which managers assure that resources are obtained and used effectively and efficiently in the accomplishment of the organization's goals.

Managerial options. Options that can be exercised to alter a project during its useful life, including the options to abandon, expand, or defer a project.

Manufactured home. A partially or fully assembled, factory-produced housing unit that can be transported to a desired location, placed on either a permanent or temporary foundation, and then connected to utilities and used as a residence.

Margin. The amount paid by a customer when using credit to buy a security, the balance being advanced by a broker. Under Federal Reserve regulations, the initial margin required in the past 20 years has ranged from 40 percent of the purchase price all the way to 100 percent.

Marginal tax rate. The tax rate that would be applied to the next dollar of income.

Margin call. A demand upon a customer to put up money or securities with a broker. The call is made when a purchase is made; also if a customer's equity in a margin account declines below a minimum standard set by an exchange or by the firm.

Margin purchases (buying). The buying of securities using some borrowed funds. The percentage of borrowed funds is limited by both law and brokerage firms.

Margin requirement. A provision that specifies what proportion of each dollar used to purchase a security must be provided by an investor.

Marked-to-market. Futures contracts are marked-to-market when daily profits or losses are settled at the end of each trading day.

Marketability discount. *See* Lack of marketability discount.

Marketable securities. Security investments that a firm can quickly convert into cash balances.

Market approach to value. An approach for establishing the value of a business or ownership holding using sales of similar businesses or ownership holdings. It may overlap in concept with the assets approach to value or the income or earnings approach to value.

Market beta. Beta of a stock when a firm is indebted; also called equity or levered beta.

Market capitalization. Market cap, for short. The market value of a company, or how much it would cost in theory to buy the company outright. A company's market cap is computed by multiplying its current per-share stock price by the number of shares outstanding.

Market equilibrium. The situation in which expected returns equal required returns.

Market maker. Person who specializes in creating markets for certain securities in the over-the-counter market by offering to buy or sell a given security at specified bid and ask prices.

Market order. An order to buy or sell stock at the best price available at the time the order is placed.

Market power hypothesis. Takeover rationale according to which the acquiring firm has a larger market share after the acquisition that may enable it to raise the price of its products.

Market rate of interest. The rate of interest paid on instruments with similar types of risk in the marketplace.

Market return. The average return on all stocks, such as those in the S&P 500 Index.

Market risk. Factors, such as changes in political, economic, and social conditions, as well as changes in investor tastes and preferences, that may cause the market price of a security to change.

Market risk (of a bond). Sensitivity of a bond price to changes in interest rates.

Market risk (of common stock). Sensitivity of a stock price to changes in general market movements. *See also* Beta (coefficient).

Market risk premium. The difference between the expected return of a portfolio of all existing common stocks and the risk-free rate. *See* Capital asset pricing model.

Market synergies. Increased revenues, beyond premerger levels, as a result of combining the operations of two or more firms.

Market value added (MVA). The difference between the market value of a firm's capital (equity and debt) and the capital that shareholders and debtholders have invested in the firm.

Market-value weights. The percentage of financing provided by different capital sources as measured by the current market prices of a firm's bonds and preferred and common stock.

Marriage penalty. Under the U.S. tax code, the increased taxes paid under certain circumstances by a two-income married couple filing a joint return compared with taxes paid by a two-income couple filing as "separate" persons.

Master account. Account from which funds are transferred to zero balance accounts when needed.

Master (comprehensive) budget. A plan of activities expressed in monetary terms that involve the assets, equities, revenues, and costs that will be involved in carrying out the plans. Simply put, a master budget is a set of projected or planned financial statements.

Matching strategy. The financing of long-term investments with long-term funds and short-term investments with short-term funds in order to minimize interest rate risk and funding risk.

Maturity. The date on which a loan or a bond or debenture comes due and is to be paid off.

Maximum capital gain. *See* Aggressive growth fund.

Medicaid. A public assistance program under Social Security that is designed to provide medical benefits for those persons who are unable to pay their own health care costs.

Medical payments insurance (automobile). Insurance that provides for payment to eligible insureds of an amount no greater than the policy limit for all reasonable and necessary medical expenses incurred within one year after an automobile accident.

Medicare. A health care plan administered by the federal government designed to help persons over age 65 and others who receive monthly Social Security disability benefits.

Merchant banks. *See* Investment banks.

Merger. A combination of two or more businesses into a single operational entity.

Mezzanine financing. Junior unsecured debt in a leveraged buyout (LBO).

Minimum payment (charge account). The minimum payment required on a charge account; usually represents a specified percentage of new account balance.

Minority discount. A discount often associated with a minority ownership holding in a business because such a holding lacks the ability to control the affairs of the business. It should be based on the relationship between the control holding and the minority holding(s), although in practice, a 15 percent to 35 percent discount is often applied to noncontrolling holdings based on averages determined by various "studies."

Minority holding. An ownership holding in a business of less than 50 percent; sometimes an ownership holding of 50 percent.

Money market. Market for short-term (less than one year) debt securities. Examples of money market securities include U.S. Treasury bills and commercial paper.

Money market certificate (MMC). Type of certificate of deposit issued by banks, savings and loan associations, mutual savings banks, and credit unions. They have six-month maturities and pay interest at a maximum rate set equal to the rate paid on the most recently issued six-month Treasury bills.

Money market deposit account (MMDA). Offered by federally insured financial institutions; basically the same as a money market mutual fund.

Money market instruments. Debt securities with maturity not exceeding one year.

Money market (mutual) fund. A mutual fund that invests in high-yielding, short-term money market instruments such as U.S. T-bills and commercial paper.

Monitoring costs. A form of agency costs. Typically these costs arise when bond investors take steps to ensure that protective covenants in the bond indenture are adhered to by management.

Monthly investment plan (MIP). An arrangement that allows investors to invest specified amounts, typically in the range of $50 to $1,000, in securities listed on the New York Stock Exchange every month or every three months.

Moody's Investors Services. A company that publishes a variety of ratings (e.g., bond ratings). The company used to publish a variety of investment reference manuals including *Moody's Manuals*. These are now published by Mergent FIS, Inc.

Mortality rate. The number of deaths per 1,000 that will occur at specified ages each year.

Mortgage. A document conveying legal interest in a property to a lender as security for payment of a debt.

Mortgage banker. A firm that solicits borrowers, originates primarily government-insured and guaranteed loans, and places them with mortgage lenders; frequently uses its own money to initially fund mortgages it later resells.

Mortgage bonds. Bonds secured by a lien on real property.

Mortgage broker. A firm that solicits borrowers and originates primarily conventional loans, placing those loans with mortgage lenders. Unlike a mortgage banker, a mortgage broker is *not* involved in servicing the loan; it merely takes loan applications and then finds lenders willing to grant the mortgage loans under the desired terms.

Mortgage life insurance. An insurance policy on the life of the borrower in which the lender is the beneficiary. If the borrower dies, the mortgage is automatically paid off.

Mortgage loan. Borrowing to finance the purchase of a piece of property.

Mortgage points. Fees charged by a lender in a mortgage loan.

Multiple earnings approach. A method of multiplying annual gross earnings by some arbitrary multiplier to determine life insurance needs.

Multiple indemnity clause. A clause in a life insurance policy that typically doubles or triples the policy's face amount in the event of the insured's accidental death.

Municipal bonds. Debt securities issued by states, counties, cities, and other public agencies. They are tax exempt.

Mutual fund. A company that uses its capital to invest in other companies. There are two principal types of mutual funds—closed-end and open-end. Shares in close-end investment trusts are readily transferable in the open market and are bought and sold like other shares. Capitalization of these companies is fixed. Open-end funds sell their own new shares to investors, stand ready to buy back their old shares, and are not listed. Open-end funds are so called because their capitalization is not fixed and they issue more shares as people want them.

Mutually exclusive projects. A set of projects that perform essentially the same task; acceptance of one will necessarily mean rejection of the others.

Mutual savings banks. Financial institutions similar to savings and loan associations whose depositors are their owners.

Naked (naked option strategy). This uncovered option strategy is an investment in which the written options are not matched with a long stock position, or a long option position that expires no earlier than the written options. The loss potential with such a strategy is thereby unlimited.

Named peril policy. An insurance policy that names the perils covered individually.

NASDAQ indexes. Measures of current price behavior of securities sold in the over-the-counter (OTC) market.

National Association of Securities Dealers (NASD). A self-regulatory organization that has jurisdiction over the NASDAQ National Market and the NASDAQ SmallCap Market, two listing systems for over-the-counter (OTC) stocks. The NASD also operates the OTC Bulletin Board. The NASD requires member broker-dealers to register, and it conducts examinations for compliance with net capital requirements and other regulations.

National Credit Union Administration (NCUA). Organization of federal credit unions that insures deposits in all federal and many state-chartered credit unions.

National Foundation for Consumer Credit. An organization that sponsors nonprofit credit counseling centers in many communities.

National health insurance. A much discussed form of insurance coverage under which the government would assume all or part of the costs of health care services.

Needs approach. Method of determining life insurance needs that considers the financial resources available in addition to life insurance, and the specific financial obligations a person may have.

Negative cash flow. A situation in which cash inflows are less than cash outflows. This is an unfavorable situation that may result in liquidity problems.

Negligent action. An action inconsistent with the "reasonable man doctrine"—the doctrine that if a person fails to act as one would with normal intelligence, perceptions, and experiences common to the community, he or she is negligent.

Negotiable. Refers to a security, the title to which, when properly endorsed by the owner, is transferable by delivery.

Negotiable certificates of deposit. Marketable receipts for funds deposited in a bank for a fixed period. The deposited funds earn a fixed rate of interest. More commonly, these are called CDs.

Negotiable order of withdrawal (NOW) account. Similar in appearance and behavior to a checking account; can be viewed as an interest-earning checking account or as a savings account against which checks can be issued. While interest is paid at the passbook rate on regular NOW accounts, no interest rate ceiling exists on Super NOW accounts.

Net assets. Total assets minus total liabilities; also called equity.

Net asset value. (1) The difference, at a particular date, between what a firm's shareholders collectively own, called assets, and what they owe, called liabilities; also called net worth, owners' equity, shareholders' equity, and shareholders' funds. Not to be confused with net assets. (2) A mutual fund's assets minus liabilities.

Net change. The change is the price of a security from the closing price on one day to the closing price on the following day on which the stock is traded. In the case of a stock that is entitled to a dividend one day, but is traded "ex-dividend" the next, the dividend is considered in computing the change. For example, if the closing market price of a stock on Monday—the last day it was entitled to receive a 50-cent dividend—was $45 a share, and $44.50 at the close of the next day, when it was "ex-dividend," the price would be considered unchanged. With a split-up of shares, a stock selling at $100 the day before a 2-for-1 split and trading the next day at $50 would also be considered unchanged. If it sold at $51, it would be considered up $1. The net change is ordinarily the last figure in a stock price list.

Net cost method. A method by which the relative cost of life insurance can be assessed. It is calculated by totaling the premiums paid over a given period, subtracting from the total the total dividends and cash values projected for the period, and dividing the remainder by the number of years in the period.

Net earnings. The earnings an employee takes home after their employer has made all required as well as requested deductions.

Net federal estate tax payable. The estate tax payable to the federal government after all credits are subtracted.

Net income. A figure representing a firm's profit or loss for a period. It also represents the earnings available to a firm's common and preferred stockholders.

Net monetary position. Monetary assets less monetary liabilities.

Net operating cash flow (NOCF). The net cash flow originating from a firm's operating activities during a period under consideration (cash inflows from operations minus cash outflows from operations).

Net operating loss carryback and carryforward. A tax provision that permits a taxpayer first to apply a loss against the profits in the three prior years (carryback). If the loss has not been completely absorbed by the profits in these three years, it may be applied to taxable profits in each of the seven following years (carryforward).

Net operating profit after tax (NOPAT). Earnings before interest and tax × (1 − Tax rate). *See* Economic value added.

Net payment cost index. The measure of cost of an insurance policy exclusive of its cash value.

Net present value (NPV). A capital-budgeting concept defined as the present value of a project's annual net cash flows after tax less the project's initial outlay.

Net profit margin. Net income divided by sales. A ratio that measures the net income of a firm as a percent of sales.

Net working capital. Current assets less current liabilities.

Net worth. Often considered the amount of personal or family wealth; it is determined by subtracting total liabilities from total assets.

New issue. A stock or bond sold by a corporation for the first time. Proceeds may be used to retire outstanding securities of the company, purchase new plant or equipment, or provide additional working capital.

New York Stock Exchange (NYSE). The largest and most prestigious organized securities exchange; it handles a majority of the dollar volume of securities transactions and a high percentage of the total annual share volume on organized securities exchanges. Also called "Big Board."

Night depository. A protected type of mail slot on the exterior of a bank or other financial institution. Deposits can be submitted in special envelopes provided for after-hour deposits.

No-fault insurance. A concept of automobile insurance that favors reimbursement without regard to negligence.

No-load fund. A mutual fund that does not charge a commission when shares are purchased.

Nominal rate of interest. Stated rate of interest on a loan or savings deposit; this rate does not necessarily represent the true rate of interest being paid on the funds.

Nominal value. *See* Face value.

Noncatastrophic loss. A loss that is not the result of catastrophic occurrences such as war, nuclear explosion, and large-scale flooding; generally speaking, losses from catastrophes cannot be safely insured by private insurance companies.

Noncontributory pension plan. A pension plan in which an employer pays the total cost of the benefits.

Noncumulative preferred stock. Preferred stock on which dividends do not accumulate. The current dividend must be paid prior to earnings being distributed to common stockholders.

Noncurrent assets. Long-lived assets that are not expected to be turned into cash within a year; also called long-term assets, fixed assets, or capital assets. It can be tangible or intangible assets as well as financial assets.

Nondiscretionary cash flows. Cash outflows that a firm is legally obliged to meet.

Nondiversifiable risk. *See* Systematic risk.

Nonforfeiture right. An option that gives a life insurance policyholder a portion of the assets that had been set aside to provide payment for the death claim that was not made. The amount, often called cash value, is given to the policyholder when the policy is canceled.

Nonoperating items. Assets owned by a business that do not contribute to the operating profits of the company, such as items owned for the personal enjoyment of the owner(s). Usually, nonoperating items are valued separately and added to the value of the company otherwise determined.

Nonparticipating preferred stock. Preferred stock on which only the stated amount of dividends is owed to the shareholder.

Nonqualified deferred compensation plan. An arrangement between an employer and employee to defer payment for services rendered by the employee. Such an agreement is most useful when an employee's future needs for funds exceeds his or her present requirements.

Normalized earnings. *See* Adjusted earnings.

Note. A debt security acknowledging a creditor relationship with the issuing firm and stipulating the conditions and terms under which the money was borrowed; also called promissory notes.

Notes payable. Bank overdrafts, drawings on lines of credit, short-term promissory notes, and the portion of long-term debt due within a year.

Not-sufficient-funds check (NSF check). Check not covered by sufficient bank balance. In preparing its bank reconciliation, the depositing entity must deduct the NSF check from the cash book balance.

N-ratio method. A formula for estimating the annual percentage rate on an add-on loan.

NYSE (Composite) Index. An index of the performance of all stocks listed on the New York Stock Exchange.

OCC. Option Clearing Corporation.

Odd lot. A quantity of fewer than 100 shares of a security.

Offer price. The price at which a person is ready to sell, as opposed to bid, the price at which one is ready to buy. *See* Ask price.

Old-age, survivor's disability, and health insurance (OASDHI). Commonly referred to as Social Security, a U.S. government program established in 1935 and providing not only retirement benefits but also payments for survivors, disability income for workers and their dependents, and health care benefits for low-income and elderly families and individuals.

Online broker. Typically a discount broker through which investors can execute trades electronically/online through a commercial service or on the Internet; also called Internet broker or electronic broker.

Online database. An Internet service, such as Dow Jones Interactive or CompuServe, providing historical financial, market, and economic information, as well as current stock market prices and financial news. Access obtained via computer modem or broadband cable.

Open account credit. A form of credit extended to a consumer in advance of any transaction. It is often referred to as a charge account.

Open-end investment company. Investment company that will sell or buy back its own shares at a price that is based on the current value of the securities the fund owns. It is commonly called a mutual fund.

Open-end (mutual) funds. A mutual fund that an investor buys shares from and sells these shares back to the fund itself. This type of fund offers to sell and redeem shares on a continual basis for an indefinite time period. Shares are purchased at net asset value (NAV) plus commission (if any), and redeemed at NAV less a service charge (if any).

Open order. An order to buy or sell a security at a specified price. An open order remains in effect until executed or canceled by the customer.

Operating cash-earnings multiple. Share price divided by earnings before interest, tax, depreciation, and amortization (EBITDA) per share; used to value a firm.

Operating cycle. Average time period between buying inventory and receiving cash proceeds from its eventual sale. It is determined by adding (1) the number of days inventory is held and (2) the collection period for accounts receivable.

Operating exposure. The effect of changes in exchange rates on a firm's cash flows generated by future and uncertain transactions.

Operating lease. A contractual commitment on the part of a firm leasing an asset (the lessee) to make a series of payments to the firm that actually owns the asset (the lessor) for use of the asset. An operating lease differs from a financial lease in that it can be canceled at any time after proper notice has been given to the lessor.

Operating leverage. A responsiveness to sales changes of the firm's earnings before interest and taxes. This responsiveness arises from the firm's use of fixed operating costs.

Operational (operating) budget. A budget that embraces the impacts of operating decisions. It contains forecasts of sales, net income, the cost of goods sold, selling and administrative expenses, and other expenses.

Opportunity cost. The loss of revenues that results from giving up an activity in order to carry out an alternative one.

Optimal capital structure. A capital structure that minimizes a firm's composite cost of capital (maximizes the common stock price) for raising a given amount of funds.

Option. A contract with three characteristic features. It allows an investor to reserve the right to buy or sell (1) a specified number of shares of stock (2) at a fixed price per share (3) for a limited length of time. There are two types of option contracts: call options and put options.

Option A contract. A contract that permits an investor to either purchase or sell a specified security at a predetermined price within a certain period of time.

Optional renewability. A contractual clause allowing an insured to continue insurance only at the option of the insurer.

Option charge account. A type of revolving charge account.

Option premium. The market price of an option.

Order imbalance. A situation where there are too many buy orders for a particular stock and not enough sell orders—or vice versa. When this occurs, stock exchanges may halt trading temporarily to allow more of the other kind of order to come in. This permits better matching of buyers and sellers and can lessen volatility in the stock.

Organized securities exchange. An institution where listed financial securities are traded by exchange members on a floor organized according to different types of securities. The largest and most prestigious example is the New York Stock Exchange.

Out-of-the-money. This term is used when the striking price of an option is less than the price of the underlying stock of a call option, or greater than the price of the underlying stock of a put option.

Overdraft. (1) Negative balance in a checking account caused by payment of checks drawn against insufficient funds. (2) Situation where a borrower draws money against a previously established line of credit. The basic cost to the borrower is the interest rate levied on the daily overdraft balance.

Overdraft protection. Special arrangement between a bank and account holder whereby the bank automatically advances money to cover an overdrawn check. The account holder is charged interest on the advance.

Overspending. When consumers spend more money or incur more obligations for future payment than they have income to cover.

Over-the-counter (OTC). Trading of securities through a broker-dealer, usually over the telephone, without using the facilities of an exchange. The securities may or may not be listed on an exchange. OTC stocks include those listed on the NASDAQ systems as well as the OTC Bulletin Board (*see* Bulletin Board).

Over-the-counter market (OTC market). The market in which the securities of smaller, less well-known firms are generally traded.

Pac man. A defensive tactic to a tender offer where the firm under attack becomes the attacker.

Paper profit. An unrealized profit on a security still held. Paper profits become realized profits only when the security is sold.

Participating policy. A life insurance policy that pays dividends which reflect the difference between the premiums charged and the premium necessary to fund the actual mortality experience of the company.

Participating preferred. A stock entitled to receive both (1) a stated dividend before the common stock and (2) part of any dividend thereafter declared on the common stock.

Participation or coinsurance clause. A provision in many health insurance policies stipulating that the company will pay some portion of a covered loss in excess of the deductible.

Partnership. A business owned by more than one person. Its income is normally taxed as the personal income of the owners, and their liability is not limited to their investment in the business.

Par value. The stated or face value of a stock or bond. (1) For a share of stock, an arbitrary fixed value set when shares are issued. (2) For a bond, the fixed amount (face value) that has to be paid back to bondholders at the maturity date of the bond.

Passbook account. A regular savings account at a financial institution.

Passed dividend. The omission of a regular or scheduled dividend.

Passively managed funds. Funds that might follow an index, a formula, or, in some cases, not change holdings at all. They simply buy and hold shares of investments found in a benchmark, such as the Standard & Poor's 500 Index.

Past due balance method. Method of computing finance charges whereby customers who pay their account in full within a specified period of time, such as 30 days from the billing date, are relieved of finance charges.

Pawnshop. A loan source that accepts certain types of goods, such as jewelry, guns, and stereos, against which it lends 25 percent to 75 percent of their established market value.

Pay-as-you-go basis. Method of paying income taxes whereby an employer deducts from employees a portion of income every pay period and sends it to the IRS.

Payback period method. A capital-budgeting criterion defined as the number of years required to recover an initial cash investment.

Payment date. The date on which a company mails a dividend check to each investor.

Payoff (on a loan). Amount required to terminate a loan.

Pecking order. Refers to the order in which firms raise capital, relying first on retaining earnings, then issuing debt before finally raising new equity.

Pecuniary legacy. Type of clause in a will that passes money to a specified party.

Penny stocks. Low-priced, often highly speculative stocks, that typically sell for $5 or less per share. According to the SEC, penny stock is any stock that is one of the following: (1) not listed on a major exchange or listing system; (2) is sold for less than $5; (3) has net tangible assets of less than $2 million if in business at least three years, or of less than $5 million if in business less than three years; or (4) has average revenue for the last three years of less than $6 million. All penny stocks are traded in the over-the-counter (OTC) market.

Pension. A fixed sum paid to a person following retirement.

Pension Benefit Guarantee Corporation (PBGC). Established by a provision of the Employee Retirement Income Security Act of 1974, this organization guarantees that certain benefits be payable to eligible workers even if their employer's pension plan has insufficient assets to fulfill its commitments.

Pension liabilities. Liabilities owed to employees and paid to them when they retire.

People planning. Estate planning that places primary emphasis on the satisfaction of human needs, anticipating psychological and financial needs for others, especially dependents with special problems or gifts and others who cannot, or do not want to, manage financial resources themselves.

Percentage of sales method. A financial forecasting tool that estimates expenses for a future period as a percentage of the sales forecast.

Performance budget. A medium- to short-range budget often used in governmental accounting. It is typical of the type incorporated by a program planning budgeting system (PPBS), but without references to long-range goals.

Performance (go-go) fund. An investment company portfolio that emphasizes performance as measured by the total return earned on its shareholders' investments; the investment strategies are speculative.

Peril. The cause of a loss.

Perpetuity. An annuity with an infinite life.

Personal article floater (PAP) policy. Insurance policy that provides for comprehensive coverage on a blanket basis for virtually all personal property of the insured.

Personal bankruptcy. A form of legal recourse open to insolvent debtors in which they may petition a court for protection from creditors and arrange for the orderly liquidation and distribution of their assets.

Personal financial planning. Planning that covers the key elements of an individual's financial affairs and is aimed at achievement of his or her financial goals.

Physicians expense insurance. Insurance that can provide coverage for the costs of such services as physicians' fees for nonsurgical care in a hospital, at home, in a clinic, or in a doctor's office.

Pink sheets. A pink-tinged publication sold by the National Quotation Bureau Inc. that lists the prices of stocks not traded on the NASDAQ systems.

Planning. The selection of short- and long-term objectives and the drawing up of tactical and strategic plans to achieve those objectives. In planning, managers outline the steps to be taken in moving an organization toward its objectives. After deciding on a set of strategies to be followed, the organization needs more specific plans, such as locations, methods of financing, hours of operations, etc. As these plans are made, they will be communicated throughout the organization. When implemented, the plans will serve to coordinate, or meld together, the efforts of all parts of the organization toward the company's objectives.

Pledging accounts receivable. A loan a firm obtains from a commercial bank or a finance company using its accounts receivable as collateral.

Pocket money. All currency and coin under the control of an individual or family. This includes cash on the person or in the home.

Point. (1) In the case of shares of stock, a point means $1. For example, if Xerox shares rise two points, each share has risen $2. (2) In the case of bonds, a point means $10, since a bond is quoted as a percentage of $1,000. A bond that rises two points gains 2 percent of $1,000 or $20 in value. (3) In the case of market averages, the word point means merely that and no more. It is not equivalent to any fixed sum of money.

Point-of-service (POS) plan. Type of HMO that allows members to go outside the HMO network for care; the plan reimburses members for nonaffiliated services at a specified percentage of the cost after a member's annual deductible has been satisfied.

Policy dividends. Payments made to participating policyholders that represent a refund of overcharges resulting from the insurance company's overestimation of its mortality experience.

Policy limits. The benefit limits described in an insurance policy.

Policy loan. An advance made by a life insurance company to a policyholder secured by the cash value of the life insurance policy.

Political risk. The risk that the cash flows from a project may be affected by changes in local regulations governing foreign investments; also called country risk.

Portfolio. A collection of securities assembled for the purpose of meeting common investment goals.

Position. (1) A specific instance of a chosen "strategy." (2) An option position is an investment comprised of one or more options.

Preauthorized check (PAC). A check written by the payee on the payor's account and deposited on the agreed date.

Preauthorized debit (PAD). An authorization given by a customer to a seller to routinely and automatically charge his or her account.

Preauthorized payment. The mechanism that allows a savings institution to make payments from a customer's account at the customer's directions.

Precious minerals. Minerals, such as gold, silver, and diamonds, that are used for investment purposes.

Preemptive right. A right entitling a common shareholder to maintain his or her proportionate share of ownership in the firm.

Preferred provider organization (PPO). Health care provider that combines the characteristics of an individual practice association (IPA) with an insurance plan to provide comprehensive health care services to its subscribers within a network of physicians and hospitals.

Preferred stock. A class of stock with a claim on the company's earnings before payment may be made on the common stock, and usually entitled to priority over common stock if the company liquidates. Preferred stockholders are usually entitled to dividends at a specified rate (when declared by the board of directors and before payment of a dividend on the common stock) depending upon the terms of the issue.

Premium. (1) A market expression carrying the idea of an excess over an expected norm. A preferred stock or bond selling at a premium brings more than its par value. A new issue that rises quickly from its issuing price sells at a premium. When the redemption price of a bond or preferred issue is higher than par, redemption is at a premium. (2) The purchasing or selling price of an option contract. (3) The increase in the value of something, usually as a percent of something. Often, a control premium. Also, elements in the "build-up" capitalization rate.

Premium (bond). The difference between the price of a bond and its face value, if the former is higher.

Prepaid card. A plastic card with a magnetic strip or microchip that stores the amount of money a purchaser has available to spend, deducting the value of each purchase; it eliminates the need to use cash.

Prepayment penalty. A penalty charged by a lender for advance payment of a loan.

Present value. The value in today's dollars of a future payment discounted back to present at the required rate of return.

Prestige card. A type of bank or travel and entertainment card that offers higher credit limits, has stricter requirements for qualification, and generally offers more features than its "regular" counterpart.

Previous balance method. A method of computing finance charges by which interest is computed on the outstanding balance at the beginning of the billing period.

Price-earnings (P-E) ratio. The ratio of current stock price to the earnings per share; also called earnings multiplier. For example, if a firm has an earnings per share of $2, and a stock price of $30, its price-earnings ratio is 15 ($30 ÷ $2).

Price-earnings valuation method. The valuation of a company or ownership interest in which a ratio determined by publicly traded stocks or sales of closely held businesses is used to value the subject business, also called multiplier method. For example, if the price-earnings ratio is determined to be 4.5, and the subject company's earnings are $100,000, the value of the company is estimated to be $450,000 ($100,000 × 4.5).

Price pegging. Buying orders placed by an underwriting syndicate manager for the security being marketed by his or her selling group. The objective is to stabilize the market price of the new issue.

Price-to-book ratio (P-B). Share price divided by book value of equity per share.

Price-to-cash-earnings ratio (P-CE). Share price divided by cash earnings per share.

Primary distribution. The original sale of a company's securities; also called primary offering.

Primary market. A market in which new securities are traded.

Prime rate. The interest rate charged by banks to their best customers.

Principal. The person for whom a broker executes an order, or a dealer buying or selling for his or her own account. The term "principal" may also refer to a person's capital or to the face amount of a bond.

Principal amount. The amount being borrowed on which interest is paid.

Principal (on an annuity). Amount paid by an annuitant or person buying an annuity during the accumulation period.

Principle of indemnity. An insurance principle that states an insured may not be compensated by his or her insurance company in an amount exceeding the economic loss.

Private mortgage insurance (PMI) program. Insurance plan for lenders that insures them against loss on certain mortgages, usually those with a low down payment.

Private placement. The issuance and sale of a firm's securities directly to financial institutions and qualified investors, thus bypassing the financial markets. *See* Public offering.

Pro forma balance sheet. *See* Budgeted balance sheet.

Pro forma income statement. *See* Budgeted income statement.

Pro forma statements. Financial statements based on estimated, or projected, data.

Probate. A process of liquidation that occurs when a person dies. The deceased's debts are collected or paid, and the remaining assets are distributed to the appropriate individuals or organizations.

Probate estate. The real and personal property a person owns in his or her own name that can be transferred according to the terms of that person's will.

Probate process. The court-supervised process of liquidation that occurs when a person dies; it consists of collecting money owed the decedent, paying his or her debts, and distributing the remaining assets to the appropriate individuals and organizations.

Processing float. Funds are tied up during the time it takes a firm to process remittance checks and deposit them in a bank.

Production budget. A schedule for expected units to be produced. It sets forth the units expected to be manufactured to satisfy budgeted sales and inventory requirements. Expected production volume is determined by adding desired ending inventory to planned sales and then subtracting beginning inventory.

Professional corporation. A corporation established by a group of lawyers, doctors, architects, dentists, or other professionals in part to allow them to set up pension and retirement plans.

Professional liability insurance. Policies designed to protect professionals, such as doctors, lawyers, architects, professors, and engineers, in the event that they are sued for malpractice.

Profitability index (PI). The present value of an investment's expected cash-flow stream divided by the investment's initial cash outlay.

Profit diagram. A graph showing the relationship between the price of a stock and the corresponding profit or loss to an investor.

Profit margin. A measure of earning capacity after taxes; for example, if a company made 20 cents after taxes on each $1 of its sales, its profit margin would be 20 percent.

Profit planning. A process of developing a profit plan that outlines the planned sales revenues and expenses and the net income or loss for a time period. Profit planning requires preparation of a master budget and various analyses for risk and "what-if" scenarios. Tools for profit planning include the cost-volume-profit (CVP) analysis and budgeting.

Profit retention rate. Retained earnings divided by net profit.

Profit-sharing plan. An arrangement whereby the employees of a firm participate in the earnings of the firm. Such an arrangement may qualify as a pension plan.

Profit table. A table showing the relationship between the price of a stock and corresponding profit or loss to an investor.

Profit taking. Selling to take a profit. The process of converting paper profits into cash.

Program trading. The term used to describe the use of computer software to generate security trading decisions. The software has built-in guidelines that instantaneously trigger buy and sell orders when differences in the prices of the securities are great enough to produce profit. Program trading is used by institutional investors, who place buy and sell orders in large blocks of ten thousand or more units. This type of large trade tends to significantly impact the prices of securities in the market. Sometimes, the program trading orders reach the trading floors from a number of firms. This impact can be seen most readily during what is called triple witching hour. The triple witching hour occurs four times annually in the hour prior to the moment when stock options, stock index options, and stock index futures all expire at once (4:15 p.m. EST on the third Friday of March, June, September, and December). During this hour, the Dow Jones Industrial Average and other indices have been known to change drastically.

Progressive tax. A tax schedule in which the larger the amount of taxable income, the higher the rate at which the income is taxed.

Projected (budgeted) balance sheet. A schedule for expected assets, liabilities, and stockholders' equity. It projects a company's financial position as of the end of the budgeting year. Reasons for preparing a budgeted balance sheet follow: (1) discloses unfavorable financial condition that management may want to avoid; (2) serves as a final check on the mathematical accuracy of all other budgets; and (3) highlights future resources and obligations.

Projected (budgeted) income statement. A summary of various component projections of revenues and expenses for the budget period. It indicates the expected net income for the period.

Promissory note. A debt security acknowledging a creditor relationship with the issuing firm and stipulating the conditions and terms under which the money was borrowed.

Property damage liability losses. Losses caused by an insured to the property of another as a result of an accident in which the insured is legally obligated to pay such property damages.

Property insurance. Insurance that provides coverage for physical damage to or destruction of property.

Property inventory. A prepared schedule of property with corresponding values noted.

Property owner association agreement. Rules and regulations for owners of condominiums and other developments in which owners share the use of a property or facilities.

Property tax. A tax levied on the value of various items of property, such as real estate, automobiles, and boats, owned by a taxpayer.

Prospectus. A circular, required by the Securities Act of 1933, that describes securities being offered for sale. Its purpose is full disclosure, especially of any adverse prospects for the issuer. It discloses facts regarding the issuer's operations, including the experience of its management, its financial status, any anticipated legal matters that could affect the company, and potential risks of investing in the corporation.

Proxy. A written statement used to assign a stockholder's voting rights to another person, typically the existing directors.

Proxy statement. Information that the SEC requires most companies to give their stockholders as a prerequisite to solicitation of proxies.

Prudent man rule. In some states, the law provides that a fiduciary, such as a trustee, may invest only in a list of securities designated by the state. In other states, the trustee may invest in a security if a prudent man of discretion and intelligence, who is seeking a reasonable income and preservation of capital, would buy it.

Public offering. The issuance and sale of a firm's securities to the public at large, not only to its existing shareholders.

Pump-and-dump. A scare in which a marginal firm's stock is hyped by phone or on the Internet until its price soars, whereupon the scam artists sell out, causing the stock price to crash.

Purchasing power parity (PPP). States that the general cost of living should be the same across countries. In the long run, exchange rates adjust so that the purchasing power of each currency tends to remain the same and, thus, exchange rate changes tend to reflect international differences in inflation rates. Countries with high rates of inflation tend to experience declines in the value of their currency.

Purchasing power risk. A risk resulting from possible changes in price levels in the economy that can have a significant effect on the prices of securities.

Put. This option contract conveys the right to sell 100 shares (usually) of a specified stock at a fixed price per share (the striking price) for a limited length of time (until expiration).

Put option. A contract that gives its holder the right (with no obligation) to sell a fixed number of shares, or a certain amount of currency, at a fixed price during the life of the option (American option) or at the expiration date of the option (European option). *See* Call option.

Puts and calls. Options that give the right to buy or sell a fixed amount of a certain stock at a specified price within a specified time. A put gives its holder the right to sell the stock; a call the right to buy the stock. Puts are purchased by those who think a stock may go down. A put obligates the seller of the contract to take delivery of the stock and pay the specified price to the owner of the option within the time limit of the contract. The price specified in a put or call is usually close to the market price of the stock at the time the contract is made. Calls are purchased by those who think a stock may rise. A call gives the holder the right to buy the stock from the seller of the contract at the specified price within a fixed period of time. Put and call contracts are written for 30, 60, or 90 days, or longer. If the purchaser of a put or call does not wish to exercise the option, the price he paid for the option becomes a loss.

Qualified pension plan. A retirement plan that meets specified criteria established by the Internal Revenue Code.

Quick asset. Current asset that can be converted into cash in a short time. Examples are cash, marketable securities, and accounts receivable. Certain current assets, such as inventory and prepaid expenses, are excluded.

Quick ratio. Quick assets divided by current liabilities; also called acid test ratio. It is a measure of liquidity.

Quotation. The highest bid to buy and the lowest offer to sell a security in a given market at a given time; also known as a quote. For example, a broker may give a quotation on a stock as "26¼ to 26½." This means that $26.25 was the highest price any buyer wanted to pay (bid) at the time the quotation was given on the exchange and that $26.50 was the lowest price at which any holder of the stock offered to sell.

r. The symbol used in the *Wall Street Journal* and similar publications indicating that there were no trades on that option that day, so there is no last quote to report.

Raider. A company attempting to acquire the assets or the stock of a target company.

Rally. A brisk rise following a decline in the general price level of the market or of an individual stock.

Rate of return. For business valuations, typically, the earnings an investor expects to receive on an annual basis expressed as a percent of the investment made in the business.

Real estate investment company. A corporation that sells its shares and uses the proceeds to make real estate investments.

Real estate investment trust (REIT). A type of closed-end investment company that invests money, obtained through the sale of shares to investors, in various types of real estate.

Real Estate Settlement Procedures Act (RESPA). A law that requires mortgage lenders to clearly disclose settlement costs, closing costs, and the annual percentage rate to loan applicants and borrowers.

Real estate tax. The dominant form of property taxes, it is typically collected by the county and distributed among other governmental bodies to finance schools and other services.

Real interest rate. The interest rate adjusted for changes in the cost of living. *See* Nominal rate of interest.

Realized yield. The rate of return earned over a period of time that is less than the life of the issue.

Reasonable man doctrine. Doctrine stating that if a person fails to act in a reasonable manner, he or she is said to be negligent.

Rebate (co-branded) credit card. A bank credit card that combines features of a traditional bank credit card with an additional incentive, such as rebates or airline mileage.

Recapitalization. The substitution of debt for equity, leaving assets unchanged.

Recession. The phase of the economic cycle during which both the level of employment and the overall level of economic activity are slowing down.

Record date. The date on which an investor must be registered on the books of a company as a shareholder in order to receive a declared dividend or, among other things, to vote on company affairs.

Recovery. The phase of economic cycle during which the employment level is improving and the economy is experiencing increased activity and growth.

Redeeming a bond. Repaying a bond's face value or call value.

Redemption price. The price at which a bond may be repurchased before maturity, or a preferred stock retired, at the option of the issuer.

Redemption value (of a bond). *See* Face value.

Redemption yield (of a bond). *See* Yield to maturity (YTM).

Refunding. The process of replacing an old debt issue with the sale of new debt.

Regional stock exchanges. Organized securities exchanges other than the New York Stock Exchange (NYSE) and the American Stock Exchange (AMEX) that deal primarily in securities having a local or regional flavor.

Registered bond. A bond registered on the books of the issuer's transfer agent. The owner receives the interest by mail rather than by coupon and must endorse the bond to transfer it.

Registered bonds/securities. Bonds/securities that identify a holder's name. *See* Bearer bonds/securities.

Registered representative. Present name for the older term "customers' man." An employee of a brokerage firm, he or she is registered with an exchange or the National Association of Securities Dealers as having passed certain tests and met certain requirements authorizing him or her to serve the firm's public customers. Also known as "customers' broker."

Registration. Before a public offering may be made of new securities by a company (or outstanding securities by controlling stockholders), either through the mails or in interstate commerce, the securities must be registered under the Securities Act of 1933. The application must be filed with the SEC by the issuer. It must disclose pertinent information relating to the company's operations, securities, management, and purpose of the public offering.

Registration statement. A lengthy document filed with the Securities and Exchange Commission containing pertinent facts about a firm planning to sell new securities.

Regulation T. The federal regulation governing the amount of credit that may be advanced by brokers and dealers to customers for the purchase of securities.

Regulation U. The federal regulation governing the amount of credit that may be advanced by a bank to its customers for the purchase of securities.

Regulation Z. A regulation (Consumer Credit Protection Act) issued by the Federal Reserve Board.

Remote disbursing. A cash management service specifically designed to extend disbursing float.

Renewable term. A type of term insurance that may be renewed at its expiration for another term of equal length.

Renewal. Right of the insured to continue coverage upon the expiration of the policy period.

Rental contract. A legal device intended to protect a lessor from nonpayment or some adverse action of the lessee. It specifies the amount of the monthly payment, the payment date, penalties for late payments, length of the lease agreement, any deposit requirements, distribution of expenses, renewal options, and any other restrictions.

Rent controls. Controls imposed by a local government that limit annual rent increases to a "reasonable" level.

Reorganization. A procedure, administered by the courts, that attempts to revitalize a firm by changing its operating procedures and capital structure.

Replacement cost. (1) The amount necessary to repair, rebuild, or replace an asset at today's prices. (2) The cost to replace something.

Report date. The date a valuation report is completed or dated.

Repossession. The act of seizing collateral when a borrower defaults on an installment loan.

Repurchase agreements. Legal contracts that involve the sale of short-term securities by a borrower to a lender of funds. The borrower commits to repurchase the securities at a later date at the contract price plus a stated interest charge.

Reserves. The accumulation of retained earnings since the creation of the firm.

Residual dividend theory. A theory asserting that the dividends to be paid should equal the equity capital left over after the financing of profitable investments.

Residual income. Net income less the minimum return on total assets.

Restrictive covenants. Provisions in a loan agreement that place restrictions on the borrower and make the loan immediately payable and due when violated. These restrictive covenants are designed to maintain the borrower's financial condition on a par with that which existed at the time the loan was made.

Restrictive endorsement. This check endorsement, by adding the word "only" after the third party's name, prevents the check from being endorsed over to a fourth party.

Restructuring. The rearrangement of a company's organization to reduce costs and improve efficiency, resulting in a reduction of shares outstanding.

Restructuring plan. Changes in a firm's assets or financing structures to improve its performance.

Retail charge card. A type of credit card issued by retailers, airlines, and so on, that allows customers to charge goods and services up to a preestablished amount.

Retail lockbox. A lockbox that collects numerous small-dollar remittances from consumers.

Retained earnings. The part of a firm's profit that owners decide to invest back into their company.

Retention rate. Retained earnings divided by earnings after tax (EAT).

Retirement goals. Goals aimed for by individuals at retirement.

Return on assets (ROA). Earnings after tax (EAT) divided by total assets. It is a measure of profitability.

Return on equity (ROE). Earnings after tax (EAT) divided by owners' equity. A measure of the firm's profitability to shareholders.

Return on invested capital (ROIC). Net operating profit after tax (NOPAT or EBIT × (1 − Tax rate)) divided by invested capital (cash plus working capital requirement plus net fixed assets). Same as return on net assets (RONA). Equal to return on capital employed (ROCE). Can also be measured before tax by replacing EBIT × (1 − Tax rate) with EBIT. It is a measure of operating profitability.

Return on investment (ROI). A general measure of profitability that refers to the ratio of a measure of profit to a measure of the investment required to generate that profit.

Return spread. The difference between a firm's, or a project's, after-tax return on invested capital (ROIC) and its weighted average cost of capital (WACC). *See* Economic value added (EVA).

Reverse stock split. A division of shares into a lesser number.

Revocable living trust. A trust in which the grantor reserves the right to revoke the trust and regain the trust property.

Revolving charge account. A type of credit that allows customers to continue to purchase goods as long as they do not exceed the credit limit established or let their account become delinquent by not making specified minimum payments.

Revolving credit agreement. An understanding between a borrower and a bank as to the amount of credit the bank will be legally obligated to provide the borrower. *See* Line of credit.

Right. An instrument that gives the holder an opportunity to purchase a specified number of shares of common stock at a specified price over a designated period of time.

Right of election. The right of a surviving spouse to take a specified portion of the probate estate regardless of what the will provides.

Rights offering. An offering of new shares of corporate stock to existing shareholders on a proportional basis relative to their current ownership.

Rights-on shares. Shares for which rights were issued and which are traded with their rights attached.

Risk. (1) A term used to describe a situation in which a firm makes an investment that requires a known cash outlay without knowing the exact future cash flow the decision will generate. (2) The chance of losing money. (3) The possible variation associated with the expected return measured by the standard deviation or coefficient of variation.

Risk-adjusted discount rate. A method for incorporating a project's level of risk into the capital budgeting process—the discount rate is adjusted upward to compensate for higher-than-normal risk or downward to compensate for lower-than-normal risk.

Risk averse (investors). Investors who would buy shares of firms with riskier projects only if they expect to earn a higher return to compensate them for the higher risk they have to bear.

Risk avoidance. Avoidance of an act that creates risk.

Risk-free rate. The rate of return of a risk-free asset, usually government securities; also called riskless rate of return.

Risk premium. (1) The additional return expected for assuming risk. (2) The difference between the expected return on a security and the risk-free rate. *See also* Capital asset pricing model (CAPM).

Rolling over the forward contract. Entering into a new forward contract after the first contract expires.

Rollover mortgage. A mortgage in which the rate of interest is fixed but the whole loan is negotiated (rolled over) at stated intervals, usually every five years.

Roth IRA. A new type of IRA, established by the Taxpayer Relief Act of 1997, that allows taxpayers, subject to certain income limits, to save for retirement while allowing those savings to grow tax free. Taxes are paid on contributions, but withdrawals, subject to certain rules, are not taxed at all.

Round lot. A unit of trading or a multiple thereof. On the New York Stock Exchange the unit of trading is generally 100 shares in stocks and $1,000 par value in the case of bonds.

Rule of 78 (sum-of-the-years-digits). A rule that is used to determine the portion of the total finance charges a lender receives when a loan is paid off prior to its maturity.

Rule of thumb valuation methods. Any valuation method unique to an industry that uses general assumptions to value a business or ownership holding. Often, a term used to discredit valuation methods used by business owners in general.

s. The symbol used in the *Wall Street Journal* and similar publications indicating that the option does not exist. The options exchange has not opened trading on that option.

Salary-reduction plan. An agreement under which a portion of a covered employee's pay is withheld tax free and invested in an annuity or other eligible form of investment.

Sale and leaseback arrangement. An arrangement arising when a firm sells land, buildings, or equipment that it already owns, and simultaneously enters into an agreement to lease the property back for a specified period under specific terms.

Sales budget. An operating plan for a period expressed in terms of sales volume and selling prices for each class of product or service. Preparation of a sales budget is the starting point in budgeting since sales volume influences nearly all other items.

Sales contract. A formal agreement to purchase a house, automobile, or other major item that states the offering price and all conditions—including repairs, inspections, closing date, and so on—required by buyer and seller. It is a contractually binding agreement.

Sales finance company. A company that purchases notes drawn up by sellers of certain types of merchandise, typically more expensive items such as automobiles, furniture, and appliances.

Sales forecasting. A projection or prediction of future sales. It is the foundation for the quantification of an entire business plan and master budget. Sales forecasts serve as a basis for planning. They are the basis for capacity planning; budgeting, production, and inventory planning; manpower planning; and purchasing planning.

Sales tax. The tax levied by many state governments on the purchase price of an item or service. Some states exempt items viewed as necessities, such as food and drugs.

Salvage value. The resale value (or scrap value) of an asset at the end of its useful life; also called residual value or disposal value.

Samurai bonds. Bonds issued by non-Japanese firms in the Japanese corporate bond market and denominated in Japanese yen. *See also* Shogun bonds.

Savings. Money that has been set aside, commonly in an interest-earning form, in order to achieve any of a number of savings or investment goals.

Savings accumulation plan. An arrangement under which an investor makes scheduled purchases of a given dollar amount of shares in a mutual fund.

Savings and loan association. A financial institution that channels the savings of its depositors primarily into mortgage and home improvement loans.

Savings ratio. Ratio of savings to income after taxes (disposable income).

Seasoned issue. When a firm returns to the market after an initial public offering for another issue of equity.

Secondary distribution. The resale of a block of stock from a major owner or owners, rather than from the company itself; also known as a secondary offering. It is generally sold through an underwriting company or syndicate at a fixed price close to the stock market's valuation of the shares, but without sales commission or odd-lot differential.

Secondary market. Market in which old securities are sold and bought. Equivalent to a used car market.

Second mortgage. Mortgage taken out after a first mortgage.

Sector (mutual) fund. A mutual fund that invests in one or two fields or industries (sectors); also known as a specialized fund. These funds are risky in that they rise and fall depending on how the individual fields or industries do. An example is Prudential Utility Fund.

Secured (and unsecured) loans. If collateral is named for a loan, the loan is secured; if none is given, it is unsecured.

Secured bond. A bond for which the issuer has provided collateral to the lender.

Secured (collateralized) credit cards. A type of credit card that's secured with some form of collateral, such as a bank CD; with these cards, the amount of credit given depends on how much collateral the cardholder can put up.

Secured credit. Sources of credit that require security in the form of pledged assets. In the event a borrower defaults in payment of principal or interest, the lender can seize the pledged assets and sell them to settle the debt.

Securities. Obligations of issuers that provide purchasers with an expected or stated return on the amount they invested. The two basic types of securities are stocks and bonds.

Securities and Exchange Commission (SEC). The federal agency created by the Securities Exchange Act of 1934 to enforce federal securities laws. This agency regulates the disclosure of information about the securities exchanges and markets in general to help protect investors.

Securities exchanges. Marketplaces—either organized or over-the-counter—in which buyers and sellers of securities can be brought together to make transactions.

Securities Investor Protection Corporation (SIPC). An agency of the federal government that insures brokerage customers' accounts.

Securities market indexes. Indexes that measure the value of a number of securities chosen as a sample to reflect the behavior of the general market of investments.

Securities markets. The marketplace in which stocks, bonds, and other financial instruments are traded.

Security agreement (security interest). A legal agreement that gives the installment lender control over the item being purchased.

Security market line (SML). A straight line that relates the expected returns on risky investments to their corresponding risk measured by the beta coefficient. *See also* Capital asset pricing model (CAPM).

Segmental reporting. The presentation of financial information (such as profitability) by a business segment, including the product, major customer, division, and department.

Segment margin. Contribution margin less direct (traceable) fixed costs.

Self-Employment Individuals Tax Retirement Act (1962). The HR-10 or Keogh Act that gives self-employed persons the right to establish retirement plans for themselves and their employees, providing them the same tax advantages available to corporate employees covered by qualified pension plans.

Self-employment tax. A tax that must be paid to the federal government by self-employed persons. The proceeds of this tax are used to provide self-employed persons with the same benefits regularly employed persons receive through the FICA tax.

Self-liquidating loans. Short-term bank loans to firms that need to finance the seasonal buildup in their working capital investment, and that bankers expect the firm to repay with the cash that will be released by the subsequent reduction in working capital.

Self-sustainable growth rate (SGR). The fastest growth rate a firm can achieve by retaining a constant percentage of its profit, keeping both its operating and financing policies unchanged, and not issuing new equity. It is equal to the profit retention rate multiplied by return on equity; also called sustainable growth rate.

Selling against the box. A short sale undertaken to protect a profit in a stock and to defer tax liability to another year. For example, when an investor owns 100 shares of ABC Company, a stock whose price has gone up, but seems likely to decline, the investor sells the 100 shares "short" and keeps them. If ABC Company stock declines, the profit on the short sale is exactly offset by the loss in the market value of the stock that is owned. If ABC Company stock advances, the loss on the short sale is offset by the gain in the market value of the stock that is retained.

Selling concession. A fee received by a selling group for its efforts to sell the securities allocated to them by the underwriter of an issue.

Selling group. A collection of securities dealers that participates in the distribution of new issues to final investors. A selling group agreement links these dealers to the underwriting syndicate.

Sell-off. The sale of a subsidiary, division, or product line by one company to another.

Sell order. An order to sell a specified number of shares of a given security.

Senior bond/debt/loan. A bond/debt/loan that has a claim on a firm's assets (in the event of liquidation) that precedes the claim of junior or subordinated debt.

Senior debts. Debts or bonds to which debentures are subordinated; these debts have a senior claim on both the income and assets of the issuer.

Series EE bond. A savings bond issued in various denominations by the U.S. Treasury.

Settlement date (currency trading). The date on which the delivery of the currencies takes place.

Settlement options. The various ways in which the death proceeds of a life insurance policy may be paid, such as interest only, payments for a stated period, payments of a stated amount, or income for life.

Settlement price (for currency futures contracts). The quote of the last trade of the day for a currency futures that is marked-to-market.

Share buy-back program. The buying by a firm of its own shares for the purpose of reducing the number of shares outstanding; also called share repurchase program. The opposite of a new issue of shares.

Shared-appreciation mortgage. A mortgage on which the rate of interest is set lower than market in exchange for giving the lender a partial—about one-third interest—in any gain in the property's value.

Share draft account. Checking account offered by credit unions. They are similar to a negotiable order of withdrawal (NOW) account offered by other financial institutions.

Share repurchase program. *See* Share buy-back program.

Shareware. Computer programs that authors have provided for others to use on a trial basis. If "adopted," users are requested to register or pay a fee. This usually includes technical support. Information about shareware programs may be obtained from various sites on the Internet.

Shark repellents. Any of a variety of legalistic means used by a firm under attack to counteract a tender offer.

Shogun bonds. Bonds issued by non-Japanese firms in the Japanese corporate bond market and denominated in any currency other than yen. *See also* Samurai bonds.

Short. (1) A transaction in which an investor sells borrowed stock, hoping to buy it back at a lower price. (2) In options, an investor who has written options has a short position in them.

Short covering. Buying stock to return stock previously borrowed to make delivery on a short sale.

Short position. (1) Stock sold short and not covered as of a particular date. On the New York Stock Exchange, a tabulation is issued a few days after the middle of the month listing all issues on the Exchange in which there was a short position of 5,000 or more shares, and issues in which the short position had changed by 2,000 or more shares in the preceding month. This tabulation is based on reports of positions on member firms' books. (2) Short position also means the total amount of stock an individual has sold short and has not covered, as of a particular date. Initial margin requirements for a short position are the same as for a long position.

Short-run financial goals. Goals set for one or two years only.

Short sale. When an investor sells a stock he or she does not own in the belief that it can be bought later at a lower price.

Short-term capital gain. The gain from the sale of a capital asset owned for one year or less at a higher price than its original cost. The gain is taxed as ordinary income.

Sickness policies. Insurance policies that cover a named disease such as cancer.

Signaling effects. Market reactions to a firm's actions, such as a drop in the firm's share price when the firm skips a dividend payment—an action interpreted by the market as a signal of weakening corporate cash flow.

Signature card. A card kept on file in a financial institution and used to confirm the validity of signatures on checks drawn on an account. Each card contains an accountholder's account number, name, address, phone number, and signature.

Simple interest method. The method by which interest is charged only on the actual loan balance outstanding.

Simple rate of return. *See* Accounting rate of return.

Simplified employee pension (SEP). An account that can be used to either supplement or replace an employee's self-selected and controlled IRA. Through employer participation, this plan can substantially increase the amount that can be credited each year to an IRA.

Simulation models. "What-if" models that attempt to simulate the effects of alternative management policies and assumptions about a firm's external environment. They are basically a tool for management's laboratory.

Single-limit automobile liability. An automobile liability policy that specifies the maximum amount paid per accident as a single lump sum rather than in terms of separate per-individual and per-accident limits for bodily injury and property damage.

Single-payment loan. A loan made for a specified period of time at the end of which full payment is due.

Single-premium annuity contract. Annuity purchased with a lump-sum payment, often just prior to retirement.

Single-premium whole life. A whole life insurance policy that is purchased on a cash basis by making a single premium payment.

Sinking fund. A required annual payment that allows for the periodic retirement of debt.

Sinking fund provision. Requires that a bond issuing firm set aside cash in a special account according to a regular schedule in order to allow the firm to redeem the bond at maturity.

Socially responsible fund. A type of mutual fund that puts social concerns on the same level of importance as financial returns, investing only in companies that meet certain moral, ethical, and/or environmental tests.

Social Security survivor's benefits. Benefits included in the social insurance provision of the social security system that are intended to provide basic support for families who have lost their principal wage earners.

Sole proprietorship. A business owned by one person and operated on his or her own behalf. Its income is taxed as personal income, and the owner's liability is unlimited.

Solvency. A firm's ability to meet its long-term cash obligations.

Solvency ratio. Ratio of net worth (assets minus liabilities) divided by total assets.

Spec home. New homes constructed by builders on speculation that a buyer will be found. They vary in price, size, and other features and can be found in various stages of construction.

Special endorsement. Check endorsement that includes a notation indicating specifically to whom the check is to be paid.

Specialist. A stock exchange member who undertakes to keep an orderly market in a specified stock by buying or selling on his or her own account when bids and offers by the public are not matched well enough to maintain an orderly market. He or she is a broker's broker in that specific stock, receiving commissions for executing other brokers' orders.

Special savings account. A savings account that offers slightly higher interest rates than a passbook account, but in exchange, the saver is required to maintain a specified minimum balance and/or to maintain that balance for a specified period of time. Certificates of deposit are an example.

Specialty fund. A common stock fund that invests in the shares of firms within a specific industry.

Speculation. The employment of funds by a speculator. The safety of principal is a secondary factor.

Speculative (day) traders. Traders who purchase stocks with the intention of gaining from their day-to-day fluctuations in price.

Speculative stock. Risky stocks that are purchased in the hope that their price per share will increase.

Speculator. One who is willing to assume a relatively large risk in the hope of significant gain. Such an investor's principal concern is to increase his or her capital rather than dividend income. The speculator may buy and sell the same day or speculate in an enterprise that he or she does not expect to be profitable for years. An example is investing in a penny stock.

Spiders (SPDRs). A slang term for the Standard & Poor's Depository Receipts (SPDRs) It is an exchange-traded fund (ETF) that represents ownership of the S&P 500 Index. Its stock ticker is SPY.

Spin-off. The separation of a subsidiary from its parent, with no change in the equity ownership. The management of the parent company gives up operating control over the subsidiary, but the shareholders maintain their same percentage ownership in both firms. New shares representing ownership in the averted company are issued to the original shareholders on a pro-rata basis.

Split. The division of the outstanding shares of a corporation into a larger number of shares. A 3-for-1 split by a company with 1 million shares outstanding would result in 3 million shares outstanding. Each holder of 100 shares before the 3-for-1 split would have 300 shares, although his or her proportionate equity in the company would remain the same, since 100 parts of 1 million are the equivalent of 300 parts of 3 million. Ordinarily splits must be voted by directors and approved by shareholders.

Split-funded pension plan. Qualified pension plan in which both a trust fund and an insurance contract are used to fund the plan.

Spontaneous financing. A trade credit and other accounts payable that arise "spontaneously" in a firm's day-to-day operations.

Spot rate. The rate at which a spot transaction is executed.

Spot transaction. A transaction made immediately in the market place at the market price.

Spread (in currency). The difference between the ask price and the bid price of a currency.

Spread (in underwriting). The difference between the price at which an issue is sold to the public and the price paid by the underwriter to the issuing firm.

Spread order. A type of order for the simultaneous purchase and sale of two options of the same type (calls or puts) on the same underlying stock. If placed with a "limit," the two options must be traded for a specified price difference or better.

Stand-alone value. Estimated value of a takeover target firm before the acquiring firm factors in any performance improvements; also called as-is value.

Standard. A quantitative expression of a performance objective, such as standard hours of labor allowed for actual production, or a standard purchase price of materials per unit. Sometimes the terms standard and budget are used interchangeably.

Standard & Poor's Corporation (S&P). The publisher of a variety of financial and investment reports and services, including *Corporation Records, Stock Guide,* and *Bond Guide.*

Standard & Poor's 500 Index (S&P 500). The 500-stock composite index calculated by Standard & Poor's. It differs from the Dow Jones Industrial Average (DJIA) in several important ways. First, it is a value-weighted, rather than price-weighted, index. This means that the index considers not only the price of a stock but also the number of shares outstanding. That is to say, it is based on the aggregate market value of the stock, i.e., price times number of shares. An advantage of the index over the DJIA is that stock splits and stock dividends do not affect the index value. A disadvantage is that large capitalization stocks—those with a large number of shares outstanding—heavily influence the index value.

Standard & Poor's (S&P) indexes. Indexes compiled by Standard & Poor's Corporation; similar to the Dow Jones Industrial Average (DJIA), but they employ different computational methods and consist of far more stocks.

Standard costs. Production or operating costs that are carefully predetermined. A standard cost is a target cost that should be attained.

Standard cost system. A system by which production activities are recorded at standard costs, and variances from actual costs are isolated.

Standby agreement. An agreement between a firm and an underwriting syndicate of investment banks such that the syndicate agrees to buy any shares that have not been sold during the period a rights offering is outstanding.

Standby fee. Fee received by investment banks for underwriting the unsold portion of a rights issue.

Stated value. An arbitrary fixed value attached to each share of common stock when it is issued.

Statement of cash flows. A financial statement, such as FASB Standard 95, that provides information about the cash transactions between a firm and the outside world by separating the transactions into cash flows related to operating, investing, and financing activities. *See* Cash flow statement.

State taxes. Taxes levied by state governments to finance their operating costs. Sources include sales tax, income tax, property tax, and licensing fees.

Static (fixed) budget. A budget based on one level of activity (e.g., one particular volume of sales or production).

Step-up trust. A type of living trust in which the trustee steps up to take the grantor's place in decision making and day-to-day management.

Stock average (or index). An average or index of a group of stocks that is believed to reflect the behavior of a given industry or the entire securities market. These averages are used to gauge the behavior of the securities market.

Stockbroker. Sometimes called an "account executive." A stockbroker purchases and sells securities on behalf of clients, to whom he or she provides advice and information.

Stock company. An insurance company that is owned by stockholders.

Stock dividend. A dividend paid in stock rather than cash. The dividend may be additional shares of the issuing company, or shares of another company (usually a subsidiary) held by the company.

Stockholder of record. A stockholder whose name is registered on the books of the issuing corporation.

Stockholders' report. A report that includes a variety of financial and descriptive information about a firm's operations during the year. Sometimes called an annual report.

Stock index futures. Futures contracts written on broad-based measures of stock market performance such as the S&P 500 Index.

Stock index option. A put or call option written on a specific market index such as the S&P 500 Index.

Stock purchase option (plans). An option given to employees of a corporation that allows them to purchase a specified number of shares of its stock at a price set above the prevailing market price when the option is granted.

Stock repurchases. The repurchase of common stock by the issuing firm for any of a variety of reasons resulting in a reduction of shares outstanding.

Stock split. A division of shares into a larger number. For example, a 2-for-1 split means two new shares are exchanged for each old share and the price is halved after the split.

Stop-loss order. An order an investor gives his or her broker to sell a security if the security's market price reaches a certain level lower than its current price.

Stop-loss provision. A cap in a major medical insurance policy that limits the insured's payment under the participation, or coinsurance, clause to a specified amount, such as $10,000.

Stop order. An order for the purchase or sale of stock or options that is placed away from the current market price; it becomes a market order if the stock or option trades at the price specified.

Stop payment. An order to the bank not to make payment on a check that has been written.

Store charges. A type of open credit account that is offered by various types of retail merchants.

Straight bankruptcy. A legal proceeding that results in "wiping the slate clean and starting anew."

Straight-line depreciation method. Depreciation method according to which a firm's tangible fixed assets are depreciated by an equal amount each year. *See* Accelerated depreciation method.

Straight term (in insurance). A term insurance policy that is written for a given number of years. Coverage remains unchanged throughout the period of the policy.

Strategic planning decisions. The implementation of an organization's objectives. Strategic planning decisions will have long-term impacts on the organization while operational decisions are day-to-day in nature.

Strategy (in options). An option strategy is one of the various kinds of option investments, i.e., long call, covered write, bull spread, etc.

Street. The New York financial community concentrated in the Wall Street area.

Street name. Securities held in the name of a broker instead of the customer's name are said to be carried in street name. This occurs when the securities have been bought on margin or when the customer wishes the securities to be held by the broker.

Stretching on trade credit. Failing to pay within a prescribed credit period; for example, under credit terms of 2/10, net 30, a firm would be stretching its trade credit if it failed to pay by the 30th day and paid on the 60th day.

Striking price. The price at which an option (call or put) can be exercised; normally that is at a price set close to the market price of the stock at the time the option is issued.

Stripped Treasuries. Zero-coupon bonds sold by the U.S. Treasury and created by stripping the coupons from a Treasury bond and selling them separately from the principal.

Subordinated debenture. An unsecured bond that carries only a secondary claim (on both income and assets) to that of other bondholders or lenders.

Subscription price. The price for which a security may be purchased in a rights offering.

Suicide clause. A life insurance clause that voids the contract if an insured commits suicide within a specified period of time after its inception.

Super NOW account. A negotiable order of withdrawal (NOW) account issued by financial institutions that may pay interest without restrictions and offer unlimited check-writing privileges. Minimum balances are required.

Supplementary medical insurance (SMI). A voluntary program under Medicare (commonly called Part B) that provides payments for extra services, such as physicians' and surgeons' services, home health service, and X-ray and laboratory services. Participants are required to pay premiums.

Surgical expense insurance. Health insurance coverage for the cost of surgery.

Survivorship benefit (on an annuity). That portion of the premiums and interest that has not been returned to the annuitant prior to his or her death.

Survivorship life insurance. A life insurance policy that covers two persons, but it only pays when the second one dies. Also known as "last-to-die" insurance.

Sustainable growth rate. *See* Self-sustainable growth rate (SGR).

Sweep account. A bank account in which excess funds are automatically transferred into an interest-earning account at the same bank.

Switching. Selling one security and buying another.

Syndicate. A group of investment bankers who together underwrite and distribute a new issue of securities or a large block of an outstanding issue.

Syndicate (real estate). A limited partnership that invests in various types of real estate and is professionally managed. There are various types of real estate syndicates—such as single property and blind pool—involved in specific kinds of real estate acquisitions.

Systematic risk. Risk that remains despite having risk-reduction through diversification. Measured with the beta (coefficient); also called market risk, nondiversifiable risk, or undiversifiable risk. *See also* Capital asset pricing model (CAPM).

Systematic withdrawal plan. A plan that allows a mutual fund shareholder to be paid specified amounts each period.

Take-home pay. The actual earnings an employee takes home after his or her employer has made all required, as well as requested, deductions.

Takeover. A transaction involving one firm that wants to acquire all or a portion of another.

Takeover premium. The difference between the acquisition price paid by a bidder for a target firm and the target firm's current market value.

Take-up fee. A discount on the price of shares offered to investment bankers engaged in a standby agreement.

Tangible assets (tangible property). Tangible items of real and personal property that generally have a long life, such as housing and other real estate, automobiles, jewelry, and other physical assets.

Target balance. The average collected balance to be maintained at a bank to compensate it for services provided to a small business.

Target capital structure. The debt-to-equity ratio that maximizes the market value of a firm's assets .

Target debt ratio. The desired proportion of long-term debt in a firm's capital structure. Alternatively, it may be the desired proportion of total debt in a firm's financial structure.

Target firm. A firm whose shares a bidder is trying to acquire in a takeover.

Taxable gift. Money or property that is subject to a gift tax.

Taxable income. The amount of income that is subject to taxes. It is calculated by subtracting itemized deductions and exemptions from adjusted gross income.

Tax audit. An examination by the IRS to validate the accuracy of a given tax return.

Tax avoidance. A legal stategy of minimizing tax payments that accurately reports a taxpayer's items of income and expenditure while using legitimate deductions.

Tax credits. A deduction, such as the child care credit, from a taxpayer's tax liability.

Tax-deferred income. Income that is not subject to taxes immediately, but will be subject to taxes at a later date.

Tax-deferred annuity. An annuity that is exempted from current income taxes.

Tax equivalent yield. The yield on a tax-free municipal bond needs to be looked at on an equivalent before-tax basis, because the interest received is not subject to federal income taxes.

Tax evasion. The failure to accurately report income, expenditures, and tax liabilities; the failure to pay taxes. Persons found guilty of this illegal act are subject to severe financial penalties and prison terms.

Tax-exempt bond. A bond that pays no federal taxes because it is issued by a state or subordinate division of a state.

Tax-exempt income. Certain types of income, such as child support payments and disability payments, that do not have to be claimed as part of a taxpayer's gross income for tax purposes.

Tax-exempt money fund. A money market mutual fund that limits its investments to tax-exempt municipal securities with short maturities.

Tax-exempt securities. Bonds paying interest that is exempt from federal, and in many cases, state income taxes. These securities are issued by various state and local governments and are often called municipal bonds.

Tax liability. The actual amount of taxes owed.

Tax preparation services. Professionals trained in the preparation of taxes, including those employed in national and local firms as well as attorneys with tax training, and CPAs.

Tax refund. The amount of money due an individual taxpayer from the IRS when their withholding and/or estimated tax payments exceeds their actual tax liability.

Tax shelter. Certain types of investments that provide tax write-offs (deductions). Tax shelters often involve real estate and oil-related investments.

Tax-sheltered college education fund. A fund in which money can be accumulated tax free and used to pay the future college education expenses of a child.

Tax write-off (in accounting). Using depreciation, amortization, and depletion to lower tax liability.

Technical analysis. The belief that security prices are solely the result of the forces of supply and demand.

Technical insolvency. A situation in which a firm can no longer honor its financial obligations. Although its assets may exceed its total liabilities, thereby indicating a positive net worth, the company simply does not have sufficient liquidity to pay its debts.

Technically bankrupt. A firm that is no longer able to pay its creditors.

Technical position. The internal factors affecting the market, as opposed to fundamental forces such as prosperity or recession.

Temporary financing. Financing (other than by spontaneous sources) that will be repaid within a period of one year or less. Included among these sources of short-term debt are secured and unsecured bank loans, commercial paper, loans secured by accounts receivable, and loans secured by inventories.

Temporary investments. A strategy of using a seasonal excess of cash to invest in marketable securities that the company intends to convert back into cash within one year. The investments produce dividend and/or interest income as well as possible capital appreciation for the company.

Temporary life annuity. An annuity in which benefits continue for the specified period only if the annuitant survives.

Tenancy by the entirety. A form of ownership by husband and wife, recognized in certain states, in which the rights of the deceased spouse automatically pass to the survivor.

Tenancy in common. A title to property under which each tenant who owns an interest is free to dispose of that interest without the consent of the other tenants.

Tender offer. A bid by an interested party, usually a corporation, for the controlling interest in another corporation.

Terminal cash flow. Cash flow that occurs in the last year of a project.

Terminal warehouse agreement. A security agreement in which the inventories pledged as collateral are transported to a public warehouse that is physically removed from the borrower's premises. This is the safest (and a costly) form of financing-secured-by-inventory.

Term life insurance. Insurance that covers the insured only for a specified period and does not provide for the accumulation of any cash values.

Term loan. An immediate- to long-term secured loan granted to a business by a commercial bank, insurance company, or commercial finance company, usually to finance capital equipment or provide working capital. The loan is amortized over a fixed period.

Term structure of interest rates. The relationship between interest rates and the term to maturity when the risk of default is held constant.

Testamentary trust. Trust created in a will.

Testator. A person whose will directs the disposition of property at his or her death.

Thin market. The market for a stock is thin when buying or selling a few shares can affect its price disproportionately in either direction.

Third market. Trading in the over-the-counter market of securities listed on an exchange.

30-day charge account. A charge account that requires a customer to pay the full amount billed within 30 days after the billing.

Thrift and savings plan. A plan established by employers to supplement pension and other insurance fringe benefits. The employer generally makes contributions to a savings plan in the same amount contributed by the employee.

Ticker. The instrument that prints prices and volume of security transactions in cities and towns throughout the U.S. within minutes after each trade on the floor.

Ticker symbol. Letters used in a ticker that identify a company for trading purposes.

Tight money. A situation in which fewer funds are made available to borrowers by lending institutions and creditors. If available, the loans carry higher interest rates.

Time deposit. A savings account at a financial institution that earns interest but is not legally subject to withdrawal on demand or transfer by check. The depositor can withdraw only by giving notice.

Time-sharing. A real estate arrangement under which buyers purchase rights to a resort condominium or hotel unit for a specified time each year; also called interval ownership.

Times-interest-earned ratio. Earnings before interest and taxes (EBIT) divided by interest expense. A ratio that measures a firm's ability to meet its interest payments from its annual operating earnings.

Time value (in options). The amount that the premium of an option exceeds its intrinsic value. It reflects the statistical possibility that the option premium will increase in value rather than finishing at zero dollars. If an option is out-of-the-money then its entire premium consists of time value.

Time value of money. The value of money at different time periods. As a rule, one dollar today is worth more than one dollar tomorrow. The time value of money is a critical consideration in financial decisions.

Tips. Supposedly "inside" information on corporation affairs.

Title check. Research of legal documents and records—usually performed by an attorney or title insurance company—to verify ownership and interest in a title to real estate.

Total leverage. A measure of total risk, referring to how earnings per share is affected by a change in sales. It equals the percentage change in earnings per share divided by the percentage change in sales. Total leverage at a given level of sales is the operating leverage multiplied by the financial leverage.

Total return. The return received on a security investment over a specified period of time. It is made up of two basic components—the dividend (or interest) yield and capital gains.

Tracking stock. A stock created by a company to track the performance of one of its divisions—typically one that is in a line of business that is fast-growing and commands a higher industry price-to-earnings ratio than the parent's main business.

Trade credit. A credit made available by a firm's suppliers in conjunction with the acquisition of materials. A trade credit appears on the balance sheet as accounts payable.

Trade-off model of capital structure. An optimal capital structure reached by means of a trade-off between the present value of the interest tax shield and the present value of financial distress costs.

Trader. (1) One who buys and sells for his or her own account for short-term profit. (2) Brokerage firm employees who buy and sell in the over-the-counter market.

Trading post. Trading locations at which stocks assigned to that location are bought and sold on the exchange floor.

Transaction loan. A one-time loan used to finance a specific, nonrecurrent need.

Transfer price. The price charged between divisions for an internal transfer of an assembled product or service.

Transit float. Funds are tied up during the time it takes for a deposited check to clear through the commercial banking system and become usable funds to the company.

Translation exposure. *See* Accounting exposure.

Transparency. Providing complete information about a firm's operations and future prospects to its (outside) shareholders.

Travel and entertainment (T&E) card. Credit cards, such as American Express, Diners Club, and Carte Blanche, that enable a cardholder to charge purchases at a variety of locations. The holder is charged an annual fee to use the card.

Traveler's check. A check that can be purchased at commercial banks and other financial institutions in denominations ranging from $10 to $1,000. When properly endorsed, they are accepted by most U.S. businesses and can be exchanged for local currencies in most parts of the world.

Treasury bill (T-bill). Short-term obligation of the federal government commonly called T-bill. Treasury bills carry no coupon but are sold on a discount basis. Denominations range from $10,000 to $1 million. The yields on T-bills are lower than those on other marketable securities due to their virtually risk-free nature.

Treasury bond. A federal government obligation, ordinarily payable to the bearer, that is issued at par. The maturity is for more than five years, and interest is payable semiannually.

Treasury inflation-indexed securities (TIPS). A type of Treasury bond that provides protection against inflation by adjusting investor returns for the annual rate of inflation.

Treasury note. An obligation of the federal government, usually issued payable to the bearer, with a fixed maturity of not less than one year or more than seven years. A note is issued at par, and a specified interest return is paid semiannually.

Treasury stock. Stock that was issued by a company but later reacquired. It may be held in the company's treasury indefinitely, reissued to the public, or retired. Treasury stock receives no dividends and has no vote while held by the company.

Treasury valuation method. *See* Excess earnings valuation method.

Triple witching days. *See* Program trading.

Trust. A relationship created when one party (the grantor) transfers property to a second party (the trustee) for the benefit of a third party (the beneficiary).

Trustee. (1) Someone appointed to enforce the indenture and protect the interest of a bondholder. (2) In the case of estate planning, a person or corporation that manages a grantor's property for the benefit of his or her beneficiaries.

Trust fund pension plan. A pension plan in which an employer places its contributions with a trustee, who is then responsible for the investment of contributions and the payments of benefits.

Truth in Lending Act. A wide-ranging law designed to protect credit purchasers. The most important provision is that both the dollar amount of finance charges and the annual percentage rate (APR) charged must be disclosed prior to extending credit. It was formally called the Consumer Credit Protection Act (1969).

Turnover. The volume of business in a security or the entire market. If turnover on the New York Stock Exchange is reported at 3 million shares on a particular day, 3 million shares changed hands. Odd-lot turnover is tabulated separately and ordinarily is not included in reported volume.

12b-1 fee. A type of fee that is charged annually and that is supposed to be used to offset the promotion and selling expenses of a mutual fund; known as a hidden load because it's often used by funds as an indirect way of charging commissions.

Umbrella personal liability policy. A policy that provides excess liability coverage for both homeowner's and automobile insurance, as well as coverage in some areas not provided for in either of these policies.

Unadjusted rate of return. *See* Accounting rate of return.

Unbundling. An approach in which a business only pays for the bank services actually used.

Uncovered. An uncovered option strategy is an investment in which the written options are not matched with a long stock position or with a long option position expiring no earlier than the written options. The loss potential with such a strategy is thereby unlimited.

Underlying stock. This is the stock specified in an option contract that is transferred upon exercise of the option contract.

Undervaluation hypothesis. A takeover rationale according to which the acquiring company has superior skills in finding undervalued target firms that can be bought cheaply.

Underwriter (in banking). An investment bank that buys the securities a firm wants to issue and then resells them to the public at a higher price.

Underwriting. (1) The purchase and subsequent resale of a new security issue. The risk of selling the new issue at a satisfactory (profitable) price is assumed by the investment banker. (2) The process of deciding who can be insured and determining the applicable rates.

Underwriting syndicate. A group of underwriting firms (that is, investment banking firms) that accepts the responsibility for selling a new security issue.

Undiversifiable risk. The portion of the variation in investment returns that cannot be eliminated through investor diversification.

Unfunded pension plan. A pension plan that allows an employer to make payments to retirees from current income.

Unified rate schedule. The graduated table of rates used for bothfederal gift and estate tax purposes; these rates are applied to all taxable gifts.

Unified tax credit. The credit that can be applied against the tentative gift or estate tax.

Uninsured motorist coverage. Insurance designed to meet the needs of innocent accident victims when involved in an accident in which an uninsured or underinsured motorist is at fault.

Unit investment trust. A closed-end investment company in which the proceeds from the sale of original shares are invested in a fixed portfolio of taxable or tax-exempt bonds and held until maturity. Like a mutual fund, a unit investment trust offers to small investors the advantages of a large, professionally selected and diversified portfolio. Unlike a mutual fund, however, its portfolio is fixed; once structured, it is not actively managed.

Universal life insurance. A type of insurance contract that combines term insurance (death benefits) with a tax-deferred savings/investment account that pays competitive money market interest rates.

Unlevered asset value. The estimated value of assets assuming they are financed only with equity capital. *See* Adjusted present value (APV).

Unlevered beta. *See* Asset beta.

Unlevered cost of equity. The cost of equity of an all equity financed firm. It can be estimated with the capital asset pricing model using the firm's asset beta.

Unlevered firm. A firm without borrowed funds, or an all equity financed firm.

Unlimited liability. Liability that can extend beyond the amount of money an investor has put into a business (for example, the liability of owners of a sole proprietorship or partnership).

Unlisted securities. Securities that are not traded on an organized security exchange.

Unsecured loan. A loan on which no collateral is required.

Unsecured personal credit line. A line of credit that is made available to an individual on an as-needed basis through check-writing privileges.

Unsystematic risk. The portion of the variation in investment returns that can be eliminated through investor diversification. These variations result from factors that are unique to a particular firm.

Uptick. A term used to designate a price higher than the preceding transaction in the stock. Also called a "plus" tick. A stock may be sold short only on an uptick, or on a "zero-plus" tick. A "zero-plus" tick is a term used for a transaction at the same price as the preceding trade but higher than the preceding different price. Conversely, a downtick, or "minus" tick, is a term used to designate a transaction made at a price lower that the preceding trade. A "zero-minus" tick is a transaction made at the same price as the preceding sale but lower that the preceding different price. A plus sign, or a minus sign, is displayed throughout the day next to the last price of each company's stock traded at each trading post on the floor of the New York Stock Exchange. *See also* Short sale.

U.S. savings bond. Bond issued in various denominations and maturities by the U.S. Treasury to assist in financing federal government operations.

Usury laws. State laws that prohibit the charging of interest above a certain limit.

Utility. The amount of satisfaction a person receives from purchasing certain types or quantities of goods and services.

VA loan guarantee. The guarantee of a mortgage loan by the U.S. Veterans Administration to lenders who make qualified mortgage loans to eligible veterans.

Valuation. The act or process of assigning a value to something; also called appraisal.

Valuation date. The date on which a property is valued, as distinguished from its report date.

Valued approach (in health insurance). The payment to an insured of amounts specified in a policy. Such payments may not necessarily bear a direct relationship to actual costs incurred.

Valued-based management. Managing a firm's resources with the goal of increasing the firm's market value.

Value Line Composite Average. A stock average, published by Value Line, that reflects the percentage changes in share price of some 1,700 stocks traded on the NYSE, AMEX, and OTC markets.

Value Line Investment Survey. A weekly subscription service covering some 1,700 of the most widely held stocks.

Variable annuity. An annuity in which the monthly income provided can be adjusted according to the actual investment experience of the insurer.

Variable life insurance. Insurance in which the benefits payable to the insured are related to the value of the company's assets that support its payment obligation.

Variance. The difference of revenues, costs, and profit from the planned amounts. One of the most important phases of responsibility in accounting is establishing standards in costs, revenues, and profit, and establishing performance by comparing actual amounts with the standard amounts. The differences (variances) are calculated for each responsibility center, analyzed, and unfavorable variances are investigated for possible remedial action. *See also* Analysis of variances.

Venture capital. A financing source for new businesses or turnaround ventures that usually combines high risk with the potential for high return.

Venture capital firm. An investment firm specializing in the financing of small and new ventures.

Venture capitalists. Investors interested in supplying capital to particularly high-risk situations, such as start-ups or firms denied conventional financing.

Vertical merger. An example of a vertical merger would be the integration of a car manufacturer with its major supplier or its major distributor.

Vesting. The right of employees to benefits in a retirement plan based on their own and their employer's contributions.

Veterans Administration (VA). U.S. Department of Veterans Affairs provides many benefits to veterans including VA home loans.

Volatility. A measure of the amount by which a stock is expected to fluctuate in a given period of time. Stocks with greater volatility exhibit wider price swings and their options are higher in price than less volatile stocks.

Voluntary remedy. A voluntary reorganization that is acceptable to its creditors.

Voting right. A stockholder's right to vote his or her stock in the affairs of the company. Most common shares have one vote each. Preferred stock usually has the right to vote when preferred dividends are in default. The right to vote may be delegated by the stockholder to another person.

Wage earner plan. An arrangement that schedules debt repayment over future years. It is an alternative to straight bankruptcy when a person has a steady source of income and there is a reasonable chance of repayment within three to five years.

Waiting period. A provision of some disability income insurance policies that requires that the insured wait a specified length of time after the disability before payment begins.

Waiver of premium. A clause that provides for automatic payment of premiums should an insurance policyholder be unable through disability to make the payments.

Warrant. (1) An option to purchase a fixed number of shares of common stock at a predetermined price during a specified time period. (2) A paper giving its holder the right to buy a security at asset price, either within a specified period or perpetually. A warrant is generally offered with another security as an added inducement to buy.

Warranty. For automobiles and other products, a contract stating responsibilities for repair and maintenance of a vehicle or product; offered by manufacturers and dealers.

Weighted average cost of capital. A composite of the individual costs of financing incurred by each capital source. A firm's weighted average cost of capital is a function of (1) the individual costs of capital, (2) the capital structure mix, and (3) the level of financing necessary to make the investment.

What-if analysis. *See* Simulation models.

When distributed. A security trading in advance of the printing of the certificate.

When issued. A short form of "when, as, and if issued." The term indicates a conditional transaction in a security authorized for issuance but not as yet actually issued. All "when issued" transactions are on an "if" basis, to be settled if and when the actual security is issued and the National Association of Securities Dealers or an exchange rules the transactions are to be settled.

White knight. A defensive tactic to a tender offer whereby an able company comes to the rescue of the firm targeted for takeover.

Whole life insurance. Life insurance designed to offer financial protection for the entire life of the individual. Cash values are accumulated under this type of insurance.

Will. A written document that allows a person, called a testator, to determine the disposition of property at his or her death.

Wilshire 5000 Index. The measure of the total dollar value of 5,000 actively traded stocks, including all those traded on the NYSE, AMEX, and OTC markets.

Workers' compensation insurance. A type of insurance paid for by an employer and designed to compensate a worker for job-related injuries or illness.

Working capital. A concept traditionally defined as a firm's investment in current assets. Net working capital refers to the difference between current assets and current liabilities.

Working capital requirement (WCR). The difference between operating assets (trade receivables, inventories, and prepaid expenses) and operating liabilities (trade payables and accrued expenses). WCR measures the firm's net investment in its operating cycle.

Write. An investor who sells an option contract not currently held (selling the option short) is said to have written the option.

Writer (of options). In an option transaction, an individual who writes the options to be purchased or sold by the option buyer.

Yankee bonds. Bonds issued by foreign firms in the United States, and denominated in U.S. dollars.

Yield. The return on an investment.

Yield spread. The difference between the market yield on a nongovernment bond and the yield on a government bond with the same maturity and currency denomination.

Yield to maturity (YTM). The annual rate of return that a bondholder purchasing a bond today and holding it to maturity would receive on his or her investment.

Zero-base budgeting. A planning and budgeting tool that uses cost/benefit analysis of projects and functions to improve resource allocation in an organization. Traditional budgeting tends to concentrate on the incremental change from the previous year. It assumes that the previous year's activities and programs are essential and must be continued. Under zero-base budgeting, however, cost and benefit estimates are built up from scratch, from the zero level, and must be justified.

Zero bracket amount (ZBA). A specified amount of a taxpayer's income to which a zero tax rate applies. A taxpayer can use this blanket deduction instead of itemizing personal expenses.

Zero-coupon bond. A bond bought at a deep discount; also called original issue discount (OID) bond. The interest instead of being paid out directly is added to the principal semiannually. Both the principal and the accumulated interest are paid at maturity.

Zombies. Companies that continue to trade despite having no product or real business activity.

Zoning laws. Laws that govern permissible uses of property. They may also control factors such as building size and appearance and site placement.

Appendix B

Financial and Statistical Tables

Table 1	**Future Value of $1 = T_1 (i,n)**
Table 2	**Future Value of an Annuity of $1 = T_2 (i,n)**
Table 3	**Present Value of $1 = T_3 (i,n)**
Table 4	**Present Value of an Annuity of $1 = T_4 (i,n)**
Table 5	**Normal Distribution Table**

Table 1

Future Value of $1

(Compound Amount of $1) = T_1 (i, n)

Periods	4%	6%	8%	10%	12%	14%	20%
1	1.040	1.060	1.080	1.100	1.120	1.140	1.200
2	1.082	1.124	1.166	1.210	1.254	1.300	1.440
3	1.125	1.191	1.260	1.331	1.405	1.482	1.728
4	1.170	1.263	1.361	1.464	1.574	1.689	2.074
5	1.217	1.338	1.469	1.611	1.762	1.925	2.488
6	1.265	1.419	1.587	1.772	1.974	2.195	2.986
7	1.316	1.504	1.714	1.949	2.211	2.502	3.583
8	1.369	1.594	1.851	2.144	2.476	2.853	4.300
9	1.423	1.690	1.999	2.359	2.773	3.252	5.160
10	1.480	1.791	2.159	2.594	3.106	3.707	6.192
11	1.540	1.898	2.332	2.853	3.479	4.226	7.430
12	1.601	2.012	2.518	3.139	3.896	4.818	8.916
13	1.665	2.133	2.720	3.452	4.364	5.492	10.699
14	1.732	2.261	2.937	3.798	4.887	6.261	12.839
15	1.801	2.397	3.172	4.177	5.474	7.138	15.407
16	1.873	2.540	3.426	4.595	6.130	8.137	18.488
17	1.948	2.693	3.700	5.055	6.866	9.277	22.186
18	2.026	2.854	3.996	5.560	7.690	10.575	26.623
19	2.107	3.026	4.316	6.116	8.613	12.056	31.948
20	2.191	3.207	4.661	5.728	9.646	13.743	38.338
30	3.243	5.744	10.063	17.450	29.960	50.950	237.380
40	4.801	10.286	21.725	45.260	93.051	188.880	1469.800

Table 2

Future Value of an Annuity of $1

(Compound Amount of an Annuity of $1) = T_2 (i, n)

Periods	*4%*	*6%*	*8%*	*10%*	*12%*	*14%*	*20%*
1	1.000	1.000	1.000	1.000	1.000	1.000	1.000
2	2.040	2.060	2.080	2.100	2.120	2.140	2.200
3	3.122	3.184	3.246	3.310	3.374	3.440	3.640
4	4.247	4.375	4.506	4.641	4.779	4.921	5.368
5	5.416	5.637	5.867	6.105	6.353	6.610	7.442
6	6.633	6.975	7.336	7.716	8.115	8.536	9.930
7	7.898	8.394	8.923	9.487	10.089	10.730	12.916
8	9.214	9.898	10.637	11.436	12.300	13.233	16.499
9	10.583	11.491	12.488	13.580	14.776	16.085	20.799
10	12.006	13.181	14.487	15.938	17.549	19.337	25.959
11	13.486	14.972	16.646	18.531	20.655	23.045	32.150
12	15.026	16.870	18.977	21.385	24.133	37.271	39.580
13	16.627	18.882	21.495	24.523	28.029	32.089	48.497
14	18.292	21.015	24.215	27.976	32.393	37.581	59.196
15	20.024	23.276	27.152	31.773	37.280	43.842	72.035
16	21.825	25.673	30.324	35.950	42.753	50.980	87.442
17	23.698	28.213	33.750	40.546	48.884	59.118	105.930
18	25.645	30.906	37.450	45.600	55.750	68.394	128.120
19	27.671	33.760	41.446	51.160	63.440	78.969	154.740
20	29.778	36.778	45.762	57.276	75.052	91.025	186.690
30	56.085	79.058	113.283	164.496	241.330	356.790	1181.900
40	95.026	154.762	259.057	442.597	767.090	1342.000	7343.900

* Payments (or receipts) at the *end* of each period.

Table 3

Present Value of $1

(Present Value of $1) = T_3 (i, n)

Periods	4%	6%	8%	10%	12%	14%	16%	18%	20%	22%	24%	26%	28%	30%	40%
1	.962	.943	.926	.909	.893	.877	.862	.847	.833	.820	.806	.794	.781	.769	.714
2	.925	.890	.857	.826	.797	.769	.743	.718	.694	.672	.650	.630	.610	.592	.510
3	.889	.840	.794	.751	.712	.675	.641	.609	.579	.551	.524	.500	.477	.455	.364
4	.855	.792	.735	.683	.636	.592	.552	.516	.482	.451	.423	.397	.373	.350	.260
5	.822	.747	.681	.621	.567	.519	.476	.437	.402	.370	.341	.315	.291	.269	.186
6	.790	.705	.630	.564	.507	.456	.410	.370	.355	.303	.275	.250	.277	.207	.133
7	.760	.665	.583	.513	.452	.400	.354	.314	.279	.249	.222	.198	.178	.159	.095
8	.731	.627	.540	.467	.404	.351	.305	.266	.233	.204	.179	.157	.139	.123	.068
9	.703	.592	.500	.424	.361	.308	.263	.225	.194	.167	.144	.125	.108	.094	.048
10	.676	.558	.463	.386	.322	.270	.227	.191	.162	.137	.116	.099	.085	.073	.035
11	.650	.527	.429	.350	.287	.237	.195	.162	.135	.112	.094	.079	.066	.056	.025
12	.625	.497	.397	.319	.257	.208	.168	.137	.112	.092	.076	.062	.052	.043	.018
13	.601	.469	.368	.290	.229	.182	.145	.116	.093	.075	.061	.050	.040	.033	.013
14	.577	.442	.340	.263	.205	.160	.125	.099	.078	.062	.049	.039	.032	.025	.009
15	.555	.417	.315	.239	.183	.140	.108	.084	.065	.051	.040	.031	.025	.020	.006

16	.534	.394	.292	.218	.163	.123	.093	.071	.054	.042	.032	.025	.019	.015	.005
17	.513	.371	.270	.198	.146	.108	.080	.060	.045	.034	.026	.020	.015	.012	.003
18	.494	.350	.250	.180	.130	.095	.069	.051	.038	.028	.021	.016	.012	.009	.002
19	.475	.331	.232	.164	.116	.083	.060	.043	.031	.023	.017	.012	.009	.007	.002
20	.456	.312	.215	.149	.104	.073	.051	.037	.026	.019	.014	.010	.007	.005	.001
21	.439	.294	.199	.135	.093	.064	.044	.031	.022	.015	.011	.008	.006	.004	.001
22	.422	.278	.184	.123	.083	.056	.038	.026	.018	.013	.009	.006	.004	.003	.001
23	.406	.262	.170	.112	.074	.049	.033	.022	.015	.010	.007	.005	.003	.002	
24	.390	.247	.158	.102	.066	.043	.028	.019	.013	.008	.006	.004	.003	.002	
25	.375	.233	.146	.092	.059	.038	.024	.016	.010	.007	.005	.003	.002	.001	
26	.361	.220	.135	.084	.053	.033	.021	.014	.009	.006	.004	.002	.002	.001	
27	.347	.207	.125	.076	.047	.029	.018	.011	.007	.005	.003	.002	.001	.001	
28	.333	.196	.116	.069	.042	.026	.016	.010	.006	.004	.002	.002	.001	.001	
29	.321	.185	.107	.063	.037	.022	.014	.008	.005	.003	.002	.001	.001	.001	
30	.308	.174	.099	.057	.033	.020	.012	.007	.004	.003	.002	.001	.001		
40	.208	.097	.046	.022	.011	.005	.003	.001	.001						

Table 4

Present Value of an Annuity of $1

(Present Value of an Annuity of $1) = T_4 (i, n)

Periods	3%	4%	5%	6%	7%	8%	10%	12%	14%	16%	18%	20%	22%	24%
1	.9709	.9615	.9524	.9434	.9346	.9259	.9091	.8929	.8772	.8621	.8475	.8333	.8197	.8065
2	1.9135	1.8861	1.8594	1.8334	1.8080	1.7833	1.7355	1.6901	1.6467	1.6052	1.5656	1.5278	1.4915	1.4568
3	2.8286	2.7751	2.7232	2.6730	2.6243	2.5771	2.4869	2.4018	2.3216	2.2459	2.1743	2.1065	2.0422	1.9813
4	3.7171	3.6299	3.5460	3.4651	3.3872	3.3121	3.1699	3.0373	2.9137	2.7982	2.6901	2.5887	2.4936	2.4043
5	4.5797	4.4518	4.3295	4.2124	4.1002	3.9927	3.7908	3.6048	3.4331	3.2743	3.1272	2.9906	2.8636	2.7454
6	5.4172	5.2421	5.0757	4.9173	4.7665	4.6229	4.3553	4.1114	3.8887	3.6847	3.4976	3.3255	3.1669	3.0205
7	6.2303	6.0021	5.7864	5.5824	5.3893	5.2064	4.8684	4.5638	4.2883	4.0386	3.8115	3.6046	3.4155	3.2423
8	7.0197	6.7327	6.4632	6.2098	5.9713	5.7466	5.3349	4.9676	4.6389	4.3436	4.0776	3.8372	3.6193	3.4212
9	7.7861	7.4353	7.1078	6.8017	6.5152	6.2469	5.7590	5.3282	4.9464	4.6065	4.3030	4.0310	3.7863	3.5655
10	8.5302	8.1109	7.7217	7.3601	7.0236	6.7101	6.1446	5.6502	5.2161	4.8332	4.4941	4.1925	3.9232	3.6819
11	9.2526	8.7605	8.3064	7.8869	7.4987	7.1390	6.4951	5.9377	5.4527	5.0286	4.6560	4.3271	4.0354	3.7757
12	9.9540	9.3851	8.8633	8.3838	7.9427	7.5361	6.8137	6.1944	5.6603	5.1971	4.7932	4.4392	4.1274	3.8514
13	10.6350	9.9856	9.3936	8.8527	8.3577	7.9038	7.1034	6.4235	5.8424	5.3423	4.9095	4.5327	4.2028	3.9124
14	11.2961	10.5631	9.8986	9.2950	8.7455	8.2442	7.3667	6.6282	6.0021	5.4675	5.0081	4.6106	4.2646	3.9616
15	11.9379	11.1184	10.3797	9.7122	9.1079	8.5595	7.6061	6.8109	6.1422	5.5755	5.0916	4.6755	4.3152	4.0013

16	12.5611	11.6523	10.8378	10.1059	9.4466	8.8514	7.8237	6.9740	6.2651	5.6685	5.1624	4.7296	4.3567	4.0333
17	13.1661	12.1657	11.2741	10.4773	9.7632	9.1216	8.0216	7.1196	6.3729	5.7487	5.2223	4.7746	4.3908	4.0591
18	13.7535	12.6593	11.6896	10.8276	10.0591	9.3719	8.2014	7.2497	6.4674	5.8178	5.2732	4.8122	4.4187	4.0799
19	14.3238	13.1339	12.0853	11.1581	10.3356	9.6036	8.3649	7.3658	6.5504	5.8775	5.3162	4.8435	4.4415	4.0967
20	14.8775	13.5903	12.4622	11.4699	10.5940	9.8181	8.5136	7.4694	6.6231	5.9288	5.3527	4.8696	4.4603	4.1103
21	15.4150	14.0292	12.8212	11.7641	10.8355	10.0168	8.6487	7.5620	6.6870	5.9731	5.3837	4.8913	4.4756	4.1212
22	15.9369	14.4511	13.1630	12.0416	11.0612	10.2007	8.7715	7.6446	6.7429	6.0113	5.4099	4.9094	4.4882	4.1300
23	16.4436	14.8568	13.4886	12.3034	11.2722	10.3711	8.8832	7.7184	6.7921	6.0442	5.4321	4.9245	4.4985	4.1371
24	16.9355	15.2470	13.7986	12.5504	11.4693	10.5288	8.9847	7.7843	6.8351	6.0726	5.4509	4.9371	4.5070	4.1428
25	17.4131	15.6221	14.0939	12.7834	11.6536	10.6748	9.0770	7.8431	6.8729	6.0971	5.4669	4.9476	4.5139	4.1474
26	17.8768	15.9828	14.3752	13.0032	11.8258	10.8100	9.1609	7.8957	6.9061	6.1182	5.4804	4.9563	4.5196	4.1511
27	18.3270	16.3296	14.6430	13.2105	11.9867	10.9352	9.2372	7.9426	6.9352	6.1364	5.4919	4.9636	4.5243	4.1542
28	18.7641	16.6631	14.8981	13.4062	12.1371	11.0511	9.3066	7.9844	6.9607	6.1520	5.5016	4.9697	4.5281	4.1566
29	19.1885	16.9837	15.1411	13.5907	12.2777	11.1584	9.3696	8.0218	6.9830	6.1656	5.5098	4.9747	4.5312	4.1585
30	19.6004	17.2920	15.3725	13.7648	12.4090	11.2578	9.4269	8.0552	7.0027	6.1772	5.5168	4.9789	4.5338	4.1601
40	23.1148	19.7928	17.1591	15.0463	13.3317	11.9246	9.7791	8.2438	7.1050	6.2335	5.5482	4.9966	4.5439	4.1659

Table 5

Normal Distribution Table

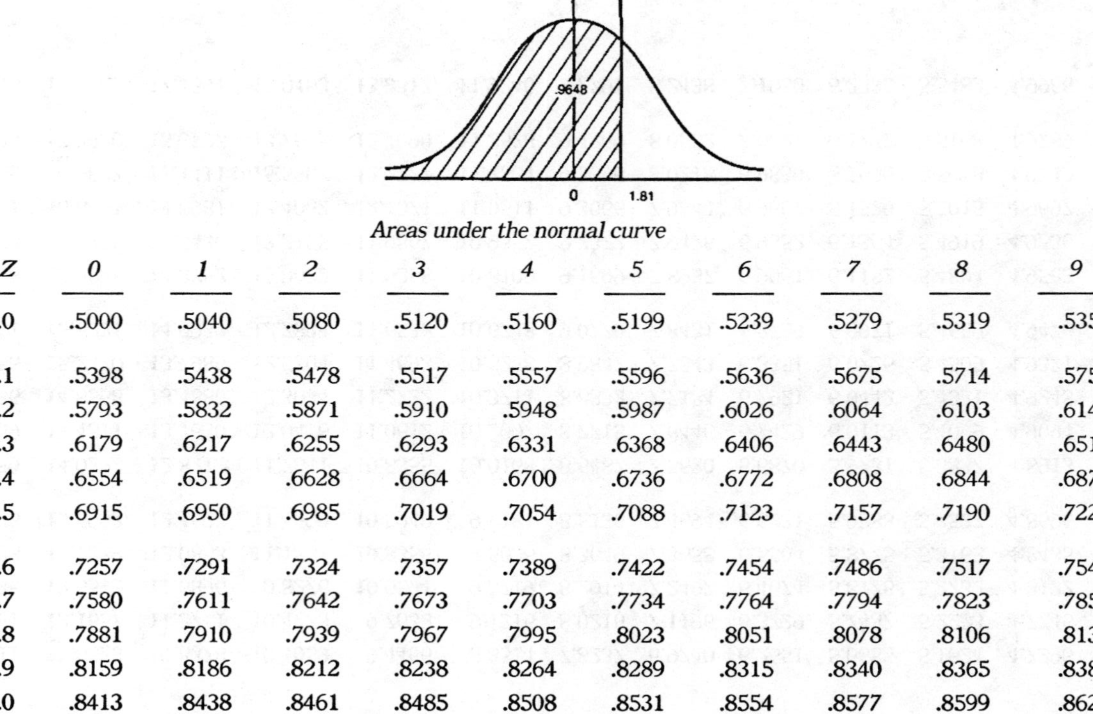

Areas under the normal curve

Z	0	1	2	3	4	5	6	7	8	9
.0	.5000	.5040	.5080	.5120	.5160	.5199	.5239	.5279	.5319	.5359
.1	.5398	.5438	.5478	.5517	.5557	.5596	.5636	.5675	.5714	.5753
.2	.5793	.5832	.5871	.5910	.5948	.5987	.6026	.6064	.6103	.6141
.3	.6179	.6217	.6255	.6293	.6331	.6368	.6406	.6443	.6480	.6517
.4	.6554	.6519	.6628	.6664	.6700	.6736	.6772	.6808	.6844	.6879
.5	.6915	.6950	.6985	.7019	.7054	.7088	.7123	.7157	.7190	.7224
.6	.7257	.7291	.7324	.7357	.7389	.7422	.7454	.7486	.7517	.7549
.7	.7580	.7611	.7642	.7673	.7703	.7734	.7764	.7794	.7823	.7852
.8	.7881	.7910	.7939	.7967	.7995	.8023	.8051	.8078	.8106	.8133
.9	.8159	.8186	.8212	.8238	.8264	.8289	.8315	.8340	.8365	.8389
1.0	.8413	.8438	.8461	.8485	.8508	.8531	.8554	.8577	.8599	.8621

1.1	.8643	.8665	.8686	.8708	.8729	.8749	.8770	.8790	.8810	.8830
1.2	.8849	.8869	.8888	.8907	.8925	.8944	.8962	.8980	.8997	.9015
1.3	.9032	.9049	.9066	.9082	.9099	.9115	.9131	.9147	.9162	.9177
1.4	.9192	.9207	.9222	.9236	.9251	.9265	.9278	.9292	.9306	.9319
1.5	.9332	.9345	.9357	.9370	.9382	.9394	.9406	.9418	.9430	.9441
1.6	.9452	.9463	.9474	.9484	.9495	.9505	.9515	.9525	.9535	.9545
1.7	.9554	.9564	.9573	.9582	.9591	.9599	.9608	.9616	.9625	.9633
1.8	.9641	.9648	.9656	.9664	.9671	.9678	.9686	.9693	.9700	.9706
1.9	.9713	.9719	.9726	.9732	.9738	.9744	.9750	.9756	.9762	.9767
2.0	.9772	.9778	.9783	.9788	.9793	.9798	.9803	.9808	.9812	.9817
2.1	.9821	.9826	.9830	.9834	.9838	.9842	.9846	.9850	.9854	.9857
2.2	.9861	.9864	.9868	.9871	.9874	.9878	.9881	.9884	.9887	.9890
2.3	.9893	.9896	.9898	.9901	.9904	.9906	.9909	.9911	.9913	.9916
2.4	.9918	.9920	.9922	.9925	.9927	.9929	.9931	.9932	.9934	.9936
2.5	.9938	.9940	.9941	.9943	.9945	.9946	.9948	.9949	.9951	.9952
2.6	.9953	.9955	.9956	.9957	.9959	.9960	.9961	.9962	.9963	.9964
2.7	.9965	.9966	.9967	.9968	.9969	.9970	.9971	.9972	.9973	.9974
2.8	.9974	.9975	.9976	.9977	.9977	.9978	.9979	.9979	.9980	.9981
2.9	.9981	.9982	.9982	.9983	.9984	.9984	.9985	.9985	.9986	.9986
3.0	.9987	.9990	.9993	.9995	.9997	.9998	.9998	.9999	.9999	1.0000

Appendix C

Financial Management Organizations (and Related Associations) and Government Organizations

American Association of Artificial Intelligence

445 Burgess Drive
Menlo Park, CA 94025-3442
Phone: 650-328-3123 Fax: 650-321-4457
Web: www.aaai.org

American Bar Association

750 N. Lake Shore Drive
Chicago, IL 60611
Phone: 312-988-5000 Fax: 312-988-6281
Web: www.abanet.org

American Economic Association

2014 Broadway
Suite 305
Nashville, TN 37203
Phone: 615-322-2595 Fax: 615-343-7590
Web: www.aeaweb.org

American Institute of Certified Public Accountants

1211 Avenue of the Americas
New York, NY 10036-8775
Phone: 888-777-7077; 201-938-3750
Fax: 212-596-6213; 201-938-3329
Web: www.aicpa.org

American Management Association

1601 Broadway
New York, NY 10019
Phone: 212-586-8100; 800-262-9699 Fax: 212-903-8168
Web: www.amanet.org

American Production and Inventory Control Society

Helmut Derra, CPIM
Haldex Brake Systems
10707 N.W. Airworld Drive
Kansas City, MO 61453
Phone: 816-801-4122 Fax: 816-880-9557
Web: www.apics-kc.org

American Society of Association Executives

ASAE Building
1575 I St. N.W.
Washington, DC 20005-1103
Phone: (202) 626-2723 Fax: (202) 371-8825
Web: www.asaenet.org

American Statistical Association

1429 Duke St.
Alexandria, VA 22314-3415
Phone: 703-684-1221; 888-231-3473 Fax: 703-684-2037
Web: www.amstat.org

Association for Investment Management and Research (AIMR)

(Formed by a merger of the **Financial Analysts Federation** and the **Institution of Chartered Financial Analysts)**

P.O. Box 3668
560 Ray C. Hunt Drive
Charlottesville, VA 22903-0668
Phone: 800-247-8132; 434-951-5499 Fax: 434-951-5262
Web: www.aimr.com

Bureau of Economic Analysis

1441 L Street N.W.
Suite 320
Washington, DC 20230
Phone: 202-606-5310 Fax: 202-606-5310
Web: www.bea.gov

Canadian Institute of Chartered Accountants

277 Wellington St. West
Toronto, Ontario M5V 3H2
Phone: 416-977-3222 Fax: 416-977-8585
Web: www.cica.ca

CMA Canada

Mississauga Executive Centre
One Robert Speck Parkway
Suite 1400
Mississauga, ON L4Z 3M3
Phone: 905-949-4200; 800-263-7622
Web: www.cma-canada.org

The Conference Board

845 Third Ave.
New York, NY 10022-6679
Phone: 212-759-0900 Fax: 212-980-7014
Web: www.conference-board.org

Conference Board of Canada

255 Smyth Road
Ottawa, Ontario K1H 8M7
Phone: 866-711-2262; 613-526-3280 Fax: 613-526-4857
Web: www2.conferenceboard.ca

Department of Commerce

14th Street
Washington, DC 20230
Phone: 202-482-2000
Web: www.osec.doc.gov

Financial Executives Institute

10 Madison Ave.
Morristown, NJ 07960
Phone: 800-336-0773; 201-898-4600 Fax: 201-898-4649
Web: www.fei.org

Financial Management Association International

College of Business Administration
University of South Florida
4202 Fowler Ave.
Tampa, FL 33620
Phone: 813-974-2084 Fax: 813-974-3318
Web: www.fma.org

Institute of Internal Auditors

249 Maitland Ave.
Altamonte Springs, FL 32701
Phone: 407-830-7600 Fax: 407-831-5171
Web: www.theiia.org

Institute of Management Accountants

(formerly **National Association of Accountants)**

10 Paragon Drive
Montvale, NJ 07645-1718
Phone: 800-638-4427; 201-573-9000 Fax: 201-474-1600
Web: www.imanet.org

Internal Revenue Service

1111 Constitution Ave.
Room 3000
Washington, DC 20224
Phone: 202-622-5000
Web: www.irs.gov

International Association of Financial Engineers

560 Lexington Ave.
11th floor
New York, NY 10022
Phone: 212-317-7479 Fax: 212-527-2927
Web: www.iafe.org

International Association of Information Technology Trainers

PMB 451
6030-M Marshalee Drive
Elkridge, MD 21075-5935
Phone: 888-290-6200; 410-290-7000 Fax: 603-925-1110
Web: itrain.org

International Economic Policy

Office of Financial Management
Herbert Hoover Building
14th Street and Constitution Avenue Northwest
Room 3866
Washington, DC 20230
Phone: 202-482-3022 Fax: 202-377-5444
Web: usinfo.state.gov/topical/econ

International Trade Administration

Office of Financial Management
Herbert Hoover Building
14th Street and Constitution Avenue Northwest
Room 4112
Washington, DC 20230
Phone: 202-482-3809 Fax: 202-377-5933
Web: www.ita.doc.gov

National Association of Business Economists

1233 20th St. N.W.
#505
Washington, DC 20036
Phone: 202-463-6223 Fax: 202-463-6239
Web: www.nabe.com

National Association of Credit Management

8840 Columbia 100 Parkway
Columbia, MD 21045
Phone: 410-740-5560 Fax: 410-740-5574
Web: www.nacm.org

National Association for Female Executives

P.O. Box 469031
Escondido, CA 92046-9925
Phone: 800-634-NAFE
Web: www.nafe.com

National Tax Association

725 15th St. N.W.
#600
Washington, DC 20005-2109
Phone: (202) 737-3325 Fax: (202) 737-7308
Web: ntanet.org

National Technical Information Service

U.S. Department of Commerce
Technology Administration
Springfield, VA 22161
Phone: 703-605-6000
Web: www.ntis.gov/products/milpubs.htm

New York Society of Security Analysts (NYSSA)

(A local of the **Association for Investment Management and Research)**

1601 Broadway
11th floor
New York, NY 10019-7406
Phone: 212-541-4530 Fax: 212-541-4677
Web: www.nyssa.org

North American Simulation and Gaming Association

c/o University of Wisconsin—La Crosse
203 Mitchell Hall
La Crosse, WI 54601
Phone: 608-785-8162
Web: www.nasaga.org

Office of Business Liaison

1401 Constitution Ave. N.W.
Room 5062
Washington, DC 20230
Phone: 202-482-1360 Fax: 202-482-4054
Web: www.doc.gov/obl

Office of the Chief Economist

Room 112-A
Jamie L. Whitten Building
USDA
Washington, DC 20250-3800
Phone: 202-720-5447
Web: www.usda.gov/oce

Office of the General Counsel

1500 Pennsylvania Ave. N.W.
Room 3000
Washington, DC 20220
Phone: 202-622-0287
Web: www.hqda.army.mil/ogc

Office of the Secretary of the Treasury

Main Treasury
1500 Pennsylvania Ave. N.W.
Room 3330
Washington, DC 20220
Phone: 202-622-2960 Fax: 202-622-6415
Web: www.ustreas.gov

Risk and Insurance Management Society

655 Third Ave.
New York, NY 10017
Phone: 212-286-9292 Fax: 212-986-9716
Web: www.rims.org

Securities and Exchange Commission

Office of Investor Education and Assistance
450 Fifth St. N.W.
Washington, DC 20549
Phone: 202-942-7040 Fax: 202-272-7050
Web: www.sec.gov/edgar.shtml

Tax Executives Institute

1200 G St. N.W.
Suite 300
Washington, DC 20005
Phone: 202-638-5601 Fax: 202-638-5607
Web: www.tei.org

Appendix D

Accounting Software Buyer's Guide

High-end accounting software

On the following 12 pages, high-end accounting software is compared by integrated functions, integraged manufacturing, integrated Internet functions, platform, pricing, and target customer. High-end packages generally target companies with revenues *over* $100 million.

Midrange accounting software

Following the high-end comparisons are 12 pages comparing mid-range accounting software using the same criteria. Midrange packages generally target companies with revenues *under* $100 million.

Part 1 of 3	ACCOUNTING SOFTWARE: High End				
	AXS-One Rutherford, NJ	**Flexinternational** Shelton, CT	**GEAC Enterprise Solutions** Atlanta	**Infinium** Hyannis, MA	**Interbiz** Fort Lee, NJ
PRODUCT NAME	Foundation Solutions	FlexiFinancial Enterprise Suite	SmartStream	Infinium Financial Management	Masterpiece/Net
INTEGRATED FUNCTIONS:					
Activity-based Costing	no	yes (via-3rd party vendors)	yes (via-3rd party vendors)	yes	yes
Complex Allocations	yes	yes	yes	yes	yes
Credit Management	yes	no	yes	yes	yes
Complex Consolidations/Roll-ups	yes	yes	yes	yes	yes
Debt Collection	yes	no	yes	yes	yes
Document Management/Imaging	yes	yes	yes	yes	no
Electronic Funds Transfer	yes	no	yes	yes	yes
Govt. Commitment Accounting	yes	no	yes	no	yes
Human Resources	no	no	yes	yes	yes
Multicurrency	yes (unlimited)	yes (all)	yes (unlimited)	yes (unlimited)	yes (up to 50 per batch)
Job/Project Costing	yes (via flexible GL chart of accts)	yes	yes	yes	yes

Source: From CFO.com © CFO Publishing Corporation 2001.

Multilingual	yes (unlimited)	yes (all)	yes (unlimited)	yes (unlimited)	yes (up to 50 per batch)
Nonprofit Accounting	yes	no	yes	yes	yes
OLAP/Data Warehouse	yes (MIS Alea)	yes (FlexiFinancial Datawarehouse, FlexiFin, Rules Engine)	yes (Cognos Power Play)	yes	NA
Project Mgmt	yes (via 3rd party)	yes	yes (via 3rd party: Microsoft)	yes	yes
Sales Force Mgmt	no	no	yes (via 3rd party: Applix)	yes	yes
Service Mgmt	no	no	yes (3rd party: Concur Tech.)	yes (via Momentum)	yes
Transaction Analysis Codes	yes	yes	yes	yes	yes
Travel Mgmt	yes	yes	yes (3rd party: Concur Tech.)	yes (via Momentum)	yes
Treasury Mgmt	no	yes	yes	no	yes
Workflow	yes	yes	yes	yes	yes

Part 1 of 3	ACCOUNTING SOFTWARE: High End				
	AXS-One Rutherford, NJ	**Flexinternational** Shelton, CT	**GEAC Enterprise Solutions** Atlanta	**Infinium** Hyannis, MA	**Interbiz** Fort Lee, NJ
PRODUCT NAME	Foundation Solutions	FlexiFinancial Enterprise Suite	SmartStream	Infinium Financial Management	Masterpiece/Net
INTEGRATED MANUFACTURING					
Discrete Manufacturing	no	no	no	no	no
Logistics & Distribution	no	no	no	yes	yes (see footnote 1, below)
MRP/ERP	no	no	no	yes	yes (see footnote 1, below)
Process Manufacturing	no	no	no	yes	yes (see footnote 1, below)
Work Orders	Yes	Yes	No	Yes	yes (see footnote 1, below)
INTEGRATED INTERNET FUNCTIONS					
Business-to-Business E- commerce	yes	In future (release 4.4)	yes	no	yes (see footnote 1, below)
Business-to-Consumer E- commerce	no	In future (release 4.4)	no	no	yes (see footnote 1, below)
Employee Self-Service	yes	no	yes	yes	yes
Customer Self- Service	yes	no	no	yes	yes

Source: From CFO.com

PLATFORM					
Servers	NT, Unix	NT, Unix	NT, HP-Unix, AIX, Sun Solaris	AS/400	NT, Unix, AS/400, S/390
Databases	SQL Server, Sybase, Oracle, Informix	SQL Server, Sybase, Oracle, ODBC	SQL Server, Sybase	DB2 Universal Database for AS/400	SQL Server, Oracle, DB2, Informix, Ingres
Source language available	yes (Escrow only)	yes (Microsoft C++)	no	yes (RPGIV/ILE)	yes (Cobol, C++, Java, HTML)
PRICING					
Price	\$40K; \$700K; \$1M	\$60K; \$300K; \$500K	\$25K; \$125K; \$250K	\$75K; \$250K; \$1M	NA
Price per module	\$40K-\$150K	NA	NA	\$50K-\$200K	NA
Available in ASP licensing model from: vendor? / 3rd party?	yes, yes	yes, yes	yes, no	yes, no	yes, yes
TARGET CUSTOMER					
Customer Size (\$Sales)	\$10M-\$200B	\$100M-\$750M	\$200M-\$1B	\$100M-\$1B	\$50M-\$1B
Principal Target Markets	Generally, \$50M-\$500M	Banking, health care, utilities, transport, financial, acctg., & mgmt. svcs.	Financial svcs., health care, public sector	Hospitality, mfg., transportation, retail, health care	All industries

[1]Through integration with interBiz's other products

Part 2 of 3	ACCOUNTING SOFTWARE: High End				
	J.D. Edwards Denver	Lawson Software St. Paul, MN	Oracle Redwood Shores, CA	PeopleSoft Pleasanton, CA	Elevon Raleigh, NC
PRODUCT NAME	OneWorld	Lawon.insight e-Business Management System	Oracle Applications	PeopleSoft Financials	Elevon 5
INTEGRATED FUNCTIONS:					
Activity-based Costing	yes	yes	yes	yes	no
Complex Allocations	yes	yes	yes	yes	yes
Credit Management	yes	yes	yes	yes	yes
Complex Consolidations/Roll-ups	yes	yes	yes	yes	yes
Debt Collection	yes	yes	yes	yes	yes
Document Management/Imaging	yes (via 3rd party)	yes (via 3rd party)	yes	yes	yes (via 3rd party; Altris)
Electronic Funds Transfer	yes	yes	yes	yes	yes
Govt. Commitment Accounting	yes	Planned for first half of 2001	yes	yes	yes
Human Resources	yes	yes	yes	yes	no
Multicurrency	yes	yes	yes (unlimited)	All ISO Standard currencies.	All
Job/Project Costing	yes	yes	yes	yes	yes

Source: From CFO.com © CFO Publishing Corporation 2001.

Multilingual	yes	yes (10)	yes (29)	yes (8)	yes
Nonprofit Accounting	yes	yes	yes (Oracle)	yes	yes
OLAP/Data Warehouse	yes	yes (via integration with Hyperion & Microsoft SQL)	yes	yes	yes
Project Mgmt	yes	yes (via 3rd party by industry)	yes	yes	yes
Sales Force Mgmt	yes (via Sieble)	yes (via integration with Siebel)	yes	yes	no
Service Mgmt	yes	yes (via 3rd party by industry)	yes	yes	no
Transaction Analysis Codes	yes	yes	yes	yes	yes
Travel Mgmt	yes (via Extensity)	yes	yes	yes	yes (via Extensity)
Treasury Mgmt	yes	yes (via 3rd party; XRT/CERG)	yes	yes	no
Workflow	yes	yes	yes	yes	yes

Part 2 of 3	ACCOUNTING SOFTWARE: High End				
	J.D. Edwards Denver	**Lawson Software** St. Paul, MN	**Oracle** Redwood Shores, CA	**PeopleSoft** Pleasanton, CA	**Elevon** Raleigh, NC
PRODUCT NAME	OneWorld	Lawon.insight e-Business Management System	Oracle Applications	PeopleSoft Financials	Elevon 5
INTEGRATED MANUFACTURING					
Discrete Manufacturing	yes	yes (via 3rd party; MACPRO)	yes	yes	no
Logistics & Distribution	yes	yes (see footnote 2, below)	yes	yes	no
MRP/ERP	yes	yes (see footnote 3, below)	yes	yes	no
Process Manufacturing	yes	no	yes	yes	no
Work Orders	yes	yes	yes	yes	no
INTEGRATED INTERNET FUNCTIONS					
Business-to-Business E- commerce	yes	In future (release 4.4)	yes	yes	yes
Business-to-Consumer E- commerce	yes	In future (release 4.4)	yes	yes	yes
Employee Self-Service	yes	no	yes	yes	no
Customer Self- Service	yes	no	yes	yes	yes

PLATFORM					
Servers	NT, Unix, AS/400, S/390, Sun	NT, Unix, AS/400, S/390	NT, Unix	NT, Unix, AS/400, S/390	NT, Unix, Novell, S/390
Databases	SQL Server, Oracle, DB2	SQL Server, Sybase, Oracle, DB2, Informix	Oracle	SQL Server, Sybase, Oracle, DB2, Informix	SQL Server, Oracle, DB2
Source language available	no	yes (4GL, Java, C++)	yes (Pl/sql, Oracle Developer, C)	yes (PeopleCode)	yes (COBOL)
PRICING					
Price	$100K– $1M	$180K- $540K	$50K- $10M	$100K; $1M; $2.5M	$100K; $500K; $2M
Price per module	NA	NA	$3,995 per user	Varies	$100K
Available in ASP licensing model from: vendor? / 3rd party?	no, yes	no, yes	yes, no	yes, yes	yes, no
TARGET CUSTOMER					
Customer Size ($Sales)	$150M-$2B+	$20M-$200M	$200M+	$50M-$1B+	$100M-$500M+
Principal Target Markets	Industrial, consumer, & svcs. organization	Health care, retail, prof. svcs., public sector, fin. svcs., telecom	Midsize to large companies	Multiple	Finance, retail, airlines, banking & insurance

[2]Low-end via 3rd party; high end via Manhattan Associates [3]Lawson.insight is classified by many analysts as an ERP system.

Part 3 of 3	ACCOUNTING SOFTWARE: High End				
	SAP Walldorf, Germany	**SSA Global Technologies** Chicago	**Systems Union** White Plains, NY	**Tecsys** Dorval, Quebec, Canada	**Walker Interactive Systems** San Francisco
PRODUCT NAME	MySAP Financials / mySAP.com	BPCS (Business Planning and Control System)	SunSystems	EliteSeries	Walker e-business Solutions
INTEGRATED FUNCTIONS:					
Activity-based Costing	yes	no	yes	yes (via 3rd party: Avcor Systs.)	no
Complex Allocations	yes	yes	yes	yes	yes
Credit Management	yes	yes	yes (with 4/1/01 release)	yes	yes
Complex Consolidations/Roll-ups	yes	yes	yes	no	yes
Debt Collection	yes	yes	yes	yes	yes
Document Management/Imaging	yes	no	no	yes (3rd party: Image Solutions)	no
Electronic Funds Transfer	yes	no	yes	no	yes
Govt. Commitment Accounting	yes	no	yes	no	yes
Human Resources	yes	no	yes (with partner Tenrox)	no	no
Multicurrency	yes (about 185; 4 simult. in GL)	yes (user definable, incl. euro)	yes (all)	yes (unlimited)	yes (unlimited)
Job/Project Costing	yes	yes	yes	yes	yes

Source: From CFO.com

Multilingual	yes (approx. 37)	yes	yes (27+)	yes (3)	yes (single-byte languages)
Nonprofit Accounting	yes	no	yes	no	yes
OLAP/Data Warehouse	yes	yes (via 3rd party: Cognos)	yes (Cognos, Accutate, Vision)	yes	yes (Hyperion Essbase, IBM DB2 for OLAP)
Project Mgmt	yes	yes (limited functionality)	yes (with Tenrox & SharpOwl)	yes	no
Sales Force Mgmt	yes	no	no	no	no
Service Mgmt	yes	no	no	no	no
Transaction Analysis Codes	yes	yes	yes	yes	yes
Travel Mgmt	yes	no	yes	no	yes (via Concur Technologies)
Treasury Mgmt	yes	no	yes	no	no
Workflow	yes	no	yes	yes (via 3rd party: Cognos)	yes

Part 3 of 3	ACCOUNTING SOFTWARE: High End				
	SAP Walldorf, Germany	**SSA Global Technologies** Chicago	**Systems Union** White Plains, NY	**Tecsys** Dorval, Quebec, Canada	**Walker Interactive Systems** San Francisco
PRODUCT NAME	MySAP Financials / mySAP.com	BPCS (Business Planning and Control System)	SunSystems	EliteSeries	Walker e-business Solutions
INTEGRATED MANUFACTURING					
Discrete Manufacturing	yes	yes	Via 3rd party	no	no
Logistics & Distribution	yes	yes	Via 3rd party	yes	no
MRP/ERP	yes	yes	Via 3rd party	no	no
Process Manufacturing	yes	yes	Via 3rd party	no	no
Work Orders	yes	yes	Via 3rd party	yes	no
INTEGRATED INTERNET FUNCTIONS					
Business-to-Business E- commerce	yes	yes	yes	yes	yes
Business-to-Consumer E- commerce	yes	no	yes	no	no
Employee Self-Service	yes	no	yes	no	yes
Customer Self- Service	yes	no	yes	yes	yes

Source: From CFO.com

PLATFORM					
Servers	NT, Unix, AS/400, S/390	NT, IBM AS/400, HP 9000	NT, Unix, Novell	NT, Unix	NT, Unix, S/390
Databases	SQL Server, Oracle, DB2, Informix, ODBC	Oracle, DB2/400, Informix	SQL Server, Oracle	Oracle, Informix	DB2
Source language available	yes (ABAP)	yes	no	yes (4GL)	yes (Java, VB6, COBOL)
PRICING					
Price	(see footnote 4, below)	$50K; $250K; $500K	$25K; $75K; $200K	Varies	$250K; $600K; $4M
Price per module	(see footnote 4, below)	$250 per user	NA	Varies	$250K-$600K
Available in ASP licensing model from: vendor? / 3rd party?	no, yes	no, no	NA	yes, yes (IBM)	no, yes
TARGET CUSTOMER					
Customer Size ($Sales)	Midsize to large companies	$200M+	$50M-$500M	$50M; $500M; $4B	$1B+
Principal Target Markets	All industries	Manufacturing and industrial	Int'l, financial svcs., energy, hospitality, high growth	Wholesale & indust. distributors, mfrs. with comlex distribution oper., self-distrib. retailers, 3PLs, & E-distrib.	Cross-industry solution

[2]Price depends on solution and other SAP installations available.

Part 1 of 3	ACCOUNTING SOFTWARE: Midrange				
	Accountmate Software Novato, CA	ACCPAC International Pleasanton, CA	Agresso Burlington, MA	Baan Barneveld, The Netherlands	Deltek Systems McLean, VA
PRODUCT NAME	Visual AccountMate	ACCPAC Advantage Series	Agresso	BaanERP	Deltek Costpoint
INTEGRATED FUNCTIONS:					
Activity-based Costing	no	yes (3rd party: Groupe A.G.I.)	yes	yes (via ProDaCapo)	yes
Complex Allocations	no	yes (3rd party: Lorge Consult.)	yes	yes	yes
Credit Management	yes	yes	yes	yes	no
Complex Consolidations/Roll-ups	yes	yes	yes	yes (via Hyperion Solutions)	yes
Debt Collection	yes	yes (3rd party: CFO Technol.)	yes	yes	yes
Document Management/Imaging	no	yes (3rd party: Perceptive Vision)	yes	yes (via StreamServe)	no
Electronic Funds Transfer	yes	yes	yes	yes	yes
Govt. Commitment Accounting	yes	yes (3rd party: Pacific Software)	yes	yes	yes
Human Resources	yes	yes (3rd party: HRIS)	yes	yes (via Meta4)	yes
Multicurrency	yes (unlimited)	yes (unlimited)	yes (unlimited)	yes (10 unlim., 3 home curr.)	yes (180)
Job/Project Costing	yes (via 3rd party)	yes (3rd party: Network Micro.)	yes	yes	yes

Multilingual	yes (3)	yes (5)	yes (12)	yes (16)	yes (1; 15 via Web)
Nonprofit Accounting	yes	yes (3rd party: MicroChannel))	yes	yes	yes
OLAP/Data Warehouse	yes	yes (3rd party: Brio)	yes	yes (via MS server, Hyperion)	yes (via 3rd party: Cognos)
Project Mgmt	yes	yes (3rd party: SoftSys)	yes	yes	yes
Sales Force Mgmt	no	yes	yes (3rd party: SuperOffice)	yes	yes
Service Mgmt	yes	yes (3rd party: Technisoft)	no	yes	no
Transaction Analysis Codes	no	yes	yes	yes (via 3rd party)	yes
Travel Mgmt	no	no	yes	yes (Big Dog)	yes
Treasury Mgmt	no	yes (3rd party: Peresoft)	yes	no	Planned for v5 (July 2002)
Workflow	no	yes (3rd party: Perceptive Vision)	yes	yes	yes

Part 1 of 3	ACCOUNTING SOFTWARE: Midrange				
	Accountmate Software Novato, CA	**ACCPAC International** Pleasanton, CA	**Agresso** Burlington, MA	**Baan** Barneveld, The Netherlands	**Deltek Systems** McLean, VA
PRODUCT NAME	Visual AccountMate	ACCPAC Advantage Series	Agresso	BaanERP	Deltek Costpoint
INTEGRATED MANUFACTURING					
Discrete Manufacturing	no	yes (3rd party: Full Capacity Int'l)	no	yes	yes
Logistics & Distribution	yes	yes	yes	yes	yes
MRP/ERP	no	yes	no	yes	yes
Process Manufacturing	no	yes (3rd party: MISys)	no	yes (via 3rd party: Baan IV)	no
Work Orders	yes	yes (3rd party: Technisoft)	yes	yes	yes
INTEGRATED INTERNET FUNCTIONS					
Business-to-Business E- commerce	no	yes	yes	yes	yes
Business-to-Consumer E- commerce	no	yes	no	yes	yes
Employee Self-Service	no	yes	yes	no	yes
Customer Self- Service	no	yes	yes	yes	yes

Source: From CFO.com © CFO Publishing Corporation 2001.

PLATFORM					
Servers	NT, AS/400	NT, Unix, Novell, AS/400	NT	NT, Unix, AS/400, S/390	NT, Unix, Novell
Databases	SQL Server, DB2	SQL Server, Oracle, DB2, Pervasive	SQL Server, Oracle	SQL Server, Oracle, DB2, Informix, any ODBC	SQL Server, Sybase, Oracle
Source language available	yes (VFP, SQL; VB [future])	yes (C++, Visual Basic, ActiveX)	no	yes (BaanERP Tools)	yes (SQL Windows, Enterprise Java Beans)
PRICING					
Price	NA	$2K; $25K; $150K	Contact Agresso for pricing	$2,500 per license	$35K; $95K; $250K
Price per module	From $995	NA	Contact Agresso for pricing	NA	Varies
Available in ASP licensing model from: vendor? / 3rd party?	no, no	yes, yes	no, no	yes, yes	no, yes
TARGET CUSTOMER					
Customer Size ($Sales)	$5M-$500M	NA	Mid-market ($50M-$500M)	$10M-$1+B	$15M-$1B
Principal Target Markets	Manufacturing, distributing, accounting	NA	Professional services organizations; high tech, consulting	Midsize manufacturers	Professional services and project-based organizations

Part 2 of 3	ACCOUNTING SOFTWARE: Midrange				
	Epicor Software Irvine, CA	**Great Plains** Fargo, ND	**Khameleon** Clearwater, FL	**Macola Software** Marion, OH	**NavisionDamgaard** Duluth, GA
PRODUCT NAME	e by Epicor	eEnterprise	Khameleon	Macola Progression Series	Navision Solutions
INTEGRATED FUNCTIONS:					
Activity-based Costing	yes (3rd party: Best/Smart)	yes (via 3rd party)	yes	no	Planned for late summer 2001
Complex Allocations	yes	yes	yes	yes	no
Credit Management	no	no	yes	yes	yes
Complex Consolidations/Roll-ups	yes	yes	yes (3rd party: FRx Financial)	yes	yes
Debt Collection	yes	yes	yes	Planned for v8 (Fall 2001)	yes
Document Management/Imaging	yes (3rd party: Watermark or other)	yes (via 3rd party)	yes (3rd party: Highland Technologies)	no	yes (3rd party: Matriks A/S)
Electronic Funds Transfer	yes	yes	yes	yes (3rd party: ACOM)	yes
Govt. Commitment Accounting	no	yes (via 3rd party)	no	no	yes (3rd party: Serenic)
Human Resources	yes	yes	yes (3rd party: Humanic)	yes	yes
Multicurrency	yes (unlimited)	yes (unlimited)	yes	yes (unlimited)	yes (unlimited)
Job/Project Costing	yes	yes (via 3rd party)	yes	yes	yes

Source: From CFO.com

Multilingual	yes (16)	yes (8)	no	yes (6)	5+ (future)
Nonprofit Accounting	yes (3rd party VARs)	yes (via 3rd party)	no	no	yes (3rd party: Serenic)
OLAP/Data Warehouse	yes	yes (via 3rd party: Knosys)	yes (3rd party: Oracle)	yes	Planned for late 2001
Project Mgmt	yes	yes	yes	NA	yes
Sales Force Mgmt	yes	yes	yes	yes	Future (3rd party: Siebel)
Service Mgmt	no	yes	yes	yes (3rd party: ServicePro Int'l)	Future (3rd party: Solution One)
Transaction Analysis Codes	yes	yes	yes	no	yes
Travel Mgmt	yes	no	yes	yes (3rd party: Unanet)	(3rd party: Paramount Tech.)
Treasury Mgmt	yes (3rd party)	yes (via 3rd party)	no	no	no
Workflow	yes	yes	yes	yes	yes (3rd party: Soft Answers)

Part 2 of 3	ACCOUNTING SOFTWARE: Midrange				
	Epicor Software Irvine, CA	**Great Plains** Fargo, ND	**Khameleon** Clearwater, FL	**Macola Software** Marion, OH	**NavisionDamgaard** Duluth, GA
PRODUCT NAME	e by Epicor	eEnterprise	Khameleon	Macola Progression Series	Navision Solutions
INTEGRATED MANUFACTURING					
Discrete Manufacturing	yes	yes	no	yes	yes
Logistics & Distribution	yes	yes	no	yes	yes
MRP/ERP	yes	yes	yes	yes	yes
Process Manufacturing	no	yes (via 3rd party)	no	yes	yes
Work Orders	yes	yes (via 3rd party)	yes	yes	yes
INTEGRATED INTERNET FUNCTIONS					
Business-to-Business E- commerce	yes	yes	yes	yes	yes
Business-to-Consumer E- commerce	yes	yes	no	yes	yes
Employee Self-Service	yes	yes	yes	yes	yes
Customer Self- Service	yes	yes	yes	yes	yes

Source: From CFO.com

PLATFORM					
Servers	NT	NT	NT, Unix	NT	NT, Unix
Databases	SQL Server	SQL Server	Oracle	SQL Server, Pervasive, Btrieve	SQL Server
Source language available	yes	yes (C++)	yes	yes (MFCobol, Business Objects)	yes (similar to Delphi)
PRICING					
Price	$25K; $110K; $250K	$50K; $90K; $225K	$50K; $125K; $200K	$30K; $50K; $80K	$10K; $40K; $125K
Price per module	Flexible	$7.5K-$20K	NA	Price based on concurrent users	NA
Available in ASP licensing model from: vendor? / 3rd party?	yes, yes	no, yes	no, yes	yes, no	no, yes
TARGET CUSTOMER					
Customer Size ($Sales)	$10M-$500M	$25M-$500M	$5M-$400M	$10M-$100M	$10M-$250M
Principal Target Markets	See footnote 1, below	Svc. orgs., E-commerce solutions, wholesale/distrib.	Products & svcs. delivery industries	Small to midsize distributors & manufacturers	Distributors, manufacturers, services, verticals

[1]Business, financial, & professional svcs; hospitality; not-for-profit; computer & software svcs; dot- coms; sports & recreation; wholesale distributors; retail; manufacturing

Part 3 of 3	ACCOUNTING SOFTWARE: Midrange				
	Open Systems Shakopee, MN	**Ross Systems** Atlanta	**Sage Software** Irivine, CA	**Southware Innovations** Auburn, AL	**Syspro Impact Software** Costa Mesa, CA
PRODUCT NAME	Traverse C/S	iRenaissance Enterprise Management Solution	Sage Enterprise Suite	SouthWare Excellence Series	Impact Encore
INTEGRATED FUNCTIONS:					
Activity-based Costing	no	no	no	no	yes
Complex Allocations	no	yes	yes	no	no
Credit Management	yes	yes	yes	yes	yes
Complex Consolidations/Roll-ups	yes	yes (via 3rd party: FRx)	yes	no	yes
Debt Collection	no	yes	no	yes	yes
Document Management/Imaging	no	yes	no	no	yes (via 3rd party)
Electronic Funds Transfer	no	yes	yes (via 3rd parties)	no	no
Govt. Commitment Accounting	no	yes	yes	no	no
Human Resources	yes	yes	yes	yes (via Essential Integrat. Data)	yes (via 3rd party)
Multicurrency	yes	yes (unlimited)	yes (unlimited)	yes (unlimited)	yes (unlimited)
Job/Project Costing	yes	yes	yes	yes	yes

Multilingual	yes	yes (12 to unlimited)	yes (1, via 3rd party)	no	yes (3)
Nonprofit Accounting	yes	yes	yes (via 3rd party)	no	no
OLAP/Data Warehouse	yes	yes (Business Objects, Crystal)	Future	no	yes
Project Mgmt	yes	yes	yes (via 3rd party: Intellisol))	no	yes
Sales Force Mgmt	yes (via Applied Business Svcs.)	no	yes	yes	yes
Service Mgmt	yes (via Genesee Info. Systs.)	yes	yes (via 3rd party)	yes	yes (via 3rd party)
Transaction Analysis Codes	yes	yes	yes	no	yes
Travel Mgmt	no	yes (via 3rd party: Clarus)	no	no	no
Treasury Mgmt	yes	yes	yes	no	no
Workflow	no	no	yes	yes	yes

Part 3 of 3	ACCOUNTING SOFTWARE: Midrange				
	Open Systems Shakopee, MN	**Ross Systems** Atlanta	**Sage Software** Irivine, CA	**Southware Innovations** Auburn, AL	**Syspro Impact Software** Costa Mesa, CA
PRODUCT NAME	Traverse C/S	iRenaissance Enterprise Management Solution	Sage Enterprise Suite	SouthWare Excellence Series	Impact Encore
INTEGRATED MANUFACTURING					
Discrete Manufacturing	no	no	yes	yes (via BTM Solutions)	yes
Logistics & Distribution	yes	yes	yes	yes (via BTM Solutions)	yes
MRP/ERP	no	yes	yes	yes (via BTM Solutions)	yes
Process Manufacturing	no	yes	yes	yes (via BTM Solutions)	yes (batch)
Work Orders	no	yes	yes	yes (via BTM Solutions)	yes
INTEGRATED INTERNET FUNCTIONS					
Business-to-Business E- commerce	yes	yes	yes	yes	yes
Business-to-Consumer E- commerce	yes	yes	no	yes	yes
Employee Self-Service	yes	yes	Planned for v6.0 (May 2001)	yes	no
Customer Self- Service	yes	yes	yes	yes	yes

PLATFORM					
Servers	NT	NT, Unix, Novell	NT	NT, Unix, Novell	NT, Unix, Novell
Databases	SQL Server, Access	SQL Server, Oracle	SQL Server	SQL Server, Sybase, Oracle, Pervasive, Informix, ODBC, Btrieve	SQL Server, ODBC; ORacle (future)
Source language available	yes (Access, Transac SQL)	yes (DML/Gembase, Java)	yes (Visual Basic)	yes (Cobol)	Possible
PRICING					
Price	$8K- $50K	$50K; $250K; $1M	$20K; $50K; $150K	$30K; $100K; $250K	$10K; $30K; $100+K
Price per module	$3.5K	$20,000	NA	NA	Varies by module, no. of users
Available in ASP licensing model from: vendor? / 3rd party?	yes, yes	yes, yes	yes, yes	yes, yes	no, yes
TARGET CUSTOMER					
Customer Size ($Sales)	$5M-$100M	$40M-$500M	$50M-$500M	$2M-$200M+	$10M-$350M
Principal Target Markets	Manufacturing, distribution, construction, service, hotel	Food & beverage, chemical, pharmaceutical, metals, paper	NA	Wholesale, retail hard goods, svc. mgmt., rental, job coast	Small to midsize manufacturers & distributors

Appendix E

Financial and Investment Worksheet Functions in Microsoft® Excel

ACCRINT. Returns the accrued interest for a security that pays periodic interest.

ACCRINTM. Returns the accrued interest for a security that pays interest at maturity.

AMORDEGRC. Returns the depreciation for each accounting period. The function is similar to AMORLINC, except that a depreciation coefficient is applied in the calculation depending on the life of the assets.

AMORLINC. Returns the depreciation for each accounting period.

COUPDAYBS. Returns the number of days from the beginning of the coupon period to the settlement date.

COUPDAYS. Returns the number of days in the coupon period that contains the settlement date.

COUPDAYSNC. Returns the number of days from the settlement date to the next coupon date.

COUPNCD. Returns the next coupon date after the settlement date.

COUPNUM. Returns the number of coupons payable between the settlement date and maturity date.

COUPPCD. Returns the previous coupon date before the settlement date.

CUMIPMT. Returns the cumulative interest paid between two periods.

Microsoft® Excel is a product of Microsoft Corporation.

CUMPRINC. Returns the cumulative principal paid on a loan between two periods.

DB. Returns the depreciation of an asset for a specified period using the fixed-declining-balance method.

DDB. Returns the depreciation of an asset for a specified period using the double-declining-balance method or some other method specified.

DISC. Returns the discount rate for a security.

DOLLARDE. Converts a dollar price, expressed as a fraction, into a dollar price, expressed as a decimal number.

DOLLARFR. Converts a dollar price, expressed as a decimal number, into a dollar price, expressed as a fraction.

DURATION. Returns the annual duration of a security with periodic interest payments.

EFFECT. Returns the effective annual interest rate.

FV. Returns the future value of an investment.

FVSCHEDULE. Returns the future value of an initial principal after applying a series of compound interest rates.

INTRATE. Returns the interest rate for a fully invested security.

IPMT. Returns the interest payment for an investment for a given period.

IRR. Returns the internal rate of return for a series of cash flows.

MDURATION. Returns the Macauley modified duration for a security with an assumed par value of $100.

MIRR. Returns the modified internal rate of return where positive and negative cash flows are financed at different rates.

NOMINAL. Returns the annual nominal interest rate.

NPER. Returns the number of periods for an investment.

NPV. Returns the net present value of an investment based on a series of periodic cash flows and a discount rate.

ODDFPRICE. Returns the price per $100 face value of a security with an odd first period.

ODDFYIELD. Returns the yield of a security with an odd first period.

ODDLPRICE. Returns the price per $100 face value of a security with an odd last period.

ODDLYIELD. Returns the yield of a security with an odd last period.

PMT. Returns the periodic payment for an annuity.

PPMT. Returns the payment on the principal for an investment for a given period.

PRICE. Returns the price per $100 face value of a security that pays periodic interest.

PRICEDISC. Returns the price per $100 face value of a discounted security.

PRICEMAT. Returns the price per $100 face value of a security that pays interest at maturity.

PV. Returns the present value of an investment.

RATE. Returns the interest rate per period of an annuity.

RECEIVED. Returns the amount received at maturity for a fully invested security.

SLN. Returns the straight-line depreciation of an asset for one period.

SYD. Returns the sum-of-years' digits depreciation of an asset for a specified period.

TBILLEQ. Returns the bond-equivalent yield for a Treasury bill.

TBILLPRICE. Returns the price per $100 face value for a Treasury bill.

TBILLYIELD. Returns the yield for a Treasury bill.

VDB. Returns the depreciation of an asset for a specified or partial period using the double-declining-balance method or other method specified. VDB stands for variable declining balance.

XIRR. Returns the internal rate of return for a schedule of cash flows that is not necessarily periodic.

XNPV. Returns the net present value for a schedule of cash flows that is not necessarily periodic.

YIELD. Returns the yield on a security that pays periodic interest.

YIELDDISC. Returns the annual yield for a discounted security (e.g., a Treasury bill).

YIELDMAT. Returns the annual yield of a security that pays interest at maturity.

Appendix F

Top Providers of Budgeting and Planning Systems

ABC Technologies

Product Name: Oros
Web: www.abctech.com

ActiveStrategy

Product Name: ActiveStrategy Enterprise
Web: www.activestrategy.com

Actuate

Product Name: e.Reporting Suite 5
Web: www.actuate.com/home/index.asp

Adaytum Software

Product Name: e.Planning
Web: www.adaytum.com

Applix

Product Name: iPlanning
Web: www.applix.com

Brio Software

Product Name: Performance Suite
Web: www.brio.com

Business Objects

Product Names: Auditor; Business Objects 5i; BI; WebIntelligence
Web: www.businessobjects.com

Cartesis

Product Names: Budget Planning; Magnitude
Web: www.cartesis.com

Closedloop Solutions

Product Names: Biz Plan Manager; SpendCap Manager; TopLine Manager
Web: www.closedloopsolutions.com

Source: From CFO.com © CFO Publishing Corporation 2002. All rights reserved. Reprinted by permission. (CFO sources were AMR Research and Buttonwood Group.)

Cognos

Product Names: Finance; PowerPlay; Visualizer
Web: www.cognos.com

Comshare

Product Names: Decision; FDC; MPC
Web: www.comshare.com

CorVu

Product Names: CorBusiness; CorManage; CorPortfolio; RapidScorecard
Web: www.corvu.com/small

e.Intelligence

Product Name: e.Intelligence Suite 3.5
Web: www.eintelligence-inc.com

Epicor Software

Product Name: eIntelligence Suite
Web: www.epicor.com

FRx Software

Product Name: FRx Forecaster
Web: www.ebudgets.com

Geac Computer

Product Names: E Series; Smartstream
Web: www.geac.com

Hyperion Solutions

Product Names: Hyperion Enterprise; Hyperion Essbase; Hyperion Financial Management; Hyperion Pillar; Hyperion Planning
Web: www.hyperion.com

J.D. Edwards

Product Name: Financial Planning and Budgeting
Web: www.jdedwards.com

Lawson Software

Product Name: Financials Suite
Web: www.lawson.com

Longview Solutions

Product Name: Khalix
Web: www.longview.com

Microsoft Great Plains

Product Names: Dynamics; eEnterprise
Web: www.greatplains.com

MicroStrategy

Product Name: MicroStrategy 7.0
Web: www.microstrategy.com

MIS-AG

Product Name: MIS Decisionware
Web: www.misag.com

NextStrat

Product Name: NextStrat Strategic Implementation Portal (NextSIP)
Web: www.nextstrat.com

Oracle

Product Names: Financial Analyzer; Strategic Enterprise Management
Web: www.oracle.com

OutlookSoft

Product Name: EAP Financial APPack
Web: www.outlooksoft.com

PeopleSoft

Product Names: Activity-Based Management; Balanced Scorecard; Budgeting; Business Planning and Budgeting; Solution; Enterprise Performance Management; Enterprise Warehouse
Web: www.peoplesoft.com

SAP America

Product Name: Strategic Enterprise Management
Web: www.sap.com

SAS Institute

Product Names: SAS Consolidation and Reporting; SAS Strategic Performance Management; SAS Financial Management Solutions
Web: www.sas.com

Silvon Software

Product Names: DataTracker; Stratum
Web: www.silvon.com

SRC Software

Product Names: Budget Advisor; I*Net Budgeting; Information Advisor; Payroll Planner
Web: www.srcsoftware.com

Index

References are to paragraph (¶) numbers

A

B

D

E

F

N

O

P